# PORTRAIT OF A NATION

# NORWAY

Translation by James Anderson, Don Bartlett, Basil Cowlishaw, Kari Dickson, Marianne Foss-Skiftesvik, Rosalind Waddams and David Worsley

DINAMO FORLAG 2004

When work on this book began in the autumn of 2002, the goal was to offer Norwegian and foreign readers a more extensive presentation of Norway and her people than that found in the many available tourist brochures. As work progressed, we realized that the need for a book like this is much greater than we had first envisioned – for business activities, public life in Norway, foreign travellers and the Norwegian public in general.

To succeed in our intention of providing a balanced view of our country that would afford a deeper insight into the character and peculiarities of Norwegian society, we asked our contributors to be personal and unbiased, but also critical, in their approach to the subject matter. Hence the reader will not find between these covers a collection of panegyric articles, but stimulating and, at times, challenging information.

Several gateways exist to this book, depending on the reader's needs and interests. The bulk of the text consists of thirteen chapters that embrace a wide range of subjects – from politics and business to cuisine and sport, from environmental conservation to education, history, art and philosophies of life. They are written by some of the nation's most distinguished writers, who have joined forces in painting a comprehensive portrait of a nation that is about to celebrate its centennial. The individual contributions primarily comprise a description of the Norway of today, but they also sketch the historical features necessary to understand how we and the nation have become what we are.

Those with more artistic interests will be able to review the book's 'art gallery', the anthology of Norwegian poetry, or seek out the pictures through which twelve of the nation's most eminent photographers each interprets one of the months of the year. In addition, fifteen literary portraits offer the reader satirical encounters with prominent personalities in Norway's history.

At the back of the book will be found an extensive statistical chapter, historical time charts and detailed indexes of names and places.

It has been a privilege to head the editorial staff behind this work, and it has been a great pleasure to cooperate with such a unique panel of writers, artists and specialists. Finally, we wish to extend our thanks to H.R.H. Crown Prince Haakon for his considerable and important participation in the Editorial Committee.

Oslo, September 2004
Tove Bull and Harald Norvik
Editors-in-Chief

# CON

NORWEGIAN HISTORY UNTIL 1814

THE NORWEGIAN PEOPLE

ADMINISTRATION AND INTERNAL AFFAIRS

FOREIGN POLICY

NATURE, RESOURCES AND ENVIRONMENTAL PROTECTION

FAITH AND PHILOSOPHIES

ARTS AND CULTURE

TRANSPORT AND COMMUNICATIONS

EDUCATION AND RESEARCH

ECONOMY AND BUSINESS

SPORT

FOOD AND BEVERAGES

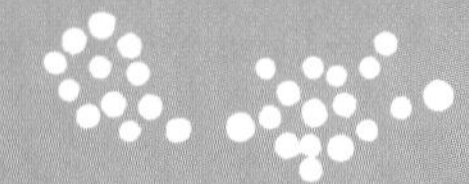

A STATISTICAL PORTRAIT

TENTS

# INTRODUCTION

# H.R.H. CROWN PRINCE HAAKON

I could barely see the prow of the ship a few metres in front of me and the dark, heaving waves below. It was snowing thick and hard and the wind was blowing. We had sailed through the night on our way back to the naval base in Tromsø, and I was tired. Then it happened: the clouds parted and for a few seconds the light broke through, illuminating the islands and coastline I had been watching on radar for hours – magnificent, naked, wild. Light is a precious commodity in northern Norway in late autumn, which is perhaps why, when something like this happens, its impact is so powerful. The sky closed over again and we sailed out into open waters, where I increased speed to 30 knots. We were returning from a routine exercise, but I felt in a way that I had witnessed something sacred.

A few years later, when I was in the United States, I gave a speech to representatives of the Norwegian-American community in the Midwest. The thrust of my message was that traditional Norwegian culture is important, something we need to preserve and show proudly to the world. But Norway has other things to be proud of too: high-tech manufacturing, modern design and information technology to mention but a few. How wonderful it would be if these resources were to become as famous as the country's fjords and folk culture. Afterwards, a Norwegian-American came over to talk to me. 'Norway is not about high-tech manufacturing and the offshore industry,' he said, 'Norway's comparative advantage is rose-painting and folk art.' This statement took me slightly by surprise, but it is a view shared by many people outside Norway; and it is one that we should bear in mind and respect. I have had the great good fortune to travel extensively in Norway

and to see the traditional farming culture, the coastal culture and the Sámi culture, all of which serve as anchors to our history and national pride. Many Norwegians now work in the service sector and offshore industry, but Norwegian folk art is still very much a part of our lives. In fact, it is an integral part of our identity.

Some time later, back in Norway, I attended the Pakistani Students Association's annual general meeting. I sat next to the Minister of Education and Research, surrounded by several hundred young Norwegian Pakistanis, one of whom had recently been elected president of the Norwegian Students Union. The venue was in Oslo and the programme included presentations of different fields of study, among them medicine, law and engineering, interspersed with sketches poking fun at 'Norwegian-ness' and what it means to be a Norwegian Pakistani. Clearly, I was sitting in a room full of resourceful young people who would help shape the future of Norway.

What is Norway? What are Norwegians like and how do they to live, so far north? The three experiences I have just mentioned go some way to illustrating the diversity of our culture. We are a small nation on the outskirts of Europe and it is not easy to describe our country. That is why projects like this book are so interesting. What will the writers include and what will they leave out? Will the reader be able to grasp the essence of Norway?

Norway is extremely elongated, extending from the North Cape in the north to Lindesnes in the south. The landscape is very varied, embracing as it does an extensive coastline, dense forests and countless mountains and valleys. This variety is reflected in the cultural diversity and myriad dialects. We are a seafaring nation with strong farming traditions and a growing urban culture. Norway, like so many other countries, is constantly changing and is now, perhaps more than ever, a complex and diverse nation, which is one of the reasons why it is so difficult to define what 'Norwegian-ness' really is.

I have been spared the most hackneyed misunderstandings about Norway. When I went to study at Berkeley in California, I often used to follow up the fact that I was from Norway with a brief explanation – telling my listeners where it was, that the capital was Oslo, and so forth. But I soon stopped giving this little lecture as I was in a highly international environment and meeting people from all corners of the world. Moreover, those I met already possessed a surprisingly detailed picture of Norway. Depending on their interests, most people had heard of the Oslo Accords, *A Doll's House*, Munch or the Nobel Peace Prize, to name but a few topics.

When tourists come to Norway, it is very gratifying to be able to show them places like the North Cape, Nidaros Cathedral and the Geiranger fjord. But it is also valuable to give visitors an insight into what is happening in the country today. The Oil Museum in Stavanger, for instance, is a prime example of modern architecture that also provides an overview of the Norwegian offshore industry. Foreign friends may also appreciate the diversity of Norwegian music, which ranges from folk and classical to more modern expressions such as jazz, pop, rock, hip hop and electronica. There is a plethora of festivals showing the scope and breadth of music in Norway. A trip to the National Museum or Momentum in Moss would give visitors an idea of what is going on in art. There are lots of interesting galleries and exhibitions too that will repay a visit; or perhaps your visitors would be happy just to sit in a café and watch the world go by.

**Hadseløya**, Vesterålen

Today it is not unusual to hear tourists talking about Norway as an exotic destination. This image has certainly been enhanced in recent years by the opportunities offered to kayak on the Sjoa, north of Lillehammer, or to scale the peaks of the Lofoten Islands – though a visit to the Sámi heritage centre in Karasjok or Valdres Folk Museum might be a slightly less challenging alternative.

Foreigners often ask about typical Norwegian food. What we eat and how we prepare it says a lot about who we are. I often start by telling them that we eat a lot of fish and potatoes, to illustrate the link between sea and land in Norwegian culture. Of course, it is tempting to describe some of the more unique Norwegian dishes such as *lutefisk* (boiled lyed cod), *smalahove* (salted, smoked and boiled sheep's head), *klippfisk* (sun-dried split cod) and *kumle* (potato dumplings). But our food culture has changed enormously in recent years. Norwegian chefs have won international competitions, and the number of restaurants in Norway has risen steeply and the range of ingredients available greatly increased. Many culinary impulses have come from abroad and Norway would be a poorer nation without them. However, dishes that were originally imported are nowadays often given a Norwegian twist.

What are Norwegians good at? The key to Norway's economic growth lies in exploitation of our natural resources. The oil and gas industry is a cornerstone of Norway's wealth, thanks to oil extraction on the continental shelf and the development of pioneering know-how in this field. But we are not interested in material development alone. We have, for example, also gained an enviable reputation in other areas, such as voluntary work, peace negotiations, sexual equality, human rights and development work, to name but a few other concerns.

Conservation has also received a lot of attention in recent years. The Norwegian people's affinity with nature goes a long way towards explaining this interest. Outdoor recreation is important to us and we have unparalleled facilities for hiking and skiing in the mountains and lowlands. Outdoor activities are equally important to city dwellers, many of whom are able to combine working in town with a walk in the woods or a boat trip on the fjord in the late afternoon.

Our country lies far to the north, so it is natural that winter sports should be particularly dear to our hearts. As the average Norwegian has become wealthier, we have invested more systematically in elite sport, and this has borne fruit in the shape of world cups, world championship titles and Olympic medals. But local clubs and voluntary work still constitute the foundations on which our broad-based interest in both elite sport and exercise rest.

The contributors to this book were asked to give a personal perspective on their particular topic and to highlight any problems and challenges in that field. The intention is not that *Norway* should define what Norway is, but rather to afford an insight into the breadth and diversity of Norwegian society, culture and the natural heritage. The book is lavishly illustrated and the photographs provide a visual backdrop to the text. There is no need to read the book from cover to cover. Most chapters can be read independently, so you can select your reading on an à la carte basis. You have a treat in store.

**Andøya**, Nordland, with Bleiksøya in the background.

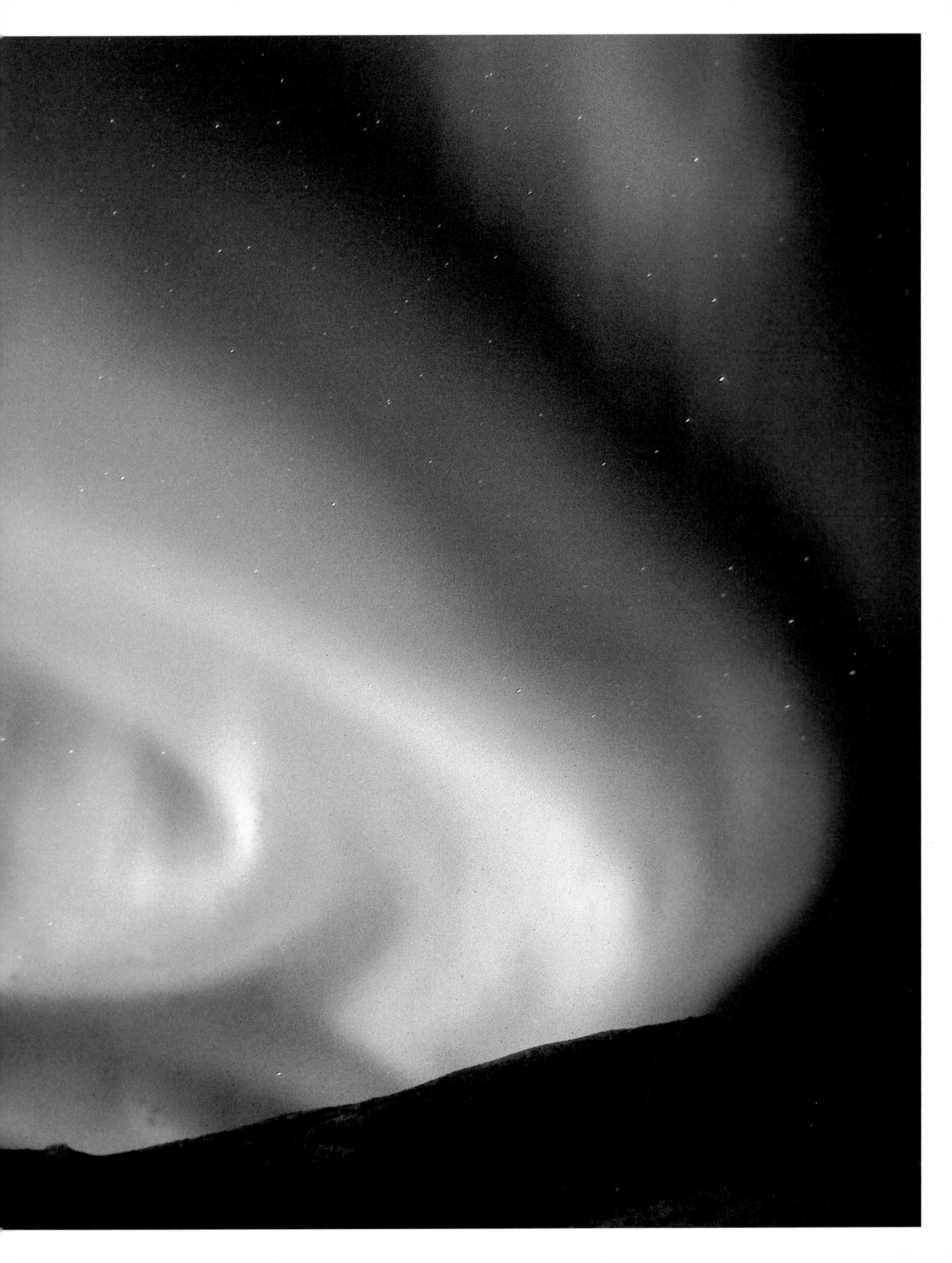

# HARALD FAIRHAIR

It goes without saying that if one is remembered as a king primarily because of one's hair, there must be many good reasons why one's reign as a whole is recalled with displeasure. Many people, including his own father, King Halvdan the Black, disliked Harald, even when he was a small boy. One reason may have been that he once helped a Sámi steal King Halvdan's and Queen Ragnhild's Christmas dinner. Worse, after their dastardly deed Harald and the Sámi sought refuge with a shaman. To feel affronted by such outrageous behaviour is only human.

Harald was only ten years old when his father fell through the ice of Randsfjord [a lake, despite its name] and drowned. He was returning from Hadeland to his home county of Vestfold and had taken a short cut across the ice – an urge to save time that cost him his life. Afterwards, there was disagreement as to where he should be buried, so as a compromise the body was quartered.

Many chieftains did their best to prevent Harald, hothead that he was, ascending the throne. However, together with his uncle, the young king quickly disposed of his rivals, not infrequently resorting to arson, with the result that many of them were burned alive. Between battles Harald fell deeply in love with a girl from Hordaland named Gyda, though his feelings do not appear to have been reciprocated. Whether they were or not, Gyda set some tough terms. She had no desire to become betrothed to a petty king like Harald. However, if he were to rule over the whole country, as the kings of Denmark and Sweden ruled over their countries, it would be a different matter entirely. Strange as it may seem, the thought of nationwide sovereignty had never occurred to Harald, who felt that being ruler of his own small kingdom was quite good enough. But Gyda had sown a seed, with the result that Harald determined to neither cut nor comb his hair until he had become king of all Norway.

With this in mind, he set out northwards with a large army. He had no intention of gambling on a charm offensive and a show of hands when he came to a strange farm. If its occupants refused to acknowledge him as their king, he simply burned the place down. He seized the land of recalcitrant farmers by revoking their freehold. Any chieftain who offered resistance was summarily cleft in two. Harald must have been constantly worried by the fear that his subjects might change their allegiance to another king, so he imposed a tax, and in order to collect it enlisted the services of a body of earls, who were obliged at all times to keep him supplied with soldiers. This enabled him to build a bigger army and accumulate more wealth than any king before him. He became so rich, in fact, that he had a royal farm built at Lade in Trondheim.

One may be forgiven for thinking that under the weight of his many duties and conquests he would have forgotten about the waiting Gyda. Be that as it may, he married Håkon Grjotgardsson's daughter Åse. The fact that her father ruled the coast north of Trondheim rather suggests that it was a marriage of convenience: one could say that he married Åse in order to win Gyda.

But was that the end of things? In a word, no. Not a few chieftains and minor kings were opposed to subjugation by this longhaired barbarian. Some of them foregathered in Sunnmøre with the intention of attacking Harald at Solskjel. According to the sagas, Harald lashed his ships together and in the ensuing battle went completely berserk. What he did was to consume large quantities of liberty cap mushrooms, the poison of which is believed to have the same effect on the central nervous system as LSD. Norway's first king may thus be said to have been something of a junkie.

No sooner had the troublemakers in Møre been vanquished than word came to Lade of insurrection in the south. King Sulke of Rogaland, the berserker Tore Haklang, King Kjøtve the Rich and a number of other leading figures had formed an alliance. The battle fought at Hafrsfjord, outside Stavanger, in about 880 was to be a turning point in Norwegian history. The minor kings were slaughtered without mercy and the rest fled in disorder. It has often been said that Harald's victory at this battle resulted in Norway's becoming a united kingdom, but this is an exaggeration, as he still exercised no control over the vast areas north of Trondheim. Moreover, many Norwegians had fled to Iceland, the Faeroes and the Shetlands. It is possible that Harald's 'drugtaking', combined with his zeal to conquer the whole of Norway, led to his inadvertently invading some key areas of Sweden as well. In general, it may be said that a lot of people were dissatisfied with their new ruler – though women found him irresistible.

Harald had four sons with Åse before he remembered Gyda's promise, whereupon he despatched a body of men to bring her to him. The two married and she bore him five children. However, Harald's appetite for land was matched by his appetite for women: at one time he had no fewer than twelve wives, though there is evidence to suggest that he was a singularly poor father. It is clear that he quite soon lost track of how many children he actually had, but it is widely accepted that it was close to one hundred.

Harald celebrated his victory at Hafrsfjord at the home of his closest friend, Ragnvald, earl of Møre. At the time the king was a sorry sight. He had not cut his hair for ten years, and in consequence was widely referred to as Harald Shockhead. It was Ragnvald who tidied him up and gave him the name 'Fairhair'. One drawback resulting from unification of Norway was that robbery was prohibited by law. Ragnvald's son Rolf the Ganger could not bear the thought of this and carried on raiding until he was outlawed. This brawny brigand then made his way to France, where he seized Normandy, which takes its name from its Norwegian conquerors. Another of Ragnvald's sons died fighting for Harald. In gratitude for his support Harald invaded the Shetlands and

Orkneys, for the sole purpose of donating them to Ragnvald – an indication of his generosity towards those for whom he felt affection. There is reason to believe that the king was as partial to women abroad as he was at home. It is said that in England alone he had no fewer than nine sons, all by different women.

Harald found life with his twelfth wife, Ragnhild, so congenial that he dismissed his other wives, Gyda included. It may have helped that Ragnhild was the daughter of the Danish king. She bore him a son, Erik, who grew up to be the apple of his father's eye – and a veritable monster to boot. For his twelfth birthday Erik was given five Viking ships, complete with the men to man them, and with these he ranged the world, pillaging and slaughtering wherever he went. Such was his cruelty that he was nicknamed 'Bloodaxe'.

The most disastrous phase in Harald Fairhair's life was when he fell in love with a Sámi girl, Snefrid. So enamoured of her was he that he neglected his kingdom. In the course of time Snefrid bore him four sons, but died young. The king had her corpse laid out on a bed of down and mourned by her side for three long years. Finally, when it became clear that the corpse had become host to both worms and frogs, Harald reacted by expelling his four sons from the country. One might say without exaggeration that Harald Fairhair never succeeded in establishing a stable family life.

The problem with Harald's numerous sons was that many of them harboured a desire to replace their father on the throne. Two of them, Halvdan and Gudrød, went so far as to set fire to a farm belonging to Ragnvald, earl of Møre, which resulted in the death not only of Ragnvald himself but also of sixty of his men, leaving Harald with no choice but to go to war against his rebellious sons. Perhaps the most peace-loving of them was Bjørn Farmann, king of Tønsberg; a merchant, he was both good-natured and popular. Returning from a Viking foray to Russia, Erik called in on Bjørn and demanded food, drink and lodging and, more especially, the taxes due to his father. When Bjørn told him that he would give the money to his father himself, Erik set fire to the house and slew everyone who tried to escape the flames – including his own brother. Not surprisingly, after that Erik Bloodaxe was highly unpopular in the east of Norway.

At the age of seventy Harald sired another son, the mother being a servant girl, Tora. The boy was given the name of Håkon. At about the same time Harald received a sword as a gift from King Athelstan of England. According to the custom of the time, such a gift meant that the recipient was to be regarded as having been conquered. Harald's revenge was to send Håkon to Athelstan, to make it clear that he regarded the king as his inferior. The remarkable thing is that Athelstan grew extremely fond of young Håkon, who was tutored by monks, schooled in the ways of Christianity, taught good manners and baptized.

Harald was about eighty when he died, which was about 940. He elected to pass on his throne to Erik Bloodaxe – an arrangement none of Erik's brothers were prepared to tolerate. Erik fled to the Orkneys, from where he conquered a part of England. It was Håkon who then succeeded to the Norwegian throne. He pledged himself to return to the farmers their allodial rights, which is one of the reasons why he has come down to us as Håkon the Good.

NIELS CHR. GEELMUYDEN

FAIRHAIR, HARALD (c. 860–c. 940), son of Halvdan the Black, originally king of Viken and Opplandene [the Uplands region]. By collaborating with the earl of Lade, Håkon Grjotgardsson, he sought to gain control of the entire coastal region north of Viken. As a result of his victory at the battle of Hafrsfjord (c. 880), Harald is traditionally accounted the first king of a united Norway.

# NORWEGIAN HISTORY
# UNTIL 1814

# AND LET THE LAW BE OUR FOUNDATION

Erling Lægreid

Television cameras sweep across the country to cover the children's parades on Norway's Constitution Day, 17 May. In Oslo the sun is shining, the trees are coming into leaf, the marching bands are playing and thousands of jubilant children in their best clothes cheer, smile and wave their flags. In the Setesdal valley, too, it is sunny and children are dressed in national costumes, *bunads*, as happy as can be amidst the flags and birch foliage. In Bergen, people carry metre-long 17 May ribbons and the drill corps march to the beat of their drums in the rain. In a small community on the arctic coast, far to the north, snow banks still line the roads and the sleet drives horizontally in the wind. Heading the parade and clutching the flag is a man in a suit, frozen to the bone. Behind him comes the school band, ten to twelve warmly dressed youngsters, followed by the rest of the local children, all waving small flags. At the end come the grown-ups, the rearguard, they too sporting ribbons. Not as long as those in Bergen, but still.

Nowhere else is the national day a children's day. Other nations celebrate their national days with a show of force and bombast, with military parades and uniforms. Military triumphs of the past are celebrated, and the day is often a demonstration of power. Here the day is a children's festival and our great spring celebration. We are still a young nation, and much remains to be done, and instead of celebrating our past, we celebrate our future, our children, who are all dressed up in their best clothes for the big day. 'We are a nation, we too, we little ones just two feet tall,' they sing.

'Happy 17th of May', we cry in response.

**Odin, God of War,** had one eye because, according to Norse legend, he had given away his right eye. Wood carving from the old quarter of Oslo.

As the glaciers slowly retreated towards the end of the last ice age some 14,000 years ago, parts of the Norwegian coastline emerged from the icy carapace that had covered northern Europe. Herds of reindeer trekked north towards the Scandinavian glaciers, and hunters followed across the Norwegian Trench and further northwards. Around 9,300 BC some of them had reached as far as Magerøya, an island near North Cape.

The hunters gradually settled on the barren coast, making a living by fishing and hunting. The coast was rich in marine animals and fish, which provided not only food but also raw materials for clothing and heating and for boats and tents made of hide. People may have settled at the river mouths that were ice-free during the winter, for such estuaries are often rich in fish. Seals and walrus hunted for salmon and sea trout entering the rivers to spawn. When the ice cap retreated further, revealing the mountains, forests spread upwards and inland until ultimately almost the entire country was forested. With the forest came birds and game, red deer, elk, wild boar and bears. Above the timberline trekked herds of reindeer and glacial waters deposited nutrients at the bottom of the fjords and on the flatlands. The reason the climate is so mild despite the latitude, is the warm and fertile Gulf Stream that caressess the coast all the way up to the Arctic Ocean, making winters along there mild and ice-free.

**With more** than 5,000 figures, the Alta petroglyphs are the largestknown collection of rock paintings and engravings in northern Europe. The work of hunters, they date from between 4000 and 500 BC and were first discovered in 1973. The most characteristic illustrations are of animals, chiefly reindeer, bears and elk. The petroglyphs were placed on the UNESCO World Heritage List in 1985.

The Norwegians started to cultivate the land in about 4000 BC, when people along the coast and inland began growing grain, keeping cattle, pigs, sheep and goats. During the Bronze Age (1800–500 BC) fields were tilled with wooden ploughs, and the horse was used for riding and ploughing. Farmers settled down and built permanent farmsteads, mainly in areas with very fertile soil – around the Oslo fjord and Lake Mjøsa, for example, and at Jæren and in Trøndelag. Crops thrived, and some farmers managed to trade for luxury items from foreign parts. These articles were probably received in exchange for furs and hides, products that were much sought after elsewhere in Europe. Finds of jewellery and decorative items in graves from this period bear witness to the new riches. Moreover, the impressive Bronze Age burial mounds are visible proof that society was becoming more stratified, and that chieftains enjoyed a high status.

In the centuries preceding the birth of Christ, temperatures fell and precipitation increased until the climate became roughly as we know it today. The change in climate meant that the farmers had to build more houses which would provide shelter and heating for both people and animals. This early period of the Iron Age (500 BC to 0) is called the *Celtic Iron Age*. The name emphasizes that it was the Celts who brought iron to this part of Europe. The new metal was produced from bog iron that was easily accessible in marshes, and people could now get hold of knives, sickles, arrowheads and other weapons and tools. The iron tools made it easier to cultivate the land, harvests improved and the population increased. More ground had thus to be cleared for farming and several generations lived under the same roof. When sons married, they remained on the farms with their wives and children. Such extended families were called clans. The clan provided security and protection for all its members. If a conflict arose between local clans because of murder, theft or farm boundary disputes, all free men assembled at the *ting*, a sacred place where all use of force was forbidden.

During the *Roman Iron Age*, the first four centuries after Christ, the Roman Empire was the economic and political power centre of Europe, and people in the Nordic regions received many impulses from it. From the Latin alphabet they developed their own form of writing, *runes*, and they adopted the weightsystem of the Romans. In the graves of wealthy farmers Roman bronze utensils, gold and silver jewellery, glassware and swords have been found. Grave finds clearly show that the clans living on the largest farms, the chieftain clans, became richer and in many areas more influential. For example, the chieftains, functioned as priests when gods such as Njord (god of navigation and trade) and Frøya (goddess of fertility and carnal love) were celebrated. At these celebrations, or *blot*, the farmers presented their chieftains with offerings. The chieftains used some of these to pay their *hird*, an army of professional soldiers. His *hird* enabled a chieftain to increase his power and subjugate other tribes.

During the restless period of migrations from 400 to 550 AD, chieftains were given increased authority to organize and lead the defence of their districts. An important part of this consisted of building simple fortresses where people and livestock could seek refuge in troubled times. Such local fortifications may have been built for protection against foreign tribes which came to the country after the breakdown of the western Roman Empire. Two place names in western Norway may indicate such migrations: *Rogaland* may be associated with the Ryger, a tribe found on the coast of the Baltic Sea, while *Hordaland* may be linked to the Hordar, a tribe from the German area of Harz.

Towards the end of the 500s, some parts of the country underwent a crisis, possibly a plague, which is mentioned in contemporaneous writings from both Gaul and the British Isles. In the south-west, many hundreds of farms were abandoned, and the population must have been drastically reduced.

**The stave churches** are Norway's oldest extant wooden buildings, and our most important contribution to world architecture. Originally, there were about a thousand stave churches in Norway, of which only 28 remain. Urnes stave church was built between 1150 and 1200 in Luster, Sogn og Fjordane. On its north wall are two beautifully decorated wall panels and a richly carved portal. The church was placed on the UNESCO World Heritage List in 1979.

**Around the year** 1000, an expedition led by Leiv Eiriksson sailed from Greenland to the coast of North America, where it wintered at a settlement now called L'Anse aux Meadows, on the northern tip of Newfoundland. The site was excavated between 1961 and 1968. Anne Stine and Helge Ingstad, who led the archaeological work, presented clear evidence that the settlement was Norse. L'Anse aux Meadows is now on the UNESCO World Heritage List.

However, in the 600s a new period of prosperity began. This sprang from developments in the land of the Franks, where the Merovingian dynasty built up a new and stable kingdom that served as a model for the tribes of northern Europe. Finds of jewellery, helmets and swords are evidence of close contact with Francia. This last part of the prehistoric period in Norway, from 550 to 800, is called the Merovingian period.

From the end of the 700s until the mid-1000s, for the first time the Scandinavian people played a major part in European history. This period, known as the Viking Age, started in 793 when the Vikings plundered the rich monastery on the island of Lindisfarne off England's northeast coast. At this time there was little difference between people from Sweden, Denmark and Norway, and there was a lot of intermarriage between the chieftain clans of these countries. The immigrant tribes from the Age of Migration had been assimilated, though it was previously claimed that there were physical differences between the broad, shortheaded people of the west coast and the tall, narrow-headed people in the eastern part of Norway. The only group to retain their language and ethnicity were the nomadic Sámi, who came from the east to the northernmost part of the Scandinavian peninsula.

From the year 800, the Vikings raided and colonized throughout western Europe, but they also sailed to the Mediterranean, the Black Sea and the Middle East. And, of course, to America: Leiv Eiriksson sailed from Greenland to Vinland (probably present-day Newfoundland) as much as 500 years before Columbus. Settlements in Vinland did not last long, as the indigenous Indians were probably as hostile to the Viking intruders as everyone else. On Greenland, however, the Vikings settled, as well as in the Faeroes, Iceland, the Orkney Islands, Shetlands and Hebrides, and in northern Scotland, parts of England and Ireland, on the Isle of Man and in Normandy. Reminders of these settlements are still found in many areas in the form of Norwegian place names.

The Vikings were among the foremost seafarers of their time. They mastered the art of navigation, and developed the best ships. The longship did not draw much water, but it had a very stout keel. And, most importantly, it was elastic and extremely seaworthy. It could sail through shallow sounds, and the crews were able to pull it across isthmuses and land and make surprise attacks almost anywhere. At this time there were no ships or seafarers that could compete with the Vikings. They also developed an efficient cargo ship called the *knarr*.

The Vikings began as traders, but soon discovered that pillaging rich monasteries and trade centres was also very profitable. Resistance was weak. Viking chieftains from all over the Nordic region would join forces in attacks. Thus they harvested great riches, which made it possible for the most successful of them to create their own realms and keep a *hird* of professional warriors. These *hirds* also included *skalds*, poets, whose task it was to entertain with odes to gods and heroes, but also to pay homage to their chieftain and in this way spread reports of his power and prowess.

The Viking was a fearless warrior with utter contempt of death, a man who revered strength, skill at arms and heroic deeds. He worshipped Odin, the god of war, whom he believed could determine defeat and victory on the battlefield. And he believed in good fortune, for if he fell in battle, Odin would lead him to Valhalla, realm of the dead. There he would fight all day and every night be served pork and mead by beautiful women. This optimistic view of death must have given the Vikings a psychological advantage in battles with the Christians. In the churches priests preached that, at worst, after death people could risk eternal damnation in Hell. The Vikings did not know of any such Hell.

Culturally, the Viking era left a permanent mark in the form of poetry. The *Edda* literature, about pagan gods and heroes, has been admired for a thousand years and almost functioned as a Germanic bible, for the pre-Christian religion was shared by the Germanic tribes. Many of the ideas expressed are in a mythical and exciting half-darkness that still generates interest, and it was in Norse mythology that the great German composer Richard Wagner found much of his inspiration. The *Edda* deals with gods and heroes, and provides an insight into pagan culture, ethics and religion. The greatest of all gods, Odin, was powerful and mystical, but also human and tragic.

This literature was transmitted orally and was remarkably resilient; at the *hird* of kings and chieftains the cult was preserved and practiced in an oral tradition that lasted for a long time, the reason being that the strict rhythmic and metric verse was easy to commit to memory and narrate. This made it possible for the Icelanders to write it down in the 1200s, when the Latin alphabet was introduced along with Christianity. It was in this way that the written Old Norse or Norse came into being, and in Iceland, Norse culture was preserved and further developed. The historical writings and the sagas of the Icelanders, based on material from heathen times, made Iceland a culturally advanced country at the time. Many of the family sagas can be regarded as the first psychological novels of European literature, and even today they serve as a model for great authors. The most prominent of the Norse authors is Snorri Sturluson (1178/79–1241). His works include the masterpiece *Edda*, which is an introduction to mythology and poetry, and *Heimskringla*, an account of Norwegian history from mythical times until 1177.

In the 800s, people all the way from the Oslo fjord to southern Troms spoke a language that to some extent differed from that of their neighbours, and although local communities were separated by mountains, forests, uplands and fjords, trading and family ties linked the different parts of the country. Because of the wealth accumulated from Viking raids, a number of powerful chieftainships developed from the 800s onwards. The most important of these seem to have been located at Borre in Vestfold, at Åker on Lake Mjøsa, in Ytre Namdalen in Trøndelag, at Karmsund in Rogaland and on Vestvågøy in Nordland. The petty kings, the richest chieftains, formed alliances, married strategically and amassed power. To a great extent this formed the basis for the economic expansion and political unification of the country that was to accelerate in the centuries that followed.

In the latter half of the 800s, a power struggle started between the chieftains. Harald Hårfagre (Fairhair), who according to Snorri belonged to the Yngling family from the county of Vestfold, allied himself with the powerful Jarle family in Trøndelag. Together they started to fight the petty kingdoms in the western part of the country. Towards the end of the 800s, Harald won a decisive battle at Hafrsfjord in Rogaland, and future kings of Norway were to be his descendants; he is the Norwegian king of kings.

Harald did not build up any large state administration. Together with his *hird*, he travelled around his kingdom; when the king and his men arrived at a settlement, the peasants had to provide lodging, food and beer. He deprived petty kings and

**On a summer's morning** in 1834, Halvor Torstensen Kvernmoen was draining a bog when he caught the glint of a gold ring on his spade. The bog subsequently yielded nearly 2.5 kilograms of jewellery, coins and beads made of glass and semi-precious stones. This hoard from Hoen in Øvre Eiker, Buskerud, is the largest collection of gold jewellery from the Viking Age found in Norway.

**Excavated at Oseberg** farm, Vestfold, in 1904, the Oseberg ship is 22 metres long and is built to accommodate 34 oarsmen. The site is believed to have been the grave of a woman of high birth, who was buried there together with her female slave and implements and accoutrements from the large farm where she once lived. **A Viking helmet** from Gjermundbu in Buskerud.

farmers of their power and exacted taxes with an iron hand. It was said that he confiscated the rights of inheritance from the farmers, some of whom fled the country and became the first settlers in Iceland.

Harald Fairhair had many sons and lived to a ripe old age. When he died, in about 940, bloody strife ensued over who should inherit the kingdom. One of his sons, Eirik Blodøks, (Bloodaxe), was a strapping warrior and Viking who spent most of his life raiding and pillaging. He was married to Gunnhild, daughter of the Danish king. She was one of many strong-minded and ambitious women of the Norse era. Eirik was not allowed to rule in peace, for several of his brothers also demanded the right to reign. On the advice of his father, Eirik killed two of them, but was finally driven from the country by his youngest brother, Håkon, in 935. Håkon made an early attempt to Christianize the country, hence his soubriquet of Håkon the Good, but was soon forced to give up.

Håkon reformed the *ting* system, strengthened the *Allting*, where the farmers met, and established *Gulating*, a representative assembly and a model for the Allting in Iceland. The Gulating law included guidelines on how to punish thieves in a society that had neither police nor prisons. For a first offence, a thief was to be beaten. If he stole again, he could be driven from the community. If he stole a third time, the tip of his nose was cut off. After that, nothing more could be done: the miscreant had been stigmatized, and people had to take care of their belongings themselves. By comparison, as late as the 1840s a poor English boy of ten who stole food was beheaded.

Håkon's *hird* was small, but he established the institution of *Leidangen*, which was a form of compulsory military service. The country was divided into districts, each with a duty to build and equip a longship with warriors who could be summoned when the country was in danger. Håkon also built cairns on mountain tops to be used for signalling purposes in case of trouble. He himself was not given any peace by Gunnhild's sons, who, with the aid of the Danes, finally managed to kill him at a battle at Fitjar in 960 or 961. After that, the Danish king and the Fairhair family continued their power struggle for a long time.

In 995, the great king, hero and Viking of the Fairhair family, Olav Tryggvason, regained power from the jarls (earls) who had reigned with Danish backing. A Christian, Olav tried but failed to put a stop to the offering of sacrifices to the heathen gods. It cannot have been easy for chieftains or ordinary farmers to give up their old faith, which had permeated daily life and festivities for hundreds of years. Many chieftains feared that Christianity would deprive them of their positions as religious leaders and heads of clans, so it was not surprising that Olav had many enemies around Mjøsa and in Trøndelag, where the old religion still had a strong hold. Only five years later Olav fell at Svolder, and the jarls returned to power.

Then came another Olav, Olav 'Digre' (Big), later Saint Olav. In 1015, the country lay wide open, and he Christianized it ruthlessly and brutally. He built up a new state and church administration, and apparently had full control. However, people were dissatisfied with his ruthless rule, and in the end he was driven out of the country. 'Digre' did not mean 'tall', but 'stout' – Olav was a short man with a pot belly. In 1030 he made another attempt to conquer the country, but fell that same year in battle at Stiklestad.

After his death, Olav's hair and beard continued to grow, and shortly afterwards he was canonized. He became the Nordic countries' principal saint, and was worshipped many places abroad. For several hundred years pilgrims made their way to his shrine in Nidaros cathedral in Trondheim, a custom that has recently been revived. Olav's death firmly established Christianity in Norway, and the Church made him Norway's eternal king.

The last of the Viking kings may be said to have been Harald Hardråde (the Ruthless), who fell in a battle against the English king at Stamford Bridge in 1066. The Norwegian Viking kings had amassed much of their income from raids and taxation in the lands to the west, but henceforward the kings' revenue would have to come from Norway. This meant higher taxes, which affected the farmers. The church, too, needed an income, and increasingly so. The country entered a period of peaceful growth. Kings and Church alike increased their power, and the population grew. During the Viking era, farmers had owned their farms, but in the 1100s a majority of them became tenants under the king, the nobility and, especially, the Church. The *odel* right – the right of descendants to inherit agricultural land – was still practised, however, and the farmers were freer than in other countries. As many as a third of them succeeded in maintaining their freehold rights, which was unique in Europe at that time.

One of the Norse kings familiar to all Norwegians is Sigurd Jorsalfare (the Crusader), *c.* 1090-1130. At the age of eighteen he assembled a fleet of longships and a large army and travelled to Jerusalem, wreaking havoc in Portugal, Spain and the Mediterranean on his way. In Joppe (Tel Aviv) he was warmly welcomed by King Baldwin. The two kings rode to Jerusalem, where Sigurd bathed in the River Jordan and visited Jesus' tomb. Then he helped Baldwin conquer Sidon, where the large fleet made a valuable contribution. This event is also recorded by Snorri Sturluson. Sigurd's triumphant arrival in Miklagard (Constantinople), however, is probably pure fantasy.

Back in Norway, the wild and adventurous Sigurd became a good and peaceful king, who established episcopalian seats in Stavanger, the Faeroes and on Greenland; according to the sagas, people had never been happier. Sigurd was prone to bouts of mental illness and died on his sickbed, which was most

**The Baldishol tapestry** is one of very few extant Gobelin tapestries from the 1200s, and the only one of its kind in the Nordic countries. It was discovered when Baldishol church at Nes in Hedmark was demolished in 1879. The horseman carrying a lance symbolizes the month of May.

**Effigy of Queen Margaret I** on her tomb in Roskilde Cathedral, Denmark.

unusual for a Norse king. His skull is still to be found at the University of Oslo's Museum of Antiquities.

Up to that time all princes – both legitimate and illegitimate – had enjoyed the right of succession to the throne, which meant that there was almost always dispute about the order of succession. This may not have been entirely bad, if it was the strongest and most capable who won. However, it could also lead to very turbulent times, as during the so-called civil-war period from 1130 to 1217. This helped the Church become an independent power, especially after Nidaros became an archdiocese in 1152. All over Europe, king and Church struggled for power. Leading the battle against the Church was Sverre; trained for the priesthood, he led a rebellious faction called the *Birkebeiners*. Sverre seized power, but had to fight against the Church to his dying day. He was excommunicated by the Pope in Rome, but never gave up. His successors, on the other hand, did. His grandson, Håkon Håkonsson, reached a settlement with the church for an unknown sum of money, but had to accept that from then on, only the oldest legitimate son (he himself was illegitimate) would have the right to the throne, and the king had to be approved by the Church.

It was during the long reign of Håkon in the 1200s that the Norwegian kingdom was at its peak. The country was Europeanized, the written language was developed, and the population increased from 150,000 in 1000 to 400,000 in 1300. In other words, this was a time of considerable growth. The country adopted European – especially French – culture: churches and fortresses were built in the French style, French literature was translated into Old Norse, and common European myths and legends quickly spread. Christian culture also gained a foothold, although the language of the Church, Latin, proved an obstacle. The Christianization of Norway took a long time, and heathen customs, traditions and beliefs proved very resilient; some, in fact, may have survived to the present day. The great midwinter *blot* became a Christian holiday, but the celebrations remained the same, although the sacrifice of horses was prohibited.

In 1319, the male line of the Fairhair family died out, and a serious decline set in. The Hansa, a powerful league of merchants from the German towns on the Baltic coast, gained control of Norwegian imports and exports, draining the country of important revenues. For several hundred years, Norwegian longships and knarrs had traded with important markets overseas, especially in England. The longships were divided into sections, with up to six men to an oar. Each group was equipped with its own food, *mat*, and was called a *mataneytr*. The word was incorporated in the Dutch language, where it became *matros*, which we reintroduced without knowing its etymology, and which now means a *sailor* or *seaman* in Norwegian. At this stage, the Hansa had developed ships technologically superior to the longships, in terms of both navigation and cargo capacity.

However, the overwhelming disaster of the 1300s was the Black Death. Brought to Bergen by an English ship in 1349, in less than a year it killed more than one-third of the Norwegian population. Minor plagues later in the century also claimed lives, and by the year 1400 the population had been reduced by 50 per cent.

It seems reasonable to assume that the Norwegian elite at all levels was decimated or sank into poverty. For people in general, however, this period was not entirely dark. After the Black Death, the farmers' situation improved. There was plenty of land, and a shortage of labour. Renting land was cheap, and taxes and dues were lowered. The local *ting* of old was revived, and farmers were able to run their own affairs in a way they had not done for a long time. The archbishop of Nidaros was now the most powerful man in the country – the widespread fear of death following the plagues enabled the Church to sell absolution and make good money. It is otherwise unclear exactly how great the Church's power over the people was. The priests were instructed to live in celibacy, but did not: 80 per cent lived with mistresses, and both women and children enjoyed full civil rights. It may perhaps be said that human nature triumphed over discipline.

At this time both Denmark and Sweden had larger resources than Norway. They were richer and stronger, and Norwegians had little say in the Nordic power struggle. Besides, the neighbouring countries had larger populations, their agricultural acreage was many times larger than Norway's and, most important of all, the Hanseatic League exercised full control over Norwegian foreign trade. In the Nordic countries, fear of the economic and political progress of the Germans grew, and it is with this in mind that the Kalmar Union must be viewed.

**In the Middle Ages,** Bergen, with its beautiful and characteristic Hanseatic quarter (Bryggen), was the largest and most important town in Norway. The 58 buildings still standing are now listed, and in 1979 they were also placed on the UNESCO World Heritage List.

In 1343 the informal union that existed with Sweden was dissolved. King Håkon VI married a daughter of the Danish king, Margrete, which antagonized Sweden and resulted in the Swedish state council electing Albrecht of Mecklenburg as king. This triggered a conflict between two dynasties as regards power over the Nordic region. Håkon and Margrete had a son, Olav, who on his father's death in 1380 inherited the Norwegian throne. Thus began the long union between Denmark and Norway, which was to last until 1814.

When Olav IV died in 1387, Margrete managed to make her underage relative, Erik of Pomerania, king of both Norway and Denmark. She attacked Sweden and deposed King Albrecht, and in 1397 the union between the three Nordic realms was sealed in the town of Kalmar. Erik of Pomerania was crowned king of the Nordic region, and Margrete herself ruled the three kingdoms with a firm hand. A German blockade and heavy taxes hit Norway hard, and both in Norway and Sweden farmers revolted. In this situation the Swedish nobility managed to withdraw the country from the union. The Norwegian state council, however, was too weak; it proved impossible to restore a separate Norwegian kingdom. After the royalty moved out of the country, the cultural centre too, disappeared. The state council was dissolved, and gradually all important administrative functions were moved to Denmark.

Norway's last archbishop, Olav Engelbrektsson (*c.* 1480–1538), was a powerful man. He tried to save both the country's independence and the Catholic Church by political intrigue, but was forced to flee the country. In 1537, King Christian III's forces reached Norway. The newly elected king was a Lutheran, and with the Reformation in 1537, the power structure changed radically: the Catholic Church was expelled and all its properties (40 per cent of all land!) and other treasure were taken over by the throne. Tax collectors and state-employed priests became the new authorities. The state was both modernized and streamlined, which weakened the nobility and paved the way for the autocracy that followed.

The Danish king who had the greatest impact on Norway was Christian IV (1577–1648). It is no coincidence that it is his statue that stands in a central square, Stortorget, in Oslo, which under his rule became Christiania. A highly intelligent and well-

educated man of unbelievable energy, he reigned for 60 years! He established the town of Kristiansand, built fortifications from Båhus in the south to Vardø in the north, and secured Norwegian sovereignty over the northern areas. He also developed Norwegian ironworks, silver mines and copper mines. In 1628 he laid the foundations of a Norwegian army. Christian IV's Norwegian law from 1604, a translation and revision of Magnus Lagabøte's (the Lawmaker's) national legislation from 1276 bears testimony to his enterprising nature. As a result, Norwegian law survived the Danish period.

Christian Quart, as he was called, was said to be a disaster for Denmark and a blessing for Norway, for his involvements in international politics were not very successful. For example, he entered the Thirty Years' War on the side of the Protestants, suffering heavy losses and ruining the Danish state finances in the process. In this country, however, he was popular and welcome. He visited Norway 30 times. He was both strict and irascible, but also paternalistic, humorous and unassuming. Christian was a workaholic and had many children. A man inclined to pleasure and festivities, he enjoyed excellent health. In addition, he had a deep interest in music and art and proved a gifted architect and engineer. Under his reign Norway made great progress, financially, administratively and militarily, so it is no wonder we thought a lot of Christian Quart.

For people in general, the Danish period was not a dark age. Taxes were significantly lower than in Denmark, and Norwegian farmers enjoyed greater freedom than elsewhere in Europe. When in 1648 Norwegian representatives paid tribute to the new king, Frederik III, in Christiania, the 712 representatives included 524 farmers! This would have been inconceivable elsewhere. Frederik introduced absolute monarchy in 1661. The state apparatus was expanded and administrative districts (counties) were formed, divided into smaller units that were administered by bailiffs. The local *ting* retained its power, but the magistrates, who initially had only a secretarial function, became sole royal judges. The judicial system still functioned well however, and it was not uncommon to successfully appeal cases all the way to the king in Copenhagen. The Sámi had their rights ratified in the 'Sámi code' of 1751; only recently has there evolved a corresponding respect for minorities. In many ways, the Norwegians were privileged, not only as far as taxes were concerned, but also because they were allowed to practise a surprisingly strong autonomous local government. The kings were interested in keeping the Norwegians happy; it would have been both costly and complicated to rule this country with a heavy hand.

**Christian IV** (1577–1648) became king at the age of eleven. This painting was made by Pieter Isaacsz shortly after the Kalmar war (1611–13).

From 1500 to 1800, the population of Norway increased from about 150,000 to 900,000, nine out of ten inhabitants belonging to rural society. Houses were still primitive. Although two-storey farmhouses had been built on some farms in the eastern part of the country by 1660, the draughty log houses with open hearths in the centre, which we know from the Middle Ages, were still predominant. The diet was simple, consisting for most people of porridge, gruel, crisp unleavened bread (*flatbrød)*, and thin pancakes (*lefser*) made from rolled dough. There was no health service that could cure or prevent diseases, and the society was vulnerable to epidemics and famines; crop failures or failing fisheries could have disastrous consequences.

From the end of the 1600s, Norwegian farmers enjoyed ownership of the soil they cultivated. With the introduction of absolute monarchy in 1661, only 20 per cent of the land was owned by the farmers themselves, whereas by 1800 the majority of Norwegian farmer families lived on their own land.

Towards the end of the Danish period, the mood was optimistic. Forestry flourished, ironworks abounded, silver and copper mines were in operation, the fisheries were doing well, and for the first time in several hundred years Norwegian shipping prospered. Thus it is no wonder that the Norwegians should have grown more self-confident and demanded, for example, a university of their own – which they got in 1811. However, Norway remained subject to the whims of the great powers. Determined to seize the large Dano-Norwegian fleet, England attacked Denmark, with the result that the Danes threw in their lot with the opposing forces and joined Napoleon. Sweden, on the other hand, did not. The Swedes wanted Norway as compensation for the loss of Finland to Russia, and were rewarded when Napoleon was defeated at Waterloo. First, though, Norway was destined to suffer years of unparalleled hardship as a result of food shortages, war, and blockade. The year 1812 is arguably the worst in Norway's history. The Norwegians survived the war against the Swedes, but the English blockade was a catastrophe.

In 1813 the Danish heir to the throne, Christian Frederik, who was sent as governor to Norway by his father, tried to save something from the wreckage. He arrived in Norway and was elected king on 17 May the following year by the National Assembly at Eidsvoll, on the same day that Norway ratified its Constitution. Shortly afterwards, however, Christian Frederik returned the throne to the Norwegian people and recommended a union with Sweden, provided that Sweden was prepared to recognize the Constitution. The most radical and modern such declaration of its day, the Constitution was based on sovereignty of the people and was largely inspired by the French constitution of 1791. Almost half of all men over the age of 25 were entitled to vote in elections to the *Storting*, the Norwegian parliament, which meant that the farmers were assured of political power. It was the newly elected Storting that formally deposed Christian Frederik and elected Sweden's Carl XIII as Norway's king. The Storting was to issue legislative Acts, make monetary grants and convene every three years. The new constitution stated that the Norwegian government should be divided into two, one part residing in Christiania, the other in Stockholm, which was where the king lived. Norway was not allowed to pursue an independent foreign policy, but the Swedish king could no longer declare war or make peace without the consent of the Storting. A Norwegian flag and a Norwegian central bank were also part of the agreement. Norwegians now considered themselves an independent people, even though they had to share a king with the Swedes.

In 1814 Norway lacked everything that other nations had. The contrast to Denmark and Sweden's magnificent palaces, castles, fortresses and cities was glaring. During the Danish period, generally only churches were built, many of them small and mean. We had been cut off from higher levels of cultural life for 400 years, and had to make do with the music, art, poetry and wisdom that the people itself created. The absence of European high culture, however, strengthened popular art and made us self-sufficient in terms of spiritual nourishment. We were seen as an uncouth peasantry living in a country where it was believed that no one could live. Foreigners turned their noses up at us, literally speaking, although they were surprised at the proud and well-fed Norwegian farmers. Christiania was a small, muddy town devoid of pavements.

Many Norwegians, however, had studied in Copenhagen, and in the Norwegian Society in Copenhagen, a Norwegian intellectual and artistic elite was already established and eager to get to work. Most people had survived the 'Four Hundred Years' Night' without harm to body or soul. Living conditions and the climate had given us a sense of solidarity, and made us rational and stubborn.

In most countries 'peasant', like 'popular', has derogatory connotations. Here, the opposite is the case. We avoided feudalism, and the people were always heard. In 1814 few people lived in towns, or even in villages. We were widely dispersed, living wherever we could find subsistence. We were forced to be self-supporting. In the rest of Europe, most people lived in towns or villages, and thus people became specialized early. Here, every family had to fend for itself. They had to make their own shoes, tools and clothes, weave, card and spin, brew beer, be blacksmiths and carpenters, turn their hand to anything. In short, they simply had to trust to their own skills and creativity in practically everything.

They also had to create their own aesthetics, compose and play their own music, do their own decorative carvings, build their own houses, pass on traditions to their successors and settle disputes – as well as collect wisdom in exquisite proverbs and legends.

The Old Norwegian word *idrott* (sports) encompassed proficiency in both sports and the art of literary creation. This is how it had been for the Fairhair family, and this is how it was for their descendants. Body and soul had to work in harmony. The Viking ship is, in a way, the symbol of the Norwegian, a fusion of aesthetics and functionality which we still admire today.

The thousand years that passed, from the time that we were visible to others and became a people, until 1814, when we became a modern nation, show a remarkable continuity. Living conditions were the same for most people, key words being self-sufficiency and independence. The able commanded respect; there was no place for the pretentious. The skilled fisherman and hunter, farmer and musician was the ideal, as was the brave warrior – but he had to be modest in speaking of his wounds.

In retrospect we have idealized the Old Norse period and been ashamed of the Danish period and the 'Four Hundred Years' Night'. This is a gross simplification. It is blind nationalism. It is un-Norwegian.

The 17th of May, however, *is* Norwegian – with jubilant children in the forefront.

**january** fin serck-hanssen **february** rolf m. aagaard
**march** herdis maria siegert **april** janne solgaard
**may** jens hauge **june** vibeke tandberg
**july** dag alveng **august** rune johansen
**september** knut bry **october** asle svarverud
**november** ingvar moi **december** per berntsen

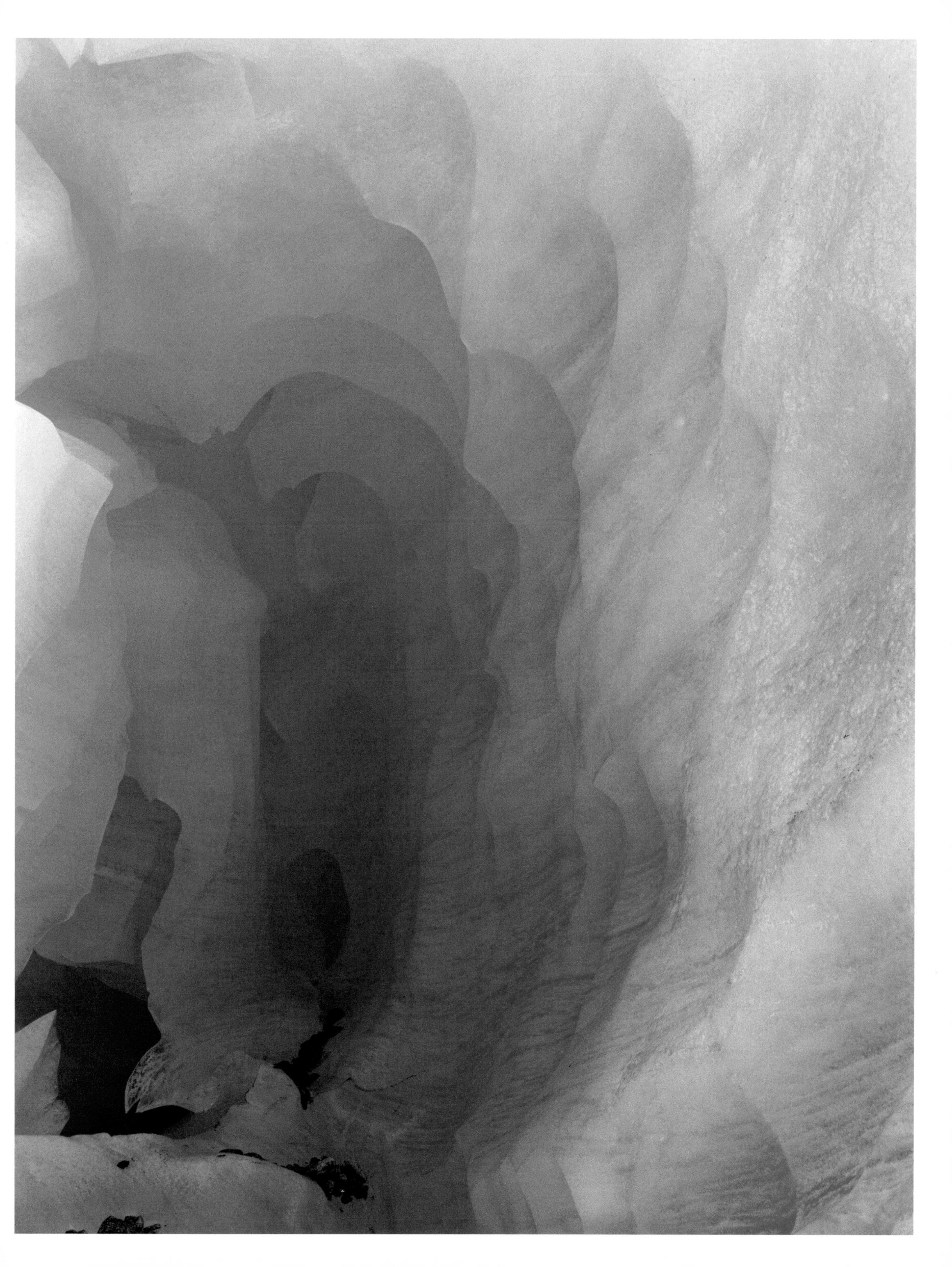

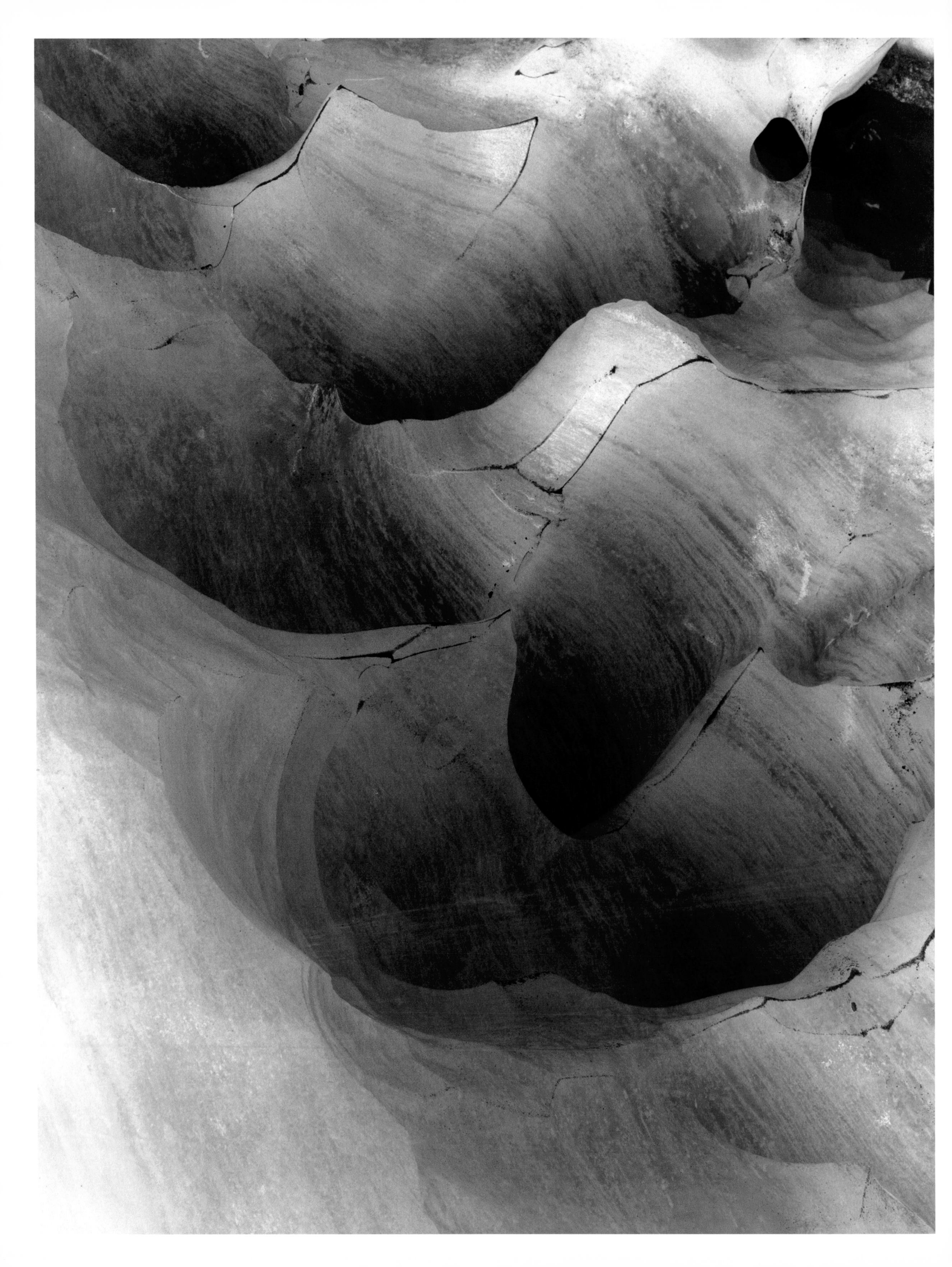

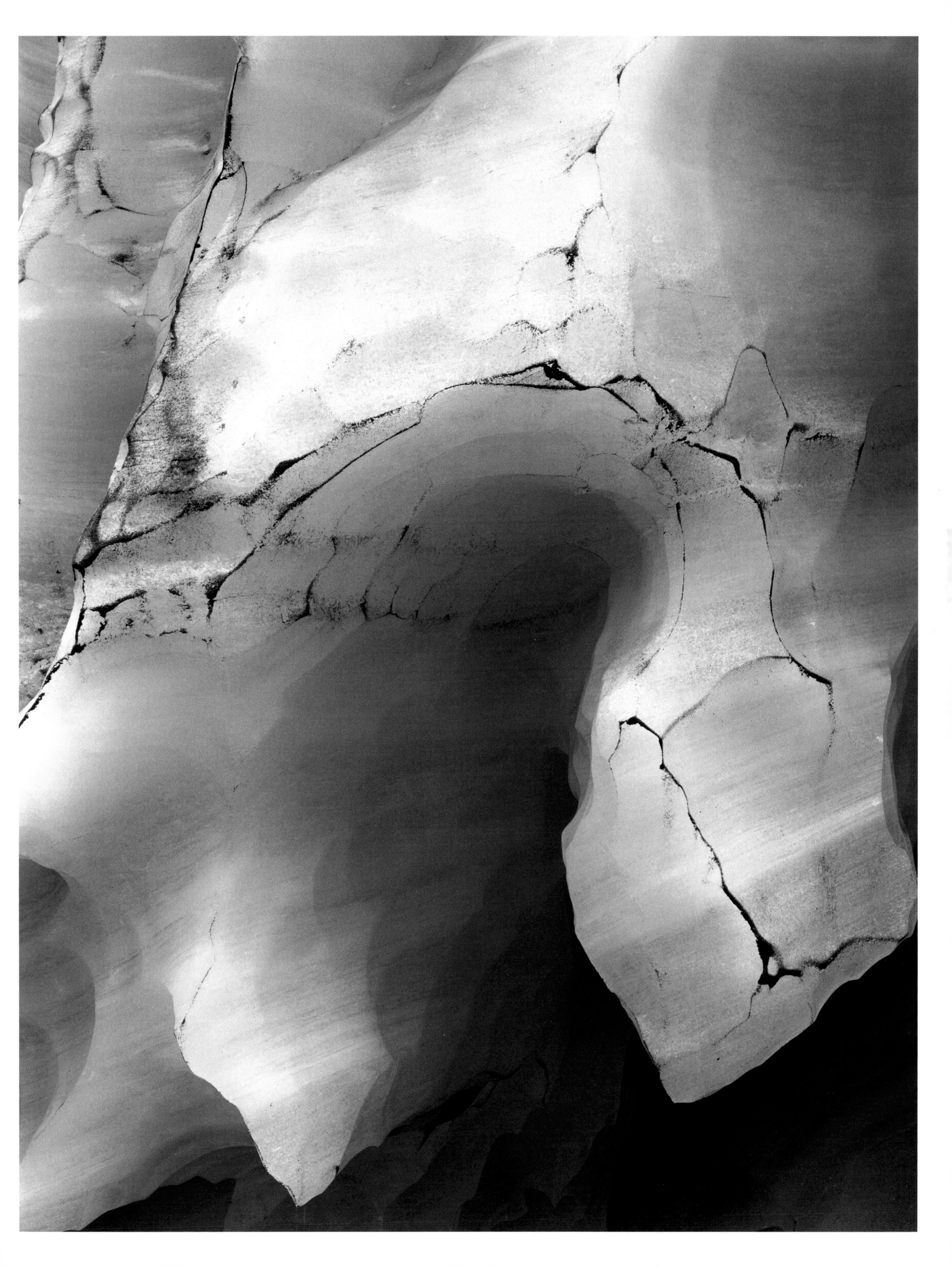

*Under Vor Haand og Rigets Segl*
*Givet paa Eidsvold, d. 19de Maj 1814*

*Christian Frederik*

# THE MEN OF EIDSVOLL

'We were intoxicated,' declared sober-minded District Governor Blom some years later. By that he meant elated, and no doubt he was correct. In Kiel on 14 January 1814 Denmark had been forced to cede Norway to Sweden. The Danes had supported Napoleon, who had lost the war that had recently raged in Europe, and this was the retribution exacted. The choice was between relinquishing Norway and accepting occupation of their own country. With the understanding of Great Britain, Russia and Prussia, King Charles XIV John of Sweden [Carl Johan (Swedish), Karl Johan (Norwegian)] was awarded Norway in gratitude for his support in the hostilities. The reason the Swedish takeover was not immediately implemented was that Karl Johan and his troops were fully occupied in expelling Napoleon from France. In the vacuum thus created, 27-year-old Danish Prince Christian Frederik saw an opportunity to seize Norway for himself, and to this end, in 1813, disguised as a sailor, he had himself set ashore there from an open boat. The following year he summoned a constituent assembly of 112 select representatives to his friend Carsten Anker's estate at Eidsvoll. Anker himself set off for England with the intention of mollifying the authorities there, only to be thrown into a debtors' gaol immediately on arrival.

It was an absurd situation altogether. While a few hundred thousand allied soldiers were entering Paris to put an end to the strife, 112 bewildered Norwegians made their way to the small town of Eidsvoll to stage their own French-style revolution in a country that now formally belonged to the victorious Swedish throne. Opposing the Eidsvoll delegates were the massed armies of Europe. There was no hope of a successful outcome, but they had to try nonetheless. They were like naughty boys running away from home in a moment of spring madness

PORTRAIT

Christian Frederik had made sure that 57 of those present were government officials, as it was in this circle that his popularity was greatest; the remainder were farmers and tradesmen. The assembly had a lot to agree upon in a very short time, and Norwegians were later to joke that it was a good thing none of the delegates from the north got there in time [the implication being that they would never have stopped talking]. In the event, many of the other delegates only just made it. The spring thaw had set in, and when they finally reached Eidsvoll not a few looked as though they had been in a mud bath. The scenario was prophetic of today's Big Brother TV programmes, with 112 people, mostly complete strangers to each other, crowded together in an out-of-the-way building. They were charged with the task of formulating a constitution with the greatest despatch – and no holds were barred. Many of them began the day with a beer and schnapps, or a glass of port. Malicious rumours were set on foot about some delegates, while others were charged with spying and treachery; Wergeland, a man of the cloth, was even accused of corruption. At the end of April District Governor Blom claimed that the assembly was made up in equal parts of madmen, wretched vermin and victims of calumny.

In actual fact, it quickly split into two irreconcilable factions. The majority, led by Falsen, Sverdrup, Motzfeldt and Christie, saw themselves as patriots and were all for independence. The minority looked upon themselves as realists and wished to make the best of the union with Sweden. Among the latter group were such well-known personalities as Wedel, Wergeland, Aall and Anker. Ominously, the first bone of contention was a picture of a reclining Venus that hung on the wall of the main hall. This gravely offended the delegates from the deeply religious western part of the country, who demanded that the abomination be removed; and removed it was. The room was decorated with branches of spruce instead, making District Governor Blom feel that he was attending a funeral.

The campaigners for freedom had been gathered at Eidsvoll for only four days when, with an overwhelming majority and a minimum of discussion, they resolved to deny Jews entry to the kingdom on a permanent basis. The decision was justified by the clergymen present on the grounds that 'Jews would corrupt the common people'. Wedel, Midelfart and Christie were among the few who vehemently protested. Greater dissension was occasioned by such issues as conscription, the nobility, voting rights and finance. The wisdom of holding the debate on financial matters on Friday the 13th may be questioned. In any case, it ended in an altercation the like of which had rarely been seen in such circumstances. In his journal one delegate reports that 'they babbled away as though at a country wedding', adding the revealing comment that 'order broke down'.

Generally speaking, the delegates had one thing in common, and that was that they had little experience of law-making and government. The most able person there was Norway's only feudal overlord, Count Wedel, but very few of those present were interested in listening to what a count had to say. It may safely be said that there was great antipathy towards the nobility. Chief Magistrate Falsen endeared himself to all present by renouncing his title, though it came as a surprise to many to learn that he possessed one. Falsen and Adler had, at least, had the foresight to prepare a draft constitution. However, this was considerably less democratic than most of the delegates had envisioned. It was finally agreed to award the vote to 45 per cent of men over the age of 25. What is interesting in this respect is that the youngest of the Eidsvoll delegates, Thomas Konow, was 18 at the time, and 12 of those present were under 30. The assembly went on to decide that the illicit distilling of liquor would result in forfeiture of voting rights – a decision that immediately prompted Chief Magistrate Koren to despatch a written warning to everyone back home!

Well aware that the French-born Karl Johan was a Roman Catholic, the constitutional assembly determined that the king of Norway should be Lutheran. Applying the same logic, they also resolved that he should reside in Norway. All manner of obstacles were put in the way of Prince Pontecorvo, as the delegates delighted in calling Karl Johan. When, early in May, Napoleon was exiled to Elba, Christian Frederik's hope that Karl Johan would suffer a similar fall from grace was dashed. Blom clung to the hope that Karl Johan would find Scandinavia too cold a place in which to live – and it really was cold that spring; the lakes near Eidsvoll were still frozen in mid-May. The count developed arthritis and Jacob Aall was confined to his bed by a bout of diarrhoea; even Sverdrup was incapacitated. Captain Motzfeld was in a far better state of health, but he had, after all, once been a prisoner of the British.

The fact is that many of the delegates were homesick. Chamberlain Løvenskiold was later to refer to the time he spent at Eidsvoll as 'the most miserable six weeks of my life' – and that was not merely because he had had to sleep on a bed of straw in the attic. Løvenskiold was so controversial a figure that Superintendent of Mines Steenstrup threatened to box his ears – and that on 17 May, Constitution Day! On 16 May Jacob Aall toyed with the idea of leaving the country altogether, it having in his opinion lost both its freedom and independence. To his wife he wrote: 'I wish to leave this hell as soon as I am able.' Johan Collett complained to his wife about the wretched bedding and that he 'had nothing to drink but a mixture of whey and water'. Wergeland, for his part, noted that the wine was as unpalatable as the times, though between them the delegates managed to down as many as one hundred bottles of wine at dinner. No one asked why the men of Eidsvoll drank so much, but it seems reasonable to suppose that they were very much on edge with the knowledge that Karl Johan and his forces were heading north.

Peder Anker proposed that choice of a king should be delayed until someone had recognized Norway as an independent nation, but his words fell on deaf ears. The constitution was signed by the delegates on 17 May, which ever since has been celebrated as Norway's national day. At the same time, by an overwhelming majority Christian Frederik was appointed Norway's first king for over four hundred years. Afterwards, Commander Fabritius got all the delegates to link arms in the courtyard, where they swore to remain united and true '*til Dovre faller*', that is, 'until the Dovre mountains collapse'. Something approaching such a cataclysm occurred the very next day, when both Russia and Prussia signalled their willingness to support a conquest of Norway.

Karl Johan returned to Sweden in the summer with a large, well-trained force, and in late July proceeded to attack Norway. Christian Frederik knew little or nothing of military strategy and allowed himself to be surrounded in Moss, whereupon he abdicated and in October returned to Denmark. Remarkably, with the battle lost Sweden still allowed Norway to retain its newly framed Constitution largely unchanged. After all, Karl Johan could always have used it as a spill to light a fire. But Jean-Baptiste Jules Bernadotte, to use his real name, had no desire to be less magnanimous than Napoleon had been. He had, in fact, begun his career as one of the Emperor's most prominent generals. The result was that Norway found itself with one of the most liberal and democratic constitutions in the world, which is why, every year on 17 May, thousands of flag-waving children parade along the capital's main thoroughfare, Karl Johans gate, to the Royal Palace.

NIELS CHR. GEELMUYDEN

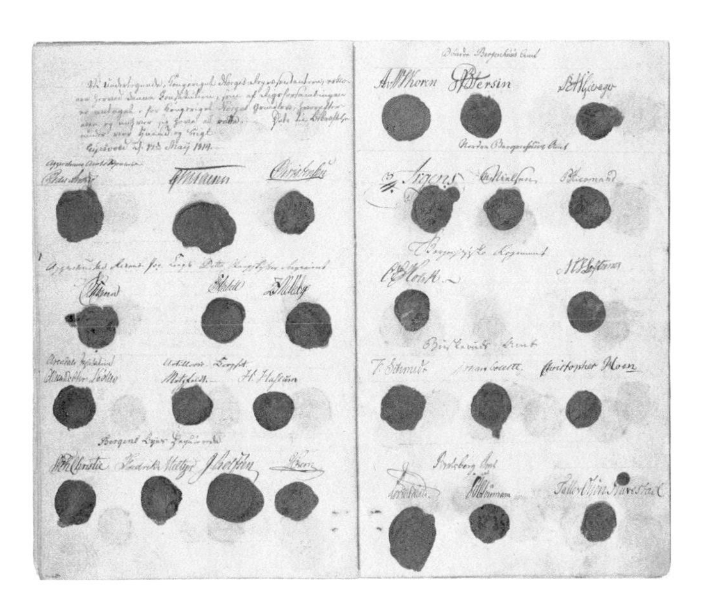

THE NATIONAL ASSEMBLY AT EIDSVOLL, the first Norwegian legislature, convened at Eidsvoll from 11 April to 19 May 1814. It comprised 112 representatives drawn from the ranks of townsmen, farmers, public and government officials, the army and the navy, selected by indirect vote. The National Assembly appointed a constitutional committee to draw up a draft constitution. Nineteen drafts were submitted and entered in the minutes. The Constitution would finally consist of 110 articles. It was based on a draft drawn up by a teacher, J.G. Adler, and a chief magistrate, C.M. Falsen.

# THE NORWEGIAN PEOPLE

# A PEOPLE APART

Marit Anne Hauan

In the north-Norwegian chieftain Ottar's account to King Alfred of England around the year 880, he described the land stretching from his home at Hålogaland in central Troms to Kaupang in the south as the land of the Northmen. When he sailed southward along the coast, he had *Norweg* to port all the time. In a French chronicle from *c.* 900 the designations *Northwegia* and *Norwegia* are used. It has been questioned whether *Norweg* was simply the name of the shipping lane or also included the inhabited hinterland. Whatever the truth of the matter, the area was important to the people referred to in Ottar's account as Northmen. According to him, other peoples, among them the Finlanders, Kvens and Biarmians, lived further to the north. In other words, by the end of the 800s the concept of a geographical region belonging to the Northmen already existed, an area that differed from the territories of other peoples. The lands within this area were controlled by a variety of rulers, but the inhabitants nonetheless viewed themselves as belonging to a distinct ethnic group, and were regarded by others as doing so. This suggests that a Norwegian territorial identity may have existed for more than a thousand years.

It is important to remember, however, that neither current national boundaries nor our modern concept of a nation existed at that time. What Norwegians of today may have in common with the Northmen of that time is, perhaps, most of all the ability to associate identity with geography, to feel a sense of community with people living inside the same boundaries.

**'Far, far away** he saw something shine and sparkle.' Painting by Theodor Kittelsen, c. 1900.

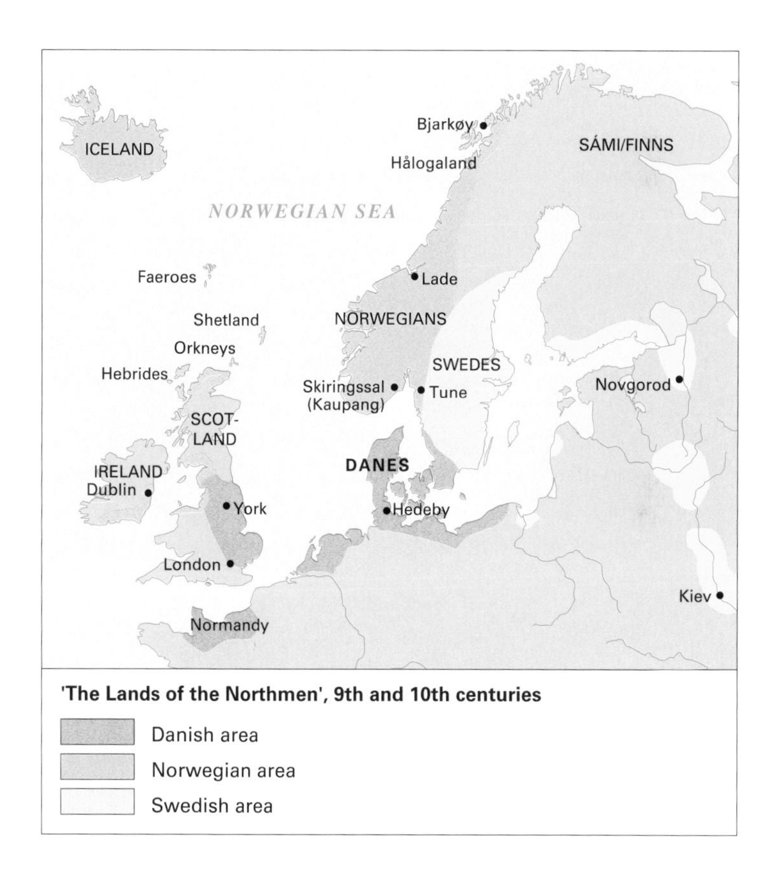


**'The Lands of the Northmen', 9th and 10th centuries**

The feeling of being Norwegian is not a conscious, permanent and explicit experience or condition. Our sense of being Norwegian is passive, but is activated by special events such as football matches and world skiing championships, and during discussions and referendums concerning EU membership. And it is probably strongest when we celebrate Constitution Day, our national festival.

**We are a nation too ...**

Once a year the abstract concept of Norway is transformed into lived and living reality. The celebration of Constitution Day, 17 May, commemorates that day in 1814, when an assembly of 112 Norwegian men gathered at Eidsvoll, and framed and signed a separate constitution for Norway.

Today's 17th of May overflows with national symbols. All over the country, wreaths are laid at selected memorials, there are children's parades, accompanied by marching bands and much jubilation, as well as citizens' parades. Participation in such parades, cheering in honour of the day, the Constitution and the country, engenders a feeling of community and a sense of being Norwegian. Speakers at monuments and statues throughout the country talk of peace, independence, freedom and wealth.

Neighbouring countries regard this special celebration with a mixture of admiration and wonder. In their finest national costumes and newly acquired Sunday best, Norwegians of all ages flock to the streets and squares to celebrate together. The 17th of May is a time of festivity and joy, ice cream and pop, hot dogs and balloons. The celebration may perhaps be seen as an expression of national complacency, but it involves only a mild form of nationalism. It embraces our 'new countrymen' and visitors, and is important in cultivating ideals of peace and freedom. Norway's Constitution Day is entirely devoid of military parades and other forms of pomp and ceremony. It is a day for the children, the people and freedom; it has nothing to do with political or military strength power, only happiness, the joy of spring, national identity and a sense of community.

**Nationalization of Norwegians**

Community feeling is not something we are born with, it is something inculcated in us. We are nationalized, and our national identity is part of a cultural-political project. In this perspective it seems appropriate to ask how old the Norwegian nation and the Norwegian identity are. Some claim that the nation is more than a thousand years old; others that a nation is a very modern phenomenon, and that a group of people becomes a nation only when it has formed a state. Opinions differ, but most agree that the formation of national identity and a national consciousness are processes that are closely related to the formation of modern nation states and political, unifying institutions.

The establishment of a free constitution in 1814 introduced a process of fundamental modernization of Norwegian society. This modernization and the struggle for independence were simultaneous and parallel processes in which the desire for, and endeavours to create, a unifying Norwegian culture were the main goal. A new and independent Norway needed a culture which offered the entire population, all over the country, a recognizable and unifying way in which to be Norwegian. It was important for the young nation state to be able to demonstrate distance and difference in relation to, most notably, Swedes and Danes. Although the state of being Norwegian may be said to be continually changing, the basis of the current Norwegian way of life is found in the development of the Norwegian national culture.

But what does this feeling of community consist of, and how is it communicated? Norwegians are given a strict national upbringing. We are, in a way, enticed, cajoled, coerced and welded into a cultural community through, for example, the school system, health service, postal and telegraph services, mass media, organizational work and working life. In addition, we define our identity in dialogue with, and in relation to, others.

Much has been written in recent years about what it means to be Norwegian. In the fields of anthropology, history, philosophy, social science and especially cultural sciences such as folklore and ethnology, this subject has been aired and debated. There may seem to be a certain agreement as to which topics and fields may provide the best illustrations of what is perceived as Norwegian values and attitudes; what makes up the Norwegian way of being. And the fact that this attitude, or identity, is based on selected building blocks from *popular* culture is a special Norwegian feature. The chosen popular culture was *rural*.

**On 17 May,** television companies broadcast running commentaries on the children's parades in different parts of the country, and always from Oslo, where, from the palace balcony, the Royal Family celebrate with the people.

**The tradition** of celebrating high-school graduation has long roots in Norway. The red cap, **russelue**, was first introduced in 1905, and ever since celebrations have grown greater by the year. On 17 May they culminate in a parade, **russetog**, marked by humorous and audacious comments on current political and social issues.

Hard Rock

### To speak and write Norwegian

*Norway is more than mountains and Munch and goat cheese*
*more than Lysholmer and stave churches*
*Norway is also the Jæren-reef lightship*
*and Liv Ullmann*
*and No to the EEC*
*and even more*
*it is, for example, the country*
*where my daughter started school*
*and learned two kinds of Norwegian*
*(which went well)*
*Norway, among many other things, is the country*
*in which two conflicting languages*
*found each other in a small Danish girl*
*and did fine side by side*

– Benny Andersen: 'I know a little about Norway' (1975)

**'The language trolls** enter Kristiania.' A drawing by Olaf Gulbransson from 1885 depicting the New-Norwegian advocate Ivar Aasen behind his fellow-poets Arne Garborg and Per Sivle.

Norway is among the few countries in Europe not named after the people who have dominated the territory. In Denmark lived the Danes, in Sweden the Sveas, and in Norway lived people. Norway, apparently, is named after a shipping lane.

Also as one of very few European countries, Norway has two variants of its own language. Norwegian is not simply Norwegian. On the one hand we have the Danish-inspired *Bokmål*, on the other the dialect-inspired *Nynorsk*, or *Landsmål* as it is also called. Today, the schools teach in both languages or language variants, and the rationality of demanding a good knowledge of two national written languages is regularly subject to energetic debate. Language was a central theme in the national-romantic idea of getting to the core of what was genuinely Norwegian and was regarded, as it still is, as a nation's common and unique spirit, the foundation of its culture. Norway did not have a national written language, which is why language became a the subject of so much discord. On one side stood the poet and linguist Ivar Aasen. After researching spoken language, especially in the western part of Norway and in the mountainous areas of eastern Norway, he published two books, *Det norske Folkesprogs Gramatik* (*Grammar of the popular language of Norway*) in 1848 and *Ordbog over det norske Folkesprog* (*Dictionary of the popular language of Norway*) in 1850. In a Norway that was searching for its distinctive character, Aasen's work was largely positively received. His books were regarded as evidence that the Norwegian language had retained some similarities with the Norse language of the sagas, and the connection between Norwegians and the Vikings was consolidated. Aasen may be said to have reconstructed a special standard for written Norwegian based on a selection of Norwegian dialects. He received a grant and gained a position which may give the impression that he was regarded as an antiquary for the Norwegian language. But his ambitions were greater: he shared with such cultural celebrities as Aasmund Olavsson Vinje the idea that a distinct language was a condition for becoming an independent nation.

On the other side of the conflict stood Knud Knudsen, also a farmer's son. His project was the Norwegianization of the Danish-Norwegian written language. What he sought as the basis for a new Norwegian language, was the 'nationally spoken Norwegian', or the 'general pronunciation of the words as spoken by persons of culture'. In 1856, Knudsen published a handbook in Danish-Norwegian language instruction, and in 1881 the dictionary Unorsk og norsk eller Fremmedords Avløsing (*Non-Norwegian and Norwegian, or the replacement of words of foreign origin*).

Whereas Aasen based himself on the countryside and set

out to restore the Norwegian language, Knudsen stuck to the 'spoken language of persons of culture', mainly in Kristiania, and was simply Norwegianizing written Danish. In addition to these two views, many people believed that by retaining the Danish language one would keep a close contact with modern Denmark, and thus with Europe. The language dispute continued and led to many humorous comments from our neighbours. Norwegians can speak seven languages, it was said, 'of which six are Norwegian.' When asked in 1919 how far the revolution had progressed in Norway, Ragnvald Blix offered the following answer in a cartoon: 'So far, we are fighting about how to spell it.'

The reason the language dispute assumed such importance was, not least, the need to create a political independence from Sweden and a cultural distance to Denmark. And the dispute did not end when, in 1885, the Storting determined that the two languages were to be accorded equal footing in the school system, thus giving *Landsmål* an official position. Later, an active, though unsuccessful, attempt was made to merge the two languages into *Samnorsk* (Pan-Norwegian). *Samnorsk* was intended to unite town and countryside, past and present. This turned out to be impossible.

The language controversy has been rekindled at regular intervals, disagreement arising over everything from spelling to inflection, orthography and everyday language. More often than in most other European countries, language has constituted part of the general political debate. What has perhaps been the most interesting aspect, however, is that the dispute has also resulted in greater linguistic diversity. Whereas in the beginning, the conflict centred on consolidation of a linguistic and cultural distinctiveness, it has also paved the way for the dialects and for an awareness of the numerous local variants of the spoken language, and of the relationship between language and identity on a local level. In this way, the diversity of Norwegian dialects has cemented their positions as the natural spoken language in all contexts.

Benny Andersen ends his poem about Norway in the following way:

*Many Norwegians don't know this*
*(and now she lives in Sweden)*
*but this is part of what I know about Norway*
*and gradually I shall learn more*
*for a country like that must be inexhaustible.*

In Andersen's interpretation, the Norwegian language dispute thus emerges as the national enrichment it probably is.

### Askeladden

In the western world, the oral tradition, folklore, is generally understood as being central to the development of national cultures. This story-telling tradition was regarded as a remnant of a glorious past that has survived in the hearts of the people because the peasant culture was so stable and unchangeable. In Norway, too, folklore was sought and found among the people. Through their choices of genre and collection areas – Ringerike, Telemark and Valdres – and their processing of the material, researchers in the 1800s refined a project which can be understood as an attempt to create Norwegian tradition and culture. Therefore, age was an important criterion; it would not be a disadvantage if the stories originated in the Middle Ages, but they also had to be beautiful and possess a certain exotic character.

The oral story-telling tradition that was chosen and regarded as especially powerful nationally, focused on poetic genres: folk tales, legends and ballads. These made great demands on the storytellers in regard to both memory and performance.

Peter Chr. Asbjørnsen (1812–85) and Jørgen Moe (1813–82), who were our first folklore collectors and researchers,

**Legends of origin** have a special task – to explain names and phenomena occurring in nature. The hole in **Torghatten** was reputedly made by a troll's arrow, and the name **Riddarspranget** (Knight's Leap) comes from the story of a horseman who abducted a beautiful woman and, when hotly pursued by another lovesick horseman, leaped over this gorge with the maiden in his arms.

**During the 19th century** the national-romantic wave also made its impact felt on pictorial art. This painting, 'Bridal Journey in Hardanger', by Tidemand and Gude (1848) is a national icon.

found proof of 'the local character of our folk tales' and compiled a set of 'Norwegian criteria' based on the contents of the tales. We share our storytelling tradition with the rest of Europe and large parts of the western world. What makes it Norwegian is primarily that it is adapted to our topography and nature, and furthermore that national, historic characters are included in the legends and ballads, and finally, that typically Norwegian storytelling styles can be recognized. Moe found a Norwegian characteristic in the connection between the sagas and folk tales, that is, the stories were told objectively and using masculine expressions.

Asbjørnsen and Moe printed the folk tales in the spirit of the people, using the Danish written language with a lot of Norwegian words to ensure broad popular acceptance of the books. According to the folklorist Ørnulf Hodne, 'few books have been read by and for more Norwegians than these collections of legends and folk tales'. In 1940, the author Sigurd Hoel wrote of Asbjørnsen and Moe's collections of folk tales:

*This is the Norwegian literary work of the last hundred years that has been of the most versatile and greatest overall importance, – to Norwegian literature and research, Norwegian national identity and self-awareness, yes, even to Norwegian everyday life.*

In what way, then, did the folk tales affect the day-to-day life of Norwegians? The compilation and publication of the oral tradition had a unifying effect on all social classes and circles in the country. Folklore provided an opportunity to experience a common Norwegian identity. Another significant factor is that in relation to both language and folklore, neither the sources nor the people were accidental. The peasant was chosen as the national reference.

The folk-tale tradition affords us an insight into the attitudes and norms of society. In this tradition, good deeds, but also undreamed-of possibilities, are themes, and the plain and simple is held up as an important quality. Legends, too, constitute a rich epic genre, but as opposed to the folk tale, the legend is presented as a true story in which place, time and, often, names convince the listener of its veracity.

The folk tales are a source of insight into the culture and society of the people. The storytelling tradition is direct and palpable. Qualities such as strength, courage, kindness and evil stand out clearly. To Jørgen Moe, Askeladden, the 'Cinder Lad', our most famous folk-tale character, was one who had a clear perception of his own power, and who would never let himself be overcome in his battles with superior forces. Besides, Askeladden was acting in keeping with the ideals of the sagas – 'he keeps silent and sleeps, asks to be allowed to try, and wins'.

The folk tale is important because it contains dreams and longings, opens up for incredible possibilities and presents the fantastic as the ordinary and *vice-versa*. It is wishful literature where good deeds are always handsomely rewarded. And Askeladden inspires dreams and wishful thinking. On the one hand, by attending to the fire and raking the ashes he has the lowest social status, but at the same time he actually controls the fire, which symbolizes the fountain of life. In the person of Askeladden, what is simple and inferior proves to be noble and valuable, dynamic and industrious. In Norway, a man who achieves something special, and who may be said to have created wealth starting with two empty hands, is often spoken of as a new Askeladd. The most recent example is perhaps the innovator and industrialist Kjell Inge Røkke.

**Those who go out, never pout**

We shall never know if our forefathers were out of their minds, but at least we know that they were out of doors, following as they did herds of wild reindeer from the German plains to the glaciers of Scandinavia more than 10,000 years ago. So maybe it is a matter of genetics. Be that as it may, the Norwegians are said to be the only people in the world who voluntarily go out walking, no matter what the weather.

**That skiing** originated from Sondre Norheim's lodge at Morgedal, Telemark, is a Norwegian truth, and the fictional Trysil Knut, who ski-jumped so brilliantly over people and houses, is regarded as a real, historical person and has become a symbol of the Norwegian people's natural aptitude for skiing.

Nature seems to be especially attractive to the Norwegian spirit: it provides primitive and simple pleasures, and mastery of the inherent qualities of the wilds – a challenging topography and rough climate for all, regardless of social status and gender. It is hardly surprising that people who live surrounded by so much nature, and who until recently earned their living from it, should have developed a close and very active relationship with it. And more than anything we use it to go walking and rambling – as well as skiing. To the dedicated, winter means skiing trips, the highlight of the season being the Easter trips, preferably undertaken from one's own holiday cabin. There are some 369,000 such cabins in Norway today, and over 40 per cent of the population claim to have access to one.

As early as the 1800s, winter and winter sports became part of the nationalistic project, which was reinforced and realized all through the century, later to give legitimacy to the Norwegians' persistent self-image as masters of the winter. The significance of skiing as a national symbol and basis of identification is due to its widespread popularity. The Norwegians practise their Norwegianness on their skis throughout the winter season and throughout their lives. With skis on their feet, the national identity is made physical.

Skis were seen as a Norwegian appliance, the proof being found in both rock-carvings and historical works, as well as in lyrical descriptions of the joys of skiing. At the national assembly at Eidsvoll it was proposed to legislate for eight days of training in gymnastics, shooting and military exercises 'on skis' as a 'national upbringing' for the nation's young men. Thus skis became an instrument in the service of the nation – young Norwegian men should be able to defend their country on skis.

The reasons why the sport of skiing assumed such a prominent national role are many, a significant one being its popularity in all social classes. From the 1860s, skiing events became increasingly common, and the sport became truly fashionable. Skiing became one of the chosen expressions of Norwegian culture, and in the 1890s found its place as Norway's national sport. Nansen's expedition on skis across Greenland in 1888 and his North Pole expedition with Hjalmar Johansen in 1895 were regarded as proof that skiing and winter activities were a field in which Norwegians displayed a special aptitude.

'The Norwegian people live and die on skis, and should a war break out between Norway and Sweden, the Norwegians will beat us back on skis,' wrote the Swedish poet Gustav Fröding in 1895. Fröding points to a serious theme of Norwegian culture, that is, the idea that Norwegians are born with skis on the feet.

Norwegians have an ongoing ability and willingness to appreciate athletes on snow and ice. The most highly rated of winter sports are cross-country skiing and ski jumping, closely followed by Nordic combined, the biathlon, and the rather dubious alpine disciplines, while freestyle and snowboard have recently become rebel variants of accepted sports. In January 2004, Tromsø launched itself as a candidate for the 2014 Olympic Winter Games, promising a spectacular winter show that would unite the entire nation. Norway has hosted the Olympic Winter Games twice before, and both events strengthened the national idea of Norway as a winter nation.

The 1952 Winter Olympics in Oslo were faithful to the national values. The Olympic flame was brought from Morgedal, Fridtjof Nansen's grandson carried the torch on its final leg, and more than half a million Norwegians turned out to watch the games. The fact that Norway emerged as the best nation cemented its position as a winter nation. The sports and organizational success of the 1994 Olympic Winter Games at Lillehammer provided further proof that the national self-image was rooted in reality.

Of course, other sports too are important in a national context, but although Petter Solberg became world rally-cross champion and was voted Norway's number one athlete in 2003, he is unlikely to achieve a position on a par with that of ski jumper Bjørn Wirkola and Nordic skier Oddvar Brå. Bjørn Wirkola was active in the 1960s, winning the Austro-German ski-jumping week three years in succession, from 1966 to 1969.

In addition, he won the world championships in 1966, in both the big and small hills. Since then, to say that something is 'like jumping after Wirkola' has become synonymous with saying that it is great challenge. Another expression Norwegians immediately understand is the question 'Where were you when Brå broke his ski pole?' Nordic skier Oddvar Brå broke his pole in the relay race in the 1982 World Championships, but nonetheless the Norwegians ended up sharing the gold medal with the Soviet team. Even if they have never watched a ski race in their lives, most Norwegians can answer the question.

When we put our skis away for the summer, we climb mountains and go for rambles in field and forest. Modern outdoor life has its origin in the peasant population's daily life. They fished, picked berries and tended livestock in the woods and mountains. At the beginning of the 1800s, wealthy city people discovered the pleasures of outdoor life, and it gradually became common to rent rooms at a hotel or farm near a suitable mountain. When the railway network was extended across mountain areas, for example the Valdres line in 1906 and the Bergen line in 1909, getting to the mountains from the capital and other towns in southern Norway became easier. The locals acted as coachmen and cooks, observing the town dwellers' new activities with wonder at the same time as providing an interesting backdrop themselves for the visitors. Not until after the Second World War did their financial situation enable the working class to follow suit. The Norwegian Mountain Touring Association was established in 1868, probably the first of its kind in the world. The association has played an important role, marking hiking trails and building lodges in the mountains. The special Norwegian *allemannsretten*, the right of public access, means that everybody can enjoy nature, though the legislation also enjoins everyone to take due care of it.

### The Norwegian polar people?

Nansen's skiing expedition across Greenland became a symbol of Norway as a polar nation. Through its fight for territorial rights to Svalbard and eastern Greenland, political Norway profiled itself as a polar nation. Norway was awarded sovereignty over Svalbard in the peace negotiations that followed the First World War, and the archipelago has been under Norwegian jurisdiction since 1925. In the case of Greenland, however, the result was less favourable for Norway: Denmark won the dispute over sovereignty in the Hague Court in 1933, and Norwegian polar ocean imperialism suffered a major setback. Nevertheless, in 1939, Queen Maud's Land near the South Pole was declared a Norwegian territory. Already in 1928, Bouvet Island had been placed under Norway's jurisdiction, and in 1931 Peter I Island followed. Interest in the polar areas was part of the national project, and Norwegian polar imperialism may be seen as one aspect of the struggle for national independence. The Norwegian desire for expansion centered on geographical areas that triggered our national talents – mastery of snow and cold. Polar expansion was also explained by our Viking nature: mastering the winter and an adventurous turn of mind were simply national qualities.

The qualities and values emphasized through sports, and especially winter sports, are parallel with the values found in the Norwegian polar stories: physical strength, endurance, a competitive instinct and boldness. Through Fridtjof Nansen and, later, Roald Amundsen and their men, Norway presented a picture of a nation ideally suited for polar deeds and research. Norwegian-Pakistani stand-up comedienne Shabana Rehman called her 2002 show 'Shabana crosses Greenland on skis'. She made a journey, a cultural collision, across the two Greenlands – the part of inner Oslo called Grønland (Greenland), known for its multicultural population, and the island of Greenland itself. This provided her with an excellent basis for comments and ironical remarks directed at Norwegians and immigrants alike, while showing that she also possessed the national skills of a true Norwegian.

However, the polar regions are not popular destinations for Norwegians. They rather represent a domestic story of traditional qualities and values. In 2002, Svalbard was visited by 46,400 people, many of them international cruise tourists. The Norwegians themselves prefer to travel south, their favoured goal being Spain. 90,000 Norwegians own second homes abroad, many of them on the Spanish coast or in the Canary Islands. In a way, Norwegians keep alive the idea of themselves as a nation of travellers. A connection can be made between the Vikings via the seafarers in the 1700s and the expeditions of the polar heroes and today's travellers, but the differences are greater than the similarities. When we conquer the world now, we do so in large, noisy groups which gather in national ghettos in warm, pleasant places with low food and alcohol prices. An occasional forgotten Norwegian polar hero or heroine may still make their way across the Arctic and Antarctic, but the rest of us prefer to traverse Spanish marketplaces en route to our favourite café.

**The annual** Constitution Day celebration (17 May) is a colourful multicultural parade.

**To dress the Norwegian way**

The formation of a Norwegian identity also concerns clothes. Round about 1900, the intellectual élite saw its main goal as giving the population of this long and narrow country a common national identity, and aimed to revitalize rustic culture. The national identity was to be based on the rural past, on peasant culture and on history. As an element in this national culture and identity scheme, the *bunad,* or national costume, assumed importance.

Hulda Garborg (1862–1934) has been called the mother of the bunad in Norway. However, even before her entry into this arena, a lively debate on national costumes took place in youth societies. The debate concerned, for example, which costumes should be used for festivities and which for everyday use. To Hulda Garborg the costumes belonged with folk dance. She claimed that in the Nordic countries, people used to dance to folk songs, and that this fascinating and beautiful tradition had been forgotten. She herself went on a field trip to the Faeroe Islands and came back with adapted and simplified 'Norwegian' versions, which became popular with the young farmers' societies. Her own dance group had its first performance in 1900, a gathering at which her husband, the author Arne Garborg, first spoke about Nordic folksong dancing. Folksong dancing was presented as a national and Nordic tradition. In the words of the art historian Astrid Oxaal, 'the bunad which came in symbiosis with the dance' had something national, almost sacral, about it.

At the same time as old folk costumes experienced a renaissance through Hulda Garborg's project, new costumes were being designed. Hulda Garborg was not afraid to simplify and change the costumes, claiming that 'many of the best costumes were so unpractical and unsuitable for present-day use, that they would soon be completely forgotten if one did not modify them a little'. She herself designed the Hulda Garborg costume, which was a simpler and more modern version of the Gol costume, made a little lighter and more elegant, but based on traditional elements. It was the rich colours, the embroidery, the materials and the artistic expression that were important to pass on as a Norwegian cultural heritage. The fact that the festive bunads so rapidly became part of the visible Norwegian culture is ascribed to Hulda Garborg's ability to communicate with everybody from the youth movement to the new Norwegian bourgeoisie. Together with the folksong dance, the epic poem and the language, the festive bunad was chosen as a symbol of Norwegian culture, and for this reason has performed a special function in the national community. It became as much a symbol of a chosen past as a manifestation of modern Norway. Through the bunads, one could present oneself as a Norwegian and look like one.

The bunad has proved viable. The two rounds of EEC/EU struggle and referenda have not least been identified as periods that revitalized the use of bunads. It is when one feels that the

**Hulda Garborg** dressed in her own 'bunad', based on traditional costumes from Gol, Hallingdal

national is threatened, that one clearly stands up for one's native country and national values. One literally dresses Norwegian.

Bunads have been, and still are, important in Norway, and special ideas of genuineness and authenticity have developed in regard to the Norwegian folk costume. In 1947, a National Council for Folk Costumes, which approved costumes right up until the end of 1967, was established. From 1967 to 1977, the Council's task was to recommend or decline to recommend designs submitted to it. It was jocularly, but not unjustly, dubbed the 'bunad police'. When businessmen with immigrant backgrounds launched the idea of having the bunads made in low-cost countries to bring down their price and make them more accessible, the 'police' were outraged; they wanted not only to keep the costumes, but also to make sure that they were made on Norwegian soil by Norwegian labour.

Today, there are some 200 different bunads in the country, and about 400 festive costumes and bunad variants. During the last century, and especially from about 1970, regional and local bunad and folk costume milieus flourished, as the national bunads were partly regarded as loans and were ascribed other values than those of the local regions. The local variants of the bunad may be regarded as part of the dismantling of the unified and homogeneous Norway. The historian Åsa Elstad has shown that the costumes designed during this period and later, are based on regional and local elements: a wave is embroidered on the Senja dress, icebergs and Arctic flowers float along the skirt edge of the Svalbard dress, while municipal symbols such as the bluebell and eagle are used as decorative elements for Kvænangen and Karlsøy dresses, respectively. The most spectacular variant is perhaps the festive costume of Vardø, which bears the town's motto, 'Darkness must give way to light', embroidered on the back of the vest. The most recent addition to the bunad flora is probably the Kven costume. This too is made according to established bunad tradition, but it also emphasizes ethnic affiliation, and so employs light colours to demonstrate the purity of this ethnic group.

Despite apparently new elements, the actual designs of the costumes remain very similar; wool fabric is essential, and blouses are generally white. It is the decorative elements that are local. While Hulda Garborg and the cultural nationalists were preoccupied with creating a common national identity which was not to reflect social, financial or geographic differences, the bunad work of the last thirty years bears testimony to national versatility and local variation.

The Sámi costumes are not thought of as bunads but as folk costumes of a living and unbroken tradition. As for the Sea-Sámi, their costumes have been reconstructed in recent years.

Bunads and festive costumes signal local affiliation, but because they are largely made in the same way and based on the same fundamental values in regard to choice of material, design and colours, many people probably consider them much alike. Whether one dresses as a person from Vardø or Bergen, one also dresses as a Norwegian. In recent years, bunads have become increasingly popular with young people. They are favourites on festive occasions in life and in the year, and many girls are given one when they are confirmed. There are estimated to be about two million bunads, mostly women's, dispersed throughout the whole country.

### With paperclips as weapons?

Not only cultural expressions and special days have been important for the building of a national identity; such dramatic events as wars have also contributed to the Norwegians' self-image. The folklorist Anne Eriksen claims that the Second World War occupies 'a very special, near-mythical, place in Norwegian culture'. War stories and war history have been transformed into collective memories. This has made it possible for each individual to perceive such memories as his or her own, and in this way the national becomes personal and alive to those who did not experience the war. We have also been keen to mark the return of peace: Liberation Day, 8 May, is an official flag-flying day. The war is a topic which offers opportunities to thematize what is specifically Norwegian. In the collective memory, Norway is depicted as a small and peaceful country that was attacked by a powerful enemy. According to Eriksen, stories like this make it possible for us to see ourselves as a non-aggressive people, rather than as unprepared and naïve. Other war memories comprise the actual national symbols that were created.

The most important symbols in the fight against German military power and the Norwegian Nazis were King Haakon VII and Crown Prince Olav. When Germany attacked Norway, the Nazis demanded that all resistance cease and that Norway accept the German occupation. The King and the government rejected

**The red stocking cap** symbolizes that the Norwegian people are 'up from the country'. During the Second World War it was also adopted as a sign of resistance to the occupying forces. Painting by Christian Tanke Andersen Bjørnaa.

these demands, which did much to encourage the Resistance movement. On 7 June 1940, the Royal Family and the government left for London, there to continue the fight. They travelled all over to boost morale among Norwegian sailors and soldiers, and helped to keep up the spirits of the people at home through radio broadcasts.

Loyal Norwegians put a paperclip on their lapels as a token of their resistance to the occupying Germans. This simple symbol suggested a peaceable and sensible people, a people whose chief ideals were simplicity and a sober lifestyle. The red stocking cap was another symbol of resistance. The occupying forces resented the use of the cap, which was regarded as part of the resistance strategy. This was a clear victory for the Resistance movement. Like the paperclip, the cap was a national symbol and in this context functioned as a sign of national solidarity and active resistance.

The Resistance movement, *Milorg* (Military Organization) and the men of *Hjemmefronten* (the Home Front), some 40,000 strong by the end of the war, were generally referred to as *gutta på skauen*, 'the boys in the woods'. The woods in question provided a training ground and hiding place for the many covert activities carried on outdoors, and further maintained the Norwegian people's close relationship with nature as an ideal. 'Boys' was linked to the Norwegian ideal of equality: in the woods, everyone is equal.

On 7 June 1945, five years to the day after he had had to

**The artist and sculptor Gustav Vigeland** (1869–1943) designed one of Oslo's most renowned and monumental landmarks, the sculptural park that bears his name. Here, over a period of 40 years, he erected more than 200 sculptures depicting all phases of human life.

leave the country, King Haakon was again able to set foot on Norwegian soil. The rejoicing was endless when the King, the very symbol of unity in the fight for freedom and democracy, stepped ashore at Honnørbryggen (Honour Pier) in Oslo. Resistance during the war years had brought people closer together, and the comprehensive reconstruction work strengthened the community feeling. This was clearly reflected when, later the same year, all the political parties stood for election on the same political platform, the *Common Programme*.

### Ola and Kari Norwegian

A child's name is often the subject of family wrangling. However, naming does not only belong to the private sphere – here too we find notions of what is genuinely Norwegian. We refer to ourselves as Kari and Ola in all contexts where the universal Norwegian is to be described. But this is only symbolic. Our real names are much more dignified and authentic. In Norwegian naming tradition, what we refer to as hereditary Nordic names, remained popular throughout the 20th century. By Nordic hereditary names we mean names that can be traced back to Norse times. In the 1900s, over 50 per cent of all Norwegian children were given Nordic hereditary names. Boys were given names such as Arne, Asbjørn, Knut, Olav, Harald and Håkon, whereas girls were named Astrid, Gerd, Hilde, Ingrid, Liv and Ragnhild. Students of names have asserted that the stable naming tradition is evidence of the fact that the young nation was suffering from a kind of 'Norse imperialism'. Genuine Norwegian names were important and gave power and legitimacy to the young nation. Therefore, the Danish Prince Carl took the name Haakon when he became king of Norway in 1905. His son, Alexander Edward Christian Frederik, became Olav, and Olav's three children all have honourable Norse names like Ragnhild, Astrid and Harald. The most recent member of the Royal Family, who was born on 21 January 2004, has been named Ingrid Alexandra.

Thus the Crown Prince and Princess continued the popular Norwegian naming tradition. The name Ingrid originates from the Norse *Ing(f)ridr*. It is made up of the name of the god *Ing* and the designation *frid*, which means beautiful. Ingrid is a common Norwegian name and was in regular use as early as the 1300s. It gained renewed popularity in the 1880s, and peaked in 1920. From then on its popularity gradually sank until the 1970s, when it increased again. In 2003, Ingrid was the ninth most used female name.

But the birth of Ingrid did not concern naming traditions only.

### A gendered nation

A female heir to the throne, and the fifth generation of our Royal Family of 1905, was born in January 2004. When the announcement was made that a princess had been born, the leader of the Labour Party, Jens Stoltenberg, announced that this was in itself an important equal rights political measure. Interpreting a royal birth in such terms is part of the gender-political rhetoric of the country, reminding us that equal rights has long been a heated topic in Norwegian public life.

The social debate towards the end of the 1800s largely concerned women's rights. Also a number of leading men championed the women's cause, and Henrik Ibsen's and Bjørnstjerne Bjørnson's plays occasioned not a little debate. However, the demands of the Norwegian Feminist Association, established in 1884, met with resistance both inside and outside the Storting, and Norwegian women were not awarded universal suffrage until 1913.

Towards the end of the 1960s, the modern feminist movement developed in Norway. The sociologist Andreas Hompland has declared the women's parade on 8 March 1971 'the official and conscious beginning of the new and rapidly growing story of the feminized Norway'. During this period, nationwide organizations such as the Marxist-Leninist *Kvinnefronten* (Women's Front) and socialist *Brød og Roser* (Bread and Roses), as well as initiatives such as the neo-feminist magazine *Sirene*, fuelled what can be described as a liberation movement. The struggle for equal status was also fought internally in the world of research, where not only equal rights, but also the right to explicit knowledge about women and topics related to women, were claimed. Today, 120 years after women were allowed to take degrees at the university in Kristiania, all Norwegian universities have their own centre for women's research, and Norway is considered a pioneer country in terms of equal rights. Lately, however, young male researchers have indignantly been referring to Norway as a 'vaginal state', in serious irritation at what they perceive as a feminized daily life and reality.

The right to self-determined abortion was a predominant issue right up to 1978 when the Act was adopted. The abortion controversy exemplified the main doctrine of the feminist movement: it concerned the right to decide over one's own body and life. The struggle for women's rights affected not only the lives of women, but also family life, and so kindergarten availability also became a political issue. With both parents working outside the home, society in general had to become more family-friendly. The women's liberation struggle implied a criticism of the establishment and of all the institutions that kept women in their traditional role. As an alternative to conventional marriage, cohabitation appeared on the agenda. Today, this way of living together is a real alternative, and more common than marriage among couples under 30. The number of cohabiting couples more than doubled between 1990 and 2004, from 102,000 to 250,000 respectively, while during the same period, the number of married couples declined from 871,000 to 835,000. Not only cohabitation, but also the massive change from church weddings to civic marriages may be interpreted as criticism of existing patterns and traditions.

Gro Harlem Brundtland is the symbol of the liberated woman and a driving force in regard to both equal status and feminist thinking, nationally and internationally. In 1981, she became the first female Norwegian prime minister, and in 1986 emphasized her political image by appointing seven female ministers out of 17 for her second government. In addition, she placed women's rights and position on the agenda in issues concerning everything from kindergarten and maternity leave to representation on boards and councils, salary policy and environmental matters. Legislation, too, has in part become more equal. Acts relating to children, divorce and abortion give mothers special rights in regard to children. The fact that the struggle for equality became so closely interwoven with political leadership and public administration is claimed to be a particularly Norwegian feature. On the one hand, it may be ascribed to the fact that during the most active period of the women's liberation movement, the Labour Party, as governing party, underwent a political renewal based on feminism. The prime minister, Gro Harlem Brundtland, made political use of the ideals of the feminist movement at the same time as she realized these ideals, and for a long time the ideals of the women's liberation movement and the social democracy overlapped. On the other hand, it might have to do with the Norwegian ideal of equality.

### Egalitarian Norway

While, for example, Spain has 36 sites on UNESCO's list of world heritage sites, Norway has five: Urnes stave church in Sogn og Fjordane, Bryggen, the old Hanseatic wharf in Bergen, the mining town of Røros, the petroglyphs in Alta and the Vega islands in Nordland. Cathedrals are almost non-existent in Norway, apart from Nidarosdomen. What we call palaces rather resemble the manors of our neighbouring countries, and cultural monuments such as the Greek Acropolis or the Roman Colosseum are non-existent. We have fishing stations, small farms, cotters' farms, settlements and a few towns; and nature: mountains and valleys, fjords and islands. Norway may be said to appear as an enormous folk museum, because of the modest size of our buildings, our homely ways and scattered houses. We are, and have been, quite equal – no élite to speak of, and with only moderate social and cultural differences.

Equality, according to the ethnologist Brit Berggren, is a passion in Norway. On the one hand, she refers to the special Norwegian industrial adaptation, a kind of multiple pursuits or Jack-of-all-trades, where flexibility in the utilization of resources, and multiple skills, ensured a living for large sectors of the population. On the other hand, there also existed an unwillingness to acknowledge that some are better than others. The socially regulated systems of voluntary communal work groups and organized communities of which everybody within

**With its old buildings,** the mining town of Røros is an example of a living cultural heritage, combining continental ideas and old, Norwegian architectural traditions.

a defined geographical area was a member, regardless of position or class, demonstrated this concept of equality.

The principle of equality also forms the basis for the development of the modern Norwegian welfare society. It is often claimed that it is *Janteloven* (the 'Jante Law') that governs us, and that our relations are controlled by its first article: 'You shall not believe that you are somebody special.' Without wishing to deprive envy of its inherent strength, we nonetheless venture to claim that the ideals of equality are rooted in political and cultural ideologies and processes, of which envy is only one ingredient.

The social anthropologist Thomas Hylland Eriksen writes in his book *Veien til et mer eksotisk Norge* (The Road to a more exotic Norway): 'We are not used to associating with people who live and think differently from ourselves.' What this probably expresses is that the ideas of social and cultural equality and the myth of a national belonging still have a defining power, and only to a lesser degree a correct picture of Norway. The Norwegian people are spoken of as a homogeneous group, but it is not as simple as that. The doctrine behind the creation of a Norwegian national identity was about defining and defending our territory as our state, and those living within its boundaries, as a homogeneous people. To feel Norwegian and to be a Norwegian citizen should be the same thing. However, not everybody has had the same opportunity to unite the two.

Until the 1980s, the *Sámi* were practically absent from

public discourse. And to the extent that a public Sámi discourse existed at all, it concerned the reindeer-herding Sámi. Through Norwegianization, the Sea-Sámi had become invisible in the public sphere, even though they lived out their lives on the coast of northern Norway. Following harsh Norwegianization measures, the Sámi language had been silenced, to be replaced by Norwegian. Nor did any visual symbols express the special nature of the Sámi population. The reindeer-herding Sámi went about their business on the mountain plateaus, and were often a colourful and spectacular element in the tourist brochures, though they were hardly looked upon as genuinely Norwegian.

The Alta hydroelectric issue seriously put minority issues and Sámi rights on the agenda in Norway. In January 1981, approximately 600 demonstrators who had chained themselves together in protest were forcibly removed from the plateau by a large police force. The campaign against development of the Alta River had then been going on for a decade. An increasing number of people and groups had become involved, protesting against the government's decision to build a power station in the heart of the Sámi reindeer grazing lands. What started as an environmental issue gradually developed into a question of the position and rights of minorities. Photographs of police officers forcibly removing peaceful, seated demonstrators went around the world. The reindeer-herding Sámi lost their river, but won the case.

The conflict forced people with and without Sámi affiliation to re-examine their attitudes to themselves and others, and it subsequently became easier to address Sámi issues. Eight years later, in 1989, the Sámi parliament was established. Today, *Sápmi* is a nation, the Sámi are recognized as an indigenous people with their own flag, museums, college, president and their own great international successes, such as singer Mari Boine and motor-cross champion Ailo Gaup. In 2004, the Sámi national day, 6 February, became an official flag-flying day in Norway, which is seen as final recognition of the Sámi people.

The Sámi are an indigenous people, whereas the *Kvens,* who came as immigrants to the northern areas from Finland, are regarded as a national minority. The Kvens too, were practically invisible in the public debate until the 1960s. When in 1977, King Olav V, together with Sweden's King Carl XVI Gustav and Finland's President Urho Kekkonen, unveiled Ensio Seppänen's Kven monument in Vadsø, the Kven town celebrated. After having been regarded as suspect for a long time because of their relations with Finland, the Kvens now received a form of public approval.

In the book *Folk uten fortid* (People Without a Past), Peder A. Pedersen from Porsanger says: 'Historically, we have witnessed the meeting of three tribes in Porsanger, but there was never any doubt about their ranking; first Norwegians, then Kvens and then Sámi.' This categorization of the ethnic groups corresponds in essence to the more official attitudes a few generations back. In the standard work *Norges land og folk* (1906) (The Country and Peoples of Norway), undisguised racist attitudes are expressed when the Sea-Sámi are said to 'be low and degenerate', the Kvens are ascribed certain virtues, such as patience and endurance, while 'the Norwegians here in the north . . . possess all the best qualities of the Germanic race'. The contempt and stigmatization of the Sámi also struck *tatere*, *splint*, and *fanter* – all terms used variously in the past in a derogatory sense for the Romany people. They too did not have the right to consider themselves a nation. On the contrary, they were accused of stealing children and were exposed to such eugenic measures as sterilization.

The 1970s marked the beginning of a new kind of immigration to Norway, mainly from Pakistan, Turkey, Vietnam, and

**The Sámi** are active in international debates and fora on the special rights, both cultural and political, of minorities. Ole Henrik Magga was elected the first chairperson of the UN Permanent Forum on Indigenous Issues in 2002. Here with the 1992 Nobel Peace Prize winner, Rigoberta Menchú.

Morocco. Ethnic, cultural and religious Norway was thus influenced, through for example, language, skin colour, dress, religions and family structures. This immigration placed 'the exotic' in our midst. The immigrants challenge our everyday attitudes and norms simply by their presence, but we cannot yet see any significant changes in the Norwegian national self-image. In the same way that Norwegians tend to congregate abroad, the people of various immigrant cultures congregate and live parallel with the Norwegian population rather than as part of it. Especially in the 1990s, political discussions have taken place on two clearly distinct fronts; criticism of the authorities' immigration policy on the one hand, and demands for rapid integration in Norwegian language, culture and way of living on the other. Norwegian national ideals have created a persistent assimilation policy – the Norwegian political and cultural ideal still seems to be 'the more equal, the better'. Nevertheless, ethnic diversity stimulates the Norwegian debate and our way of thinking and living, and gives us another opportunity to think and act internationally. Ethnic minorities that refuse to allow themselves to be moulded by Norwegianization, in fact make Norway larger.

### A country tactfully out of step?

Peer Gynt, the legendary character who inspired one of Henrik Ibsen's greatest successes, has been interpreted in many ways. As an example of a wasted life, as a dreamer and liar, as a man of nature and as a child who loses its will to its dreams. And perhaps as a Norwegian? At any rate, Ibsen drew on national-romantic sources, but when Peer Gynt makes his great buck ride, perhaps it is the meeting with modernity we are given an insight into? Peer Gynt represents the country's contact with international society. He is a Norwegian by birth, but a world citizen by disposition, as Ibsen once put it. The buck ride is perhaps both a mental leap and a leap in time.

The Norwegian people have also made some 'buck rides' since the formative period of nationalism and romanticism. Technological innovations have provided us with new opportunities, and post-war growth and wealth have turned Norway into a knowledge nation. Exploitation of the oil resources in the North Sea, in particular, has cemented our position as one of the world's wealthiest nations. We are the rich people in the Land of Happiness – and the transition from a developing country to our present wealth has been very rapid.

After having repeatedly chosen a position outside the European community, the term *Annerledeslandet*, the land that is different, has frequently been used about Norway. Rolf Jacobsen's poem with this title from 1985 declares that '. . . we are not as well-trained as our neighbours'. By a constant reminder that Norway is the 'Otherwise Land', the notion that the country is out of step is maintained with tenacity and obstinacy. At the beginning of the 1990s, the government, after sustained pressure, lifted the moratorium on minke-whale hunting. Amidst wild protests from large international and small national environmental organizations, Norwegian whale hunting was resumed. The Norwegian reply to the accusations of barbaric murder of intelligent animals included, for example, T-shirts with *Barbarians eat intelligent food* emblazoned on them. The right to manage their own resources and continue traditional hunting was more important to both people and government than the massive opposition which such hunting aroused – and this despite the fact that whale hunting is insignificant in terms of the gross national product.

From several quarters it is claimed that nation states and national cultures as such are under pressure, and that the values and norms on which national identity is based are no longer satisfactory. Through all the cultural impulses received from all over the world through the media, the Internet, international partnerships and tourism, and through the competence and cultural diversity engendered by immigration, Norwegians too are being forced to ask critical questions regarding their national community and their stories of triumphs in the glorious Viking Age, their close relationship with nature, etc. A deconstruction is taking place, it is claimed, of Norwegian nationalism, whereby we Norwegians are being challenged to understand identity as being relational and dependent on the situation, and subject to constant negotiation and change.

In January 1991, King Olav died, he who had come to Norway in 1905 as little Alexander. His death touched a whole nation, and in a very short time the palace grounds were transformed into an improvised site of ritual mourning. People flocked there to light candles, lay down flowers and leave

**There are seven** different Sámi costumes in Norway. These are part of a living and exploratory tradition in which silver is a central element.

personal greetings in the form of letters, drawings and photos. The king's death became an opportunity to express both personal mourning and a national feeling of community, was one of very few occasions on which Norwegians have had the opportunity to feel that they belonged to a community and be part of one another's lives. The King's death had nothing to do with a system of government or politics, but provided an opportunity for emotional fellowship and a demonstration of common norms and values.

Thus, although we may now agree that hardly any organic connection exists between a people and its country, one should perhaps still dwell on the question of whether national belonging has lost its significance as an individual or collective bond in modern times. Or are national ideas and values tenacious constructions with which we find it hard to part? Our cultivation of nature, the principles of equality and our obstinacy are characteristics which it will probably take more than one generation to change. As Andreas Hompland says: 'Askeladden remains our guardian angel.' And if we maintain that he is a character who has a clear perception of his own power, who will never let himself be overcome in a fight against a superior force, it may take some time.

Being tactfully out of step is, perhaps, what suits Norwegians the best.

**Norwegians love** this photograph of King Olav V, dressed for skiing, buying a ticket on the Holmenkollen suburban railway during the oil crisis of 1973.

**january** fin serck-hanssen **february** rolf m. aagaard

**march** herdis maria siegert **april** janne solgaard

**may** jens hauge **june** vibeke tandberg

**july** dag alveng **august** rune johansen

**september** knut bry **october** asle svarverud

**november** ingvar moi **december** per berntsen

HH

# SIGRID UNDSET

It is often said that a dark thread runs through Sigrid Undset's literary works – the same dark thread that can be found in her own life. Early in his life her father, Ingvald Undset, a well-known archaeologist, contracted syphilis, which eventually affected his spine. His gradual enfeeblement and the years he spent on his deathbed were to have a very considerable effect on his eldest daughter as she grew up. From the age of six, Sigrid's family life was dominated by her father's approaching death. She used to read to him from the sagas, and as a result developed a lasting interest in the Middle Ages. When her father died five years later, her mother did not receive a widow's pension, and things looked very bad for her and her three daughters. Their furniture and books had to be sold, and all four women were forced to sleep in the same room. As Sigrid later wrote in a poem, life in Steensgaten in Oslo was 'vile and grey, I learned to long for everything I could not have'.

Undset declined to sit the final school exam, despite the fact that she was offered a free university place. At the age of seventeen she got an office job in order to help her mother and sisters. Her sense of duty led her to take work as a secretary – a position in which she was unhappy. For a widely read, imaginative and artistic soul with a considerable talent for drawing, it must have been an ordeal to transcribe estimates for turbines year after year. She referred to her colleagues as her 'fellow slaves', had no friends and considered suicide as a way out. She became an introvert early in life, and it was only in her writing that she was able to find any escape.

PORTRAIT

In 1900, when she was just seventeen, she started work on her first novel. Writing at night, she struggled with this book, which was to be the precursor to *Kristin Lavransdatter*, for five years, only to have it turned down with the harsh words: 'Do not attempt any more historical novels, because you are no good at them.' Instead she went on to write the contemporary novel *Fru Marta Oulie*. This was likewise rejected, but Sigrid's younger sister re-submitted it and this time the book was accepted. And so, in 1907, Sigrid Undset made her debut as an author. However, it was not until her second book, *Den lykkelige alder*, that the breakthrough came. This book too was dominated by grey streets, loneliness and dismal boarding houses.

After working for ten years as a secretary, Sigrid Undset handed in her notice to go travelling with the one thousand kroner she had saved up. Her destination was Rome, the city that had so absorbed her father. She stopped off at the headquarters of the AEG company in Germany in order to meet the people with whom she had corresponded during her years at the company's Norwegian branch. But the visit proved a disappointment, and only served to reinforce the aversion to Germany and the Germans that she retained for the rest of her life.

It was in Rome that she made her first friends ever. It was here too that she wrote the novel *Jenny* about a woman who embarks upon an erotic relationship with a father and his son. When it was published it was regarded as grossly immoral and scandalous, with the result that sales went through the roof! In the Eternal City she developed a taste for the good life. She partied and smoked and fell in love with a painter, Anders Svarstad. At 27, Sigrid Undset had never been in love with a person before – though she had fallen love at an early age with a Florentine plaster bust from 1461 on display in Norway's National Gallery. She talked of it as 'my heart's sole passion'. Svarstad reminded her of this sculpture. Like Undset, he was drawn to the melancholy; it was a case of two recluses who had found each other. He already had three children from an earlier marriage, all of whom were in an orphanage.

Undset and Svarstad lived together clandestinely for two years until he became legally divorced from his former wife. They spent six months of this time in England, a period biographers often refer to as the only happy time in Sigrid's life. She was pregnant and at the same time sewing her wedding gown. Her love affair with England began then, and was to endure for the rest of her life -- something that fortified the tense relationship between her and her fellow writer, the Anglophobe Knut Hamsun.

Back in Rome in 1913 she gave birth to a son. She wanted to have only sons, as she believed that a woman's lot in life was far too tragic. Her son, however, was sickly and constantly lost weight, so she took him home to Norway. At first she lived with her mother, before renting the ground floor of a house in Ski, outside Oslo. Once her son had recovered, she decided that she wanted to build a proper home for her little family. But her husband often left her alone for long periods. She decided to take on all three children from his first marriage, one of whom was mentally handicapped. Everyone, especially her publishers, advised against this, but she was determined. To add to her woes, in 1915 she herself gave birth to a handicapped daughter.

The burgeoning family then moved to an apartment in the east of Oslo. During this period, she described her nerves as 'rotten sewing thread'. It is therefore all the more impressive that between 1913 and 1919 she should have published four books. Her lifestyle was, to put it mildly, difficult. Once the children were in bed, she set herself up for the night, equipped with coffee and cigarettes; she also consumed alcohol in increasing quantities. She ended up, exhausted, at a sanatorium, before falling pregnant for the third time. Immediately after the delivery, the family was evicted from the apartment. The marriage had been going badly for a long time, and Svarstad, the first and only man in Undset's life, had also turned out to be fanatically anti-Semitic. The two went their separate ways, and later in life, when she had settled in at Bjerkebæk, a cluster of houses near Lillehammer, Undset wrote that the time she spent at Sinsen had been like living behind a barbed-wire fence.

Undset made a name for herself as an astute commentator of social mores. It could almost be said that she was, without exception, a fierce opponent of her own time. She campaigned against women's rights, emancipation, divorce and sex education. She firmly believed that the man should be master. What makes this even more astonishing is that, at the time, very few women lived or behaved as independently as Undset; she was always the one who held the purse strings.

In 1920 she began work in earnest on her masterpiece, the trilogy centred on Kristin Lavransdatter. The books were a great success in terms of sales, both in Norway and abroad. The critics wrote that Undset showed in this work how little significance a woman has in a man's world. Undset converted to Catholicism in 1924, once she had completed the trilogy – a move that was, to some extent, an expression of her anti-modernism. Her conversion would cost her dear in that she would lose her best friend, the writer Nini Roll Anker, as a result.

In 1928 Undset was awarded the Nobel Prize for Literature, only the third woman to be so honoured. Several thousand people bearing torches gathered in the small town of Lillehammer to greet her when she returned from Stockholm with the prize. She donated the cash prize, which in modern terms was equivalent to three million kroner, to an endowment fund for mentally retarded children and destitute Catholics. Altogether she evinced immense compassion for every living creature, a concern that found expression in her providing financial assistance to friends and strangers alike. She also devoted a lot of her spare time to gardening, and it was not unusual for her to feel closer to plants and flowers than to people. For most of her life she was reluctant to be photographed or interviewed. It was only in the company of other authors that she would let her hair down for a while, and she was twice elected president of the Norwegian Society of Authors. Books continued to flow from her pen – there would be thirty-five in all.

The year 1939 was in every way a desperate time for Sigrid Undset. Not only was she profoundly depressed by Europe's imminent destruction, which in her eyes the world war threatened to bring about, but her mentally disabled daughter died after twenty-four years in her mother's care. As if that were not enough, her long-suffering mother passed away at Bjerkebæk after years of being nursed by her eldest daughter. Sigrid Undset's urge to care was so strong, however, that she immediately took in three Finnish refugee children.

When the Germans occupied Norway in April 1940, Undset fled the country – with very good reason. She knew that Goebbels had banned all twenty-two of her books that had been translated into German. Her flight was arduous and took its toll on her health, which was already poor. The worst blow, though, was to be told, once she was safely out of the country, that her eldest child, her son Anders, had been shot and killed by German soldiers in the battle to defend Lillehammer.

It was a broken woman, mother and author who fled to the USA, where she remained throughout the war, working as an 'information officer'. She would never again return to writing fiction. That is to say, she tried, but without success, her book *Om Catharina av Siena* being rejected. When she returned to Bjerkebæk, the home the Germans had occupied and turned upside down, the light had for ever gone from her eyes. The final years of her life were characterized by despondency, rheumatism and illness. Sigrid Undset died from pyelitis, completely alone, on 10 June 1949.

NIELS CHR. GEELMUYDEN

UNDSET, SIGRID (1882–1949), author. Made her debut with **Fru Marta Oulie** (1907), a novel about a marriage. Her breakthrough came with **Jenny** (1911), a novel centred on the setbacks suffered by a female artist. Many of her novels and short-story collections from 1912 to 1918 bear the stamp of her social indignation and marital problems. In the period 1920–22 she published the trilogy **Kristin Lavransdatter**, a historical novel set in the 14th century. In her mediaeval novels, **The Master of Hestviken** (1925) and **Olav Audunssøn and His Children** (1927) (published in English as **The Axe, The Snake Pit, In the Wilderness** and **The Son Avenger**), heathen self-assertion confronts Christian humility. She was awarded the Nobel Prize for Literature in 1928.

# ADMINISTRATION AND INTERNAL AFFAIRS

# THE COUNTRY WITH NO FOCAL POINT

Per Egil Hegge

Governing Norway from one place, from one centre, has never been possible and has hardly ever been attempted, certainly not since the French-born king of Sweden, Karl Johan Bernadotte, gave up in the 1820s after valiant, but not particularly protracted attempts. The distances were too great, the capital too remote, and the mountains that separated the valleys, too lofty for success.

For us Norwegians, geography and topography are expressions of a mentality. Our own ability to realize this is one thing. But we are not alone; the Danish poet Piet Hein also conceived 'a relationship between the soul and nature's power: it is the inflexible Norwegian mind that makes their mountains tower'.

One might almost suspect Hein of having read the 1821 proposal of the Norwegian Storting's Constitutional Committee, in which with enormous care it justifies its rejection of King Karl Johan's suggestion for a law on the dissolution of parliament, which he favoured in order to ensure more power for himself in his tussle with the democratic representatives:

*... In addition, although nature has in no way poorly endowed our beloved Norway, nevertheless it gravely and rigorously enjoins the inhabitants to persistent and unceasing efforts, as well as waging a hard battle with the harshness of the elements and other local difficulties, in order that they may live tolerably in it. The resultant fixedness of mental purpose and calm, even temperament and thoughtfulness, does not easily cause any apprehension that such people, occupied as they are with the necessities of life, or their native-born national representatives, would harbour any tendency to unjustified impatience in the execution of public affairs, which is rather more to be expected in peoples whose milder climes leave more time for an idle, carefree and easy life, as well as heedless thoughts of their country's perceived good.*

So Piet Hein, poetic humorist that he was, reversed the relationship between cause and effect. But barely 150 years earlier, Norway's parliament had made itself every bit as clear to the King, and that with sombre, Norwegian earnestness: the severer the climate and the harsher the environment, the firmer the ideas, the calmer the mood and the more equable the thought. The proposal is a quite unsurpassed political and social analysis, even though it clearly reflects a self-image rather than any measurable reality, either in 1821 or 2004.

Karl Johan suffered defeat on a few more points in his endeavour to bolster the monarchy. His adversary was a Storting that had graciously been allowed to survive the union with a much more powerful Sweden, which, with solid support from the other great European powers, had been forced on an impoverished and backward Norway in 1814. But yet again Norway distinguishes itself from the rest of Europe at that time. The King wanted the prerogative of nominating a peerage, but this would have been directly contrary to the Constitution ratified at Eidsvoll in May 1814, in which the egalitarian principle was enshrined in one single sentence: 'Hereafter, no personal or hereditary privilege is to be granted to anyone.'

In diametrical opposition to the King's plan and wish, in 1821 the Storting was bent on passing, for the third time, the law that would abolish the remnants of the aristocracy that still existed in Norway. The King had twice refused his sanction, but

**The lion is** not part of Norway's fauna, but two stately examples of the breed guard the Storting from Løvebakken. In the national coat of arms they have an extra Norwegian touch: they wield Viking axes.

**King Karl Johan Bernadotte** (1763–1844) wished to amend the Norwegian Constitution, preserve the aristocracy and limit freedom of expression after he became king in 1818. He soon gave up the attempt.

on its third reading the law would be passed without his assent. Now he threatened – rather emptily, but he threatened nevertheless – that the other great European powers would declare war on Norway if the nobility were abolished. After all, there was aristocracy everywhere else, it was a part of the national and social order. What would happen if others began to follow Norway's example?

The aristocracy *was* abolished. It happened less than thirty years after the Terror in France, and it happened without a single drop of blood being spilt. Was this a manifestation of 'Firmness, level-headedness and an even temperament'? Perhaps there was a more important reason why the European countries did not let it bother them.

So to the other battles that the King lost in the early 1820s, and which were to set the tone for the biggest bone of contention of the century: how much power should the Storting have? At whose expense should its powers increase?

The King wanted an absolute veto in order to block any resolution from the Storting that he did not like. That would have secured him his nobility, or at least he would have kept the remnants of what existed – but he did not achieve that. He proposed a limitation on freedom of the press, enshrined in a key section of the Constitution of 1814 and modelled on the first American Constitutional Amendment and the proclamations during and after the French Revolution. Naturally, the King's motives were of the purest: he wanted to prohibit deleterious comments about Sweden and the Swedes, as they might harm the union, and *that* was not in anyone's interests. The proposal was phrased in such a way that even a joke at the Swedes' expense – foolish or otherwise – might, in the worst case, have landed its wayward author in court and incurred a severe sentence.

The Constitutional Committee argued against notions of this kind on grounds both of principle and practicality. In its principles the Storting had moved quite a long way towards constitutional conservatism, and that in an amazingly short time: the Constitution was regarded as something that was not to be tampered with. On purely practical grounds, the King's proposed statute was open to an unacceptable level of arbitrary interpretation. This latter point was particularly emphasized in the committee's negative response.

Section 1 of the King's proposal read:

*It is hereby prohibited to print anything in Norway that directly or indirectly contains an affront to or attack on the Swedish nation, the character of its administration, laws, burghers or general establishment.*

Were anyone to suggest dissolution of the union in print, the author would 'be punished as a traitor'. Set against this was Section 100 of the Constitution that said that comments on 'the nation's governance and any other subject shall be permitted by any person'. And that stood.

Some fifteen years later, in 1837, the Local Committees Acts (*Formannskapslovene*), which set up town councils and local councils and created a solid foundation for local self-government, were passed. Historians are divided about their importance. It is possible to regard them as a logical, sensible and relatively undramatic evolution of the old administrative partitioning that can be traced right back to the Viking Age. We know from the sagas that what is today called Norway was then divided into districts which made, revised and exercised their own laws; these included the Gulating, Frostating and Eidsivating. The lesser units were called *fylker* – some of which were so small that a couple of them would fit into the area of a present-day municipality.

### The Peasant Parliament

The Local Committees Acts were passed after the farmers' representatives became more numerous and skilful – the so-called 'Peasant Parliament' elected in 1832 transferred quite a lot of power from the official classes in parliament to the newcomers. The regulations concerning local autonomy can also be seen as another blow at central authority and for the local principle: that people should themselves have the decisive say in matters that most directly affected them, for the simple reason that they knew best. The feeling of distrust for those who wanted to govern remotely from a distant capital, and who therefore could have no grasp of detail, of 'how we always do things here', was linked to longstanding scepticism about the people in the next valley or on the other side of the fjord. Such attitudes were difficult to adjust to for a French-born monarch who was used to being guided by Napoleon's centralist principles.

In more nationalistic historical archives the Local Committees Acts have been held up as important local policy reforms, curbing central power and increasing the farmers' influence. This was also how they had been conceived by those who had promoted the Bills in 1827. Their architect was Jon Neergaard, one of the farmers' leaders, and a man who had mastered sufficient English to make himself acquainted with Scottish municipal law. For some years these Bills were drafted by an unofficial group which became known as 'the Farmers' Secret Management'. But in 1830-31 Europe was riven by revolutions and attempted revolutions, and the Secret Management's meetings were reported to the police – who considered interrogating some of the participants, as there was a fear that they might not be loyal to the Constitution, and certainly not to the King.

From the way in which the Acts took shape in these discussions we can glimpse the outlines of one of the classic contrasts in Norwegian community life, culture versus administration; perhaps also in the national psychology – periphery versus the centre. Nationalistic historical accounts place much more weight on the psychological than what is measurable, practical and factual: the fact that participation in the first local council elections after 1837 was extremely low, is often disregarded; in some places as little as 15 percent of the electorate turned out. If there was any euphoria over the establishment and legalization of local self-determination, there is little to suggest that it spilt over to the grass-roots in the regions. But local government in its modern form had taken root and became one of the most vital tools, perhaps the most vital, in the struggle to prevent those at the centre from assuming too much power. It helped, too, to transform officials into the servants of local government. And more than anything else: the new local councils would deal with questions that directly affected the everyday lives of the people, and which therefore interested and concerned them far more than goings-on far away in the capital. It was further decided that local councils would control the financial purse-strings, and those of a more optimistic kidney conjured up visions of falling expenditure.

But the battle line between the periphery and the centre was not merely drawn between the largest urban communities and the rest of the country. It also ran right through the middle of the Storting, where the farmers were in an inferior position to representatives of the official classes in numerical terms, in education and in political and administrative training. In 1833 a Peasant Parliament took office, far more farmers having been elected than ever before.

The farmers had never really found their place in the seat of power before: they were not suitably qualified and did not understand the tortuous legal language. They were quite literally country bumpkins, not even cultured ones at that, lost in an urban environment. Moreover, lacking as they did experience, the King might easily have been able to trick them. In 1832 a columnist in the newspaper *Morgenbladet* wrote: 'It is a very remarkable phenomenon that so many farmers have been elected to the Storting. This has been the subject of conversation in every circle and a cause of apprehension among the country's greatest men.' There were so many of them indeed that there was reason to fear that they would 'prostitute the nation and sully our Constitution, at which our enemies will for ever gleefully be able to rub their hands'.

In his biography of Ole Gabriel Ueland (1799–1870), who was later to become the farmers' leader, and who was first elected in 1832, the historian Arne Bergsgård puts it this way: 'The farmers were come to a foreign country when they arrived at the capital and the Storting.' Their qualifications were also rather modest: many of them were 'beneath contempt, even as regards the expectations of a farmer's representative of the time. They were of the usual type from the 1820s and quite inadequate in the chamber.'

But by 1833 the farmers had grown so in number and accomplished enough to gain the majority in the upper house of the Storting, the Lagting, where they occupied 13 of the 24 seats. This gave them a veto in all legislative matters, and should there be a Court of Impeachment (*riksrett*), they would also wield an influence they had never enjoyed before. Furthermore, despite the high social barriers, there were certain representatives of the official classes who 'displayed a kindly interest in the farmer members'. The farmers also had associates and admirers among some of the younger and more colourful inhabitants of the capital: the poet Henrik Wergeland found it 'difficult to see a farmer in national costume without going into raptures'. He went so far that on one occasion, after a chance meeting with Ueland in the street, he insisted on taking the Storting representative to a restaurant and treating him to a 'farmer's breakfast', accompanied by schnapps and Norwegian-brewed beer. The waiters had no idea what a 'farmer's breakfast' was, and neither had Wergeland. Things were not helped when Ueland, acting as gastronomic interpreter, prescribed oat porridge and sour milk, or oatmeal flatbread with butter, sharp cheese and sweet whey cream cheese. Needless to say, the establishment was unable to provide these, so in the end the two would-be breakfasters drained their glasses and made to leave. As host, it was up to Wergeland to pay, but he hadn't enough money. When talk of 'putting it on the slate' was rejected – this was in 1839, and the 31-year-old poet had certainly become known to Christiania's (Oslo's) restaurants – he borrowed the rest from Ueland.

1844, the year Karl Johan died, is a natural point at which to take provisional stock of the effects of the Constitution, as the King's demise coincided with the Eidsvoll legislation's reaching 30-year-old maturity. This period laid the foundations for the mind-set of modern Norway, and it did so before poets and artists appeared on the scene to entrench it, more than shape it, by their contributions.

In 1814 the great powers of Europe had decided to move the country, like a pawn, from Danish to Swedish control. Norway was lost to Denmark as punishment for the Danes' having taken the losing side in the Napoleonic War, and we were awarded to Sweden, which had been on the winning side. But the Swedes clearly did not have such high hopes as the Danes: they did not talk about twin realms, but about 'brother peoples', a slightly more distant relationship, therefore, but close enough for them to feel duty bound to help their little brother in whatever way they could, and just a bit more than he sometimes thought he needed. When the unruly Norwegians got together, formed a Constitution, elected a king and declared their desire for independence, the Swedes prevailed upon their victorious allies to read the Riot Act loud and clear, to the background accompaniment of war-drums. Sweden started a war that could have inflicted Balkan conditions on many generations to come, had not the newly elected king, 27-year-old Christian Frederik, capitulated, abdicated and returned home to Denmark.

**Henrik Wergeland** (1808–45) was a nationalist and romanticized rural culture. He was a prime advocate of celebrating the anniversary of the Constitution on 17 May.

**In 1814**, as a 27-year-old, Christian Frederik (1786–1848), felt forced to abdicate after only five months as Norway's king.

It is characteristic of the way historians' assessments are influenced more by current trends than past facts, that Christian Frederik was sharply criticized for his lack of pugnacity, his near cowardice, in Sverre Steen's book about 1814. Written in 1947, it is suffused with the author's proximity to five years under German occupation. Whereas Karsten Alnæs's historical novel *Flyktende kongers følge* (Fleeing Kings' Retinue), written 35 years later, praises the King for his understanding and desire for peace, and for letting the weapons lie and instead manoeuvring Norway and Sweden out of a bloody war that would have burdened and possibly poisoned the relationship between the two neighbours for generations to come.

What the Norwegians were allowed to keep, was their Constitution. And amazingly, it acted as an anchor against the Swedish King's pressure as he tried, again and again, to get his way shortly after ascending the throne in 1818. At the same time the whole legal tradition, as clarified during most of the long Danish rule, stood unchanged. Local and central government was administered by Danish-educated officials. A university sprang up in Christiania, but most graduates' degrees were from 'Royal Copenhagen'. (No one ever used the term 'Royal Stockholm'.)

During the first few years of the union the Swedes spoke of amalgamating, alloying, binding, merging the two realms into one. This policy was abandoned, although no specific date can be given – it was a seamless transition towards indulging the inflexible mind and the lofty mountains. With hindsight it almost seems as if the Swedes had given up around 1830. It was not even possible to prevent those stubborn Norwegians from starting to celebrate 17 May, which they continued to do even though it most definitely was not a Swedish holiday.

**Parliamentary Government**

The struggle between royal prerogative and the influence of the Storting thus characterized most of Karl Johan's reign (1818-44), and it was not the king who won. Next came the question of how authority was to be divided between the government and the Storting. Once again it was royal power that suffered.

'Government by Storting' is an expression we are familiar with from discussions about the weak position of minority governments in modern times – in situations where the government, owing to its lack of majority support, can be instructed by the Storting to act against its own inclinations and manifesto. A rather similar state of affairs is apparent if we look at the dramatic twelve-year period from 1872 to 1884, during which the Storting forcefully gained, or manoeuvred its way into, the power that would become part of the apparatus of state and an unwritten rule of the Constitution, via the Court of Impeachment ruling against the Selmer ministry in 1884. This instituted parliamentary government, the system that lays down that no government can remain in power if it has a majority of the Storting against it.

The episode began on the night of 16 May 1872. That evening the Storting adopted – with 47 votes against – the following address to King Carl XV:

*The Storting of Your Majesty's Council does not find the recognition of the Storting's constitutional position, or the consideration of the Storting's efforts to provide an effective and vital co-operation between the powers of state, which alone can enable a government to fulfil its heavy responsibilities . . .*

**Presumably the** very first illustration of the Storting's new chamber – taken from **Skilling-Magazin** in 1866.

Behind this resolution lay disagreement as to who should decide how long parliamentary sessions were to last. The King wanted this prerogative, and it became even more important to him after 1869, when Frederik Stang's government had accepted that the Storting could meet annually instead of every third year. Stang was not a despot by any means, but he reasoned that, compared to the people's representatives, he was more than ably equipped to govern, without interference from them, for as long possible. The struggle against the annual parliament was abandoned in 1873, in the first year of Oscar II's reign. The other bone of contention concerned privy counsellors' access to the Storting. The proposal that they could appear had, against the will of the King, received a constitutional majority in March 1872. Two months later the King refused to sanction the bill. The King and prime minister wanted to prevent the Storting having too much influence on the government, its policies and its composition. Such influence would blur the distinction between two of the most important powers, the legislative and the executive. In his book *Det norske storting gjennom 150 år* (150 Years of the Norwegian Storting) Rolf Danielsen says that government critics in the Storting early in the 1870s had no purposeful strategy and wanted 'a far less radical solution than the one that finally emerged from the long struggle'. But if one was going to adjust things, it could not be done 'without a certain distortion of power in the Storting's favour, in such a way that representatives . . . not only gained influence over the government's policies, but also over its composition'. The first, and possibly biggest and most decisive, step along the road to the introduction of parliamentary democracy as a system had therefore been taken as early as 1872. 'Now at last the time seemed to have arrived for a stocktaking, and this confirmed that the Storting was the moving spirit in Norwegian governance,' Danielsen writes.

But the Storting, with Johan Sverdrup at its head, had no real strategy. There is little to suggest that Sverdrup had set himself any goal at this point – it only gradually came into focus – and his map took shape as he progressed. Prime Minister Stang, on the other hand, had his basic plan clear. He was not going anywhere, he merely wanted to hold on to power. Certainly he was fond of power, but he was also convinced that he could still achieve great things. For us who know the final result, it is easy to see that this was a regime riding for a fall.

The final and highly dramatic phase began with the resolution of 9 June 1880, in which the Storting withdrew the King's right of veto in constitutional matters. Three months earlier the Storting had framed its third constitutional proposal for privy counsellors' access to parliament. The King refused to sanction it, as he wanted the distance between his privy counsellors and the people's representatives to be maintained. The refusal to sanction was attached to the minutes without debate, and thus it was clear that the election of 1882 would be about one thing: Court of Impeachment or no Court of Impeachment, and the faction that gained the majority could count on getting its way.

The question now was what did a court of impeachment mean: was it to be regarded as part and parcel of the criminal law? The government's defence lawyers maintained that the Court of Impeachment should be regarded as a court which 'handed down judgments about official malfeasance' (in other words, it could not be employed against politicians who had done nothing more than disagree with the Storting), whereas Jakob Sverdrup, a close and soon to be troublesome relative of the later prime minister, maintained that such a judgment would be a moral reaction, not a criminal judgment. The privy counsellors would still be 'honourable men', even if the Court of Impeachment found that they had acted improperly. On 23 April 1883, after a landslide election victory that bolstered Johan Sverdrup's point of view, the lower chamber of the Storting, the Odelsting, decided to file impeachment proceedings against Selmer's ministry. The pre-trial review was put in the hands of what was called an Action Committee, with Johan Sverdrup as one of its five members.

Early on, this lengthy impeachment case demonstrated that the process was a stage in a political battle and did not represent any kind of legal problem. The people who most wanted to emphasize this were the legal members – the Supreme Court judges who, together with the Lagting's representatives, constituted the Court of Impeachment – and they never let an opportunity pass to point out that using the Court of Impeachment in such a dispute was to abuse justice and the law. 'Complete nonsense' and 'a wild notion' were just two of the characterizations that these roughshod lawyers used of the prosecution's views and process. At the heart of such contrasting views was also, of course, the fact that the Constitution was ambivalent and unclear. There was room in it for interpretation. It had become a far more flexible tool than many of its Eidsvoll authors had

**Johan Sverdrup** (1816–92) was the driving force behind impeachment of the Selmer ministry and the introduction of parliamentarism in 1884. But as party leader of the Liberals and prime minister from June 1884, he was not a unifying force.

envisioned two generations earlier. And when it was a matter of searching for flexibility that gave room for manoeuvre, Johan Sverdrup proved that he had considerable skill, an eagle eye and an almost animal instinct for where he was going and how to get there.

This is how Rolf Danielsen describes the advantages of flexibility:

*The Constitution's ambivalence . . . made it an El Dorado for its interpreters. But it was precisely its imperfection that made it a serviceable framework for political development in this situation. It is beyond doubt that both the prosecution and the defence, like the powers behind them, felt an overwhelming need to avoid a breach of the law. Here, the Constitution, with all its flaws, suited them perfectly. It made it possible to keep the struggle within the confines of the law, despite all the conservatives' talk of revolution and the cynical disregard of the people's sense of justice.*

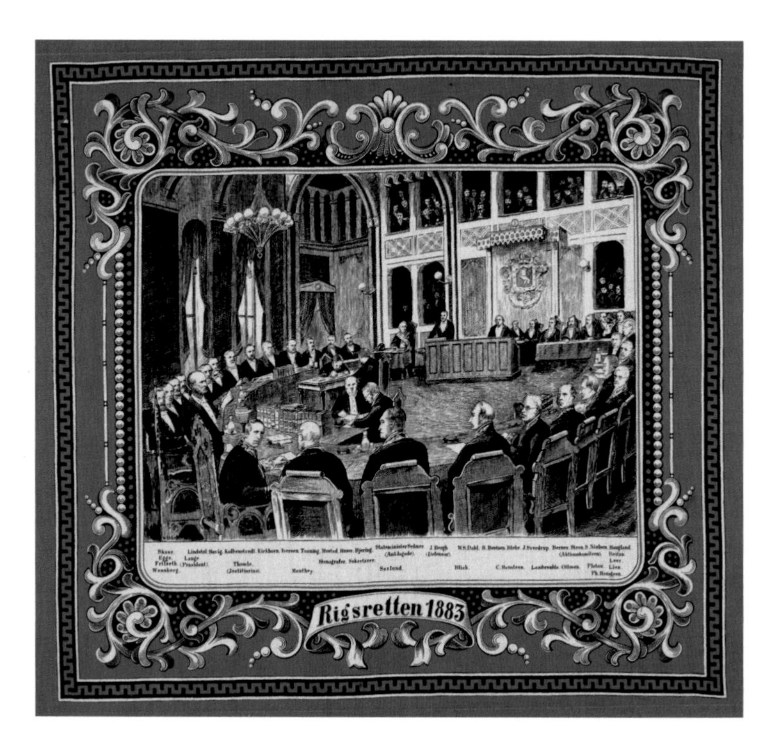


**The Court of Impeachment's** ruling on Christian August Selmer is handed down on 27 February 1884.

The impeachment proceedings were quite complicated, legally as well as politically. The main points concerned the King's constitutional veto and his budgetary veto. It could have been turned into an ideological issue, but this was not what the tactician and pragmatist Johan Sverdrup had in mind: 'The most important thing for the Storting's majority under the leadership of Johan Sverdrup was . . . not to arrive at a legally binding demarcation between the two divisions of government, but to bring about a systemic shift that would provide a practical solution to these contentious questions,' writes Rolf Danielsen. Like so many Norwegian politicians both before and after him, Sverdrup was far more of a craftsman than an ideologue.

On 27 February 1884 the Court of Impeachment handed down its judgment on Prime Minister Christian August Selmer. He was sentenced to forfeit his official position and pay 18,000 kroner in costs. A further six privy counsellors were sentenced to lose their positions, while three escaped with a fine and costs. Thirteen days later, on 11 March, the King accepted the Court of Impeachment's judgment *de facto* through a resolution on the prime minister's departure, and although the government still believed that its rights over the Storting were intact, the outcome was clear: royal prerogative had capitulated to parliament on the most important political issue since 1814. Despite this, King Oscar did not appoint the victor, Johan Sverdrup, to head a government until 26 June – and even then only after abortive attempts had been made to have two interim administrations installed. These attempts were prevented by the Storting's threatening further impeachment proceedings, partly because the more bellicose of its members wanted to cast some light on the military preparations that had been started as the impeachment drew to its close. This was something King Oscar wanted to avoid, and so did other leading Swedish politicians.

According to the terms of the Court of Impeachment, the representatives from the bench of the Supreme Court had to take part in the negotiations. Amongst the more book-learned, traditional and conservative lawyers of the court, and in the circles around the institution, there was little cause to celebrate the Court of Impeachment. It was impossible to say which was worse: the result itself, or the way it had come about. But the victors, losers and critics could all agree on one thing: this was politics not law. And it was the politicians, in this case Sverdrup's Liberals (*Venstre*), who held power and could use it to cut a new swathe, and in reality alter a key principle of the Constitution and alter the balance of power between the Storting and the government.

**'We aren't facing a situation ...'**

'Government by Storting' underwent a renaissance of sorts in the 1920s and up until the formation of the Labour (*Arbeiderparti*) government in 1935. Dissatisfaction with weak governments and frequent government crises led to the creation of an extra-parliamentary organization, *Fedrelandslaget* (The Patriotic Union), in 1925. Its leading men were the former prime minister, Christian Michelsen, who had lived in voluntary exile in Bergen after he left office as prime minister, and Fridtjof Nansen, who had never had much taste for the parliamentary system along Norwegian lines, and certainly not for compromises and political haggling.

But Michelsen died in 1925 and Nansen was not a man keen on organizations; and despite a large membership – it had 100,000 members at its height in 1930 – *Fedrelandslaget* never became a political nucleus of power. Naturally enough, the non-Socialist parties regarded it as an unwelcome competitor in their own fief, while the Socialists saw it as an ideological opponent. At that time *Fedrelandslaget* espoused a clear non-Socialist, and sometimes anti-Socialist, ideology that was opposed to the Soviet Union and the Labour Party. When Vidkun Quisling founded the National Union Party (*Nasjonal Samling* or *NS*) in 1933, some of the leading men in *Fedrelandslaget* defected to it, causing many people to brand the party a precursor to fascism in Norway. *Fedrelandslaget* was dissolved in 1940.

Cooperation across party lines was always problematic, but the Labour Party and the Agrarian Party (*Bondeparti*) broke new ground with an agreement in 1935 which allowed the former to form a one-party government with support from, but not with members of, the Agrarian Party. After the Liberation a coalition government was formed that remained in office until the election in the autumn of 1945, when the Labour Party was returned with a clear majority, which it retained until the election of 1961. In this period, during which Einar

**The Norwegian** and Swedish delegations averted war at their negotiations at Karlstad in September 1905 and laid the foundations for a peaceful resolution to the union conflict. This is a postcard from 1905.

Gerhardsen was premier for most of the time, two comments were made which, satirically but succinctly, sum up the political situation in which Labour was the dominant party: 'We aren't facing a situation, we have a majority,' declared the Leader of the House, Nils Hønsvald in 1958. And in his famous lecture on the one-party state at the Norwegian Students' Union in the autumn of 1963, the historian Jens Arup Seip said of the Storting that it had been 'in exile from Elverum to King's Bay'.

Seip was here referring to two highly important events: the first was the Elverum Mandate of 9 April 1940, with which the Storting, fleeing from the German invasion forces together with the Royal Family and government, empowered the latter to exercise power until parliament could reassemble; the second was the government crisis in the late summer of 1963, when the Labour government was toppled after a debate about responsibility for a serious mining accident at King's Bay on Spitsbergen in the autumn of 1962. The subtext was that the Labour Party had governed without needing to worry overmuch about the Storting.

The party returned to government office after only one month. But the short-lived non-Socialist government demonstrated that the non-Socialist parties were capable of working together, and after the election victory of 1965, the Conservatives (*Høyre*), Christian Democratic Party (*Kristelig Folkeparti*), the Liberals and the Centre Party (*Senterparti* – the new name for the Agrarian Party) formed a coalition government which remained in office until the late winter of 1971. It eventually broke up and had to step down, but the coalition laid the foundations for a new non-Socialist power takeover after the election of 1981, this time with the Conservative parliamentary leader Kåre Willoch at its head.

The year 1981 was an unusual one in Norwegian politics, as in it the country was served by three prime ministers. A generation that had started school, been confirmed and married under Einar Gerhardsen, suddenly found itself with rather a lot of prime-ministerial names to keep track of. For a few months Gro Harlem Brundtland was Norway's first female head of government and, at the time, one of the youngest in modern times. When she returned to power after the Willoch government's fall in 1986, she really did make history: of the government's seventeen cabinet ministers, seven were women, a much more powerful female contingent than could be fielded by any other cabinet in the world.

It had now been seventy-three years since women had first been granted the vote in Norwegian parliamentary elections, so the pace of change was not all that impressive. But the feminist rebellion of the 1970s and much greater demands for equality in politics, the workplace and the home, placed women's interests much higher up on the agenda of social debate. For radical women, the proposal for abortion on demand was a touchstone issue. After a long and, at times, bitter battle, in 1978 the Storting agreed to abortion on demand. It was three years after the Supreme Court of the USA had declared that there were no grounds in the American Constitution to refuse a woman's request for termination of pregnancy.

Gro Harlem Brundtland made her entry into national politics as Norway's Minister of the Environment in 1974, and in a speech made during a prime ministerial visit to the USA told of how lonely a woman could feel in political forums. One of her first tasks was to represent the government at a large national environmental conference in Norway. There were about a hundred delegates, and she was the only woman. 'It struck me,' she said, 'that such a ratio is hardly a natural environment!'

**Gro Harlem Brundtland's** second government was appointed on 9 May 1986. She set a world record with seven female cabinet ministers. From the left: Anne-Lise Bakken (Minister of Consumer Affairs and Government Administration), Kirsti Kolle Grøndahl (Minister of Church and Education), Vesla Vetlesen (Minister of International Development), Sissel Rønbeck (Minister of the Environment), Prime Minister Gro Harlem Brundtland, Tove Strand Gerhardsen (Minister of Health and Social Affairs), Helen Bøsterud (Minister of Justice), and Gunhild Øyangen (Minister of Agriculture).

The Women's Liberation movement brought with it the struggle for longer pre- and post-natal leave and more playschool places. The right to six months' maternity leave after childbirth was increased in 1993 to either 42 weeks with full pay and the legal right to return to the same or an equivalent job, or 52 weeks with 80% pay and the same rights. For fathers, an arrangement was brought in to allow them to take four weeks' paternity leave, an allowance that could not be transferred to the mother.

Naturally it is hard to prove a direct correlation, but it seems reasonable to assume that the relatively high birth rate in Norway – with Catholic Ireland as the only comparable country ahead of us – has an obvious link with leave arrangements and financial benefits, which are well in excess of what is on offer in Denmark or Sweden. Between 50,000 and 55,000 children are born annually in Norway. This figure sank somewhat at the turn of the millennium, from almost two children per woman to about 1.7. In Catholic southern Europe, Germany and the Baltic States it was close to one. The magic demographic birth rate in a modern society with a healthy population and a good health service is 2.11 , which means, in statistical terms, that a woman must give birth to an average of 2.11 children during her fertile lifetime in order to keep the population stable.

Kjell Magne Bondevik's first non-Socialist coalition government introduced a controversial measure when it took office in 1997. Fulfilling a Christian Democratic Party´s manifesto commitment, a so-called cash support scheme was introduced that ensured families with small children a monthly payment from the start of the child's second year until it reached the age of three, provided its parents did not take up a playschool place. The measure was criticized by the Labour Party as a retrograde step for policies of equality, their reasoning being that it would encourage women to stay at home instead of stimulating them to go out into the job market. But the party did not attempt to tinker with these cash payments when it returned to power again for eighteen months from the spring of 2000 until the election of 2001.

### The Supreme Court

To the extent that it was necessary, the Court of Impeachment negotiations and their result also helped put the Supreme Court in its place. The judges voted unanimously against a guilty verdict for Selmer's ministry, and they lost to the politicians. In the Norwegian context it was initially unclear just how strong a position the country's highest court had vis-à-vis the other powers of state. In contrast to its American counterpart, it seldom used its position to act as a constitutional court by declaring or viewing Storting motions as constitutionally unlawful. But provision for this had been established, more or less as a result of the American example, as early as 1840. And in a judgment from 1866, Chief Justice Peder Carl Lasson of the Supreme Court formulated the principle of the Court's right to review, and therefore its potential to set aside, a law that contravened the Constitution: '. . . inasmuch as one cannot expect the courts to judge using both laws at once, they must of necessity favour the Constitution.' In certain situations, therefore, the Supreme Court does not have to abide by the Storting's decisions, but may disregard them if it finds them at variance with the provisions of the Constitution.

The right to review has remained. It is seldom used, but the best example in modern times is found in what became known as the Kløfta ruling of 1976. The Supreme Court, in plenum and with a majority of ten to seven, overrode a statutory provision with reference to paragraph 105 of the Constitution, which conveys the right to full compensation for expropriation. The newer provision that the Supreme Court set aside, was revoked by the Storting in 1984.

Almost twenty years after the Kløfta case, the Chief Justice of the Supreme Court, Carsten Smith, assessed the importance of this judgment so that the court could make a tripartite division, weighting or ranking, of Constitutional rules:

*Concerning provisions dealing with the protection of an individual's personal freedom or security, great weight must be given to the Constitution. As to provisions regarding the protection of financial rights, the Storting's interpretation must play an important role for the Supreme Court. Finally, with provisions that regulate the operation of other divisions of government or reciprocal jurisdiction, the courts must to a large extent respect the Storting's own view.*

Ranking or no – the Supreme court had earlier, at one of the most vital crossroads in Norway's history, taken a stand by demanding retention of its right of review. If we go back to the time just after the German attack on Norway in the spring of 1940, we see that fifty-five years before Carsten Smith's assessment, the Supreme Court was willing to raise the stakes to protect the individual's personal freedom and security. The govern-

**The leader of the** Nasjonal Samling, Vidkun Quisling, gives the Nazi salute before the Royal Palace in Oslo at a farewell parade in 1942 for soldiers who were bound for the eastern front.

ment and Royal Family had gone into exile in June after the country's military defeat on its own soil, and the Supreme Court had appointed the Administrative Council (*Administrasjons-rådet*), which began negotiations with the Germans about how the country was to be governed. These negotiations were brought to naught by Reichskommissar Josef Terboven at the end of September 1940, when he proscribed political parties and dissolved the Council. Barely three months later, on 21 December 1940, the judges of the Supreme Court resigned en bloc. They did this in protest at a letter from Terboven which said that the courts did not have the right to test the legality of, or set aside, decrees originating with him or the commissarial cabinet ministers, the NS cabinet ministers. In formal terms it was the right of judicial review that the Supreme Court judges were using as a touchstone for the German occupying powers. If this were taken away, the court would have no function at all.

A letter to this effect was despatched on 12 December 1940. It read in part:

*We wish to point out that according to Norwegian constitutional law the courts have a duty to test the legality of legislation and administrative decrees. During a military occupation the courts, when considering the legal issues thrown up by a case, must in our view – and to the extent that international law allows – determine the validity in international law of decrees emanating from the organs of the occupying power.*

*We cannot accept the view of the court's authority as set out in the Reichskommissar's letter, without dereliction of our duty as judges of the Norwegian Supreme Court.*

*We therefore find it impossible to continue in our offices.*

Resistance, under the leadership of Nygaardsvold's exiled government in London, already had a political basis in the Elverum Mandate of April 1940; now it also had a legal foundation. One of the judges reportedly said to a colleague after their decision: 'We could be shot for this.' His colleague replied: 'Yes, people are shot in war.'

Chief Justice Paal Berg of the Supreme Court was later to become the Norwegian Resistance movement's clandestine leader and the man who issued and signed the victory proclamation in May 1945. When the Supreme Court was able to hold its first session after the Liberation on 14 May 1945, Berg opened the proceedings by repeating the historic first words spoken in the Supreme Court in 1815: 'Injustice must be banished. May right prevail and true civic freedom live in our land.'

The person who has most clearly advocated an extension of the Supreme Court's role in Norwegian state practice is Carsten Smith, who was Chief Justice from 1991 to 2002. In an article he wrote in 1975, in his period as an academic, some sixteen years before he entered the Supreme Court, he held that the court 'ought to take a more active role in the ordinary development of justice. Our highest court ought to make clear that its most important task is not to decide particular cases, but to lay down guidelines for the future.' He conceded that his ideas did not meet with enthusiasm amongst the country's judges.

Smith also promulgated rather unusual views when, shortly after his appointment, he ordered closer scrutiny of judges' activities, in particular their special assignments. He also advocated more openness towards the media, and was unorthodox enough to hint that the field of recruitment to the Supreme Court was possibly somewhat limited – in plain language, that too few members were recruited from outside the Ministry of Justice's Legal Department, meaning people who had, or at least had had, rather close ties to the Executive.

As far back as 1964, i.e., very early on in his career as a legal academic, Smith had also spoken out in favour of incorporating the European Convention on Human Rights into Norwegian law. Towards the end of his term as Chief Justice a number of Supreme Court judgments were overruled by the European Court of Human Rights in Strasbourg, particularly in matters of freedom of expression and defamation legislation. This court went considerably further than was the practice in Norway, in the direction of creating more room for critical expression, even when it was directed at people who might have reason to consider themselves defamed. After one such overruling in Strasbourg in 2000, in which a surprising and much-criticized ruling from the Supreme Court in 1994 was set aside, Smith issued a press statement in which he made it clear that a more liberal interpretation of freedom of expression had to be regarded as established practice, and that it would form the basis of the Supreme Court's rulings in future. His words were:

*The Supreme Court regards itself as bound by the decision of the Court of Human Rights in Strasbourg. This is both in respect of the individual case and of the interpretation employed by the Court of Human Rights. Where the court interprets the convention differently to the Supreme Court, the latter must accept the consequences thereof.*

**A portrait by** Håkon Gullvåg of Carsten Smith, Chief Justice from 1991 to 2002.

From a constitutional point of view the consequences were very wide-ranging indeed, as Chief Justice Smith explained – in a press release at that! – that section 90 of the Constitution had, in effect, been set aside by an international court on the Continent. This is the section that states that the Supreme Court is the final instance and its judgments cannot be appealed against. As Norway had signed the European Convention on Human Rights, the country had also accepted the Convention's pre-eminence over Norwegian legislation. Smith's successor, Tore Schei, followed this up after his appointment in 2002 by urging the Storting to alter the laws on defamation so that they would be more in harmony with the articles of the Human Rights Convention. This suggestion was logical enough after what had happened, but it is a very rare thing in Norwegian practice that the Chief Justice applies to the Storting for legislative changes of such a substantial nature.

### The break-up of the Union

Two things about the dissolution of the union between Norway and Sweden in 1905 made it unique in world history, and one of them remains unique to this day. In the first place it passed off peacefully, and the like of this would not be seen in Europe until the federal state of Czechoslovakia underwent its so-called Velvet Divorce in 1993 and separated into Czech and Slovak republics. But Norwegians are unique in having managed the constitutional trick of staging a national coup by means of a subordinate clause. State coups, revolutions and the undoing of unions often occur through the agency of hard-hitting main clauses, and not uncommonly with the use of soldiers and firearms as well. Here, too, Norway was to show itself to be a rather different country.

When contention over a separate Norwegian Consular Service reached its climax in 1905, the prime minister, Christian Michelsen, staged an insoluble government crisis, insoluble because King Oscar would be unable to get any politician to form a new Norwegian government. This subtle and well-staged ploy provided the basis for the Storting's coup-like resolution of 7 June, in which the retiring Norwegian government was given authority to exercise royal authority in keeping with the Constitution and relevant legislation, 'with any changes necessitated by the association with Sweden under one king having been dissolved, pursuant to the King's ceasing to function as the Norwegian sovereign'.

This wording was not only a constitutional, but also a grammatical insult. The resolution embittered the King, who genuinely felt himself to be Norway's head of state, and who from an early age had even taught himself a reasonably passable Norwegian. Because Michelsen had got the political elite to agree to a man not to be persuaded to form a government, the King found it impossible to select a new prime minister. And because he was unable to do so, he had 'ceased to function as the Norwegian sovereign'. Was this to be all the thanks he was to get after almost thirty-three years on the Norwegian-Swedish throne, years of endeavour in the interests of the 'brother nation'?

It was indeed. For Norwegians, independence was naturally, the most important aspect of 1905, but there was a new constitutional element creeping in at the same time, even though it had no place in the Constitution of 1814, which built on a representative, not on a direct, democracy. But now a new principle had come into being: the consultative plebiscite. Two such plebiscites were held, only three months apart. The first, on 13 August, was to approve dissolution of the union; only 184 voted to continue the liaison. The next was on 12 and 13 November as the royal candidate, the Danish Prince Carl, grandson of the ruling Danish king, Christian IX, had realized that republican sentiments existed in Norway. Before saying yes to the Norwegian throne he therefore demanded incontrovertible proof that there was a democratic majority for a monarchy. 259,563 people voted in favour of a monarchy, 69,264 opted for a republic. Then the Constitution's machinery began to roll again: the throne was vacant, as Oscar II had finally, and very unwillingly, approved the 7 June resolution as a *fait accompli*, and the Storting had to choose a new king.

### The Royal Family in the 20th Century

One man was highly sceptical of the royal candidate's insistence on a referendum, and he tried his hardest to persuade him to drop the idea. He was against the idea that important decisions should be taken at street level, in what are usually called referendums, and he could point to the fact that the Constitution was quite clear on this point: it was the Storting that should choose the king, not the people. Prince Carl insisted, and the sceptic had to give in. His name was Fridtjof Nansen. And there were to be more referendums in the course of the 20th century.

The newly elected king was to reign for almost 52 years, and today, one hundred years later, it is his grandson, King

**On 17 April 2004**, Norway's first female heir apparent was christened in the Chapel Royal. Here, on the palace balcony after the ceremony, are King Harald, Crown Princess Mette-Marit with the newly christened Ingrid Alexandra on her arm, Ingrid Alexandra's elder brother, Marius Borg, Crown Prince Haakon and Queen Sonja.

Harald V, who is on the Norwegian throne. In common with his grandfather and father, King Olav V, he took for himself the watchword *Alt for Norge* (All for Norway), and continued along the same path as a constitutional monarch and ceremonial head of state without political power.

But constitutional monarch or no, at two periods of crisis King Haakon was forced to assume the role of leading politician. The first occasion was during a government crisis in 1928 when, against the advice of the non-Socialist parties, he summoned the Labour politician Christopher Hornsrud and requested him to form a government. At that time the Labour Party was still revolutionary and had the dissolution of the monarchy as one of its most important manifesto commitments, but it was the largest party in the Storting. That government did not remain in office for more than a fortnight, but the episode made the Socialists view the King and royal power in a slightly different light. The King is said to have remarked. 'I'm also King of the Communists' – a phrase which has become part of the myth surrounding him, and which has the historical status of an undocumented 'fact'.

The second episode strengthened him far more and won him cross-party support and admiration, if we exclude National Union Party members: his refusal to accede to Nazi Germany's ultimatum shortly after the German attack in April 1940 was in line with the Labour Party's wishes, but it was the King's own decision. After five years of exile in London during the Occupation, he could return to his country as a dearly loved and respected monarch.

His son, Crown Prince Olav, had been Chief of the Defence Staff during the war, and was known to be a person with real military and historical abilities – and an almost legendary memory. His more than 33 years on the throne (1957-91) passed without constitutional crises.

A royal family in such an egalitarian society, a society devoid of aristocracy, as is the Norwegian, may easily be seen as a foreign element and an anachronism. Nevertheless, those politicians who, in principle, favoured a republic had a difficult job. It was impossible to call for removal of the monarchy by citing a popular consensus, and the Royal Family had won a position that made them hard to criticize. When in 1968 Crown Prince Harald obtained government permission to marry a Norwegian 'commoner', Sonja Haraldsen, the monarchy's most ardent supporters found it harder to accept than did those who had ideas about turning the whole Royal Family into private citizens in a newly formed republic.

A generation later, in August 2001, the heir-apparent, Crown Prince Haakon, married Mette-Marit Tjessem Høiby. There followed a debate about the future of the Royal Family based on the fact that she was a single mother with a turbulent youth behind her. But times had changed. While still unmarried the two had moved in together, something that had become common in Norwegian society during the 1970s. (Amongst the Norwegian peasantry it had been common since the Middle Ages, regardless of what the Church had to say about the practice.) And now a far more intrusive mass media followed the couple at close quarters – whereas the lengthy relationship between the then Crown Prince Harald and Sonja Haraldsen during most of the 1960s had been little discussed before their engagement was announced in March 1968.

With the birth of an heir-apparent, Princess Ingrid Alexandra, on 21 January 2004, a great-great-grandchild of King Haakon and Queen Maud was in the royal succession, 98 years and two months after the couple had stepped ashore in Kristiania. The Constitution had been amended in 1990 to allow women right of succession to the throne.

### Nation Building

Nation building in Norway was a romantic project. The return to the ancient sagas, to the Viking heroes (descriptions that dwelt less on their rampages and rather more on their many heroic deeds and wise words), the worship of national poetry and music and short, terse, telling sentences – these were all part of the formation of Norway. Less lyrical, but no less important, was the developing economy, burgeoning industry and the foundations for an expansion of shipping.

Some became nation builders because they thought ahead. Christian Michelsen, prime minister during the break up of the Union, was one such. Some were nation builders almost in spite of themselves and before they had realized it. Fridtjof Nansen (1861–1930) is the foremost example of this type. The contrast between the two, the flamboyant Bergen businessman and the purposeful, ever inquiring explorer eccentric, makes it even more amazing that they pulled so well together throughout a decisive period in Norwegian history. In certain matters they remained in tandem even after they had both lost most of their political influence, right up until Michelsen's death in 1925.

At the age of 26 Nansen interrupted, although he did not give up, a promising career as a zoological neurologist. He wanted instead to cross Greenland on skis, which he did in 1888. Then he hatched the madcap idea of exploring the Arctic Basin by allowing a specially constructed ship to freeze fast in the ice and drift – or be carried – from Siberia to somewhere north of Spitsbergen. The fact that he survived the foolhardy attempt to reach the North Pole on skis in 1895, when he left the *Fram* accompanied by Hjalmar Johansen, borders on the incredible. But both men came home; not only were they alive, they were also in good health. Norwegian polar explorers generally managed this, unlike their Danish, British, Italian, Czechoslovakian, Russian and American counterparts. This was a clear competitive advantage when working in the field.

Enthusiasm along the coast after the thirteen members of the *Fram*'s crew returned to Vardø and Skjervøy in August 1896 knew no bounds, and when Professor Geir Hestmark very pithily described the ceremony in Nidaros Cathedral in Trondheim as an acclamation for 'a leader and his twelve disciples', one can envisage something of the degree to which they were worshipped. But it was only when the *Fram* arrived at Bergen at the beginning of September, that the political dimensions and potential of the journey were realized. The two who understood and interpreted them were the Mayor of Bergen, Christian Michelsen, and a short, temperamental and deeply nationalistic

**At the end** of Rosenkrantzgate in Oslo a troupe of athletes formed a three-storey triumphal arch to herald the Fram's return in September 1896.

composer by the name of Edvard Grieg. These two gave the main speeches in honour of the *Fram* and the expedition's men on the quay of their home town, and underlined that the journey was to be used to strengthen Norway's place in the union with Sweden, and perhaps even to dissolve it.

Michelsen was the first to realize that the *Fram* expedition, notable scientific achievement that it was, could be exploited for far more than travelogues and scientific papers. It could serve to put Norway on the map, and it would be an independent Norway: the voyage of the *Fram* showed that 'this small nation . . . has . . . strengths and abilities that accord it a natural right to live its own, independent life and add its deeds to those of other peoples'. In a national and nationalistic euphoria such attitudes formed the core of the celebrations held in the capital, Kristiania, a few days later. The city more or less shut up shop for five days. King Oscar came from Stockholm, held a banquet at the Palace, handed out distinctions en masse and praised the members of this 'expedition which was Norwegian through and through'. (There was one Swedish participant, but he wisely changed his name from Petterson to the more Norwegian-sounding Pettersen.) Then the king was packed off back to Stockholm, and the celebrations, a party for the Norwegians themselves, continued. By this time even Nansen had glimpsed the political dimension. But for the time being the scientific ramifications were of most importance for him, as well as the proceeds accruing from book sales and lecture tours.

In 1905, during the run-up to the controversy with Sweden, Michelsen was the prime minister and strategist. Nansen was one of his foot soldiers, and used the position he had built up in Great Britain to put Norway's case to her top politicians during the dramatic weeks when war almost broke out with Sweden, and when it was vital to win the new, small and perhaps immature nation sympathy and hopefully support from Europe's dominant power.

Nansen succeeded in this because he had taken to his skis and set out on a bold voyage in a mystical ship right out of the pages of an adventure story, a ship that looked like a tub and tossed about even worse than one, but that could travel on sea and on 'land'. Furthermore, it had a name that was an imperative. All this counted for far more than the fact that Nansen had written an important, but at that time not very well known or acknowledged, doctoral thesis on the nervous system of animals of the lower orders, a pioneering work in the history of medicine, a foundation of 20th-century neurology.

Athleticism's sovereignty over science in Norway did not emerge with the television age. When the artist Erik Werenskiold set out to depict the athletic king Olav Tryggvason, the man who walked on the oars of the Viking ships, he gave him Nansen's features. The link from the present was made to the heroes of the past.

Fridtjof Nansen serves as an illustration, this time without artists' brushes, for yet another vexed question in Norway; and again it is the contrast between the periphery and the centre that stands out – now in educational policy.

### The institutions

Christiania – or Kristiania as the name was spelt from the 1870s – had long had its university, it having been established before 1814. But nearly a century later an institute of marine research was to be set up, and the Storting decided it should be situated in Bergen. Nansen was indignant and intimated that he was against the idea purely on principle: such institutions ought to be in the capital, he thought. He had forgotten – though barely 30 years had passed – that it was in Bergen that he had benefited from an extremely exciting and challenging research environment in the 1880s which had turned him into a scientist. He was even more annoyed when a new technical college was built in Trondheim; also this was too far away from the centre of things.

But not even the education system in Norway could be centralized. With Bergen Museum at its core, the city eventually acquired a university. The National College of Technology in Trondheim was amalgamated with other teaching institutions and became NTNU, the Norwegian Scientific and Industrial University, and in 1968 the first university north of the Arctic Circle, the University of Tromsø, was given the go-ahead.

Since then the national colleges have emerged as a link in academic decentralization, also fully in line with Norwegian regional policy. At the turn of the millennium there were 26 state-run colleges, two art colleges, six scientific colleges and four universities. In addition we have 23 private colleges. The setting up of seats of learning is accompanied by the usual discussion: isn't the money earmarked for education too thinly spread if we have so many institutions dotted about our strange country with its great distances? Even those inclined to answer yes know only too well how this kind of discussion ends in Norway: no region must suffer discrimination in the enjoyment of benefits.

## Concession Laws and the Outside World

Christian Michelsen continued as prime minister after the break-up of the union, but only for a couple of years. He was the man of the heroic moment, the dramatist and director who had out-manoeuvred the Swedes, averted war and written himself into Norwegian history books as the man who gained for us independence after 500 years of foreign dominance, if not exactly oppression. But then the party ended, and normality returned – in the shape of vast, deadly dull piles of drafts of concessionary laws. This was too much, and as early as the autumn of 1907 Michelsen handed over the reins to his foreign minister, Jørgen Løvland, and returned home to Bergen.

The country's first foreign minister had not been overworked. Foreign policy was easy enough once the threat of war with Sweden was averted early in October 1905. After that Norway was to have no foreign policy, that was something only great powers dirtied their hands with: Norway would have nothing to do with such things. But the country had to be protected against one thing: foreign interests were to be prevented from exercising control over our natural resources, and the detailed and wide-ranging concessionary laws set extremely tough limits on foreigners owning them. Contact with the outside world and Norway's right to administer it with her own consulates was the motivation and the key problem in the process that led up to dissolution of the union. But Kristiania, a fairly small administrative seat in a remote land of two million inhabitants, was hardly overrun by a deluge of foreign diplomats: by 1907 nine countries had set up their own embassies in the Norwegian capital. Seven were self-evident, they were neighbours or great powers: Sweden, Denmark, Great Britain, Russia, Germany, France and the United States. (Finland did not become an independent state until a decade later.) Viewed from our vantage point almost a century later, the two remaining ones, Cuba and Mexico, are rather more surprising. Cuba was important because of the sugar trade, however, and because a group of Norwegians had established a colony on the island's eastern seaboard. Mexico was an American power that Norway also did a considerable amount of trade with.

One type of contact with foreign lands was to assume a surprising level of importance – surprising, because the connection was not obvious: God and Mammon in extraordinary interaction. The key word is Stavanger, and the city can throw light on an important and complex aspect of Norwegian psychological history.

The Norwegian Missionary Society, which opened its school for missionaries in Stavanger in 1859, took the New Testament's admonition 'Go ye therefore, and teach all nations' literally. The school and the Society's headquarters were located in a part of the country where Christianity was regarded as so strict, joyless and hostile to enlightenment that people from other places turned up their noses and shook their heads over it, even those who were far from antipathetic to the Church.

It was to be more than a hundred years before the oil boom arrived, and the wealth it has brought with it has, with reasonable certainty, contributed more to the flood of money, increased consumption and greater materialism, than to greater godliness. But gradually people all over the country began to realize that there were other things besides geographical proximity to the oil fields of the North Sea that made Stavanger a natural centre for the new industry. The oil business has marked international features and links – and Stavanger had a tradition for both of these. God moves in a mysterious way . . .

## The Trade Union Movement

Few elements in Norwegian society are so surprising as the so-called Basic Agreement of 1935. It was concluded in the same year that the Labour Party gained power after several years of crisis marked by almost irreconcilable ideological differences. This was to a large extent caused by the diametrically opposing views of the extreme political wings on the subject of the Russian Revolution. In addition, and of more basic concern to Norwegian society, was the unemployment, bitterness, strikes, and even something resembling a real battle between workers and soldiers. For the first and only time in Norwegian history the army was deployed by the government in what became known as the 'battle of Menstad' near Skien in June 1931. Some workers were arrested and sentenced, but no one was killed.

The two parties that put their signatures to the Basic Agreement only four years later were the trade unionists' organization, the Norwegian Federation of Trade Unions, and the Norwegian Employers' Confederation. This agreement formed a framework for later negotiations on binding agreements about wages and conditions, and it ensured that the two main parties in industry had control over their individual organizations and members. As a compromise agreement bridging a social and economic gap during a period characterized by conflict and hostility, it is quite unique in European history. It is no less unique

**In his fresco** in Oslo City Hall, the artist Reidar Aulie's social realism depicts the Norwegian labour movement's development from revolutionary class warfare to social-democratic reform policies.

in a land where Henrik Ibsen's contentious hero in *Brand* has often set the tone with his 'The spirit of compromise is death'. But this spirit of compromise led rather to peace in industry, with a framework that for once ensured that something could be directed and controlled from the centre, and embodied a procedure so successful that outsiders who have studied it use it as a paradigm. They also use it as an argument to refute the contention that Norwegians are so rigid in their love of battle that the art of the compromise is almost totally foreign to them. The agreement, which was renewed for the first time in 1947, meant that Norway enjoyed well-organized and predictable industrial relations in the difficult period of reconstruction after the German occupation. In contrast, in the 1940s and throughout most of the 1950s, countries such as France and Britain had to contend with wildcat strikes and rampant unrest among employees and employers alike.

**Foreign policy awakening**

'All politics are local politics' is an aphorism attributed to the American politician Thomas ('Tip') O'Neill. For Norwegians this was true from the moment Norway acquired its own Foreign Service in 1905: the country's foreign policy was based on 'not having a foreign policy at all'.

This worked quite well until April 1940. Norway became a member of the League of Nations in March 1920, and even raised its profile when Fridtjof Nansen became the League's first Commissioner for Refugees. But Norway played no major part in the unsuccessful attempts to avert or solve international conflicts in the 1930s. The war, however, forced the exiled Norwegian government in London to adopt a foreign policy. Not only did it have to adopt a standpoint towards the sides in the conflict, it also had to consider how, in the longer-term, postwar international cooperation was to be organized.

After its liberation in 1945, Norway viewed itself as a bridge-building nation amongst the great powers, and because it is hard to change the overall course of a foreign policy, the country continued on this course, even after the Cold War began to undermine the foundations on which this policy rested, and the differences between the Soviet Union and the western allies, with the USA, Great Britain and France at their head, became more pronounced. Then, in February 1948, came the coup in Czechoslovakia.

It is difficult to explain to non-Norwegians why the Communist takeover in this central European country should have had a much profounder effect, and greater psychological and political consequences, in Norway than in any other European state. Pangs of conscience resulting from the feeling that Czechoslovakia had been betrayed in 1938 at the Munich Agreement entered into between France, Britain and Nazi

Germany, was one factor; but they should have been felt more by the British. Perhaps the relationship can better be explained as a result of a diffuse, but nonetheless powerful, Norwegian-Czechoslovakian cultural bond, across what seems to be an insurmountable cultural and linguistic barrier. Tomáš G. Masaryk (1850–1937), the philosopher and historian who became the new Czechoslovakia's first President in 1918, was a figure of international standing. As an author and patriarch he was familiar in Norwegian cultural circles, especially in the people's colleges (*folkehøgskolene*). His son, Jan (1886–1948), was foreign minister in the government that fell when the Communists took power. He did not have his father's stature, but Jan Masaryk, too, was a more than competent politician who had very close contacts with western European, including many Norwegian, politicians. When, only a fortnight after the takeover, he was found dead, having jumped out of a window in his flat in the Foreign Ministry in Prague, the new regime was stigmatized in western European eyes – either the Communists were directly responsible for his death or he committed suicide because he could not bear being a non-Communist member of a government which, from its first day in power, had shown highly unsympathetic and anti-democratic traits.

**Norway and NATO**

The Czech Communists had seized power in close liaison with, and with political support from, Moscow. In the course of just a few weeks the new rulers had fully adopted the Soviet Union's Stalinist policies, at home as well as abroad. At the same time, the Soviet Union exerted strong political pressure on Norway's Scandinavian neighbour, Finland, and drew the country into a Friendship, Co-operation and Mutual Assistance Pact that placed tangible and worrying restrictions on Finnish sovereignty. The fear that the Communists' taste for power would grow the more they got, was widespread. An abortive attempt to set up a Scandinavian defence union with Denmark and Sweden, resulted in each of the three countries having to make a choice. Memories of occupation strongly influenced Norway and Denmark to cooperate with the USA and they joined the NATO Alliance in 1949, whereas Sweden, which had had quite different experiences as an unoccupied country from 1940-45, remained officially neutral.

In Norway at that time, the ruling Labour Party had a clear majority in the Storting. Because the NATO Alliance was a treaty much disliked by the Soviet Union, accession was a difficult matter for the party, especially those who belonged to its left wing, and had regarded the revolutionary Soviet regime with considerable sympathy. As for the eleven Communists in the Storting (out of 150 members) all loyal to the Soviet regime, NATO membership was rather like pushing the country over a capitalistic, imperialistic and militaristic precipice.

The split between the Communist and Labour parties in Norway had taken place a generation earlier, in the 1920s, and then too it had been caused by the attitude to Moscow and the Soviet Union. The same people who had engineered the schism were still in place at the heads of their respective parties. As a consequence, the settling of scores was charged with a good deal of long-pent-up and well-nurtured bitterness.

It is possible to recognize features of the ideological controversies of the 1920s in the equally insult-laden contention about NATO in 1948–49. In its admiration for the Bolshevik revolution, in 1920 the Norwegian Labour Party had ratified the Communist International's 'Twenty-one Points'. These assumed that all national Communist parties would be accountable to Moscow and be organized along strongly centralized principles. But just as for the country itself, it was too much for a Norwegian political party to allow itself to be run from somewhere abroad, and that a mere 15-20 years after the break-up of the union. Irrespective of the socialistic ideology and the principles of the International and the Revolution, it was a tall order to take commands from a capital that was twice as far away as Stockholm. Neither were the Labour Party leaders over-endowed with modesty: Erling Falk, one of its leading intellectuals, was not slow to give the tyro Soviet rulers directives and advice on how to govern their country. During a visit to Moscow he irritated them so thoroughly that Karl Radek, later to become a victim of Stalin's terror regime, exclaimed that 'Erling Falk should have every bone in his body broken before being thrust into his grave'.

As Moscow had been ditched as the mentor of Labour Party policy in the 1920s, there was no very persuasive argument for allowing the Russians to have anything that smacked of too much influence 25 years later – especially with Stalin's horrifying dictatorship to point to. Prior to the Storting giving its approval to NATO membership, the Labour Party held an extraordinary national conference, at which the delegates voted overwhelmingly for the motion proposing membership. Labourites who could not accept the new move towards NATO and the cooling of relations with the Soviet Union, formed a clique around the left-leaning Socialist weekly *Orientering*. This group formed the kernel of the Socialist People's Party (*Sosialistisk Folkeparti*), which was set up in 1961 and won two Storting seats in the election that same year. The party's two representatives wielded considerable influence, as they held the balance of power between 74 Labour Party members and 74 non-Socialists; they thus became a barometer of left-wing intellectuals' grievances about western defence cooperation and a defence policy with a long stop in Washington.

For opponents of Norwegian NATO membership it was scant comfort that the Norwegian government had taken steps to pacify Moscow: Norway did indeed join NATO at its founding in 1949, but placed unilateral military and strategic limitations on herself. This was not the result of negotiations with the Russians, and therefore not part of any specific agreement, but occurred after a relatively acrimonious exchange of diplomatic notes with the Soviet Union. Norway wanted special treatment within NATO and stipulated that Allied forces were not to be stationed permanently on Norwegian territory except in time of war, or unless there was a threat of war. Nor were atomic weapons to be deployed in the Norwegian area, and no allied military operations were to take place east of the 24th degree of longitude, which crosses western Finnmark. If this lessened Moscow's worries, as the Norwegians hoped, it certainly was not apparent in the intense Soviet propaganda against both NATO and Norwegian membership of it. The attacks subsided a little after the Soviet dictator Josef Stalin died in March 1953, and the climate grew a little milder, even internally. The Communists, who had had eleven representatives in the Storting at the election in 1945, lost all their seats in the election period 1949–53.

These unilateral limitations from the Norwegian side found little opposition in non-Socialist quarters, not even from those who had traditionally regarded the Soviet Union and the Communist system in a far more critical light than did the ruling party. Viewed with the benefit of hindsight, these measures must be deemed impressively astute moves. On many occasions, and over a number of years, the Soviets referred to them as if they were constituents of a bilateral 'agreement', which they were not. The reason the Russians employed this term may have had some connection with their desire for the limitations to gain force in international law. But in theory they allowed sufficient freedom of action for Norway to request Allied help, or warn that such help would soon be requested, should the Soviet

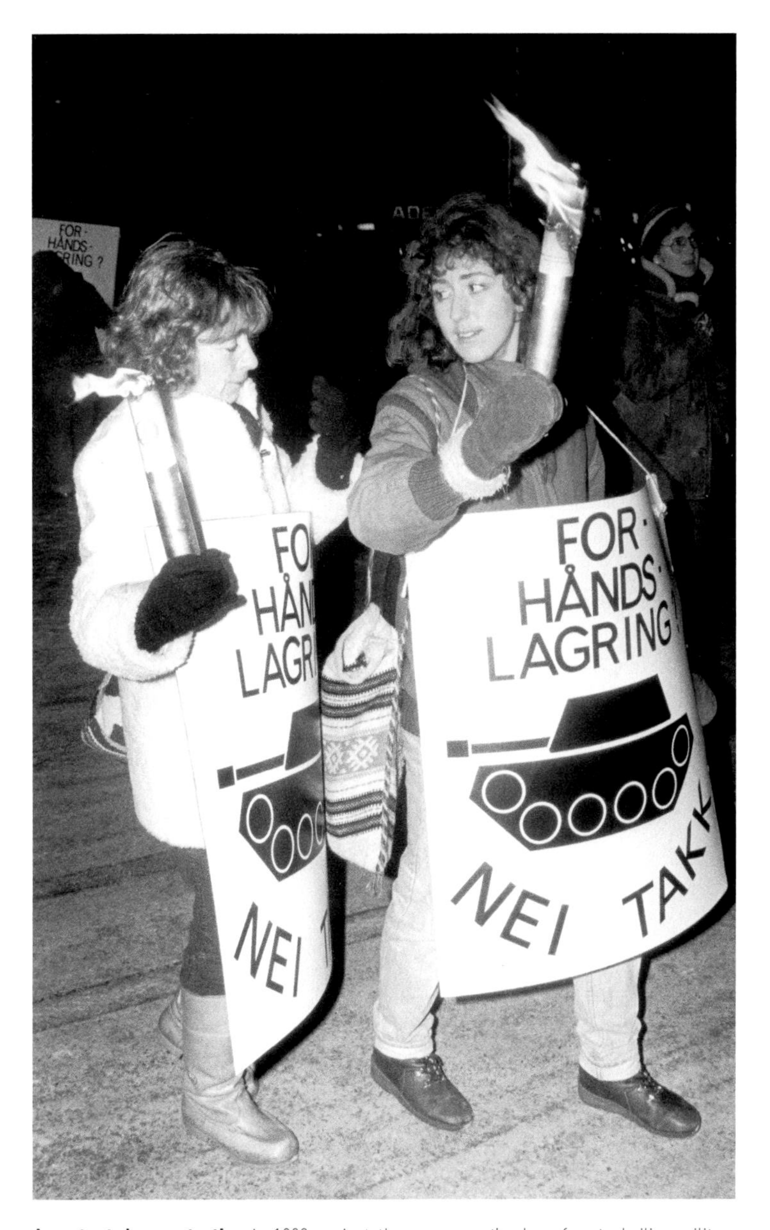

**A protest demonstration** in 1980 against the government's plans for stockpiling military hardware in Norway.

Union try to put undue pressure on the country. To this extent they helped create stability and predictability in a region at the interface of two military alliance. The Warsaw Pact was only set up in 1955, but the Socialist countries were engaged in a close and highly constrictive, Soviet-dominated military cooperation long before that. And stability and predictability were things the Russians were very much interested in after all they had been through, not least during the war with Nazi Germany.

The Norwegian NATO debate flared up from time to time, often in connection with international crises. In 1968 a group of intellectuals and artists founded the organization 'Norway out of NATO'. The main impetus behind it was the increasing opposition to America's war in Vietnam. The organization was never very influential, and encountered strong opposition in the same year, when castigation of the Americans was for a time eclipsed by bitterness at the Soviet invasion of Czechoslovakia.

A new debate on Norway's attitude and contribution to NATO arose after 1990, when the Soviet Union and the Warsaw Pact collapsed and there was no longer any military threat from the east. NATO now revised aspects of its policy and was drawn into operations outside the territory of its constituents.

This first occurred in the Balkans, where dissolution of the Yugoslavian Federation proceeded anything but peacefully, and where NATO first threatened and then instituted a military campaign against Serbia in 1999 to end attacks on the Albanian population in Kosovo. The opponents of NATO found themselves in a tactical and strategic bind here because they were against Norway taking part in military actions, and certainly those outside NATO's own boundaries. On the other hand, the Serbian attacks on Muslims in Bosnia in the mid-1990s were a terrible example of what could happen if an organization such as NATO stood by and did nothing.

For the left wing, and for people much closer to the political centre, it was easier to express scepticism when the USA demanded – and received – support from the whole of NATO in an offer of help after the terrorist attack on New York on 11 September 2001. Resistance increased markedly when such help was drawn on in the form of military assistance in Afghanistan, as a stage in the war against the Islamic Taliban, which had sheltered the terrorist leader Osama bin Laden, the self-proclaimed head of al-Qaeda. Concern grew even greater when the USA, Britain and certain other allies prepared a military strike against the regime in Iraq in the autumn of 2002. The USA's motives were that Saddam Hussein's regime constituted a threat to the rest of the world because of his weapons of mass destruction, and that he ought to be punished because he had helped al-Qaeda. None of this was proved in a way that assuaged the opponents of the war plans, and before, during and after the campaign in March/April 2003 critics of NATO had their arguments against participation in the alliance's military operations strengthened.

**European Co-operation**

There has hardly been any aspect of domestic policy that has remained so enduringly inflammatory as Norway's links with Europe – something which until well into the 1990s was synonymous with western Europe. After a lengthy debate, Norway applied to join the Common Market, the EEC, in the summer of 1962. The application is a document which at great length, but also very informatively, sets out the conditions that make the country rather different to the other western European nations, and necessitate a number of special provisions.

European cooperation was based on the Treaty of Rome of 1957 and consisted, at that time, of six countries: Italy, France, West Germany and the Benelux countries – in other words Belgium, the Netherlands and Luxembourg. Norway was a partner in the free trade organization EFTA, and the government decided to apply in 1962 because Great Britain – which had not signed the Treaty of Rome when it was concluded – had now changed her mind. The British were barred by France's President Charles de Gaulle, and thus there were no meaningful negotiations for Norway's part, either.

After de Gaulle's departure in 1969 the opportunity arose once more, and Britain, Denmark and Norway commenced membership negotiations. The membership debate was a classic periphery-versus-centre argument for Norwegian domestic politics, and it was largely representatives of the primary industries, agriculture and fisheries, that made up the picket troops of the No campaign. From March 1971 the Labour Party headed a minority government following derailment of a non-Socialist coalition, principally caused by underlying internal disagreements about relations with the European community. The Common Market question influenced Norwegian domestic politics much more than any other political issue, and was to continue to do so for the remainder of the century. But the Labour Party was split, too. The death-knell of the party leadership's campaign for membership sounded when the Minister of Fisheries, Knut Hoem, resigned because he could not agree to negotiate fisheries settlements based on the conditions the government had stipulated. Nor did it help when the prime minister, Trygve Bratteli, made it known that his government would resign if there was not a majority for membership: party discipline had gone the same way as nostalgia in Simone Signoret's famous book: it wasn't what it used to be.

In line with the principles established in 1905, a consultative referendum was held. There was a majority for joining the

**The referendum of 1972** resulted in a majority vote against membership of the Common Market (later the EU). Fishermen voted massively against.

Common Market, or EEC, only in Oslo and its immediate environs, and in Bergen. In the rest of the country the No camp was in the majority, and in some remote places along the coast and in northern Norway the No vote was as high as 90 per cent. On a national basis the result was 53.5 per cent no. Commitment was near-total, the turn-out being 77.8 per cent.

The Common Market battle of 1972 had two important, long-lasting consequences: the country's first political party, the Liberals, which had been founded after the introduction of parliamentarism in 1884, split over the issue and was reduced almost to nothing in elections during the remainder of the century. The press, 90 per cent of which had supported membership, had to face the fact that its influence had been greatly overrated – and that maybe it was time to loosen the newspapers' traditional links to political parties. Most obvious were the links in the Labour press – its chief organ, *Arbeiderbladet*, was in the unique position of having its editor-in-chief elected at the party's national conference. But also newspapers that had other political affiliations gradually but completely freed themselves from party loyalties of varying strengths.

This occurred at about the same time as the press in the USA assumed, or fell into, a new role, after President Richard Nixon was forced to step down as a result of the Watergate scandal. The reverberations from this event were strong all across western Europe, including Norway. And with additional impetus from the youth rebellion and radicalization, the mass media's scepticism of elites, leaders and authority became much more pronounced than anyone could have imagined, even a decade earlier.

At the start of the 1990s, when a new referendum about joining the European project was in the air, radicalization had noticeably declined as a result of the collapse of European Communism. The countries now applying for membership of the European Union, the EU, included Sweden and Finland. But those who imagined that a Swedish sign-up in particular would pull Norway in too, were mistaken. The referendum result in November 1994 was an almost exact duplicate of that in 1972: an overwhelming no in northern Norway, so vehement indeed that the three most northerly counties, with a mere 10 per cent of the population, turned a 50/50 outcome in the rest of the country into a collective no majority of more than 52 to 48 per cent.

The electioneering prior to the referendum of 1994 was, however, marked by much less acrimony and fanaticism than in 1972. Then, the two camps were sharply defined, and from both sides there rained down dire predictions of doom and destruction should the other side win. In 1994 there was a greater sense that tomorrow was another day, even if one was unfortunate enough to lose. Since oil extraction was providing Norway with a firm financial foundation, it was difficult to put across the view that Norway needed EU membership to survive. Neither had the dismal economic predictions from the 1972 battle come true. Part of the argument also harked back to 1905: we had broken out of a union and gained our independence – was it now to be given away to a new and larger union? Wasn't it called the European *Union*, and weren't more and more things being decided there?

Paradoxically, Norway, through its affiliation to the European Economic Area in 1994, had to accept the same directives from the EU as the member countries, but without having an input into them. Prior to the enlargement of the EU in May 2004, when five former Warsaw Pact countries, three former Soviet republics plus Malta and Cyprus were given membership, there were signs of a new EU debate. But the problem was, firstly, that Kjell Magne Bondevik's non-Socialist coalition government had far less than half the members of the Storting behind it. Secondly, two of his three coalition parties were anti-EU; the third, the Conservative Party, was pro-membership, but knew that the government would fall the moment the matter was broached, for which reason it hardly could, nor should, be raised before the election in September 2005. This position was undermined by the decision to enlarge the EU, not merely by bringing in countries that had been in the Warsaw Pact, but also three former Soviet Republics. If this did not make an impression on the parties in government, at least not sufficiently for them to change their minds, it certainly did on the electorate: popular polls during the autumn and winter of 2003-04 showed a clear majority in favour of EU membership.

**Administrative Challenges for a Rich Country**

When, in 1970, it was announced that oil had been found in the Norwegian sector of the North Sea, the first reaction of leading politicians was that it would not alter the fundamental principles of Norwegian social organization. A surfeit of money would not be injected into the economy and settlement patterns would not change, at least not to any large extent.

Right from the start there was an overarching strategy that the international oil companies were not to wield too much power over Norwegian oil policies. The Norwegian authorities would decide the pace of oil extraction, and for this purpose the Statoil company was set up, with its headquarters in Stavanger. There was something approaching consensus on both sides of the Socialist and non-Socialist divide, that the biggest part of the oil resources was not to be handled by foreign oil companies, and that these were to be taxed relatively heavily. The ideological views that had underpinned the concessionary laws at the start of the 20th century were still very much alive and kicking.

This modest lifestyle did not fare so well in the shadow of the ever-growing pile of money. Even in the mid-1970s, before noticeable amounts of oil had been pumped up, we had begun to take an advance on our oil money, in a manner that was inflationary. In only a few years this caused the earnings and prices index in Norway to rise to Danish and Swedish levels. At the dawning of the oil age, this inter-Scandinavian differential had been so marked that a local council educational psychologist in Denmark was earning the same annual salary as the Norwegian prime minister, roughly NOK 110,000. Einar Gerhardsen's annual salary in 1965, the year he stepped down as head of government, was NOK 70,000. From the start of 2002, the prime minister's salary was NOK 925,000, about three times the rate for a Danish educational psychologist.

This very limited set of figures cannot give a comprehensive idea of the change, but it shows at a glance how the oil economy brought with it higher wages, and thus also higher costs for industry, especially exporters. This rise had effects that rippled out into the rest of society.

Economists had held a very influential position in the Norwegian social hierarchy ever since the 1930s, and this was in no way lessened when two of their grand old men, Professor Ragnar Frisch and Professor Trygve Haavelmo, were awarded the Nobel Prize for Economics in 1969 and 1989 respectively.

It was important for the economic experts to counter the popular feeling of demand that said that oil money could be used – the more and faster the better as far as society was concerned: there was no lack of unsolved problems, whether in transport, health or education. It was a difficult task, educationally, to explain that the injection of large sums of money would send inflation rocketing and contribute to further unemployment because the export industry would price itself out of the market. The oil revenues were instead put away and invested abroad as oil capital, and by the turn of the millennium the politicians had thrashed out a code for its distribution: the capital would not be touched but managed as an oil fund; however the profit, i.e. the increase in value plus interest, could be drawn upon in the national budget. By 2004 the oil fund had climbed to some NOK 1,000 billion.

### Immigration Policy

When the present railway to Bodø was opened as far as Lønsdal in Nordland in 1947, the Oslo newspaper *Aftenposten* carried a headline that read: 'the Northern Line Opened – Negro Aboard.'

A person with a different skin colour to the pale Norwegian variety was such a rarity as to warrant a note in a headline. The word was also quite innocuous at the time, and it was not until about 1990 that younger people began to regard it as a racist and condescending characterization.

In 2004, roughly one-fifth of Oslo's population had been born in a country other than Norway; the proportion for the under-20s was one-quarter. This, for a country which in 1814 had laid down in section 2 of its Constitution that Jews and Jesuits were debarred from entry, is quite a sweeping change. The prohibition on Jews was rescinded in 1851, that on Jesuits was lifted following a constitutional debate on 31 October 1956. The date affords a good illustration of how Norwegian politics is not always very outward-looking: the rest of the world was at that time more concerned about the revolution in Hungary and the British-French-Israeli invasion of Egypt.

In their 2003 book *Norsk innvandringshistorie* (A History of Norwegian Immigration), the authors concentrate on the Hungarian refugees who came to Norway after suppression of the Hungarian revolt. This period also saw the beginnings of economic immigration, more and more people entering the country from Pakistan, and early in the 1970s came the first requests for a curb. There were 110 Pakistani employees in Norway in 1970, 990 in 1971, and 1,240 the year after. In 1972 the collective total of foreigners working in Norway was 19,472, by far the majority Swedes and Danes.

It was at this time that the first investigations were made into the living standards, especially housing standards, of the new, non-European workers. There was a feeling that Norway was not managing to integrate the newcomers properly, and a one-year moratorium on immigration from 1974 to 1975 was proposed. All parties supported this, but it was only to be temporary, it was said, until the matter had been rectified.

During the 1970s an increasing number of political refugees and asylum seekers began to arrive. Some were the Vietnamese 'boat people', others political refugees from General Augusto Pinochet's dictatorship in Chile. There were more than

**In 2001 Afshan Rafiq** (Conservative) became Norway's first permanent Storting representative with an Asian immigrant background.

**Vietnamese boat refugees** arrive in Norway in 1978.

enough brutal regimes in the world to maintain the flood of refugees. The administration had constantly to adjust to new demands and new arrivals, and from 1 January 1988, refugees and immigrants came under the aegis of a new department, *Utlendingsdirektoratet* (the Directorate of Immigration).

The phenomenon of immigration now became a party political issue. Sceptical about immigration, the Progress Party (*Fremskrittspartiet*) regarded a large part of the asylum seekers as economic migrants and demanded a much higher fence around the country to make it harder to get in. The numbers of asylum seekers rose rapidly during the 1980s: 829 in 1985, 2,722 in 1986 and 8,613 in 1987. That year the immigration problem – for it had by now become a problem – was an item on every party's manifesto, and it played a part in local elections.

The historian Grethe Brochmann sums it up thus:

*Although it was the Progress Party that raised immigration as an issue in the run-up to the 1987 [local] election, and although it was the Progress Party that profited from the negative attitude of voters, it was a Labour government that effected a*

**An immigrant-owned shop** in Oslo's Grønland district, with a large selection of fruit and vegetables.

*tightening-up of immigration policies at the end of the 1980s, and which laid the foundations for a root-and-branch change in asylum policy.*

In the 1990s the Yugoslavian Federation began to fall apart, and the ensuing conflicts resulted in a stream of refugees, especially Muslims from Bosnia and Kosovo. No fewer than 8,000 asylum seekers arrived in Norway in the third quarter of 1993, a year in which all Bosnian refugees who came were automatically given leave to remain for six months, a period later extended to one year. When there was talk of sending some of them home, a number sought sanctuary in churches. The percentages of those granted right of residence fell consistently: 20 per cent of applications in 1985, five per cent in 1990, and 0.5 per cent in 1994-95.

Discussion on how immigrants should be integrated, was generally rather messy and complex all through the 1990s. Did they really want to be integrated? How important was it for them to retain their religion? Very important, replied all the Pakistani Muslims who were asked. How tolerant were they of

Norwegian society's more liberal laws? Fairly tolerant, most of them. But not the fanatics, and while Norwegians critical of immigration pointed at these extremists and the signs of serious and hard crime in certain immigrant communities, the immigrants launched an equally sharp critique of the Norwegian community's moral laxity. The multicultural element was never the less even more in evidence by the turn of the millennium, in the shape of a range of restaurants and shops that would have been inconceivable only twenty years before.

The people who perhaps did more than any others to reduce the tension between immigrants and ethnic Norwegians, were artists – not only musicians, but comedians as well. 'Shabana Rehman crosses Greenland on skis' became one of Oslo's great cabaret successes of 2002, casting as it did a sidelong, satirical glance at both Norwegian and Pakistani-Norwegian pigheadedness, and at Norway's national heroes. Shabana Rehman, born in 1976, lived at Holmlia on the outskirts of Oslo and summed up cultural disparities by saying: 'Whenever we sat down to watch a Pakistani film on the video, the Norwegians would come along and want us to help with things that needed doing on the estate.'

**The Welfare State**

The beginnings of the growth of a national welfare ideology can presumably be traced back to the immediate postwar period, once it was possible to see the end of the task that everyone agreed had to take priority: reconstruction after the Occupation. Sickness benefits, industrial injury benefits, child allowances and the old-age pensions had been partially instituted prior to the war, but introduction of these measures was completed during the 1950s. They were founded on a concept of equality, together with general acceptance of collective responsibility, the wish to build and secure a welfare system in which no one would fall through the net. The authors of *Norsk idéhistorie* (A Norwegian History of Ideas), published in 2003, quote a 1974 article by the then prime minister, Trygve Bratteli, with the title 'The philosophy behind the welfare state':

*For the good of all, the welfare state has accepted responsibility for fulfilling people's primary needs such as work and income, housing, education, health, and security during illness or old age . . . Few people today would view it as desirable to throw the individual back on to his own resources, to shoulder alone responsibility for whether he sinks or swims.*

In this quotation it is easy to perceive some of the major ideas of Norway's great 20th-century health and welfare ideologist, Karl Evang, who stepped down as Director-General of Health in 1972. Evang stamped his personality on much health education work, stressing the need not merely to cure, but also to prevent illness. As a young doctor he had been controversial both because of his left-wing Socialism and his indefatigable educational efforts on behalf of sex education and contraception. But he was also a force behind vaccination programmes and the dissemination of information about hygiene and nutrition. Throughout the whole of his career he was on the left wing of the Labour Party, until towards the end of his life he broke with the party and ended up in the Socialist Left Party (*Sosialistisk Venstreparti*). He was the embodiment of a powerful postwar director-general of health, a strong character with little talent for compromise, with the result that his work had about it a sense of guardianship.

Evang had retired by the time the next set of problems emerged. How were these primary human needs to be met at a time when medical technology was developing so fast and making it possible to cure, or at least minimize the effects of, diseases that previously no one had been able to do anything about? Technically it might possibly be managed, but what about the cost?

Now two things came together at once: ever greater costs associated with the Health Service meant higher taxes at a time when the winds of right-wing change came blowing in from the west, after Margaret Thatcher became prime minister in Britain in 1979 and Ronald Reagan was elected president of America the year after. These two conservative leaders were pugnacious critics, and indeed actual opponents of collective solutions, especially if these had a Socialist link or provenance. And they believed, in contrast to our own Bratteli, that individuals could be spurred on to extra personal efforts if they were not completely insured against going under. Sweden, which had in many respects been a model for Norway in the postwar period, provided statistics which showed that the welfare state there had developed to the point where a family with children, in which

**The care sector** was the object of exhaustive debate in the 1980s and '90s.

the two parents were unemployed, could live better on benefits, housing allowance and other entitlements than if the mother and father went out to work for a basic wage.

Keeping pace with this trend was also a reaction to what critics called the therapy society: the notion that therapy and good will could turn even the most brutal and unrepentant criminal into a responsible member of society, whereas court judgments and prison sentences would have the reverse effect.

This clash of ideas was strongly represented in the ideological debate about the Progress Party's basic tenets. The party had been founded in 1973 by Anders Lange under the name 'Anders Lange's party for the drastic reduction of taxes, duties and bureaucratic meddling', and before it was six months old, it had four representatives in the Storting. Anders Lange died only a year later, and following the example of its Danish sister party, his heirs adopted the name Progress Party. The discussion surrounding private hospitals went right to the heart of the ideological divide. The Labour Party vehemently maintained that publicly owned hospitals had to be brought up to the requisite standards, and that private hospitals should be prohibited because, first, they would drain resources from those in the public sector. Secondly, they would represent sheer social injustice because, if it became possible to buy medical services, wealthy people would be in a privileged position.

The riposte from the Progress Party, with its new leader, Carl I. Hagen, as spokesman, was that people were at liberty to spend their money on ruining their health, so why shouldn't they be allowed to use it to purchase medical treatment and improve their health? As it was possible for the more affluent to travel abroad for treatment, irrespective of whether private hospitals were permitted in Norway or not, it was hard to maintain the opposition to private clinics.

### Right-wing swing and Socialism

The principled ideological resistance to such reforms from Socialist quarters became something of a burden for the parties of the left, as was evidenced when the Conservative Minister of Government Administration, Astrid Gjertsen, campaigned for shops to stay open longer and adopted the slogan 'a more open society'. When this battle had been lost, one of the Oslo Labour Party's leaders, Rune Gerhardsen, was honest enough to admit that 'I spent a year of my life fighting to prevent people being able to buy bread on Saturday morning'.

When Kåre Willoch's non-Socialist government fell in the spring of 1986 and the Labour Party returned to power, there was never any talk of reinstating the old opening times. The belief in the most traditional Socialist solutions fared poorly in the ideological winds that blew during the 1980s. A reaction to the move to the right came at the end of the decade, when the so-called yuppie mentality had gone a little over the top and it became clear that unbridled and untamed capitalism did not have the answers to everything. But those on the left also had to check their direction as, by 1989, the disintegration of Soviet-dominated eastern Europe had culminated in the fall of the Berlin Wall and dissolution of the Warsaw Pact. The nations of central and eastern Europe made it clear that the only Socialism they were interested in was anti-Socialism. The law of pendulum swing caused an adjustment when it became clear that Margaret Thatcher – who had become a political pensioner in 1990 – had a somewhat simplistic solution to the former Socialist countries' transitional problems: 'Bring in capitalism, then all the problems will be solved.'

As far as political thought in Norwegian society was concerned, only a few marginal groups had failed to take a critical view of 'real-life Socialism', whether that meant the Soviet-dominated regions of Europe or special cases like the corrupt despotism of Albania.

It is too optimistic to assume that any country is immune to totalitarian tendencies, be they imports or home-grown ideas. But the chances of such a centralist and dictatorial doctrine taking root in a Norway still hallmarked by 'fixedness, even temperament and thoughtfulness', were no better then than when Karl Johan Bernadotte tried it a century and a half earlier with his French-inspired notions. When it fell apart, they decided to commend themselves to self-irony – for they crossed to the benisons of capital and the capitalistic society.

Every country has a capital city, and in most of them it is in this metropolis, or within its institutions, that decisions are made. But in Norway decentralization is rather more than just an administrative method – it is more like an article of faith, and it goes back at least a thousand years. The gut reaction of most Swedes on hearing that an institution in Stockholm has made a decision, or of the French about some resolution passed in Paris, is 'I see' and 'Well, all right'. Usually the latter.

In Norway the reaction is more likely to be: 'Really? So that's what you lot think down/over there in Oslo, is it?' To this day 'the inflexible Norwegian mind' is unique.

**january** fin serck-hanssen **february** rolf m. aagaard

**march** herdis maria siegert **april** janne solgaard

**may** jens hauge **june** vibeke tandberg

**july** dag alveng **august** rune johansen

**september** knut bry **october** asle svarverud

**november** ingvar moi **december** per berntsen

# CHRISTIAN MICHELSEN AND 1905

Rarely does a nation succeed in liberating itself from another state's dominance without resort to armed conflict. That Norway was able, through negotiation, to secede from the union with Sweden in 1905 is mainly due to the prime minister, Christian Michelsen. Many people have said that the most prominent, and perhaps most decisive, of Michelsen's characteristics was that, as a person, he was never much of a politician.

Certainly, as a young boy he was supposed to have said that his ambition was to become a member of parliament – which, like his father before him, he succeeded in doing. But Michelsen never fitted into any one party; in fact, he never cared much for the party system at all. As a conservative radical, he joined and then left most of the parties of the day. He was an unpredictable politician who allowed uncertainty to prevail until the last moment. Remarkably, this became his strength as head of state and negotiator at the defining moment in the nation's history. This indecisiveness made him a figure around whom others gathered: he represented something of value to everyone.

Peter Christian Hersleb Kjerschow Michelsen was a remarkable person. He was born into the Bergen middle class in 1857. At school he was one of the poorest pupils in his class. The prime minister-to-be failed his exams and had to repeat a year. He went on to study law in the capital, but without ever becoming a lawyer of note; he said himself that he was far too lazy to be a good lawyer. Instead he set up as a shipowner, taking a leading role in the transition from sail to steam. Michelsen quickly became one of Norway's biggest shipowners, and his shipping activities made him rich and independent. His business dealings also meant that he was closely involved with what became known as the 'consulate question', which caused difficulties in Norway's relationship with Sweden in the years prior to 1905. In 1902 he used part of his wealth to found a newspaper, *Morgenavisen*, in Bergen.

PORTRAIT

In many ways Michelsen must have been different from other shipowners. He was unmusical, colour blind and had little understanding of art. He spoke no foreign language, seldom read books and was totally uninterested in sport. The only thing in which he was really interested, other than business and politics, was the theatre. Right up to his death, he would remain involved in the management of Den Nationale Scene in Bergen.

Throughout his life, Michelsen suffered from obsessive-compulsive neuroses. In particular he displayed great reluctance to travel. It has been suggested that his first journey abroad, apart from the time he spent in the cabinet offices in Stockholm, was when, at the age of 48, he travelled to Karlstad in Sweden to negotiate the terms of the secession.

Generally speaking, wherever he was, he missed Bergen. Given the opportunity, he would go straight back home and often stay there for longer than the politicians in the capital appreciated. At times he could become so fed up with politics that he would want to go back to Bergen for good; next minute he would decide that he wanted to be prime minister, as he did in March 1905, after he had brought about the fall of the Hagerup government – a government in which he was Minister of Finance. This changeable side of his nature made him unpredictable and lively. The political world is full of people who blindly adhere to doctrine, and these people are seldom responsible for creating peace. Michelsen's lack of principles made him attentive and flexible – qualities that are needed more than any others at the negotiating table.

He was also well known throughout his life for his penchant for cutting remarks. In 1897, Michelsen declared that he would rather be governed by Russia than by Sweden. He would often have cause to regret his impulsive outbursts. What is beyond question is that, as a speaker, he was outstanding; he must have had a gift for diplomacy, too. When he was mayor of Bergen and King Oscar II was about to pay him a private visit, Michelsen had trouble deciding which flag to raise. If he went for the union flag – popularly known as the herring salad – it would be seen as deference, whereas if he raised the Norwegian flag, it would be a breach of royal protocol. In the event, he flew Bergen's own flag.

As mayor, Michelsen gained the reputation of being lazy and imprecise. A lot of people disliked his innate reluctance to familiarize himself with procedural documents. The strength inherent in this weakness was that he preferred impulses that had their origins in real life, and he tended always to see the big picture. Some felt that Michelsen lacked gravity, determination and a sense of responsibility; others considered him charming and an eloquent humorist. This was a man who certainly presented a wealth of contradictions. By conviction he was a social Darwinist, though, more than any other politician, he was also able to mix with a broad mass of people without difficulty. Socially he was cheerful and easy-going, though privately he was always a gloomy and solitary person. Michelsen was that rare beast, an untravelled man of the world.

In May 1905 the Storting put before the King an Act providing for a separate consular system. The King refused to sanction it, with the result that the Norwegian government resigned. Michelsen interpreted the King's failure to appoint a new government to mean that the union was in practice dissolved, and he managed to convince the majority of Storting representatives of this. On 7 June 1905 the Storting decided that Oscar II's failure to procure a government for Norway meant that he had ceased to function in his role as King of Norway. When this was found to be in contravention of the Norwegian Constitution, it was announced, in the form of a minor clause, that the union with Sweden was considered to be at an end.

The Swedish Riksdag (parliament) was furious when it became known that Norway, under the leadership of Michelsen, had deposed the ageing king, after first having branded him a criminal. 30,000 Swedes spontaneously gathered outside the royal palace and swore allegiance. The Swedish press called for war. Perhaps the most astute idea from the tactician Michelsen in this situation was to offer the Swedish king the opportunity to appoint a prince from the Bernadotte family as the new king of an independent Norway. In this way he cooled tempers in Sweden, calmed the outside world and won the sympathy of the Conservative party. The offer was rejected, however, and instead negotiations were started with Prince Carl of Denmark.

The Swedes insisted on a plebiscite in Norway on the question of union – an absolute gift in the light of the spirit of nationalism then prevailing in town and country. The count revealed that 368,208 Norwegians had voted for secession, only 184 voting against. Of the latter, 13 were Sámi who erroneously believed that they had voted 'no' to continued union. It was an overwhelming result for both parties.

Michelsen led the subsequent negotiations in Karlstad with prudence, charm and dignity. On the decisive day, when the Act of Dissolution was to be sealed, it transpired that he had left his seal behind in Norway. It would have been deplorable had the country's liberation foundered on something so mundane. Michelsen's solu-

**Christian Michelsen** welcomes Prince Carl of Denmark to an independent Norway in 1905. The prince ascended to the Norwegian throne under the name of Haakon VII. On his arm is the infant Crown Prince Olav.

tion was to borrow a seal that had belonged to Karlstad's late mayor, Carl Moberg, a supporter of the union and a man whom fate had given the same initials. Once again Michelsen provided evidence that he was first and foremost a practical businessman.

If Norway had been led at the time by an obstinate ideologist and formalist, there is reason to believe that the parties would have clashed on the battlefield, as there was a strong appetite for war in both countries. Troops were on alert from June until November, so Michelsen's popularity in the months that followed the peaceful outcome to the conflict was tremendous. Unfortunately he allowed himself to be prevailed upon to continue as prime minister. In this role he attempted to promote the idea of coalition, but in the face of reality failed utterly. Michelsen resigned as prime minister for health reasons in the autumn of 1907, by which time he had more or less lost his former position as father of the country. He resumed his occupation as a shipowner and was appointed the first president of the Norwegian Shipowners' Association. Michelsen was involved in founding the *Frisinnede Venstre* party (Independent Liberals) in 1909, attempted to set up a coalition government in 1919, and in the autumn of his years, together with Fridtjof Nansen, was a mainstay of the Fedrelandslag (a pan-political anti-Communist party).

In his private life Michelsen was never a happy person. For much of his life he suffered from physical and mental health problems. Following a relatively successful marriage, his wife died in 1910 and he lost his son in 1921; his daughter remained childless. Upon his death in 1925, in the absence of an heir he left most of his fortune to the Christian Michelsens Institutt for Videnskap og Åndsfrihet (The Christian Michelsen Institute for Science and Intellectual Freedom). His home in Bergen, Gamlehaugen, has since become national property.

NIELS CHR. GEELMUYDEN

MICHELSEN, CHRISTIAN (1857–1925), businessman and politician. Storting representative for the Norwegian Liberal Party 1891–94, member of the government 1903–05, prime minister 1905–07. Implemented dissolution of the union with Sweden in 1905. Involved in founding Frisinnede Venstre 1909 and Fedrelandslaget 1925. In his will (1924) he bequeathed his estate to the Christian Michelsens Institutt for Videnskap og Åndsfrihet.

# THE NOBEL PEACE PRIZE

# THE NOBEL PEACE PRIZE, NORWAY AND THE WORLD

Geir Lundestad

*The Oxford Dictionary of Contemporary World History* describes the Nobel Peace Prize as 'the world's most prestigious prize'; not, it should be noted, as just the most prestigious peace prize, but as the most prestigious prize of all. That, to many Norwegians, is exactly what the Prize is, and what it should be. But the fact that the Nobel Peace Prize has achieved the status accorded it by the *Oxford Dictionary* is a minor miracle.

Each year, when the winner of the Nobel Peace Prize is announced on a Friday in October, the award generates a worldwide storm of conflicting opinions. Presidents, prime ministers and leading newspapers across the globe comment on the Norwegian Nobel Committee's choice. Some applaud, others are critical. But why should they be interested at all in what a committee of five relatively unknown Norwegians decides? Norway accounts for less than one-thousandth of the world's population. Its people live in a country far to the north, close to the ice and snow of the Arctic and remote from the central regions of the world. There are now some three hundred peace prizes in existence, and representatives for many of these have found their way to my office. They all ask the same questions: 'Why does the Nobel Peace Prize occupy this unique position?' and 'How can we achieve a similar status for our own prize?'

**Alfred Nobel** (1833–96)

I think there are four or five key reasons why the Nobel Peace Prize enjoys the position it does. First of all, it has existed for no fewer than 102 years. This gives it a considerable historical edge over most other peace prizes, the majority of which came into being after the Second World War.

Second, the Peace Prize is a part of the Nobel family of prizes, which gives it an extra cachet. It may be argued that it receives more attention than all the other Nobel prizes put together, but if it does, this is undoubtedly to the advantage of the whole family. For our part, we in Oslo are proud to be related to the more scientifically oriented Nobel prizes awarded in Stockholm.

The Nobel Peace Prize is awarded in Oslo because in 1895 Alfred Nobel so decreed in his will. He gave no reason for doing so, but presumably he was influenced by a number of factors. At the time Norway was in union with Sweden and he may have felt that his country's 'little brother' ought also to be given responsibility for a prize. He may also have been sceptical of Sweden's hierarchy and historically more aggressive stance compared with that of the more humanitarian and peace-oriented Norway. In particular, he may have been swayed by the interest displayed in the 1890s by the Norwegian Storting (parliament) in conciliation, arbitration and peaceful conflict resolution. Finally, Nobel was a great admirer of the Norwegian author and playwright Bjørnstjerne Bjørnson, a leading peace activist of the time.

The third reason is that the Norwegian Nobel Committee has built up a solid reputation since the Peace Prize was inaugurated. Mistakes have, of course, been made, some of them serious. Among those who have not received the Prize, Gandhi is in a class of his own. It is most regrettable that the twentieth century's leading spokesman for non-violence did not receive the Peace Prize. The Committee did, in fact, decide that Gandhi should be awarded the Prize in 1948, but that same year he was assassinated. This naturally created a problem, although the Prize can in certain circumstances be awarded posthumously. Among the 110 people and organizations that have received the Prize, we can all call to mind some who, perhaps, should not have done so. But this is a sensitive subject, even for an outspoken Committee Secretary. However, the point is not that mistakes have been made; everyone makes mistakes. The real wonder (and to this I shall return) is that there have been so few.

The fourth reason is that the Prize has proved to be relatively adaptable. The peace concept has expanded over time, human rights, in particular, having been accorded a more central place in recent years. And although it took time – too much, some may say – the Prize has become increasingly global. Prior to 1960, only one representative of the 'Third World' had received the Nobel Peace Prize; not until the 1970s did the Prize become truly global. Over the years the Prize has also been awarded to a growing number of women, and there are now eleven female laureates. It is true that this is nothing to boast about, but a total of eleven women (as compared to seventy-nine men and twenty organizations) is far more than can be claimed by any of the other Nobel prizes.

Finally, some people may contend that the position of the Nobel prizes today is attributable to the size of the prize money. But the sum involved, SEK 10 million (approx. 1.2 million Euros), has not always been so high, and some of the other peace prizes carry more money than does the Nobel Peace Prize; the statutes of one, in fact, even state that the amount awarded shall at all times be higher than that accompanying the Nobel Peace Prize!

**Bridge building**

It may well be asked how the Norwegian Nobel Committee has managed to avoid making more serious mistakes in the last 102 years than it has. I think it would be misleading to point to the Committee's understanding of international affairs as a determining factor, be it on the part of the chairman, the secretary or its members. There have, of course, been many exceptional people from all levels of society who have served on the Committee, but there have also been plenty with a more limited outlook. Ideally, the Norwegian Nobel Committee should, perhaps, represent 'the best and brightest' of Norwegian society, but more often than not appointments to the Committee have been rather arbitrary. The Norwegian Storting appoints the Committee members, and it has ruled that the Committee's composition should reflect the standings of the various political parties in parliament, which means that anything can happen.

I think a better explanation is to be found on a more structural level: in the Norwegian and, in part, general Scandinavian approach to international affairs. In an international context Norwegian and Scandinavian politics tend to be 'to the left of centre'. This is the perfect place for a peace prize, which should represent a blend of idealism and realism. The ultimate aim of the Prize should be a better world, though without losing touch with the world as it is today.

If there is one concept that Norwegian politicians delight in, it is 'bridge-building'. Norway was part of the West bloc, but continued to build bridges to the East; and as, in the North, Norway became ever richer, she continued to nurture a fervent desire to build bridges to poorer countries in the South. Norway was very pro-Israel, but gradually became more committed to extended contact with the Palestinians in particular and with the Arab world in general. This may seem something of a schizophrenic approach, but potentially it constitutes an excellent vantage point from which to award a peace prize.

The moral-idealistic stance that is so characteristic of Norwegian and Scandinavian foreign policy has been of even greater importance. Whereas major powers can base their policies on force, smaller states naturally prefer to rely on legislation and the rule of law. In Scandinavia, where conflicts have been few and far between, and relatively small-scale, at least in recent times, there is an undying belief that organization and democracy are the only roads to peace on both a national and international level. The world has to become more like Scandinavia: well-organized (hence the many prizes awarded to pioneers of the Inter-Parliamentary Union, the League of Nations and the UN), democratic (*vide* the increasing number of human rights prizes) and a champion of social equality (the prizes awarded to people fighting poverty) – coupled with a dream to do away with all weapons that we do not have ourselves, as is evidenced by the many prizes awarded to nuclear-disarmament activists.

As everything is so simple here, we tend to believe that things must be equally simple in the rest of the world, too. This is, of course, a rather naïve view; but the Peace Prize *should* embody a measure of naïvety. It is when the Peace Prize has come up against *Realpolitik* that problems have arisen – for example, in connection with the awards to Roosevelt (1906), Kissinger and Le Duc Tho (1973), Begin and Sadat (1978) and Arafat, Peres and Rabin (1994).

The moral-idealistic tradition is, needless to say, not confined to Norway and Scandinavia. Had it been, the Peace Prize would soon have become very parochial. The tradition has strong roots also in many other western countries, most notably the USA and UK. This is an important factor in explaining why precisely these two countries are special in terms of the number of prizes they have received. The USA can claim twenty Nobel laureates and the UK fourteen; no other country can boast more than seven. Although there have been a number of departures in a more realistic direction, most of these prizes have been awarded to representatives of the moral-idealistic tradition. As democracy spreads to more and more countries, the basis on which

**The most glaring** sin of omission: Mahatma Gandhi (1869-1948) was never awarded the Nobel Prize for Peace.

the Peace Prize rests is being increasingly widened and reinforced.

The strength of the Nobel Peace Prize is, therefore, that it has been based on a tradition that may well be Norwegian and Scandinavian, but that is also international – though at times it may seem that the Prize rests exclusively on Norwegian premises. For example, there were undoubtedly many reasons why Gandhi never received the Peace Prize, but one may have been Norway's close relations with Britain, another an inability to appreciate something as alien and seemingly anti-modern as Gandhi's politics, particularly his resolute adherence to the principle of non-violence (especially as Norway had, in popular opinion, recently fought so gallantly against Nazi Germany).

There is, however, one area in which the Norwegians have shown themselves to be provincial, and that is in relation to

European integration. In the interwar period the Nobel Committee awarded several prizes to champions of Franco-German reconciliation. But since 1945, when integration has really taken on political significance, no such prizes have been awarded, with the exception of that given to Willy Brandt in 1971, which was primarily for his *Ostpolitik*. Everyone knows the reason: a prize for European integration would split the Norwegian Nobel Committee down the middle, owing to its members' differing positions on Norwegian membership of the EU. No one would want to face up to this, though there can be no denying the EU's peace-promoting effect.

In an essay on the Nobel Peace Prize a few words must be said about the influence the Prize exerts on international affairs. Many people have a rather exaggerated perception of this. The Peace Prize is no magic wand. It goes without saying that in an international context five relatively unknown Norwegians cannot exert any appreciable influence on international politics.

What is surprising, however, is not that the Peace Prize has limited influence, but that it has any influence at all. Because it does. Metaphorically speaking, it would be more appropriate to talk of a microphone than of a magic wand. It is amazing to witness how, almost overnight, receipt of the Peace Prize can catapult a comparatively unknown person on to the world stage. The Prize awarded to Shirin Ebadi in 2003 is the last in a long list of examples – or perhaps it should be viewed as a door-opener. Many laureates have told me that most doors were open to them after they were awarded the Peace Prize. Or the Prize may be looked upon as a protective device, as both Andrey Sakharov and Lech Walesa have confirmed. Hopefully, Burma's Aung San Suu Kyi too has enjoyed similar protection as a result of her being awarded the Nobel Peace Prize.

Only rarely, when the time is ripe, can the Prize actually influence the course of international politics. The best example of this is, perhaps, when it was awarded to Bishop Carlos Belo and José Ramos-Horta in 1996. It was profoundly moving to witness their firm belief that East Timor would gain its independence as a result of their receiving the Peace Prize. Not a few of us tried to temper their expectations, but today East Timor is indeed an independent country. And although the primary explanation is the political and economic disintegration of Indonesia in 1997-98, the Peace Prize awarded to these two men made a supplementary contribution to this surprising turn of events.

Normally, the Peace Prize is but one of many factors that influence broad historical processes. It contributed to the successful fight against apartheid in South Africa, to the strengthening of democracy and human rights in many different parts of the world and, though with less success, to the struggle for peace in the Middle East.

**Awarded the Peace Prize** in 2003, Shirin Ebadi was the first Muslim woman to be so honoured and the eleventh female recipient of the Prize.

What is truly noteworthy, therefore, is not the many natural limitations of the Prize, but rather what I regard as two great wonders. The first is that the world cares about the Nobel Peace Prize at all; the second, that the Prize brings more than laurels to its recipients.

# PRIZE WINNERS

(The years when the prize was reserved and/or allocated to the Nobel Institute's Special or Main Fund have been omitted from the list)

1901: The prize was divided equally between **Dunant, Jean Henri,** Switzerland, 1828–1910. Founder of the Red Cross, Geneva. Initiator of the Geneva Convention and **Passy, Frédéric,** France, 1822–1912. Founder and President of the first French peace society (Ligue internationale et permanente de la paix, later known as Société française pour l'arbitrage entre nations).

1902: The prize was divided equally between **Ducommun, Élie,** Switzerland, 1833–1906. Honorary Secretary of the Permanent International Peace Bureau, Bern and **Gobat, Charles Albert,** Switzerland, 1843–1914. Secretary General of the Inter-Parliamentary Union, Bern.

1903: **Cremer, Sir William Randal,** Great Britain, 1838–1908. Member of Parliament. Secretary of the International Arbitration League.

1904: **Institut de Droit International** (Institute of International Law), Gent, Belgium (a scientific society founded in 1873).

1905: **Suttner, Baroness Bertha Sophie Felicita von, née Countess Kinsky von Chinic und Tettau,** Austria, 1843–1914 (born in Prague, then part of Austria). Writer. Honorary President of the Permanent International Peace Bureau, Bern. Author of the book *Die Waffen nieder* ('Lay Down Your Arms').

1906: **Roosevelt, Theodore,** USA, 1858–1919. President of the USA. Drew up the 1905 peace treaty between Russia and Japan.

1907: The prize was divided equally between **Moneta, Ernesto Teodoro,** Italy, 1833–1918. President of the Lombard League of Peace and **Renault, Louis,** France, 1843–1918. Professor of International Law, the Sorbonne, Paris.

1908: The prize was divided equally between **Arnoldson, Klas Pontus,** Sweden, 1844–1916. Writer, former member of the Swedish parliament. Founder of the Swedish Peace and Arbitration League and **Bajer, Fredrik,** Denmark, 1837–1922. Member of the Danish parliament. Honorary President of the Permanent International Peace Bureau, Bern.

1909: The prize was divided equally between **Beernaert, Auguste Marie François,** Belgium, 1829–1912. Former Prime Minister, member of the Belgian parliament, member of the International Court of Arbitration, The Hague and **d'Estournelles de Constant, Paul Henri Benjamin Balluet, Baron De Constant de Rebecque,** France, 1852–1924. Member of the French parliament. Founder and President of the French parliamentary group for international arbitration. Founder of the Commitee for the defence of national interests and international conciliation.

1910: **The Permanent International Peace Bureau (Bureau International Permanent de la Paix),** Bern. Founded in 1891.

1911: The prize was divided equally between **Asser, Tobias Michael Carel,** the Netherlands, 1838–1913. Lawyer, Cabinet Minister. Initiator of the Conferences on International Private Law, The Hague and **Fried, Alfred Hermann,** Austria, 1864–1921. Journalist, founder of the peace journal *Die Waffen Nieder* (later renamed *Die Friedenswarte*).

1913: The prize for 1912: **Root, Elihu,** USA, 1845–1937. Former Secretary of State. Initiator of several arbitration agreements.

1913: **La Fontaine, Henri,** Belgium, 1854–1943. Member of the Belgian parliament. President of the Permanent International Peace Bureau, Bern.

1917: **The International Committee of the Red Cross,** Geneva. Founded in 1863.

1920: The prize for 1919: **Wilson, Thomas Woodrow,** USA, 1856–1924. President of the USA. Founder of the League of Nations.

1920: **Bourgeois, Léon Victor Auguste,** France, 1851–1925. Former Minister of Culture, Minister of Justice and Prime Minister, President of Parliament, President of the Council of the League of Nations.

1921: The prize was divided equally between **Branting, Karl Hjalmar,** Sweden, 1860–1925. Prime Minister, Swedish delegate to the Council of the League of Nations and **Lange, Christian Lous,** Norway, 1869–1938. Secretary General of the Inter-Parliamentary Union, Brussels.

1922: **Nansen, Fridtjof,** Norway, 1861–1930. Explorer, scientist and humanitarian. Norway's delegate to the League of Nations. Initiator of the Nansen Passport (for stateless refugees).

1926: The prize for 1925 was divided equally between **Chamberlain, Sir (Joseph) Austen,** Great Britain, 1863–1937. Foreign Minister. A negotiator of the Locarno Treaty and **Dawes, Charles Gates,** USA, 1865–1951. Vice President of the USA. Chairman of the Allied Reparation Commission and originator of the Dawes Plan.

1926: The prize was divided equally between **Briand, Aristide,** France, 1862–1932. Foreign Minister, a negotiator of the Locarno Treaty and the Briand-Kellogg Pact and **Stresemann, Gustav,** Germany, 1878–1929. Former Chancellor, Foreign Minister. A negotiator of the Locarno Treaty.

1927: The prize was divided equally between **Buisson, Ferdinand Edouard,** France, 1841–1932. Former Professor at the Sorbonne, Paris. Founder and President of the League of Human Rights and **Quidde, Ludwig,** Germany, 1858–1941. Historian, professor honoris causa, member of the Bavarian parliament, member of Germany's constituent assembly 1919, delegate to numerous peace conferences.

**1930**: The prize for 1929: **Kellogg, Frank Billings,** USA, 1856–1937. Former Secretary of State. Negotiated the Briand-Kellogg Pact.

**1930**: **Söderblom, Lars Olof Jonathan (Nathan),** Sweden, 1866–1931. Archbishop, leader of the ecumenical movement.

**1931**: The prize was divided equally between **Addams, Jane,** USA, 1860–1935. Sociologist. International President of the Women's International League for Peace and Freedom and **Butler, Nicholas Murray,** USA, 1862–1947. President of Columbia University, promoter of the Briand-Kellogg Pact.

**1934**: The prize for 1933: **Angell (Lane), Sir (Ralph) Norman,** Great Britain, 1872–1967. Writer. Member of the Executive Committee of the League of Nations and the National Peace Council. Author of the book *The Great Illusion*, among others.

**1934**: **Henderson, Arthur,** Great Britain, 1863–1935. Former Foreign Secretary. Chairman of the League of Nations Disarmament Conference 1932–34.

**1936**: The prize for 1935: **Ossietzky, Carl von,** Germany, 1889–1938. Journalist (with *Die Weltbühne,* among other publications), pacifist.

**1936**: **Saavedra Lamas, Carlos,** Argentina, 1878–1959. Foreign Minister, President of the League of Nations, arbitrator in the dispute between Paraguay and Bolivia in 1935.

**1937**: **Cecil of Chelwood, Viscount (Lord Edgar Algernon Robert Gascoyne Cecil),** Great Britain, 1864–1958. Writer. Former Lord Privy Seal, founder and President of the International Peace Campaign.

**1938**: **The Nansen International Office for Refugees,** Geneva. An international aid organization established by Fridtjof Nansen in 1921.

**1945**: The prize for 1944: **The International Committee of the Red Cross,** Geneva. Founded 1863.

**1945**: **Hull, Cordell,** USA, 1871–1955. Former Secretary of State. One of the initiators of the United Nations.

**1946**: The prize was divided equally between **Balch, Emily Greene,** USA, 1867–1961. Former Professor of History and Sociology. International President of the Women's International League for Peace and Freedom and **Mott, John Raleigh,** USA, 1865–1955. Chairman of the first International Missionary Council in 1910, President of the World Alliance of Young Men's Christian Associations.

**1947**: The prize was divided equally between **The Friends Service Council,** London. Founded in 1647 and **The American Friends Service Committee (the Quakers),** Washington. The society's first official meeting was held in 1672.

**1949**: **Orr of Brechin, Baron John Boyd,** Great Britain, 1880–1971. Physician, nutritionist, leading organizer and Director General of the UN Food and Agricultural Organization, President of the National Peace Council and the World Union of Peace Organizations.

**1950**: **Bunche, Ralph,** USA, 1904–71. Professor at Harvard University, Cambridge, Mass., Director of the UN Division of Trusteeship, mediator in Palestine in 1948.

**1951**: **Jouhaux, Léon,** France, 1879–1954. President of the trade union CGT-Force ouvrière, President of the International Committee of the European Council, Vice President of the International Confederation of Free Trade Unions, Vice President of the World Federation of Trade Unions, member of the ILO Council, delegate to the UN.

**1953**: The prize for 1952: **Schweitzer, Albert,** France, 1875–1965. (Born in Kaysersberg, Alsace, then part of Germany.) Physician and missionary, founder of the Lambarene Hospital in Gabon.

**1953**: **Marshall, George Catlett,** USA, 1880–1959. General, President of the American Red Cross, former Secretary of State and of Defense, delegate to the UN, originator of the Marshall Plan.

**1955**: The prize for 1954: **The Office of the United Nations High Commissioner for Refugees, Geneva.** An international aid organization established by the UN in 1951.

**1957**: **Pearson, Lester Bowles,** Canada, 1897–1972. Former Foreign Minister, President of the UN General Assembly 1952.

**1958**: **Pire, Georges,** Belgium, 1910–69. Dominican, head of the aid organization for refugees L'Europe du coeur au service du monde.

**1959**: **Noel-Baker, Philip John,** Great Britain, 1889–1982. Member of Parliament. Campaigner for international cooperation and peace.

**1961**: The prize for 1960: **Lutuli, Albert John,** South Africa, 1898–1967. (Born in Southern Rhodesia.) President of the South African liberation movement the African National Congress.

**1961**: **Hammarskjöld, Dag Hjalmar Agne Carl,** Sweden, 1905–61 (awarded the Prize posthumously). UN Secretary General.

**1963**: The prize for 1962: **Pauling, Linus Carl,** USA, 1901–94. California Institute of Technology, Pasadena, California. Campaigner especially for an end to nuclear weapons tests.

**1963**: The prize was divided equally between **The International Committee of the Red Cross,** Geneva. Founded in 1863 and **The League of Red Cross Societies,** Geneva.

**1964**: **King, Martin Luther, Jr.,** USA, 1929–68. Leader of the Southern Christian Leadership Conference, campaigner for civil rights.

**1965**: **United Nations Children's Fund (UNICEF),** New York, established by the UN in 1946. An international aid organization.

**1967**: One-third of the prize money for 1966 was transferred to the Main Fund, and two-thirds to the Nobel Institute's Special Fund.

**1968**: **Cassin, René,** France, 1887–1976. President of the European Court of Human Rights.

**1969**: **The International Labour Organization (ILO),** Geneva.

**1970**: **Borlaug, Norman Ernest,** USA, b. 1914. Led research at the International Maize and Wheat Improvement Center, Mexico City.

**1971**: **Brandt, Willy,** West Germany, 1913–92. Former Chancellor, initiator

**The struggle to end** racial discrimination has run like a scarlet thread through the history of the Nobel Prize for Peace. Nelson Mandela and Frederik Willem de Klerk were awarded the Prize in 1993.

of West Germany's *Ostpolitik*, embodying a new attitude towards eastern Europe and East Germany.

1973: The prize was divided equally between **Kissinger, Henry A.,** USA, b. 1923. Former Secretary of State and **Le Duc Tho,** North Vietnam, 1911–90. (Declined the prize.) Jointly negotiated the Vietnam peace accord in 1973.

1974: The prize was divided equally between **MacBride, Seán,** Ireland, 1904–88. President of the International Peace Bureau, Geneva. UN Commissioner for Namibia and **Sato, Eisaku,** Japan, 1901–75. Former Prime Minister.

1975: **Sakharov, Andrey,** the Soviet Union, 1921–89. Campaigner for human rights.

1977: The prize for 1976 was divided equally between **Williams, Betty,** Northern Ireland, b. 1943. Co-founder of the Peace People and **Corrigan, Mairead,** Northern Ireland, b. 1944. Co-founder of the Peace People.

1977: **Amnesty International,** London. A worldwide organization for the protection of the rights of prisoners of conscience.

1978: The prize was divided equally between **Al-Sadat, Mohammad Anwar,** Egypt, 1918–81. President of Egypt and **Begin, Menachem,** Israel, 1913–92. Prime Minister. Jointly negotiated peace between Egypt and Israel.

1979: **Mother Teresa,** India, 1910–97. Leader of the Order of the Missionaries of Charity.

1980: **Pérez Esquivel, Adolfo,** Argentina, b. 1931. Architect, campaigner for human rights.

1981: **Office of the United Nations High Commissioner for Refugees,** Geneva.

1982: The prize was divided equally between **Myrdal, Alva,** Sweden, 1902–1986. Former Minister, diplomat and delegate to UN disarmament conferences and **García Robles, Alfonso,** Mexico, 1911–91. Diplomat and campaigner for disarmament.

1983: **Walesa, Lech,** Poland, b. 1943. Founder of Solidarity, campaigner for human rights.

1984: **Tutu, Desmond Mpilo,** South Africa, b. 1931. Bishop, former Secretary General of the South African Council of Churches.

1985: **International Physicians for the Prevention of Nuclear War,** Boston.

1986: **Wiesel, Elie,** USA, b. 1928. Author, humanitarian.

1987: **Arias Sánchez, Oscar,** Costa Rica, b. 1941. President of Costa Rica, initiator of peace negotiations in Central America.

1988: **The United Nations Peace-keeping Forces.**

1989: **The 14th Dalai Lama, Tenzin Gyatso,** Tibet, b. 1935. Religious and political leader of the Tibetan people.

1990: **Gorbachev, Mikhail Sergeyevich,** the Soviet Union, b. 1931. President of the Soviet Union, helped to bring the Cold War to an end.

1991: **Aung San Suu Kyi,** Burma, b. 1945. Opposition leader, human rights advocate.

1992: **Menchú Tum, Rigoberta,** Guatemala, b. 1959. Campaigner for human rights, especially for indigenous peoples.

1993: The prize was divided equally between **Mandela, Nelson,** South Africa, b. 1918. Leader of the ANC and **de Klerk, Frederik Willem,** South Africa, b. 1936. President of the Republic of South Africa.

1994: The prize was divided equally between **Arafat, Yasir,** Palestine, b. 1929. Chairman of the PLO and **Peres, Shimon,** Israel, b. 1923. Foreign minister of Israel and **Rabin, Yitzhak,** Israel, 1922–95. Prime minister of Israel. Awarded for their efforts to create peace in the Middle East.

1995: The prize was divided equally between **Rotblat, Joseph,** Great Britain, b. 1908 and **Pugwash Conferences on Science and World Affairs,** b. 1957. For their efforts to diminish the part played by nuclear arms in international politics.

1996: The prize was divided equally between **Belo, Carlos Filipe Ximenes,** East Timor, b. 1948 and **Ramos-Horta, José ,** East Timor, b. 1949. For their work towards a just and peaceful solution to the conflict in East Timor.

1997: The prize was divided equally between the **International Campaign to Ban Landmines** (**ICBL**) and **Williams, Jody,** USA, b. 1950.

1998: The prize was divided equally between **Hume, John,** Northern Ireland, b. 1937 and **Trimble, David,** Northern Ireland, b. 1944. For their efforts to find a peaceful solution to the conflict in Northern Ireland.

1999: **Doctors Without Borders** (**Médecins Sans Frontières**). In recognition of the organization's pioneering humanitarian work on several continents.

2000: **Kim Dae Jung,** Republic of Korea, b. 1925. For his work for democracy and human rights in South Korea and in East Asia in general, and for peace and reconciliation with North Korea in particular.

2001: The prize was divided equally between the **United Nations** and its Secretary General, **Annan, Kofi,** Ghana, b. 1938. For their work for a better organized and more peaceful world.

2002: **Carter, Jimmy,** USA, b. 1924. For his decades of untiring effort to find peaceful solutions to international conflicts.

2003: **Ebadi, Shirin,** Iran, b. 1947. For her efforts for democracy and human rights, especially the rights of women and children, in Iran and the Muslim world in general.

2004: **Maathai, Wangari,** Kenya, b. 1940. For her contribution to sustainable development, democracy and peace.

**january** fin serck-hanssen **february** rolf m. aagaard

**march** herdis maria siegert **april** janne solgaard

**may** jens hauge **june** vibeke tandberg

**july** dag alveng **august** rune johansen

**september** knut bry **october** asle svarverud

**november** ingvar moi **december** per berntsen

# FRIDTJOF NANSEN

Fridtjof Nansen is, and will for ever remain, Norway's greatest hero. In his day he was looked upon as a superman, endowed as he was with an exceptional intellect, great artistic talent and extreme physical strength. Moreover, he possessed a will of iron. Nansen grew up in affluent circumstances in the capital and, like most upper-class Norwegian children, in winter spent much of his free time skiing. Even as a youth he gained a reputation not only as an above-average sportsman but also as an incorrigible skirt-chaser. He was fond of having his picture taken in athletic poses and would early give his name to a close-fitting, muscle-enhancing garment known as the Nansen suit.

He elected to study zoology, and on graduation spent some time as curator of Bergen Museum. However, the indoor life was not for Nansen. His relationships with penpushers and stick-in-the-muds were always strained. He signed on with a sealer, the *Viking*, for an expedition to Jan Mayen Island, something he enjoyed far more than working in a museum. Inspired by Adolf Erik Nordenskiöld's Greenland expedition, he planned to cross Greenland on skis – and without dogs. Forty Norwegians applied to join him on this 670-kilometre-long trip across territory that was at the time still unexplored. Nansen selected five of them and set about making preparations for the journey, at the same time as he took a doctorate in zoology, specializing in the hagfish.

PORTRAIT

As is only to be expected, the expedition was not without its dramatic moments. Nansen followed up the crossing by spending a winter among the Eskimos, for whom he developed a great liking; he subsequently did much to bring their way of life to the attention of the world. Upon his return he was made a Knight of Denmark's Order of Dannebrog and at home he was welcomed as a national hero. His 700-page book *På ski over Grønland* (The First Crossing of Greenland) became a best-seller. It seems that only then was it brought home to the nation what indomitable stuff it was made of. 'I could never compete in popularity with a man who has crossed the inland ice cap,' said a rueful Knut Hamsun.

In 1884 Nansen read a newspaper article that was to have far-reaching consequences. It stated that the ice at the North Pole was in perpetual drift from east to west. Thus was born the idea of journeying to the North Pole on board a vessel held in the grip of the ice. Nansen's aim was the imperial one of planting the Norwegian flag on the pole itself. The Storting made a grant of NOK 200,000 towards the project. The vessel Nansen chose was the *Fram* ('Forward') and it reached the edge of the ice north of Novaya Zemlya on 20 September 1893. It has been said that it was no accident that he decided to take exactly twelve men with him. The vessel also carried thirty-three

Samoyed dogs, large quantities of bock beer, an organ and an ample supply of tobacco. This was something more than an expedition mounted by a band of adventurous young men, as it embodied patriotic parades in the icy wastes on Constitution Day. By the following autumn Nansen had realized that the *Fram* would never reach the North Pole, so he decided to leave the ship, together with a companion, Hjalmar Johansen, and make his way there by dogsled. In this he was unsuccessful, but the two men penetrated further north than anyone had done before. On 8 April 1895, prior to setting out on what was to prove an appalling return journey, at the northernmost point of their trek they planted flags. On their way back they killed and ate their team dogs, one by one, warded off attacks from polar bears and walruses, and constantly found themselves floundering in the sea between ice floes. By August Nansen could see that they would have to spend the winter in the ice. They built a hut from bearskins and to keep warm shared a sleeping-bag. On New Year's Eve, after ten months in the same sleeping-bag, Nansen suggested that in addressing each other they should use the familiar form of address, *du*, in place of the more formal *De* they had used hitherto. When, in June 1896, they again made contact with human beings, their clothes were stiff with animal fat and blood.

Never had Norway's capital witnessed such scenes as when Nansen, now reunited with the crew of the *Fram*, sailed into the Oslo fjord on 9 September that same year. That his achievement coincided with Norway's struggle for independence from years of Swedish rule made him the very symbol of the people's inherent strength and pride. There were Nansen marches and Nansen songs, as well as Nansen aquavit and Nansen beer. He became every boy's hero and every woman's dream – a living icon. The fearless conquerer of the Arctic Ocean accepted an appointment as professor of zoology, though with no obligation to teach. He published an account in several volumes of the *Fram* voyage and embarked on a worldwide lecture tour. These activities brought in so much money that he designed and had built his own palatial residence at Lysaker, on the western outskirts of Oslo. It was inevitable that when the time came to draw the mediaeval king Olav Trygvason to illustrate the Icelandic chronicler Snorri Sturluson's Royal Sagas, Nansen should be the model.

In 1905 it seemed that Nansen, together with Christian Michelsen, was to be the nation's saviour. Acting entirely on his own, he succeeded in turning the mood in Britain to Norway's advantage – which helped towards peaceful dissolution of the union with Sweden. Nevertheless, the playwright and great patriot Bjørnstjerne Bjørnson thought that the explorer had a tendency, both in writing and in speech, to go a little over the top. 'There is just too much of the polar bear in him,' he said. Many found Nansen too stubborn and unyielding. On his expeditions he, and he alone, took photographs, with the consequence that he never appeared in any of them; instead, he had his image inserted into polar landscapes at a photographic studio on his return.

Nansen was proposed as presidential candidate in the newly independent Norway, though he was actually a fervent monarchist and, as a negotiator, contributed to the Danish prince Carl's acceptance of the Norwegian throne as Haakon VII. He accompanied the royal couple on their first tour of the country and, most importantly, taught them how to ski – a skill which, by virtue of his life and work, was to become synonymous with being a true Norwegian.

It may be claimed that Nansen was less successful as a politician. One reason for this was his dislike of the party system and all its works. He dismissed party politics as 'dry fish, bagatelles and personal issues'. He may have been instrumental in forming the breakaway *Frisinnede Venstre* (Independent Liberal) Party, but that was mainly in protest against Gunnar Knudsen's *Venstre* (Liberal) government. The newspaper *Dagbladet* recommended that he be appointed prime minister, and Michelsen did in fact offer him a seat in his government, but Nansen turned it down – he still had far too much to do elsewhere.

He was also beset by problems in his private life. Shortly before setting out on his Greenland expedition he began an affair with a singer, Eva Helene Sars. On the eve of his departure on board the *Fram*, when Eva was

heavily pregnant with their first child, he made the surprising declaration that he had 'only one love, the North Pole'. In the event he was to have a great many loves – far more than his marriage could withstand. The couple separated when, in 1906, Nansen left for London as Norway's ambassador. However, the diplomatic life, with all its formalities, was anathema to him. The following year Eva died, and he became something of a recluse.

Nansen dreamed of being the first man to reach the South Pole, so he evinced considerable generosity when, in 1909, Roald Amundsen asked to borrow the *Fram* for an expedition to the North Pole. Amundsen learned en route that Robert Peary had reached the pole, so he changed his plans and set a course for the South Pole instead, to the undying disappointment of the man who had lent him the ship. Nansen subsequently mounted expeditions to both Siberia and Spitsbergen, but they earned him little in the way of further laurels.

After the First World War Nansen accepted an appointment as Norway's representative to the League of Nations, in which capacity he did sterling work. It is believed that the aid he provided for famine victims in the Soviet Union saved the lives of some seven million people. Also of value was the assistance he gave to Greek, Russian, Turkish and Armenian refugees. He is the only person in history to have been authorized to issue passports in his own name. For his humanitarian activities Nansen was awarded the Nobel Prize for Peace.

Nonetheless, he was disappointed by the lethargy and adherence to doctrine that he encountered among Europe's politicians. In 1925 he helped establish *Fedrelandslaget* (a pan-political, anti-Communist party), which constituted a clear counter to Socialism and the class struggle. The newspaper *Tidens Tegn* advocated formation of a non-Socialist coalition government with Nansen at its head, but the political parties rejected this solution.

Nansen retained his passion for the great outdoors and physical fitness well into old age. Characteristically, the last article he wrote was on the gliding properties on snow of various kinds of wood. To the very end he dreamed of borrowing the airship *Graf Zeppelin* for a scientific polar expedition, but by then his health was failing. He developed a heart condition and died in the garden of his home on 13 May 1930. Four days later, on Norway's Constitution Day, his funeral cortege through the streets of Oslo was followed by 12,000 mourners. In accordance with his wish as a free thinker, his ashes were spread on the wind.

NIELS CHR. GEELMUYDEN

NANSEN, FRIDTJOF (1861–1930), zoologist, polar explorer and humanist. In 1888 crossed Greenland by ski from east to west. 1893–96 led the Fram expedition to the Arctic and, by ski, penetrated further north than anyone before him. Norwegian minister in London 1906–08. From 1920, directed the League of Nations' endeavours to repatriate prisoners of war and introduced the 'Nansen passport' for stateless refugees. In 1921 directed aid work during the famine in the Soviet Union and, in 1922, the exchange of Turkish and Greek minorities, as well as work among Armenian refugees. Awarded the Nobel Peace Prize in 1922.

# FOREIGN POLICY

# SMALL COUNTRY, BIG WORLD

Espen Barth Eide

*On 13 September 1993, Johan Jørgen Holst, the foreign minister of Norway, was standing on the White House lawn in Washington together with President Bill Clinton, PLO leader Yasir Arafat and Israel's Prime Minister Yitzhak Rabin. Thanks to Norwegian mediation, the Israeli Government and the Palestinian political leaders had worked out the so-called* Oslo Accords, *which were now to be signed. This agreement, which outlined a course towards a final solution to the Middle East conflict, was largely a product of the 'Norwegian channel': a negotiation and facilitation effort conducted by the Norwegian authorities in deep secrecy through the early 1990s. The Norwegian foreign minister had become a central player in a global political drama of notable dimensions. Since the end of the Cold War, considerable progress had been made in resolving several international conflicts. Would the highly divisive Middle East conflict now become a thing of the past? The apparent breakthrough marked by the Oslo agreement was celebrated as one of the greatest and most remarkable achievements ever for Norwegian diplomacy.*

*In retrospect we know that the process failed to develop in the way that the architects of the Oslo Accords had hoped. Central players passed away, while extremist groups on both sides managed to undermine the peace process. Today the Middle East is in deep crisis. Some will claim that the belief that this agreement would lead to peace in the region was unrealistic from the start.*

**US President** Bill Clinton thanks Norwegian Foreign Minister Johan Jørgen Holst for his contribution to the signing of the 'Oslo Accords'. The White House lawn, Washington D.C., 13 September 1993.

*In the context of this chapter, the question is a different one: What had brought the Norwegian foreign minister into this situation? How did little Norway manage to chisel out a niche for itself as a facilitator here and – during the years that followed – in so many other international peace processes as well? Can the reason be found, as many Norwegians believe, in Norway's peripheral role as a small nation with no colonial background or hidden agendas? Or, quite the reverse, was it Norway's close relationship with the USA, Israel and the other central players that made possible this special role? Was the tight interaction between voluntary organizations in Norway and the Norwegian state a prerequisite for the 'Norwegian model' – or was it a combination of all these factors, plus an element of happenstance, that resulted in the foreign minister's presence on the White House lawn with the US president that September day? What can this episode tell us about Norway's international role?*

Like any other state, Norway is constantly influenced by changing international circumstances to which it tries to adapt as best it can. *The way* in which any country adapts to these external conditions is determined largely by the experiences, ideas and priorities that have evolved within the framework of its own foreign policy traditions. This may involve balancing between different business interests, or between political principles. In the case of Norway, foreign policy choices are also influenced by the national 'identity debate'. The nation's self-perception and, not least, the question of how Norway and Norwegians wish to be perceived by others, have always been central issues in Norwegian politics. Inherent in the Norwegian self-image are several paradoxes: for example, nationalism, patriotism and self-righteousness exist side by side with a strong internationalist tradition. 'We would like to save the world out there, but don't you get too close to us here at home,' is the watchword.

It is a common perception in Norway that the country's political choices are shaped by its peripheral location in Europe. The true Norwegian is seen as a kind of Isak Sellanraa, the Hamsun character who tends his meagre plot of land way up north, and whose interests are incompatible with the sophisticated societies of the outside world. 'Oslo is far away, but it's even further to Brussels,' was the slogan during the EC referendum debate in 1972. On the other hand, Norway may also be viewed as a global lottery winner. Today it is one of the world's wealthiest nations, with recognized rights to exploit enormous sea areas rich in natural gas, oil and fish: not least as a result of Norwegian efforts to secure the rights of coastal states. From being a poor fringe country on the outskirts of Europe, Norway has become a highly successful operator in today's global economic realities. This is more the result of the country's unique access to raw materials and energy than the product of an advanced industrial culture. However, the Norwegian authorities have played their cards well, especially when it comes to national control of natural resources. The combination of wealth, rich natural resources, and the prevailing self-perception as a 'fringe country' seems to be an important part of the key to understanding Norway's relations with the rest of the world.

Throughout the hundred years that Norway has pursued an independent foreign policy, various phases have been accorded differing degrees of 'prominence' – if not stated explicitly, then at least in practice. During the first years after 1905, it was important for the new establishment to prepare for Norwegian participation in international trade in the best possible way, and otherwise remain undefiled by greater political considerations and ambitions. This led to a primary focus on trade policy, or so-called *low politics*. The distance to continental Europe was to be converted into positive capital. Indeed, non-alignment until 1914 enabled Norway to remain neutral throughout the First World War. During the interwar period Norway endeavoured to contribute to promoting international arbitration and rule of law through the League of Nations. At the same time it was expected that Great Britain, out of self-interest, would want to protect Norway's independence, even though the latter was formally non-aligned. The Nazi German occupation in 1940, however, gave the kiss of death to the belief that this alone would keep Norway outside major political conflicts.

During and after the Second World War, security policy was given primacy in Norwegian foreign policy. The political elite believed that Norway would have to hold a steady course in the progressively harsher political climate, squeezed as it was between the Soviet Union and the USA. Norway actively participated in establishing the United Nations in 1945. The UN has since been described as a 'cornerstone' of Norwegian foreign policy. After some years of attempts at 'bridge-building', Norway finally opted to join the Atlantic Pact in 1949. Together with Marshall Aid, this security-motivated choice of the 'West' was to become central to Norway's commercial as well as political orientation in the decades that followed. Throughout the Cold War, much of the security policy tightrope consisted in striking the right balance between participation and shielding, or deterrence and reassurance, vis-à-vis the Soviet Union. The aim was to increase the credibility of the allied defence of Norway should the country be attacked, but at the same time to avoid fostering Soviet apprehensions of possible Western attacks being launched from Norwegian territory.

Now that the Cold War is over, it is no longer obvious that security policy should maintain this overarching primacy in Norway's foreign relations. Several innovative moves have been made over the past ten to fifteen years: a new policy for the Northern Areas and Russia, through the Barents regional cooperation programme; an active Norwegian policy of mediation and reconciliation in conflict areas throughout the world; and a change in defence policy – away from defence against invasion and towards international participation. In other areas, however, Norway has continued along familiar paths, and a more general debate on Norway's place in a changed world has been slow in coming. The 100th anniversary of the dissolution of the union with Sweden – and thus of an independent Norwegian foreign policy – should present a natural opportunity for launching such a debate. First, let us take a closer look at some main features in the history of Norway's foreign policy.

## 1905–1940: NEUTRALITY AND FRINGE ROLE

On 7 June 1905 Norway declared itself independent from Sweden after a prolonged conflict between the Norwegian Parliament and King Oscar II in Stockholm over the degree of self-government in the union. A central issue had been the demand for a separate Norwegian consular service, one which would represent Norwegian rather than Swedish commercial interests. Norwegian trade and industrial interests were active internationally, in fishery and timber exports and in shipping, but Norwegians did not feel they received the requisite support from the union's Swedish-dominated Foreign Service. The Foreign Service, it was claimed, focused far too much on political squabbles in continental Europe and was shaped by Sweden's international political traditions and ambitions. As early as in 1896 the Norwegian poet and activist Bjørnstjerne Bjørnson had written in the newspaper *Verdens Gang,* pointing out that a future independent Norway would be better off 'having no foreign policy'.

When the declaration of independence was a fact in 1905, Jørgen G. Løvland, the country's first foreign minister, presented a similar argument: 'If one looks at the international situation, one always says emphatically: we will not have any foreign policy.' However, neither Bjørnson nor Løvland meant to suggest that Norway should isolate itself totally from the outside world. What they were expressing was instead a deep scepticism to 'the European warrior states' and their power games. Now that the union had been dissolved, people were well aware of the precarious position of the young Norwegian state, trapped in a 'power triangle' between the naval power of Great Britain to the west and the continental powers of Germany and Russia to the south and east. Individually, each of these states was mightier than even a united Nordic region could ever be. Norway therefore sought to distance itself from the tensions between the Great Powers of the time by utilizing its peripheral position in Europe as a basis for remaining neutral.

Therefore it was vital that the dissolution of the union,

**This contemporary postcard** offers a humorous comment on the events surrounding Norway's secession from Sweden, the choice of government and the appointment of a king in 1905.

**In connection** with Norway's declaration of independence, mobilization took place on both sides of the border, and many people feared a Norwegian–Swedish war. Seen here is a Norwegian frontier-guard company in the summer of 1905.

and thus Norway's independence, should be accepted quickly and not itself become the object of a Great-Power conflict. Norway would not be able to match Sweden militarily, so it was important to consolidate the independence resolution of 7 June through international recognition. Norway's newly established Foreign Service worked actively to achieve this. The need for international recognition also served as an independent argument in favour of the new Norwegian state becoming a monarchy rather than a republic. Around 1905 the central states in Europe were largely monarchies, so it was assumed that acceptance would be more readily granted for a Norwegian kingdom than for a republic. This project was successful, and Great Britain, Russia and Germany chose to signal to the Swedish king that Sweden should leave the recently proclaimed independent Norway in peace instead of creating a conflict. The first state to recognize the new Norwegian state was Russia, and others followed in rapid succession.

The choice of a monarchic government, in other words, had clear international political overtones. Then, when Danish Prince Carl (who took the name Haakon VII) was chosen as the Norwegian king, this, too, had international political implications. In choosing Prince Carl, Norway also chose his wife Maud, the daughter of British King Edward VII, as queen. The Norwegian authorities believed this would form the basis for a close and good relationship between the new Norwegian state and Great Britain – which indeed proved to be the case. The historian Olav Riste has argued that Norwegian neutrality after 1905 was some kind of 'cover' for the implicit British security guarantee.

The period following dissolution of the union in 1905 was characterized by considerable unrest on the international scene. Tensions between the European Great Powers culminated in 1914 with the outbreak of the First World War. Norway succeeded in remaining neutral throughout the War, although there is no doubt that sympathy lay mainly with the western alliance. Nevertheless, with its active merchant marine, Norway was seriously affected by the war. Several thousand Norwegian sailors lost their lives, many of them when their ships were sunk by German U-boats.

Even before 1914, the Norwegian government had been involved in establishing international arbitration systems to prevent recourse to war. After the First World War, US President Woodrow Wilson proposed the establishment of a League of Nations, in order to unite the nations of the world in binding international cooperation. In keeping with its attitude in the prewar years, Norway actively supported this work and, together with most other European states, joined the new world organization. Even though the League of Nations was originally a US concept, President Wilson's proposal for American membership was turned down by the US Congress in 1919. Without US participation, and bedevilled by various structural weaknesses, the League found itself unable to alleviate the tensions that developed in the 1930s and that gradually led to the outbreak of the Second World War.

Two Nordic countries, Norway and Denmark, set a good example for international arbitration when, in 1933, they allowed the sovereignty dispute over Greenland to be settled by the International Court in The Hague. Norway lost, but respected the Court's ruling – which, at the time, was the exception rather than the rule in international relations.

Humanitarian efforts were to become a central element of Norway's foreign policy and national identity. An early example is Fridtjof Nansen's work for refugees and former prisoners of war as High Commissioner for the League of Nations after the First World War, during the famine in the Soviet Union and after the Greek-Turkish war of 1919–22. Nansen was awarded the Nobel Peace Prize in 1922 for his extensive humanitarian work.

**During the Nazi occupation,** Norway's legitimate government continued to operate from London. King Haakon VII and Crown Prince Olav are seen here presiding over a wartime meeting of ministers in the British capital.

### 1940/45–1990: OCCUPATION, BRIDGE-BUILDING, ALLIANCE AND COLD WAR

The combination of non-alignment and the implicit guarantee from Great Britain did not prevent the German Nazi attack on Norway on 9 April 1940. After a few months of armed resistance, all of the country was under Nazi control. Thanks to the Norwegian Parliament's 'Elverum authorization' granted to the Government under dramatic circumstances on 9 April, and the evacuation of both King and government, the Norwegian state was, however, able to continue to operate as a sovereign actor: throughout the occupation, Norwegian foreign policy was managed by the Norwegian government-in-exile in London. Norway as a *state* had succeeded in ending up on the side of the Allies, even though its *territory* was under Axis control. The merchant marine, now controlled through the state organization *Nortraship* (Norwegian Shipping and Trade Mission), ensured continued revenues to the Norwegian state. Nortraship organized the approximately one thousand Norwegian merchant marine vessels that were outside Norwegian territorial waters when the country was occupied. In this way, 'free Norway' was able to take an active part in the Second World War from Allied territory.

The international political experience gained during the war provided the basis for a far more clearly expressed Western orientation, and this was to be decisive for postwar Norwegian foreign policy. It was felt that Norway belonged with 'the North Atlantic population', together with Great Britain and the USA, rather than to continental Europe.

The central choices that were made during the period 1945 to 1949 still characterize Norway's international orientation and affiliations. This period also illustrates how political choices are made in the interface between external events and a country's experience and inherited way of thinking. It took four years, however, before this reinforced Western orientation became a

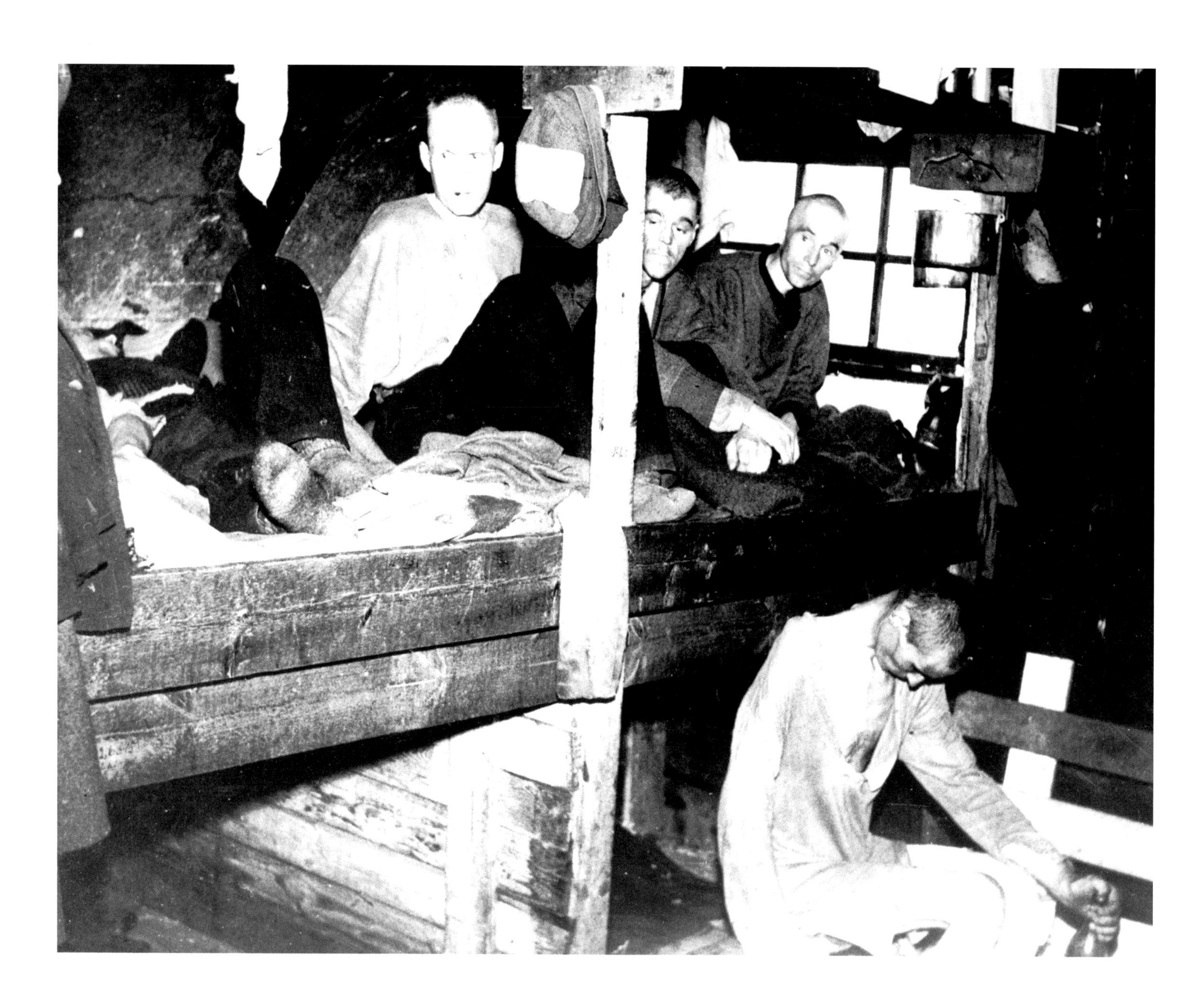

**Soviet prisoners of war** in a slave-labour camp in Norway during the Second World War. The local population did its best to help prisoners from both the Soviet Union and Yugoslavia. Towards the end of the war, Soviet troops liberated northern Norway from the Nazis, which may explain the postwar popularity of the Soviet Union in many quarters in the north.

political reality: first came participation in a new attempt to organize the world through a collective security organization.

During the Second World War, US President Franklin Delano Roosevelt took the initiative to call an international conference to provide the basis for a new world organization after the war. At a meeting of the Allied foreign ministers in Moscow in 1943, he succeeded in gaining the support of the Soviet Union and Great Britain, and the foundation stone of the United Nations was laid. The USA and its allies had great ambitions for this new organization, which was envisaged as forming the basis for a future international order based on international law, collective security and mechanisms for peaceful settlement of conflicts. The new world organization would learn from the mistakes of the League of Nations, and this time the USA would also participate.

From day one, the idea of the establishment of a new, powerful world organization was met with great enthusiasm in Norway. First, it was considered a logical continuation of Norway's interwar commitment to international arbitration and law. Secondly, the UN was seen as an instrument for ensuring good relations among the new superpowers, especially between the Soviet Union and the USA. Even at this early stage, the Norwegian authorities realized that this could become a crucial issue for Norway, given the country's proximity to the Soviet Union and its close political ties with the West. (In fact, even during the Second World War, Norway had anticipated the danger of the Soviet Union and the USA, allies at the time, becoming opponents in the future.) A future East/West conflict would place Norway in an extremely vulnerable situation. At the San Francisco conference where the UN Charter was negotiated in the spring of 1945, Norway's foreign minister and head of delegation, Trygve Lie, eagerly sought a conclusion that would be acceptable to the superpowers. In this way, he thought, they would take the organization seriously, once it had finally been established. Norway henceforth assumed a 'realistic' political attitude in relation to the new organization. For example, the fact that Norway was sympathetic to the superpowers' being granted a right of veto in the Security Council attracted the attention of other small states. Norway chose to serve as a 'bridge-builder' between the superpowers on several other issues as well. Indeed, it was due not least to Trygve Lie and his bridge-building policy that he was found acceptable to both the Soviet Union and the USA when the UN's first secretary general was to be appointed.

Norway's relations with the Soviet Union were especially important during the initial postwar years. Popular feeling towards the Soviet Union was relatively positive. After all, Soviet troops had driven the German Nazi forces out of northern Norway during the final winter of the war. At times Norway was regarded by other Western quarters as being excessively preoccupied with appeasing the Soviet Union: in some international contexts, for example at the 1946 Paris Peace Conference, Norway more than once voted with the Soviet Union and (the future) Eastern bloc against proposals from the Western states.

This bridge-building attitude may be seen as another expression of the general desire for some form of non-alignment in Norway's immediate surroundings, combined with the belief in a 'better-organized world' on the international level. However, this policy also had its critics, and at times the much-exalted Norwegian bridge-building role consisted primarily of keeping a low profile.

Towards the late 1940s, relations between the West, led by the United States, and an increasingly recognizable Eastern Bloc, led by the Soviet Union, turned sour. The Cold War had begun. Norway had based itself on a policy of local non-alignment and global collective security through the UN. Now it had to adjust to these new realities: an international security policy based on good relations between the superpowers was no longer relevant in an increasingly polarized situation.

**The Norwegian government** firmly supported the establishment of the UN in 1945, and Norway's Trygve Lie became the organization's first Secretary General. This 1952 photograph shows Lie signing an agreement for financial aid to India.

**Norway, as one of the Allies,** participated in the postwar occupation of Germany. The Norwegian Brigade was included in the British occupation zone, where it was stationed from 1947 to 1953. This 1947 photograph shows the Norwegian medical corps parading through the main street of Northeim in West Germany.

The Communist takeover of Czechoslovakia in 1948 and the impression that the Soviet Union had imposed Communist regimes in the East European states liberated by the Red Army in 1945 created uncertainty in Norway as to Soviet intentions. For this reason the Labour Party government under Einar Gerhardsen initiated an internal review of its relations with the Communist Party. Several of the architects behind the bridge-building policy adopted after the Second World War eventually decided that it was time for Norwegian security to become more closely linked with the Western powers. This was especially the case for the defence minister, Jens Christian Hauge, previously sceptical to certain aspects of US foreign policy.

The Labour Party had an absolute majority during the period 1945 to 1961, in practice defining Norway's foreign policy throughout this period. However, there was generally broad agreement among the other parties in the Storting – the Norwegian Parliament – with the exception of the Communist Party. Norwegian membership of the North Atlantic Treaty Organization was an important issue at the annual Labour Party Conference in February 1949, where the pro-NATO faction won a resounding victory.

Norway joined NATO in March 1949, as did two of its neighbours, Denmark and Iceland. Like Norway, Denmark had been occupied by Germany. Iceland was not independent in 1939, but had had a British military presence during the war. These countries continued their wartime alliances by opting to become members of NATO. Sweden, which had been neutral in the Second World War, decided to continue its non-alignment policy after the war. In 1948 Finland signed the Agreement of Friendship, Cooperation, and Mutual Assistance with the Soviet Union, primarily to prevent the forced assumption of an East European position. Thus, the concept of a closer Nordic or Scandinavian defence union, mooted in Nordic political circles for some years, had come to naught. Instead, from the 1950s onwards, close Nordic cooperation developed in other areas, especially within the framework of the Nordic Council and gradually also the Nordic Council of Ministers. Through active cooperation, the Nordic countries maintained close contact, despite the potentially divisive effect of the Cold War. In several areas – for example, the common labour market and the Nordic passport union – the Nordic countries were far in advance of integration efforts in continental Europe.

For Norway, as for many other countries that joined NATO, it was important to emphasize that the Atlantic alliance

**After the Second World War**, Norway received substantial material support through the US military aid programme, which contributed to rapid development of an independent Norwegian defence capability. This was not altogether uncontroversial, however. The Norwegian Communist Party organized a separate May Day parade with a home-made American tank – which, in the opinion of the party, was 'not an instrument of peace'.

was a *defence* pact, not an alliance with aggressive intentions towards the Soviet Union. Norway did not want its NATO membership to conflict with previous commitments made in relation to the UN. The Atlantic Pact itself makes this point clear. Article 5 emphasizes that NATO is an alliance in which the members prepare to exercise the form of collective defence authorized in Article 51 of the UN Charter. This article was included at the 1945 San Francisco conference after some dispute, but with the support of Norway. The article established that UN member countries would continue to have the 'inherent right to self-defence', and that such self-defence could be exercised alone or together with others. The Atlantic Pact expressly states that in no way will it change the rights and duties of the parties as members of the UN, and that it will not undermine the Security Council's primary responsibility for maintaining international peace and security.

This was important to the Norwegian authorities for two reasons. First, the Soviet Union was to be *deterred* from attacking NATO members, at the same time as assurances would be given that NATO did not represent a threat of some kind. Secondly, there was a great concern to protect the recently established UN. No one wanted to give the impression, either internationally or in domestic politics, that Norway was abandoning its fundamental belief in the world organization. Thus, we can see that from 1949 Norway combined a belief in genuine collective security through the UN, at least as a long-term ambition, with participation in concrete preparations for collective defence through NATO.

A long-term foreign policy compromise based on the views of the Norwegian Labour Party developed in the years around 1949. The belief in non-alignment and neutrality, which had characterized Norwegian foreign policy thus far, was to be replaced by an *Atlantic* defence and security policy together with an *active global commitment* through the United Nations. In general terms, the 'internationalists' thus chose to accept 'Atlanticism', whereas the 'Atlanticists' accepted a continued commitment to international law and cooperation through the UN. Most Norwegian political parties endorsed this compromise in practice, and organizations – *Den norske Atlanterhavskomité* (the Norwegian Atlantic Committee), *Folk og Forsvar* (People and Defence), *FN-sambandet* (the Norwegian United Nations Association) and others – were established to ensure popular support for the international political choices that had been made. Political opposition continued nevertheless, culminating in the establishment of the *Sosialistisk Folkeparti* (Socialist People's Party) in 1961. Still, this was the exception that proved the rule. The consensus course of Norwegian foreign policy was confirmed by several non-Socialist governments from 1965 onwards, without any dramatic changes in direction.

### NATO and Norwegian defence policy

With NATO membership and the increasing tensions of the Cold War, it became important to build a strong Norwegian defence – one that could function as a first-line response to a possible Soviet invasion and retain as much territory as possible until allied help arrived.

Foreign and defence policy experts, headed by Minister of Defence Jens Christian Hauge, originally wanted a particularly close relationship with Great Britain within the NATO framework. This, they felt, would represent a continuation of the long-term tradition from 1905 when Norway based itself on an implicit British security guarantee, and of the more recent experiences of the Norwegian government-in-exile in London. However, Great Britain was weakened after the war and involved in many international problems, not least those relating to the surrender of its colonies, and had neither the financial nor political strength to provide any significant support to Norway. Instead, the USA gradually took over this role, and US aid became an increasingly important factor in Norway's military build-up. Northern Norway was central in this context. It was important to ensure a certain *holding time* in case of invasion, and a realistic ability to receive allied supplies quickly was essential. The main part of Norwegian defence strategy was concentrated on the county of Troms and *Brigade Nord* (Northern Brigade). The open landscape of Finnmark county was considered difficult to defend against a possible Soviet invasion. Instead, the strategy was to confront the Soviet forces at the 'Lyngen Line' in northern Troms. The idea was to lure an invading Red Army to spread itself out across a vast territory, with the supply and refuelling difficulties this would entail. A number of military bases, airfields and quays were built in the years that followed, many of them jointly financed through NATO budgets.

The Gerhardsen government placed great emphasis on Norway's military ability while strongly emphasizing the reassurance aspect. This led to the development of a special Norwegian military base and nuclear policy: foreign military bases would not be allowed on Norwegian territory, nuclear weapons would not be accepted in peacetime, and allied military exercises would not be permitted in eastern Finnmark.

The question of Franco-Spain's candidacy for membership in NATO was a central topic in Norwegian politics for many years. Here, the Norwegian government placed itself at the head of the resistance to Spanish membership. It became a central moral issue to prevent Spain, whose dictator Francisco Franco had been a *de facto* ally of Hitler, from joining the alliance. Norway's efforts to exclude Spain from NATO, completely counter to explicitly stated US interests, were successful until Spanish democracy was re-established after the death of Franco in 1975. The reason was probably that the USA was more concerned with supporting Norway, a country flanking the Warsaw Pact countries, than Spain, which would be relatively far from any front.

At the start of the Cold War, Norway was still seen as a peripheral player on the sidelines of the actual line of confrontation in central Europe. During the decades that followed, the role of the northern areas was to change – from being

**Concurrently** with Norway's entry into NATO, peaceful relations with the Soviet Union remained a central aim of foreign policy. During a state visit in 1964, Soviet leader Nikita Krushchev joined in a display of Norwegian folk dancing. Norway's long-term prime minister, Einar Gerhardsen, is on the left.

**British soldiers** with Scorpion reconnaissance vehicles undergoing winter training in Norway in March 1976, during the NATO Atlas Express exercise.

peripheral and a 'flank' to becoming an international front line. This reflected both political and technological developments. The shortest air route between the USA and the Soviet Union crossed the polar regions. As the Cold War continued, the strategic significance of nuclear-powered submarines also increased on both sides. The ability to retaliate after an effective nuclear attack, the so-called *second-strike capability*, became a major element of the balance of terror. Technological advances made it possible to ensure such second-strike capability by stationing strategic submarines under the polar ice, where it was particularly difficult for an enemy to pinpoint their location. Accordingly, the maritime areas around Norway became increasingly central in nuclear strategy, and a number of monitoring and warning stations were installed on Norwegian territory. These stations were operated by Norway, but were closely connected to global US networks.

The supply lines across the Atlantic Ocean were also important to Norway's strategic position. If the Soviet Union were to attack Europe, the European allies would depend entirely on supplies from the USA – and such supplies would have to come mainly by sea. Soviet control of Norway's many ice-free harbours would make it much easier for the Soviet Union to cut off these supply lines, so such a situation would have to be avoided at all costs. Various scenarios were developed, all showing that it was unlikely that Norway would manage to stay out of a major war.

This situation led to the desire to make the American security guarantee as visible as possible. Norway continued its military base and nuclear policy with its 'self-imposed restrictions', but this was combined with firm evidence of the US presence through frequent visits by naval units and exercises on and around Norwegian territory. Moreover, in the early 1980s an agreement was reached for pre-positioning of US material in Trøndelag county, in order to facilitate the reception of large American units early in a possible war. Generally speaking, this was a period characterized by strong Norwegian ties with the USA on many levels, often exceeding the formal prerequisites of alliance membership.

For Norway, the Cold War represented 40 years of security policy stability. It was relatively easy to explain Norwegian security policy on Norway's home ground. Close relations with the USA and NATO could be combined with continued 'national' justification of the Norwegian defence model: most of the citizenry saw it as a matter of Norwegians being prepared to defend Norway in Norway, or at least close to Norway, while her allies prepared to come to the rescue. The *de-facto* internationalization of Norway's defence, a logical consequence of joining NATO in 1949, meant that for four consecutive decades the country became a net importer of security. To the people of Britain, the Netherlands, Denmark, Canada, the USA and a number of other allies, the situation was different: in case of war against the Soviet Union, their soldiers would be fighting in foreign lands – for example in Turkey, Germany or Norway. For the generations of Norwegian officers and politicians who grew up during this period, this was the 'normal' situation in NATO. This is probably why, when the Cold War finally came to an end, it took longer for Norway to understand the new realities than it did for many of its allies.

However, the Cold War agreement on security policy was not all-encompassing. Even within the large 'Atlanticist' majority in Norwegian politics opinions differed, and the balance between deterrence and reassurance led to political tension on several occasions. Large political groups in Norway were sceptical towards the role of nuclear weapons in NATO defence strategy throughout the postwar period, and from 1979 an extensive protest movement developed against NATO's deployment of (additional) nuclear weapons in Europe. With well over 100,000 members, the 'No Nuclear Weapons' organization became one of the largest political movements of the time. The immediate cause was the process that resulted in NATO's so-called *double-track decision* in December 1979, which involved deployment of medium-range Pershing II missiles and simultaneous negotiations with the Soviet Union for bilateral disarmament of these missiles and Soviet SS-20 missiles. The movement was part of an increasing Western European anti-nuclear weapons movement, inspired not least by West German political thinking. Leading leftist and centre politicians concurred with the fundamental ideas of the movement, while the Conservative and Progressive parties disassociated themselves from 'unilateral western disarmament', which they believed the movement would lead to.

The Labour Party, under Gro Harlem Brundtland, made an attempt to meet the opposition on its own ground by proposing a nuclear-free zone in the Nordic countries as part of a larger European disarmament solution. The plan did not meet with much enthusiasm in the USA, to put it mildly, and the meeting between foreign ministers Alexander Haig and Knut Frydenlund on 14 May 1981 is described as one of the toughest Norwegian-American political meetings ever. Mr Haig made it abundantly clear he could not recommend the US president to send reinforcements to Norway if such a zone were to be established,

**From the signing** of the 'Grey Zone Agreement' in 1978. L to r: Jens Evensen, Minister for the Law of the Sea; his secretary, Arne Treholt; an interpreter; and the chief Soviet negotiator, Aleksandr Ishkov. Seven years later Treholt was arrested for espionage on behalf of the Soviet Union and Iraq and was subsequently sentenced to 20 years' imprisonment; in 1992 he was pardoned and released.

a statement that made a very deep impression on Mr Frydenlund. The defence-policy radicalization of the Labour Party spread after the party went into opposition in 1981. Public opinion regarding Norwegian foreign policy was further tested in the dispute over President Ronald Reagan's 'Star Wars' initiative in 1983. However, the most dramatic test of Norway–US cooperation was probably the KV-Toshiba case in 1986, when it emerged that Kongsberg Våpenfabrikk (a state-controlled munitions and armaments concern) had been involved in producing control systems that made possible the development of very quiet-running Soviet submarine propellers. The Americans held that this made it difficult to monitor the Soviet Union's submarine-based second-strike capability and thus significantly reduced Western security. The US Congress, in particular, employed very strong language against Norway and Kongsberg Våpenfabrikk. Finally, however, a deeper political crisis was averted when Prime Minister Brundtland succeeded in convincing the Americans that both countries would benefit by putting an end to the matter.

In broad terms, however, general consensus around the Atlanticist project dominated throughout the period. The Cold War had led the flank country Norway into a close alliance with the USA, and the Norwegian population's support of both Norwegian defence policy and NATO was among the highest in the alliance throughout the postwar period.

Relations between Norway and the Soviet Union during the Cold War were heavily influenced by the northern area's becoming a highly political deployment area. The relationship was correct, but restrained. Trading and other contacts between Norway and the Soviet Union in the north were limited. Territorial boundaries remained fixed and were not disputed. However, much of the political contact concerned clarification of the offshore boundary line, with negotiations continuing more or less uninterruptedly from 1967. In 1977 a provisional grey zone or 'disputed area' was delineated in the Barents Sea and a fisheries protection zone was defined around Svalbard. In other respects a *modus vivendi* was reached in Soviet–Norwegian relations on Svalbard, where the Soviet Union recognized Norwegian sovereignty while Norway accepted Soviet coal mining and permanent settlement at Barentsburg and Pyramiden. For decades, both the Soviet Union and Norway subsidized mining operations on Svalbard to demonstrate their commitment to maintaining a significant presence on this Arctic archipelago.

### Global commitments and Norwegian aid policy

The other side of the coin in terms of political compromise that developed after 1949 concerned a continued Norwegian commitment to the UN and international fair play and social justice. In 1952 the Storting established the Aid Fund for Underdeveloped Countries, which later became NORAD. The first Norwegian aid projects were directed towards impoverished fishermen in Kerala in southern India, and consisted in helping to provide more modern vessels and fishing technology. Norway was a pioneer in modern international development cooperation, gradually becoming one of the world's leading donors in per capita terms. (In certain sectors it has even been one of the world's major donors even in absolute terms.) Norwegian authorities subscribed to long-term aid programmes, focusing on a few selected priority countries. Together with the authorities of these countries, ambitious and resource-demanding plans were drawn up to develop infrastructure and industry. The aim was to raise them from poverty in the same way that Norway had itself developed some decades earlier. A considerable share of the development assistance budget was channelled through multilateral organizations and programmes. In this way, Norway exercised a relatively significant influence on global aid policy in the postwar period, and also enjoyed a certain prestige in the Third World. By the 1980s and 1990s, however, Norwegian authorities had to admit that the model for international aid developed in the postwar period had not always produced the desired results and that in some cases it even served to encourage aid dependency rather than real economic progress.

Norwegian development assistance involvement received broad political support, most of it from the Labour Party and the Christian Democratic Party, along with the ecclesiastical and labour organizations in this field. Despite their somewhat disparate starting points, they were united in wanting Norway to provide substantial development assistance and work actively for greater international justice. Public interest, however, focused more on the scope rather than the content of such assistance: whereas there was strong public support for a high volume of aid in terms of its share of the GDP, decisions regarding its content and direction were reserved for more specialized circles. From the 1970s, corporate elements developed through increasingly close cooperation between the state (through NORAD) and voluntary organizations which became active in Norwegian aid policy.

**Norwegian development assistance** began with the Indian-Norwegian Kerala fishery project (1952-62), which became an important part of Norway's aid to India. Norway aimed to secure a better life for poverty-stricken Indian fishermen by providing them with modern, motorized fishing vessels. Regrettably, at the time it was not realized that the project actually deprived the traditional fishermen of their living. Not everything has turned out as planned with Norwegian development assistance.

A conspicuous feature of Norwegian development assistance policy is the extent to which it has been detached from commercial policy. Attempts have been made to encourage Norwegian investment in developing countries, but Norway itself has been one of the most closed markets as regards access for developing countries. Imports from such countries have largely remained static at about one-tenth of total imports to Norway.

In addition to its assistance to developing countries, Norway also involved itself in a number of international conflict issues during the Cold War. This *involvement policy* led to extensive Norwegian political efforts vis-à-vis Central and South America – including opposition to the dictatorial regimes in Chile and Argentina in the 1970s and active support to Jamaica under Michael Manley during the same period, and then to Nicaragua under the Sandinistas in the 1980s. The Norwegian Labour Party in particular here saw a 'third way' between Communism and US-oriented market liberalism. The Nicaraguan policy led to tensions between Norway and the

USA, who under the presidency of Ronald Reagan actively sought to bring about the fall of the Sandinista government by supporting the so-called *Contra* forces.

The apartheid regimes of southern Africa also attracted considerable attention at an early stage, and the anti-apartheid movement met with great popular sympathy in Norway. From the late 1970s this became a domestic policy issue when the UN encouraged an oil boycott of South Africa – and much of the oil was being transported by Norwegian-owned ships. The Norwegian Council for Southern Africa gathered Norwegian parties and youth organizations in systematic work towards majority rule in South Africa and against Norwegian oil transportation. At times this created considerable problems for the Norwegian authorities, who tried to shift attention to the oil-producing countries and otherwise compensate with other measures against South Africa, Southern Rhodesia (later Zimbabwe) and Namibia. In the 1980s and early 1990s Norway worked actively in South Africa in support of the ANC and other internal apartheid resistance movements, partly on the borderline of what is considered traditional diplomatic practice. Funds allocated as 'help to apartheid victims' were in fact channelled to oppositional South African organizations, and money was sent by diplomatic bag so that it would not be traced by the South African apartheid authorities.

**Europe – a source of much strife**

Whereas there was relatively broad agreement on both NATO and UN policies in the postwar period, Norway's financial and political relations with Europe were much more disputed. The question of membership in the EEC, later the EU, has been the most harrowing issue in recent Norwegian political history.

While the Second World War was still raging, the idea of an extensive European union once peace returned was formulated, to stimulate postwar economic reconstruction and to establish a political order that could avoid the mistakes made after the First World War and the misery of the 1930s. The Hague conference on large-scale European political integration in 1948 did not bring about the desired results, and six continental states chose instead to begin functional integration based on the European Coal and Steel Community (ECSC), formally established in 1951. France, Germany, Italy and the Benelux countries continued working together on the issues of non-military utilization of nuclear power (Euratom) and a general European common market (EEC), both formalized in the 1957 Treaties of Rome. In establishing the EEC, the treaty stated that the goal was 'an ever-closer union of the people of Europe' through gradual sectoral integration.

Great Britain did not take part in these efforts. London supported the idea of free trade between the European states, but did not share the long-term political ambition built into the Rome Treaties. Britain therefore took the initiative to form a competing organization, the European Free Trade Association (EFTA), established 1960. EFTA was to facilitate free trade in products between member countries, but without establishing a joint customs union toward external states in the way that the EEC intended to do. Norway chose to join the British in EFTA – an expression of its traditional orientation towards Great Britain and of its scepticism towards continental Europe ever since 1905. Norway saw itself more as a member of an Atlantic society than as part of a continental European tradition. Moreover, the apolitical free-trade focus corresponded to the trade-political logic that had characterized Norwegian foreign policy in the years after 1905 and dissolution of the union with Sweden. Both Norwegians and Britons were free traders, and were comfortable in that role. Thus in 1960 Halvard Lange, Norway's Minister of Foreign Affairs, signed the *Stockholm Convention* establishing EFTA, together with Austria, Denmark, Portugal, Sweden, Switzerland and the UK.

On the European continent, the experience of the Second World War and the threat of new political unrest and a possible Communist takeover in Western Europe led to a strong desire for long-term political and economic stability through extensive European integration – but not in Norway. Norwegian security policy focused more on the Barents Sea and the Kola Peninsula, and on the relationship between the superpowers, than on internal conditions in Western Europe.

Although Great Britain had originally launched EFTA as an alternative to the more far-reaching European integration process, it soon became apparent that EFTA would not emerge victorious from the struggle to become the dominant economic organization in Europe. Under Prime Minister Harold Macmillan, Britain opted in 1961 to apply for membership in what had become the European Communities. Norway followed Britain's example and applied for membership in April 1962.

However, President Charles de Gaulle of France saw Great Britain's application as an attempt to gain control of – and put brakes on – the European integration process. In 1963 he vetoed British membership, and with this the idea of Norwegian membership also collapsed. The same thing happened again in 1967. After de Gaulle resigned in 1969, however, it again became possible for the British to apply for EC membership. Together with Denmark, Ireland and Norway, Great Britain negotiated a membership agreement in 1972, aiming for membership from 1 January 1973.

### The EC dispute of 1972

There was disagreement about Norwegian EC membership in the early 1960s, but the issue became even more controversial from the late 1960s and into the 1970s. A sizeable movement, across party lines, developed against Norwegian membership. To remove all doubt concerning popular support for EC membership, the Labour Party government under Trygve Bratteli decided to hold a referendum on the issue in March 1972. As a majority in the Storting, the labour unions and the employers' organizations, along with most of the media, all favoured membership, the government assumed that it would get a majority. In the event it failed to do so. After one of the most dramatic political proceedings ever in Norway, on 25 September 1972 a majority (53.5%) of the electorate voted against membership. Although the referendum was merely advisory, the government decided to withdraw its application, and so Norway did not follow when the other three applicant countries joined the European Community on 1 January 1973. Bratteli treated this issue as a vote of no confidence, with the result that it was the new Conservative coalition government of Lars Korvald that came to negotiate a free-trade agreement between Norway and the EC in 1973.

The question of Norwegian EC membership was put on hold for almost 15 years, while the players in the dispute licked their wounds and chose to focus on other issues. As Knut Frydenlund, Norway's Minister of Foreign Affairs from October 1973 until 1981, later pointed out, after the referendum it was feared that Norway would be seen as drifting towards neutralism. Thus it became necessary to compromise by further strengthening ties with the USA in the 1970s and '80s.

The years that followed were marked by oil crises and economic stagnation in large parts of Western Europe. This also affected EC cooperation, which went into 'eurosclerosis' until well into the 1980s. Europe's position in the world economy was weakened, and unemployment rose.

**The EEA agreement** between the EFTA and EU countries is the most comprehensive international legal agreement ever entered into by Norway. Its initiators were EU President Jacques Delors and Norwegian Prime Minister Gro Harlem Brundtland.

Headed by former French Minister of Finance Jacques Delors, the EC gained renewed impetus. In 1985 the so-called *1992 Project* was launched, to prepare for a true *internal market* by removing non-tariff obstructions between member countries. The project consisted in implementing 300 concrete resolutions by the end of 1992 to facilitate the unobstructed flow of products, services, capital and labour throughout the EC area. The project breathed fresh life and enthusiasm into the EC during the second half of the 1980s.

### The EEA agreement in the making

Revitalization of the European Community raised the question of the other West European countries' relationship with the organization. Together with Norway's Prime Minister Gro Harlem Brundtland, Jacques Delors advocated talks between the EC and the then six EFTA countries – Finland, Sweden, Austria, Switzerland, Norway and Iceland. The idea was to expand the internal market to cover all of Western Europe. Although the EC was far larger than EFTA, EFTA was its major trading partner. Together, the twelve EC countries and six EFTA countries would make up the world's largest internal market, and in practice cover all of Western Europe. The EFTA countries stated that they wanted 'to further strengthen our special relationship with the EC based on a balance between rights and

**The civil war** in Bosnia and Herzegovina evolved into the most savage conflict in Europe after the Second World War. In 1993 Thorvald Stoltenberg was appointed UN mediator in the Balkans. He is seen here at the UN-controlled airport in Sarajevo.

obligations'. They said they were prepared to 'consider ways together with the EC in which to achieve a more structured community with joint decision-making processes and administrative institutions with the aim of making cooperation more efficient'. The approach would use 'reciprocal approval of equal legislation and joint decision-making processes', the aim being to develop a balanced system with a large degree of reciprocity.

These ideas developed before the fall of the Berlin Wall, at a time when East European membership in the EC was still inconceivable. In other words, the EC and EFTA largely constituted the whole European integration potential. The idea of EC-EFTA cooperation was also attractive because four EFTA members – Austria, Finland, Sweden, and Switzerland – were non-aligned or neutral countries. In this way they could participate in the 1992 process without having to join the EC, which they considered incompatible with their non-aligned status as long as the framework of the Cold War defined their activities.

The foundations for negotiations on a European economic cooperation area were laid in Oslo in February 1989. Negotiations continued until 1992, and the agreement was signed at the beginning of 1993. The European Economic Area – EEA – was established one year later, on 1 January 1994. The then EEA members were the twelve members of the EC (now EU, the European Union) and all the EFTA countries except Switzerland, which had rejected the EEA in a referendum in 1992. As we shall see in the next section, this was to be a short-lived situation.

## NORWEGIAN INTERNATIONAL POLICY AFTER THE COLD WAR – FROM 9.11 TO 11.9

The fall of the Berlin Wall and the end of the Cold War were the major historical events in Europe – and in Norway – since the formative years between 1945 and 1949. The time that followed was characterized by both uncertainty and optimism. It was characterized by uncertainty because the old framework disappeared and a new way of thinking had to be introduced in several political areas. The Soviet Union was dissolved and a new Russia was emerging. The Balkan wars proved that Europe was not to be spared war and unrest, as many people had hoped, and it took many years before hostilities were halted in south-eastern Europe. The Western security community came under pressure. However, the period was also characterized by a fundamental optimism. The West had won the Cold War, and values like democracy, human rights and a free market economy enjoyed a more prominent position than ever. A financially and politically united Europe was no longer a utopian dream. For most of this period the Clinton Administration governed the USA, and many Europeans discovered that the USA and Europe had common goals for the world beyond the Cold War. Nuclear weapons did not disappear, but the fear that they would be used was noticeably reduced. In the early 1990s the UN was again flourishing, and several ambitious new peace-keeping operations were initiated. Many envisaged that a world no longer marked by East/West conflict could finally focus on the real global challenges, such as the poverty gap and environmental issues.

For simplicity I will call this period 'the 1990s', although this is not entirely accurate: in reality it encompasses the time between 9 November 1989 and 11 September 2001. Several limiting factors disappeared together with the Cold War, and new opportunities arose. Some opportunities were quickly seen, while others took longer to develop – simply because of the blinker effect of the long and unbroken tradition of a specific security-political viewpoint.

### Norway and Europe – alone on the outside?

One important line of development in Norway's foreign policy during this period was the replay for EU membership.

Although the EEA negotiations from 1989 to 1992 led to the desired result, the basic idea was taken over by the wide-ranging historical events that finally ended the Cold War. The foundations were laid before the fall of the Berlin Wall, at a time when it was not envisaged that neutral and non-aligned states like Finland, Sweden, Austria and Switzerland would apply for EC/EU membership as such. However, Mikhail Gorbachev's *glasnost* and *perestroika* in the late 1980s signalled a significantly milder climate in Eastern Europe, after several East European countries had begun to relax their domestic policy and border controls. On 9 November 1989, the Berlin Wall was torn down by deliriously happy East Berliners, without interference by the authorities. From then on, it was only a question of time before the division of Europe into blocs would be a thing of the past. In rapid succession, Germany was reunited on the premises of the Federal Republic, the Warsaw Pact was dissolved and the Soviet Union was split up into its individual states.

To the EC it now became both possible and necessary to further develop its existing, mainly economic, cooperation into a more politically oriented community. The international and security political 'surroundings' of the EC were changing rapidly, and the community could no longer have a purely economic focus. The idea of an economic and monetary union was supplemented by the idea of a political union. The two were combined in the Maastricht Treaty in 1992, which established the European Union, a direct consequence of the removal of the Iron Curtain in Europe. The Maastricht Treaty entered into force in November 1993, and thus the EC became the EU.

Suddenly, East European membership of the EU was no longer inconceivable, and the neutral and non-aligned countries could reconsider their relationship with the West European cooperation. While EEA negotiations were still taking place, Sweden, Finland, Austria and Switzerland chose to apply for EU membership, which Norway also did, in the autumn of 1992.

Once again the question of membership was fiercely debated, now complicated by the ongoing EEA negotiations. Some supporters regarded the EEA as a natural step on the road towards full membership; others considered it a bulwark against EU membership. The EEA agreement gave Norway, as an EFTA member, access to most areas of the internal market without affecting the country's agriculture and fisheries.

Norway did not have to participate in the economic and monetary union, nor make commitments to the more political ambitions of the European Union. Norway's Christian Democratic Party and the left wing of the Labour Party, especially, had many members who supported the EEA, but not the EU. By contrast, the (originally agrarian) Centre Party and the Socialist Left Party were opposed to both the EEA and EU, arguing that they were two sides of the same coin. The Conservative Party and the majority of the Labour Party led the supporters of the EU.

Norway held a referendum on 28 November 1994, as the last country of four (Austria, Finland and Sweden had already voted 'yes' earlier that year). The result was very similar to that of 1972. This time, 52.2% voted against membership, and the proposal fell. From 1 January 1995, the EU was expanded by the addition of Austria, Finland and Sweden. EFTA membership in the EEA was correspondingly reduced, now consisting only of Norway, Iceland and Liechtenstein (which had joined EFTA in 1991). In view of the situation six years earlier, when the EEA negotiations were initiated, this was rather paradoxical. From being the EC's largest trading partner with close to 30 million inhabitants, EFTA now had slightly over 4.5 million inhabitants. And with the exception of the mini-state Liechtenstein, two NATO allies (Norway and Iceland) remained outside the EU, while three of the four non-aligned applicant countries had joined. Switzerland chose to participate in neither the EU nor the EEA, but many years later negotiated an extensive set of bilateral agreements similar to the EEA agreement in content, but without the institutional 'balance' and formal dispute mechanisms embedded in the EEA agreement.

The two-pillar system of the EEA had been retained, despite the obvious difference in size between the two sides. The EU member states are monitored by the European Commission, and Iceland, Liechtenstein and Norway by the EFTA Surveillance Authority, while formal political cooperation is pursued through the EEA Council and the EEA Committee, among other channels. In this way, Norway, Iceland and Liechtenstein have a far more 'balanced' situation, institutionally speaking, than could have been dreamt of today, if the agreement were to be renegotiated without the larger EFTA countries. On the other hand, regarding political realities, the agreement is highly unbalanced. In practice, the agreement has become a method of unilateral adjustment by EFTA to EU resolutions. The EFTA states' right of reservation against adopting new EU legislation has never been put into practice.

Why did Norway say 'No' once more, even in a situation where its closest neighbours, Finland and Sweden, had already opted to join the EU? There is no simple answer to this question. Some point to Norway's petroleum assets – that the country had simply become so rich and financially independent as to be exempt from the 'laws of nature' that others had to observe. It is also worth remembering that the difference in voting between Norway and Sweden was relatively small: while the result was 52.2% *against* the EU in Norway, 52% voted *for* the EU in Sweden. Can the difference simply be explained by Sweden being in the midst of a financial crisis in the early 1990s, while this was a period of prosperity in Norway? Others describe the 'No' of the majority as a successful mobilization of the 'nation' against the 'state'. They claim that the 'No' side managed to exploit the traditional scepticism to 'the rulers in Oslo' acting in collusion with foreign powers – in the same way as during the Danish period and the union with Sweden, or when the Norwegian King Sverre spoke out against Rome, 763 years before the Rome Treaty. In some quarters it was also asserted that the successful Winter Olympics held at Lillehammer in the same year, with all the Norwegian medals and national symbolism that followed, had given new impetus to a belief in everything Norwegian and a corresponding scepticism to anything foreign.

Did any of this have any real significance? Or was it simply sectoral interests that were allowed to dominate? Agricultural interests were generally united in claiming that EU membership would lead to serious pressure on Norway's generous farming subsidies and strict import restrictions, while the fisheries feared forfeiture of national control of the country's rich ocean areas. These sectors were very prominent on the 'No' side, and also contributed much of the financing. Was this decisive?

The truth is probably that all these factors had a bearing, and that it is difficult to gauge the relative influence of each one. What is clear, however, is that the Norwegian EU debate differed from that of the other applicant countries, also because Norway had already had a corresponding debate in 1972. Interestingly, the views and arguments of the radical 1970s reappeared in the café and Interrail culture of the 1990s, having hibernated since the last round. It has also been suggested that the EEA agreement actually contributed to Norway's remaining outside the EU, in that it provided the security attendant on the country's being part of the internal market anyway – so one could vote against EU membership without any great economic risk.

While the Bratteli government resigned after the defeat in 1972, the Brundtland administration chose to remain in power after the result of the referendum in 1994. Already the following day Prime Minister Brundtland indicated that Norwegians would have to roll up their sleeves and make the best of the situation. Norway already had the EEA agreement as a platform, and was concerned with maintaining it despite the imbalance. The EEA agreement included Norway in the main elements of EU economic cooperation, through what EU jargon calls pillar I (the community area), but not with the economic and monetary union. In the 1990s, however, much of the development in the EU took place in pillar II (common foreign and security policy) and pillar III (justice and home affairs). The government, therefore, also sought to develop bilateral agreements with the EU in these areas. Norway set about adjusting to the EU joint international policy, and as a general rule associated itself with most of the EU joint comments and statements in international fora. It also started preparations for providing armed forces for the EU's common security and defence policy, ESDP. Thirdly, Norway and Iceland applied for membership in the Schengen cooperation for common external border control of people's movements. Although this cooperation was originally restricted to EU members, Iceland and Norway succeeded in convincing the Schengen states that it would be easier to exercise surveillance over the Union's external border along the well-controlled (and relatively short) Norwegian-Russian border than along the long and very open Swedish-Norwegian border. Furthermore, a Nordic passport union had already existed for more than 40 years, and would have to be dissolved if Schengen borders were to be established between the Nordic countries.

It is worth noting that these active accommodations have taken place not only under the Labour Party governments of Gro Harlem Brundtland, Thorbjørn Jagland and Jens Stoltenberg, who were all pro-EU, but also under the 'No-government' of Kjell Magne Bondevik (1997–2000) and Bondevik's coalition government (2001–), which had its self-declared 'suicide clause' linked to the question of EU membership. The policy has received broad support in the Storting. Only the Centre Party and the Socialist Left Party have taken a stance as opponents of the adjustment policy. However, as to the former, its resistance was not so strong that the party could not be part of the first Bondevik coalition government, which oversaw Norway's final accession to the Schengen agreement.

Today, Norway is the EU's closest cooperation partner outside the Union itself. No country in the world is more integrated with the EU without actually being a member; Norway participates actively in the internal market, in judicial policy, and in the areas of defence and foreign policy.

Debate on the status and future of the EEA agreement did not begin until recently. By 2004 it was becoming increasingly difficult for Norway to achieve 'special arrangements', first and foremost because the European Commission for its part has had to stick to the straight and narrow path in relation to requirements from a group of countries that actually wanted full membership, but first had to make significant changes themselves. The problems of Norway, Iceland and Liechtenstein simply carry less weight. Even if the EEA does not become outdated, the question is how long it can be used as a permanent platform for Norway's europolitical challenges. It is difficult enough to evoke an understanding for Norway's special 'problems' among the traditional West European EU states, and it will not be easier among new member states who have had to undergo a comprehensive and painful adjustment process in preparing for membership. The expansion of the EU from 1 May 2004 has made even more obvious the imbalance between the EU and the EFTA sides of the EEA.

### The Norwegian model: 'Travellers in peace'?

During the Cold War, parties to local conflicts were often associated with one side or the other. Whether right or wrong, this meant that superpower interests 'infected' many local conflicts, thus preventing progress. In the far more favourable international climate that developed after 1989, this 'superpower influence' disappeared, and several previously locked conflicts could now be reopened and resolved – or at least steered back on course. There was great optimism, especially in the early 1990s. Norway attracted international attention by making an important innovative move: the new Norwegian peace initiative. Although its roots are older, this policy has flourished especially after the end of the Cold War.

This climate provided proper scope for Norway's 'special mediation services'. Ministers of foreign affairs during this period – Thorvald Stoltenberg, Johan Jørgen Holst, Bjørn Tore Godal, Knut Vollebæk and Thorbjørn Jagland – all indicated a political willingness to offer mediation or mediation facilitation in several international conflict areas. The sum total of the Norwegian involvement has not necessarily been the result of an

**Modern civil wars** leave in their wake enormous numbers of mines and undetonated explosives which may kill and mutilate long after peace returns. Here, trained personnel from the Norwegian People's Aid organization are seen clearing mines in Ucua, Angola.

overall plan, and Norway has often become involved in a particular conflict area by chance. All in all, however, 'peace activism' has become something akin to a trademark of Norwegian diplomacy since the Cold War, and Norway is constantly being asked to contribute in new, specific situations. Areas of conflict in which Norway has so far been involved, whether as mediator or facilitator, include Aceh (Indonesia), Bosnia-Herzegovina, Colombia, El Salvador, Ethiopia and Eritrea, the Philippines, Guatemala, Israel and Palestine, Cambodia, Kosovo, Croatia, Cyprus, Macedonia, Mozambique, Namibia, Serbia and Montenegro, Sierra Leone, Sri Lanka, Sudan and South Africa, to mention the most important.

However, there has not been complete agreement in political circles on this as a Norwegian focus area. On several occasions, Nils Morten Udgaard, foreign editor of the influential Oslo daily *Aftenposten*, has pointed out the danger of overemphasizing peripheral problems a long way from Norway instead of attending to Norway's 'real' interests. Before the change of government in 2001, Conservative Party leader Jan Petersen often criticized this form of foreign policy, which in his opinion was conducted at the expense of more important topics nearer to home. On becoming Minister of Foreign Affairs from October 2001, however, Petersen too pursued the Norwegian mediation policy, and thus it became more accepted. One clear side-effect of this activity is a high profile for Norway among the main actors in, for example, the USA and the EU. The conflicts in the Middle East, Sri Lanka and Sudan have proved good door-openers for Norwegian foreign-policy makers – although this does not necessarily mean that the Norwegian authorities know what to do once they have become involved in any particular conflict.

As mentioned, in per capita terms Norway is among the world's largest contributors to development assistance programmes. Roughly speaking, Norway has been on the same level as, for example, Sweden and Denmark in this field. Interestingly, Norway has set aside a significant proportion, about 20% of the OECD-approved aid budget, for more flexible political use. These funds are spent independently from the more long-term, programme-based NORAD appropriations, and have, for example, made it possible to 'lubricate' the machinery in various peace processes on a day-to-day basis and to provide so-called *support to democracy*. Whether this has involved organizing a meeting at short notice, supplying observers or facilitating so-called *quick impact* or start-up measures, this flexibility has been of immeasurable help to Norwegian foreign-policy officials. Again, this has been possible because of general agreement within the Storting as to the importance of these activities, and because the Storting has been confident that the money is spent in keeping with the overall objectives of Norway's aid and foreign policy.

Another special feature of Norwegian foreign policy is the interaction with the non-governmental sector. Several of the peace processes in which Norway is involved originate from many years of presence by voluntary organizations. Alert key persons have spotted the opportunities, and because of the direct communication between the voluntary organizations and the diplomats, the road to official Norwegian involvement has often been short. For example, Petter Skauen's long-term involvement in Latin America for the Norwegian Church Aid was instrumental in bringing about the peace process in Guatemala, where Norway acted as midwife. This in turn led to the signing of the peace agreement between Guatemala's authorities and the guerrillas in Oslo City Hall in 1996.

Norway's long-term involvement in the Middle East is another example. What Norway did here was to facilitate an informal channel between the Palestinians and Israelis in a situation where an official channel also existed (including the Madrid Conference in 1991). The creation of an atmosphere that facilitates a mutual search for constructive opportunities, far from the conflict and domestic political realities, has gradually become a Norwegian 'mediation strategy'. After the Oslo Accords were signed in 1993, Norway followed up with financial and political support to the implementation process, including financing of the new Palestinian Authority.

The Oslo Accords would hardly have been possible had Norway not enjoyed a good relationship with both Israel and the USA from the outset. In this case the key was not Norway's independent position, but rather its close relations with two main actors. After the Second World War, Norway developed a very good relationship with Israel, and until well into the 1980s, Norway's Middle East policy remained markedly more Israel-friendly than was common elsewhere in Western Europe. Then, during Knut Frydenlund's terms as foreign minister (1973–1981 and 1986–1987), contact was established with Yasir Arafat and other Palestinian leaders, and gradually Norway also developed good relations with the Palestinians – especially between the Labour parties of the two countries – without this affecting its close bonds with Israel. Precisely for this reason, Norway became an attractive communication channel. The Norwegian authorities were heard by both Israel and the USA, and thus also became a meaningful partner for the Palestinians, even if other European countries were more vociferous about the Palestinian situation. It was against this historical backdrop that Norway's Terje Rød-Larsen could manage to organize a meeting between the Israeli academic Yair Hirschfeld and PLO's Abu Ala in London in December 1992. This formed the basis for the real Oslo Peace Process. Johan Jørgen Holst inherited the Oslo Peace Process from Thorvald Stoltenberg, and during his term as foreign minister made extensive efforts to achieve a decisive breakthrough.

Both before and after the breakthrough, the Institute for Applied Social Science (FAFO) was central in the Oslo process. FAFO's survey of living conditions in Gaza, later expanded to cover the entire region, illustrates another characteristic of the process, in that the Norwegian Ministry of Foreign Affairs worked closely together with independent institutions for applied research, in practice making them participants in the political process rather than external analysts. This close interaction was not above criticism. In particular, Professor Terje Tvedt at the University of Bergen has criticized this in his report on 'the Norwegian model'. In his opinion, 'the Norwegian Samaritan' must be critically examined and one should look at what he calls a 'national corporate system' in which authorities, organizations and researchers have developed a 'close southern-political community' exempt from general democratic control.

**In 1983 Norway** appointed its first Development Aid Minister, Reidun Brusletten of the Christian Democratic Party. She is seen here visiting Sidamo province in Ethiopia together with Ethiopian Foreign Minister Goshu Wolde (second to the left of Brusletten).

Another area, in which Norwegian authorities have worked closely together with civilian society, and with a clear political profile, is the Balkans. Here too, in addition to physical reconstruction, Norway has been especially concerned with contributing to the development of democracy and reform of the security sector. Using the model from South Africa a decade earlier, Norway, during Knut Vollebæk and Thorbjørn Jagland's terms as Ministers of Foreign Affairs (1997–2001), directed its humanitarian aid to the opposition to the Milosevic regime in Yugoslavia. This aid was not delivered to the opposition parties as such, but was distributed so as to support the activities of the democratic opposition, especially on the municipal level and within free and independent media. Again, Norway balanced on the borderline of traditional diplomatic custom, and without the consent of the state in question. However, this was consid-

**Over the years,** more than 55,000 Norwegians, here represented by Norwegian soldiers of the UNIFIL force in Lebanon in 1988, have participated in UN peacekeeping operations.

ered acceptable in Norway, because both South Africa under apartheid and rump-Yugoslavia under Milosevic were formally boycotted by the UN anyway, and Norway wanted to show that it was possible to support South Africans and later Serbs without supporting the states as such. Here, Norway exploited its role as a small nation to do things larger states would have had great difficulties doing. As far as Serbia is concerned, Norway was also able to draw on the particularly good historical relationship between Norwegians and Serbs that dates from the Second World War, when large numbers of Yugoslavian prisoners of war were sent to Norway by the Nazis. This special relationship made it difficult for the authorities in Belgrade to crack down on Norwegian activity, but a series of warnings were issued. Norway's efforts attracted international attention and became a foreign-policy trump card for Norwegian authorities in relation to both the EU and the USA. Since the change of regime in October 2000, Norwegian authorities have developed a close relationship with the new leaders.

### New Northern Area policy

The end of the Cold War opened up for major changes to Norway's Northern Area policy. For more than 40 years, Norway's relations with the Soviet Union had been almost entirely defined by security-policy concerns. NATO membership, close ties with the USA, a Norwegian defence focusing on northern Norway, and the self-imposed military base and nuclear restrictions – these had been the main elements of Norwegian deterrence and reassurance policy. The relationship between Norway and the Soviet Union had largely been one between Oslo and Moscow.

The resolution of the East/West conflict led to a certain détente also in the North, although this was not as pronounced as in the more central parts of Europe. One reason was that the new Russia had lost many important naval bases, especially in the Baltic Sea and the Black Sea. As a result, the strategic importance of the Kola military base became even greater for Russia than it had been for the Soviet Union, and northern Norway was still only a few kilometres away from the major naval installations of the world's second-largest nuclear power. Furthermore, it soon became apparent that different sectors of Russian society were adjusting to the new situation at different rates – and the powerful Russian Northern Fleet was not the first to adjust. In the economic sector, however, a new openness ruled. The change from a socialist economy controlled by a *nomenklatura* to a Russian version of capitalistic freedom was so rapid as to occasion some disquiet.

Foreign Minister Thorvald Stoltenberg recognized the new potentials and opportunities of this situation. On 11 January 1993 he summoned eleven countries and representatives of the EU Commission to a meeting of Foreign Ministers in Kirkenes in Finnmark county, to launch the *Barents regional cooperation initiative*, with the establishment of the Barents Euro-Arctic Council. This cooperation should be seen as a local version of the general European trend of focusing on cross-boundary regional cooperation – as in the Baltic, the Black Sea and eventually also the Euro-Med region, as well as the Barcelona Process, for EU cooperation with the rest of the Mediterranean area.

Regional cooperation in the northern areas held several

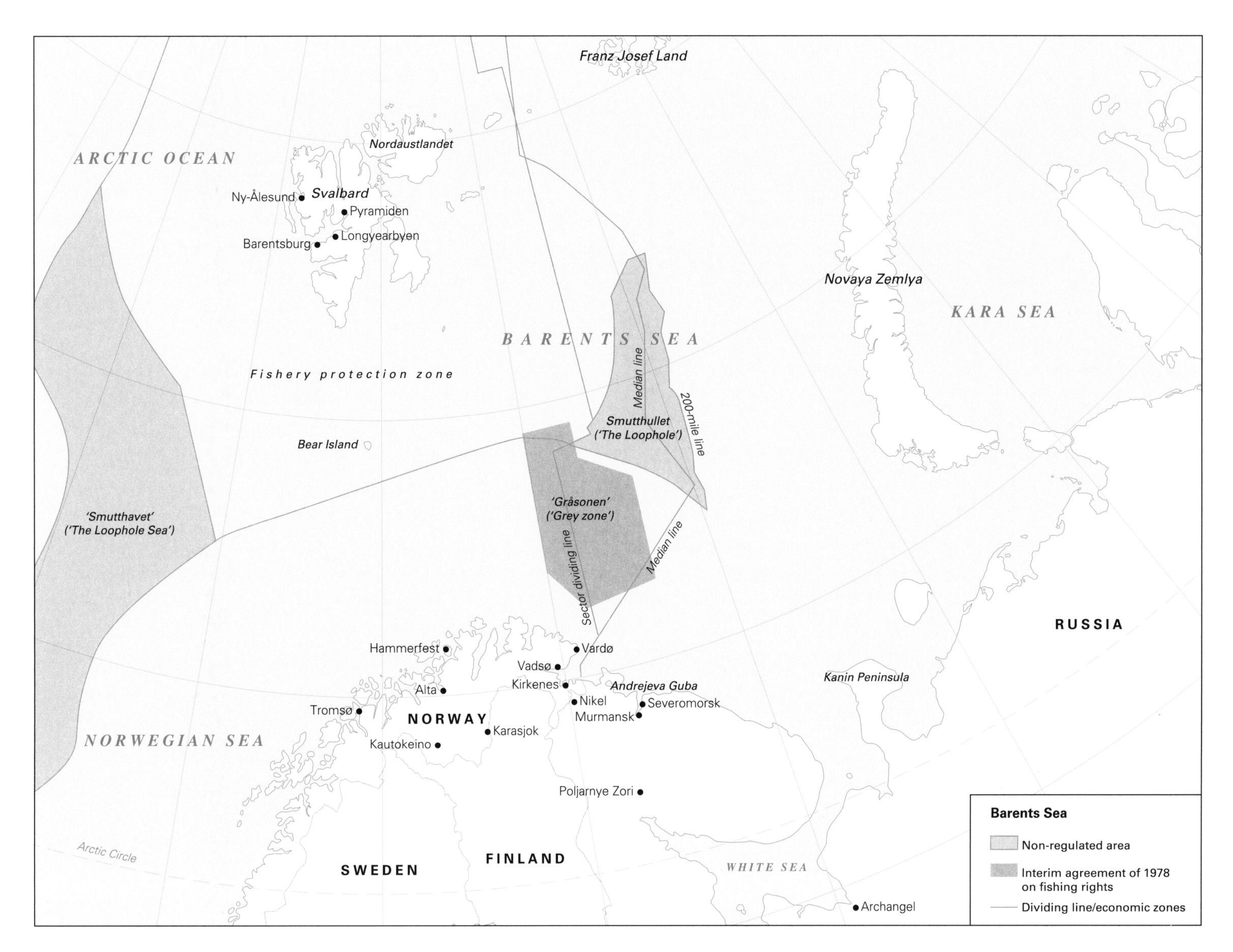


**Map** of the Barents Sea

attractions. The political framework could be based on increased trade and contact across the old Iron Curtain, and at the same time be presented as a European project, not merely a bilateral Norwegian-Russian one. The Barents initiative aimed to facilitate investments and trade, but also to promote person-to-person contact and cooperation in the north. However, the economic upturn in northwestern Russia was slow in coming, and the rouble crisis of 1998 saw the collapse of many investment projects. Not until later was the true economic potential of the Barents initiative to become apparent.

The person-to-person cooperation experienced greater success. Exchanges between a large number of organizations, cultural and educational institutions and indigenous population groups helped to bring about a major upturn in contacts across the Norwegian-Russian border. This in turn had positive effects on the tourist industry and retail trade on both sides. And – one in every four marriages in eastern Finnmark involves a Russian partner.

With the disappearance of the Iron Curtain came greater attention to environmental hazards in the northern areas. Heavy metalliferous clouds had long been drifting in over the

Southern Varanger Peninsula, creating fear of serious environmental and health damage, and Norwegian authorities were urged to become involved in the environmental situation on the other side of the border.

Together with the USA, EU and certain European countries, Norway took part in the work of cleaning up the remains of the Soviet Navy's many years of activity on the Kola Peninsula. Several discarded nuclear submarines (and civil nuclear icebreakers), as well as the spent nuclear fuel from these vessels, were being stored under highly inadequate conditions at several military facilities on Kola. Norwegian authorities worried about the radiation risk, especially possible leakage into the Barents Sea.

A special Norwegian action plan for nuclear issues with Russia was adopted in 1995. This involved safety measures at Kola nuclear power plants, mapping of radioactive contamination and implementation of priority clean-up projects. It was recommended that the fuel should be transported to the recycling plant at Majak in the eastern Urals – which, however, created the impression that Norwegian authorities were primarily concerned with getting the nuclear waste as far away as possible from their own borders. After heavy involvement by, among others, Norway's Bellona Environmental Foundation, Norwegian authorities agreed to the storage of used nuclear fuel in the northern regions, provided that this could be done under safe conditions.

Also the USA was interested in Russia's spent nuclear fuel. The fear that some of it would fall into terrorist hands explained the US involvement, while Norway was more concerned with the environmental dangers. Regardless, this provided the basis for the special Arctic Military Environmental Cooperation (AMEC) arrangement involving the Defence Ministries of Norway, the USA, the UK and Russia from 1999 on.

Nuclear cooperation with Russia has been proceeding for a decade now, and has become an important part of cooperation in the North. However, it has also been plagued by many difficulties caused by the current Russian bureaucratic maze.

Norway's active involvement in nuclear clean-up can illustrate the development of security policy after the end of the Cold War. Stated in the extreme, until 1989, Soviet nuclear submarines were feared because of their military effectiveness and their unlawful intrusions into Norwegian fjords. In the 1990s, however, it was the Russian submarines that were no longer operative that posed the greatest threat, whether they were laid-up and rusting or, like the strategic nuclear submarine *Kursk* in the autumn of 2000, lost at sea.

Several problems have remained unsolved. Agreement has not yet been reached on boundaries in the Barents Sea. Russia is constantly hinting that Norway is trying to force her out of Svalbard, and repeatedly expresses her dislike of Norwegian and allied military exercises near her borders. Critical questions are repeatedly posed concerning the use of the *Globus II* radar station in Vardø. After Vladimir Putin assumed the presidency in 2000, the reins have been tightened in Moscow, and this has also been felt in Norway.

All things considered, the upheavals in Russia have led to better relations with Norway, and new opportunities have gradually emerged in the bilateral relationship. In a somewhat wider perspective, however, there is a potentially more problematic aspect. During the Cold War, Norway could, with its close relationship to the USA, play its 'security trump card' to seek US support against Russian moves, should the need arise; the Svalbard policy, for example, was tolerated rather than accepted by Norway's Western allies.

Now Norway no longer has any such guarantee. Moreover, energy-sector cooperation between the USA and Russia is on the rise. Thus the changes in Russia have also led to changes in the Russia–USA axis and in Norway's relationship

**The Globus II** radar in Vardø has been a repeated source of friction between Russia and Norway.

**Norwegian security policy** is no longer what it used to be. Norwegian F-16 fighters in action over Afghanistan during Operation 'Enduring Freedom'.

with this axis. Norway's security trump card no longer exists – and this implies an entirely new set of challenges for Norwegian regional policy.

### Defence-policy restructuring

It took some time for defence-policy circles in Norway to come to terms with the new challenges that arose after the fall of the Berlin Wall. After all, the entire Norwegian defence structure was based on one scenario that had remained stable for a very long time. Without the threat of Russian invasion, many now feared that the very foundation of the Norwegian defence system would crumble. Thus it is not so strange that suggestions that Russia might once again pose an invasion threat were promulgated by high-ranking Norwegian officers, MPs and northern Norwegian politicians, years after the rest of Europe had adjusted to the new reality.

In fact, a series of defence restructuring projects had been initiated in the early 1990s, but these were minor adjustments rather than a fundamental reorientation in a completely changed framework. Norway's defence investments and structural plans remained basically the same, even though NATO had begun positioning itself away from emphasis on exhaustion tactics and 'holding time' towards the concept of manoeuvres with small, mobile units with considerable firepower.

Not until 2001 did Norway finally declare that there was no longer any ambition of *counter-invasion defence.* At this point, this mainly involved stating already existing facts: counter-invasion defence policy was an illusion, regardless. The proposals of Bill No. 45 to the Storting (2000–2001) concerning reorganization of Norwegian defence, and the 'defence settlement' adopted by the Storting in the summer of 2002, indicate a completely different defence policy for Norway. Resources have now moved away from maintaining a large military organization in peacetime, prepared for mobilization, and towards a smaller, but at least as effective, mobile and flexible structure. Much more targeted to allied participation abroad than before, this new structure is intended to protect Norway's interests in her own region in what is called 'the lower to middle end of the conflict spectrum'. There is to be a focus on 'niche capabilities', which are meaningful primarily when operating together with allied forces.

An extensive restructuring has taken place, not only of the defence forces, but also in Norway's international military involvement. After the 9/11 terrorist attacks in the USA, Norway has participated in offensive military operations in Afghanistan and in the stabilization forces in Iraq under US-British command. At the same time, Norway has greatly reduced its participation in more traditional peacekeeping missions through the UN and to some extent NATO.

The question about where Norway should participate militarily in the world, however, is independent of the defence policy restructuring from 2001–02. The modernization of the defence forces as such does not specifically define where, and with whom, Norway will participate internationally. Together, however, the two processes point towards a radical reorganization of Norwegian military efforts. The first shifts the focus from home defence against invasion to assignments abroad, the second from peacekeeping missions through organizations of which Norway is a member, to 'coalitions of the willing' within the framework of more offensive, US-headed military operations.

Not until after the war in Iraq in 2003 was the post-restructuring role of the defence forces discussed in Norway. It will probably take some time for the Norwegian public to come to terms with the reorientation. In Norway, popular support for the defence forces has been among the highest in NATO. Without a public debate on the purpose of the restructuring, however, this support may soon diminish.

## INTO A NEW CENTURY

As we have seen, the 1990s brought about several innovative changes to Norwegian foreign policy, but these changes have not yet been included in any overall debate on Norway's future direction. For a long time, this seemed unnecessary: on the one hand, one could fall back on tradition, and on the other there was an eagerness to meet new, pressing challenges.

The terrorist actions in New York and Washington created a new security policy agenda, at least in the USA and Europe. Suddenly it became clear that the traditional concepts of predictability, strategic depth, terror balance and deterrence were no longer relevant. They had been replaced by asymmetric threats from diffuse terrorist networks, national collapse and religious fanaticism.

Immediately after the attacks, the USA received a historically high level of sympathy. Also Norway was quick to emphasize its solidarity with the USA and its support for the 'fight against terrorism'. Initially, the USA also largely behaved in the way desired by the world around it. During the autumn of 2001, the Bush Administration established a global coalition against terrorism before opting to take recourse to force. When military force was employed, it was restricted to the removal of the Taliban regime in Afghanistan. There was broad international agreement as to the justice and legitimacy of the Afghanistan war. What did give rise to some concern, however, was that the USA did not want to seek assistance from its NATO allies, even though the alliance had declared that the attacks on the USA were to be considered an attack on all alliance members, in keeping with Article V of the NATO charter. 'The task defines the coalition,' was now the stance taken by Washington. The USA would include the allies that it needed, and no other countries.

Early in 2002, new tones were heard. In his State of the Union address on 30 January 2002, George W. Bush's main enemy was no longer diffuse, international terror networks but the states in the so-called *axis of evil.* He especially pointed to Iraq, Iran and North Korea, emphasizing the danger of terrorists gaining access to weapons of mass destruction through these nations. Later the same year, a heavily revised national security strategy was presented, which stated that the USA must be entitled to launch *pre-emptive strikes* in order to remove potential threats, even if they had not yet materialized. As in the rest of Europe, Norwegian support for the war against Iraq was far lower than it had been for the war in Afghanistan. Many

Europeans considered the USA's war against Taliban rule in Afghanistan legitimate because it had come in response to an attack by the al-Qaeda terrorist network, which had in turn received support from Afghanistan's Taliban leaders. By contrast, the attack on Iraq took place without a UN mandate, and without the world having been convinced that Saddam Hussein's Iraq posed an immediate threat to international peace. A great many leaders and peoples in Europe considered the attack unlawful and in conflict with international law.

The war against Iraq in the spring of 2003, and its prelude and sequel, placed the issue squarely on the agenda. Traditional allies opposed one another in the UN Security Council on the questions of Iraq's presumed weapons of mass destruction and what should be done about Saddam Hussein. NATO almost fell apart during debates on possible support for Turkey should an attack on Iraq lead to an Iraqi counter-attack on Turkish territory. A transatlantic rift seemed to be opening; also within Europe, views were strongly divergent.

In the months preceding the war on Iraq, Norway's position remained unclear for a long time. Gradually, however, the government and most of the opposition rallied to the 'UN course': Norway would support an attack on Iraq if, and only if, this were explicitly authorized by the UN Security Council. As a member of the Security Council until December 2002, Norway sought to assume a middle position between the USA and Great Britain on the one hand and the major opponents of the war – Germany, Russia and France – on the other. When the British-US proposal to attack Iraq failed to receive majority support, Norway was forced to choose between its long-standing relationship with the USA on the one hand and the weight it had traditionally placed on the UN and international law on the other. In the end, Norway opted for the UN and abstained from supporting the Iraq war. The position Norway and several other allies took has subsequently been reiterated by Mr Kofi Annan, the UN Secretary General.

The decision received broad political support from the Storting, and even more so among the general public in Norway. Resistance to the war in Iraq resulted in the largest popular involvement in a foreign-policy issue since the EU dispute, as opinion polls clearly showed. From the point of view of international politics, the choice was right: Norway chose not to be in the front line among the 'Atlanticists'. However, NATO members Denmark, Great Britain, Italy, Poland and Spain all supported the war.

This has been an important experience for Norway. The position assumed by the government of Kjell Magne Bondevik during the war in Iraq seems justified by subsequent events. Norway's handling of the Iraq crisis has also shown that it is possible for Norway to support a different view from that of the USA in an important international conflict. Norway's prime minister is still welcome at the White House, and cooperation between Norway and the USA continues on a range of central international issues.

**In Norway,** as in Europe as a whole, there was strong opposition to the Iraq war in the spring of 2003. This photograph was taken at a demonstration which drew 60,000 people to Youngstorget Square in Oslo on 15 February.

The next time, the threshold for signalling disagreement with the USA may well be lower. Part of the reason may lie in the fact that, with so many other countries joining the EU, which in turn is steadily becoming politically more cohesive, the USA is not interested in becoming further distanced from Norway. Moreover, the disappearance of the once-unifying threat from the East has made it easier for Washington's European allies to steer a more independent course than was possible during the Cold War, when US interests and protection were the major security policy objectives.

On the other hand, during the spring and early summer of 2003, Norwegian authorities also worked to prevent any weakening of relations with Washington because of Norway's decision not to support the war on Iraq. Despite its opposition to the actual war, Norway was quick to contribute forces for the stabilization of Iraq after the fall of Saddam Hussein's regime. On 16 May 2003, Prime Minister Bondevik visited the White House, where he was assured by President Bush that friends and allies could have differing opinions without being penalized for holding them.

Transatlantic relations have improved somewhat after the Iraq crisis: Americans and Europeans have realized that there are more issues that unite than divide them. The Americans need their allies; the Europeans have to relate to a new landscape of threats. The large number of international challenges can be resolved only through binding, international cooperation. This, however, does not overshadow the fact that Europe, first and foremost the EU, and the USA have quite different views on the value of international regimes as such.

### Central challenges at a centenary

On the centenary of Norwegian independence, Norwegian international policy is facing a series of major challenges. These will be dealt with only briefly below:

**Relationship with the USA.** Given Norway's location, economic basis and international orientation, the country has every reason to continue its good relationship with the USA. This relationship should, however, be adapted to a new age. As internal national security is no longer the primary element defining Norwegian international policy, this will have consequences also for transatlantic relations. The Soviet Union and the Warsaw Pact no longer exist, nor do the traditional reasons for a particularly close *security policy* relationship with the US. Neither Norwegian emigration to America in the 19th century nor Marshall Aid after the Second World War can in themselves provide a sufficient basis for re-establishing a close relationship with the USA in future generations. On the other hand, the USA is now the world's sole remaining superpower, with a very important and dynamic economy and an unrivalled capacity for research, development and education. Norway's strategy towards the USA, therefore, should focus on developing cooperation in these fields, with a good balance between interaction and distance vis-à-vis an influential, but disputed, superpower.

**Northern Area policy and relations with Russia, the USA and the EU in the North.** The fact that the Cold War is over does not mean that being the small neighbour of a great power like Russia has suddenly become unproblematic. Certain aspects of this relationship can still be quite tense. However, the traditional threat of invasion has been removed, and with it the main threat that had structured Norwegian defence and security policy for so long. The new task consists in finding a platform for working together with Russia, a platform which can take into account the fact that the traditional security framework no longer applies. A changed relationship between the USA and Russia, with confrontation replaced by energy cooperation and shared targets in the fight against terrorism, also forms part of this picture. Throughout the Cold War, the USA sought to keep Russian energy exports down for strategic reasons. Today, the current situation is exactly the reverse: the USA wants to reduce its dependency on Arab oil resources. By 2020, as much as 20% of the USA's oil and gas imports may come from Russia, most of which will be shipped past northern Norwegian coastal areas. In the even longer term, sea routes between Russia and the USA may become increasingly navigable, especially if parts of the polar ice cap melt. At the same time, forces in both the USA and Russia support the transport of as much nuclear waste as possible to Russia for storage or reprocessing. This traffic will go in the opposite direction to the oil, but still past vulnerable Norwegian coastal areas.

In the USA-Russia-Norway relationship, Norway must come to terms with the fact that its security trump card no longer exists, and will need to find ways of adjusting to this new reality. Should Norway with its technological expertise endeavour to play a more important role in the Russian energy sector? Do Norway and Russia have common interests in the manage-

**After the end** of the Cold War focus shifted from Soviet submarines as a military threat to the environmental threat of the Soviet fleet's stocks of spent nuclear fuel. This photograph is of Seida Guba, Kola, where reactor parts from 52 nuclear submarines are stored.

ment of the Northern areas? Will it be possible to arrive at final solutions to the still-unresolved issues of the disputed zone in the Barents Sea and Svalbard within a strictly bilateral relationship with Russia? Or will this become a decisive question in future discussions of Norwegian security and resource policy within the framework of the European Union?

**Role in the UN.** The period following the Iraq crisis has shown that the United Nations is still very much alive and well, despite predictions from many neo-conservative hawks in Washington. Activity in the UN is greater than ever, and several new operations have been launched following the Iraq crisis. At the same time, competition for resources has never been fiercer. The Iraq crisis, however, has also demonstrated that the UN must be rejuvenated in order to meet this new set of challenges. During the General Assembly sessions in 2003, therefore, Secretary General Kofi Annan took the initiative to start an in-depth examination and discussion of the UN's structure and possible courses of action.

Ever since its establishment, the UN has been described as a 'cornerstone' of Norwegian foreign policy. It is important to seize the opportunity now that the UN is in the middle of an extensive reform debate. What should Norway's UN policy be in this situation? How can belief in multilateral solutions to common problems be maintained at a time when the very ability of global organizations to tackle the problems of our time has been questioned? What should Norway's views be in the debate on today's global challenges and how to meet them?

**International military involvement.** Norway has participated in the UN's peacekeeping operations since the beginning, over 50 years ago. Extensive Norwegian international involvement abroad has come to stay. In 1993, however, Norway had almost 2,000 armed men and women in international peacekeeping operations – a far greater number than today. Norway participated when NATO replaced the UN as peacekeeper in the Balkans, and again when the EU subsequently took over. Recent years have seen an increasing emphasis on 'coalitions of the willing', largely led by the USA. The US agenda also involves Norway militarily in the 'expanded Middle East' – so far this has taken Norwegian troops to Afghanistan, Iraq and also to Kyrgyzstan.

NATO is not what it used to be. Although the commitments of Article 5 still formally apply, NATO is on the way to becoming a niche organization for use only in those cases where European and US security interests and perspectives coincide. If they do not, it is more likely that the EU will coordinate itself on the European level and that the USA will continue to form its so-called coalitions of the willing, independent of former alliance commitments. The risk is that NATO will end up as no more than an instrument in the US toolbox. To prevent this from happening, NATO will have to be re-established as a real political decision-making forum.

For several years Norway has voiced its support of reform of UN peacekeeping operations, but has yet to follow up with action. Norwegian participation in UN peacekeeping operations is lower than for many decades. It is probably time to take a closer look at how Norway supports UN operations, and what kind of capacity Norway might contribute in an important phase of restructuring the world organization.

**Role in the 'new' security-policy context.** Traditional security policy must also be weighed against the 'new' security policy, with its greater emphasis on non-military aspects. This may range from increased police cooperation across national borders to assistance in preventing conflicts. After the terrorist attacks in Madrid on 11 March 2004, we saw how the EU, and not NATO, engaged in several new initiatives. What is Norway's position in this context? And is it possible that conflicts might arise between Norway's role in this field and the country's military involvement otherwise? Or, on the contrary, might such roles be used to complement one another?

**Relationship between energy policy and foreign policy.** When, in the early 1970s, it became clear that Norway would become a major supplier of oil and gas, the prevailing opinion was that this issue should be de-linked from the country's foreign policy and treated in the most 'technical' and unpolitical way possible. A politicized superpower role here, it was felt, could have a disturbing effect on both Norway's security policy and its close relations with Israel, as it was obvious that Norway's material interests would correspond closely to those of OPEC. For several decades, therefore, Norway has had (at least) two 'ministries of foreign affairs': the one now called the Ministry of Petroleum and Energy, which handles the country's primary source of income, and the Ministry of Foreign Affairs, which handles the rest. In addition come trade and commerce, whose political bureaucracy had led a constantly wandering existence between various ministerial constellations. This division was in many ways logical when, in the midst of the Cold War, Norway emerged as a major energy nation. But should this still be the case? Or should Norwegian authorities acknowledge that certain sectors do exist in which Norway actually *is* a significant global player, and act accordingly? Should foreign, commercial and energy policies continue to lead separate lives in Norwegian officialdom, or has the time come to view everything in a broader context?

**Middle East policy.** Norway gained international status and expertise through the work that led to the Oslo Accords and subsequent efforts to implement them. Today, the Middle East is marked by considerable political turbulence, and any peace between Israel and Palestine is long in coming. At the same time, the Middle East has become the focus of international politics, not least in the fields of security and energy. It remains at the top of Washington's global agenda; and following expansion of the EU, the Middle East will also be high on the Union's agenda. As for Russia, the Middle East borders on its turbulent southern flank. What, then, should be Norway's role? Should Norway try to move away from the Israel/Palestine course, which at times has looked more like a dead-end than the road to regional peace, and instead chisel out a broader involvement in the entire region?

**The challenges of globalization.** The meeting of World Trade Organization (WTO) in Cancun in the autumn of 2003 can be seen as a constructive breakdown. It heralded a more aggressive and collective attitude of the Third World in international trade negotiations, in which the Third World turned the industrialized world's argument in favour of free trade back on the West itself. 'If you think free trade is so good for all of us, how come you don't remove protective duties and export subsidies from agriculture?', developing countries have begun asking in increasing unison. Speaking at the World Economic Forum on 24 January 2004, UN Secretary General Kofi Annan stated that establishing a truly balanced world market is the most important development-political issue facing the world today. Real access to Western markets is more important than development aid for long-term global equalization, especially in the food sector. As far as Norway is concerned, this directly affects several domestic compromises. Like most countries, Norway has both aggressive and defensive trade interests. Within the fisheries industry, for example, most actors want to pursue an aggressive Norwegian free-trade policy, whereas in agriculture the desire is to protect domestic production to the greatest extent possible. Here, national and international political goals are in direct conflict. How should these conflicts be handled?

**Relationship with the EU.** The most important issue Norway will have to deal with in the years ahead, however, is its relationship with the EU. Norway is facing another membership debate – in a greatly changed reality. The relationship between Europe and the USA is rapidly changing, and there is much to indicate that the two main blocs in international economy and politics are sliding apart. The EU has been expanded and strengthened. On 1 May 2004, ten new countries became fully-fledged members of the Union, which now totals 25 members. Most European countries already are, or want to become, members of the Union. Rather than becoming a Western 'rich men's club', the EU has evolved into an all-European community. The extent of integration is increasing. The common euro currency was introduced in the most comprehensive currency reform ever. Extensive cooperation in justice and home affairs has been launched. Integration of security policy is increasing apace, and the EU has carried out its first independent peacekeeping operations.

Norway has more than ten years' experience with the EEA. Technically, the agreement has fulfilled expectations: Norway, Iceland and Liechtenstein have gained access to the EU internal market, except in areas explicitly omitted from the EEA agreement. However, in many ways the EEA represents EU membership without any political influence. The most important decisions relating to Norwegian everyday life are made in fora in which Norway is not represented.

The EEA agreement has often been referred to as the large national compromise, the lowest common denominator. Rhetorically, one could easily argue the opposite – that the EEA gives Norway the worst of both worlds, compared with what people voted *in favour of* in 1994. Many of those who voted *for* EU membership did so because they wanted to participate in the decision-making in Europe. This they have not been able to do.

**EU membership** again rejected: the 'Queen of the No-to-the-EU movement', Centre Party leader Anne Enger Lahnstein, on referendum night in 1994. Note the EU 'barometer' in the background.

Many 'No' voters have explained that they voted *against* EU membership because they wanted a different political course in Norway than that pursued in the EU. Since then, Norway has in fact adapted more rapidly to the EU than many of the member states. This is not only a consequence of the EEA: many of the measures have been voluntary. For example, deregulation of Norway's domestic economy has been at least as extensive as that within the EU.

At the same time the EU has continued to develop. The Union has long outgrown its trade-policy framework, whereas the EEA has retained its affiliation with the internal market. Whether this is an advantage or a disadvantage depends on one's point of view. What is certain is that all these questions will again come up in the new EU debate that will soon be launched.

Fishery issues have had a special status in all of Norway's EU debates to date. There is every reason to believe that this will also be the case now. The most important questions here, how-

**The Low Church** movement has been a strong driving force in Norway's international involvement, and missionary work has long occupied a special place. This 1927 photograph shows Rødøen women's club, whose members are seen busily knitting mittens and socks in aid of the Norwegian Missionary Society's work.

ever, concern the balancing of *resource access* and *market access*: Which is the more important – the right to one's own marine resources, or duty-free access to the most important markets? Almost all export markets in Europe are now members of the EU. The development of the EU's fishery policy and the possibility that Iceland may apply for EU membership will also influence these issues in the years to come.

## FOREIGN POLICY – NORMS AND INTERESTS, FORM AND CONTENT

One hundred years after dissolution of the union with Sweden, Norway is still a small country in a big world. We may have the same neighbours as in 1905, but we have changed from being one of the poorest to one of the richest countries in Europe – with an economy still based on raw materials and oriented towards a global export market. The bipartisan Europe of the second part of the last century no longer exists. Norwegians still prefer free trade to more solid political cooperation in Europe, and we have chosen the EEA instead of the EU. Norwegian authorities are still seeking to strike a balance between integration and protection, and still trying to contribute to the peaceful settlement of world conflicts.

And yet, the nature of international politics has changed considerably in the course of those one hundred years. Norway is a member of several hundred international organizations and a party to equally many agreements. Bilateral diplomacy has largely been replaced by ongoing multilateral cooperation. Norwegian interests have fared well in many of the major initiatives for justice based on international law. The Law of the Sea negotiations until 1975 formed the basis for a 200-nautical-mile economic zone around Norway as a coastal nation, with enormous consequences for energy and fisheries. This again demonstrated that it is possible to pursue a policy that satisfies both commercial interests and political values. Norway's involvement in international law has in many ways been prompted by both self-interest and altruism.

Today, it is not clear how to distinguish between domestic and foreign policy. Traditionally, foreign policy has been defined as involving those aspects of a nation's policy that concern its relations with other states – diplomacy, alliance policy, participation in international organizations, defence policy, trade policy, currency policy, etc. There was a time when foreign policy, at least in theory, had a life of its own, being the purview of statesmen, diplomats and experts who acted as gatekeepers for the nation, 'mediating' between the 'inside' of the state and relations with 'outside' states.

In an increasingly globalized reality this picture is no longer particularly accurate. Today, Norwegian firms are trading on the world market. Norwegian students, employees and tourists cross national boundaries more than ever before; our everyday culture is permeated by international influence at all levels. Norwegian professional and industrial bodies and voluntary associations operate in close contact with international colleagues, and Norwegian political parties participate actively in European and global party groupings. Regions, counties and municipalities engage in formal and informal political cooperation with corresponding sub-national units in several countries. Practically all of Norway's government ministries now have their own international departments and work directly with their counterparts in the administrations of other countries, often without going through diplomatic channels. Paradoxically, this means that the more Norway is internationalized, the less the relative importance of the Foreign Service in forming Norway's international relations.

Norway has a broad international political environment in which civilian society and the state interact more closely than is the case elsewhere in Europe. Especially as regards development assistance, much support is channelled through non-governmental organizations. These organizations become 'co-owners' of a kind in Norwegian foreign policy, since they contribute to shaping public opinion and at the same time carry out important aspects of this policy themselves. Two important movements in Norway are central carriers of Norwegian internationalism: the Low-Church movement with its tradition of altruistic missionary work, and the labour movement with its emphasis on international solidarity. When the two converge in formulating Norwegian foreign policy, they tend to be on very firm ground.

National sovereignty does not mean the same today as it did in 1905. Retaining sovereignty means maintaining political control of at least some of our surroundings. This takes place in the tension-interface between an inherited state system with a focus on its own right to make arrangements, and an integrated world economy which fosters specialization and integration. We are moving from a modern to a post-modern international society, quite different from the Westphalian state model that has formed the basis for international relations since 1648 – although the nation-state has remained the cornerstone of the system. As far as I can see, we are only beginning to realize the contours of what this will mean for a country like Norway in the long term, and for maintaining relations with the world around us. *Formal* foreign policy has an inherently conservative nature, and this may make it difficult to absorb this global change of system.

The hard lines of the Cold War created a deep-rooted culture of consensus in Norwegian foreign policy. A small country in a vulnerable situation is strongest if it stands united – that was the feeling at the time. Many a Foreign Minister has opened his foreign policy report in the Norwegian Storting with the following statement: 'Norwegian foreign and security policy remains unchanged,' after which the assembly would breathe a sigh of relief. This adjuration that Norwegian policy would remain unchanged continued long after the rest of the world had moved on. The question today is whether this consensus culture is still necessary. Not that disagreement is a good thing in itself – but as a *compulsive idea*, consensus may hinder innovation and alternative perspectives. In many ways the world is more complex and unpredictable than ever, but at the same time Norway is located in one of its most peaceful corners. There are no immediate threats to Norway's survival as an independent nation, other than the threats that in principle apply to any

**No foreign-policy issue** has divided the Norwegian people more than that of EU membership. There are strong indications that Norway is heading for yet another debate on this issue. The photograph is from the EU referendum campaign of 1994.

country in the world. This gives Norway both significant freedom of action and considerable outward responsibility.

The expanded foreign affairs and constitutional committee of the Norwegian Storting, *DUUK*, has been a very useful instrument when it comes to developing consensus across party lines, also in delicate foreign policy topics. DUUK includes members of the Standing Committee on Foreign Affairs and parliamentary leaders. DUUK decisions are made behind closed doors, as opposed to the open parliamentary deliberations that are exposed to media scrutiny. However, a new era makes new demands. In countries like the USA, Great Britain and Denmark, the war in Iraq has resulted in far greater demands for openness on the part of the authorities. Today it is far less easy for national authorities to hide behind 'the safety of the realm', saying 'trust us, we know what's best for you', than only a few years ago. Generally, this is a positive development, and one with which the political system will have to come to terms.

Foreign policy, like all other political areas, must relate to this new openness and to the increasing requirements for speed. Today, policies are formulated by mass media as much as by parliamentary decision. Rather than denying this new reality, both the voters and the elected must learn to handle it. Modern terms like *flow* and *just in time* are better concepts than the traditional, slow-negotiating diplomacy, where official standpoints are kneaded out in a laborious, hierarchical process.

Today, long-term political 'branding' is as important as communiqués from ministerial meetings. Norm development in itself has become a political field. Countries like Norway may position themselves as *norm developers* and enter into alliances with non-government players, the way Norway, working together with Canada and others, did in 1997 in the work for a global ban on landmines.

The active international political portfolio that Norway has built up in recent years gives the country prestige – at least among those out there who actually know that Norway exists, which should in no way be taken for granted. A recent British evaluation of Norway's official diplomatic activity concludes that the country's biggest problem is invisibility: to the extent that people outside Norway's national boundaries are at all aware of Norway as an international actor, the associations are generally positive. The survey recommends that Norway should be more active in publicizing some of the work that is already being carried out, for example its peace and reconciliation involvement. This is described as a kind of 'positive capital', supported by the fact that Norway both displays an innovative ability and maintains a long-term involvement in the various peace processes. Indirectly, to some extent this 'positive capital' may compensate for the impression that Norway does not want outsiders to get too close where, for example, its rich oil, gas and fishery resources are concerned.

Norway today is a fully internationalized nation. The broad scope of its involvements has resulted in complexity, with the associated risk that the country may lose the ability to set priorities. The task of future foreign policy will no longer primarily consist in acting as a 'gatekeeper' between internal and external affairs, but rather to form some kind of a whole and maintain consistency in a highly diversified picture. The country's national interests must still be weighed against principal perspectives on international issues. However, the contrast between the two seems to be blurring; Norway now shares most of its overall interests with other countries.

Now, at the nation's centenary, the debate on Norwegian foreign policy should focus on what international policy in general ought to be, and on how Norway can contribute toward creating what former Foreign Minister Knut Frydenlund described as a 'better organized world'.

**january** fin serck-hanssen **february** rolf m. aagaard
**march** herdis maria siegert **april** janne solgaard
**may** jens hauge **june** vibeke tandberg
**july** dag alveng **august** rune johansen
**september** knut bry **october** asle svarverud
**november** ingvar moi **december** per berntsen

# EINAR GERHARDSEN

Gaunt and angry, during the nationwide strike of 1921 he stood on the back of a truck outside the editorial offices of the Oslo newspaper *Aftenposten*. Surrounded by a hundred revolutionary supporters, he ranted that the best solution would be to blow the lot to kingdom come. Chairman as he was of Veivesenets Kommunist-forening (The Highway Authority's Communist Association) he was, of course, immediately taken into custody. Shortly afterwards he was sentenced to 24 days in prison for having exhorted people to steal food and employ violence against strikebreakers. The strange thing is that, in the fullness of time, this selfsame firebrand would become the longest-serving prime minister in Norway's history and, more than anyone else, the man most closely associated with the accolade 'Father of the Nation'.

'Einar can be a little difficult,' his primary school teacher once said. This particular trait found expression in such escapades as, in his sixth year at school, running away with a friend; the two were found a few days later on an island in the Oslo fjord. In all fairness, however, it should be pointed out that his friend had been severely beaten at home. Solidarity was never just an empty phrase for Einar Gerhardsen: it was his philosophy of life. He saved the little he was given to buy sweets on 17 May, Constitution Day, to ensure that his family had something for dinner when times were hard. Times were always hard, and Einar would be there, ready to hand, with a pail of rice pudding. Class distinctions were anathema to him, and it did nothing to help matters when his elder brother died of typhoid fever in 1915. His loathing was further fuelled when, as an errand boy in Oslo's west end, he gained an insight into the standard of living enjoyed by the more well-to-do.

With the offer of a five-kroner reward, his boyhood friends once tried to inveigle him into downing a glass of schnapps. Einar resisted the temptation, as he was to do for the rest of his life. There was a time when this ascetic young man used to sleep out in the woods, alone, to toughen himself up. At a meeting of the Christiania Workers' Association, of which he was deputy chairman, he spoke in favour of dispensing with the 'bourgeois' dance that customarily followed the proceedings, with the result that attendance at the annual general meeting promptly fell from 322 to 36. Much to the despair of his roadworker father, hanging on the wall of his room at home Einar had a heroic picture of Lenin. In 1920 he made a pilgrimage to Moscow. His avowed intent was 'to make the blood of the upper classes run cold from fear'. However, as is often the way with young revolutionaries, much of his energies were expended on internecine strife, not least when the party was divided by the Comintern's demand for absolute submission. In the Youth Association the battle was fought with guns and sledgehammers. From then on Gerhardsen always feared the same kind of schism as had afflicted the Labour party in the 1920s.

A turning point in his life came in 1922 when, as a 25-year-old roadworker, he was invited to become a full-time shop steward in Norsk Kommuneforbund (Norwegian Union of Municipal Employees). All night long he roamed the streets of the capital, pondering the proposal. His fear of becoming the kind of person who might take advantage of such a position was so great that he wrote a letter to himself in which he swore to remain true to his roots and the working class from which he sprang.

Gerhardsen demanded a great deal of himself in his years as a shop steward. In 1931 he published a book, *Tillitsmannen* (The Shop Steward), in which he discoursed on how a person should conduct himself to prove worthy of the confidence placed in him. One basic rule was always to be an example to others. He regarded his time as secretary of the Oslo Labour Party from 1925 to 1936 as the happiest of his life. It was then that he married Werna, fifteen years his junior, whom he met through his work for the party.

**Norway's 'national shop steward'** and his wife Werna on their way to a state visit to Moscow in the autumn of 1955. Gerhardsen's relations with the Soviet Union underwent dramatic changes in the course of his life.

In 1939 Gerhardsen was promoted to deputy chairman of the Labour party and deputy mayor of Oslo. There was nothing to indicate that he would soon supersede both of the men who had promoted him. The fact was, however, that they sought refuge in Britain and Sweden during the German occupation. In their absence Gerhardsen allowed himself to be appointed party chairman and mayor. When the occupying forces banned political parties and removed him from mayoral office, he became a roadworker and joined the Resistance. In the autumn of 1941 he was apprehended by the Germans and subjected to torture. He was sent to Sachsenhausen concentration camp in Germany, where he soon became a leader. On the whole, the war years created a sense of solidarity that transcended former lines of conflict – something that made a permanent impression on Gerhardsen. His younger brother, Rolf, prevailed upon the Swedish prime minister to use his influence to have Einar transferred to a Norwegian prison camp, Grini, on the outskirts of Oslo. His transfer there in 1944 meant that he was already a prominent figure when Norway was liberated in May of the following year. As mayor of the capital, it fell to him to welcome King Haakon VII on his return to Norway; his speech on that occasion marked his breakthrough as a national leader.

However, when he was appointed prime minister in 1945, most people had no idea of who Gerhardsen was: he had never been a cabinet minister or a member of parliament, and his retiring nature meant that he had always remained a background figure. 'You'll have to go to the back of the queue,' a Bergen policeman told him when, as Norway's newly appointed prime minister, he visited the town to address a meeting.

Both his parents lived to see their son become prime minister. They found it hard to believe that it was true:

after all, he had had no education to speak of. This was a problem for Gerhardsen, as he had never learned English, with the result that his meetings with Kennedy, Nehru and Ben-Gurion were not all they might have been.

It came to be a characteristic of Einar Gerhardsen that he rarely used the first person singular, but always said 'we' and 'us'. In practice Norway found itself with a prime minister who, in essence, regarded himself as a national shop steward. His lifestyle remained as Spartan as it had always been and he continued to live in the same flat. He usually walked to and from work, but when he didn't he took the tram, which enabled him to keep in touch with ordinary people. One of the most enduring pleasures in his life was to go for walks in the woods and countryside, an activity that he not infrequently combined with picking berries to take home with him. In 1947, on his fiftieth birthday, Gerhardsen confided to a reporter that he didn't like his job as prime minister and would have preferred to have remained anonymous – something that was probably more than just talk.

In a famous speech he held on the island of Kråkerøy in 1948, this former Communist, who once had toed the Moscow line, came across as strongly opposed to Communism. He was very keen to form a Nordic Defence Alliance in order to be better armed against Stalin to the east. When nothing came of the alliance he made sure that Norway joined NATO. In 1951 Gerhardsen resigned as prime minister, claiming that he felt tired. His successor, Oscar Torp, was far from popular with the public, so Gerhardsen decided to stand for another term from January 1955. Support for the prime minister and his party in the 1957 election was a record 48.3 per cent. Now, more than ever, he had acquired the status of Father of the Nation and its anchor; however, this may have had something to do with the death of King Haakon while the election campaign was in progress. But power had its darker democratic aspects, and it was not always easy to know what went on behind the scenes. Gerhardsen would often justify political decisions by simply saying, 'the matter has been discussed'.

The late 1950s are considered to have been Gerhardsen's golden age. This was a time of all-round economic growth, and after the Soviet Union's invasion of Hungary the Norwegian Communist party faded into political insignificance. However, an icy relationship would develop between Gerhardsen and the party secretary, Haakon Lie, over foreign policy and the question of whether nuclear weapons should be deployed on Norwegian soil. Gerhardsen was afraid of a division in the party, and his fears were borne out when, in 1961, the Sosialistisk Folkeparti (Socialist People's Party) won two key seats in the Storting.

All his life Gerhardsen was passionate about solidarity and joint action. During Norway's postwar period of reconstruction he helped to promote a sense of collective endeavour which many people look back upon with longing.

The non-Socialist parties' 1965 election victory signalled the end of the Gerhardsen era. By then, Einar Gerhardsen had been prime minister for seventeen years. Many people refer to this period as one of 'slow revolution'. Viewed in this light, there is a link between the young hothead on the back of the truck and the elder statesman who devoted much of his retirement to writing his memoirs, which ran to four volumes. He donated the proceeds to a variety of scholarship foundations.

NIELS CHR. GEELMUYDEN

GERHARDSEN, EINAR (1897–1987), Labour politician. Secretary of the Norwegian Labour Party 1923–26 and 1936–39, deputy chairman 1939, chairman 1945–65. Mayor of Oslo 1940 and 1945. Imprisoned by the occupying Germans 1941–45. Prime minister 25 June to 5 November 1945, 1945–51, 1955–63 and 1963–65. Member of parliament 1945–69, president of the Storting 1954. Awarded the Borgerdådsmedalje, a medal for outstanding public service, in 1972 and published comprehensive memoirs.

# NATURE, RESOURCES AND ENVIRONMENTAL PROTECTION

# NATURE'S OWN COUNTRY

## Gro Harlem Brundtland and Ole Mathismoen

Magnificent, awesome, breathtaking . . . Countless visitors and artists have turned to such vivid and emotive language to describe the Norwegian landscape. A land of soaring mountain peaks, deep fjords, enchanted forests and rugged coasts, Norway is still near-virgin and unspoiled compared with most of Europe. Rich and industrialized yet still relatively pristine, it was formed by a succession of ice ages and weathering extending over thousands of years.

But things could have been different, very different. In the 1970s, when I was Minister of the Environment in Labour governments, warning lights began to flash. Some people saw them, sounded the alarm and Norway woke up.

Three major events made us change course: a dying lake, a blowout on an oilrig and an endangered mountain plateau.

### Mjøsa 1976: a dying lake

Lake Mjøsa, Norway's largest lake, was in danger of becoming choked with weeds and dying. Algae flourished and fish stocks were suffering from the sewage, fertilizers and industrial pollutants entering the water. This led to the largest clean-up operation ever. In my capacity as Minister of the Environment I was authorized by the Treasury to spend NOK 1bn of public money on rectifying matters. The fact that a country was prepared to invest so much money to save a lake created an international sensation. Combined with new and strict regulations, the operation brought about dramatic changes. Consumers gradually stopped using detergents containing phosphates, farmers, albeit reluctantly, changed their ways, manufacturing industry put its house in order and, once the money was on the table, local councils came on board and environmentalist groups set the agenda. Between 1976 and 1981 no less than NOK 1.4bn was devoted to, among other things, the construction of 42 water-treatment plants, and in 1991 Lake Mjøsa was certified as being as clean as it had been in the 1950s. But in recent years a different threat has arisen. The world's heaviest concentration of a new and insidious toxic substance has been recorded in trout in the lake, proving that in today's industrial society there can be no let-up in the fight against pollution.

**Tumbling and thundering** down the mountainsides, for more than 200 years Norway's waterfalls have drawn visitors from all over the world. With the harnessing of water power a lot have lost their former glory, but many remain, among them magnificent Hesjedalsfossen.

### The 1977 Bravo blowout

In the spring of 1976 a fierce debate raged in Norway as to whether drilling for oil should be permitted north of lat. 62

**In April 1977** occurred what conservationists had long feared: an uncontrolled blowout on the Bravo oil platform in the North Sea. In its aftermath Norway introduced the strictest environmental laws in the world.

degrees North. Given the equipment available at the time for checking spills and limiting damage to the environment, I concluded that drilling would be unwise. It was not a popular stance to take, and opinion in the Labour party was divided. In the end the government put off making a final decision. At the time renewed efforts were being made to introduce nuclear power plants in Norway; it was felt that a country without such power was not a truly industrial nation. I found support for saying no in the party's parliamentary committee, but the energy question was a thorny one. Those in favour of drilling for oil in northern waters believed that the risk of an uncontrolled blowout was negligible. Alas, one year later, in the evening of 22 April 1977, it happened. I received a phone call in the middle of the night to say that there had been an uncontrolled blowout on the Bravo platform in the North Sea. Before the engineers managed to staunch the flow one week later, 12,700 cu.m of crude oil had spilled into the sea. After that, the debate surrounding growth, conservation and environmental safety was taken very seriously – years before most other countries followed suit – and the Ministry of the Environment was granted extensive powers, which was likewise unique in an international context.

Little wilderness remains

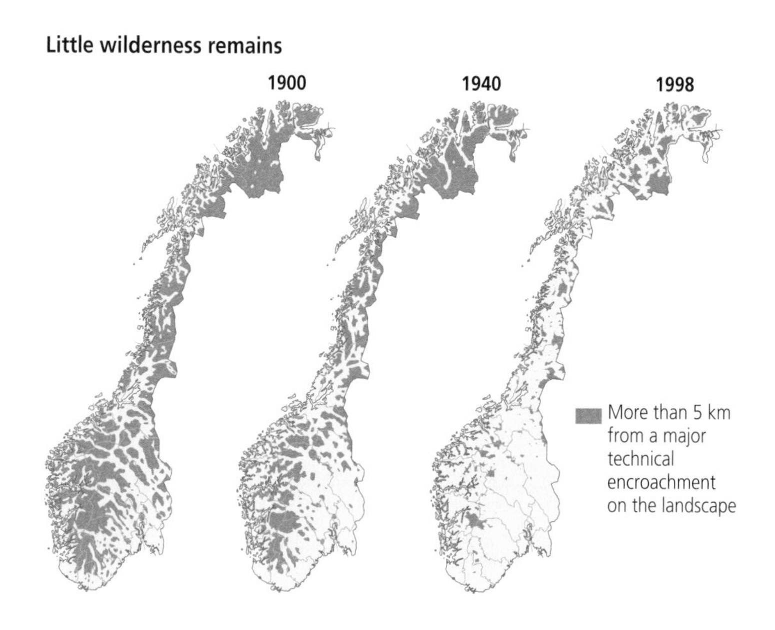


**Like most** industrial countries, Norway has been heavily developed and built up over the last hundred years. With the advent of paved roads, dams and powerlines, even some of the country's most extensive open tracts of land can no longer be classed as wilderness. The green patches represent areas that are more than five kilometres from a sign of human intervention. Not much is left untouched.

### Hardangervidda 1977: an endangered mountain plateau

Norway achieved prosperity by developing its sources of hydroelectric power. Rivers and waterfalls were harnessed to provide industry and private consumers with cheap electricity. Conservation plans for the Hardanger plateau had been discussed and studied for some years before, in 1977, developers sought to harness the Veig and Dagali rivers. Previously, all major conflicts between conservationists and developers had ended in favour of the latter. In the Labour party the issue was hotly debated: it was the first time the slogan 'growth *and* conservation' had been put to the test. The party's National Conference wanted to protect the plateau, but in practice left the fate of the two rivers to the government and Storting. I was warned that the fledgling Ministry of the Environment might lose the battle, but was convinced that conservation simply had to win and that I had to pull out all the stops. A tense meeting of the parliamentary committee concluded with the Labour party opting for conservation by a single vote. It was the greatest victory of my life! Shortly afterwards the Storting passed a resolution to establish the Hardangervidda National Park, a tract of mountain moorland some 3,422 sq.km in extent.

### Nature helps to transform Norway into an industrialized nation

Norwegians lived off the land for thousands of years. They evolved from hunters to farmers, and when the Industrial Revolution swept through Europe, Norway long remained a poor peripheral outpost. Only when it began to exploit its natural resources on a large scale did this agrarian country in the north come into its own, contributory factors being mining, hydro-electricity and fishing.

At the start of the twentieth century Norway was still one of the poorest countries in Europe. The previous century had been marked by growing nationalism resulting from the framing of the Constitution in 1814 and the work of prominent writers and artists, who did much to inspire the country and its people. These spurs, and the establishment of a National Assembly, the Storting, intensified the desire for full independence.

A large country with abundant space, Norway was heavily dependent on the land, the forces of nature and, not least, the riches of the sea, fjords, forests and mountains. Industrialization did not get into its stride until the latter half of the nineteenth century. But when, in 1891, Hammerfest in the far north

**The summer of 1970** saw the first major confrontation between conservationists and the authorities, the former resorting to civil disobedience in an endeavour to halt development of the Mardøla watercourse. Seen here is Professor Arne Næss, a prominent philosopher, being forcibly removed from the scene by the police.

became the first town in Europe to install electric streetlighting, Norway proved that it, too, could lead the way. The country's natural resources were exploitable in many ways, and opportunities for growth and development abounded.

Developments in the new century were greatly influenced by breakthroughs in science and technology. Norsk Hydro embarked upon the manufacture of nitrogen fertilizers in 1905. The process required enormous quantities of electricity, and the watercourses of the surrounding county of Telemark were extensively developed. A new era dawned, bringing power-hungry manufacturing industries and new workplaces to sparsely populated rural areas. Economic growth, a greater degree of local democracy and a new wave of optimism swept the country. Norway's natural heritage could clearly provide more than minerals, timber, meat and grain.

Decades were to pass before anyone voiced concern or misgivings about the marked changes in the countryside and environment resulting from such intensive industrialization. Not until the 1970s did people start to protest and public attention focus on the need to protect the remaining unspoiled regions of the country. In 1900, about half of Norway was wilderness, that is, more than five kilometres from any major encroachment on the landscape; by the 1970s this share was down to 15 to 20 per cent. The decline has now levelled off, however, and today, based on the same critera, about 12 per cent of the country is classed as wilderness. In the south, where the population is densest, only 5 per cent of land is wilderness.

### Dissension precipitates a change of course

The 1970s saw the start of a long and, at times, acrimonious dispute between advocates of growth and champions of conservation that resulted in some of the most stringent environmental legislation of the day. The EU and a number of other countries have since introduced even stricter laws in certain areas.

In the summer of 1970 protests against development of the Mardøla waterfall in north-west Norway, one of the highest waterfalls in the world, heralded the start of a twenty-five-year period in which were fought some of the bitterest and most groundbreaking political battles over environmental conservation in the history of modern Norway. For the first time environmental activists succeeded in bringing construction work to a halt by civil disobedience. The Mardøla waterfall was ulti-

**The very special,** near-magical atmosphere of a wild, primaeval forest is rarely to be experienced in Norway nowadays. One-third of the country is forested, but only about two per cent of this may justly be termed pristine.

**The Svalbard archipelago** is the very essence of arctic Norway. It is the home of animals that for most of the year need, and thrive in, severe cold: polar bears, walruses, Svalbard reindeer and many species of bird — all denizens of a majestic landscape of towering, snowclad mountains, rugged coasts and deep fjords. As a consequence of widespread hunting and trapping since the 18th century, many species have found themselves under threat of extinction. The discovery of vast coal deposits early in the 20th century heralded the start of a campaign to preserve the archipelago's natural resources. Norway has enjoyed sovereignty over Svalbard since 1925 and controls and administers the archipelago. In recent decades large areas have been placed under government protection, and most species of wildlife are now secure. Wind-borne air pollution from countries further south constitutes a new threat, however, large concentrations of PCB, among other toxins, having been found in polar bears, arctic foxes and glaucous gulls. It is feared that this will adversely affect these creatures' capacity for reproduction and thus endanger them anew. Svalbard's population currently stands at about 2,500, but several thousand tourists visit the islands every summer.

mately developed, but in 1973 the ensuing debate resulted in formulation of the first conservation plan for Norwegian rivers.

The two conflicting ideas of, on the one hand, establishing new national parks and, on the other, developing the nation's watercourses, became symbolic causes linked to the debate on Norwegian autonomy.

Between 1979 and 1981 local communities, political parties and families were divided by protests against development of the Alta river in northern Norway. Feelings ran high, and the struggle to decide the fate of Norway's national heritage was a hard-fought one. These passions were subsequently rekindled, and reflected in the two opposing sides, in the debate on Norway's relations with the European Union, which dominated the nation's politics from 1987 to 1994.

The yearning for freedom and an unspoiled natural environment spawned by the National Romanticism of the nineteenth century, dissolution of the union with Sweden in 1905 and idolization of the polar explorers Fridtjof Nansen and Roald Amundsen as national heroes in the early twentieth century all provided an important backdrop to this debate and the strong feelings aroused by the campaign to improve environmental conservation. There was growing realization that the very things for which Norway was internationally renowned – its virtually pristine landscape and the manner in which its natural resources were exploited – were in danger.

### First wealth, then sustainable development

In the decades following independence in 1905, Norway often looked north, to Spitsbergen (Svalbard), to the polar regions at large, and across the sea to Greenland – in short, to the trackless, snow-covered expanses of the Arctic. This constituted a central element of our culture, but also of our international image. We raised the Norwegian flag on vast tracts of land in the polar regions, far from our own borders, and named them after members of the Royal Family. Small it might be, but Norway had a voice that linked us to these boundless regions on the world map. The voice was that of Fridtjof Nansen, whose international renown rested on more than polar exploration and his scientific achievements. As a result of his mission to succour the hungry and deprived of Russia, Norway's powerful neighbour in the east, Nansen came to symbolize humanitarian values. It was in this way that Norway's role as a country with a voice in the international arena slowly took root. In the century that followed Norway's voice and image were to become increasingly important. Our respect for, and love of, nature and the outdoor life, along with sports such as ice-skating and skiing, helped to form the image of Norway the world holds today, an image enhanced in so many ways by the Winter Olympics held in Lillehammer in 1994. Both at home and abroad the Games were seen as a show window – an expression of untrammelled joy and exhilaration, a rich natural and cultural heritage and the product of a vibrant, open democracy.

This sense of solidarity with the poor and repressed was already an established fact and an important element in the way the world viewed Norway. But the fight against poverty and repression, coupled with that for a clean and healthy environment for future generations, presupposes sustainable development. By the end of the twentieth century this global analysis was well-established and explicity stated in the UN's thousand-year plan.

Norway played a part in this. We were afforded an opportunity to influence ideas and results in connection with international work in this area. And we were heard, among other things thanks to our leadership and support of the World Commission for Development and the Environment (1984-87) and follow-up measures prior to the World Summit in Rio de Janeiro in 1992 and the World Summit on Sustainable Development in Johannesburg in 2002.

Norway is closely associated with Fridtjof Nansen and Trygve Lie (the first Secretary General of the UN), and with endeavours to resolve conflicts in the Middle East, Latin America and Asia in the 1980s and '90s. The image of Norway as a peace broker is clearly enhanced by the nation's development policy, various voluntary organizations and commitment to sustainable development, and I was very fortunate to be able to contribute to this work in the 1980s and '90s.

Norway was able to assume this role because of its urge to care for people, as is illustrated by its protection of exploited groups of industrial workers, the Acts of 1915 relating to children and the gradual introduction of a welfare system. I believe the building of a welfare state to be a crucial and integral part of a process leading to sustainable development. This is as true for Norway today as it is for poorer countries. That people should enjoy a fair measure of security and opportunity for advancement, education and hope for the future is a prerequisite of sustainable development.

The Occupation of 1940–45 brought Norwegians closer to each other. Traditional geographical and class barriers were broken down, with a resultant narrowing of the differences between political parties in the protracted period of postwar reconstruction. Efforts to improve welfare and social security continued, with the provision of better housing, more workplaces and improved health as a result.

### Conservation becomes an ideal

Following a sustained period of economic growth in Norway and Europe as a whole, towards the end of the 1960s new ideas began to make their appearance. Protest movements sprang up in developed countries, and in Norway, by the early 1970s, political parties across the board were influenced by such radical impulses, resulting in a call for more democracy, greater decentralization and equality, further reforms and an increase in environmental conservation. The Labour party, the biggest political party in the country, proposed a whole raft of radical new laws, among them an Outdoor Recreation Act, a Working Environment Act, a Product Control Act and a new Planning Act; it also drew up a plan for the establishment of national parks. In 1972 Olav Gjærevoll was appointed Norway's – and the world's – first Minister of the Environment. This Labour politician, a professor of botany, made his mark as, among other things, head of the Norwegian delegation to the first UN international conference on the environment, which was held in Stockholm in 1972.

Owing to various changes of government, in the space of only a few years the new ministry was headed by ministers from a broad range of political parties. This led to the rapid acceptance in Norwegian politics of environmental issues as a cross-party concern.

When I was appointed Minister of the Environment in the Labour government in September 1974, the foundation had thus been laid for a very active period in the Ministry and in government offices in general. My predecessor, Tor Halvorsen, former secretary of the Norwegian Confederation of Trade Unions, moved to the Ministry of Social Affairs. Given my background in public health and his in chemical manufacturing, along with his familiarity with the effects of pollution on both the internal and external environments, we were both somewhat surprised by the prime minister's choice with regard to our respective posts. Today, however, I can say that my experience as a medical practitioner specializing in public health, together with his background and experience from the Ministry of the Environment, gave us twice the power in our stimulating and important task of formulating Norway's environmental policy. In most matters I could count on the support of an important government minister, as could the Minister of Social Affairs, once I had gained experience in highlighting the cross-sector issues that the Ministry of the Environment needed to focus on. Work continued to identify links between the internal and external environments, and the foundations were laid for a policy that would gradually resolve the environmental problems of ageing Norwegian industrial enterprises. The operation mounted to save Lake Mjøsa had taught me how to achieve this: by a combination of public funding and legislation on the one hand and a responsible manufacturing industry on the other.

All the while environmental pressure groups were gaining strength and increasingly making their presence felt. Norway was ready to embark upon the process leading to what came to be known as sustainable development. Most people supported the idea, though it would inevitably entail some tough decisions in which workplaces and wealth would be pitched against environmental issues. The key was to strike a balance between conservation and growth, and to prove that it was possible to develop Norway as an industrial nation while preserving the country's priceless natural heritage.

### Science as a guideline

Norway has also had to fight on an international front to prove that environmental conservation and the sustainable husbanding of resources can proceed hand in hand. This was never more true than in the late 1970s, when our sealing and whaling activities were used against us in an attempt to detract from our international reputation as a lobbyist.

Norway has a long history as one of the world's foremost whaling nations, and accordingly has had to assume a large share of responsibility for the fact that many of the larger species of whale are now extinct in some parts of the world's oceans. But Norway was also an active member of the International Whaling Commission, and as such campaigned for a ban on the hunting of endangered species. However, the move to stop whaling entirely evolved into a symbolic cause for international activists, who enlisted the aid of politicians and governments, largely from countries with no tradition in whaling. For this reason their arguments were more often based on gut reaction than on scientific facts.

**Norway came in** for severe criticism from many countries when the hunting of lesser rorquals for scientific purposes was inaugurated in the 1980s. Although the culling was sustainable, the Norwegian government was subjected to extremely heavy pressure by the United States and a number of European countries to induce it to desist. Strong and emotionally inspired boycotts, most notably on the part of Germany and the US, markedly affected Norwegian exports. This notwithstanding, such whaling is still permitted.

In 1982, when the International Whaling Commission instituted a moratorium on commercial whaling with effect from 1986, Norway reserved the right to go her own way. In the late 1980s Norway resumed the hunting of lesser rorqual whales for scientific purposes. Several countries called for a boycott of Norwegian goods and Norway was subjected to severe political pressure. My stance as prime minister was not widely supported. The Ministry of Foreign Affairs, together with the media and the business community, was of the opinion that to continue whaling would prove detrimental to Norway and Norwegian interests. But I was convinced that we were doing the right thing: big countries should not be allowed to override smaller ones merely because they disagree with their policies. It is crucial that international law and international management of natural resources be based on, and developed in the light of, scientific facts, not feelings. If Norway were to knuckle under, it would be doing the world a disservice in regard to the global rule of law. Norway continues to hunt whales, but to a limited extent, and international criticism has largely subsided. It has been proved that the lesser rorqual population in the waters off the Norwegian coast is large enough to tolerate a sustainable yield.

Scientific fact must be the common international language in any discussion of the management of natural resources. If the battle for the right to continue whaling made my government popular with the fishing industry, in 1986-87 scientific evidence made us equally unpopular. Research had shown that a dramatic reduction in cod-fishing quotas was essential in order to save stocks. There was a tremendous outcry when we made the recommended cuts. When the Minister of Fisheries reported on the situation and expressed his concern, all I could do was to apologize; there was no option – quotas simply had to be reduced. We now know that it was the right decision: today, Norway manages one of the most important stocks of cod in the world and is the world's tenth-largest fishing nation. Fish account for 4 per cent of Norway's total export revenue.

**Wild and beautiful** mountain ranges, snowcapped even in midsummer, are among Norway's premier attractions. The Jotunheimen massif is one of the most imposing ranges of all. Summer and winter alike, tens of thousands of Norwegians make their way there in search of peace and quiet in unspoiled natural surroundings.

**White in winter,** brown in summer, the arctic fox is one of mainland Norway's most endangered mammals. After decades of unrestricted hunting, the arctic fox was placed under protection as early as 1930, but despite this its numbers have continued to decline, though the populations of all other predators that have been similarly protected in Norway have strongly increased. Scientists cannot say for certain, but believe there are several reasons why no similar increase has occurred in the number of arctic foxes, among them the great distances that separate the few communities that exist, which results in in-breeding, strong competition from the red fox and climate changes that have adversely affected the foxes' habitats. In 2003 cubs were found in only two out of 209 dens studied.

**Rich and powerful – but the conflicts never cease**

Norway has come a long way and we currently pursue a very strict environmental policy, but the process towards sustainable development is by no means completed. There are battles still to be fought. In more than one area Norway is exposed to more pollution than humans, animals and plants can withstand; many species are threatened with extinction, and the debate on how to meet energy demands is as intensive and divisive as ever. Should Norway build natural-gas plants? How much of the nation's natural heritage should be preserved? It is true that we now have a number of large national parks, but a conservation order has been imposed on only one-quarter of the area of productive pine forests recommended by scientists to preclude extinction of endangered species. Imposing a conservation order on a bare mountain is less controversial than doing so on a forest. And how many predators should Norway be home to?

Norway's four largest – the bear, wolf, wolverine and lynx – are today either threatened with extinction or classed as endangered species. And does the world's richest population consume too much? Each Norwegian household currently spends some NOK 290,000 on consumer goods annually; adjusted to its present-day value, the corresponding figure in 1950 was only NOK 107,000. There are still many problems awaiting solution.

Not without reason, Norway is noted for its mountains and fjords; two-thirds of the country are what most people would call mountainous. But considerable variations exist in both scenery and geology. There are wide, windswept plateaus (Hardangervidda is one example), regions of gentle, undulating moorland too high above sea-level and too exposed for trees to grow, except where the topography affords some shelter. Nevertheless, delightful little flowers and sturdy shrubs do grow and flourish there. Then there is the wild landscape of the Jotunheimen range, with its jagged peaks and inhospitable habitats, where only the hardiest plants and animals are able to survive. There are also the rugged mountains of the west, where steep, fertile slopes plunge into the fjords that cleave their way far into the interior and rivers hurl themselves into the sea from heights of up to 300 metres. Thousands upon thousands of tourists from Norway and abroad are drawn to the region each year, to marvel at the combination of wilderness and tiny farms clinging to the mountainsides. This is the realm of the sea and golden eagle, both species once in danger of becoming extinct but which now boast a robust, viable population.

But inland, in the counties of Trøndelag, Norway also possesses unique moist, rainforest-like habitats supporting shrubs and species of moss rarely found elsewhere in Europe. The long, more rounded valleys of eastern Norway are rich in mixed deciduous and pine forests, small farms, slow-flowing rivers and tumbling streams where dippers stand poised, cocking their stubby tails. The Oslo fjord is bordered by woods thick with centuries-old oaks and resonant with the song of birds. There are dense forests, too, forests that have not heard the ring of an axe for years. These provide the setting for many ancient folktales, stories in which venerable pine trees, their wizened branches festooned with lichens, are transformed into trolls and, in the dusk, the wraiths of mist above the lakes and tarns turn into dancing elves. There are also wetland deltas along the broad rivers, where patient herons fish and, on the north and west coasts, precipitous cliffs and birdrocks, where myriads of seabirds rend the air with their raucous cries.

Norway is also rich in ancient farmland, a reminder of the long association between its people and the land, of the time when the wilderness was tamed and the land put under the plough. This region is home to a wide variety of flowers, birds and insects, all of which, over centuries of farming, have become an integral part of the nation's heritage. Some of these species are now under threat, however, as nature reclaims her own. To its detriment, modern agriculture has taken over the best farmland; elsewhere, what remains of this once so piously cultivated land is reverting to its original state, as farming it no longer pays; as pine and birch take over, some species may disappear completely.

**3,000 endangered species – but conservation is gaining ground**

Compared with the estimated 13 million species (of which only 1.8 million have so far been 'discovered' and named) in the world today, it goes without saying that only a fraction are able to survive in Norway.

Until quite recently the Norwegian habitat was, in fact, widely believed to suffer from a paucity of species. But although the number of animals and plants able to withstand the rigours of such an arctic environment is limited, naturalists continually come across new species.

When, in 1992, the authorities drew up what is known as a red list, a survey of endangered and vulnerable species, it was estimated that Norway supports some 33,000 species of plants

National parks, national reserves and national scenic areas, by number and area. 1975-2002

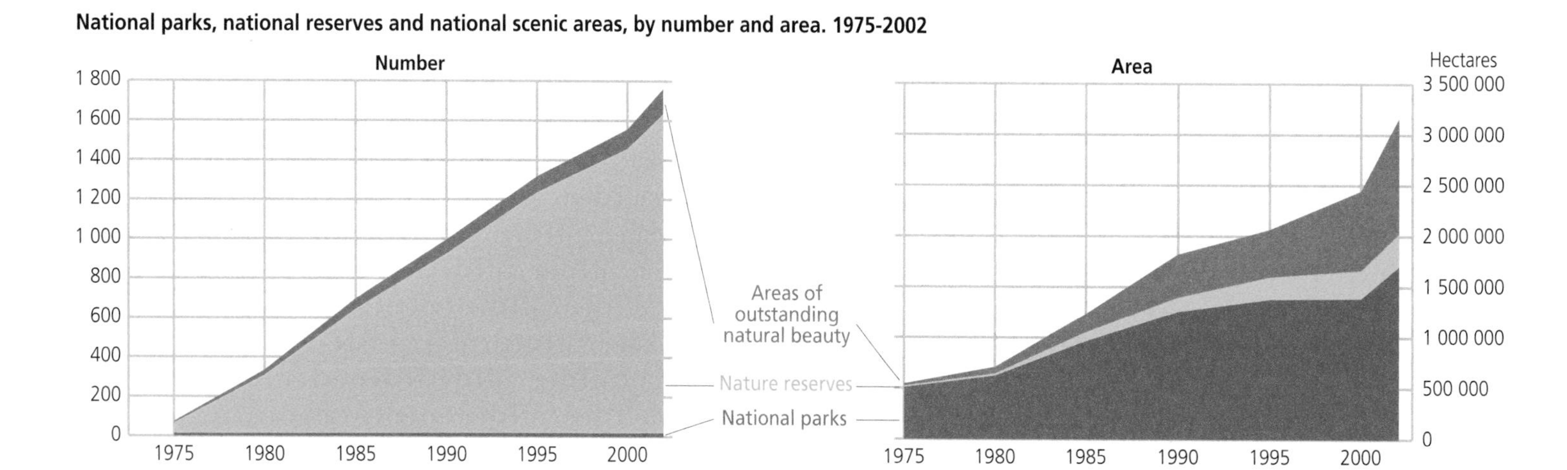


**More and more** areas in Norway are being placed under protection, and before long 12 per cent of the countryside will in some way or other have been secured for future generations. But much remains to be done. In particular, species that live in productive coniferous forests and on ancient farmland are in need of more protected habitats.

and animals (and that excludes marine life), though scientists were in a position to assess the standing of only some 12,000 of them. Now, however, those selfsame scientists put the number of species found in Norway at some 38,000 – and if marine life is included, the figure almost doubles to 60,000.

At the last count 15,000 species were assessed in terms of vulnerability. Of these, it was concluded that at least 100 had already been lost, and that a further 300 were in imminent danger of extinction. Norwegian scientists believe that a total of 3,000 indigenous species of plants and animals are under threat and will eventually die out unless something is done to safeguard their habitats.

Recent research has revealed that in a European context and, indeed, also globally, Norway bears responsibility for the survival of certain species.

Nature conservation embodying a ban on destructive inroads into the natural environment is nowadays taken for granted, which is more than it was in 1872, when the US Congress voted to establish the world's first national park, Yellowstone. Many years were to pass before statutory protection of the environment gained acceptance in Norway, where most people, justifiably, it must be said, reasoned that the Norwegian landscape was virtually unspoiled anyway.

But only two years or so after Norway gained her independence in 1905 a change occurred. A group of scientists began to worry about the way things were going, and a professor of botany warned that 'the original community of animals and plants is being destroyed, or changed, because their living conditions are in process of transformation'.

This stirred things up and people began to revise their opinions. Norway's first nature conservation organization, Landsforeningen for Naturfredning i Norge (The National Society for Nature Conservation in Norway), now Norges Naturvernforbund (Norwegian Society for the Conservation of Nature, or Friends of the Earth), was established in 1914. This marked the beginning of a movement that has subsequently done a great deal to ensure that Norway currently provides protection to 12 per cent of its mainland area.

This notwithstanding, for many years industrialization was accorded priority, and not until 1954 did the Storting pass the Nature Conservation Act, which provided for protection – or conservation, as the process had by then become known – of extensive areas of unspoiled countryside. But a further eight years were to elapse before Norway was to open its first national park, Rondane, which was established in December 1962. This was a red-letter day, although it was almost one hundred years after America had shown the way!

After that, conservation proceeded apace. Nineteen sixty-four saw the adoption of the first National Parks Plan, and in the decades that followed several hundred nature reserves were established to safeguard specific types of forest, wetlands and bird and other wildlife habitats. Then, as now, though, such measures were not without their problems. Clashes with forestry interests, power companies and landowners on the one

**Its characteristically** tufted ears alert, Norway's only wild cat, the lynx, slinks smoothly and silently through the forest; only rarely is it seen by man. Midway through the 20th century the lynx was close to extinction, but strict protection has resulted in steadily increasing numbers and the lynx has now spread to new areas. Today, it is the most widely distributed of the four large predators native to Norway, the others being the bear, wolf and wolverine. In the mid-1990s there were marginally more than 400 lynxes in Norway, and hunting was reintroduced under strict licensing. Scientists put the present population at between 250 and 270; between 30 and 50 lynxes are shot annually.

hand and conservationists and ramblers on the other continued to give cause for debate.

Following a prolonged period of research and reporting activity, conservation has in recent years regained its momentum. Between 1998 and 2002 the area of land (excluding Svalbard) under protection increased by no less than 48 per cent, mainly thanks to implementation of the National Parks Plan approved by the Storting early in the 1990s. The number of protected areas increased from 345 to 1,940, which amounted to something in excess of 30,000 sq.km. Some 12 per cent of the land area will eventually be protected in the shape of national parks, nature reserves and scenic conservation areas, once plans already sanctioned are fully implemented, which will be around the turn of the year 2004/05.

The autumn of 2003 saw the establishment of Norway's twenty-first national park, Dovrefjell National Park, realm of the musk-ox. At the same time the country's oldest such park, Rondane, was greatly enlarged – and it was agreed to protect several more scenic locations and establish further wildlife reserves. As a consequence of these measures the Dovre/Rondane region is now Europe's largest protected area for wild reindeer.

To supplement these new and imposing national parks, in recent years the government has made provision for a large number of reserves to safeguard specific biotopes.

Norway acceded at an early stage to a number of international agreements designed to safeguard biological diversity, and when in 1992 world leaders appended their signatures at the Rio conference, did much to ensure that the UN Convention on Protection of Biological Diversity was as strict as it is. The Storting has agreed that an end shall be put to the ongoing loss of biological diversity by 2010. But more than a target date is needed to achieve success. In common with many other countries, Norway is finding it difficult to strike a balance between growth and conservation and between political aims and practical politics.

### Ancient forests: a source of dissension

Among other things, the controversy surrounding conservation of utilizable forests has shown that it is easier to hold an opinion on protection of rainforests on the other side of the globe than on concrete issues at home; and it is easier to protect mountains and moorlands than productive forests. Norway has accorded protection to only about one per cent of her utilizable forests. That is only a quarter of what our Nordic neighbours have protected and of what scientists deem necessary to save the close on one thousand species that inhabit the nation's forests and are under threat of extinction. Each year the Storting allocates new funds earmarked for conservation purposes; but purchasing productive forestland is an expensive business. In recent years a number of Norwegian environmentalist organizations have campaigned for increased protection of the nation's forests and more than once brought felling to a standstill by civil disobedience. Along with the controversial subject of drilling for oil off the coast of northern Norway, it is in the forests that the most relentless struggle is being waged.

Norway's capital is surrounded by forest. Thousands of its inhabitants use the city's environs (Oslomarka) for walks and recreation and to pick berries and mushrooms. Winter and summer alike, the ski-trails and paths that interlace the area are thronged with people. But although the forest's proximity to Oslo makes the city unique among Europe's capitals, little in Oslomarka is reminiscent of virgin woodland. Decades of intensive forestry and clear-cutting have left their mark. The forest is relatively poor in terms of the number of species to be found there, though skiers and ramblers often encounter elk, foxes, badgers and many species of bird. Wild, primaeval forests in which fallen and half-rotten trees make progress difficult, and whose floors are carpeted with expanses of bright-green moss – the eerie, magical backdrop to so many Norwegian folktales – are a rarity. Where forests are concerned, the bone of contention in Norway is how much of what remains of such untouched woodland should be handed down to future generations in its present pristine state.

In the last ten years Norwegian landowners have done a great deal to introduce environment-friendly operations. As a result, among other things many of them have now engaged to leave in place key biotopes that support rare species, and also to protect brooks and streams and leave more tall trees standing than was customary in the past. A nationwide scheme is currently on foot to register such key biotopes. The timber industry is also advocating voluntary conservation, meaning that landowners are encouraged themselves to suggest areas deserving of protection. Because most Norwegian landowners possess only small areas of forest, government protection has often hit some of them hard and led to bitter altercations. Not infrequently, protection deemed necessary in the light of Norway's international obligations has divided families, local communities and political parties.

Despite increasing conservation and international commitments, some species are still endangered in Norway, and the natural balance is not everywhere as it should be. A case in point is the elk population. Since 1970 the number of elk in the country has increased sixfold and now stands at close on 130,000 animals. Never have more elk been felled than at present – 40,000 are culled each year – but overall their numbers continue to rise. The elk population is, in fact, so large than in some places it is beginning to affect the biological diversity, such deciduous trees as the rowan, goat willow and aspen having all but disappeared as a result of over-grazing; severe damage is being done to young pine trees, too. In some localities – southern Norway is a case in point – rapid growth of the elk population has resulted in malnutrition and a rising incidence of deficiency diseases among the animals. There are many reasons for this population explosion, one being widespread extermination of the elk's natural enemies, among them the wolf.

Changes in habitats determine which species find it hard to survive in the modern world, as they result in plants and animals either disappearing or buckling under from sheer weight of numbers.

One of the principal reasons the number of species is declining is that wetlands, virgin forests, estuaries and farmland have all been subjected to change, cut back or completely destroyed. Because of this, Norway's natural environment is losing much of its diversity. Most in decline are species that have difficulty in holding their own in the face of competition from rival plants or animals, or that need special conditions to survive. More adaptable species, on the other hand, are rapidly increasing. In the forests, for example, many mosses, lichens and fungus have already been lost, as they depend for survival on moist biotopes rich in old, dead and rotting trees. In a modern plantation, in which all the trees are of more or less the same age, such species are chanceless. So are many species of owl and woodpecker, both of which likewise need dead trees in which to find food and nest; furthermore, they require relatively large tracts of virgin woodland over which to range. Mosses dry out and die if the protected areas in which they live are reduced, with a resultant change in the stable environment to which they are accustomed.

Some species, on the other hand, have no difficulty at all in accommodating to a more modern, homogeneous environment. Crows can overcome radical changes in their surroundings and adapt to almost anything. The same is true of foxes and badgers, which readily adapt to new environments and are now appearing in growing numbers in residential areas and even in town centres. Then there is the elk, which, thanks to the prevalence of plantations and the practice of clear cutting, has, in a manner of speaking, been served a whole plateful of fresh and ready-made feeding grounds!

The species really in trouble in Norway are the denizens of natural forests, wetlands and long-cultivated farmland.

**Crying wolf: Norway's dilemma**

As in many other countries, in Norway too predators are a source of conflict. The prime reason is the head-on collision between their need for food and the time-honoured practice of allowing sheep to graze freely in the forests and mountains in summer.

Four large predators – the bear, wolf, lynx and wolverine – are indigenous to Norway, and for centuries a never-ending battle has been waged between them and man. This is particularly true of the wolf. In the first half of the nineteenth century wolves were found in large numbers throughout most of the country. In 1845 this prompted the authorities to introduce a bounty scheme with the object of reducing their numbers, and in the decades that followed thousands of wolves fell to the bounty hunters' guns. From 1940 to 1973, when protection was introduced, it is unlikely that there were more than forty or fifty wolves in the whole of the Scandinavian peninsula. When a wolf was killed in Norway in 1963, it was thought to have been the last of its kind in the country. But it wasn't. Every so often sightings were reported, and by the end of the 1970s it was apparent that there was still a small pocket in the deep forests of the Trysil/Värmland area on the frontier between Norway and Sweden.

Throughout the 1980s a few roving individuals were shot, or killed on the roads, at different places in southern Norway, and it eventually became clear that a new Norwegian-Swedish pack had established itself and was ranging ever further afield. Heated clashes again occurred when the Storting approved the establishment of core areas in which the country's large predators would be afforded greater protection.

It is difficult to estimate the number of wolves currently at large in Norway. Some thirteen to twenty animals may be permanently resident in the south-eastern region, and to them should be added about twenty from packs that haunt the borderland with Sweden. Old antagonisms are revived whenever

**Norway's centuries-old** farmland is rapidly being reclaimed by nature and becoming overgrown, as here at Valle in the county of Aust-Agder. **1992:** Spruce saplings spring up on what was once pasture, but the remains of the cultivated fields of yore are still plainly visible. **2002:** The spruce trees have now taken over altogether, the last traces of the former arable land are no longer to be seen and species that once grew so prolifically in the ancient meadows are fast disappearing.

the number of wolves increases. The authorities have remained firm in their decision to protect these dedicated core areas, however, so it attracted international attention when, in the winter of 2001, a new, viable pack that had established itself outside one such area in the Østerdal valley was hunted down and exterminated. Wolves settle in without as much as a by-your-leave, and this particular pack had made the wrong choice, with the result that ten animals were gunned down from a helicopter. The Norwegian government had to answer many pointed questions from abroad about how it could have condoned this massacre of a near-extinct species. As in the past, the answer was that a balance has to be struck between conservation and other interests.

From the closing years of the 1990s, and since the turn of the millennium, scientists have repeatedly reported new litters. When, shortly before Christmas 2003, the government introduced a new environmental management plan in which it was laid down that Norway should support viable stocks of, among other animals, wolves, it again created a furore. Sheepfarmers and hunters think Norway can do without wolves, and perceive the government's policy as a threat to their livelihood. Environmentalists, on the other hand, believe the government is too wishy-washy, owing to its failure to set clear targets for a bigger increase in the wolf population. The government's response is that as both sides are equally dissatisfied, it seems to be nearing a golden mean – like the policy on predators adopted by Parliament in the spring of 2000.

### Farmland and coral reefs – new areas in need of conservation

The population of Norway is still widely dispersed, and thanks to an active and, by the standards of continental Europe, near-unique regional policy, farming is still carried on practically everywhere. But thousands of farms have been abandoned, and the way in which many of those that remain are run has radically changed in recent years. Every day in the last forty years about nine farms have been given up. In 1959 there were 198,315 working farms in Norway, a figure which by 2003 had fallen to 58,800! Much pasture has been lost, though overall the area of cultivated land remains the same as in 1950, i.e. about 10,000 sq.km.

Throughout the thousands of years that people have lived in Norway, in many places the original landscape has been partially or totally transformed. Forests have been cleared, land has been put under the plough and people have grown their own food. Unlike natural landscapes, cultivated land, be it ploughland or pasture, needs to be cared for and utilized if it is to retain its character. Few such cultivated landscapes have been preserved in Norway, though in recent years large areas have been accorded special protection as scenic conservation areas.

The farming methods in use until only a few decades ago were the product of a tradition extending thousands of years into the past. For centuries they constituted an eminently stable way of farming that provided habitats for many hundreds of highly distinctive species of plants and animals. It is the farmer who is principally responsible for maintaining this ecological system, and if he throws in his hand because he can no longer make a living from small fields bordering on forests, or from pastures tucked in between hills and rocky outcrops, natural environments disappear with him. Once the cattle have gone and the plough has been sold, it takes only a few years for nature to reclaim her own.

There are various reasons why we wish to preserve such cultivated landscapes. If the thousands of tourists who make their way into Norway's fjords by cruiseship, or traverse her valleys by road and rail, are to enjoy the sights promised them in the travel agents' catalogues, the land must not be allowed to revert to its former wild state. Most important, however, is, perhaps, the fact that, owing to changes in farming practices that have led to the disappearance of pastureland – either because of the introduction of new methods or because the most unproductive fields have been left untended or untilled because it no longer pays to farm them, and in consequence have returned to the wild – many hundreds of plant and animal species are slowly becoming extinct. One-third of the species currently threatened with extinction or classed as endangered live on such cultivated land. Many species of plant are especially at risk, and the situation is, in fact, so acute that numerous grasses and flowering plants may soon disappear for good. In recent years scores of fungi that for centuries have remained undisturbed on ancient pastureland and in the mountains have come to light and been identified, among them waxcaps, entoloma fungi and earthtongues. Although these are species few people have ever heard of, they nonetheless have their place in the Norwegian ecology – and we have, after all, pledged ourselves to safeguard all species on our soil.

**A priceless** discovery of recent years: vast coral reefs, protected when scientists became aware of their existence. The hermit crab is one of the numerous marine creatures that live on these reefs. Norway boasts the world's largest concentration of cold-water coral reefs, though scientists believe that as much as half of those that once existed may have been destroyed by trawling and from other causes.

Who knows, perhaps some such microscopic fungi, grasses and flowers harbour secrets that may one day solve a medical puzzle. A fungus discovered by chance on Hardangervidda proved to contain a substance that revolutionized transplant surgery. It keeps the body's defence system at bay, thus giving the new organ time to establish itself.

To safeguard these species conventional conservation methods will not suffice, as the areas concerned will simply revert to their former state. For this reason the government has introduced purpose-oriented programmes, and spends millions each year to ensure that many thousands of decars of old, 'unprofitable', cultivated land continue to be farmed.

In recent years it has also been revealed that Norway's coastal waters conceal what was, until then, literally a deep secret. Between two and four hundred metres below the surface scientists have discovered extensive coral reefs. They had long known of the existence of coral, but had never realized that it was present in such vast quantities. Only in the 1980s did it become clear that there was far more than had been imagined. On one expedition alone, undertaken in 2003, nearly 1,500 new reefs were charted. Unlike tropical corals, which thrive best close to the surface, the Norwegian variety is happiest in the stygian blackness of the depths.

Provisional estimates suggest that 30 to 50 per cent of these reefs have already been destroyed, in the main by bottom trawling; this has impelled the government to launch a crash programme to save what is left. In 1999 an emergency regulation was introduced providing for a ban on trawling in certain designated areas where there are known to be coral reefs, and since then reefs off the coast of central Norway have enjoyed protection.

In the spring of 2002 a gigantic coral reef was discovered off the Lofoten Islands. It proved to be no less than 45 kilometres in length and two to three kilometres wide, which makes it ten times bigger than any other known Norwegian reef. This totally unsuspected natural formation was discovered with the aid of an RUV (Remote Underwater Vehicle). Some months after discovery of the reef, which is now known as the Røst Reef, trawling was banned in the surrounding area.

The largest Norwegian coral reefs may be as much as 8,500 years old, meaning that they began to form soon after the last Ice Age. Scientists have identified more than 600 species of fish, sponges, crustaceans and other organisms in the offshore reefs. And a stunned Ministry of the Environment has had to face the fact that, in terms of biodiversity, these hitherto unknown natural formations are among the richest habitats in the country. Similar coldwater reefs are found in many places throughout the world, but nowhere in such abundance, and none are as large as those in Norway's coastal waters.

**Pollution from within and without**

In the last century Norway has, then, lost much of its original natural environment, with a consequent impoverishment of plant and animal life. But pollution has also contributed to a deterioration in the living conditions of the country's flora and fauna and, indeed, of society at large.

Nonetheless, the situation is far more favourable in Norway than in many countries on the Continent. Norwegian industry was made subject to the provisions of a strict Pollution Act quite early on, and in many areas domestic pollution has been greatly reduced in recent years. Despite this, because of the prevailing winds and ocean currents, if the deleterious effects of pollution are to be alleviated, Norway is totally dependent on her European neighbours emulating her.

In the decades immediately following the Second World War reconstruction and development were spearheaded by engineers and technologists. It was to them the nation looked for innovative industrial projects, more jobs and a higher standard of living. Only a few people evinced concern over the fact that many rivers, fjords and wetlands were being destroyed in the process. In the 1960s, however, the question increasingly arose of whether the campaign against pollution and destruction of the environment was not of equal importance to the country. There was little point, it was said, in establishing national parks if the animals and plants in them were dying. Furthermore, it became apparent that the Norwegian people themselves were beginning to suffer from the increasingly poor quality of the air they breathed and the water they drank, as well as from pollution of the seas surrounding them.

Nineteen seventy-four saw the setting up of the Norwegian Pollution Control Authority (SFT), an organization staffed by professionals and, in part, idealists and charged with responsibility for leading the way in clean-up operations over the next few years.

Whereas the 1960s had been devoted to increasing public awareness of the threat posed by pollution, the 1970s were, in the words of SFT's own published history, a time of policy making. Various reports and parliamentary bills were put before the Storting, and the ranks of those in favour of stricter controls swelled. I myself was fortunate in being enabled to contribute to the framing of several of these bills, and to help push them through. But environmental awareness in industry was not overly great, and many industrial enterprises did their best to avoid taking action. By contrast, nowadays most Norwegian companies have introduced strict internal environmental-control regulations. In fact, the majority have procedures for themselves reporting discharges and emissions in excess of what is permissible. Things were far different in the 1970s. The breakthrough came with the operation undertaken to save a badly polluted Lake Mjøsa from becoming overgrown with weeds. For the first time it became necessary to view the problem as a whole. To close a tap here and a valve there was of little avail: everything, from the housewife's use of washing-powders containing phosphates through sewage and the farmer's excessive use of fertilizers to industrial emissions had to be considered as part of the whole.

After a time, besides providing for a reduction in toxic emissions SFT was entrusted with new responsibilies in the shape of product controls and contingency plans to cope with acute discharges of industrial effluents.

A bitter battle was fought over the question of who should pay for clean-up and purification operations. The management of Norway's biggest industrial undertaking, Norsk Hydro, fought to the end against the principle that the company responsible should pay. For some years recourse was had to interim solutions, but today the principle is generally accepted. No less than five per cent of the capital investments made by Norwegian industrial companies in 2000 was directed towards environmental-protection methods. That same year a total of NOK 78m was spent on reducing discharges. One-fifth of the metal industries' capital investments was devoted to environmental protection, as was one-quarter of the wood-processing industry's. This proves that industry is spending more on the environment; but it also shows that much has yet to be accomplished.

There is no justification for calling it a day and declaring that the job is done. Inspections undertaken in recent years have revealed that 80 per cent of industrial enterprises discharge more than is permissible by law. However, such violations are usually not unduly serious, and in only three per cent of cases has the Pollution Control Authority considered prosecution.

**In the 1960s** and '70s acid rain depopulated hundreds of lakes, most notably in southern and western Norway, of fish. Vast sums of money have been expended on liming in an attempt to save trout stocks and to reintroduce fish in once-moribund lakes. Tens of millions of kroner continue to be spent on liming annually, although a substantial reduction has occurred in acid precipitation over Norway.

### Acid rain kills

In the 1970s and '80s acid rain was widely viewed as one of our gravest pollution problems. In large areas of southern Norway sulphur dioxide and nitrogen oxides practically emptied lakes of fish; the problem of dead and blighted forests, on the other hand, which attained catastrophic proportions on the Continent, was not as great in Norway.

There was considerable disagreement among scientists about whether the depleted fish stocks in many of the country's lakes were really attributable to acid rain, and for many years this lack of consensus made it difficult to reach full agreement on effective countermeasures. This notwithstanding, in time we came to spend vast amounts of money annually on liming, to neutralize acidity. Light aircraft and helicopters releasing tonnes of white lime over idyllic mountain lakes came to symbolize the struggle to save the environment.

Strict regulations providing for reductions in emissions and discharges were imposed on industrial manufacturers, but as almost 90 per cent of the acid in the rain falling on Norway came from abroad, every attempt was made to enlist the support of neighbouring countries. For many years securing a reduction in emissions from coal-fired power stations in Britain was one of the Norwegian Minister of the Environment's principal tasks. In the event, a breakthrough was achieved at top level when, on a visit to Norway in 1986, the British prime minister, Margaret Thatcher, acknowledged that the time had come for a change of course.

The results are there for all to see: acidification is declining, primarily because of a reduction in sulphur emissions. Norway herself has already met the requirements of the Gothenburg protocol, an annex to the Convention on Long-Range Transboundary Air Pollution. But this is no reason to relax. The reduction in Norwegian emissions in recent years is largely ascribable to cutbacks in industrial activity and not to the success of the campaign alone.

As has been pointed out, the sulphur emissions that are a problem for Norway mostly have their provenance in other countries, but in the last twenty years there has been a 50 to 80 per cent reduction in sulphur-laden precipitation. The greatest improvements have been seen in eastern Norway, where trout stocks in many mountain lakes are now regaining lost ground without recourse to artificial liming. Overall, areas in which acidification is greater than the environment can stand have diminished by more than one-third over the last twenty years. But the critical load is still too great in some parts of southern Norway and in the far north, in eastern Finnmark. The prime source of the sulphur affecting Norway's natural environment today is Russia's nickel plant on the Kola peninsula. The Norwegian government has allocated considerable sums of money to help curtail these discharges. Discharges from Nikel are actually greater than Norway's total emissions, and it is thus deemed highly cost-effective to help the Russians reduce them. But this poses a new problem: if Russia's nickel industry is modernized, the life of its plants will be prolonged, and, *ipso facto*, the emissions, as they can never be entirely eliminated. On the other hand, if emissions continue unabated, the natural environment of eastern Finnmark may be irreversibly harmed. Many square kilometres of mountain landscape around the nickel plant on the Russian side of the frontier are, to all intents and purposes, dead, providing clear proof of the deleterious effect on nature of heavy and long-standing pollution.

Norway's battle against acid rain is a textbook example of the fact that pollution is not only a national concern. Pollution can be as damaging in a neighbour country as in its country of origin, so to solve the problem it is necessary to work together. Just as Germany could never have saved her forests had not industry been modernized in some of the countries of central and eastern Europe, we would have been unable to save the fish in our lakes had not Britain reduced her sulphur emissions. It should be borne in mind, however, that one of the prime reasons for the reduction in acid rain is industry's collapse in eastern Europe in the 1990s.

Both Norway and the rest of Europe are, however, up against far more serious problems when it comes to reducing emissions of nitrogen oxides (NOx), which also result in acid rain. Nitrogen oxide pollution mostly emanates from motor vehicles and ships. In this field Norway has managed to achieve only a minimal reduction, and emissions need to be drastically reduced if we are to meet the international targets to which we have pledged ourselves. But even if we and the rest of Europe do manage to reach our targets and bring about the agreed reduction by 2010, some seven to eight per cent of the country will continue to suffer from more acid rain than the environment can cope with. Despite the installation of catalytic converters in cars and more environmentally friendly engines, the level of $NO_x$ emissions shows just how difficult environmental conservation can be in the face of modern society. In the last twenty years the volume of traffic on Norwegian roads has tripled: at the turn of the millennium a total of 33 billion road kilometres were being notched up annually, for the most part by private motorists.

Although the impact on the environment is still too great, scientists have noted some positive changes. For example, the living conditions of several kinds of arboreal lichens have improved, and in recent years these lichens have become more widespread – due, it is believed, to a reduction in acid rain.

The quantities of heavy metals and other toxic substances in rain have similarly declined, in some cases by as much as 80 per cent. Nonetheless, Norway is still paying for past sins. Many such metals have been absorbed by nature and will remain *in situ* for years to come. The concentration of lead is up to ten times more than the 'normal' level, notwithstanding a reduction in emissions of more than 50 per cent since 1990. The pesticide DDT, once regarded as a panacea, was banned in Norway in 1970. But owing to its continued presence in the food chain, not a few birds of prey, among them the merlin, still lay eggs that are too thin-shelled to take the weight of a sitting bird. This is a good example of how future generations of animals and humans will continue to suffer from past pollution and destruction of the environment. They will also have to adapt to what is known as biological pollution, that is, to new species introduced by man. A good example is the king crab, which originally came from Russia.

**The power problem**

Norway is very much an energy nation. In 2002 we generated nine times as much energy as we used, mostly thanks to offshore oil and gas production. In Norway electricity is primarily generated by waterpower – in fact, we produce more hydro-electric power per capita than any other country in the world. And although the harnessing of the country's rivers and waterfalls has always been a controversial issue (as, indeed, it still is), the fact remains that waterpower is a renewable, non-polluting source of energy – though there is a limit to how much more of the nation's water resources can be harnessed, as a good 60 per cent of the potential has already been developed.

Despite this, energy production is Norway's greatest headache as regards living up to its commitments and promises to reduce its contribution towards possible climate changes. When, in the late 1980s, the danger of an increase in the greenhouse effect became recognized as an environmental hazard, Norwegian politicians were among the first to call on the global community to take action. Some political parties went so far as to include substantial cuts in Norwegian emissions by the close of the millennium in their manifestoes, though most of them have since considerably modified their promises. One reason is that it soon became clear how difficult it is to reduce emissions in a country that obtains the bulk of its electric power from a renewable source. Something in excess of one-quarter of Norway's emissions of the most important of such toxic gases, carbon dioxide ($CO_2$), stems from oil and gas extraction, motor vehicles being the principal source. Private-car ownership in Norway has risen dramatically, so much so that at the turn of the millennium the total volume of vehicular traffic on the roads was 33 per cent up on the 1980 figure.

Norway has been a driving force in securing international commitments, and in 2002 ratified the Kyoto protocol. However, we are still far from reaching our agreed target, which allows for an increase in emissions in the next ten years of only one per cent in relation to the base year, 1990. This includes any gains obtainable through international quota trading and other mechanisms designed to encourage the most effective possible use of financial resources. Our problem is that, as early as 2002, emissions were already five per cent up on 1990. Although this is little compared with a 35 per cent increase in Spain and one of 14 per cent in the United States, it nevertheless represents a problem for Norway – both because it makes it harder to obtain a hearing in international bodies and because it is becoming increasingly difficult to reach the national targets.

Other countries in Europe have achieved substantial reductions simply by modernizing old coal-fired power stations or by replacing oil with natural gas. Things aren't that simple in Norway, however, and in consequence we have often been unjustly accused of supporting international quota trading simply to avoid meeting our own obligations. But campaigning for more cost-effective methods in pursuance of common environmental aims is not unethical; quite the reverse, in fact. In any case it must be permissible to press for an improved global environment even if one is finding it difficult to reach one's own targets.

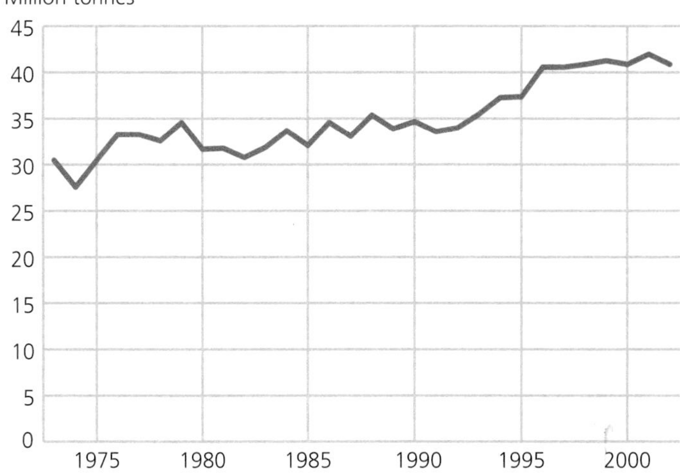


**Although Norway** has been a forerunner in endeavours to have adopted an effective international climate convention, the country's $CO_2$ emissions continue unabated. In 2003 alone emissions increased by 1.8 million tonnes (2%). If the Kyoto protocol comes into force, $CO_2$ emissions will be something of a headache for Norwegian politicians, regardless of international quota trading and other cost-effective measures.

Since 2002 Norwegian $CO_2$ emissions have declined somewhat, but this is primarily owing to an industrial downturn and resultant factory closures. UN estimates suggest that Norway is one of the countries that will find it hardest to meet the requirements of the Kyoto protocol. The government has warned the Storting that, failing the introduction of new technologies, Norwegian emissions of greenhouse gases will be as much as 26 per cent higher in 2010 than they were in 1990.

The fundamental problem is that the agreement fails to take sufficient account of the fact that conditions in the signatory countries differed widely when it was signed.

In Norway, as elsewhere, there has been considerable debate about the scientific evidence for climate changes. It has been asserted forcibly in the country's scientific and university circles that the threat of such changes is greatly exaggerated and, to some extent, has been played up by scientists out for funding. Not a few people believe that the global warming of

**Preceding page:** Magnificent, beautiful, majestic, unspoiled – the adjectives are limited only by the viewer's own imagination and emotions. Many are the superlatives called upon to describe Norway's mountain realm, a part of which, Bukkeskreden in the county of Møre og Romsdal, is seen here.

the last ten years may be a perfectly normal phenomenon, and that, even if the climate-change theory should prove correct, its harmful effects are not of such magnitude as to warrant major social reforms. However, in recent years discussion and criticism have to some extent subsided, as most of the world's leading scientists and universities have come to the conclusion that 'something serious' really is happening.

For many years now Norway has been riven by heated discussions on the advisability of building natural-gas plants on Norwegian soil. Many people think it ludicrous that an energy-producing country of Norway's standing should not itself process more of the energy it produces, but instead export its gas untreated. Matters came to a head in the latter half of the 1990s, culminating in the resignation of the coalition government under Prime Minister Kjell Magne Bondevik following the Storting's sanctioning, in the spring of 2000, of the construction of two natural-gas plants. However, neither of these has so far materialized, mainly because the money has not been forthcoming. Discussions on the subject between environmentalists, who wish to wait pending the introduction of technology that will ensure pollution-free plants, and those in favour of building with present-day technology, have nonetheless continued unabated.

Research is proceeding to determine how we best can fulfil our international obligations. Some environmentalists and industrial interests envisage a solution whereby carbon dioxide would be pumped back into drillholes in the North Sea. This would make it possible not only to dispose of considerable quantities of the gas, but also to extract more oil. The Storting has already agreed that, together with neighbouring countries, Norway should introduce a scheme based on what are known as green certificates. This would involve an obligation on the part of industrial and power companies to invest each year in the development of new, renewable sources of energy, even if doing so would not be profitable at the time. The underlying concept is that it would encourage more rapid development of renewable energy sources than would be the case if the market were left to its own devices, and that development would proceed at a faster pace than has proved possible so far with government aid.

**The Alta dam** is a symbol of one of the most hard-fought campaigns in the history of nature conservation in Norway. Civil disobedience, a Sámi protest movement, a large body of policemen and a rancorous political debate were all part of the struggle.

The discussion in Norway surrounding emissions of greenhouse gases shows with all desirable clarity that close international collaboration is essential if countries are not to lose heart and throw in their hand. It shows too that such fundamental problems go to the very heart of our modern industrial society. Cutting off an isolated source of pollution, protecting a forest or prohibiting release of a gas destructive of the ozone layer may be easy. But it is a different matter entirely when a threat to the environment calls for radical changes in our way of life and entails reduced energy consumption and restrictions on the use of private cars, at the same time as development of non-polluting alternatives is insufficiently advanced.

It will be interesting to observe what eventually sparks a change. Will it be new technology that revolutionizes power production? Or regulations and prohibitions? Or will the impetus once again come from the grass roots, as it did when Lake Mjøsa was in danger of dying? Norway's environmental policy in the early 1900s was increasingly based on the use of financial measures in the shape of a wide range of new and higher 'green' taxes. But after a time people began to jib. Interest in environmental issues declined, and the government did not dare to impose taxes that were high enough to make a real difference.

More than half a million Norwegians currently suffer from noise pollution, mainly resulting from road traffic. And, especially on cold winter days, in towns and urban areas tens of thousands of people are affected by what is, at times, severe air pollution – that too primarily caused by road traffic. The number of people in Norway designated allergic has increased steeply in the last few decades, so more people's deteriorating health may lead to the realization that something will have to be done about the many cars on the road. Only then will it be politically feasible to introduce the measures necessary to enable us to honour our international environmental pledges.

**Vast quantities** of radioactive waste are stored on the Kola peninsula in Russia, where they constitute a major threat to Norway's natural environment. Their removal and destruction are proceeding slowly, and Norway is helping to speed up the process, as here, where a decommissioned atomic submarine is being broken up.

**The Kola peninsula: an environmental time bomb**

As I have already pointed out, some threats to our environment are beyond our control. Even if we were to reduce our own emissions to nil overnight, we could still do nothing to halt the climatic changes that threaten us. Nor could we have stopped acidification of Norway's natural environment without the help of our neighbours.

In the last ten years Norway has led the way in doing something about the enormous quantities of nuclear waste left strewn about in what was once the Soviet Union. When the Iron Curtain fell and the Soviet Union disintegrated, it was revealed that the nuclear power plants in the east were in an even worse state than had been envisioned. Admittedly, the Chernobyl disaster in 1986 had provided an indication that standards left a lot to be desired – radioactive fallout necessitated the destruction of large quantities of reindeer meat and mutton – but Communism's fall some years later disclosed the presence of countless radioactive environmental time bombs.

Norway has expended tens of millions of kroner on improving safety at the nuclear power plant on the nearby Kola peninsula, as have other western countries on similar plants elsewhere. But rendering such assistance has given rise to other problems, as it has prolonged the life of many of the former East bloc's outmoded nuclear power plants, which would otherwise long ago have been decommissioned.

But the dumps of radioactive waste that are a legacy of the Cold War arms race are just as great a threat as the nuclear power plants. The way in which the former East-bloc countries dealt with such waste illustrates these regimes' total disregard for both the natural environment and the well-being of their own citizens. While the Cold War was still in progress large quantities of radioactive waste and disused reactors, with and without their fuel rods, were unceremoniously dumped in the sea off the islands of Novaya Zemlya at the eastern end of the Barents Sea. Vast quantities of spent rods and other waste products are still carelessly stored at former and existing military bases on the Kola peninsula. Some of this waste is stored in rusted hulks that are on the verge of sinking, some in ramshackle old sheds and some even in the open, protected only by rusting fences; and many decommissioned nuclear submarines are laid up all over the peninsula.

The dumps of spent fuel rods in Andreva Bay, fifty kilometres from the Norwegian frontier, illustrate the scale of the problem. The old naval bases in the bay account for only a fraction of the total quantity involved, but the level of radioactivity recorded in the area is 100 million curies, the equivalent of what would be released by the explosion of 5,000 atom bombs of the same power as that dropped on Hiroshima towards the end of the Second World War!

As long as this waste remains undisturbed, it is not an imminent source of contamination as far as Norway is concerned. In the long term, however, it is very much a potential danger, not least because a leak would go straight into the Barents Sea, our most important fishing ground. The question has also been raised in recent years of whether these installations, poorly safeguarded as some of them are, might present a tempting target for terrorists in search of materials with which to manufacture 'dirty' bombs.

Following three serious accidents in these waters involving Russian nuclear submarines, and increasing international concern over nuclear waste on the Kola peninsula, however, many people in Norway are now as worried about the psychological effect on international purchasers of Norwegian fish as they are about the very real threat of radioactive contamination. For this reason, in the last few years more than NOK 1bn has been expended in an endeavour to help Russia put her house in order. For one thing, Norway has paid for the scrapping of two nuclear submarines, and a number of other countries, among them the USA, Great Britain and Germany, have also played their part. But the mountain of radioactive waste is so huge, and the costs involved so great, that for many years to come it will remain a major threat to Norway's natural environment. That a clean-up by the Russians themselves is not without its hazards was made all too clear in the autumn of 2003, when a nuclear submarine that had outlived its usefulness, complete with reactors and fuel rods, sank under tow to the breakers.

**Sellafield: a greater problem**

The traces of radioactive contamination still to be found in Norway today are primarily attributable to the exploding for test purposes of 135 atom bombs in the atmosphere over the northern regions in the 1950s and '60s. The biggest new source of contamination in the last decade has not been the Kola peninsula but the British nuclear reprocessing plant at Sellafield on the Irish Sea coast. The primary source is technetium-99, large quantities of which are discharged into the sea and borne northwards by the current along the Norwegian coast into the Barents Sea and right up to Svalbard. Since 1996 increasing quantities of this substance have been recorded, not only in the water but also in seaweed and crustacea in Norway's coastal waters.

For this reason, for many years now successive Norwegian Ministers of the Environment have done everything in their power to prevail upon the British to put an end to these discharges and store the waste on land instead. They have been backed up by Norwegian environmental organizations and fishing interests, who have also staged demonstrations on the spot at Sellafield. Not until the summer of 2003, however, did the owners of the plant and the British authorities yield and promise to postpone the emptying into the sea of a large storage vat until they had tested a new method of treatment. In the winter of 2004 it became clear that a satisfactory new method had been developed, which the British decided to adopt.

**Crystal-clear streams: billions expended on sewage treatment**

Norwegians have long been been accustomed to enjoying pure water. Without giving it a thought, they have quenched their thirst in babbling brooks and placid lakes; and fish and shellfish have gone straight from sea to table, as, indeed, they still do. But not everywhere. When the public eventually woke up to the true state of affairs, serious concern was evinced about the environment. In the decades immediately following the devastation of the Second World War, when the country was in process of rehabilitation, the sea, fjords and watercourses were regarded as convenient dumping-grounds for waste resulting from the much-vaunted programme of industrial development. And in time, as flush toilets became increasingly common, the nearest river or fjord lent itself admirably to sewage disposal.

But the environment itself finally blew the whistle. One fjord after another was found to be badly polluted, and people were increasingly advised not to eat fish taken from them or to bathe in them; and industrial enterprises were ordered to cease their indiscriminate discharging of effluents into the water. But who was to foot the enormous bill for sewage treatment? Local governments certainly did not have the means and when, early in the 1970s, it was estimated that it would cost at least NOK 40bn to rectify matters, resignation set in. The situation seemed hopeless: the bill was astronomical, and far beyond the means of local authorities.

But the politicians had to find a solution. By this time the matter had become a public issue and the demand to do something had spread far beyond the environmental lobby, which was, after all, comparatively small. People's health began to suffer, so much so that it was estimated that between 50,000 and 100,000 working days a year were being lost due to impure drinking water, mainly the result of discharges of untreated sewage from neighbouring districts. Toilet paper and residual sewage were washed ashore on bathing beaches, and rats were a not uncommon sight on the foreshore near towns.

In 1974 the Storting passed a new Bill providing for a sewage charge to be levied on all Norwegian households. The culprits, the polluters themselves, were to be made to pay! The principle ultimately adopted by the international community at the Rio Summit in 1992 had thus already been an integral part of Norwegian law for twenty years. A scheme was also introduced under which the Norwegian government pledged itself to contribute by means of direct grants, and in the decades that followed tens of billions were devoted to sewage treatment. People living in the interior of the country, in common with those resident on the shores of narrow, confined fjords, all agreed that this was both necessary and only right and proper, but there was considerable dissension about whether the billions expended on sewage treatment plants along the coast was money well spent; many people thought the sea was quite capable of coping with sewage.

Discussion more or less ceased, however, when, in the late 1980s, on more than one occasion myriads of algae made their appearance in the Skagerrak and North Sea. This was widely regarded as decisive proof that the time when the North Sea could safely be used as a dumping-ground was past, though scientists still disagree as to the real cause of these sudden algal proliferations. They may have resulted from specific temperature conditions. Nothing of the kind has occurred in the area in recent years, although there have been times when the concentration of nutrients in the water has been considerably greater than it was in the 1980s. Whatever the truth of the matter, the fact remains that the introduction of sewage treatment plants did result in cleaner local environments. It was, in a manner of speaking, a pre-emptive strike.

Norway did much to induce the countries bordering the North Sea to sign what is known as the North Sea Agreement, one of the aims of which was to halve the overall discharge into the sea of phosphorus- and nitrogen-based nutrients between 1985 and 1995. Some of the signatory countries found themselves unable to meet their obligations, however, with the consequence that the period was extended to the end of 2005. Such nutrients are an important cause of over-fertilization in rivers, lakes and coastal waters, which in turn encourages the growth of algae.

Norway's emissions of nutrients deriving from sewage and agriculture are quite modest in comparison with those of many of the countries bordering on the Baltic Sea, Skagerrak and North Sea. The large-scale construction of treatment plants, the most expensive environmental project Norway has ever embarked upon, has paid off. On the south coast phosphorus emissions are down by 60 per cent and emissions of nitrogen have fallen by 38 per cent. The greatest decline has been in terms of sewage, but pollution from the agricultural and industrial sectors has also been substantially reduced.

In recent years pollution emanating from fish farms has likewise declined following the introduction of strict regulations in 1979, though in coastal areas the fish-farming industry remains the biggest single polluter in terms of nutrients, being responsible for 68 per cent of phosphorus emissions and 34 per cent of nitrogen emissions.

Because of the ocean currents that flow along its coasts, Norway also 'imports' considerable quantities of man-made phosphorus and nitrogen. The total quantity of nitrogen entering Norwegian waters in this way is currently 5 per cent higher than it was in 1985, and in the case of phosphorus 37 per cent higher. This applies to the full length of coastline, that is, to far wider areas than those covered by the North Sea Agreement. These figures are further proof that a country, in this case Norway, cannot resolve serious environmental problems alone.

Every year we expend more than NOK 4bn on sewage treatment, and large sums continue to be invested in new treatment plants and methods. In countless fjords and, not least, in the hinterland the environmental situation has greatly improved in recent years. Hardly anywhere is it now possible to find traces of untreated sewage, and people are again able to slake their thirst with little fear of the consequences in lakes and streams that once were a health hazard. But there is still work to be done. For one thing, many waterworks still find it difficult to meet the EU's strict regulations governing intestinal bacteria levels in the water supply.

**Pollutant emissions to air**

| | Lead | Cadmium | Mercury | Arsenic | Chromium | Copper | PAH-total | Dioxin |
|---|---|---|---|---|---|---|---|---|
| | | Tonnes | | | kg | | Tonnes | Gram |
| 1990 | 186 | 1 644 | 1 704 | 3 098 | 12 797 | 21 882 | 156 | 130 |
| 1991 | 143 | 1 573 | 1 583 | 2 997 | 12 718 | 19 010 | 143 | 98 |
| 1992 | 126 | 1 567 | 1 421 | 2 968 | 12 595 | 19 290 | 140 | 96 |
| 1993 | 86 | 1 637 | 1 120 | 3 151 | 12 348 | 19 303 | 144 | 95 |
| 1994 | 23 | 1 182 | 1 171 | 3 558 | 11 654 | 17 848 | 141 | 94 |
| 1995 | 21 | 1 012 | 1 088 | 2 896 | 11 367 | 18 648 | 141 | 70 |
| 1996 | 9 | 1 052 | 1 118 | 2 999 | 11 438 | 18 887 | 146 | 49 |
| 1997 | 8 | 1 073 | 1 130 | 2 823 | 12 374 | 19 375 | 152 | 41 |
| 1998 | 8 | 1 138 | 1 097 | 3 285 | 11 886 | 20 363 | 145 | 35 |
| 1999 | 7 | 978 | 1 155 | 3 286 | 11 287 | 20 530 | 138 | 39 |
| 2000 | 6 | 725 | 996 | 2 457 | 8 814 | 19 329 | 138 | 34 |
| 2001* | 5 | 696 | 950 | 2 165 | 7 083 | 19 658 | 143 | 34 |

### Moribund fjords

Many of our fjords, too, still present local environmental problems. At regular intervals the public health authorities issue warnings that the fish and other marine creatures in twenty-eight fjords up and down the coast are unfit for human consumption. In some places such warnings are required all year round, especially where children and pregnant women are concerned. The sediment on the seabed is in many places heavily polluted, a legacy of earlier sins. The Pollution Control Authority (SFT) has estimated that it will cost at least NOK 25bn to put things right. The government spends NOK 50-60m annually on clean-up operations, meaning that it will take several hundred years to complete the task. However, the Storting has expressly directed the government to obtain a clearer picture of the situation and, where possible, to enjoin the companies responsible to rectify matters themselves. The problem is, however, that many of the culprits have long been defunct.

Many experts believe that the best course is to let sleeping dogs lie and leave the polluted sediment where it is, as to disturb it may well do more harm than good. When the inner reaches of the Sandefjord fjord were dredged in the summer of 2003, for example, large quantities of particulate environmental toxins were stirred up and found their way to other parts of the fjord. It might have been better to have left things as they were.

While the heated debate over sewage was at its height all over the country, great efforts were being made to reduce emissions of other pollutants too, and statistics show that emissions of many environmentally harmful chemicals have indeed declined. Thanks to the imposition of strict requirements, Norwegian industry has made considerable progress in this regard, and not a few big companies now practise internal control procedures that are even more stringent than the official ones. But it has been a long haul.

**Thousands of tourists** visit Norway to admire the fjords, the deep ravines that cleave their way far inland from the rugged coast. On some days they are as rough as the sea without, on others dead calm, mirroring the precipitous mountain walls that tower above. A small rock surmounted by a cairn separates the Kjøsnes fjord from Lake Jølster in the county of Sogn og Fjordane.

### Environmentalists get tough

Although the Storting regularly has ordered the State Pollution Control Authority to introduce still stricter standards, there is no denying that the environmentalist organizations have played a very important role in Norway. The best example is probably provided by the Titania incident, which concerned the question of where waste from the Titania company's ilemnite plant at Sokndal, on the shores of the Jøssing fjord, should be dumped. This was the first major victory to result from the use of more activist means. Ever since the early 1960s waste from the Titania plant had been dumped in the fjord, and as early as 1961 fish taken in the fjord were of such poor quality that a ban was placed on commercial fishing there. By the mid-1970s there was hardly room for more such waste, which prompted the company to seek permission to dump its waste in the Dynga Deep close to the mouth of the fjord. The State Pollution Control Authority granted temporary permission, but the company was also enjoined to start looking for an alternative site on land. This heralded the start of a bitterly fought battle that was to rumble on for many years at varying levels.

Mainly because of the expense involved the company wanted to put off for as long as possible having to store its waste on land. The local community was a house divided against itself. On one side stood those who were fighting for their jobs, on the other the fishermen whose livelihood had been destroyed. There was also disagreement among the pundits, that is, between the Marine Research Institute on the one hand and the scientists and consultants hired by the company on the other, as to how harmful the debris really was. The dispute put the Labour Party in a difficult position, torn as it was between the interests of the trade unions and the need to protect the environment.

**In 1983** a youth organization, Natur og Ungdom, campaigned against discharges from the Titania ilmenite plant in the Jøssing fjord. This campaign marked the beginning of a far more activist approach on the part of conservationists. The youngsters depicted here later founded Bellona, which has evolved into one of Norway's most active and influential environmental organizations.

In the summer of 1983 the Titania company received a visit which both it and certain sections of the local population could well have done without. Members of two local branches of an environmental pressure group, Nature and Youth, set up camp in the neighbourhood and chained themselves to the pipeline through which it was planned to convey the waste to the dumping ground. This was the start of a ten-year battle. It was fought in the name of these two local organizations, as at the time such actions were still controversial, even in the eyes of the radical youth section of the Norwegian Society for the Conservation of Nature.

The Titania case was a headache for more than one Minister of the Environment. Because the young conservationists kept the pot boiling and the issue in the public eye through a spate of articles in the press, neither the politicians nor SFT could play it down. In 1986 Bellona, an environmental foundation, was formed and given a free hand to campaign against the dumping. They protested, drew attention to procedural errors and even occupied the Minister's office. They too made active use of the press and television to get their message across. Until the Titania case hit the headlines, the environmentalist organizations and the government had to a certain extent acted in concert, standing shoulder to shoulder in confrontations with industry and landowners. But now everything changed: the protesters were as sceptical of the government's handling of the Titania case as they were of the company itself. As SFT says in its historical review: 'Thenceforward the Pollution Control Authority was no longer alone in determining which problems and issues were to be accorded priority.' The issue was not resolved until 1990, when the government ordered the company to cease dumping waste in the Dynga Deep by 1994; the land repository has been in use since 1992.

## Oil: a mixed blessing

Oil and gas, which since the early 1970s have been pumped up from the bed of the North Sea, are the main reason why, in monetary terms, Norway is one of the richest countries in the world. But extraction has its price: marine life has undeniably suffered as a result, though in what ways and how badly scientists are still far from certain.

Since the Bravo blowout in 1977 Norway has been spared major critical spills resulting from the offshore petroleum activity. This is because the authorities have imposed extremely strict standards of safety on the operators, who themselves have expended considerable sums on research and capital investments.

Despite this, in the thirty years Norway has been an offshore oil producer, operators have been permitted to discharge large quantities of pollutants into the sea from their platforms. The production process itself involves release into the water of substantial amounts of polluted sand and what is known as produced water, water that comes up with the oil from the ocean depths. Emissions rose dramatically in the 1990s, one reason being that there was less oil left in the wells, meaning that more polluted water was pumped to the surface.

The actual drilling process requires the use of considerable quantities of chemicals, all of which, until 1992, were discharged straight into the sea. However, when deposits of chemicals and oil had been discovered on the seabed and in organisms in the vicinity of the platforms, severe restrictions were imposed on this practice, with the result that 98 per cent of the chemicals in use today are considered a negligible threat to the environment.

The authorities have introduced further strict regulations and laid down that from 2005 onwards there are to be no discharges whatsoever from the offshore oil activity. Polluted sand and water are to be pumped back into the drillholes or transported ashore for treatment and disposal there.

This, coupled with promises of further strict requirements in respect of offshore operations and improved contingency measures to deal with acute problems, constitutes the authorities' strongest argument in favour of year-round oil extraction in the northern regions. When the proposal was shelved in the 1970s, it was purely because the government institutions responsible for the environment convinced the Storting that the risks involved were too great.

A united Norwegian environmental front has warned that it will contest drilling in the Barents Sea and off the Lofoten Islands to the last. In all probability, in the decade ahead the right to drill in these offshore regions will prove the most hard-fought-over environmental issue yet.

### The downside of consumerism

The rich nations of the world are responsible for most pollution and bear responsibility for the bulk of its environmental problems. Moreover, the wealthiest are also the world's prime consumers: 80 per cent of the world's private cars are found in OECD countries.

In every decade since the Second World War the graph charting Norwegian consumption has soared ever more steeply. This means not only that the gap in standards of living between Norwegians and the people of Africa is continuing to widen, but also that the Norwegian 'refuse heap' is growing at record speed. To take one example, in the last two decades of the twentieth century the amount expended on consumer goods by Norwegian families rose by no less than 60 per cent!

In 2002 every Norwegian discarded 354 kilos of household waste – 20 kilos more than in the previous year. In the early 1970s each of us disposed of only 174 kilos. Although this increase is less than in other industrial countries, it still says a lot about the extent to which Norway, wealthy as it is, is depleting the earth's resources. Altogether, we produce marginally less than 9 million tonnes of refuse annually.

In the first postwar decades waste was considered to be an unavoidable by-product of economic growth and success. Few people concerned themselves with the ways in which industry disposed of chemicals and other waste products, a lot being either buried in the ground or stored with no thought for the consequences. However, early in the 1970s it gradually became manifest that this was resulting in serious pollution of the soil, rivers and fjords; moreover, refuse was increasingly seen as a resource. It did not take long thereafter for the Ministry of the Environment, then in its infancy, and its offshoot, the State Pollution Control Authority, to draw attention to the problem refuse and industrial waste represented. In 1973 the first official committee was formed in Norway to assess the feasibility of recycling refuse. In the event, many years were to pass before a smoothly working system was in place, but the idea had at least been mooted. The committee concluded that recycling should be the guiding principle behind refuse disposal, not only in order to reduce pollution but also to husband resources. It also advocated organized collection of paper, cars that were no longer roadworthy and, most important of all, toxic waste.

In my capacity as Minister of the Environment, in 1975 I placed before the Storting a report on the problems posed by the increasing quantities of pollutants entering the environment. In this report I said, among other things: 'Little control is exercised at present over the way in which such waste is disposed of. There is no organized system of waste collection and storage.'

As a result of this report, in the next few years more than one hundred collection points for environmentally harmful waste were set up. At the same time SFT launched the idea of instituting a 'cradle to grave' principle whereby manufacturers would be made responsible for their products, also when the time came to discard them when they had outlived their usefulness. Today this line of thought is integral to Norwegian legislation as it relates to waste. People can now return used car batteries, free of charge, to any sales outlet that sells them, and similar facilities are available for tyres, for example, and many kinds of packaging. Tens of thousands of tonnes of such waste are now collected in this manner. In most places in Norway it would be unthinkable to dump a discarded refrigerator on a refuse tip; in any case, it is against the law.

Although Norwegians are using and discarding consumer products as never before, waste management is very much a success story. From 1985 to 2002 the volume of waste rose by 18 per cent, but at the same time the volume that was recycled or used to generate energy increased by no less than 40 per cent. Virtually all municipal refuse dumps now operate a recycling system. People can bring their refuse and pay a small fee to dispose of it, but have themselves to sort it into its component parts – metal, wood, plastic, etc. – and place it in the relevant containers. In some places also household waste has to be similarly sorted prior to collection; to discard toxic waste along with other refuse is strictly prohibited.

This initiative has been successful for a number of reasons. For one thing, the authorities have introduced strict regulations governing waste disposal and also made it easier for people to sort their refuse themselves. This is an area in which most people can contribute by simple means. In many places minimizing waste has become something of a fun thing. Not a few municipalities reduce refuse-collection charges if organic waste is converted into compost. There is something ironic about the fact that the very symbol of our extremist consumption, i.e. waste, should also be a plank of what is arguably the most successful environmental programme in the country!

But despite the success of the scheme, refuse remains an environmental problem. No less than 7 per cent of Norway's emissions of greenhouse gases derive from old and existing landfills. And large quantities of the most toxic waste products still disappear without trace. A little less than 700,000 tonnes of pollutants are generated in Norway every year. The bulk (95 per cent) is collected and appropriately dealt with, but several tens of thousands of tonnes continue to disappear annually. Where do they go? The increase in toxic waste continues to keep pace with increases in consumption, making it extremely important that also this unaccounted-for tonnage be collected. Norway's fragile natural environment has more than enough to cope with as it is, in the shape of the thousands of tonnes of toxins that have been allowed to pollute it in the past.

Carried by air and ocean currents, considerable quantities of pollutants still reach Norway from abroad. Studies undertaken in recent years have revealed that large tracts of land in southern Norway are contaminated, in some places badly, by pollutants originating in other countries. Scientists have found traces of such toxic substances as PCB in polar bears and other denizens of the Arctic – thousands of kilometres from their supposed provenance. Concentrations of PCB in Norwegian polar bears are six times as great as in the bears' Canadian cousins. Emissions of some substances have declined, only to be replaced by new hazards. We make use of incredible quantities of chemicals: close on 10,000 different chemical substances are in daily use in Norway alone, and new ones are continually being added. It is by no means certain what the consequences are in terms of health and the environment when these chemicals find their way into rivers and fjords. But it certainly came as a shock to both the authorities and the public at large when, in 2003, it became known that the trout in our largest lake, Mjøsa, contained one of the world's highest concentrations of a brominated fire retardant (BDE), a substance added to certain products to make them less flammable.

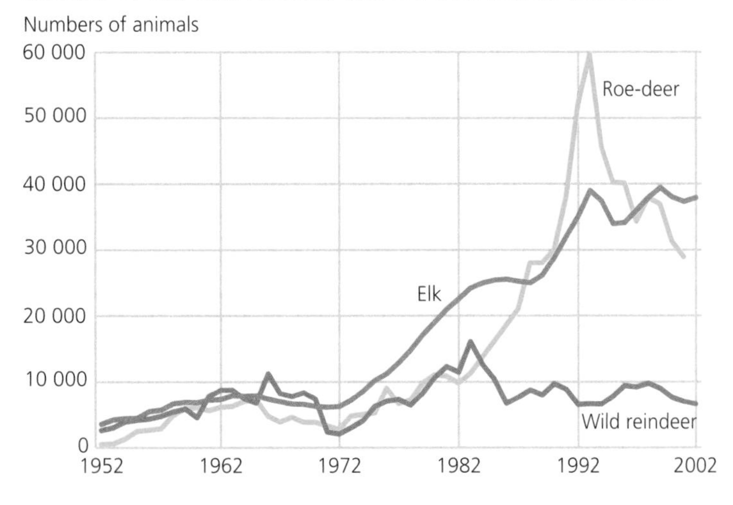


**Norway's elk**, deer and roe-deer populations have dramatically increased in recent years. In not a few places there are too many elk, and the more than 56,000 Norwegians who hunt them are unable to fell all those they are permitted to by law.

### Nine out of ten Norwegians make active use of the countryside

The Norwegians' early awareness of the dangers of pollution, and their determination to do something about it, may be traced back to their strong affinity with, and close proximity to, nature. Oslo is unique as a capital in virtue of its situation amid dense forests that reach down to the city's very suburbs. Recent studies reveal that Norwegians look upon their access to unspoiled countryside as one of the most important criteria of the good life.

We have exploited nature for thousands of years. Our forebears hunted and trapped, picked berries and mushrooms and kept their animals alive through the long, cold winters on leaves and bark. But it was left to foreign visitors to teach us how to delight in nature for its own sake, to find tranquillity and peace of mind through woodland rambles and mountain walks – outdoor pursuits that nine out of ten Norwegians continue to enjoy today.

**Two intrepid female** pioneers picking their way down the boulder-strewn side of Mount Galdhøpiggen in 1909 and (below) a group from the tourist ship Polarstar bound by rubber boat for a ramble on Spitsbergen nearly a century later. For more than 150 years tourism has been an important source of income for many rural communities in Norway. Tens of thousands of foreign tourists visit the country every year, attracted by the wildness of the landscape and its untrammelled accessibility.

Claus Helberg, a writer and mountain climber, once wrote that Europe first realized how unique the Norwegian landscape was when, in 1810, Jens Esmark, an official stationed in the mining town of Kongsberg, submitted a report on the Rjukan waterfall to the Danish deputy governer of Norway. He declared that it was 'the highest waterfall not only in Europe but even in the whole of the known world'. Word of this wonder spread, and the waterfall, along with the surrounding Gausta mountains, was for many years the country's prime tourist attraction. But before that foreign naturalists had long roamed the Norwegian countryside to record and classify its flora and fauna. As early as the 1750s the Dano-German botanist Georg Chr. Oeder had been in Norway collecting plants for his *Flora Danica* – no doubt to the amazement of many a local farmer.

The first hikers, people who enjoyed walking for walking's sake, found their way from the sprawling cities of the Continent and Britain to the Norwegian mountains in the 1830s and '40's. As urbanization spread throughout Europe, it became fashionable among the more well-to-do to 'return to nature'. Only the upper classes could afford to make the long and expensive journey to the impoverished northern outpost that Norway then was. Norwegians were largely viewed as a primitive people, an impression that was further strengthened when National Romanticism swept the Continent. The movement found reflection in the works of Norwegian authors and playwrights such as Henrik Wergeland and Henrik Ibsen, painters like Adolph Tidemand and Hans Gude, and composers like Edvard Grieg.

Wealthy Germans and members of the British upper class were the principal visitors. They made their way up-country by boat and the rough, winding roads, walked and climbed in the mountains, shot ptarmigan and reindeer, and fished for salmon in the fast-flowing rivers. On returning home they wrote lengthy accounts of their travels, and their books sold well, encouraging more tourists to follow in their footsteps.

One British aristocrat, Lord Garvagh, who visited Aurland in the fjord country of the west in the 1850s, eventually made his way to the mountainous region north of Hallingskarvet, a ridge separating Hardanger from the Hallingdal valley. Entranced by this mountain realm and the magnificence of the Hardanger plateau, he built a number of small log cabins in the area; there, keen sportsman that he was, he was able to hunt and fish to his heart's content. He returned almost every year thereafter, right up to his death in 1871. The stone shack in Folarskaret is still known as 'Lordehytta', the Lord's Cabin. Lord Garvagh and his son taught the mountain farmers of northern Hallingdal to enjoy the wonders and beauty of nature, as did their compatriots elsewhere in the country.

In the wake of these visitors from abroad small hotels and boarding-houses sprang up in the mountains. As the nineteenth century drew to a close, members of Norway's own upper class decided that the time had come to emulate their foreign counterparts' example. Thomas Heftye, a wealthy businessman, set about building his first country retreats, one of which, Frognerseteren, set among the wooded hills of Nordmarka, on the outskirts of Oslo, is still very much a going concern.

Eighteen sixty-eight saw the foundation of Den Norske Turistforening (The Norwegian Mountain Touring Association). The Association's aim was to make it easier for people to get out into the countryside, and also to encourage conservation of Norway's unique natural environment. Slowly but surely, mountain rambles and woodland walks began to gain in popularity among people of all social classes, successors to the first pioneers. Today the Association administers 350 cabins and is responsible for a network of marked trails covering a total of 18,000 kilometres! It boasts close on 200,000 members, all of whom are at liberty to put up in the cabins while on walking holidays in the mountains.

At weekends and in their holidays whole families set out, on skis or on foot, eager for exercise and a breath of fresh air; in autumn, some also go picking berries or mushrooms. In winter, at cafés in clearings in the woods outside the towns or located at intervals along marked trails in the mountains, as they notch up the kilometres on their skis children can get the booklets they carry stamped, to qualify for a silver or gold badge. There are thousands of kilometres of paths for cycling, and the Boy Scouts and Girl Guides associations, in common with other children's and youth organizations, make extensive use of the forests and mountains for their outdoor activities.

In recent years a number of new activities have made their appearances as alternatives to the more traditional rambles and walking tours, among them such action (and more hazardous) sports as rafting and mountain climbing, which appeal especially to the young. Studies reveal that 80-90 per cent of the population engage in some form of outdoor pursuit. Fifty per cent of Norwegians occasionally fish, and almost as many go berry picking.

**Norwegians love** their cabins. Time was when cabin life was synonymous with a holiday spent under rather primitive conditions that included an outside privy and paraffin lamps. In the last ten years or so, however, cabin communities of an entirely different kind have sprung up in which the accommodation is more luxurious than most people enjoy at home. The contrast is well illustrated by these photographs of a huddle of cabins in Romsdal (left) in the 1950s and (right) a similar group at Hafjell in the 1990s.

## Life in a log cabin

I was myself brought up to appreciate and take advantage of all that nature had to offer. Summer and winter alike, my parents used to take us for walks in the woods and mountains. Our summers were spent by the sea, bathing and fishing, and in the winter we went skiing in Nordmarka. I have many happy memories from those days, when we had time for each other and for physical pursuits.

We Norwegians aren't content only to pay nature a visit every now and again: we each want to have a slice of it for ourselves, a holiday cabin. In Norway the number of such cabins per head of population is the highest in the world – between them, 4.5 million Norwegians own 369,000 cabins and summer cottages. When outdoor recreation was in its infancy and, in fact, right up to the Second World War, ownership of such second homes was mostly confined to those with money and time to spend it. But in the 1950s, which saw the advent of longer holidays and the five-day working week, along with an increasing number of private cars on the roads, the building of holiday cabins was given new impetus. As a result of greater affluence and more leisure, nearly 4,000 new cabins are now being built each year. This unprecedented increase in numbers is making inroads on the environment and beginning to endanger Norway's still unspoiled countryside – so much so that such cabins have become a major threat to the herds of wild reindeer in the south. This is because when a cabin is built a road is needed to get to it, with the result that the reindeer are finding themselves cut off from many of their winter grazing grounds.

Our 'cabin culture' – the way we like to live when we visit our cabins to get away from it all – is also changing. In the 1960s and '70s cabin life was synonymous with tranquillity and simplicity. Cabins tended to be small and, as they lacked electricity, were dimly lit by paraffin lamps and candles. Many remain unchanged in this respect, but nowadays a higher standard is demanded of the new generation of cabins. People tend to insist on plenty of space and all the modern conveniences and creature comforts to which they are accustomed in their homes.

Although several central government and local authorities are striving to restrict the building of cabins to specific areas, and to ban holiday cabins from certain large tracts of country altogether, pursuance of such a restrictive policy also poses problems. Cabin owners constitute a valuable source of revenue and provide jobs for the local population. At a rough estimate, every year we Norwegians spend some 14 million nights in our cabins.

So far, the presence of cabins in the mountains has done little to restrict the public's right to roam, but the same cannot be said of cabins on the coast. Since 1965 the Planning and Building Act has imposed severe restrictions on building in a 100-metre-wide swathe along the shoreline. But exceptions are all too frequently made, so much so that between 1985 and 2003 1,666 kilometres of shoreline were developed and built on, thus denying the public access to 1.4 per cent more of the coast. Overall, more than 23 per cent of Norway's coastline has been thus developed, and in some counties, among them Oslo and Akershus, more than two-thirds of the coast has been affected in some way by building activity!

The Storting has resolved to clamp down on the granting of exemptions from building restrictions, and in recent years has increased funding to provide for the setting aside of more large areas of countryside for recreational purposes.

**Difficult choices**

As we have seen, it is often difficult to strike a balance between economic growth and conservation. Almost daily, politicians – in both central and local goverment – are compelled to make choices which, in one way or another, have an impact on the country's natural environment.

The principles of sustainable development and preventive action enjoy the support of the majority of Norwegians. But when it comes down to practical politics things are not always so simple.

The conflict surrounding exploitation of the oil and gas deposits in our northern waters is a good example. On the one hand the country's politicians are eager to boost Treasury funds, one reason being that they need to ensure that there will always be enough money available to cover pension payments. (The number of old people in Norway is rising steeply, and with it the bill for pensions.) On the other hand they have to take into consideration the fragility of the areas concerned and also our international commitment to a reduction in emissions of carbon dioxide. Oil production in the Barents Sea must necessarily be accompanied by an increase in such emissions. Furthermore, no matter how strict the regulations imposed and how effective the precautions taken, there will always be the risk of a spill.

Although in principle it is important to be prepared, being so is by no means easy in practice. An example is provided by the many new chemical products that appear on the market almost daily. As with drugs for medical purposes, it is almost impossible to foresee their long-term side effects. Only after they have been in service for many years does it become apparent how dangerous some very useful chemicals really are. It is extremely difficult to safeguard ourselves against such things, but it does show that we can never afford to relax our vigilance.

Another difficulty is deciding how to make the best use of the natural environments we protect. Their value in terms of recreational facilities is one important reason why large expanses of Norway's unique mountain regions are preserved the way they are. Moreover, the mountains are one of the country's major tourist attractions. But overuse can do untold harm. A case in point is Besseggen, a sharp-edged ridge in the Jotunheimen mountains that is showing clear signs of wear because so many people are traversing it. The time has come to consider how much such traffic should be permitted. Extensive national parks are usually able to cope with large numbers of visitors; smaller reserves established to protect one or two individual species are, however, best left undisturbed.

Norway is in a fortunate position. We still possess vast expanses of unspoiled countryside capable of sustaining widespread usage by the local population and visitors from all over the world. The safeguarding of such areas for future generations is a common task. All my experience as a Norwegian tells me that the only way to do this is by cooperation – between the authorities and business circles, between local communities and environmental activists and between nations bound by their commitments to each other.

**january** fin serck-hanssen **february** rolf m. aagaard

**march** herdis maria siegert **april** janne solgaard

**may** jens hauge **june** vibeke tandberg

**july** dag alveng **august** rune johansen

**september** knut bry **october** asle svarverud

**november** ingvar moi **december** per berntsen

# THOR HEYERDAHL

There was nothing in the cards to suggest that Thor Heyerdahl would ever become a world-famous seafarer and adventurer. He was, after all, a boy who had to have extra tuition in gymnastics, and who, at the age of twenty, could neither swim nor dance and was too shy to chat up girls. His fear of water stemmed from the time when, as a young boy, he nearly drowned in midwinter in Herregårdsdammen, a lake where his father, who owned the local brewery, was engaged in hewing out blocks of ice. His father tried, sometimes with the help of hired coaches, to teach his timorous only child a few swimming strokes, but in vain; in fact, this adventurer-to-be did not learn to swim until, at the age of twenty-three, he fell into the water on an island in the Pacific.

It is virtually inconceivable that this reserved insect collector from the small fjordside town of Larvik would later become the author of the world's next-best-selling book after the Bible. His account of the Kon-Tiki voyage was translated into some seventy languages, and he became the holder of Norway's first and only Oscar for the film from the same epic voyage – a film which, to date, has been seen by more than 600 million people.

But what of Heyerdahl himself, the child of a broken home who fainted from embarrassment when his teacher asked him why he had drawn palm trees and monkeys on the covers of his school books? Nowadays he is required reading everywhere as a result of his having redefined the history of the world on a number of critical points. He must have had a singular childhood, growing up as he did in the tension between his mother's atheist Darwinism and his father's simple Christian faith; it was an upbringing that must have been a constant source of amazement. One of the few things that his parents could agree on was the importance of their son's getting fresh goat's milk every morning. It has been suggested that this explains both his stubbornness and his rather husky voice.

'If I had completed my studies in zoology, I would probably have spent the rest of my life counting the hairs on the back of the fruit fly,' Heyerdahl said in his later years. Instead, he gave up his studies and in 1936 made his way as a newlywed to Fatu-Hiva. On paper he was going to investigate the origins of animal life on a volcanic Pacific island, but in practice Liv and Thor were planning to escape from civilization, which they both despised, in order to return to nature, possibly remaining there for the rest of their days. They lived entirely alone in a bamboo hut, wearing neither clothes nor shoes; but it was not to be the paradise for which they had hoped.

Heyerdahl early began to wonder how the islands had been populated. He found a rock carving of a vessel with a curved hull and high bow, very much like the reed boats he had seen in Peru. As a biologist, he knew that papayas, sweet potatoes and pineapples originated in South America.

**In 1947** Thor Heyerdahl and his companions amazed the world by sailing across the Pacific Ocean from Peru to the Raroia atoll on a balsa raft, 'Kon-Tiki.'

His discoveries on Fatu-Hiva set him on a trail that he was to pursue for the rest of his life, this being that ideas, people, seeds and civilizations had been carried over the oceans of the world much earlier than was believed at the time. It was an accepted scientific belief that the oceans had remained invincible obstacles right up to the time of Columbus and a firmly held conviction that the Pacific islands had been populated from the west. But Heyerdahl challenged such accepted truths. He attached importance to facts, among them that most ocean currents flow from east to west.

The president of the Explorers Club had nothing but scornful laughter for this Norwegian dilettante. 'You can try sailing from Peru to the Pacific islands on a balsa raft yourself,' he said. The idea slowly evolved that such know-alls should be taken at their word. In spring 1947, the Kon-Tiki raft put to sea from Peru. The crew was deliberately made up of landlubbers, most of them men whom Thor knew personally from his service as a parachutist and saboteur in the Second World War. Specialists the world over agreed that the frail-looking craft would sink within fourteen days, assuming that the lashings had not come apart long before then. But the raft, which consisted of nine balsa logs, remained afloat for 101 days through storms and in waves as high as a house – until it was reduced to matchwood on the Raroia reef, with Heyerdahl clinging to the mast for dear life. His success made a minimal impression on scientists around the world, but among ordinary people there was immense interest, and President Truman, eager for a firsthand account of the voyage, invited Heyerdahl to the White House.

There is a major difference between Thor Heyerdahl and other western explorers, and that is that he always made friends with the native population. This stood him in particularly good stead on Easter Island, where countless expeditions before his had fruitlessly attempted to explain the origin of the huge and enigmatic sculptures found on the island. Heyerdahl was the first person to ask the long-eared mayor about them, and he got an answer. Time after time, he showed that social intelligence could reveal far more than re-hashed book learning.

It was only natural that Heyerdahl should eventually start to wonder how America had been populated;

after all, there were no apes from which humans could have descended. There were also a great many common features between the civilizations of America and Africa. Pyramids, hierarchical dynasties and identical knowledge of stone structures were to be found on both sides of the Atlantic. Heyerdahl wanted to find out if it was possible to cross the Atlantic on a reed boat of the kind depicted in the Egyptian pyramids. He christened his craft *Ra*, the name given to the sun in ancient Egypt, Polynesia *and* Peru. Twenty-two years after crossing the Pacific on nine logs, he was now proposing to cross the Atlantic on a haystack. As before, heads were shaken – except that this time the doubters were to be proved right.

After covering 5,000 kilometres in eight weeks the *Ra* foundered. The Atlantic is about 3,000 kilometres across at its narrowest point, and even though they were so close to succeeding that their sinking vessel was surrounded by birds that had flown out from South America, Heyerdahl immediately decided to mount another expedition. This reed boat, *Ra II*, which was ten feet shorter than its predecessor, set out from Africa in May 1970, reaching Barbados 58 days later; there the mariners were met by Heyerdahl's second wife and the couple's three daughters. And so it was proven that people could have crossed the Atlantic Ocean thousands of years before Columbus. The film of this expedition was also nominated for an Oscar.

On the last of his famous ocean voyages, Heyerdahl decided to investigate whether the three major civilizations of the ancient world could have shared a common origin. It was known that 3,000 years before Christ, three civilizations suddenly evolved simultaneously at the mouths of the Nile, Euphrates and Indus. The *Tigris* had been at sea for five months when Heyerdahl resolved to set fire to it outside Djibouti on 3 April 1978 in protest against the wars then raging in the region.

Heyerdahl was inundated with honorary doctorates and knighthoods all over the world. He was Indira Gandhi's guest of honour, he was repeatedly kissed by Anwar Sadat, became best friends with Fidel Castro and was hand-picked by Gorbachev to lead the global environmental conservation organization, Green Cross. Wherever he went, he was met with fanfares, celebrations and dancing masses of people – except in his home country. Here, he was regarded mainly as a vagabond who had somehow managed to find fame by sunbathing on the quarterdecks of a series of anachronistic craft. In reality he had expended most of his energy on fieldwork, excavation and scientific dissertations. His archaeological work in Peru, the Galapagos Islands, Tenerife and the Maldives is held in particularly high esteem, having provided still more corroboration of his theories.

Heyerdahl lived in Italy for many years. Here he became increasingly perturbed by the way the local country people slaughtered small birds, so, pro-active problem-solver that he was, he induced them to change their ways by raising and introducing more worthy prey. He spent his later years on Tenerife.

At the age of 87, this indomitable adventurer was planning a major archaeological expedition to Samoa when he died in the spring of 2002. Both the *Kon Tiki* raft and *Ra II* can now be seen in the Kon-Tiki Museum in Oslo, where Thor Heyerdahl also founded an institute for archaeological and cultural studies.

NIELS CHR. GEELMUYDEN

HEYERDAHL, THOR, (1914–2002), ethnographer and explorer. In 1941, proposed the theory that Polynesia had been populated from South America. In 1947, sailed from Peru on a replica of an ancient Peruvian balsa raft, Kon Tiki, to the Tuamotu archipelago. Mounted expeditions to the Galapagos Islands (1953) and to Easter Island (1955–56). His Ra expeditions of 1969 and 1970 proved that the Atlantic could be crossed by reed boats. The Tigris voyage in 1977 took him from Iraq to Djibouti. He also carried out excavations on the Maldives, the Canary Islands and in Túcume in Peru.

# FAITH AND PHILOSOPHIES

# FAITH – FROM TYRANNY TO TOLERANCE

Gunnar Stålsett

Faith needs time: philosophies of life, beliefs, change but slowly. It was thus that Christianity came to Norway in the 11th century – slowly. The 16th century transition from Roman Catholicism to Lutherism also took time to accomplish. For those involved, these changes must have been hard to understand. The same is true today. At the start of a new millennium, change is in the air: the Norwegian landscape of faiths and philosophies is again in flux.

The process began with secularization. But when did secularization begin? Or it may have been with the coming of modernity. But when was that? We now say that we live in a post-modern society. Categorizations of this sort are imprecise, but they do attempt to capture the changing trends in faiths, beliefs and values.

Secularization of the state is an ongoing process in legislation and social life. Multiculturalism has become more in evidence in our streets and public places. Religious and philosophical variety are visible in our schools, and the media bear witness to the triumph of pluralism over a uniform culture. But strong ties still exist between the Church of Norway and the Norwegian people, and there remains a close relationship between Church and state, so any discussion of faith and philosophies in contemporary Norway must of necessity centre on the Church of Norway. When, as in Norway, a Church encompasses the great majority of the population (85.7% in 2002, down from 86.6% in 2000), and when the Christian faith has long been a pillar of values and culture in the national structure, the institutions and religious history of that Church needs must occupy an important place. History embodies codes that can be used to interpret the present. But the Norwegian landscape of faith and philosophies at the turn of the millennium is a patchwork with constituents of many shapes and colours. Churches are struggling to understand themselves in a situation characterized by a wide variety of values. This is taking place in dialogue with other religions and philosophies of life, and engenders unity of action across widely divergent cultures. A Church with a universal vision should feel at home in the age of globalization, not estranged from it.

My attempt to present this landscape will consist of a thematic dip into history and a glance at the contemporary scene, together with a stroll through what I have called the capital's, i.e. Oslo's, 'beliefs quadrant'.

**The Klepp Cross.** Stone crosses are among the oldest remnants of the Christianization of Norway. They point to Christian influence from the west, across the sea from England. This cross is from Klepp, Jæren.

## Church buildings as landmarks

No traveller in Norway can fail to notice the churches. The stone churches and cathedrals bear testimony to the country's thousand-year history of Christianity and the characteristic stave churches typify Norwegian culture and religiosity. These many churches represent a long thread of memory in Norwegian history and testify to strong influences from other lands and traditions. Numbering more than 1,600, they constitute the most important buildings in the nation's cultural history.

The Vikings' thirst for conquest, together with missionary zeal, helped, each in its own way, to bring the Christian Church to Norway. The ancient stone church at Moster, the island off the west coast where Olav Tryggvason came ashore and celebrated mass in a tent in 995, reminds us that Christianization

**The Selje monastery** on the west coast bears witness to strong ties with Iceland and the island kingdoms to the west. The former Roman Catholic archbishopric of Nidaros linked the realms and islands of the North Sea.

and nation-building went hand in hand. In 1024 or thereabouts canon law was proclaimed at the Mosterting and applied to what was eventually to become the kingdom of Norway. But it took many years to build and Christianize that kingdom. The memory of St Olav is kept alive as a religious folk legend in the shape of a national celebration of his death 'in the cause of Christianity' at Stiklestad on 29 July 1030. He is revered as a saint by both the Roman Catholic and Orthodox Churches. Forgotten are the horrors attendant upon Christianization.

Closer to the sea lie the ruins of Selje monastery, a memorial to Norway's associations with Iceland and the island kingdoms to the west. This old Catholic archbishopric linked the islands and kingdoms of the North Sea region: Norway, Iceland, Greenland, the Faeroes and the Orkneys. In 2003 Nidaros (now Trondheim) celebrated its 850th anniversary as an episcopal see. As St Olav's city, in the Middle Ages it was the most northerly destination for pilgrims, who made their way on foot from Santiago de Compostela in Spain to Olav's shrine in central Norway. In our own time the pilgrim urge has found renewed resonance in modern religiosity's yearning for the sacral. The only true cathedral in Norway, Nidaros cathedral is looked upon as part of the national heritage by virtue of its history, architecture and the use made of it. It was here, in 1906, that Norway's elected king, Haakon VII, was crowned after Norway had regained its status as an independent kingdom the year before. The ongoing process of restoration is financed by the Treasury.

At Grense Jakobselv in the far north, close to the border with Russia (and in geographical terms as far to the east as Istanbul), stands a simple chapel that tells of the links with the land of Russian Orthodoxy. In Kautokeino church on the Finnmark plateau, the Sámi foregather for religious celebrations in their own language. Hammerfest boasts the world's most northerly Roman Catholic church, and in Tromsø the modern Arctic Ocean Cathedral is a prized tourist attraction and the municipal logo. The many ecclesiastical buildings to be found all over the country bear witness to a prioritization that modern Norway, wealthy though it is, cannot match. The material decay of these buildings threatens valuable cultural treasures. More anonymously, thousands of meeting and mission halls testify to the variety of religious life resulting from the tensions between lay beliefs and the traditions of the Church of Norway.

The new church at Mortensrud in Oslo, which I consecrated in 2002, has attracted much international attention. Its architecture draws together the cathedral's long historical perspective and the postmodern experience of life. Eight hundred years ago, the rise on which the church stands once belonged to a monastery on Hovedøya, an island in the Oslo fjord. Where the congregation now meets for communion was once a resting place for pilgrims bound for Nidaros. Set in the midst of one of Oslo's most multicultural quarters, surrounded by shopping malls and an ice-hockey stadium, the church stands like a creative expression of the interaction of nature, culture and the spirit. Built of steel and stone, glass and wood, in its communion with nature it is a living miracle of light and darkness, sun and shadow. The altarpiece embodies stones from Nelson Mandela's Robben Island prison and from the equally detested Berlin Wall. In their simple way these stones tell us something about how even the most tragic conflicts in history can be transfigured. A stone from Jerusalem, a city sacred to Jews, Christians and Muslims alike, mutely testifies to the impossibility of achieving peace before tolerance is reached between these three faiths. Mortensrud church has become a shrine for architects and offers a breathing space for people in search of an experience of holiness in this highly pressurized world. It puts faith and worship at the very heart of daily life.

The worldwide Christian Church is one Church, 'the holy Catholick Church' as the Apostles' Creed puts it. As such, the Church is what it has always been, a communion of believers who carry on the preaching of Christ from the time of the Apostles. It is a living organism that has retained its identity through changing historical eras, independent of external circumstances. But the Church is also an organization with a congregation, employees, finances and leaders. As such, it will always have a relationship with the political processes that govern the public and private spheres of society. Both as an organization and as an organism, the Church of Norway has enjoyed monopoly status for almost the whole of its thousand-year history, so changing the mentality shaped by this history is a painful process. It is never easy to relinquish privileges, not even for the Church.

**Consecrated in 2002,** Mortensrud church in Oslo has been described as a sacral masterpiece of brick, stone, concrete, glass, steel and wood. The firm of architects responsible, Jensen & Skodvin, has won wide acclaim in professional and Church circles for a building characterized by both tradition and renewal.

### The darker side of history

Latin American liberation theology has argued that the most important changes emanate from the darker side of history. People who are marginalized and oppressed must shape history themselves. A history written from 'above', from a position of authority and through the eyes of a majority, can be misleading, which is why accounts from 'below' are so necessary. Perhaps those who have experienced, and continue to experience, the Church's Janus face, have the truest account to give. On one side mercy and charity, on the other condemnation and repression. Ecclesiastical history in Norway concerns an institution on the side of power: its social position has been dictated by the roles of bishops and priests. In many respects it was a class church. Intolerance was its hallmark, and it still exists in many ecclesiastical subcultures.

The witch trials of the 16th and 17th centuries are amongst the darkest chapters of Norwegian history. Anyone who was different, be it physically or mentally, received short shrift at the hands of society and the Church. Suicides were denied burial in hallowed ground and the poor and the outcast often sought sanctuary from the king's clergymen – in vain. Women who bore children outside marriage have been stigmatized right up to our own times and their children have had to live with the label 'illegitimate', a practice the Church helped to preserve. People who could not read were not confirmed. In 1786, when a deaf girl in Kristiansand evinced a desperate desire to be confirmed, only the King, who was then resident in Copenhagen, could authorize such a breach of ecclesiastical procedure.

The Church's misdeeds, well up to modern times, also include its dealings with the Romanies or Gypsies, a nomadic people of unknown origin with its own linguistic, cultural, social and religious identity. The Romanies, or Travellers as they also call themselves, were regarded as unwelcome aliens in town and village alike. Their free lifestyle brought insecurity to the highways and byways. In the name of 'mercy', and with the connivance of the Church, steps were taken to forcibly integrate the Romanies into Norwegian society. Children were taken from their parents and adults compulsorily sterilized; some unfortunates were even confined in mental asylums and lobotomized for no other reason than they had protested against such

BEDEHUSET

inhuman treatment. There are many Romanies alive to this day who never received any schooling and who do not know where their now adult children are. The attitude of society and the Church to the Romanies was suffused with racism and a desire for ethnic cleansing. Both Church and society have formally asked for forgiveness, but many victims still bear painful wounds resulting from destruction of their own lives and those of their children. Politicians and the clergy have got off too lightly with this crime: the story cries out for a truth commission and legal settlement.

The Church acted as one of the Norwegian state's tools of oppression on the Sámi people too. The colonial masters – the state and its Church – thought that in this indigenous people they could discern a primitive paganism that had to be Christianized and civilized. Centuries of systematic oppression left many Sámi with an enduring sense of shame in respect of their own culture and identity.

Today, after a long battle with the majority society, the Sámi are recognized as a native people, and they now have their own flag and parliament. The 6th of February 2004 was a red-letter day for the rights and status of the Sámi people in Norway, as it was designated Sámi Day and marked by official flag-flying. A few years ago the Church of Norway officially asked the Sámi people for forgiveness for its part in their oppression and forceful integration in Norwegian society. In the question of Sámi rights, Church and state have so far come down on different sides. In 2003 the Synod gave its full support to the Sámi parliament and Sámi Church Council (*Samisk kirkeråd*) in the debate surrounding the Finnmark Act, which relates to the management of land and water resources in this traditional Sámi heartland.

In regard to many other minorities within Norwegian society too, the Church is only slowly catching up. Not without reason, many people are asking what wisdom the Church has gleaned from its history, as it learns so very slowly from its past mistakes and omissions.

**Top:** A simple meeting house on the island of Veidholmen, Smøla. **Bottom left:** The magnificence of Nidaros cathedral is a reminder of the breadth of Christian life in Norway. **Bottom right:** King Oscar's chapel at Grense Jakobselv on the Russian-Norwegian border.

### A view from without

Accounts from 'without', from other faiths and philosophical standpoints, are important in constructing a true picture of the Church of Norway. It is not only its inner spiritual force that has given this church a leading place in society: state privileges and the power of office are also an integral part of it. Neither the established Church nor the state is desirous of competition in matters of politics or the winning of souls, so many minority faiths spent a long time knocking in vain at the nation's and Church's common portal. The Church of Norway's history is also one of deliberate exclusion of freethinkers and people of different faiths.

For reasons of power politics, the absolutist Danish-Norwegian kings demanded uniform religious practice; for some of them, this was also an article of faith and personal conviction. It well suited the Church's theological and institutional interests. Not until 1842 were peripatetic preachers permitted to hold meetings without clerical supervision. Three years later, Christian minorities were allowed to organize themselves into their own religious communities; they were labelled dissenters. This defined them, not with reference to their own identity, but as deviants in relation to the 'Great Church'. The Dissenters Act was, nevertheless, a turning point in Norwegian religious policy. Being Norwegian was no longer synonynous with being a Lutheran Christian, but just a Christian. The Constitution of 1814 had determined that Evangelical Lutheranism should remain the state religion, while at the same time it excluded Jews, Jesuits and monastic orders from the country.

Even in this area modifications were slow in coming. In no case did the Church push for change. Jews were allowed into the country in 1851 and monastic orders in 1897, but over half a century more was to elapse before the ban on Jesuits was lifted. The Act of 1956 that gave them access was passed against the votes of the Christian Democratic Party (*Kristelig Folkeparti*) and half of the Agrarian Party (*Bondepartiet*); in other words, the parties that were most strongly committed to the Christian faith. Not until the 150th anniversary of the Constitution was religious freedom enshrined within it. Even today the Roman Catholic Church can still be employed as a bogeyman in discussing Norway's place in Europe; and anti-Semitism is as obdurate a problem in Norway as elsewhere in the world.

A steadily increasing leavening of immigrants with a strong religious allegiance to Islam has imparted a more challenging tone to religion. Over the past thirty years Muslims have become the largest non-Christian religious community in Norway. They are struggling to find their rightful place in Norwegian society. The public perception of Islam is characterized by generalizations and nightmare images based on the most fundamental versions of the religion. The traditional Norwegian distrust of strangers is bolstered by the labelling of many vicious practices as Muslim, without their having any connection with the religion as such. Cases in point are forced marriage, honour killings and genital mutilation. Debate often conceals the fact that Islam is also a wide-ranging faith. This is much the same mistake as is made when Christianity is castigated on the basis of fundamentalist trends within certain Christian religious sects and organizations, and their patent abuses of human rights.

There was long a reluctance among Christians to regard humanist values as of equal validity as their Christian counterparts. Today, few people react when official political jargon speaks of 'Christian and humanist values'. Here we glimpse a paradigm shift from a pietist Christian tradition to a cultural Christianity which to a greater degree unites the personal and social. The peculiar Norwegian habit of referring to people as 'personal Christians' and the pietist tradition of emphasizing culturally conditioned injunctions and norms have made it hard for many members of the established Church to acknowledge their Christian identity. This seems to be changing in the face of other religions and beliefs, however. On visits to schools in Oslo I have found pupils introducing themselves by their religion or belief. In one inner-city school in the east of Oslo I was greeted by a class of twelve-year-olds with: 'We're twelve Muslims, eight Christians and one Humanist'.

A local curate who visited a school to meet potential confirmation candidates, returned emptyhanded from a class of twenty-seven Muslims and two Catholics. The growing Muslim presence in certain quarters of the capital has meant that others, too, are having to redefine their faith or philosophy of life.

**Members of faith and belief communities outside the Church of Norway. 1990 and 2003**

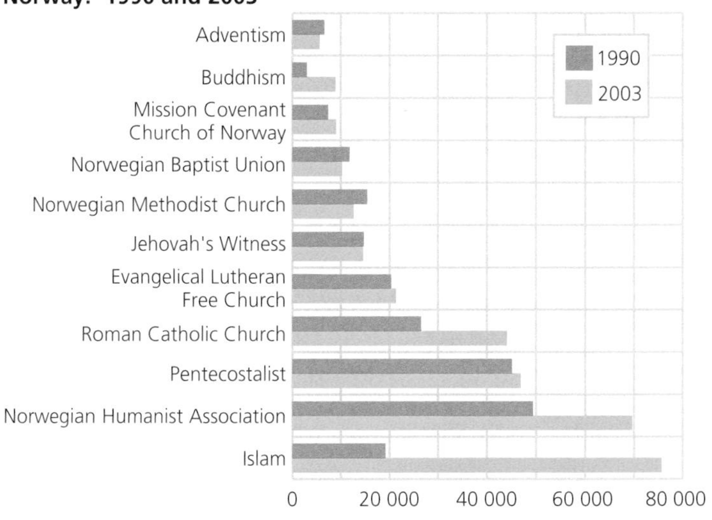


### State and Church – reform or revolution?

The 1969 Act on religious denominations helped to make it clear that the Church of Norway is a religious community and not 'the religious arm of the state', as it is defined in the Constitution. A slow process of ecclesiastical reform throughout the 20th century has gradually endowed the Church of Norway with an internal, democratically elected consultative structure ranging from parish councils through diocesan councils to the Synod. The dominating official line of priests and bishops has found its parallel in a synodal structure. The reform process has given the Church of Norway independence in important areas associated with doctrine and life, services and appointments. Even revenue accruing from national and municipal budgets is administered by the Church's own organs. Various public and ecclesiastical commissions have contributed to this reform process over the last century without altering the state-Church system.

The relationship between Church and state is again the subject of discussion by an official commission, which is scheduled to deliver its report in 2005. Unlike several earlier commissions – the first of which dates from 1908 – the future of the state Church will not be determined only by members of the Church of Norway. Other Christian religious communities, Islam and the Norwegian Humanist Association are all represented on the commission, which will also reflect the political composition of the Storting. Most political parties seem intent on a radical change in the relationship between Church and state, but as this will entail major changes in the Constitution, the result is not at all certain. It is expected that the commission will advance alternative proposals. It is doubtful if a commission appointed to submit proposals on relations between Church and state would be qualified to present proposals that redefine the role and power of the monarch. Regrettably, the suggestion of a commission to update the Constitution for its bicentenary in 2014 has not been adopted. Such a commission would have had the right format to enable it to discuss the constitutional aspects of changes to the state-Church system which affect the monarchy. According to the Constitution, the monarch is linked to the Evangelical Lutheran faith as formal head of the Church of Norway. To disestablish the Church would be to give the monarch, along with most other Norwegians, a free choice of faith and philosophy of life. None of these matters are insoluble in a modern democracy, but they involve more than a mere ecclesiastical adjustment.

It is hard to envision the established Church retaining its present status in a society that has gradually come to think of itself as a multicultural state with pluralistic values. The place occupied by religious freedom in Norwegian legislation, and to which the country is committed through international conventions, is also creating increasing pressure for change. The decisive question will be whether it is possible to arrive at a different relationship that continues to promote the Church of Norway as an open and inclusive popular church. Earlier arguments suggesting a break between Church and state have not attracted enough support on the congregational level, or generally among the population, precisely because this issue was not adequately addressed. If there are calls for disestablishment of the state Church, it should be possible to hold a consultative referendum. This was done before the break-up of the union with Sweden and introduction of the monarchy in 1905, as well as in regard to Norwegian membership of the EEC in 1972 and the EU in 1994.

The relationship between Church and state is something that has long historical roots. It concerns an identity and values that are meaningful for far more people than those who are the most active churchgoers.

**The Church of Norway. Church activity. 1995-2003. Number of people**

| | Baptised | Con-firmed | Married in church | Interred | Joined the church | Left the church |
|---|---|---|---|---|---|---|
| 1995 | 50 342 | 39 857 | 13 502 | 42 104 | 1 130 | 5 857 |
| 1996 | 50 067 | 39 122 | 13 837 | 41 352 | 1 071 | 5 000 |
| 1997 | 50 294 | 39 083 | 14 049 | 42 417 | 1 392 | 4 955 |
| 1998 | 48 462 | 37 870 | 13 189 | 42 002 | 871 | 4 831 |
| 1999[1] | 48 049 | 37 408 | 12 744 | 42 436 | 943 | 4 416 |
| 2000 | 48 023 | 37 330 | 14 041 | 41 369 | 843 | 4 519 |
| 2001 | 46 135 | 37 427 | 12 091 | 41 313 | 1 239 | 3 866 |
| 2002 | 44 136 | 38 250 | 12 690 | 41 531 | 854 | 3 759 |
| 2003 | 43 916 | 40 184 | 11 440 | 40 115 | 856 | 3 603 |

[1] The figures do not include ecclesiastical activity in institutions (hospitals, prisons), the Church for the Deaf, Army Chaplain Corps etc. which have their own church registers.

### Philosophies of life and religion – pluralism and freedom

In Norway, all religious communities and communities with a non-religious philosophy are financially and legislatively linked to the state. Communities of the latter type are also governed by a special Act. It is uncommon for a state to assume such a broad economic responsibility for registered religious communities and those of a different outlook.

The Storting introduced a faith education reform in 2003 that clearly shows how much importance it attaches to faith and philosophies of life in the community. The state finances religious and non-religious education for all children and young people from birth until the age of 18. This scheme encompasses all faiths and secular philosophical communities.

Along with faith and other philosophies, despite – or perhaps precisely because of – increased secularization, *religion* has become an important concept in everyday life. The government and Storting are having to deal with matters of religious policy quite differently from the way to which they were once accustomed. The bounds of religious freedom are constantly being tested in political debates. This implies adjusting the boundaries between religious freedom, which protects a religious community against interference with its 'internal concerns', and other fundamental human rights. In politics, for example, the principle of religious freedom is set above the demand for gender

**On Domkirkeodden** (Cathedral Point), Hamar, the ruins of the old cathedral are glassed-in for protection. A more vivid expression of the Church's vulnerability would be hard to find. Work on the original cathedral was started in 1152-53. Designed by Kjell Lund, the protective glass carapace was formally inaugurated in 1998.

HAN·GIR·DEN TRETTE·KRAFT

Velkommen tilbak

equality. A notably problematic area is that of whether society is entitled to demand more of the Church of Norway than of other religious communities precisely because of its relations with the state. Some politicians want to make continuing state support for individual faiths contingent on the extent to which their followers respect human rights within their organizations. Such a policy would preclude state support for a number of religious communities – Christian, Muslim, Jewish and others.

During the debate surrounding amendment of the Occupational Environment Act of 2004, religious freedom came to the fore in Norwegian politics. Many religious communities and a number of organizations within the Church of Norway are averse to employing former partners or divorcees who have remarried, or homosexuals living in same-sex partnerships. It was expected that prevailing opinion in the Storting, which is against such attitudes, would make use of the legislative amendment to put an end to such discrimination. But even representatives of parties that disagree with discrimination of homosexuals supported the law, arguing that priority had to be accorded to religious freedom. This is not an expression of acceptance of discriminatory views, but an admission that, in a democratic society, the battle to bring about a change in such views in a particular religious community must be waged in a different way. Changes will take longer to bring about. This is the painful price of religious freedom. But discrimination in the name of God will never be respected in a society that rests on Christian and humanist values.

Religion has also become a more prominent factor in foreign policy, which is predicated on a broad agreement embracing targeted efforts for peace and reconciliation. A new political and diplomatic competence is required where conflicts are not merely political or ethnic, but also have a fundamentally religious dimension. There is also need for such expertise in defence policy. In 2004, Norwegian forces took part in peace-building operations among people with a Muslim culture – in Kosova, Afghanistan and Iraq. In the conflict between Israel and the Palestinians, Norwegians are having to relate to Islam, Judaism and Christianity. Neither in the Middle East nor in Sri Lanka, where Norway has long been involved in the peace process, can lasting peace be established unless, for good or ill, the role of religion is taken seriously. More clearly than ever before, the local, the national and the international are interwoven in a global community in which religion is a vital dimension.

**Top left:** The Church's City Mission holds gatherings for the homeless in its congregational centre in Tøyen church and **(top right)** services that include Communion in streets and squares. **Bottom:** The largest anti-racist demonstration ever held in Oslo filled this square, Youngstorget, and adjacent streets to overflowing after the murder in January 2001 of a young boy, Benjamin Hermansen.

### The Church's socially critical voice

The Church of Norway has become a purveyor of ethical premises in a number of important contemporary social areas, a motivator in respect of poverty, aid and development strategies, and environmental protection. The prolonged battle against discharges from the atomic power station at Sellafield, which threatened marine life in the North Sea area, was brought to a successful conclusion in 2004. The British government was ultimately forced to give way to pressure from a broad Norwegian coalition of shifting governments, local grassroots protests, not least in the Lofoten Islands, countless environmentalists and wide Church involvement. The Church of Norway has been a leading force in making the government's asylum and refugee policies more humane. The Church is also unequivocal in its criticism of a state centralization policy that undermines viable local communities. It opposes the lowering of taxes and heightened consumption at the expense of development aid to poor countries. Church representatives warn against the liberal market economy that threatens to rob society of political and moral direction, and in so doing weaken democracy.

In this context Norwegian Church Aid plays a leading role as the common ecclesiastical organization for international welfare. The major humanitarian and Christian aid organizations are important in endeavours to make the world a more compassionate and just place to live in. It is in this area, too, that the new action model based on local and global network-building has proved itself. Through 'networks of networks' people – irrespective of faith or philosophy – can join together to campaign for a better world. This is, perhaps, the most exciting and promising such project at the start of the 21st century.

The Church's socially critical and prophetic voice cannot be said to be weakened by its close ties with the state; these ties may even give added weight to its critical views of official policies. But because the vast majority of Norway's present politicians are members of the established Church, and because, as an organization, that Church is an integral part of the country's economic and political system, it is also vulnerable. In many key ethical areas the Church is in this sense 'a house divided against itself'. The injunction not to throw stones when one is oneself in a glass house is an important caution for the Church of Norway. Gradually, the Council of Norwegian Christians (*Norges kristne råd*), which brings all the Christian communities in the country together, has begun to involve itself in social questions of a political nature. But there will be no broad commitment in the area of social ethics without dissenssion within religious communities, or among them.

### The pure words of scripture

The deepest cause of conflict between the various religions and philosophies is not principally the result of differing views of God, Yahweh and Allah, but their attitudes towards human beings and interpretation of a particular religion's holy scriptures. Within the Christian faith it is the various ways of reading the Bible and the interpretation of its ethical guidance that today result in the widest divisions. The term 'the pure word of God' is often used in debate as a clinching argument, one which ignores an obvious diversity of voices in the Bible. Such varied interpretations may concern anything from cohabitation to the conflict between Israel and the Palestinians. A Christian fundamentalist reading of the Bible has much in common with the relationship some Muslims have with the Koran. It is therefore of great importance that, in its discussion of the gay issue, the Church of Norway's Doctrinal Commission has attached great significance to understanding biblical authority and usage. It is a matter of clarifying how biblical texts have provided the basis for major interpretive changes in matters such as women's leadership role and their ordination as priests, as well as in questions relating to cohabitation. In all these issues arguments have been adduced that place varying constructions and weightings on biblical passages. The Reformation may itself be regarded as an expression of two different ways of reading the Bible. Since then, various biblical interpretations have provided the basis for many a new religious community and sect, and further subsects within them. It is precisely in its multiplicity that the Bible is most unambiguous.

### The postmodern person

Other winds of change are also making their effects felt on religious and non-religious communities.

A special characteristic of many western societies at the start of the new millennium is the strong emphasis placed on individualism and privatization. Values such as solidarity and communality have lost much of their former significance. At the same time existential and real emptiness has become a well-defined theme in literature, drama, poetry and the cinema. So-called postmodern individuals question the meaning of life with less embarrassment than their parents did. Faith is no longer a taboo subject, be it as a means towards understanding one's personal life or in society at large. But the quest for a meaning in life is not necessarily synonymous with a quest for God: the spiritual yearning of the age remains open and unaddressed.

The Church as the sole agent of beliefs and norms is definitely a thing of the past. Human beings have become autonomous also in the religious sense. Individuals wish to decide for themselves what is good religion. Neo-religiosity's non-institutional ideals are blooming. Theories of reincarnation derived from Buddhism fascinate people who have renounced the Christian concept of everlasting life. Certain religious communities are quite revitalized when they focus on the subjective and appeal to the individual's self-satisfaction. The modern world order, characterized as it is by the globalization of markets, culture and communications, is leading to a global religious marketplace. Non-religious, atheist and materialist attitudes are the hallmarks of spiritual poverty, while at the same time the institutional churches are suffering from a kind of spirituality that is all too lack-lustre. Charismatic 'one-man shows' are constantly popping up with new gimmicks to put new life into the Church. These, too, represent a form of spirituality centred on the individual. This in turn is wedded to reactionary attitudes to social questions of the familiar fundamentalist type.

### From ideology to global values

Ideologies were long surrogates for religious faith. This was especially true of the political left, where visions of a Communist utopia had unmistakable religious overtones. But the right, too, encompasses political trends redolent of religious pathos. The language of National Socialism and Fascism was unequivocally religious. The heritage of these movements is recognizable in neo-Nazi subcultures and in party political tendencies that appeal to racist and xenophobic traditions. One day it is the Jews who are the target, the next, the Muslims.

Following the demise of ideologies and the end of the Cold

War, which was symbolized by the fall of the Berlin Wall, an interest in values has increasingly manifested itself. The current picture of the world is dominated by frontiers other than those that dominated the Cold War. Some draw parallels between different civilizations in which religion is the main component, while others see the wide gulf between rich and poor as the most dramatic demarcation of all. If there is sufficient food available to feed the whole population of the world, they argue, it is profoundly immoral to distribute it unevenly. This is the very crux of the debate about how the inhuman face of globalization might be changed. Can a neo-liberal market system ever be made humane?

The subject of faiths and philosophies of life has thus assumed a forward-looking, global direction. This is of decisive importance in the worldwide battle for human worth and justice. A heartfelt moral duty must lead to a binding global contract between rich and poor. The impoverished must be allowed a say in negotiations relevant to their own situation and future. Making room for them at the table of the rich and powerful is one of the biggest ethical and political challenges of our time.

The United Nations' ambitious millennium targets are, in many ways, faith projects. By 2015 the number of the world's most poverty-stricken, 1.4 billion, is to be halved and the number of people starving, 800 million, is likewise to be brought down by a half. Every child is to have access to elementary schooling and the spread of HIV/AIDS and malaria is to be halted; climate change is also to be arrested. The number of people without access to clean drinking water is to be halved. Human rights are to be strengthened, with particular reference to torture and maltreatment. The same applies to protection of refugees, asylum seekers and efforts to stamp out human trafficking.

A critical glance at the budgets and policies of individual nation states after these targets were solemnly agreed upon by the world's leaders in the year 2000 reveals that, with the current national priorities, it will be a hundred years before the poverty reduction goal is reached. But instead of the rich countries showing that they mean business and are sincere in regard to fulfilling their commitments, it is once again being said that the problem lies with the poor countries themselves, as they are not doing enough to combat poverty!

A growing culture of corruption in the international community – and in our own country – has given the question of ethics and morals new and current relevance. In the international market the ethical profile of an industrial undertaking or financial institution is becoming increasingly important. Corruption is costly; trust and integrity sell. For this reason, faith- and philosophy-based values belong in the workplace, the boardroom and on the stock exchange, if for no other reason than that of informed self-interest.

**From dialogue to diapractice**

There are also clear signs in Norwegian society of growing tolerance and a willingness to cooperate across boundaries of faith and philosophy. Many important political campaigns have brought Christians, Muslims, Jews and Humanists together on the same platform or on the same protest march. In multireligious and multicultural Norway, xenophobia and racism clash head-on with ideals such as solidarity and equality. In this battle it has been important that people of differing faiths and philosophies have made common cause.

It took many years to build a collective platform for all Christian churches and faiths in the country. Relations with the Roman Catholic Church were a problem for evangelical communities in particular. Not until 1992 was the Council of Norwegian Christians established, decades after similar bodies had been set up in the other Scandinavian countries. All this notwithstanding, it proved surprisingly easy to establish a broad forum for all faiths and philosophies in which Muslims, Humanists and others were also included. The Joint Council for Faiths and Philosophies (*Samarbeidsrådet for tro og livssyn*) was created in 1996. Through such collaboration, minor religious and non-religious communities were also enabled to play an important role in civil life. The secret of the Council's success was a new acceptance of, and desire for, mutual respect, coupled with a need for concerted action. Dia*practice* has become as necessary as dia*logue*. Two examples may serve to illustrate this.

The neo-Nazi-motivated murder in January 2001 of Benjamin Hermansen, a 15-year-old boy with an African father and Norwegian mother, led to the biggest antiracist demonstration ever seen in Norway. Some 45,000 people assembled to voice their indignation in an Oslo square, Youngstorget.

On another cold winter evening, in 2003, 60,000 people filled the same square and surrounding streets to demonstrate against America and Britain's war on Iraq, which contravened international law. Never before in Norway had so many people gathered for a demonstration. On this occasion it was in protest at the flouting of international law and in support of the UN.

The protest had a decisive effect on the Norwegian government's attitude to the invasion. Both these occasions reflected a widely felt commitment from people right across the political, religious and philosophical spectrum.

Nevertheless, such concerted action cannot disguise the fact that a deep rift over human rights and worth runs clear through society. Fundamental values such as freedom and equality are accorded different interpretations and importance. This variance is especially apparent in matters relating to the body, sex and sexuality, which are bound up with both religion and culture. At the same time, Islamic and Christian fundamentalist attitudes towards women have much in common. The fear of secularization and modernity leads many Pakistani Muslims to select a Christian free school for their children rather than a state school – unless they have already decided to send them back to Pakistan to be educated.

## A CAPITAL FOR FAITHS AND PHILOSOPHIES

Karl Johans gate, Oslo's main street, which runs between the central railway station and the Royal Palace, provides an introduction to Norway as a land of divergent personal philosophies. In an area of only one square kilometre, on the axis of the capital's main thoroughfare, are to be found the meeting places of power and impotence, faith and values, politics and ideas. This 'beliefs quadrant' affords an interesting picture of tradition and change. Only churches are less to the fore than in the rest of the country as orientation points in a quest for faiths and philosophies of life, though here too they are a dominant feature of the townscape. Cultural and religious diversity is nowhere more in evidence than in Norway's capital city. The scene that greets one on leaving a train at Oslo Central Station clearly shows that faiths and philosophies are not perceived only in the shape of churches and other religious edifices. The city's many public buildings symbolize its wide range of values and emphasize how closely interwoven religion and society are.

But it is not only buildings that bear witness to a country in flux. From the station, across the adjoining square and all along the main street are to be seen people whose colour and costume impart something of an exotic flavour to the scene. Nowhere are so many languages spoken as in Europe's railway stations. Knots of young men hang about the station for hours, as if waiting for something to happen, as if happiness will arrive with the next train or as if hoping for a chance to travel to somewhere better. Some have come because Norway needed labour; others have fled persecution, violence and poverty. Others again are seeking refuge and protection from religious persecution. Many are unemployed – and most are Muslim. They know that many church communities are critical of Norway's asylum policy and have even been willing to engage in acts of civil disobedience by affording sanctuary to people in need.

As far as the traveller is concerned, the sight of old and young so obviously taking drugs in the very heart of the city brutally shatters the image of Norway as a model welfare state. An atmosphere of profound social distress hangs over the square fronting the station. The ongoing sale of goods and services is there for all to see. The low-key police presence testifies to a greater degree of tolerance than is the case in many big cities in Europe. What a visitor is likely to see are City Mission (*Bymisjonen*) and Salvation Army people who actively care for the drug addicts and prostitutes. They, together with representatives of other ecclesiastical and humanitarian organizations, are a compassionate presence in the brutal life of the streets. Perhaps that very evening there will be Communion service for the street people. Sometimes a tourist will also stop and take part in the service because he recognizes the words and symbols of a universal church. As if in an amphitheatre, immigrants, both young and old, sit on the steps on one side of the square and look on with respect.

On the other side of the square *Kirkens Hus* (Church House) has recently moved in. This is the headquarters of the Church of Norway and its highest parliamentary organ, the National Council of the Church of Norway. The Sámi Church Council, the Church of Norway Council on Foreign Relations, the Church of Norway Commission on Theology and the Committee on International Affairs manage the Council's wide and varied areas of responsibility. It is here that links with the worldwide brotherhood of churches, which includes the World Council of Churches, the Lutheran World Federation and the Conference of European Churches, are forged. Work directed towards Christian unity long faced an uphill struggle in the

**Children learning** the Koran in an Oslo mosque. The Storting has voted for a programme providing for religious instruction for children up to the age of 18 that applies to all registered religions, persuasions and philosophies. This is additional to the KRL (Christianity, religion and life philosophy) taught in schools.

Norwegian ecclesiastical landscape; today, however, the Church of Norway is a driving force within the ecumenical movement.

The Stock Exchange directly across the street is at the hub of the country's financial strength and an expression of its close association with the global market. Here, the Church of Norway's portfolio is as subject to the vagaries of the market as any other portfolio. What is known as the Enlightment Service Fund (*Opplysningsvesenets fond*) is currently worth some NOK 1.4 billion, and to that must be added the value of extensive property holdings. This may form the 'divorce settlement' when the time comes for Church and state to part company. Consequently, management of the fund is studied with keen interest by the institutions of the Church. Before the Church approached the Stock Exchange it had been decided that its money should be invested in an ethically unimpeachable way. The Church was not to enrich itself by, for example, investing in child labour, pornography, tobacco, liquor, gambling, atomic weapons or other weapons of mass destruction. Perhaps the Church's incursion into the Stock Exchange has contributed to a growing awareness of markets and ethics. The younger members of the Church, in particular, keep a close watch on its 'share speculations'.

A few hundred metres from the station and Stock Exchange stands the cathedral, which many elderly people still refer to as Our Saviour's church. The history of the cathedral has been closely linked to that of the city for almost a thousand years. The ruins of Oslo's first cathedral, the 12th-century St Hallvard's church, are still used for commemorative services on St Hallvard's Day, 15 May. The second cathedral in the city's history was consecrated in 1639, but it stood for only a few decades before being destroyed by fire. Our Saviour's church was consecrated in 1697. This building, which is now more than three hundred years old, has opened its doors to the homeless, to modern society's destitute and lonely, and to busy business people seeking a quiet moment of devotion. The cathedral is the most-visited public building in the country, averaging a thousand visitors a day. Its central position on one of the city's oldest squares, just off the main thororoughfare, makes it readily accessible to all, and services and other events held there are invariably well attended. The devotional music is of a high standard and contributes greatly to the cultural life of the city. The cathedral is the principal setting for an annual festival of church music which, with support from private sponsors and contributions from local and national government, brings eminent singers and musicians from all over Europe to perform before appreciative audiences. In 2003 the government published a cultural report which, for the first time, referred to this event as an important element in the nation's cultural life; in response, the Storting acknowledged the festival's importance.

The cathedral stands out clearly as the church of both the capital and the nation. Members of the Storting foregather here for the annual service that marks the opening of parliament. On 10 December, when the Nobel Prize for Peace is awarded, a service celebrating peace and human rights is held in the church.

**Crown Prince Haakon** and Crown Princess Mette-Marit were married in Oslo cathedral by Bishop Gunnar Stålsett on 25 August 2001. The city's most-visited building, the cathedral offers a programme which includes services to mark important events in the life of Church and nation, intercessional services for peace and reconciliation, services of unity with marginalized members of society, and regular church services. The cathedral's liturgical and musical activity is an important element in the cultural fabric of the capital.

On World AIDS Day, 1 December, we mark our solidarity with HIV and AIDS victims. At times of national and international tragedy the bishop and chapter hold an intercessional service, often in collaboration with other denominations. Sometimes representatives of other religions also take part. A service of mourning was held on the outbreak of the Iraq war and one of remembrance after the attack on UN headquarters in Baghdad later the same year; these may serve as examples of how the Church lives out the day-to-day drama of war and peace. Representatives of the state, royal family, Storting, government and Supreme Court, along with the defence chiefs, take part in these memorial services as and when appropriate. On such occasions representatives of the Diplomatic Corps also find their way to the cathedral. This key ecclesiastical function has become a subject of discord in the Collaborative Council for Faiths and Philosophies of Life. The Norwegian Humanist Association believes that expressions of public grief should be neutral in form and accordingly be held outside the Church. The solution to this conflict will probably be to do both, as after the terrorist attack on the USA on 11 September 2001. On that occasion, in addition to church services a large meeting, attended by people of many faiths and philosophies, was held in the University lecture hall.

**The Salvation Army** is in the front line when it comes to providing Christian care for sufferers from alcohol and drugs abuse and victims of other social problems. The organization is highly respected for its social work and enjoys wide support from, among others, the media, musicians and other artists, who, at Christmas, willingly take part in street concerts in support of the less fortunate.

The cathedral is also the focal point of other important events in the life of the Royal Family, a case in point being the marriage of the Crown Prince in August 2001. After royal deaths, the last of which was that of King Olav V in 1991, the coffin is transported down Karl Johans gate from the Chapel Royal to the cathedral. The annual pre-Christmas church parade of the King's Lifeguards, in which the King himself takes part, serves as a reminder that he is constitutionally head of the armed forces as well as of the Church.

Further along the street, which is now reserved for pedestrians, is the parliament building, the Storting. Here is administered the political heritage laid down in the Constitution of 1814, supplemented by parliamentarism from 1884 and democracy from 1905. The Storting enacts the laws that govern all religious faiths and secular beliefs. It bears special responsibility for legislation relevant to the Church of Norway and approves budgetary grants thereto. This also entails making similar per-capita grants to other religious communities and to communities with other philosophies of life. The political parties display a largely positive attitude towards such communities and to upholders of Christian and humanist values. In their manifestos, most parties accept Christianity as a basis of social values. the Christian Democratic Party (*Kristelig Folkeparti*) merits special mention in this context, as it builds its policies on Christian values. Up to now, in forming governments it has sought cooperation with the right. Its bedrock is composed of the free churches and evangelical and missionary factions of the Church of Norway. In outlook, the party is opposed to secular humanism, which is largely represented by the Socialist Left Party (*Sosialistisk Venstreparti*). This is especially in evidence in matters relating to abortion, homosexuality and family policy. The issue of the status of human rights in free churches and Christian organizations is a vexed one for the Christian People's Party. In view of its name the party finds it hard to make a distinction between theology and politics. On the question of disestablishment of the state Church, the Labour Party (*Arbeiderparti*) and Centre Party (*Senterparti*) have been the staunchest defenders of the status quo, whereas the Christian People's Party has moved in the direction of disestablishment, in line with the dominant voter voice in the free churches and the views of organizations critical of the state Church.

The prime minister's office in the tower block in the centre of the administrative district enjoys panoramic views of the capital. From here, heads of state and other prominent visitors from abroad are afforded their first panoramic view of the metropolis. They can see that the faiths of the capital are attested to not only by church spires but also by the tower of a mosque in the heart of the old quarter. At the foot of the government building stand the Swedish Margareta church and the Anglican St Edmund's. Together with a growing number of smaller churches for immigrants from Asia and Africa, they are reminders of the importance of being enabled to attend divine services held in one's native tongue. The churches contribute to the social cohesion that results from a sense of ethnic identity and common traditions.

Also visible is the Roman Catholic cathedral, St Olav's, arguably the most international of all the churches in the country.

**The Norwegian Seamen's Church** has evolved into a Church for all Norwegians abroad and its services and social and cultural events are well attended. Seen here is a packed church at a thanksgiving service held to mark the 75th anniversary of the Norwegian Seamen's church in London.

The church's nearest neighbour is the headquarters of the Adventists, and only a stone's throw away are the headquarters of the Salvation Army and Filidelfia, the Pentacostal Congregationalists' meeting hall. The Methodist church is also situated in the city centre. St Olga's Russian Orthodox church, consecrated in 2004, has found a home in a disused chapel in the graveyard of Our Saviour's church. The chapel houses a beautiful icon of St Olav. Somewhat more anonymously in the Christian map of the city, gay men and women find a meeting place under the auspices of the Open Church Group (*Åpen Kirkegruppa*), where they regularly celebrate divine service according to the Church of Norway liturgy.

Not far distant from the prime minister's office are the headquarters of such large voluntary organizations devoted to missionary work at home and abroad as the Norwegian Lutheran Mission and Norwegian Mission (*Normisjonen*). They represent a powerful spiritual trend in the Church of Norway's history, emphasizing as they do the preaching of the gospel and humanitarian work in connection with schools, hospitals and vocational training. Norwegian missionaries have contributed to popular education and liberation in countries in Africa, Asia and Latin America. In recent years they have been active in Europe, most notably in the former Communist countries. These organizations are rooted in the revival movements of Hans Nielsen Hauge's day and in other 19th-century evangelical and social movements. The Norwegian Universities and Schools Christian Fellowship also has its home here. This is the largest Christian pupil and student organization with an emphasis on revivalist Christianity and mission work. It has played a major role in recruitment to the priesthood and Christian organizational life throughout most of the 20th century.

The biggest missionary organizations operate with budgets that run into hundreds of millions of kroner. Their operations are financed partly by contributions from their own members and partly from offertories; these are augmented by substantial grants from the national budget for social causes, schools and other aid work. A number of Christian organizations and church communities work under the aegis of the Aid and Development Council (*Bistandsnemda*) to disburse funds from the Norwegian Agency for Development Cooperation (NORAD) and the Ministry of Foreign Affairs. The support thus provided has been questioned in public debate. But the organizations are making a good case for themselves by claiming that their work is carried on along clear social lines, just like all other development work, and that their grants are no different from similar publicly funded support for humanitarian organizations, which are likewise not value-neutral. The instances in which public funds have been directly employed for evangelistic purposes have been acknowledged as breaches of the guidelines to which such organizations are obliged to adhere and which they do, in fact, respect.

Throughout their history, these voluntary organizations have displayed critical solidarity with the Church of Norway, though in many areas – and increasingly – they are a long way from the Church's official views. Within their ambit can be found basic fundamentalist philosophies whose attitudes to the Bible, the Church and society at large reflect a deep-rooted scepticism of modernity. In recent years organizations of this nature have moved more in the direction of becoming independent ecclesiastical communities within the Church, in some cases with their own baptismal, communion and confirmation ceremonies. In many ways this development has been influenced by charismatic movements originating in the USA. These are predicated on a different concept of the Church than the state-Church model that characterizes the Church of Norway, one more in line with a free-church view. This gravitation towards free-church status is often ascribable to 'rejection' of the Church of Norway because of its attitude towards the gay question and the ordination of women priests. Criticism of the state-Church system can be vehement, especially as bishops of the Church of Norway are appointed by the King and cabinet. This has, at times, emerged as the thorniest question in ecclesiastical politics. The government, almost without exception, follows the Church's vote and appoints one of the three candidates with the highest number of votes in the episcopal ballot.

The criticism such organizations level at the Church has just as much to do with their disquiet over the fact that the Church of Norway is an open and inclusive people's church in which everyone is both equal and an equally empowered member by virtue of having been baptized into it. However, members of these organizations do share responsibility with the Church of Norway on a local level in parish councils. They do a great deal of work on behalf of children and young people and are active in the Church's instructional and welfare programmes. They are also well represented in such central bodies as the National Council and Synod of the Church. An open question for the next decade is whether these organizations' demands for autonomy *within* the Church of Norway will lead to autonomy *outside* it. If they do, the ecclesiastical landscape of Norway will be decisively altered – far more drastically, in fact, than it would be by a possible rift between Church and state.

**A Bible study group,** a weekly event in the home of Greta and Svein Strand, a missionary family working for the Norwegian Lutheran Missionary Union (**Norsk Luthersk Misjonssamband**) in Kobe, Japan.

The Norwegian YMCA and YWCA, which represent a more culturally all-embracing form of Christianity, also have their headquarters in the 'beliefs quadrant'. These movements are marked by a non-pietistic, socio-ethical tradition with the emphasis on human rights and protection of the Creation. The international Ten Sing movement, which focuses on rhythm, song and dance, has long provided a popular low-threshold sphere of activity for teenagers. Extensive solidarity work in the Third World, coupled with a strong anti-racist commitment and support for the Palestinians, is an important part of the YMCA/YWCA's image. These twin movements have much in common with the work of the Norwegian Christian Students Movement (*Norges Kristelige Studenterbevegelse*), which, despite its modest membership, has been a significant player on the ecclesiastical front as a culturally open and socially critical movement for students and academics. Most Christian student and youth organizations are national branches of international movements.

The tower block housing the prime minister's office is surrounded by several ministries of importance to the faiths and philosophies of the country. The King's ecclesiastical responsibilities are administered by the Ministry of Culture and Church Affairs. In the course of the last decade many of the Church

**Akershus Castle** has played an important role in Norwegian history, as it has in the life of the people. It is used by the government on ceremonial occasions, including state visits. The castle houses the Royal Chapel of Rest, the burial chamber of a number of Norway's kings. During the Second World War the castle was the headquarters of the occupying power, and many members of the Resistance were imprisoned and executed there. Regular services are held in the castle church.

Affairs department's prime responsibilities have been devolved to the Ecclesiastical Council structure or to the bishops. The department continues to administer the Church's budget and the terms of service of priests, deacons (*diakoner*) and bishops, and is responsible for preparing for the government's appointment of deans and bishops. The administrative functions devolving on the King pursuant to section 16 of the Constitution are performed by the Minister for the Church and are dealt with in cabinet. The minister must belong to the Church of Norway, and what is known as the Ecclesiastical Cabinet includes only members of the government who belong to this church; they must constitute at least half of the government. The Ministry of Education and Research is responsible for theological colleges and deacon-training establishments, all of which have most of their budgets met by the state. Post-2003, the political green light was given for more state-subsidized private schools, right down to primary level. These include not only religious schools but also schools based on secular philosophies. The Ministry of Health and Social Affairs looks for support to many of the Church's institutions devoted to care of the sick and elderly and the treatment of alcoholics and drug addicts, and underwrites their finances. The Ministry of Local Government and Regional Development is responsible for financing local church administration. The Ministry of Finance oversees the extensive support measures extended to all aspects of Norway's religious communities and communities of other persuasions.

The Supreme Court holds sway in an august building on the edge of the administrative district. Over the past fifty years it has handed down important interpretations of the state's commitment to Christian values. It has held that the Constitution's injunction that 'the Evangelical Lutheran religion shall remain the state religion' and that 'the King shall always profess it' does not mean that the Norwegian state is bound by Church doctrine in legislative matters. Also, the question of to what extent the Christian object clause applicable to state schools was in breach of the Constitution was answered in the negative by the Supreme Court in a case brought by the Norwegian Humanist Association. Nor was the Norwegian state-Church system found to be in contravention of Norway's obligations as set out in various human rights conventions incorporated into Norwegian law. But the idea that, in a modern society, state policies in regard to religion must preserve the human rights of one and all has been enhanced.

From their plinth before the country's principal theatre, the National Theatre, the writers and dramatists Henrik Ibsen and Bjørnstjerne Bjørnson may reflect upon what characterizes present-day Norwegian culture. It may be asked what resulted from the cultural conflicts that marked the closing years of the 19th century, a time when these giants of Norway's intellectual life were instrumental in critically questioning the Church's attitude to society and women. Their endeavours saw the meeting between Christian faith and modernity begin to find important literary expression. In the National Theatre's repertoire little time has ever elapsed between the staging of plays that address fundamental questions relating to the meaning of life, faith and impotence, heaven and hell. It may be true to say, even today, that the theatre is the most vital interface between faith and doubt, and between a Christian view of humanity and materialism.

The University on Karl Johans gate also housed the Faculty of Theology before shortage of space forced most activities to move to new premises on the outskirts of the city. The dispute surrounding liberal theology in the faculty that raged early in the 20th century led in 1907 to the founding of the Free Faculty of Theology. To start with this faculty was financed by donations and collections from voluntary organizations within the Church and the offertories of congregations. After a time it was permitted to examine candidates and award doctorates in theology; more important still, its finances were underwritten by the state.

For a long time the conflict between liberal and conservative interpretations of the Bible formed the great divide in the debate surrounding faith and philosophies of life. The terms 'liberal theologian' and 'humanist' were used insultingly. The acrimony came to a head in the 1950s in what came to be known as the 'hellfire debate', and the government was ultimately forced to take a stand on interpretation of the ecclesiastical doctrine of damnation. Even in the matter of women's place in the Church and society, the two faculties were at loggerheads. It all had to do with fundamental differences in their approach to scripture and theological method. The faculties have now drawn closer to each other and their adversarial image is largely a thing of the past. Today, their rivalry centres more on the institutions' survival strategy in terms of resources, students and academic prestige.

On the opposite side of the street stands the City Hall, which houses the municipal administration. The 1996 law on churches greatly reduced the Municipal Council's responsibility for church affairs, but most town and local councils regard churches as important partners in the social and cultural sphere. This is especially true of preventive work among young people. Oslo City Hall is also the traditional venue for the city's civic confirmation ceremony. Organized by the Norwegian Humanist Association, this important rite of passage for young people thus has an appropriately dignified setting for a festive ceremony that carries considerable cultural kudos.

**Julius Paltiel** from Trondheim, one of the few Norwegian Jews to survive the Holocaust, in which he lost his entire family. The number tattooed on his arm in the concentration camp is still visible.

Next to the City Hall is the building housing the County Governor, whose office is the central registration and administrative point for non-Christian religious communities. These have to be officially approved before they can be accepted as faith communities and it is from here that public support for them is administered. Many mosques are on the small side, as they are based on ethnic divisions, so it is a daunting task, not least linguistically and culturally, to administer grants on the basis of membership rolls.

Around the corner, across the harbour, looms Akershus Castle, which in some parts is built of stone from the mediaeval churches and monasteries of ancient Oslo. The castle conjures up some painful memories of war and famine. At its foot is the old prison, one of whose inmates was the lay preacher Hans Nielsen Hauge (1771-1824), who was incarcerated there for his illegal preaching activities. During the Second World War the castle served as headquarters of the German occupiers. Many Norwegian patriots and Resistance fighters were executed within its precincts. The old prison chapel bears witness to priests' service and care for the souls of criminals, social agitators and champions of peace. The Resistance Museum is an important reminder for generations to come of the price paid for our country's freedom and independence.

The Church of Norway's leaders played an important role in the Resistance. A near-unified Church refused to follow the dictates of the Nazi regime, and its leaders stood down. An interim church leadership put internal divisions aside for a while and became a moral force among an occupied people. The confessional tract entitled *The Church's Foundation* (1942), in which the Church took a principled stand against the illegal governing power, will live on in history. The good will earned during the war later soured for a time when the Church protested against imposition of the death penalty for collaboration and traitorous activities. The Church's foremost figure during and immediately after the war was Bishop Eivind Berggrav (1884-1959). A man of considerable international standing, Berggrav helped found the World Council of Churches, the Lutheran World Federation and the United Bible Societies.

In the grounds of Akershus Castle is the headquarters of the Corps of Chaplains. The Corps celebrated the fiftieth anniversary of its foundation in 2003, but the chaplaincy service is a centuries-old tradition. The organization of the modern Corps of Chaplains is a further expression of the close links that exist between the Church of Norway and the state, although the Corps now includes priests of other denominations. It is led by a chaplain who is under the military command of the Chief of the Defence Staff and ecclesiastically under the supervision of the Bishop of Oslo. The Corps of Chaplains is versed in ethical matters relating to war and peace and takes part in the training of defence personnel and in counselling the Defence Staff. In the same way as the priesthood in hospitals, nursing homes and prisons, the chaplains organization raises important questions relating to treatment of religious communities and those of other persuasions.

Below the castle, close to the water's edge, at the spot where Norwegian Jews were brutally shipped out to extermination camps in occupied Poland, a monument has been erected to remind future generations of the tragedy and to encourage new generations to take an active part in repudiating anti-Semitism. When the Nobel Peace Prize Centre opens in nearby Vika in 2005, a 'Peace Path' will be marked out from the Holocaust Centre on the Bygdøy peninsula, just across the bay, via the Peace Prize Centre, to the Resistance Museum in the castle grounds. The terminal point, the Castle Church, may serve to focus people's minds on religion as a cause of war or source of peace. Confrontations with history must help us build bridges between religious and other persuasions in today's conflict-ridden world.

Paradoxically, Humanism's House (*Humanismens Hus*) is situated in a street that bears the name of the saint-king Olav, and is next door to the building that for many years housed the Free Faculty of Theology. When the Norwegian Humanist Association was founded in 1956, it was largely as a reaction to the faith espoused by the Free Faculty. Only Great Britain has a higher percentage of Humanists than Norway. The Norwegian Humanist Association has been actively critical of Christianity, directing its censure mainly at the Church of Norway. It has targeted its recruitment campaigns, which are partly financed from the same public funds that provide support for religious and similar communities, at passive (i.e. non-practising) members of the Church of Norway. Today, the Association's most penetrating criticism is reserved for Islam. The Association represents a major philosophical alternative for those who attach importance to fundamental ethical values but eschew a religious interpretation of life. It has created its own rites of passage for children and young people, as it has for marriage and burial. The Norwegian Humanist Association enjoys considerable support for its civic confirmation ceremony, especially in large cities. A new service is the organization it runs as an alternative to hospital chaplains.

There are several television and radio studios in the centre of the city, and the majority of the national newspapers also have their offices close to the main street. The media give valuable expression to how questions of faith and belief are viewed in modern Norway. Pluralism of values has in many ways helped to alter the image of the Church as portrayed by the media. Tabloidization, with its emphasis on personalities and news stories that sell, is a poor means of promoting an understanding of philosophies of life or debates on values.

The national Norwegian Broadcasting Corporation (NRK) has radio slots for daily prayers that still command high listening figures. A church service is broadcast every Sunday, as on other public holidays. The Corporation's television channels likewise offer church services. Such services are less frequently seen on TV2, financed as it is by advertising. Other programmes dealing with beliefs remain part of the repertoire of the national channels. In topical discussion programmes, representatives drawn from religious and other cults and sects are often in demand. The nationwide television programmes designed to raise money for humanitarian purposes do much to enlist support for the needy. Local congregations play their part in conjunction with many such events by holding church services, organizing collections and so on.

The daily press finds room for the Church's voice when it is seen as relevant to a specific situation. The newspapers have largely discontinued their once-regular Sunday sermons, but some continue to advertise services for all Christian sects. The great Christian festivals are accorded space in virtue of their status as important social and cultural events, and in many papers leading articles comment on the significance of such occasions. But ecclesiastical journalists, who once constituted what was akin to a fraternity in their own right, are now an endangered species.

Developments in the media in recent decades reflect the pluralism of culture and belief in society. The media strategy of Christian organizations has led to the appearance of dedicated publishers, bookshops, newspapers and radio and television channels. This may have contributed to a decrease in religious and related material in other media and thus helped to promote the secularization of society.

We shall round off our tour at the Royal Palace, which stands at the top of Karl Johans gate. As noted earlier, the Constitution places the King at the head of the Church of Norway. The Royal Family has always shown an interest in the life of the Church. In their many visits to places all over the country, divine service often forms part of the official programme. The King and Queen participate in a number of church anniversaries. The King is always present at the ordination of bishops and, together with the Queen, gives an annual dinner for the House of Bishops. To an increasing extent the monarchy is represented at other events than those held under the auspices of the Church of Norway. The interest of the King and Queen in the role played by religion in promoting peace and reconciliation is manifest. The palace, too, bears witness to the close connection between King and Church. When the palace was built, the first stone was laid where the Chapel Royal would later stand. Consecrated in 1849, the chapel has been used for royal baptisms and confirmation services, as well as for other services attended by the Royal Family and palace servants; on occasion, deceased members of the Royal Family have lain in state there. On Sundays the chapel is used for the student congregation's service of worship. It was refurbished in honour of Princess Alexandra's christening on 17 April 2004. An amendment to the Constitution in 1990 opened the way for

**In 1993** the Church of Norway appointed its first female bishop, Rosemarie Köhn. Ordained in Hamar cathedral, she is seen here, surrounded by well-wishers, outside the building after the ceremony.

a female heir apparent, so Princess Ingrid Alexandra may one day be Norway's first reigning queen.

No description of faiths and persuasions in Norway would be complete without mention of two outstanding debates. The relationship between the Church and schools has long been a recurring theme in political debate, and matters relating to legislation on cohabitation and sexuality have aroused a great deal of controversy in the course of the last fifty years. In conclusion, then, it may prove worthwhile to devote a section to these subjects.

### Conflict and cooperation in schools

In 1969 the Storting decreed that the Christianity taught in schools was not to be regarded as synonymous with the Church's baptismal instruction; this entailed severance of the link between Church and education that went back to 1739. Over the last thirty years the time-honoured school subject of Christianity has undergone a succession of changes. This has occurred in tandem with society's growing uncertainty about the relationship between Church and school. A strong humanist movement began to demand exemption from Christian teaching for its members' children. This was accommodated by introducing instruction in philosophies of life as an alternative to traditional Christian teaching. The divisions this caused among pupils benefited neither school nor children. A growing influx of children from other religions, especially in urban areas, necessitated rethinking of the schools' function as a purveyor of values in a pluralistic society.

The answer, a subject that brought together instruction in Christianity, other religions and philosophies – known in Norwegian by its initials as KRL – was introduced in 1997. After a period of trial and error which included determining whether it should be permissible to opt out of the subject altogether, as could be done in regard to other subjects, KRL has proved itself a sound educational innovation. It teaches common values and provides a common structure for today's children and youth. The younger generation should be better equipped to combat xenophobia and racism than were their parents and grandparents. Nor has it escaped the notice of politicians that a prerequisite for tolerance is security in one's own belief, and that for this reason it is in the state's interest that schools should continue to teach children about religious faiths and other beliefs.

The controversy over schools' Christian object clause has proceeded in parallel with discussion of Christian instruction. Here, too, the Norwegian Humanist Association has been the driving force, but sections within the Church have also lent their support. The intention has been to formulate fundamental values that will not offend those who do not subscribe to the Christian faith, as the object clause does. Several constructive attempts have been made to arrive at a wording more in line with the realities of today's schools and society. A majority of parties in the Storting appear to favour a change in the object clause at a politically opportune moment.

From the outset, women's struggle for equality was condemned by the Church. Long after the battle had been won in society at large, sexual discrimination continued in Christian organizations and church communities. Norway's first female priest was ordained in 1961. Forty years on, resistance to female clergy has largely been laid to rest in the Church of Norway, and all of its bishops now ordain women. At the start of the 21st century, 17 per cent of the Church of Norway's priests are women, and there are two female bishops. The priesthood is in the process of becoming a women's occupation, as about half the students of theology are currently women. It is highly unlikely that a person opposed to the ordination of women would be appointed a bishop in the Church of Norway, at least not as long as the state-Church system remains in force.

### Cohabitation and sexuality

Questions surrounding marriage, sexuality and cohabitation have always been of concern to religious groups and institutions. To start with the Church was opposed to modern sexual enlightenment: there was no telling what horrors might follow in its train! In 1947, when the armed forces expressed a wish to provide Norwegian soldiers serving in occupied Germany with condoms, more than 440,000 people signed a petition in protest. In 2003 the Synod declared that condoms were not only ethically defensible, but were an essential part of a responsible sex life. This was said in the context of the looming AIDS pandemic, which is claiming millions of lives. The statement was clearly aimed at the Vatican, which forbids the use of condoms, even within marriage and even if a partner is infected. This is one of the greatest ethical problems facing ecumenical unity today.

In the matter of abortion the Church was opposed in principle, basing itself on the view that a foetus is a human being from its very conception. The foetus-killing terminology, which was very much to the fore also in the first clash between paganism and Christianity in our country, was given new currency. One nightmare vision was that abortion would become the new contraceptive, thus further eroding sexual morals and leading to increased promiscuity. Advocates of abortion on demand carried their argument to political victory by linking the abortion issue with Women's Lib. It was a woman's prerogative, they said, to demand an abortion. The argument over a woman's right to exercise control over her own life meant that a time-limit had to be set for when this became not merely a matter of the woman's life but also concerned the foetus she was carrying; in the event, the limit for elective abortion was set at the twelfth week of pregnancy.

The Church of Norway has not officially lent its support to the current abortion legislation, but neither did it stand in the front rank in opposing abortion on demand once the battle was lost. The unyielding sides in the dispute have stifled wider social debate linked to more recent developments in gene and biotechnological research. Fearing a reprise of the debate relating to abortion on demand, many people are reluctant to address the problems arising from more recent research, problems that impinge on some of the same matters of principle as did the abortion issue. To a large extent the debate surrounding the ethical dilemmas of biotechnology is carried on in the political sphere without the wider participation of theological and philosophical professionals.

The Church's position on the gay issue is unclear. After a total repudiation of homosexuality, which was also in line with society's criminalization of homosexual cohabitation, the Church has moderated its official view. A distinction is now made between leanings and practice. Homosexuals can become priests on condition that they remain celibate. In 1997 the Synod, in a compromise motion, raised the possibility that homosexuals with same-sex partners might be permitted to occupy unordained positions within the Church. It can therefore be claimed that, in principle, opposition to homosexual cohabitation has been abandoned by the Church of Norway. Discussion still continues about the doctrinal basis, as it does about the right to make special demands of those who hold ordained positions within the Church, among them priests, deacons, catechists and cantors.

The House of Bishops is divided over the gay issue. A minority accepts homosexual partnership for priests and persons in other ordained posts. In 2003 the matter was put before the Church of Norway's Doctrinal Commission and an opinion

**The Arctic Ocean Cathedral** in Tromsø, seen here in moonlight, is one of the country's most striking buildings.

is expected in 2005. It will then be up to ecclesiastical bodies, the Synod and the House of Bishops to draw the administrative consequences. According to current canon law, none of these can prevent a bishop ordaining a homosexual for service in the Church, provided the person concerned is employed by a diocesan council or by the Joint Church Council. Up until 2004 only the diocesan councils of Oslo and Hamar had engaged priests living in gay partnerships. On their independent supervisory responsibility the bishops on these councils have ordained priests and deacons who live in homosexual partnerships. There is no evidence to suggest that this conflict will be of shorter duration than that surrounding women priests. The arguments adduced in both debates are very much the same.

The question of remarriage of divorcees used to be a thorny ecclesiastical topic, but following a period of massive opposition, since the 1950s an increasing number of priests have begun to marry divorced persons and the debate has gradually subsided. Today there are many priests who have been divorced and remarried, for which reason most people believed this was an area in which general agreement existed within the Church. However, in connection with amendment of the Occupational Environment Act in 2004 it emerged that a number of organizations within the Church still refused to employ people who had been divorced and subsequently remarried. On the question of cohabitation rather than marriage the Church favours marriage, which it believes affords the best protection for children. High divorce figures among both married and cohabiting partners are giving cause for concern both in the Church and in society at large.

**Epilogue**

Faiths and philosophies of life are ways of interpreting life. While faith is a religious phenomenon, 'philosophy' (or 'persuasion') can be applied to a non-religious interpretation of life's relevance and meaning. Some people who claim to have a Christian outlook on life would not describe themselves as believers in the traditional sense.

In matters of fundamental values and norms there is, despite the many differences that exist, broad assent in modern Norwegian society in regard to the commandments not to kill, lie, steal or abuse one's own or another's sexuality, as well as to respect marriage and other forms of union, to labour and to rest. Even people who reject faith in a god can respect what is sacred. It is not always easy to distinguish between what is based on faith and what on reason: people without a defined religious belief may also have a feeling for rites, symbols and spiritual fellowship. The commandments carry authority not only because they are a part of holy writ but also because they are sensible.

To a very great extent the three monotheistic religions, Judaism, Christianity and Islam, possess a common understanding of what Jesus called the first and great commandment, viz.: *Thou shalt love the Lord thy God with all thine heart, and with all thy soul, and with all thy might.* He then added that the second, *Thou shalt love thy neighbour as thyself* was 'like unto it'. It goes without saying that no one who precludes a religious understanding of the world can warm to the first commandment, and it is equally clear that if this universal injunction to love were confined to the first sentence, to love God, it would be a recipe for fanaticism. That is why it is so important that the commandment to love God is paired with love of one's neighbour. It is then that love is truly put to the test. To love one's neighbour is to show love to all, regardless of race, religion, culture and all else that determines an individual's personality. But there is an equally important reminder in the two words 'as thyself'. This means that self-respect, which includes being content with oneself, is a good thing. Never mind that the Danish humorist Piet Hein has warned against that particular commandment by maintaining that no one can cope with so much love! Loving oneself means that self-respect is fundamental to all human beings: it is both a gift when it comes in the shape of the love of others and a prerequisite for showing love towards others.

Even without the religious foundation of a belief in God, Allah or Yahwe, love of one's neighbour, coupled with love of oneself, is of decisive importance as a fundamental tenet and moral practice. Where believers start with gods, Humanists begin with a belief in mankind. In their dealings with other people, benevolence and tolerance are tested in them both. Perhaps this stroll through the Norwegian landscape of faith and philosophies has shown that fellowship's multiform arena requires various interpretations of what life is. That faiths and philosophies are able to work together in a pluralistic society shows just how important tolerance is in a truly humane society. Respect for one's own identity and the identities and values of other people is the most important expression of tolerance. To search for recognition of one's own belief in another person's ideas and one's own ideas in their belief, is an exercise in the art of tolerance.

**january** fin serck-hanssen **february** rolf m. aagaard

**march** herdis maria siegert **april** janne solgaard

**may** jens hauge **june** vibeke tandberg

**july** dag alveng **august** rune johansen

**september** knut bry **october** asle svarverud

**november** ingvar moi **december** per berntsen

# HENRIK IBSEN

'A rather small and unprepossessing chap, with neither behind nor chest.' These were the words used by the writer Bjørnstjerne Bjørnson to describe his contemporary, the playwright Henrik Ibsen. For Ibsen it was nothing new to be referred to in such unflattering terms: ever since childhood he had been teased and tormented by his fellows. He had even given his classmates money so as not to have to accompany them on his way to and from school. People would shout insults such as 'scarecrow' and 'ugly mug' after him. We have his sister's word for it that Henrik was never a very likeable boy and that 'he had no sporting ability whatsoever'.

There is reason to believe that Henrik Ibsen came into the world as the result of an extra-marital affair. His biological father is thought to have been a Telemark writer and politician, Tormod Knudsen, with whom his mother fell passionately in love. Scholars have found evidence in support of this belief both in his physical appearance and in the fact that no one in the Ibsen family composed as much as a single line of poetry, whereas the Knudsens did little else. Henrik followed in the family tradition in that, while an apothecary's apprentice in the small south-coast town of Grimstad, he had a child with the maid – a son whom he was never to meet.

When Ibsen was eight, his familial father went bankrupt, with full distraint as a result. The shame and concomitant loss of social status left an indelible impression on him, both as a person and as a writer. At the age of fourteen he was sent out to make his own way in the world. As for his brothers and sisters, one died when Ibsen was small, one was an invalid from the time a maid dropped him on the floor, two emigrated to America, where they both died relatively young, and the remaining three joined a sect led by a fire-and-brimstone preacher named Lammers in which the reading of fiction was proscribed. It would seem, therefore, that no one in Ibsen's family ever read any of his works or saw them staged. After leaving his hometown of Skien in his early teens, the famous dramatist had practically no contact with his family.

Ibsen remained an apothecary's apprentice for six years, studying in the evenings for what would be only an average degree. Increasingly, he became convinced that the prevailing social order had to be overturned. He was within a hair's breadth of being thrown into prison when, in 1851, the police stormed the offices of a weekly paper published by the followers of a short-lived movement founded by a firebrand named Marcus Thrane. At the last moment the printing-shop foreman swept Ibsen's manuscripts off the table on which they were lying on to the floor, where the police took them for waste paper. The newspaper's editor, a close friend of Ibsen, was sentenced to seven years' imprisonment with hard labour. This notwithstanding, Ibsen continued to work for

the paper, writing articles and verse for the new editor until he too was arrested in September of the same year.

Inspired by the February revolution in Paris and his own circumstances, in 1848-49 Ibsen wrote a tragedy, *Catiline*, under the pseudonym Brynjolf Bjarme. An enthusiastic childhood friend drew on his inheritance to have the play printed, but his enthusiasm was not shared by the public at large and he was compelled to sell the unsold copies to the corner grocer for use as wrapping paper. It would be another thirty-one years before the play was premiered – in Stockholm. Another of the aspiring dramatist's plays, *Lady Inger of Østråt*, was staged, but it was badly received and closed after two performances. The theatre manager, a man named Borgaard, never even took the trouble to read *The Vikings at Helgeland*; and the best that *Love's Comedy* achieved was that Det akademiske kollegium (the Executive Committee of the University) opined that the author deserved a thrashing. The newspaper *Christiania-Posten* was equally scathing, writing: 'As a dramatic writer Mr Ibsen is a nonentity around whom the nation cannot, with any show of warmth, plant a protective hedge.' It is not surprising, then, that Ibsen's son, Sigurd, was wont to say that his father was King of the Apes and his mother a Negress.

When he applied to study at university, Ibsen was turned down. He was booed off the stage as a dramatist in Bergen and sacked as theatre manager in the capital – and parliament found him undeserving of a writer's stipend. He was twice rejected when he applied for a travel grant. Even close friends described his writing as 'inane trash'.

He was, quite simply, enervated by persecution and poverty. At the age of thirty-six, his reputation in Norway was based mainly on his skill as a lyricist. For Christmas, all he could afford to give his wife, Suzannah, was a banknote he had designed himself. When his fortunes were at their nadir he dressed in no more than a woollen blanket full of holes, and on his sockless feet he wore rubber galoshes. More than once he created a disturbance in the streets of the capital, and he even tried to take his own life – as he had also attempted to do in Bergen when, drunk, he threw himself off a wharf in mid-winter.

'The important thing is to get away from Norway while I still possess a trace of humanity,' Ibsen said in explanation of his departure from his homeland in 1864. In his absence, all his belongings, all his manuscripts, letters and certificates, the paintings he had done when he was young, not to mention the folktales he had so laboriously collected in the Gudbrandsdal valley, were disposed of at a forced sale by order of the Attorney-General, a man named Dunker. It would be two years before Ibsen found out what had happened to his possessions. Long after the playwright's death, a resident of Bergen got his pocket watch back from a watchmaker wrapped in Ibsen's birth certificate. His university diploma was found by the engineer of a steamship in the Canary Islands. Ibsen kept a live scorpion in an empty beerglass on his desk in Italy to remind him of the country of his birth.

'I shall not return until Norway calls me,' he wrote. But Norway did not call him, and Ibsen remained abroad for twenty-seven years. It was during this period that he wrote *Peer Gynt*, *Brand*, *A Doll's House* and most of his other masterpieces. In Norway his plays were largely received with the vilest of abuse. Jeers greeted *The League of Youth*, but the strongest response was to *Ghosts* in 1881. The play was banned from all Norwegian theatres as it was interpreted as encouraging incest, nihilism and prostitution. Many people maintained that the dramatist should be brought before a court and punished – a reaction that would form the basis of his next play, *An Enemy of the People*. 'In Norway, writers are regarded as vermin and treated accordingly,' the dramatist declared. Ibsen retained his revolutionary zeal all his life. Towards the close he wrote to the Danish man of letters Georg Brandes that 'the state is the curse of the individual, and the state must go'. At his desk, Ibsen was always brave, but in company he could be downright cowardly. His mother-in-law described him as 'a shy little marmot'.

His works received an entirely different reception abroad. In Berlin, *Pillars of Society* was staged at five different theatres at the same time, and it was this play that was to earn him an international reputation. Foreign writers wrote books and monographs about him in his lifetime, and many countries showered him with orders and honours. Paradoxically, and possibly as a consequence of his ignominious childhood experiences, the anarchistically inclined Ibsen invariably displayed a childish pride on receiving such distinctions. It was with no less delight that he received an invitation from the Egyptian viceroy to attend the opening of the Suez Canal as a guest of honour. Few other Norwegians have made such an impact on world culture as this puny little man from the small town of Skien; ultimately, he would even enjoy recognition in his native Norway. Ibsen was finally awarded a lifetime writer's stipend and the Order of St Olav, and he even attended the unveiling of his own austere, full-length statue outside the National Theatre in Oslo. However, he remained afraid that he would die without having known the love of warm, living human hearts. 'It is as if I am separated by a wide, endless waste from God and from humankind,' he wrote.

In country after country Ibsen would find himself revered as greater than Shakespeare. In Norway, at the height of his career, he was offered a position as deputy customs officer. In the alpine town of Gossensass one of the main squares would be named Ibsen-Platz in his presence. But in the capital of his native land, after his death the authorities turned down the gift of the apartment he occupied on his return in 1891, on the grounds that the interior was not tasteful enough. Only as a result of private initiative and collections has the apartment been opened to the public in recent years. Twenty-six years after his death, one of Oslo's most undistinguished streets was named after him. And to add insult to injury, sixty years later still his name was also given to the city's ugliest multi-storey carpark.

NIELS CHR. GEELMUYDEN

IBSEN, HENRIK (1828-1906), playwright. Made his debut with **Catiline** (1849), followed by the national-romantic works **Lady Inger of Østråt** (1855), **The Vikings at Helgeland** (1858) and **The Pretenders** (1863). His first drama of ideas, and his breakthrough work, was **Brand**. He went on to write **Peer Gynt** (1867) and **Emperor and Galilean** (1873), and bourgeois dramas such as **Pillars of Society** (1877), **A Doll's House** (1879), **Ghosts** (1881), **The Wild Duck** (1884), **Rosmersholm** (1886), **Hedda Gabler** (1890) and **John Gabriel Borkman** (1896).

poetry

# 200 YEARS OF NORWEGIAN POETRY

Translation by Robert Ferguson

This selection of Norwegian poetry ranges over a period of two hundred years, from Henrik Wergeland to the present day. Had space permitted, the selection might well have presented Norwegian poems from the last thousand years. The period before 1814 and Wergeland was rich in scaldic poetry, folk ballads, baroque hymns, and verse in Dano-Norwegian and in Latin.

In other words, this is a selection of modern Norwegian poetry. Rather than presenting the poems in chronological order by year of publication, I have arranged them alphabetically by the authors' surnames. This should emphasize the contrasts in perception and sensibility between the different centuries and decades, at the same time as it highlights those overarching similarities that transcend them. The historical background against which these poems were composed has probably played a more important role in our reading of them than it did for the poets themselves in the act of composition.

Among other things, we can see that modern Norwegian poetry can hardly be divided into an early period, characterized by bound form, and a later period in which this was not the case. Nineteenth-century poets like Wergeland and Obstfelder write without end-rhyme and in irregular metre, anticipating the dominant form of written poetry in Norway over the last fifty years. And song-lyricists of the last fifty years take up the tradition of a more sonorous type of verse that is characteristic of many of the poems from the first century in this selection.

More space has been given here to spoken poetry than is usually the case in such selections. This is in recognition of the central role played by oral poetry in an age before the book became a mass medium, a role it has reassumed with the rise of the music industry.

As regards written poetry, considerations of space have dictated a concentration on single poems of relatively limited scope. This selection is therefore not representative of the kind of conceptual poetry that finds expression in large cycles of verse.

As editor, I have taken account of the fact that the selection will be available in translations into English, German, French and Spanish.

HÅVARD REM

**Astrid Hjertenæs Andersen (1915–85)**
**THE HORSES STAND IN THE RAIN**

When my mind fills with dreams
darker and more distant
than my thought can explain,
wilder and hotter,
than my heart can fathom,
I want only to stand in the rain
the way horses stand in the rain,
on some long lush pasture slung
between solid mountains, as here.

Stand and feel the body soak up
the strong, soothing wetness
that surges in swift streams
across face, hair, hands.
Be like the forest, suckling
at heaven's breast,
like the pasture, drenched in sweetness,
trembling with the lust of innocence.

The way horses stand in the rain,
hunched over, their flanks wet,
and let the scent of earth and rain
drift strong and sweet through the mind,
I want only to stand and *be*
and let the heavenly sparkle fall
until thought, free from fever,
follows dreams to clarity
in still and steady calm.

**Jens Bjørneboe (1920–76)**
**ISCARIOT**

They paid silver pieces, counting out thirty.
And I, sensing behind this some larger plan,
took their money, and showed them the man.
How could they have done it without me?

It was dark in the garden when they
took him, those villains, in the weary night.
But pale as he was, his footstep was light.
And I took my money and went my way.

It was spring. Heavy with bloom was the branch
I chose. And there we hung, he and I,
fruit the two of us, dangling on high.

It was before Passover; the houses were marked.
Before the Sabbath this had to be done:
we alone remained. The others had run.

**Bjørnstjerne Bjørnson (1832–1910)**
**SONG FOR NORWAY**

(National Anthem)
Translated by Arthur Hubbell Palmer

Yes, we love this land that towers
Where the ocean foams;
Rugged, storm-swept, it embowers
Many thousand homes.
Love it, love it, of you thinking,
Father, mother dear,
And that night of saga sinking
Dreamful to us here

This the land that Harald guarded
With his hero-throng,
This the land that Haakon warded,
Hailed by Eyvind's song.
Olaf here the cross erected,
While his blood he shed;
Sverre's word this land protected
'Gainst the Roman dread

Peasants whetted axes carried,
Broke th' invader's blow;
Tordenskjold flashed forth and
harried,
Lighted home the foe.
Women oft to arms were leaping,
Manlike in their deed;
Others' lot was naught but weeping, –
Tears that brought their meed.

Many truly were we never,
But we did suffice,
When in times of testing ever
Worthy was the prize.
For we would the land see burning,
Rather than its fall;
Memory our thoughts is turning
Down to Fredrikshald!

Harder times we bore that tried us,
Were cast off in scorn;
In that crisis was beside us
Blue-eyed freedom born.
That gave father-strength for bearing
Famine-need and sword,
Honor death itself outwearing,
And it gave accord.

Far our foe his weapons flinging
Up his visor raised;
We in wonder to him springing
On our brother gazed.
Both by wholesome shame incited
Southward made our way;
*Brothers three*, in heart united,
We shall stand for aye!

Men of Norway, high or lowly,
Give to God the praise!
He our land's Defender Holy
In its darkest days!
All our fathers here have striven
And our mothers wept,
Hath the Lord His guidance given,
So our right we kept.

Yes, we love this land that towers
Where the ocean foams;
Rugged, storm-swept, it embowers
Many thousand homes.
As our fathers' conflict gave it
Vict'ry at the end,
Also we, when time shall crave it,
Will its peace defend.

**Mari Boine (b. 1956)**
**I COME FROM THE OTHER SIDE**

(from *Eight Seasons,* Gávcci Jahkejuogo)

Your words scented
filled with unspoken invitations
me forever searching
My ice breaks, cascading
your strict prohibitions
Always these unmarked paths

If you would only say my name

Your words scented
filled with unspoken callings
me forever searching
My ice breaks, cascading
your murky worlds
All these unmarked paths

If you would only say my name

Within a shadow of fear
witnessed by a lightening sky
I confess my love
Under your blanket of stars
I let myself go with the wind
You the prince of my heart

If you would only say my name.

**Emil Boyson (1897–1979)**
**REST BY RUNNING WATER**

The heart is not tired,
but evening is not far away.
We stop. Through our silence
sounds the water's roaring play.

In the river-rush
we hear eternity close by.
We were born to this earth. We met.
We loved each other, you and I.

'Soon we will hear nothing
– that is the All we know.
But on through all eternity
runs water's bubbling flow.'

**Paal Brekke (1923–93)**
**AS IN A CINEMA**

As in a cinema, but not
knowing how I got here
and in the middle of the film
What's it about? Sshh
But what's it called? Sshh
And the usher lights me, peers at me
with his shaded torch
Why don't you sit down? What are
these suitcases?
They're mine. Sshh, he shoves me.
Have you been drinking?
Quiet now, or you'll be out again.

And a faint memory of didn't I once
protest? Shout out? Stamp my feet
I can't remember, just stumble on up
stairs numbered in
green light towards the Exit (red)
and afraid. Voices from the screen
behind me, metallic shrieks bellow,
whispers as of creaking winches
and the darkness of the grave around me
just the faces barely, palely above
the seatbacks, and when I speak to them
Sshh! then out you go,
headfirst through the door, out
but only into another cinema, exactly
the same, and the same film
Are they showing this forwards or backwards
Sshh. Then the usher and the whole business
all over again, up the stairs
out again, but always just in again.

**Olaf Bull (1883–1933)**
**METOPE**

Just *you* is what I would capture!
You, deeply and forever preserve
in poetry's eternally young alabaster!
You sun-kissed dreamer!
With forehead maidenly turned to the evening's pale gold,
one heaven's mild turning to face another –
as light and tender, its secrets as untold!
My worldly store of verse would I surrender gladly,
had I but craft enough for this: to shape
in memory's stubborn stone a soft metope
to limn your tender inscape.

You listen out, as we wander the damp shore,
to the airy splashing of the summery seaplay.
Hushed, we sense the evening silence withdraw,
its sounding bounds fading ever further away!
The air rings with the slow decline of fading sound,
beyond the golden church spire, the reddening copse.
Celestial waves of evening light roll down,
streams of sunlight falling from the mountain tops.

The hills turn blue. The stars draw nigh!
The day's last clouds answer the homeward call.
There is Evensong on the meadow, and from the tidemark in the sky
Arcturus rises! Supple, through the silver-grey fur of the rye,
a wind breathes beyond the grey stone wall.
A warmth of ecstasy flits across your face –
suddenly, in its blue depths, the eye will unmask
a damp sheen of honey, a palpable trace.
'My love, what are you thinking of?' I quietly ask.

'Of evenings like this one, by the sea,
when I am no longer here.
Of fields that foam with ripening corn, without me!
A host of tiny things: seeds that open;
a wake in the water; a pale sail out there;
waves rushing towards the shore, but without me!
Life that goes calmly on, my love. The everyday things,
these are what I think of, the deep and the blue
of all the summer garden evenings
to come, without me, without you.
How it wells in my eyes like a tear!
I grow alone, afraid, as though about to cry!
Everything that is ours, on this evening, here –
until, beyond every swift and intoxicating year,
a moment when the mists clear, and all is revealed to our eye!
Oh how deep the tide's dark mark, my sweet!
How empty the sands, when the waters were taken!
Maybe that dreadful night is near, when we must greet
a bleaker beach than this, by *everything* forsaken?

And yet it is a miracle, both tender and sweet,
that these fields, the corn and trees in azure air,
these rolling mountains in fathomless retreat,
should at *our* short seconds' gazing seem complete.
How *ours* things are – that beech tree there!
The fence! The old farmwagon – see –
still lying in the grass! The drying poles that lean
propped against the rowan tree.
And as bright this year as every year, the ditch's glowing green.

Ah sweet, if the depths of the grave one could but sway
I would become this grassy sloping here, aye,
or the mountain, or the beech tree there, with stars arrayed,
to shield, somehow, from all decay,
this, our holy garden. Because, to die –!
Oh touch me, love, and hold me! Your touch
is almost all of hope that's left for me to know,
that fleeting charge of light, its heat is such
that it wakes in me *another* eternity's glow!'

And I – a man alive to all earth's charms,
a man of solid flesh and blood from head to toe –
I sense, dizzied and shy, held within my arms,
a thing made up of glance and mood and mind alone,
a suspension in fear and haunted sorrow!
Lonely one! I offer mutely all I can, my hand
to stroke your scented hair. You hold onto me,
and thus we stand, eye to eye, Psyche and Pan,
bathed in starlight before a wheaten sea!

**Lars Saabye Christensen (b. 1953)**
**STAMPS V**

the dead
stand on another shore

chained to the same light

our memory is made of

**Arnold Eidslott (b. 1926)**
**HYMN**

I have studied solitudes
and name the dead by name
Job I love as my father
his boils are my heirlooms
Never did I pass the grottoes by
but clambered to the depths alone
to count the martyrs' bones.
Abba you were a harsh teacher
whispering at my side
but on my knees I thank you
for solitudes and winds
and dead days on punishment's leash
Those in distress are your children
the unhappy those you love
The heralds of light are born in darkness
and their suckle is melancholy
I studied solitudes and found
at the bottom of all, your love.

**Svein Ellingsen (b. 1929)**
**THE DARKNESS AROUND US IS THE DARK BEFORE DAWN**

The darkness around us is the dark before dawn!
Angels bring tidings of the joy of God:
In the midst of our darkness, He is among us!
Let none on earth be alone any more.

The radiance of angels fades in the night.
Those who were called make ready to leave,
wander in darkness and find God's dwelling.
Let none on earth be alone any more.

No dark is too dark for the eyes of God.
He who is Love is by our side.
Unscathed by darkness, He is among us
Let none on earth be alone any more.

The radiance of angels fades in the night.
The tidings they brought will always be with us,
Tidings of He who has come to the world!
Let none on earth be alone any more.

Hope shall take hold of the dawn that is coming!
The praises of angels will shatter our darkness.
See, here amongst people is God's own dwelling!
Let none on earth be alone any more.

**Henning Kramer Dahl (b. 1962)**
**HOARFROST**

I never saw light so frost-splintered
above fields of sculpted mud
– hoarfrost in late November
time has stood still
and the forest holds its breath, trembling
what is it waiting for, the dead-still winter desert
life's business here is finished

the lush green summer grasses
and nectar-brimming flowers
long for the liberation of decay
yet are pitilessly preserved
beneath a gauzy shroud
of virgin-white fronds of frost
none here believe any more
the lie about the warm spring coming
a stranger with icy fingertips
has passed through the love-kingdom of my youth
and turned my blood to stone
two crows struggle up
from the rimming horizon of ragged spruce
they flap away with all certainties of time
croaking hoarsely at the fleeing pink sun

Come love
let us walk together through cathedrals
of shimmering dead ice

take my hand beneath these glassy domes
and I'll tell you something
you ought never to have known.

**Kolbein Falkeid (b. 1933)**
**THERE IS A LOCKED ROOM**

I long for you.
There is a locked room in my body.
All your things are there, and the prints
of your short life, fleeting
as shadows on moonlit snow.
I have the key and enter
at intervals of seconds. I touch everything
and speak in silence to the emptiness,
a chronic listener.

I long for you
as well for you were most like me. Without you
I am alone with my twisted self.
All that was best in me and now fades
you bore like the early summer's day, a good
long-range forecast. My depressions too,
off in the west, could build up in you.
Now and then
our fronts collided and the downpours
and sun-seeking breezes clashed head-on. But mostly
our days hung in harmony,
matching pearls on the same necklace.

I long for you.
Neither weather nor time passes any more.
And the emptiness never answers.

**Claes Gill (1910–73)**
**MARIA**

You are dead.
Living men
have long since turned the violence of their hands
and strew the wild beauty of their dreams
elsewhere.
For you are dead.

And forgotten for any old glass of water.
But your fading words on the wages of life
breathe on in the misty billowing of a hidden autumn cataract:
about dying
spinning there.
from a play of shadows on running water.

* * *

November is already here:
trees in a bristling madness of torture
stand against strips of rain; and where
you are death alone knows. – Scorched
embittered intellectual, in a fevered joke
passion waters the ashes, thus in smoke
swathed arrogantly mocking
death's signs of pain,
laughing, like yonder madman plucking
up and down on strings of rain.

* * *

And still your sensations: fugitive
hoarse cries in the grey dawn. Fire
lit in an empty window lights
extinguished by chill steps in the sand
along the way visions of shadows rise
in hurried flight across the pillow's drab linen
glimpsed in vague outline your mouth
half-open for words that
in life unsaid leave an emptiness: Spleen!
o spleen in the impotent droop of fountains.

**Cathrine Grøndahl (b. 1969)**
**THE SUNDIAL'S PHILOSOPHY**

The sundial's philosophy –
show only the bright hours

The shadow will lengthen
one fine day,
with none
to wipe it out –
and time that passes
be visible
and luminous –
like a child

**Inger Hagerup (1905–85)**
**A LITTLE VERSE**

And so my hand empties again.
It always almost did contain
the things I would hold onto.
I never dared to close it fast.
When will one surely do, at last,
the things one so dearly wants to?

Again, and once again – defeat.
How green it is, the spring, how sweet,
– could I leave you on such a day?
Noted then in memory's book,
the dark that flickered through your look,
the thing you didn't say.

Another spring with trees and flowers,
the chestnut's silent host of stars,
the beech-tree's flaming fiery red,
the beat beat beating of a heart
that cannot understand the part …
no, best to leave the thing unsaid.

My heart's a fool from time to time.
Here – take this empty hand of mine.
Too little, much too little.
But who was coming, who was leaving,
who was giving, and who receiving –
that remains a riddle.

**Knut Hamsun (1859–1952)**
**THE ISLAND**

Now the boat glides
towards the skerry,
an isle in the sea
with green strand.
Here flowers live
for no-one's eyes,
they stand so strange
and see me land.

My heart becomes
a fabled garden,
its flowers like those
of the isle.
They talk together,
whisper strangely.
Meeting like children
they curtsy and smile.

Perhaps once before
I was here
at the dawn of time,
– a white spiraea.
I know that scent
from a far past. I stand,
caught in an old memory,
trembling here.

My eyes close.
Distantly recalling,
I lay my head
on one side.
Over the isle
night thickens.
I hear the sea's soughing tumble,
Nirvana's rumble.

**Olav H. Hauge (1908–94)**
**KUPPERN* SKATING AT SQUAW VALLEY**

I've won a skating prize too, I came
fourth in a school race when I was eight,
behind that Leiv.
But the others had steel-shod skates,
mine were only iron.
I bought them at the watchmaker's,
chose those with the curliest blades.

Now Kuppern's skating at the Squaw Valley Games!
I'm not about to go any 10,000 metres myself,
but my words speed up,
and the old girl's grip tightens on her stick.

* Kuppern (Knut Johannesen) is a champion speedskater.

**Gunvor Hofmo (1921–95)**
**FROM ANOTHER WORLD ...**

One sickens of the cry for reality.
I was much too close to things,
burned a way right through
and stand now on the far side,
where light and dark are not divided,
where no borders exist,
only silence that casts me into a
universe of loneliness,
of incurable loneliness.
See, I freshen my hand in the cool grass:
now that is reality,
real enough for your eyes;
but I am on the far side,
where blades of grass are chiming bells of grief
and bitter anticipation.

I hold a human hand,
look into human eyes,
but I am on the far side,
where what is human is a lonely fog of fear.
Oh if I were a stone,
that could contain the weight of this emptiness,
if I were a star
that could drink the pain of this emptiness,
but I am a human cast out into a twilight zone,
and I hear the rushing of silence,
the roaring of silence
from worlds deeper than this one.

**Henrik Ibsen (1828–1906)**
**THE MINER**

Mountain, groan and break below
at my heavy hammer blow!
Ever downward to the core,
to the calling of your ore.

Deep within the mountain night
buried treasure glints with light,
gems and jewels in layered bed
between the veins of golden red.

In the darkness peace is found,
peace eternal, underground;
break on, hammer, as you're bidden,
reach the heart of what lies hidden!

In boyhood days I found delight
in counting heaven's stars by night,
walking springtime's flowery ways,
the peace of childhood filled my days.

I left the glories of the day
for midnights in the tunnelled way,
forgot the meadow's singing sweet
in holy mineshaft's hammer beat.

The first step that I took down here,
to innocence t'was all so clear:
with spirits of the deep as guide
life's riddling path lay open wide.

But still no spirit yet has taught me
how to riddle what has caught me;
still no ray of light arisen
dissolving dark within the prison.

May it not – was I mistaken –
lead to truth, this path I've taken?
Yet if I search for truth on high,
The light above just blinds my eye.

No, downward is the way to go;
eternal peace lies deep below.
Break on, hammer, as you're bidden,
reach the heart of what lies hidden!

Hammer, beat the hammer's way,
beat on and on to life's last day.
Morning sunlight nowhere spreads,
its ray of hope is nowhere shed.

**Rolf Jacobsen (1907–94)**
**THE SILENCE AFTERWARDS**

Try to be done with it now,
the provocations and the sales statistics,
the Sunday breakfasts and the incinerators,
the military parades, the architectural competitions
and the triple rows of traffic lights.
Get it over with. Be done
with organizing festivals and analyzing market trends,
because it's late,
it's much too late,
be done and come home
to the silence afterwards
that greets you like a jet of warm blood against the
forehead
and like thunder coming
and like the sound of mighty bells
that make the eardrums ring
because words are no longer,
there are no more words,
from now on everything speaks
with the voices of stones and trees.

The silence that lives in the grass
beneath each blade
and in the blue spaces between the stones.
The silence
that follows the shots and follows the birdsong.
The silence
that blankets the dead
and waits on the stairs until all have gone.
The silence
that folds itself like a fledgling between your hands,
your only friend.

**Georg Johannesen (b. 1931)**
**JEWISH PARTISANS' SONG**
**In memory of the Warsaw ghetto uprising in the spring of 1943**

This light is not the sun, this light's a fire
This is smoke and not a cloud that's climbing higher
This is ash it isn't dirt on which we're walking
This song is just an act, it isn't talking

Not on heather but on barbed wire's where we lie
Not Sing! but Fire Away! the conductor's cry
It uses guns and not batons, our serenade
It's not a branch this in our hand but a grenade.

The thunder comes from canons, not from storms,
the flashing is the people's uniforms
but these people aren't the people, they're what's left,
and it's people kill the people, not the pest.

This song is only blood, it isn't words,
this people cannot fly away like birds
This is not a war that might bring peace:
we rose up, and now we're beaten to our knees

**Eldrid Lunden (b. 1940)**
**THE MUSEO ACADEMICO IN FLORENCE (5 November 1998)**

From a distance it's the vulnerable elegance

of the hips and belly we note. Then,
approaching slowly,
the gaze is seen,
compelling ours.

He doesn't take off. Not yet.
The nostril wings
are
still nostril wings

and quieter sex has never yet been seen.

He holds the sling over his shoulder, the stone secreted in the
right hand, the muscles
listening

the pulse in the
throat is all we see
move

in Michelangelo's 'David'.

**Tor Jonsson (1916–51)**
**THEN RISE UP IN ME, LONELINESS**

Then rise up in me, loneliness,
and storm the last bastion of my earthly life,
crush my consumptive dream of happiness here.
You dizzying, abyssal earth,
were you a different world
you would give up all your secrets
in this translucent morning moment,
in this hour before death's great day,
when lonesome voices summon me once more
to a rebirth elsewhere.

Now loneliness storms towards its limits.
My life was a dream, in which nothing was ever
quite certain. And now I own the earth no more –
but life itself I shall never miss, no, never –

**Stein Mehren (b. 1935)**
**I HOLD YOUR HEAD**

I hold your head
in my hands, as you hold
my heart in your love
as everything holds and is
held by something other than itself
As the sea lifts the stone
to its sands, as the tree
holds the ripe autumn fruit, as
the globe is lifted through the space of globes
so are we both held by something
                                        and lifted
to where a riddle holds a riddle in its hand.

**Kurt Narvesen (b. 1948)**
**FROST**

The great frost is upon him:
don't argue too much with him,
don't push him too far –

At a time like this he does both
best himself

**Rudolf Nilsen (1901–29)**
**THE CALL OF THE REVOLUTION**

Give me the strong, the true and the proud who would dare,
with patience and courage and willpower to spare,
to fight to the death for my great idea, and not sell out.

Give me the cool heads, who know my world, the wisest few,
who don't *think* they believe but *know* that they do.
For promised love is a word in the sand, and is gone as quickly too.

Give me the stubborn and bitter, those with no fear in their eyes.
Give me the proudly godless, who disdain the mysterious lies,
and would rather a heaven on earth that is *human* in shape and size.

Give me burning hearts, that never surrender to doubt,
nor are felled by reversals, nor wearied by grief and worn out,
but smile on as disaster and triumph wheel about.

Yes, give me the best among you, and from me you shall have my all.
For none can know, till the battle is won, just how urgent was the call.
It may be a question of saving our earth. The best among you – stand tall.

**Olav Nygard (1884–1924)**
**TO MY SON**

Beyond blue infinities you slept, fateless,
where time and thought's bright trace
are never seen; from moons of dreaming bliss
a mild-eyed silver beam floated out into space.
It was not night, heavy with the life of memory,
more the first hint of morning's fire,
that in the soft peace of eternity
wrapped cool linen around you, son of my desire.

A rushing, as of migrant flocks in flight,
swirled round and filled the trackless deep;
on bluish waves you floated, flowerlight,
rocked by the dreamgoddesses of sleep –
lily-like, swathed in sleep-eyed night,
you laid your elfin cheek in trusted resting
on lapping waves, as the bright light
of heaven's care stood by in blessing.

I walked the dales, deeply daydreaming,
while the mountains and falls taught me to grow.
Oh sky of my youth! Sunhot, spinestreaming,
chest-burning sunhot glow.
All swaddling loosed in the spring of love,
as though I swam in song and sunhaze
up mountainsides to peaks above
while time span through the infinite days.

Longing lay like blue nights at the core of love,
hid joyoars in its bosom for the journey;
I sensed in dreamstill depths of ether move
the hidden life that made longing burn. –
Crossing blue infinities my youthful spring strode on
through life's wondrous precessions;
while longing drank of life from ether's secret song
beneath the cycled moons and seasoned suns.

And from its fjords, longing rowed out,
and learned the long rhythms of the water,
raising its voice in muted thundershout
until all your dreamhomes began to stir.
The ether parted at its breathlight bounds,
gravity slipped in, held you fast,
and earthwards you drifted, in circling rounds,
falling, warmcheeked, to the cradle at last.

**Kate Næss (1938–87)**
**TERREO**

Walk along the shore
Don't see you
Squat down by craters
You never come up

Laid mines on public beaches,
wanted to wipe life out.
Only friends got killed

Making your getaway
you took a false step on the water
Your legs turned to jelly
Your arm let go the clouds

You tried to row and put out an oar
The waves stiffened in formation
And cracked

To put off death you tripped
Down a crater
The heart sprang a leak
Blood boiled over

You're still moving
Somewhere down in the earth
I tremble
And you laugh

**Sigbjørn Obstfelder (1866–1900)**
**I SEE**

I look at the white sky,
I look at the blue-grey clouds,
I look at the bloody sun.

So this is the world.
So this is the home of the planets.

A raindrop!

I look at the tall houses,
I look at the thousand windows,
I look at the distant steeple.

So this is the earth.
So this is the home of the people.

The blue-grey clouds mass. The sun disappears.

I look at the well-dressed gents,
I look at the smiling ladies,
I looked at the hunched horses.

How heavy they are, those blue-grey clouds.

I look, I look …
I must have come to the wrong planet!
It's all so strange here …

**Steinar Opstad (b. 1971)**
**PROHIBITED AREA**

The park is locked at night
and God is in there.
The prophet sleeps outside in the dark
in a smock that was once white
as a culprit's hands,
or a murderer
who was never caught.

I stroke the prophet's back,
for I act when I write:
I create, but I'm not a creator.
My eye isn't on God.
Jesus and a fence divide us
and someone asks
if not even God can save me.

'No, not even God,'
I write and smile,
for the innocent I know without
keeping their company.
The company I keep are criminals
who write words upon words,
and paint paintings upon paintings.

**Ole Paus (b. 1947)**
**KAJSA'S SONG**

Kajsa's song is of fences,
it's a song about walls and trees.
In the big white house where Kajsa lives
no sound disturbs the peace.

Words can't live in Kajsa's mouth.
Hers is a silent song.
She's seen and she's heard enough now.
She's quiet. She's screamed too long.

Kajsa, see the stars!
Nighttime follows day.
The earth spins round and round itself,
you spin around the same way.

Kajsa walking in the grounds.
They call, and she obeys them.
Peace comes with food:
Hibanil, nocinan and valium

Kajsa goes to bed,
and soon she's far away.
Kajsa is a star,
the star has lost its way.

Starless night tonight.
and dreams that hover near.
Kajsa's song was of fences.
Kajsa's song ends here.

**Alf Prøysen (1914–70)**
**ON THE ROCKY SLOPE ON THE HILLSIDE**

The sun shone down, the day's work was done
on the rocky slope on the hillside.
The dog-roses bloomed on every stone
on the rocky slope on the hillside.
I whistled and sang and gazed up at the sky,
and saw a young lassie who chanced to come by,
so slender and fair 'midst the flowers and rye,
on the rocky slope on the hillside.

I stopped her and said: 'What are you doing here,
'On the rocky slope on the hillside?'
'I've come to pick berries,' she answered so clear,
On the rocky slope on the hillside ...'
To this lassie I said , 'I'm a full grown-man,
but don't be afraid, come, give me your hand,
for I know each place where the berries do stand,
on the rocky slope on the hillside.'

Then I showed her the berries and gathered them up,
on the rocky slope on the hillside.
I emptied them into a rosy cup
on the rocky slope on the hillside.
For a joke I asked her to be my bride
'Are you off to the dance at Li?' she replied,
'for I see you each Saturday passing by
on the rocky slope on the hillside.'

'Ah but you're fooling, 'tis too well I know you,'
she said with her head to one side.
'Drunk every Saturday, that's what you do,'
– an ant climbed her skirt and she brushed him aside.
I swung my hat high and laughed in delight,
then danced and drank all the livelong night,
and woke up sober at day's first light
on the rocky slope on the hillside ...

**Lars Lillo-Stenberg (b. 1962)**
**IS THERE A WOMAN**

Is there a woman, who's just right for me
Strict, because I'm stubborn – occasionally
When bad things happen she's to hold my hand
try to make me laugh and sort of understand

Is there a woman, who's just right for me
Who'll buy me presents and call me sweetie
Tell me I'm the handsomest man around
And treat me to the cinema and dinner in town

She might have a job that pays quite a lot
Because I only play guitar, and that does not
Now I'm a self-centred type, when push comes to shove
But I'll see she gets plenty of a thing called love

a thing called love
a thing called love
a thing called love
a thing called love

Is there a woman, who's just right for me
Who'll buy me little presents and call me sweetie

**Espen Stueland (b. 1970)**
**AT RANDOM**

Passing a garden
we heard the flapping
of a tarpaulin
stretched taut across a boat

no footprints in the snow led
to a raw smell wafting from the cabin,
that was the only place we found
to undress each other

**Helge Torvund (b. 1951)**
**IF WE'RE MAKING A WOODPILE**

If we're making a woodpile
We have to start at the bottom
Lay thick runners on the
ground to keep it dry
Set supporting struts at one end
Now we can start
Pile smell of wood upon smell of wood
Earthy and airy at the same time
Touch the tree, bark and skin
The tree's love of light must be strong
My love is strong
With all that's of me between hair and earth I know
the tree understands light better than I do
Let's build a woodpile together
so the tree's love of light
can burn through the winter

**Tor Ulven (1953–95)**
**(TRIAL)**

A fault,

and the streetlamps
have gone out. Only now
do I see

how dark it is
in November,

and was, before
the streetlights came, and in

the pinewoods
before these hills

were peopled.

**Halldis Moren Vesaas (1907–95)**
**WORDS OVER A GATE**

I approach as close as your inmost gate,
and that is as close as you come to me.
Beyond these gates we are both alone
and so shall we always be.

Never to force a way closer
was the law that bound the two of us
whether meetings were often or rare
what we shared was respect and trust.

If one day I came and found you not there
I'd just turn and walk away,
standing there first, looking awhile
at the house, thinking, this is where you stay.

As long as I know that you'll sometimes come
– as now, crunching the gravel, I see you –
happy and smiling to find me here
then I know that my house is a home too.

**Aasmund Olavsson Vinje (1818–70)**
**BACK TO ANTIQUITY**

Oh, I was tired of the artful life, and longed again for those ways,
familiar and beloved, that I knew in younger days.
That art was just artful, false and mean, with all of its snares.
Hard to unravel now, that tangled skein, the knotted and twisted hairs.
For Venus should stand as she formerly stood, naked and fine,
not in chignon, nor with shawl nor train, nor in hooped crinoline.
In power and courage would I see a man dressed, from his head to his toe,
not a 'bloke' in his 'Sunday best' and all that show.
Learning exalts what's fair and great, it's clothing enough for the wanderer.
Show me now what the Good Lord made, and not some entrepreneur.
That new way of speaking, that new art of babble and bluff
it clothes the thought like the bust of man in a shirt that is mostly stuffed.
Shakespeare and Goethe play with ideas, they spin and can make them turn,
but to Homer and Edda you must, you know, in the end return.
In saga and folktale a lost self you'll find,
when you've wandered in novels too long and dizzied your mind.
They thresh that corn till it's crackling and dry, the love as well as the hate.
The heart dries up and thought runs astray with all of that empty prate.
Loyalty, that's what I seek as I make my round. With people is where I'll begin.
So give me a Human, and I'll sound him, both outside and in.
For wherever you go, the knack of the thing is the same: truth wins.
If you're looking for life, go back to the cradle – that's where your search begins.
And when grown to a man, recall these words more than once in a while:
'Ye shall not enter the kingdom of heaven, without ye become again a child.'

**Aslaug Vaa (1889–1965)**
**WAITING AND WATCHING**

Hey you, what shall I do
with all these nights?
- Sleep just the one
then turn on the lights!

But the days never end
- they go on and on!
- Then wait out the many
and live for the one!

**Jan Erik Vold (b. 1939)**
**DECEMBER LIGHT (SILENT FILM ON WERGELAND'S WAY)**

– This woman
who stops me on the pavement and says
she's met me once before,
with her husband, whose name she tells me, her own
she must have told me
already, this woman stands there with a small
boy safely sleeping in a pushchair, his mouth
collapsed around sleep – and around us
is a clear December morning, this woman –
talking about all sorts of things I can't quite
follow, partly the cars swishing by along Wergeland's Way, partly
her pure young girl's face is so strong and clear
in the morning light, the only thing
I understand is that her husband is in a monastery
somewhere in Belgium, working on a
research project, she talks
some more, I'm standing on the pavement
a little confused, listening, but can't seem to collect
myself so I reach up and stroke her cheek
with my hand – and she takes warm hold of
my hand then. Maybe this touching (I've thought about this
since) was what she was talking about all the time, out there
on the pavement, in December light, yes I'm certain
it was a silent film –

**Nils Yttri (1947–80)**
**THE PEACE OF THE PRIVATE LIFE IS AN OPEN WOUND**

You touched the whole universe
You were a sun
I thought would never set
Your mouth was a half-moon
That never hid behind a cloud
You roamed the solar system
Turned the Milky Way
Into a dead-end street
You were a sun
That gave eclipses
inferiority complexes
Now that you've gone to shine
In another mind
I wear sunglasses in the rain
The half-moon shines over the buddha
I'll never know his peace

You were a sun
Without a system
You shine brightest at night
I was a rowboat without tholes
Drifting with no harbour
I didn't know the stars
The Milky Way wasn't a dead-end street
But a brilliant confusion
One night you shone brightly in my dream
I saw you set for the first time
The way children draw the sunset
I had been a sick child
Didn't realize the half-moon
Could smile a crooked smile.

**Henrik Wergeland (1808–45)**
**TO THE SPRING**

Oh Spring! Spring! Save me!
None has loved you so tenderly!

Your first grasses are worth more to me than amber.
Your anemones I call the glory of the year,
though I know well, the roses are yet to come.

How often in passion they twined themselves after me.
It was like being loved by princesses.
But I fled them: Anemone, spring's daughter, had my heart.

Bear witness then, Anemone, before whom in passion I have knelt!
Witness, despised Dandelion and Coltsfoot, that I have prized you
more than gold,
for you are the children of spring.

Witness, Swallow, that I kept open house for you, as for
a lost child returning, for you were the harbinger of spring.

Seek out the Lord of these clouds and pray, that they cease
to shake needles down into my chest from their cold blue openings.

Witness, ancient Tree, whom I have worshipped as a god,
whose buds I have numbered each spring more keenly than pearls!

Bear witness, you, whom I have so often embraced
with a great-grandson's respect for his great-grandfather.
Ah, how often have I not wished to be a stripling maple,
offshoot of your eternal root and mingle my crown with yours!

Witness for me, Old One! None will doubt you.
Yours is the worthiness of a Patriarch.

Pray for me, and I shall water your roots with wine
and heal your scars with kisses.

Already your crown will be showing its fairest pale green,
your leaves be already rustling out there.

Spring! the Old One cries out for me, though he is hoarse.
He raises his limbs heavenward, and the Anemones,
your blue-eyed children, kneel and beg you to
save me – I, who love you so tenderly.

**Arnulf Øverland (1889–1968)**
**HERE, WANDERING**

Here, wandering,
I finger random things,
familiar to my touch:
an old pipe and candlestick,
a blue-painted ladle I once hid away;
these the oldest of the lot, I daresay.
Their moments return, I hear them tick.

I touch the chair, where so often I sat,
midnight brooding on this or that.
And time is something, I suddenly sense,
which is gone, in the far past tense.

Evening is nigh.
I touch the things, say goodbye.
I look at our children. I look at her.
I feel I'd like to say so much,
but can't; so walking past I touch
and softly stroke their hair.

**Ivar Aasen (1813–96)**
**THE NORSEMAN**

Between mountains and hills, by the sea
the Norseman has chosen his home;
he cleared the land of stone and tree
and built there a house of his own.

He looked out on the rocky coastline;
he was first, none had built there before.
'Let us clear the land, and its limits define,
so none shall dispute us our shore.'

Out at sea where the wild winds blow,
he saw danger in travelling that way.
But fish played down in the deep below
and he wanted to see them play.

The mid-winter's cold could test his love,
make him long for a land that was hot.
But when spring's sun burst in the hills above
he gave thanks in his heart for his lot.

And when hayfields with flowers are ablaze,
and the meadows all clothed in green,
when nights are as bright as days
no lovelier land has he seen.

"A"
2840
Wilse. Eneret
Oslo

# KNUT HAMSUN

'I enjoy being reckless, making good people stand open-mouthed and gaping,' Knut Hamsun declared early in his life. He must have enjoyed himself, because good people would gape at his doings as long as he lived – as, indeed, they still do, more than fifty years after his death. Hamsun is the greatest novelist Norway has ever fostered. There are even those who believe he is the greatest in the world – yet during the Second World War he was branded a traitor.

He felt betrayed himself when, at the age of nine, he was forced to live with a disabled and malicious uncle in the north of Norway. Every night for five miserable years he would go to bed hungry. It is said that his only pleasure was to escape to the local charnel house and whittle figures from the bones he found there. His uncle was so vicious and unkind that in the end the boy hacked his own leg with an axe to get away from him. The only education Hamsun ever received was the five years he spent at the local school. The son of a tailor, he grew up in such wretched conditions that he early developed the habit of wearing newspapers inside his clothes to keep warm. In the event he was destined to become no more than a wanderer on the face of the earth, and as such was closely related to many of the characters in his novels.

PORTRAIT

Hamsun eked out a living as a shop assistant on the island of Tranøy, as a country policeman in Bø, a cobbler's apprentice in Bodø, a road worker in Toten, a postmaster in Aurdal, a school teacher in Hjørundfjord, a farmhand in North Dakota, a clerk in Elroy and a streetcar conductor in Chicago; he also did brief stints as a bricklayer, bookkeeper, pigkeeper, auctioneer and arsonist. There is reason to believe that wherever he went, he was searching for himself and for Laura Walsøe, the aristocratic girl with whom he had fallen so impossibly in love as a youth. Sigrid Undset, who disliked Hamsun's writing intensely, once said that all of his books were about a poor man trying to seduce a rich woman. If you strip away everything else in his works, it is easy to concede the point to Undset, but then you also strip away all the vibrant life that Hamsun captured with a surer hand and style than any novelist before him. It was, after all, his style, with its adventurous freshness and incomparable humour, more than the content that eventually seduced readers all over the world.

He said of himself, 'I am on very bad terms with everyone and everything.'

His roommate during his first stay in America often found Pedersen, as Hamsun called himself at the time, sleeping with a cigar and a knife laid out on his bedside table. Beside them would be an elegantly written invitation to his roommate to smoke the cigar and then stab him through the heart. Hamsun contracted sycosis, sciatica, neurasthenia, haemorrhoids and rampant consumption. He was close to dying from the latter, but recovered and resumed his life as a wanderer. Hamsun early exhibited extremist tendencies. The police kept him under surveillance when he returned from America, as he wore a black armband as a token of his sympathy with some anarchists who had been executed in Chicago. During this period he changed his surname five times.

It is hard to say whether it was brass neck or bad manners or both, but as an aspiring young writer who had yet to make a name for himself, Hamsun embarked upon a lecture tour of Norway, in the course of which he abused Henrik Ibsen and sundry other great Norwegian writers. He displayed some of the same foolhardy lack of good manners when he visited Adolf Hitler during the Second World War. It is said that no one took the dictator so to task and displayed so little restraint as did Hamsun, who treated the scrawny despot as if he were no more than some young brat.

In his first ten years as an author, Hamsun plagiarized stories of country life from Bjørnstjerne Bjørnson, the great writer of the time, though Bjørnson quite rightly considered Hamsun's writing mediocre. Hamsun, however, was such an imposing figure that Bjørnson advised him to try his hand at acting in Christiania, the capital. These were hard times for Hamsun: he had been rejected by the theatre and was living with a Jewish hair-buyer in the slums, the setting of his 1890 breakthrough novel, *Hunger*. At thirty years of age, he had no home, no family, no reputation and no money; he had even pawned his overcoat.

**Knut Hamsun** photographed together with his wife, Marie, at Nørholm in 1951, the year before he died. By this time he was a broken man, hard of hearing and convicted as a traitor to his country.

Hamsun was interested in 'the poetry of the nerves, the fractions of thought and the vague mimosas of feelings – in a word: Emotions'. He wanted to write of people in whom inconsistency was a basic characteristic. His books are populated by protagonists without parents, hometowns or backgrounds – people whose lack of roots reminds the reader of the author himself. The same mixture of coarseness and delicacy that characterizes his writing can be found in his personality; even at the time of his confirmation it was said that he could beat up whole pews of his contemporaries. After years of what he referred to as 'clenched-fist books', he turned from writing lyrical-romantic psychological literature to more socio-realistic novels. It is thought that on Bjørnson's death in 1910 Hamsun felt himself called upon to carry on the deceased writer's political work. This was a task for which he was unqualified, one reason being that in newspaper debates he sometimes went so far as to threaten his adversary with hanging. In 1920 Hamsun was awarded the Nobel Prize for Literature for his authorship, which by then included *Growth of the Soil*. In this work the wanderer settles down, thus emulating the author, who had just bought the property of Nørholm in the small south-coast town of Grimstad.

Hamsun was an exceptionally complex person, and in a way it was his writing that kept him together. He was the modernist who despised modernity, the fugitive who held that people should stay in the place where they were born. Hamsun was of the opinion that city women were no more than 'sawdust and theatre songs' – but then he went and married an urbanite, an actress. Although he wrote several himself, he dismissed plays as 'the very worst kind of pretentiousness'. Hamsun loved northern Norway, but made his home in the south. There have been many advocates of the view that Hamsun was always an uncultured person, which makes it all the more remarkable that this boy from the wrong side of the tracks should so often have searched for noble souls.

In his writing Hamsun was always critical of ostentation and wealth, which he associated with the English; nonetheless, whenever he was in the capital he himself behaved in a singularly English fashion. Few dressed and deported themselves with more elegance than he, and no one tipped more generously. But as a life partner and father, Hamsun was an abject failure, even leaving home for long periods before and after the birth of each of his children. The very person who had always revered youth, grossly neglected his own offspring.

The world, however, was at his feet. Hemingway, and many others, found in Hamsun a lifelong model. Hamsun's writing was particularly well received in Russia. It was said that after the Second World War, Molotov, the normally ruthless foreign minister, implored Norway's Minister of Justice to show Hamsun as much leniency as possible, a request which prompted the minister to a unique observation: *'You're too soft, Mr Molotov.'* The Norwegian people were filled with hatred for the writer. A few days before the Liberation, Hamsun even managed to have an admiring tribute to the recently deceased Adolf Hitler published in the Oslo newspaper *Aftenposten*, the capital's principal broadsheet. Desertion was definitely not his style: even as a traitor he held nothing back. After the war, at Nørholm, people threw their old Hamsun books over the fence.

Some have tried to explain his support for the occupying power by saying that he had become hard of hearing and senile, while others believed that Hamsun's character had already been well prepared when Hitler came along and sowed the seed. At his trial after the war, it was found that Hamsun suffered from 'permanently impaired mental faculties'. He escaped with a fine – but in 1949, at the age of ninety, he produced proof that his faculties were anything but impaired by writing his last book, *On Overgrown Paths*. Throughout his life he had an aversion to old age and old people, even having himself sterilized in 1921 in the belief that this would halt the ageing process. 'As a rule, an eighty-year-old has already been dead for twenty or thirty years – it is just that he has not been buried,' he wrote. Paradoxically, he would live longer than most people.

'All will be forgotten in a hundred years' time,' he wrote in one of his poems, though in this he was to be proved wrong. Hamsun was accused of betraying his own country, but he never betrayed the art of writing. His books still shine with undiminished brilliance, providing inspiration for countless readers and writers throughout the world. The enigma that was Hamsun never ceases to fascinate, and new theses and papers on him are published every year. His complex personality is such that the world will never weary of him.

NIELS CHR. GEELMUYDEN

HAMSUN, KNUT (born Knud Pedersen) (1859–1952), author. Achieved his breakthrough with **Hunger** (1890). This was followed by **Mysteries** (1892), **Pan** (1894), **Victoria** (1898) and **The Growth of the Soil** (1917), among other books. Awarded the Nobel Prize for Literature in 1920. Went on to publish the trilogy **Wayfarers** (1927), **August** (1930) and **Men livet lever** (**But Life Goes On**) (1933). Tried for treason after the Second World War, in 1948 Hamsun was found guilty on account of his publicly declared sympathy for Nazi Germany. In 1949 he published **On Overgrown Paths**, a novel in diary form from this time.

# ARTS AND CULTURE

# A VIEW FROM PARADISE

Hege Duckert

*A view of paradise. A view of a normal day in Norway's welfare state. It had scarcely roused itself from the winter night. The light was still tentative; both Adam and Eve were still asleep. Soon, however, people would rise, rub the sleep from their eyes and begin to function. I took a deep draught of hot tea and reached for the telescope.*

Norway, 'birthplace of giants', adores the little man. The anti-hero is the man for us. We sing his praises and we see ourselves in his image. He appears again and again in a myriad Norwegian cultural expressions, however modern or sophisticated they may be. The character of Elling in Ingvar Ambjørnsen's novel is a recluse, a voyeur, a psychiatric patient, yet in the last decade he has received more media coverage than any other fictional character in Norway. The first time we meet him he is looking at the world through a telescope: at the housing co-operative, the shopping centre and the streets and squares of the suburb seventeen minutes by underground railway from downtown Oslo. Life for this most timid of men is frightening, but he can deal with it if it comes in small packages. Be it in the book, film or play, Elling touches the heart of all true Norwegians. A social democrat through and through, he idolizes Gro Harlem Brundtland politically, socially and erotically. Elling is a good and a timid person in equal portions, pure and innocent to the core. In the end, he teaches himself to live with what we still fear most in this sparsely populated country: other people.

**Defying wind** and weather, they sing with gusto and enthusiasm to make life more livable in an out-of-the-way corner of Norway. The stalwarts of Berlevåg Male Voice Choir embody all the heroic elements of the Norwegian character.

**Elling,** here portrayed by Per Christian Ellefsen, lives alone and is both a Peeping Tom and psychiatric patient. But he is more: the dearly loved anti-hero of a whole raft of books, plays and films.

The anxious, misunderstood oddball with a potential for greater things is a recurring figure in Norwegian stories. Men who have great dreams but little possibility or talent to realize them fascinate us. We see the sublime in failure. The main characters in Henrik Ibsen's *Peer Gynt* and Knut Hamsun's *August,* fabulists and dreamers, have captivated Norwegians for generations. One only has to mention the first-person narrator in Hamsun's *Sult* (Hunger) who lives as an outcast, apart from other people, observing from a distance. Or Nagel in Hamsun's *Mysterier* (Mysteries), who is as much of a lost soul in his yellow suit in a small town in the south of Norway as is the hero of *Sult* in the capital city. Or the students in Arne Garborg's writing whose spirits are broken when the values of humble folk are lost. Or Amalie Skram's female characters, who find their expectations of life unfulfilled and who are let down by society and, not least, by men.

The aim of this chapter is to look at the stories that are told in Norway today and see how, if at all, they differ from those of other countries. So this is not a complete history of culture but a snapshot of the arts in Norway in the early 2000s and a glimpse of what lies behind them.

A natural starting point might be the folk tales of our country, the collection of stories by Asbjørnsen and Moe that revolutionized the Norwegian language by its use of popular words and expressions. Let us look at one character in particular, Askeladden. Living as he does on the margins of society, he is a person of whom no one has high expectations; but still he comes through all kinds of tests – confrontations with mighty trolls and pernickety princesses – by using the imagination, resourcefulness and creative ideas he has gained from being on the outside. When a Norwegian Language Director was appointed in 2004, one of the main challenges in his first interview was to find a good Norwegian expression for 'underdog'. Norwegian heroes have created themselves. They have never received anything free: when they win, the prize is not material goods or gold, but a friendly word or a bowl of porridge. The simple life is the good life. We are proud of our 'stars' but we are equally proud of those who are misunderstood. Aksel Sandemose formulated what he called the *Jantelov* (a 'law' that says, 'Don't think you're something special' -- in other words, don't get too uppity), which Norwegians still invoke when they set out to describe the kind of people they are. The greatest compliment you can receive in many parts of Norway is that you are 'just an ordinary person'. As for our writers, they often write about oddballs, people who make off into the forest, there to sit on a stone and become geniuses. In *Det store spelet* (The Great Game) Tarjei Vesaas describes the protagonist, Per Bufast, as someone who goes to sleep at night with the certainty that he will never live anywhere else. We have a community spirit in places where, in the words of the old song, 'no one could believe that anyone could live'. The members of the male choir in the northern town of Berlevåg, shown to perfection in the film *Heftig og begeistret* (Cool and Crazy), are all true-to-life, resolute Norwegian heroes.

Norway is a young state. Its cultural life and cultural policy still bear traces of a nation-building mentality. We are a small country with a uniform educational system and few private schools, a state Church and, until quite recently, a limited number of TV channels. Norway has had no nobility since 1821 and accordingly no culture of arts patronage, no royal theatre and no court poet. Norwegian businesses are more comfortable sponsoring sport. Although the Church began to put money into cultural initiatives in the 1700s, for nationalistic reasons, the first arts grants did not appear until the 1830s. A feature of the late nineteenth century was the heated controversy surrounding the proposal to award lifetime grants to writers – most notably, to Alexander Kielland. Henrik Ibsen and Bjørnstjerne Bjørnson left their marks on the cultural life of the nation for a long time. Bjørnson, in particular, was inextricably linked with the concept of nationhood. The author of the national anthem was every Norwegian's ideal of a writer; strong, proud, an idealist in the fight for justice and independence, committed in every way; and he ensured that a wide range of issues came up for discussion.

The fact that language-based literary forms rose in popularity was due to the struggle for linguistic identity between Danish, *nynorsk* (neo-Norwegian) and the native dialects. In the period prior to Norway's independence in 1905, literature and theatre were closely bound up with nation-building, and they still receive the largest state subsidies of all. Other art forms, among them modern art and classical music, do not assume the same national importance; popular music is generally left to market forces and physical art forms, such as ballet, are eclipsed by sport. We are a nation of readers but the focus on books, publication politics and writers far exceeds the number of books actually bought. The Bjørnsonian ideal or expectation that something extra is required of writers, that they have to leave their mark on the Norwegian nation, stands out as a literary imperative. Indeed, some of the fury in the legal battle fought over Knut Hamsun after the Second World War was brought about by the expectation that a writer was supposed to fight for good causes and educate the people.

### The Culture of health

In the postwar years the state played a big part in fostering Norwegian cultural life. To this end it has used culture – and culture has used the state. Norwegian cultural policy rests firmly on the belief that culture is healthy and good for the people. In a court case against Agnar Mykle, who was accused of obscenity in his novel *Sangen om den røde rubin* (The Song of the Red Ruby) in the 1950s, the Director-General of Public Health was called as an expert witness. The marching band represents a good healthy model in that it effectively combines music and sport; what is more, the musicians develop their skills in the open air. Culture flourishes in Norway in the summer months, festivals and outdoor performances being held all over the country. We can enjoy a cultural experience and at the same time be outside in the sun in natural surroundings. Plays are staged in quarries and on beaches; music is played on islands and grassy slopes. If one is fortunate one can enjoy open-air theatre in northern Norway at temperatures of twenty degrees below zero. It can be so cold that the audience has to be moved around on animal hides so that they do not freeze to the ice.

When Norwegians hear the word 'culture' they tend to put on their skis and head for the mountains. Holiday brochures from 2001 present Norway as a sanatorium, an antidote to illnesses brought on by modern lifestyles. A trip to Norway regenerates stressed-out, lifestyle-weary Continentals and overweight Americans. Norway is the 'green' prescription for tourists. Unlike the Danes and Finns, who have a high profile in design, architecture and technology, the Norwegians' cultural treasures are carved in rock. Nature itself is the artist. When Princess Märtha Louise and her writer husband, Ari Behn, were photographed for the sophisticated American magazine *Vanity Fair,* they were shown wearing original Norwegian knitted sweaters and sitting on fur rugs in the snow.

National culture is inextricably linked with the welfare state in its social-democratic ideology of equality. After the war, the political parties acted in concert to democratize culture, to break down the elitist barriers that prevented the people from enjoying art. Culture could be used to give meaning to people's increasing amount of leisure. The state set out to encourage sporting and cultural activities, to help individuals exercise their right to self-realization. Important national cultural projects were started in the postwar years – with the founding of Riksteatret (National Touring Theatre) in 1948, Riksgalleriet (National Touring Gallery) in 1952, Rikskonsertene (National Touring Concerts) in 1967, the Norwegian Broadcasting Corporation's national television service in 1960 and the Norwegian Writers' Centre in 1968. Art was on the move. Providing information and education for the people was at the heart of these initiatives. Culture was an integral part of the Social Democrats' aspirations in regard to social levelling, fair shares for all, welfare and democratization.

**At arm's length**

The state's cultural policy was set out in parliamentary reports – *kulturmeldinger* (Cultural Affairs Reports) as they came to be called. At the outset the state was more concerned with the provision of culture than with its content. The aim was to provide individuals with access to culture regardless of where in the country they lived. On a social level this policy has been a great success, with a high level of participation in cultural activities in both town and country. However, as a result of remuneration agreements and grants the state gradually evolved into a major customer for producers of art, music and literature, so someone had to take responsibility for content. *Norsk Kulturråd* (Norwegian Arts Council) was set up in 1965 to distribute funding over and above the state budget. Based on an idea developed by Britain's Arts Council, the 'arm's-length' funding principle is an important one in Norwegian cultural policy. Politicians make funding available; the artists – through councils and organizations – distribute the money. This has given arts organizations greater political and practical power than in many other countries. In recent years, however, the policy of supporting the arts without necessarily questioning the result has been the subject of some debate.

Tension between town and country led to the building of arts centres all over Norway. Stages, concert halls and libraries burgeoned, spreading both happiness and headaches. Arts centres are difficult institutions to manage, and it is not always easy to say what they should be used for. A notable feature of the culture debate in Norway is that it tends to turn on localizing issues: which town should host the Ibsen Museum, where did Hamsun really come from and where in Oslo should the Opera House and museums be situated?

Scepticism of elitism in art permeates Norwegian politics. Major public investment in the Opera House and symphony orchestras is more controversial than spending money designated for culture on local sports teams. This lack of faith in the value of culture is reflected in the organization of the Ministry of Culture and Church Affairs. Dealing with the arts is not seen as a worthy full-time occupation for a senior minister, and accordingly the minister's time is dispersed over several areas of responsibility, including the Church and sport.

**In a superficial age,** author Dag Solstad defends the right of literature to pose questions of great moment. In his novel **Genanse og verdighet** (Shyness and Dignity), Elias Rukla, a teacher feels himself a subordinate figure in his own life.

There was great disillusionment in the sixties when it was discovered that information was not enough to convert people into enthusiastic patrons of the arts. Although people had the time and money, they did not automatically go to galleries and the theatre. In the seventies, there was growing concern that the system for grants and funding influenced the content of culture. The 1973 'Cultural Affairs Report' introduced an extended definition of culture, which meant that almost all leisure activities, from swimming to youth clubs, were defined as culture. It was an attempt to adapt to what people actually did in their free time rather than an attempt to say what they should do. This extended definition of culture had some bizarre consequences, as when, in the eighties, Gran local authority twice bestowed the Culture Prize on a horse and, as late as 1997, the county of Østfold awarded a football coach its annual Culture Prize.

Nineteen seventy-five was the year that artists were welcomed into normal society. The Storting (parliament) awarded benefits to people who made their living in the arts, along with the right to negotiate their working conditions on a par with other professional groups. Artists may have been demystified but many such also found themselves much better off. Some five hundred people currently receive a stipend from the state that guarantees them a minimum sum for life. The 1983 'Cultural Affairs Report' linked culture and business and encouraged private funding. In 1991 the Report set out to bring cultural and business policies still closer together and the word 'quality' was used for the first time. Now it is no longer elitism but market forces that give politicians in the Ministry of Culture and Church Affairs the greatest cause for concern.

Reading, listening to music, support for art galleries and theatres, even support for Norwegian films, are on the increase, though people do not always exhibit good taste. The administrative role of the state comes under attack if state theatres with 85 per cent backing put on a lighter repertoire than private theatres, or when Norwegian films are made in English. One political development is 'Den kulturelle skolesekken' (The cultural schoolbag). The idea behind the 'schoolbag' is that all Norwegian schoolchildren shall have the right to attend performances by professional artists on a regular basis and that such performances will be financed by state-sponsored lotteries and similar means. There are plans to expand the programme in the period to 2005 and NOK 180 million has been earmarked for the 'schoolbag' annually. In a Norwegian cultural context this is a considerable sum of money.

### Literature: The Fury of the Minor Character

*In the break he stood out in the schoolyard at Fagerborg High School, trying to open his umbrella. But he couldn't. Hundreds of children were milling around him and some of them must have noticed him. Now he had had enough! He stormed over to the water fountain and in his fury belaboured it with his umbrella.*

Elias Rukla, a character in Dag Solstad's novel *Genanse og verdighet* (Shyness and Dignity), is a teacher in his fifties with a fondness for the bottle. He is the awkward anti-hero who loses his grip on both the bigger and smaller issues in life. In a moment of insight he captures the deeper meaning of a dialogue in Ibsen's *Vildanden* (The Wild Duck), but is sidetracked by noisy, inattentive pupils who have no interest in their literary heritage.

Dag Solstad's basic storyline is reminiscent of one of Agnar Mykle's novels about an insecure man who does not know how to behave with people. *Genanse og verdighet* has been described as the story of a minor character. Elias Rukla is obsessed by one of Ibsen's minor characters, Dr Relling, perhaps because he is one himself. Dag Solstad's novels illustrate a clear line of development in Norwegian literature. From writing strongly committed political novels in the seventies, around the turn of the millennium Solstad turned his attention to portrayal of this disillusioned man who still has his dreams. Rukla feels superfluous in society and delves deeply into himself to examine his soul. Although the story has specific resonance for a particular generation and social milieu, it also has a universal meaning. *Genanse og verdighet* may be seen as a commentary on intellectual life, or the lack thereof, in Norway. Solstad's novel fulfils literature's duty to ask critical questions in a superficial age. Its author was awarded the Nordic Council's literary prize, but his name is noticeably absent from the group of most-translated Norwegian writers. At a time when Norwegian literature is blossoming and such varied writers as Jostein Gaarder, Linn Ullmann, Lars Saabye Christensen and Jan Kjærstad have been translated into several languages, Solstad communicates best with Norwegians.

At the beginning of the new millennium Norwegian literature is thriving in a way that the literature of its Scandinavian neighbours is not. We like to read, and we have strong story-

**Linn Ullmann's authorship** ranges far and wide and displays a willingness to tackle serious issues. In her novel **Nåde** (Mercy) she discusses what it means to die a 'dignified' death.

**To show** where the power lies, in many of her novels Hanne Ørstavik explores family relationships.

telling traditions. Hamsun, Ibsen, Garborg, Skram and Mykle are more than just obligatory reading at school. If we are to believe the column 'På nattbordet' (Bedside Reading) in the business newspaper *Dagens Næringsliv*, large numbers of Norwegian business people burn the midnight oil re-reading Hamsun. Unlike in many other countries, the top positions in the bestseller list are occupied by national writers, and when a café in Stavanger invited writers to read their complete novels aloud, people turned up in droves to listen, staying until the early hours of the morning.

*Tiden det tar* (The Time It Takes) is the title of a novel by Hanne Ørstavik, and perhaps there is something in the title. Here on the peaceful fringe of Europe we still have a little time, the time required for reading. There is a Sámi story about a man from the city who is waiting for a man from the tundra. When he arrives two hours late, the city dweller says: 'I haven't got much time. Why are you so late?' The Sámi replies: 'If you're so busy, why didn't you come yesterday?'

We read, then, more than people in other countries. One of the reasons is the book club system, which distributes quality literature to members' homes. If the major book clubs buy a novel, the writer is assured of being read. A second reason is the network of financial support, of which the state purchasing agreement for literature is the cornerstone: the Norwegian Arts Council buys in what is adjudged to be quality literature and distributes a thousand copies of each title to libraries up and down the country free of charge. This agreement guarantees access for the reading public and security for the publishers, who are thus enabled to take chances with smaller authorships. The publishing industry, however, is at present experiencing a time of great change. The purchasing agreement, VAT exemption and fixed prices are all the subject of keen debate. Three large publishing houses dominate the market, supplemented by the group De Norske Bokklubbene, which is owned by two of the three. Small, enterprising publishing houses are being bought up by the bigger companies. A third reason may be the writing courses run by newer educational institutions that have spawned and inspired at least one generation of writers. On top of that, we are a small nation with one, or rather two, minority languages, and we are constantly striving to understand ourselves in relation to others. The fact that we have two languages may divide our literature, but it also enriches it. Two different traditions exist side by side, reminding us daily that Norway is a long, narrow strip of land composed of mountains that divide us and fjords that unite us.

In an allusion to four older writers (Ibsen *et al.*), Dag Solstad, Jan Kjærstad, Kjartan Fløgstad and Herbjørg Wassmo were called 'The New Big Four' in the nineties, and this generation of writers still has an enormous impact on the literary scene in Norway. They are writers who describe various aspects of Norwegian life: from the smelters of the west and floods in the east to the fate of strong women in the north and the dream that could link the southern suburbs of Oslo to Samarkand.

Living in paradise is fine, but it is also rather dull. Ibsen had to go to Italy to write and there is a direct line out into the world from Kjartan Fløgstad's Latin America, via Axel Jensen's Sahara and Ola Bauer's Northern Ireland, to Ari Behn's fascination with gay bars in Tangiers. We are what Arne Garborg calls 'jærbuer og europeere'. We look for thrills in the crime genre, which is particularly popular in this quiet, affluent country, a vicarious drama imbued with social criticism and social realism. Crime fiction has become a kind of modern regional writing, with the hero and the plot very much part of the local scene. 'Queen of Crime' is now a recognized concept in Norwegian in the wake of such international crime successes as Karin Fossum, Unni Lindell and Anne Holt.

Many of the new generation of writers have chosen to write about family and personal relations in preference to writing about society. The children of the '68 generation use everyday ultra-realistic details to tell their stories in a near-claustrophobic style. Powerful descriptions of growing up permeate Norwegian literature, with Per Petterson, Niels Frederik Dahl and Lars Amund Vaage as recent award-winning examples. More recently there has been a renewed tendency to link literature more closely with politics. Furthermore, there is a keenness to discuss bigger issues, such as death. Linn Ullmann's *Nåde* (Mercy), Merete Morken Andersen's *Hav av tid* (Oceans of Time) and Jon Fosse's *Dødsvariasjoner* (Variations on Death) came out at more or less the same time in the nineties.

### The play: When Someone Comes

HE:
You and I alone
SHE:
Not just alone
but alone together
Our house
In this house we can be together
you and I
alone together
HE:
And no one shall come

A man and a woman travel deep into the country to be 'alone together', although they are in constant fear that 'someone will come'. They share the feeling of being alone; and both of them are indeed alone: though they are together, each of them is alone within the relationship. They nurture the romantic dream of fusing into the other person entirely but they both know that this will not happen – because someone will indeed come.

Jon Fosse gives the eternal triangle, that old dramatic construct, a new language in which the unsaid is as important as what is said. We may aim for perfection in our lives but Fosse demonstrates the splendour of failure. Every sentence, every scene, is about not achieving one's aim, not getting through to the other person. The words become ritual incantations and function in the same way that music does. Fosse's characters feel shut out and invite loneliness to join them; they strive to repair relationships without knowing what has gone wrong. Jon Fosse describes to perfection the Norwegian sense of loneliness, the reticence of western Norway, where pauses and repetition have their own significance. At the same time he appeals to something universal in us. In fact, he has been translated into 24 languages and his plays are currently being performed on 115 stages in Europe. Regional writing has gone international.

Jon Fosse is the hater of theatre who became the King of Drama in the short span of ten years. He made his debut at Den Nationale Scene in Bergen in 1994 with *Og aldri skal vi skiljast* (And Never Will We Be Parted). His first play, *Nokon kjem til å komme* (Someone Will Come), was performed at Det Norske Teater immediately afterwards. Fosse has been hailed as the new Ibsen, and from a thematic point of view the two dramatists do

**In the works** of author and playwright Jon Fosse, what is not said is often just as important as what is said. He draws attention to the nobility inherent in failure and touches on the Norwegian sense of loneliness.

**Nature provides** the background for many of the pageants and festivals that are a feature of Norway in the summer. The pageant at Stiklestad, where King Olav II Haraldsson (St Olav) was killed, is an annual event.

have obvious similarities: for example, both frequently deal with family relationships. However, whereas Ibsen sets his plots in a social context, Fosse seems only to be interested in the inner drama. His style may appear gloomy but he is fundamentally a humanist and there is often an open ending. Beckett portrayed people waiting, possibly for death, while in Fosse's plays someone does comes. It is possible to see a development from Fosse's earliest plays to his more recent ones: characters talk to each other instead of to themselves; they seek out someone instead of withdrawing; they allow themselves to be seen instead of hiding. His plays are about the fate of individuals, but their fate is determined by chance occurrences, by isolated fragments of time. Thus his dramas are quite different from the psychological, conflict-based plays that have dominated the stage, particularly in Scandinavia and northern Europe.

Norwegian theatre has a long tradition of psychological realism, much like its literature. The complicated relationships between parent and child, man and woman, lie at the heart of it. There is little political theatre. However, Ibsen, chastiser of society, has bequeathed the imperative that issues have to be taken up and dealt with; plays should have teeth and targeted energy. Henrik Ibsen has left an indelible mark on all Norwegian writing, which is littered with allusions to *livsløgner* ('life-lies'), *gennemsnittsmennesker* (average people), *bøyger man går udenom* (obstacles one circumvents), *sådant gjør man ikke* (one doesn't do that kind of thing) and *den står sterkest, som står alene* (he stands strongest who stands alone). Hedda, Nora and Peer have become archetypes of our narrative tradition. Ibsen's influence on Norwegian theatre can be seen in the use of the retrospective narrator and linguistic realism. He showed that tragedies could occur in middle-class sitting rooms and were not confined to the kings and heroes of Greek drama. A biannual Ibsen Festival is held at the National Theatre and his plays continue to be performed regularly on all Norwegian stages.

The standard Anglo-American repertoire also appears on our stages, interspersed with classic European drama. Shakespeare has been successfully transposed, notably into *Nynorsk*, and there is something about Chekhov's birch trees and loneliness that appeals to Norwegians. Modernist trends in European theatre have had little impact in Norway. It is remarkable that theatre, which in itself is a meeting place between differing modes of expression and genres, is the most isolated of all arts in Norway. There are few visiting productions from abroad and there is little indication on the stage of the multicultural changes that are taking place in Norwegian towns.

Modern writers have to a large extent abandoned the theatre. Younger writers more often write for the screen. Today the theatre is primarily an arena for actors and directors. In the first ten years of the National Theatre's existence, between 50 and 100 per cent of performances were premieres or relatively new Norwegian plays. A hundred years later that figure is down to 5 per cent, which means that the theatre has lost the nation-building function it previously shared with literature. However, the labour movement has a strong tradition of theatre, and what remains of the general educational ideal is to be found in school performances for reluctant teenagers. The postwar educational ideology is reflected in children's theatre: Karius (Caries) and Baktus (Bacterium) taught children to clean their teeth; robbers had to become good people and conform to the laws of Cardamom Town; and a clever little mouse in Hakkebakke Forest was able to cajole a fox into eating a carrots.

Institutionalization of theatres has been stronger in Norway than in neighbouring Scandinavian countries, where independent theatre companies developed alongside the permanent theatres. The main reason for this is that five regional theatres were founded in the seventies – in Tromsø, Molde, Skien, Førde and Mo i Rana – and run with idealism and a passion for innovation. Smaller stages for experimental drama were also opened in

**Never overly popular** in Norway, modern dance was practised by only a handful of enthusiasts until Bergen-based Carte Blanche brought about a change and began to attract a wider audience.

the institutional theatres. Radical new trends were addressed and touring companies were despatched from the plush auditorium of the flagship itself, the National Theatre. Regional theatre was established under collective management and had its roots in the community. Newly written plays had titles written in the local vernacular. The result of this revitalization of institutions was that there were very few independent drama groups in Norway. By way of comparison, in 1970 there was only one such group in Norway while there were seventy in Sweden. Competing with the institutions for state funding was like David fighting Goliath. This was felt most keenly by the dancing profession because the central institution, Den Norske Opera (The Norwegian Opera), had not been through the same modernization process as the theatres had. Anyone trained in modern dance had to turn to independent companies, at least until Carte Blanche was formed in Bergen in the 1990s.

But people do go to the theatre. Today in Oslo there are approximately 3,000 seats in private theatres and 4,500 in state-owned theatres, including Black Box, an experimental theatre. Three private theatres have opened in Bergen in recent years and Fredrikstad, Tønsberg, Sandefjord and Stavanger all have seasonally run private theatres. Home-grown humour is a crowd-puller. 'Oluf', a much-loved comic figure in Norway, was created by Arthur Arntzen, who has been appointed Professor of Humour at Tromsø University. Debates about humour are front-page newspaper material, and stand-up comedy can be found on the smallest of stages in basement theatres. TV comedians have set new standards for what is acceptable language on

**Bent Hamer's film Salmer fra kjøkkenet** (Hymns from the Kitchen) centres on the inadmissible friendship between two elderly men, one a visiting Swede come to study kitchens, the other a rural loner.

the stage, and faint traces of our multicultural population are now beginning to appear in the relatively homogeneous Norwegian cultural landscape.

The average Norwegian's innate scepticism of elitism in culture manifested itself in the debate that rumbled on for many years prior to the decision to build a new opera house in Oslo. 'Should we have opera at all?' it was asked. 'Should we spend billions of public money on a new opera house? If so, for whom?' 'Wouldn't the money be better spent on expanding the road network in the west?' The dramatic nature of opera runs counter to Norwegian perceptions of popular culture – though having said that, there is a ninety per cent uptake of tickets for opera performances in Oslo generally and opera in Kristiansund has a broad social appeal. The opera controversy has been as much about local politics and traffic planning as about culture. There is more discussion of the plans for regulating traffic around the building site for the opera house than there is of the inaugural performances. For Den Norske Opera, however, the move to a new home means that they can triple the number of performances they put on, increase the ensemble and expand the repertoire.

There is similar resistance to modern dance. This may be traceable to traditional Christian attitudes, which regard dance as sinful; or perhaps we find it difficult to accept the refined aestheticism of ballerinas in a culture where our heroines are marathon runners or skiing champions. The idea that physical development is healthy is accepted in all areas of life, but aesthetics takes second place. Nevertheless, in recent years creative new choreographers have made their mark in areas such as musicals, drama, classical ballet and pure modern dance in the style of Merce Cunningham and Martha Graham. Our narrative tradition has also influenced several modern choreographers: Kjersti Alveberg has used old Norse legends for her ballets, while Jo Strømgren found inspiration in football and has lent physical expression to characters from Ibsen.

### Film: Kitchen-sink Surrealism

*Two men in an old kitchen. One of them makes coffee, drinks it quietly and smokes a pipe. The other man watches him from a high stool in the corner and records his movements on a diagram. Swedish kitchen research has come to a rural Norwegian community to observe local bachelors.*

*The results will be used to maximize the efficiency of the housewife's movements so that she does not have to 'walk to Africa' in the course of a year to serve up food; instead she will only have to 'walk to northern Italy'.*

In Bent Hamer's film *Salmer fra kjøkkenet* (Stories from the Kitchen), a small Norwegian community in the fifties is woken up by the sound of people arriving. They are Swedes. They break the stillness of a deserted country road as they drive in convoy towing caravans. The Swedes are the strangers, the outside world. There is a premonition of a culture clash in the arrival scene when the leader of the Swedish research team feels faint and ill; he is, after all, used to left-hand driving. Hamer's film is one of the highpoints in a heyday of Norwegian cinema. It is a highly individual, deeply personal film, portraying the fragile friendship between lonely old men, the same theme as in the director's debut film, *Eggs*.

The anti-hero has always played a key role in Norwegian films, as in Norwegian literature, from cartoon characters like Reodor Felgen, Solan and the fearful Ludvig via children's films in which the hero is the girl who stands alone and through to figures like Roy, the strange, insignificant postman in *Budbringeren* (Junk Mail) and Stig Inge in *Buddy*, the computer nerd who is wary of venturing further than his local shopping centre. There is a little of Elling in them all. Life is a struggle as they deal with their own psychological problems and with conflict with others. In the thriller-like *Insomnia*, the spotlight is as much on the detective who cannot sleep in a Tromsø bathed in the light of the Midnight Sun as on the crime he is investigating. Even Norwegian TV ads, which regularly attract international prizes and are what most film directors live off, focus on the anti-hero. 'People think life is less complicated in smaller places,' Jonny Vang, the earthworm breeder in the eponymous film, says. 'They're wrong. You still have to make choices, and if you make a wrong choice, you're in trouble.'

Norway came late to film-making. We have had no Ingmar Bergman to found a film school. Both the Swedes and the Danes were quick to adapt to the new medium, building prestigious training institutions and introducing state funding. It took time for this Hollywood-dominated mass medium to find its place in Norwegian cultural policy. For a long time profits from popular films were used to finance schools and leisure activities. Despite the efforts of early pioneers such as Arne Skouen and Edith Calmar, and successful comedies and thrillers, Norwegian films have suffered from a bad reputation among cinema-goers. It was not easy for them to make their own mark with untrained directors and actors when Hollywood had so much of everything, and attempts to describe everyday life in Norway met with a mixed reception. In his lampooning *Nytt fra norsk film* (Norwegian Film News) satirist Ole Paus summed up the typical Norwegian film in these words: 'Father sits on a sofa from Ikea, hitting Mother.'

Norwegian cinema is not like that any more. Confidence has increased along with an awareness of form and greater technical expertise. There is no ambition in Norwegian films to change the world, as there is in Swedish cinema, and there are few political films. Our films have more in common with Finnish cinema, which tends to feature disoriented and insecure people in alien surroundings, though Norwegians do not share the Finnish proclivity for melancholy. The description of life in the country in Norwegian films has been criticized for falling into one of two traps: Bjørnsonian peasant romanticism or the narrow-minded yokel. More recently, however, films about country people have shown more sophistication. *Jonny Vang* is a portrayal of a wayward, intrinsically optimistic person from a scenic but claustrophobic rural community who tries to unravel the tangles in his life by stumbling through relationships, each more complex than the last.

Modern Norwegian cinema first emerged in the seventies. The film historian Peter Cowie puts the date of its birth as 1 March 1971, which was when Anja Breien's *Voldtekt* (Rape) was released. Perhaps it was only to be expected that the film would take its theme from an area in which Norway has led the world – sexual equality. The films from this era were notable for socially committed directors like Anja Breien, Vibeke Løkkeberg and Laila Mikkelsen. The *Hustruer* (Housewives) trilogy drew on women's issues spanning three decades. Nowadays, such strong, multi-faceted women generally appear in historical epics based on novels, such as Kristin in Liv Ullmann's film version of Sigrid Undset's *Kristin Lavransdatter*, Dina in *Jeg er Dina* (Dina's Book), which was based on Herbjørg Wassmo's novel, and Petra the fisher girl in Bjørnson's novella *Det største i verden* (The Biggest in the World). All three women rebel against society's expectations of women and to some degree become outcasts: Kristin has to cope with Erlend's deceit; Dina is blamed for her mother's death and is rejected by her father; and Petra has to flee town after unfortunate associations with three men.

Although many Norwegian writers write directly for film, there are few substantial roles for women in contemporary drama. Children's roles are better – the typical children's film features children as complete characters with some depth, frequently outsiders. Stories about children growing up, as in Lars Saabye Christensen/ Erik Gustavson's *Herman,* show the problems of being slightly different in a homogeneous society like Norway.

Documentaries are very popular with younger filmmakers. Personal experiences of gender and of family life have been themes of films that have reached wider audiences.

One would imagine that nature would play a significant part in Norwegian films, but it is predominantly used simply as background. On occasion, nature sets the scene for the action, particularly in larger productions such as the films of Hamsun's work. There is hardly a rock on Hamarøy, where Hamsun spent his childhood years, that has not been filmed. Nils Gaup's *Veiviseren* (Pathfinder) was considered exotic by Norwegians and non-Norwegians alike. Made in the style of a Western, it was about a Sámi boy in northern Norway and included elements of shamanism. It was as much a fantasy tale to Oslo filmgoers as it was to filmgoers in New York. The capricious and brutal sides of nature come to the fore in the films of Knut Erik Jensen. Finnmark plays a major role in both his documentaries and feature films. Hence human beings are vulnerable and at the mercy of nature; they live far from the seat of power and are marked by the past. What they want, though, is not revolt, but respect and acknowledgement. *Heftig og begeistret* (Cool and Crazy), a documentary about the Berlevåg men's choir, was as much a portrait of a coastal community as of the choir's colourful characters. By comparison, hardly any films have been made about Oslo. The town/country debate may seem typically Norwegian but it is also universal: civilization is contrasted with wilderness in westerns, thrillers and dramas the world over.

The blossoming of Norwegian film has led to debate about financial support and the circumstances surrounding film production. It is important to maintain a certain volume, as public interest increases according to the number of good films around. Norsk filmfond (Norwegian Film Fund) was set up in 2001 and replaced the state film-production company, Norsk Film A/S. This constituted a modernization and professionalization of the Norwegian film industry – rumour had it that only Norway and Albania still maintained state film-production companies. Independent film producers receive direct funding, on a 50/50 public–private basis, and film consultants who assess individual applications have seen their workloads reduced. Belated though it was, the founding of a film school in Lillehammer was very welcome and has led to a perceptible improvement in all aspects of film work. Audiences have noticed a new lightness in Norwegian cinema and a broader view of the world. Multicultural issues are finally making their appearance in Norwegian films.

**Bjarne Melgaard** uses powerful, personal forms of expression in his art, which encompasses paintings, drawings, videos and structures of various kinds.

## Art: Identity and Passion

*A German said to me: But you don't have to suffer with your pains. I answered: They belong to me and my art. I wish to retain my suffering.*

Edvard Munch

In modern Norwegian art Munch's legacy has been to influence the choice of subjects rather than a set of attitudes, and perhaps the artist who today has inherited most of Munch's passion is Bjarne Melgaard. He exposes his spiritual and sexual life and merges sex with death, sex-related crime and pain. Melgaard is a maximalist, maintaining that minimalism is to blame for everything that has gone wrong in his life. Going to a Melgaard exhibition is a visual shock. Everything is to excess. The walls are plastered with photographs, handwritten notes, plastic bags and cuttings from magazines. Sculptures lie prone on the floor, or stand still packed in their boxes. There are objects everywhere: books, coconuts, underpants, Gucci suits. Like many contemporary artists he likes to play with his identity and calls himself Casanova, Joey Stefano and Rudolph Valentino. He rebels against the white walls of museums, he scribbles and doodles, recruits sponsors and wastes not a moment on grants. Although Melgaard is very precise about his compositions, they look unfinished. As a spectator, you feel yourself a voyeur looking at the uncomfortably intimate details of a stranger's life.

Bjarne Melgaard's work is so powerful that he has been reported to the police in three countries; he is a rebel who has broken with what is artistically acceptable. He feels like an outsider, outside of polite society (although he is adored as a genuine *enfant terrible*) and lonely in a crowd. Paradoxically, Melgaard's explosive art has made him Norway's most successful contemporary artist on the international scene. Reactions to his work have been similar to the reactions to Munch's work in the previous century. Looking at Munch's pictures is like reading a disturbing and personal diary. It is a '*blottelse av sjelelige fenomener*' (baring of the soul), as Munch himself expressed it, and the Munch museum is one of Oslo's biggest tourist attractions. When '*Skrik*' (The Scream) was stolen, it was as if the nation had lost a child. Melancholy, discord, fear and an ability to condense human life are features of Munch's painting that have a profound impact on Norwegians, yet modern art is one of the few areas that still creates controversy in Norway. People become very heated about public art and even stalk out of galleries in disgust. The 'Cultural Affairs Report' in 2003 tried to anticipate this reaction by asking the rhetorical question: *Is it art?*

*When abstraction reaches the point where a couple of paint strokes represent a finished piece of work, many will seriously question whether it can be called art. In addition, art has moved even further towards phenomena that have nothing to do with painting or sculpture, such as performance art, installation art and so-called concept art. These can challenge anyone's idea of what art is.*

When the Ministry of Culture and Church Affairs, which is the designated provider of public funding for art, expresses itself in this way, it is not surprising that people living a long way from the capital are occasionally ruffled. One of the biggest public art projects in Norway's history, 'Kulturlandskap Nordland' (Cultural Landscape of the North), was started in 1988 and attracted international attention. Every local authority in the region was offered a sculpture by a recognized contemporary artist. Thirty-three local authorities accepted. Many sculptures were placed in natural settings, others in town centres. In some areas local people felt so patronized by the élite's idea of art and mass education that they campaigned to have the sculptures removed. In other areas, the works of art were well-received, especially if they had a naturalistic theme. This reflected the general view that it should be easy to see what a sculpture represents. Ten years later, one hundred rusting men were placed on a long sandy beach outside Stavanger, marching into the sea. The sculptures were metal casts taken from Anthony Gormley's body and were intended as a comment on human rights issues before a big oil conference in 1998. Local people threatened to pepper the sculptures with their shotguns, but passions eventually cooled; more than one hundred thousand people went to see the display. The sculptures are no longer threatened by controversy, but by lack of local-authority funding.

The eighties saw a new direction in stone sculpture. Granite acquired a different status after being associated for many years with Vigeland's sculptures in Oslo and war memorials. Many Norwegian sculptors went to Italy to work with marble and a number of architects began to use natural rock to embellish public buildings. Kristian Blystad, Bård Breivik and Nico Widerberg's sculptures are now a feature of many squares, lobbies, palatial buildings and even ocean liners.

**Artist Jan Groth** draws a simple line with the intention of making it 'vibrate'.

The Nordic light is special. In the nineties an exhibition, *Nuits Blanches*, was organized in Paris with light as its theme. Norway's links with the sea and forests are still apparent in art, long after the demise of such romantics as J.C. Dahl, Adolph Tidemand and Hans Gude. Kåre Tveter uses light and the colours of light in his abstract paintings. Ørnulf Opdahl painted in his atelier with large windows overlooking the island of Godøy outside Ålesund and the shifting shades of light at the mouth of the fjord are still to be seen in his work. Kjell Nupen draws on the sea, nature and elements of old Norwegian handicrafts in his modern paintings. Perhaps there is also something peculiarly Nordic about Ida Lorentzen's 'portraits' of deserted space. Per Inge Bjørlo's installations of crushed glass and strong

light link thematically with both Norwegian landscapes and Munch's sense of unease. With a nod to Munch, who did the same, the painter and sculptor Kjell Erik Killi Olsen hung his paintings out to dry and harden. The difference is that Killi Olsen lived on a small island in the Oslo fjord and ended up having to fish his pictures out of the sea with a landing-net!

A common quirk of several contemporary artists is to include allusions to the work of other artists in their own. Mari Slaattelid, the first female artist to have her own exhibition in the prestigious Astrup Fearnley Museum in Oslo, photographs Lars Hertervig's romantic landscape paintings and gives them a new focus with the reflection of the flash in the picture. Slaatelid plays with such expressions of femininity as cosmetics advertisements; she photographs her daughter wearing a facemask and associates the red of the lipstick with her body and shame. As with most forms of expression, the search for identity is an obvious feature of recent Norwegian art. The photographer Vibeke Tandberg, for example, consistently appears as someone else in her work. Using digital manipulation techniques, she places herself in a parodying role: as a bride, as pregnant, as a labourer, as twins and as an old man. She plays with the idea of the photograph as a representation of reality. Video art, which made its breakthrough in Norwegian art in the nineties, often deals with how we relate to our bodies, gender and identity. Many artists use their own bodies in their work and question our perception of reality and the world as we see it.

With his paintings of hermaphrodites, amputated bodies, women relieving themselves and a portrait of himself with an erect penis, Odd Nerdrum is an extreme and highly provocative figure in Norwegian art; not, primarily, because of his choice of subject but on account of his mode of expression. Nerdrum distanced himself from the leading trends in modern art and went back to Caravaggio and Rembrandt. He soon became the best-known anti-modernist painter in Norway and formed his own school. He is constantly in opposition and has been subjected to severe criticism. However, when the Astrup Fearnley Museum painted the walls olive green and filled all its rooms with

**Like Edvard Munch**, Kjell Erik Killi Olsen left his paintings outside to dry and weather. **The work of Anthony Gormley**, this rusting iron man on Sola beach is one of a hundred making their way into the sea. **Kjell Nupen's painting** incorporates elements drawn from the sea and skerries he knows so well.

**Odd Nerdrum** is a controversial painter, primarily because of his form language, which in the debate surrounding him tends to overshadow his dramatic choice of subjects.

Nerdrum's pictures, a record number of visitors attended the exhibition. Nerdrum achieved his breakthrough in the USA in the mid-eighties, the main topic of discussion there being the content of his pictures. In Norway it is still the artistic expression that causes offence. He has now moved to Iceland – the landscape is recognizable in his pictures – a kind of echo of the Viking rebels of old who fled as far west as possible.

Artists' organizations are strong in Norway. They have run their own subsidized galleries around the country, sat on financing committees and up until a few years ago were quite vociferous about which works of art should be purchased for the large art institutions. Norwegian visual artists are both the poorest and the richest proponents of culture in Norway. As independent entities living in a country without any culture of patronage worth mentioning, they are utterly dependent on grants and their own market value. Art institutions are in a period of flux, as the new National Museum of Art – a conglomeration of the National Gallery, the Museum of Contemporary Art, the Museum of Applied Arts and the Architecture Museum – has been given the go-ahead and will be built on one of the country's most exclusive sites, now a car park, in the heart of Oslo. The museum, which is scheduled to open in 2008/09, will encompass a thousand years of Norwegian art and cultural history, the idea being that old and new can be mutually inspiring. Discussions on the national aspects of the gallery are still ongoing. At a time when art has become global, the concept of what is national (not to say nationalistic) is problematic: some claim that art transcends everything and is not nation-building.

### Architecture and Design: Building and Serving the Nation

What builds nations is buildings. The capital of Norway is undergoing an unparalleled period of development; the whole of its southern face to the fjord is being renewed. Norway does little to market its architecture and design, but most visitors arrive at the magnificent airport of Gardermoen. If they are going on to Oslo, an ultra-modern train takes them into the city centre. With the experience of Gardermoen behind them, a consortium of Norwegian architects called Aviaplan won an international competition to design a large airport in Hyderabad, in India. Snøhetta, a company of architects, has attracted worldwide attention for the library in Alexandria, Egypt. A common feature of Norwegian architecture is the use of natural materials and respect for the natural environment of the building. Snøhetta put windows on three sides of the Fisheries Museum in Karmøy so that the fishermen's workplace, the sea, would dominate the rooms. The Nestor of Norwegian architects, Sverre Fehn, achieved fame by elevating Norwegian architecture to 'poetic modernism'. He made a name for himself at the World Exhibition in Venice by building the Nordic Pavilion around real trees. He built the Glacier Museum in Fjærland in Sogn at the foot of the adjacent glacier and used the glacier to form a kind of altar. There are steps, a sort of Jacob's ladder, that one has to climb to reach the observation terrace at the top. The intention is to place the focus on nature. When Fehn was building a house on the edge of a forest on the outskirts of Oslo, he built bridges over the surrounding bilberries so that they would not be harmed.

Denmark, Sweden and Finland have all achieved fame for their modern, clean-cut designs. When Norway hosted the Olympic Games in Lillehammer, runes and rock carvings were what constituted the visual impact, a clear indication that we have more faith in our cultural heritage than in modern design. Such traditional crafts as woodcarving, knife-making, old-style silver jewellery and 'rose painting' live on in traditional craft environments, particularly in the county of Telemark. Our lack of interest in modern design may be accounted for by our always having concentrated on raw materials and because we see design as something 'extra'. Norwegian designers tend to be concerned with solving problems rather than with aesthetics, as functionality enjoys a higher status than appearance. We do not produce as many designer products as our Scandinavian neighbours, nor do we have a national promotional plan, though we do have some high-profile industrial designers who have produced classics such as Cherrox boots and Trip-Trap children's chairs. With support from Queen Sonja, Norsk Form and Norsk Design are endeavouring to change attitudes and increase awareness of the importance of design. The success of teams of designers such as Norway Says has helped to enhance our image and increase our self-confidence.

Per Spook, a fashion designer involved in haute couture in Paris in the eighties and nineties, inspired Norwegian clothes designers. Spook took the Norwegian sporty women's look to Paris and astonished Parisians. Low heels, comfortable clothes, functional femininity – is that *comme il faut*? Pia Myhrvold, one of the next generation in Paris, prioritized functional clothing that was strongly influenced by her background as an artist. Her garments told stories: her French coats, for example, bore prints of Bergen's decorative manhole covers. In her modern collections Julie Skarland used elements from the story of the fairytale princess who lived in the Blue Mountain. However, Norway has no real fashion industry to speak of. Danish designers dominate the market, the Italians, French and Americans supplying the more exclusive garments.

Top: **Bibliotecha Alexandrina** brought the firm of Norwegian architects whose design it was, Snøhetta (Snowcap), to the notice of the world. Bottom: **The design team Norway Says** was awarded the Norwegian Design Committee's Good Design Prize for its 'Hal' suite. The work of **Sverre Fehn**, the Glacier Museum at Fjærland itself stands at the foot of a glacier.

The theatrical rock band **Turboneger** has made a name for itself that extends far beyond Norway's frontiers. **Annbjørg Lien** combines traditional Norwegian music with modern tones. For many people, the sounds brought forth from his saxophone by **Jan Garbarek** are the very epitome of the frozen North. A musician of international repute.

Sámi **Mari Boine** combines her people's chants (joik) and drum with her own distinctive mode of expression to create her highly individual music.

## Music: The Sound of the Great Outdoors

*They lived in a strange land where there was snow both winter and summer, where the sun shone throughout the night in the middle of summer and where, in the middle of winter, the darkness of the night continued through the day. Strange was the land and strange were the people ...*

That is how Ernst Manker describes the mysterious Sámi people on the cover of Mari Boine's CD, *Gávcci jakhejuogu* (Eight Seasons). Boine has given a voice to the frozen north and warmed hearts in the south and west. Her vocal expression is strongly inspired by 'joiking' (monotone Sámi chanting) and overtone singing. Combined with sounds from European, Latin American and African traditions it has become world music. Her voice is often described as pure, authentic, unspoiled and primal. She is Norwegian but critical of things Norwegian. Norwegian is the language of oppression for the Sámi. Mari Boine refused to be an exotic trapping for the Olympic Games in Lillehammer but she did sing 'joiks' and a hymn in Sámi at the wedding of the Crown Prince.

'Joiking' was originally unaccompanied; then came the drum, the beat of which reverberates through Mari Boine's music. There is a basic five-tone scale that we know from many folk tunes, and this gives the music a ritual feel. The 'joik' is a social commentary, the voice of the oppressed. While the integration of multiculturalism has mostly taken place on paper and, where the stage and literature are concerned, has proceeded no further than good intentions, in music it is real and naturally crosses borders. As world music came to Norway via Mari Boine, so she came to Norway via the world; for every record she sells at home, she sells five abroad. Mari Boine takes every opportunity that offers to say that home is not Oslo or Tromsø, but Karasjok in Finnmark or perhaps Paris. Her songs always take the outsider's or the oppressed people's point of view; she is driven by anger, love for her people, nature and a longing for freedom.

After the Olympic Games in 1994 Norwegian romanticism in music blossomed. Herborg Kråkevik became a bestseller with her old Norwegian songbook evergreens and the golden voice of Sissel Kyrkjebø was the very image of the pure mountain stream. These singers may have a touch of international class but there are also many like them out there. The distinctive Norwegian quality is becoming less and less apparent in popular music. Edvard Grieg formed a school in Europe based on his use of folk tunes, and he still occupies a revered place in our musical awareness thanks to his abilities and renown. Indeed, folk music has been the source of many musical meetings. Nowadays on Norwegian radio, however, the music is inspired by American jazz, soul, rock and hip-hop, as is the case in many other countries. The sound of 'Norwegian-ness' is more of a feeling, as in the tones of Jan Garbarek's saxophone, Agnes Buen Garnås' calling songs, Annbjørg Lien's fiddle playing and Röyksopp's lyrical electronica music.

In the late sixties it was only possible to pick up pop music on the radio if you twiddled the knobs feverishly to find Radio Luxembourg. Today, the plethora of channels that exists has changed the musical scene in Norway. 'Norwegians think that commercial, professional, superficial and blatant pop music is the work of the devil while in fact it actually sounds like ABBA,' says the sociologist Kjetil Rolness. While ABBA gave Swedish pop music a shot in the arm, it was ten years before a-ha made it big. They had successes almost all over the world in the 1980s and paved the way for musicians to leave Norwegian shores. The front man, Morten Harket, was uncharacteristic in his posing and behaviour, but a-ha became teenage idols even though the Norwegian ideal has always been to gain recognition from a handful of male guitar-pickers, not adoration from thousands of screaming teenyboppers. As archetypes they were an interesting trio: Harket with his exotic pop-star aura, Magne Furuholmen with his energy and boyish charm and the artistic introvert, Paul Waaktaar Savoy. Anti-heroes have also influenced pop music in their own way, not so much in terms of musical themes but in terms of characters: Norway is the country where Idol-contestant Kurt Nilsen, the plumber with oddly spaced teeth, became a pop star.

a-ha found success abroad and are one of the reasons why English is the primary language for Norwegian singers. A generation with their roots in traditional songs in the eighties created a feel for songs with Norwegian lyrics, featuring names like Lillebjørn Nilsen, Jan Eggum, Åge Aleksandersen and Anne Grete Preus. This encouraged bands like deLillos and the Dum Dum Boys to sing in Norwegian in the 1990s. Kaizers Orchestra has developed an original, offbeat sound as Norwegian texts compete with oil barrels used as drums. The influence of Anglo-American music has always been present, but trends are detected more quickly now on MTV, commercial radio and in an avalanche of magazines; and websites make it easier to pick up new sounds. Lene Marlin, from Tromsø, is popular both in Norway and abroad, yet there is nothing particularly Norwegian about her music. Many musicians have done well abroad: the theatrical band Turboneger has toured the USA and Röyskopp, an electronica band, has won MTV awards for its cool, arctic sound. One oddity is Norwegian bands' ability to distinguish themselves in the unusual niche genre of Black Metal. Confidence among Norwegians is on the up and has enabled bands such as Motorpsycho and Madrugada, and glamorous pop-star types like Morten Abel, to make their mark.

We are a country of music festivals. The Quart festival is Norway's biggest cultural event and packs the southcoast town of Kristiansand with young people holidaying in tents for a week in July. It is followed by Norwegian Wood and the Øya festival. Traditional jazz festivals, like Molde and Kongsberg, live off extensive open-air events. Bob Dylan is reputed to have been so enthusiastic about the tar-smelling log rooms of Romsdal Museum in Molde that doubled as changing rooms for the musicians, that he wanted to take them home with him. Jazz has a much more Norwegian feel to it than rock. Very early on, Germany's Manfred Eicher and ECM, his record company, built a bridge to the world for Norwegian jazz musicians and, strangely, this helped to shape their own music. ECM chose to record Jan Garbarek, Terje Rypdal, Arild Andersen, Jon Christensen and, later, Ketil Bjørnstad and Nils Petter Molvær. What they had in common was a desire not to re-create American jazz but to do something of their own based on improvisation and ethnic inspiration, Norwegian and European folk music and elements of classical music. Garbarek's soprano saxophone and Rypdal's guitar, with their clean-cut tones and clear, simple melodies, inspired reviewers to write about the Northern Lights, ice floes and eagles. Some snigger and call it mountain jazz. Others, British musical reviewers for instance, refer to musicians like Jaga Jazzist, Bugge Wesseltoft and Christian Wallumrød simply as 'Norwave'. The jazz course at Trøndelag Music Conservatory produced an explosion of talent in the late eighties. What is certain is that Norwegian jazz has developed its own sound, unlike Danish jazz. American jazzmen regarded Copenhagen as a sanctuary and influenced Danish jazz to such a degree that it is still marked by American styles such as be-bop. However, despite the international success that Norwegian jazz has enjoyed, this music is still seen as somewhat elitist and does not reach a wider audience in Norway.

One swallow may not make a summer, but one star can make a festival. In the 1990s Norwegian classical musicians made a breakthrough on the international scene. The leading lights, pianist Leif Ove Andsnes and cellist Truls Mørk, brought huge talent and vitality to classical music in Norway. The chamber music festivals in Stavanger and Risør, along with the festival organized by charismatic Arve Tellefsen in Oslo, have become meeting places for top musicians from all over the world. Inspired by the Marlborough festivals in the USA in the 1950s, the chamber music festivals have become events where musicians gather to play together. Attendances are large and the atmosphere youthful and responsive. The Norwegian Chamber Orchestra has had enormous success with a style that is full of

**Classical soloists,** among them Leif Ove Andsnes, made their international breakthrough in the 1990s and continue to attract both performers and audiences to their chamber music festivals.

verve and passion. The small format also allows the audience to have a better appreciation of the soul of each musician. The Oslo Philharmonic was given a tremendous lift when Mariss Jansons became its artistic director and conductor. Thanks to his powerful personality and lofty artistic ambitions, the orchestra moved up several leagues. It is characteristic of Norway that talent can emerge from any corner of the country. The network of local music schools, conservatories and colleges picks up anyone with musical talent and the nerve to make a go of it.

**So that was the view . . .**

*I found myself in a flat I had dreamt about once. A perfectly ordinary block of flats of the type that is often the background for a humdrum life in a small country in the far north.*

What does Elling see through the window? Can he really see paradise?

A hundred years after dissolution of the union, Norwegian cultural life no longer stands in the shadow of Sweden but has an unresolved relationship with Europe and is strongly influenced by the USA. Everyday life in Norway's welfare state produces art that mixes genres and cultivates blends. We have writers who write film manuscripts and play in rock bands, painters who use film and sounds to express themselves, musicians who look for Norwegian roots in African tribal music. This is the global reality reflected in the local community.

And the anti-hero?

Askeladden's descendants live on in Norwegian myths. Suddenly they turn round, hold up what one least expects to see, and triumphantly proclaim:

Here it is, see? I found it!

**In the far north** of Norway, the landscape forms art and art forms the landscape. In 'Skulpturlandskap Nordland' (Sculptural Landscape Nordland) contemporary art blends smoothly into the rugged scenery of northern Norway.

**january** fin serck-hanssen **february** rolf m. aagaard

**march** herdis maria siegert **april** janne solgaard

**may** jens hauge **june** vibeke tandberg

**july** dag alveng **august** rune johansen

**september** knut bry **october** asle svarverud

**november** ingvar moi **december** per berntsen

Gi oss
vårt

Sonola

# EDVARD MUNCH

It was not unusual for the painter Edvard Munch to be seen walking through the streets of Norway's capital city with his eyes strangely narrowed, prompting some of the more courageous passers-by to ask him why he was squinting so.

'I am saving my eyes for something worth seeing,' would be the reply. Munch spoke from painful experience. When he was growing up, he witnessed much that he should have been spared. At the age of five he watched his mother die of tuberculosis. Then, when he was fourteen, his elder sister succumbed to the same disease – something that would haunt him for the rest of his life. He was also often sick himself, plagued by frequent bouts of rheumatic fever and a fear of death and mental illness. He was later to write: 'Illness, madness and death were the dark angels that kept watch over my cradle.'

His father, who fell into gloomy religious meditation after his wife and eldest daughter passed away, wanted Edvard to specialize in hydroelectric engineering, so the boy enrolled at a technical college. But it was not for him. Supported by his aunt, who had stepped into his mother's shoes, he broke off his studies and in 1880, at the age of seventeen, decided to become a painter. Under the influence of Christian Krohg he began as a naturalist, and it was only after visiting Paris in 1885 that he became the Munch the world knows and reveres today. He painted *The Sick Child* as if seen through a veil of tears, and in so doing introduced an entirely new style of painting. It did not catch on – to put it mildly. The newspapers wrote that he painted 'brutish pictures' and 'humbug paintings'. Learned society at the time described his art as 'tasteless and shoddy', 'ugly and unfinished'. Again and again he was rejected by polite society. Close up, anyone could see that it was not rubies, but matchstick heads that the doctor's son had used to do up his shirtfront. When, some years later, in the small town of Åsgårdstrand, Munch encountered one of those who had rejected him, the painter pulled a revolver on the man and forced him to accompany him back to his studio to model for him. 'I just wanted to paint a frightened man,' he explained.

Munch, who customarily carried a gun, was arrested by the police in Oslo's Palace Park, which is open to the public, after threatening with a revolver a crowd of people who were bothering him. On another occasion he took aim and fired at his close friend and colleague, the colourist Ludvig Karsten. By his own account Munch may have missed him by as little as an inch. The capital's bohemians were among the very few who helped and supported him at this time. Munch became an active part of this coterie, soon earning the soubriquet of 'Norway's Bizarro'.

His father's death in 1889 was to be a turning point in his life, as afterwards the painter went to live abroad for some years, mainly in Berlin and Paris. During this period he produced many of his most important paintings, among them his Expressionist breakthrough work *The Scream* (1893). His woodcuts were also considered to be revolutionary. In all, he would go on to produce as many as 700 graphic works. In retrospect people would happily talk about the 'evocative lyrical splendour' and 'musical resonance' in his work, but at the time he was accorded few words of recognition, especially in Norway.

'Had I been compelled to live only in Norway, the Norwegians would most likely have been the death of me before I reached thirty,' Munch declared. He reserved especial contempt for the Oslo newspaper *Aftenposten*, fuming: 'That damned bourgeois rag will certainly never tire of vilifying me.'

The women in Munch's life were far from run-of-the-mill. Strindberg and he fell in love at the same time with a Norwegian woman who was married to a Polish poet, a situation immortalized in Munch's picture *Jealousy*. The conflict was resolved shortly afterwards when the lady in question was shot dead. Later, when he posed for Munch, Strindberg had a concealed revolver to hand for safety's sake. For a while, in Berlin, Munch shared both a garret and a girlfriend with the Norwegian sculptor Gustav Vigeland. This arrangement came to an end when Vigeland tried to kill Munch by throwing a bust down the stairs at him. Thereafter Munch specified on his tax returns for the rest of his life that not a penny of the tax he paid should go to Vigeland.

In 1902 a woman by the name of Tulla Larsen shot off two joints from a finger on Munch's left hand, an episode that was the beginning of an unfortunate phase in the painter's life. He did not dare cross the road without having three stiff drinks inside him, and if he saw a young girl carrying a brown parcel he was convinced that it contained the corpse of a child. He developed the quirk of assaulting people in the street at random.

There is no doubt that the crass criticism, arrests and many scuffles that were his lot contributed to his eventual descent into alcoholism, which was accompanied by paranoia and a nervous breakdown. In 1908 he had himself admitted to Daniel Jacobson's Clinic in Copenhagen for seven months. His health and lifestyle both benefited greatly from his stay there, but many people feel that his art deteriorated in the years that followed. The filmmaker Lars von Trier, who has always found inspiration in Munch, is one of many who think that Doctor Jacobson destroyed Munch as an artist.

What is certain is that his art took a new direction. He began to celebrate life's constructive and progressive forces far more than he had done before. After a fierce dispute, he was commissioned to decorate the Aula (Assembly Hall) of Oslo University, a venue that for many years provided the backdrop to the Nobel Peace Prize award ceremony. His mural there is considered to be one of the most significant works in Norwegian monumental painting.

Munch was never overly fond of his home city, and if he had to travel south, to avoid the capital he would take a boat across the fjord to Moss. When he learned that an Oslo businessman had bought one of the canvases at a showing in London, he immediately closed the exhibition and recalled all the pictures. Thus it was that his well-intentioned words in questionable English at the opening ceremony – 'I wish the exhibition hell' (*hell* is 'luck' in Norwegian) – were destined to come true. His artistic temperament was always unpredictable. Having painted a portrait of the writer Gunnar Heiberg, he proceeded to sell it in Copenhagen for the token sum of 50 øre following a row with the model.

'I paint people as they are, not as they appear. That is why I am branded as immoral,' he explained.

Munch never married. He thought married men tended to end up as soup and gruel; in fact, he saw marriage as a direct threat to a man's life. When taxed about his views, he would say that it was no coincidence that his younger brother had died only six months after getting married. Edvard Munch became an eccentric and solitary man during his years at Ekely, the house on the outskirts of Oslo to which he moved in 1916. Six years might pass before, albeit reluctantly, he would consent to attend a social event, and on such occasions he would feel as if he were in prison. If his housekeeper spoke to him more than once in a month, she would be dismissed.

Munch was very absent-minded, of that there can be no doubt. It was not uncommon for him to turn on the gas stove and then forget to light it. Sometimes he even failed to notice that his model had left. When he went to his country houses in Åsgårdstrand and Hvitsten, he often forgot to take his keys, so at both places he would turn to trusted locals to break in for him. In Åsgårdstrand he would amuse himself each time by asking the man to choose between 25 øre and a picture; unfortunately for his descendants, the man invariably opted for the money.

The interior of Munch's house, like his immediate surroundings, showed that the only thing that meant anything to him was art. At Ekely there were no curtains and none of the light bulbs had shades. His radio would often be left on, crackling with the noise between two stations. In the absence of lids for his pots, he would use his own pictures. Munch got into the habit of opening only those letters he thought would be pleasant to read. This meant that most of his bills went unpaid, with the consequence that his electricity, gas and telephone were often cut off. He sold the white horse that was his only grass cutter on the grounds that the animal had been painted often enough.

Passers-by would often see that Munch had hung paintings in his apple trees, where he left them all winter. In his opinion the pictures could do with a little sunlight, dirt and rain. He often described the treatment as a 'drastic remedy', a medicine he prescribed to his naughtiest children – because the recluse always described his pictures as his children. He treated them as if he were their father, raising, admonishing, punishing and rewarding them. The attic was packed with his 'sleeping babies', while others could be so 'naughty' that he would kick them so hard that they were ruined; and some were so 'impossible' that he did not dare let them go until they were thirty years old.

Munch died during the German occupation at the age of eighty. However, he had numerous 'children' and they are still in the best of health. And very, very slowly, Norwegians began to realize that their creator was indisputably an artist of international standing.

NIELS CHR. GEELMUYDEN

MUNCH, EDVARD (1863–1944), painter. Known for his symbolistic style with expressionistic features. Famous works include **The Sick Child** (1886), **Spring** (1889) and the **Frieze of Life** (22 pictures, including **The Kiss**, **Jealousy**, **The Scream**, **Ashes** and **Madonna**) from 1902. Decorated the University Assembly Hall in Oslo (1910–16). Portraits include **Strindberg**, **Obstfelder** and **Gunnar Heiberg**; also **Self-Portrait: The Night Wanderer**. Bequeathed his substantial collection of his own works to the city of Oslo, where they are housed in the Munch Museum, which opened in 1963.

# ART GALLERY

An exhibition that spans – and is meant to span – the years from the Middle Ages to our own time, may well seem confusing. Although all of these works are works of art, art takes many forms. Consider the statue of St Olav: not only does it portray the saintly king, but to ordinary people visiting Fresvik church in Sogn it was also a figure of wisdom to pray to and talk with. This interactive aspect vanished when the statue was elevated to art and ended up in a museum.

With the change in direction of artistic viewpoint that occurred in the 18th century, the dual function of a work of art became increasingly clear. A painting should illuminate its subject, like the clouds of J.C. Dahl, the mountains of Peder Balke and the open-hearth dwelling of Adolph Tidemand in our selection: but it should also represent pure art in the sense of an orderly and beautifully composed canvas.

From the beginning of the 20th century, Christian Krohg and Edvard Munch exemplify artists who continued to emphasize their subjects (and even provoked the bourgeoisie with their choice of subject) but at the same time accentuated the painted surface – which can only be perceived by the senses, and accordingly is called aesthetic (perceptible). While the subject was easily recognizable, it was not equally easy to understand the aesthetic form – even though that was what made the painting 'art'. Ludvig Karsten, indeed, goes further in the weakening of subjects to the advantage of the painted surface, and in the work of Jacob Weidemann and Synnøve Anker Aurdal the aesthetic has taken over completely – only the titles now provide a frail connection to the world outside the painting.

But can art be merely a beautiful surface? After the Second World War, many reacted to the one-sided cultivation of the aesthetic. There was a desire to re-open art to both the abstract and the real, and that, it was thought, could only be done by shattering the beautiful, aesthetic surface that had become so overwhelming that it enveloped all else.

In Norway this counter-reaction did not always go as far as in, for instance, the USA. In the works of Niclas Gulbrandsen, Kristian Blystad, Carl Nesjar and Per Kleiva the form is intact, but it is nevertheless impossible to ignore the intention, the idea – although it can be both vague and multifaceted, often alarmingly so. This also goes for Olav Chr. Jenssen, Gro Jessen, Sigurd Bronger, May Bente Aronsen, Mikkel McAlinden and Børre Larsen. When Børre Larsen shows us a stuffed bird stuck in a shuttlecock, we immediately ask ourselves what on earth it is supposed to mean; then we begin to reflect on it. We communicate once again with the work of art, just as churchgoers did in Sogn, seven hundred years ago.

GUNNAR DANBOLT

PEDER BALKE (1804–87)
*Stedtind in fog*, 1864
Oil on canvas, 71 x 58 cm
National Museum of Art/National Gallery, Oslo

JOHAN CHRISTIAN DAHL (1788–1857)
*Studies of clouds*, dated 27 February 1829
Oil on paper, 17.7 x 21.1 cm
Bergen Art Museum/Rasmus Meyer Collections

ANONYMOUS ARTIST
*Olav frontal from unknown church, Sogn, c.* 1320-40
Painted oak, height approx. 160 cm
University Museum of Cultural History, Oslo

ADOLPH TIDEMAND (1814–76)
*Open-hearth house at Sogneskar in Valle*, 1848
Oil on canvas glued on plate, 36 x 38.5 cm
National Museum of Art/National Gallery, Oslo

CHRISTIAN KROHG (1852–1925)
*The Seal Ground*, 1898,
Oil on canvas, 144.5 x 200.5 cm
Bergen Art Museum/Rasmus Meyer Collections

LUDVIG KARSTEN (1876–1926)
*The Blue Kitchen*, 1913
Oil on canvas, 54 x 69 cm
National Museum of Art/National Gallery, Oslo

OLUF TOSTRUP (1842–76)
*Tiara* (A gift to the actress Laura Gundersen in celebration of her 25 years on stage), 1875
Gold and freshwater pearls, star with 25 large and small diamonds, length 16.5 cm/width 14.5 cm
National Museum of Art/Museum of Applied Arts, Oslo

GUSTAV GAUDERNACK (1865–1914)
*The Libelle Bowl*, *c.* 1908
Gilded silver, mirror and window enamel, diameter 16.5 cm
National Museum of Art/Museum of Applied Arts, Oslo

EDVARD MUNCH (1863–1944)
*The Sun*, 1916
Oil on canvas, 455 x 780 cm
Oslo University Aula (Assembly Hall)

FRIDA HANSEN (1855–1931)
*The Milky Way*, 1898
Tapestry, 260 x 330 cm
Museum für Kunst und Gewerbe (Museum of Art and Applied Arts), Hamburg

EDVARD MUNCH (1863–1944)
*Portrait of Sigbjørn Obstfelder*, 1897
Etching and dry point on copper, 18 x 14 cm
Bergen Art Museum/Rasmus Meyer Collections

SYNNØVE ANKER AURDAL (1908–2000)
*The Room and the Words*, 1977
Tapestry, 200 x 600 cm
National Library, Reykjavik, Iceland

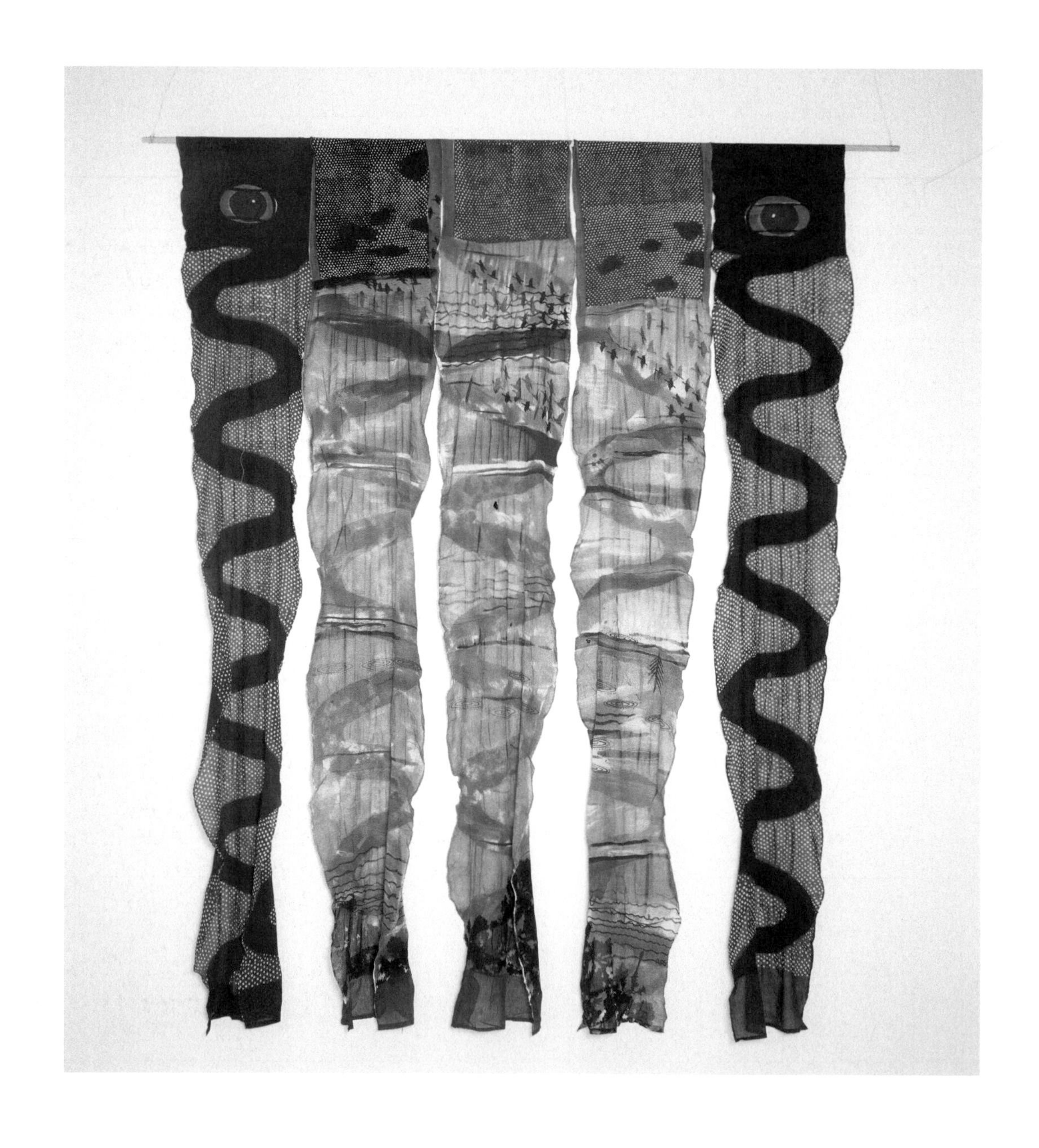

GRO JESSEN (b.1938)
*Sidsel's Landscape*, 1980
Print on fabric, 250 x 240 cm
National Museum of Decorative Arts, Trondheim

JACOB WEIDEMANN (1923–2001)
*Fog in Gethsemane*, 1965,
Oil on canvas, 200 x 225 cm
The Henie Onstad Collection, Oslo

CARL NESJAR (b.1920)
*Water and Ice Fountains*, 1971
Rust-free and oxidized steel, height approx. 7 m
National College of Agricultural Engineering, Ås

PER KLEIVA (b.1933)
*Page from the Diary of Imperialism*, 1971
Middle part of three-piece silk print, 59.7 x 59.7 cm
National Museum of Art/National Gallery, Oslo

KRISTIAN BLYSTAD (b.1946)
*Bathing II*, 1994
Red granite, 100 x 163 x 21 cm
Bergen Art Museum

MIKKEL McALINDEN (b.1963)
*The Evil Cottage*, 2000
Photo, 160 x 288 cm
Bergen Art Museum

ERIK PLØEN (b.1925)
*The Urn*, 1968
Stoneware with coating of clay glaze, height 22 cm
National Museum of Decorative Arts, Trondheim

NICLAS GULBRANDSEN (b.1930)
*Beethoven's Frühling Sonata*, 1998
Wood engraving. 30 x 43 cm

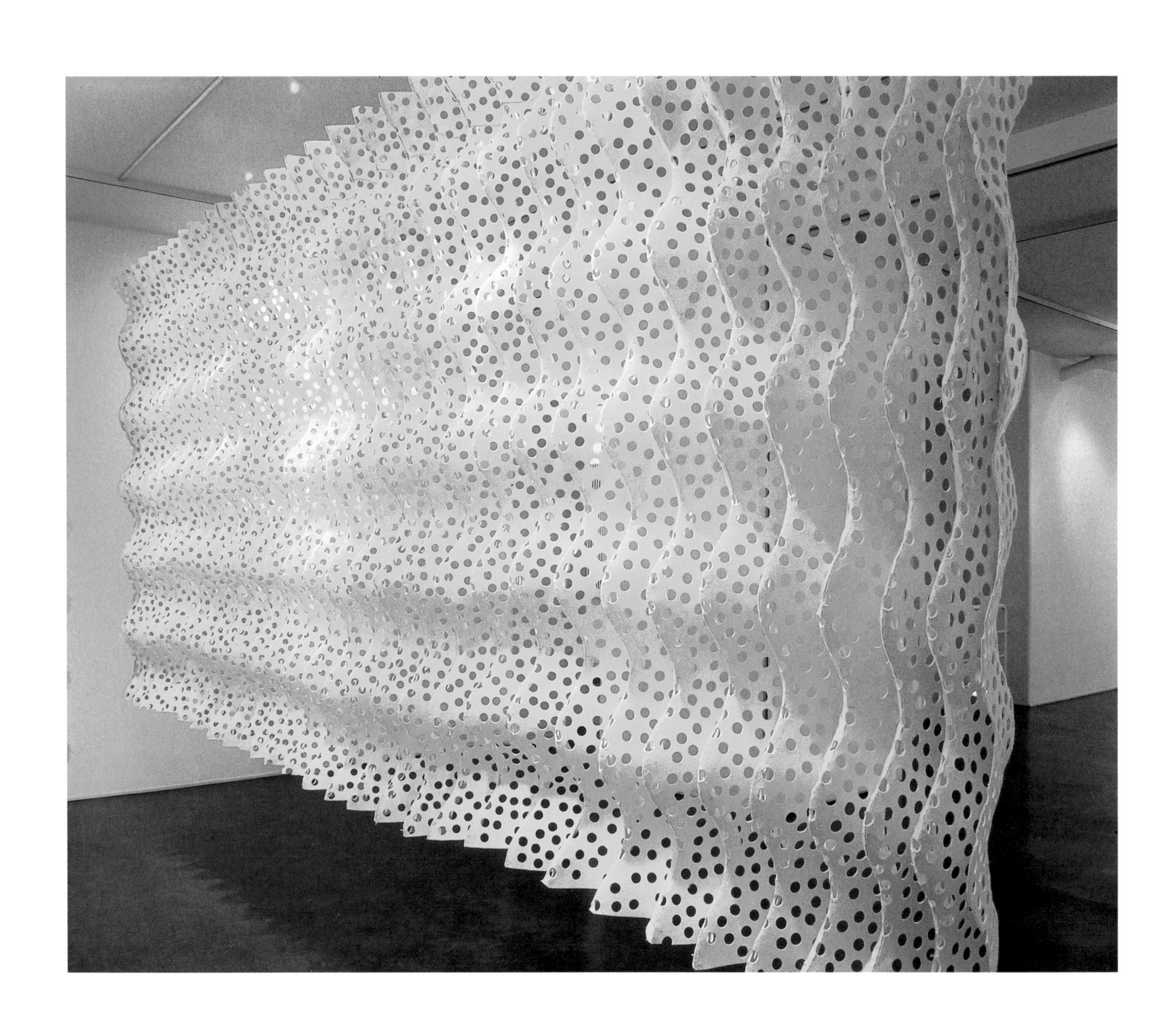

MAY BENTE ARONSEN (b.1962)
*Wave, Coral*, 1999,
Felt, 185 x 450 x 15 cm

OLAV CHRISTOPHER JENSSEN (b.1954)
*The Thinking Bells*, 2002
Ceramics, varying heights, approx. 150-170 cm

BØRRE LARSEN (b.1952)
*Shuttlecock*, 1999/2002
Multimedia

SIGURD BRONGER (b.1957)
*Ring*, 1994,
Silver, varnish, Citatool, 4 x 1 cm
National Museum of Art/Museum of Applied Arts, Oslo

# EDVARD GRIEG

Life was a trial for Edvard Grieg, beginning with his schooldays in his hometown of Bergen – and not just because he had to repeat his third year. Every day he was persecuted and beaten up by his fellow pupils. His teachers played their part too, pulling the slightly built boy by his hair and beating him for composing his own songs. At the age of ten there were only two things in the world for which Edvard had any fondness, auctions and funeral processions, and he attended as many as he could; he also enjoyed giving dramatic accounts afterwards to his father, a fish exporter.

Grieg had originally planned to enter the priesthood, but his father's childhood friend, the violinist Ole Bull, suddenly decided that the boy should be sent to Leipzig as a fifteen-year-old to become a musician. He had heard Edvard play the piano and was hugely impressed. In Leipzig, the boy was again bullied by the other students and abused by his teachers. They rocked him like a baby, laughing the while their very German laughter. For the first few months, he wept continually. Later he would say that his time in Leipzig left him with nothing but tuberculosis and painful memories; one of his lungs was permanently damaged, and at the graduation concert his entry was rejected.

PORTRAIT

On his return to Bergen he applied to the King for a travel grant, but his application was turned down and it seemed he would have to lower himself to stacking boxes of fish for his father. However, a private loan enabled him to travel to Copenhagen, where he met the girl who was to be his life partner, Nina. 'We played Schumann duets together and became engaged,' as he himself expressed it. Nina was Grieg's cousin, and in his early years Schumann was his idol. Copenhagen was also where he met the composer Rikard Nordraak. It was Bull and Nordraak who exorcized Schumann from the timorous boy, filling his mind instead with trolls and giants, ravines and snowstorms. Bull opened his eyes to folk music and Nordraak introduced him to the national spirit. Grieg and Nordraak were members of a revolutionary group called Euterpe, which campaigned for new sounds in the broadest sense. Grieg had at last found a true friend. His reaction was therefore one of rage when, shortly afterwards, Nordraak contracted tuberculosis and died.

Grieg resolved to follow his late friend's calling. He settled in Norway's capital, but here he was mostly accused of 'butchering' music. He applied for a position as conductor at the Christiania Theatre, but was turned down. He also tried to rescue the Philharmonic Society orchestra, only to be boycotted and accused of profit-mongering, despite the fact that he was scarcely able to feed his wife and himself on the little he earned as a piano teacher. There was not a publisher in Norway willing to publish his famous *Piano Concerto in A Minor*. He persevered for ten years before finally deciding to get away and 'write from the heart, regardless of whether it was Norwegian or Chinese'. His eventual breakthrough came in Copenhagen.

In a last desperate attempt to prevent Nina marrying her penniless composer cousin, his future mother-in-law wrote: 'He is a nobody, he has nothing, and he writes music that no one wants to hear,' but her warning went unheeded. Grieg's parents were equally opposed to the match. The marriage was to prove a stormy one, beset as it was with trials and tribulations. Their only child, a daughter named Alexandra, died of meningitis just over one year old. The couple's life together was also periodically blighted by adultery, depression and illness. Nina suffered from breast cancer, kidney stones and a 26-foot tapeworm. Grieg was plagued by rheumatism, gastritis, nervous disorders, anaemia, gout, asthma and recurring bronchitis in his one remaining lung.

He first met Henrik Ibsen in Rome at Christmas in 1865. The dramatist was very drunk, but Grieg was not overly sober either on the day he climbed to the top of the dome of St Peter's, where he claimed he could hear the sound of angels. It is said that the composer went on such a huge drinking spree that he was ill for some thirty months afterwards. Grieg wrote the music for *Peer Gynt*, but disliked it so much that he refused to attend its premiere in 1876. Nor did he go to the rehearsals, and he never bothered to have the score printed. He could not bear to listen to 'In the Hall of the Mountain King', which he thought sounded like 'cow pats and trollish self-sufficiency'. It is, everything considered, a stylistic pleasure to read his many articles and letters; as a writer, he was superior to most.

It is beyond doubt that 'Vardo', as his friends knew him, had an unusual relationship with his home country. He could not bear it, but at the same time he had an inordinate love for it. Typical in this respect was 'Troldhaugen', the house in Bergen that he designed himself and where he lived from 1885. Though supposed to be built in the Gudbrandsdal style, it gradually evolved into a Victorian edifice. One moment he could say 'Only fearless bundles of muscle seem to have any success in this barbaric country', then go on to assert, 'I love Norway, precisely because it is so poor.'

Grieg was notoriously outspoken. He once shouted at a conductor, calling him 'a swine', and condemned an oboist for being 'a clumsy moron'. Bjørnson compared the composer to the Rauma river in that it was hard to stop him once he got going. Kings and emperors tried, but to no avail. The republican in him offended more royalty than most people ever get to meet. He sneaked past Louis II in Bayreuth, rebuked King Edward VII of England and failed to keep engagements with Denmark's Queen Louise. After breakfasting with Emperor Wilhelm II and lunching with Queen Victoria, Grieg declared that he liked them both – despite their rank. Towards the end of his life he even induced Norway's King Haakon VII to swear that he would never put on regal airs. The composer was as unruly as the country from which he came, and would be deliberately provocative whenever he thought it appropriate. He treated himself with no more respect, however, dismissing his collected lyrical pieces as 'lice and fleas'.

Behind his temperamental facade, Grieg was a considerate and kind-hearted person. This is illustrated by, among other things, the many charity concerts he gave for the benefit of the unemployed and victims of leprosy. Both as a conductor and as a pianist, what he liked best was to perform music for ordinary people, as he saw them as being less corrupt than the ruling classes. He was invariably kind to children and, strangely, atheist though he was, superstitious. At concerts he always carried a rubber frog in his pocket, which he squeezed whenever he felt the need.

'I don't care about criticism, as long as the concert goes well and my hips hold out,' he is reported to have said.

In the world at large Grieg was lavishly praised, his fellow composers being particularly enthusiastic.

**Edvard Grieg and his wife,** Nina, often appeared together on the stage. They are seen here, she with her music in her hand, he, as always, with his talisman, a rubber frog, in his pocket.

Liszt lauded his works, and for many years attended his concerts. Rachmaninov declared that he did not know of any piano concerto more beautiful than Grieg's. Dvorák and Bruckner likewise showered their Norwegian colleague with praise. Wagner invited him to his house as a guest of honour and Richard Strauss visited him when he was ill. On one occasion, in 1887, Grieg spent New Year's Eve seated at table between two of his admirers, Brahms and Tchaikovsky. It promised to be a very pleasant evening – and so it was until Brahms demanded all the strawberry jam for himself!

The composer could scarcely travel abroad without returning home laden with honours and orders, though he himself dismissed them as 'humbug, court stuff and bits of metal'. Where he wanted to be was in Norway with his own kind, though he found that his art was not accepted there. Grieg was awkward when he walked, awkward physically, awkward, in fact, in every respect, except in his belief in the genuineness, truth and purity that imbued his music. It is incredible how this diminutive 50-kilogram figure (he was barely 156 centimetres in height) makes most musical greats sound like salon composers: only Grieg could make his listeners 'hear the fall of dew'. The music he created was lyrical, immediate, powerful and universal.

Grieg's health was always poor. He suffered from chronic gastric catarrh and was compelled to spend much time in sanatoriums. When his depression was at its worst, he considered suicide as a way out. He took opium and a whole arsenal of daily medicaments. After the age of sixty he was never in good health.

'You are really two people,' his wife is reported to have said to him when he was on his deathbed – and engaged in planning a major concert tour of England. 'No, I am just one struggling human being,' was his response. He died on 4 September 1907 with a remarkably majestic valedictory bow from his sickbed.

NIELS CHR. GEELMUYDEN

GRIEG, EDVARD HAGERUP (1843–1907), composer. Trained in Leipzig 1858–62 as a pianist and conductor. Lived in Oslo from 1866. Married his cousin, the singer Nina Hagerup (1845–1935) in 1867. Moved in 1885 to Troldhaugen, near Bergen. Among Grieg's most important works are **Sigurd Jorsalfar** (1872), **Peer Gynt, Suites I** and **II** (1876–91), **Spring** (1880–81), the **Concerto in A minor** (1868), the **Holberg Suite** (1884) and his **String Quartet** (1877–78).

# TRANSPORT AND COMMUNICATIONS

# IT IS LONG, THIS LAND

Andreas Hompland

THE OTHERWISE LAND

It is long, this otherwise land.
Northward it stretches, northward without end,
Rimming islands that blue endlessly out to sea.
We gather where'er there is soil and a living,
crowding into narrow valleys.
But beyond them the solitudes soar
– a European Tibet, heaven-high and silent,
near-infinite, like thoughts.

Rolf Jacobsen, from *All my poems*, 1990

**The main road** across the Sogne mountains early in June

This is a story about 200 years of nation building – a historical project to unite geography and love and create identification with the country across its divided landscape. What was separated by fjords and mountains, forests and long distances, yet, politically speaking, constituted a state, was also to become a communicative system and an active economic and cultural society. Traffic arteries were to link social and economic activities in rural and urban areas and in different parts of the country. The other side of the project consisted of developing communications media to spread information and education throughout the country and in all sections of the population. The Royal Norwegian Society for Rural Development endeavoured to establish local reading clubs and libraries with the aim of developing community spirit and a national identity.

The underlying driving force behind the evolution of Norwegian society since its national rebirth in 1814 has been to unite all that was once dispersed. The underlying fear, one hundred years after national independence in 1905, is that everything that has been united will once more be dispersed.

## The national building project

Norway is a small nation in terms of population (4.5 million), but large in terms of area (323,758 square kilometres, excluding Svalbard). Hence there are on average 14 inhabitants per square kilometre. By comparison, Denmark, for example, has 125 inhabitants per square kilometre and the Netherlands as many as 394. The distance from south to north Norway equals the one from Oslo to Rome. Much of Norway consists of mountains, glaciers and other unpopulated areas, with many islands and considerable distances between habitations. These are the topographical conditions facing transport and communications in Norway.

The country has always been a producer of raw materials. Long a producer of fish, ore and timber, in recent years its production has mostly centred on oil and gas. These raw materials are today found outside administrative centres and elsewhere in the country than the population centres. These are the geographical and historical conditions for creation of wealth in Norway.

The country has a democratic tradition in which the geographical periphery has enjoyed a strong political position and exercised great power. Our sense of justice has demanded that, in order to achieve legitimacy and enlist widespread support, public measures should have an integrating and equalizing effect. These are the political conditions for the development of communications and cultural infrastructure in Norway.

In the 19th century, the national project was directed against Danish and, more especially, Swedish dominance. It was built on ethnic homogeneity, aiming to unite different regional economies and cultural traditions in one Norwegian society. Broadly speaking, communications were a central part of the political-democratic and national structure. With the topography of the country and its great distances this was necessarily costly and demanding, and often impossible. Around the year 1800 there were no organized regular coastal shipping routes for goods and passenger transport. Travellers had to wait for chance rides, often for weeks. In Finnmark there were no roads at all, and in the rest of northern Norway there were merely tracks from which the biggest obstructions had been removed. The so-called postal express took 14 to 16 weeks on the round trip between Trondheim and Finnmark.

In 1814, when the constitutional assembly met at Eidsvoll to frame Norway's Constitution, the northernmost representative came from Nærøy in northern Trøndelag. Summons did not arrive in time for the people in northern Norway to organize an election. In Finnmark the election was held after the assembly had concluded its work on 17 May. Such stains on the principle of democracy set an important agenda for the new nation.

### The coastal route

The Norwegian name of the country is *Norge/Noreg*. The original meaning of the word, however, is clearer in English and German: *Norway* and *Norwegen*. Norway is the route northwards along the coast, the sea being the main communication artery.

The event referred to as the unification of the realm was a sea battle traditionally thought to have been fought at Hafrsfjord near Stavanger around the year 900. During the civil wars in the centuries that followed, both regional petty kings and anyone aspiring to the throne of a unified country had to secure their position with the aid of a fleet. To gain time to gather crews and make adequate preparations should enemies approach, they developed a warning system that was a visual forerunner of the telegraph service. Cairns were built on clearly visible mountain tops, where beacons could be lit in case of danger. In this way, news travelled from summit to summit faster than a messenger could row or sail, and continued with message sticks sent from farm to farm. However, it took seven days for news to travel from Lindesnes to Nordland.

Contact between Norway and important foreign countries was by sea, and the art of boat-building was highly developed. The elegant and highly seaworthy Viking ships enabled plundering and trade further south on the European continent, and especially westward to the British Isles. Whereas the border with Sweden in the east moved back and forth and the Russian border in the north remained indeterminate until the mid-1700s, the Faeroes, Iceland, Greenland and the islands north of Scotland were part of the Norwegian realm during the centuries following the year 1000. The North Sea was practically a Norwegian inland sea.

The first 800 to 900 years in the life of the nation were essentially a maritime era. Hunting and fishing were carried on at sea, imports came by sea, goods were transported by sea and exports, not least – timber, stone, metal and fish – also went by sea.

Commercial fishing was carried on by full-time fishermen and fishing-farmers in small, open boats on the western coast and in northern Norway. During the large-scale seasonal herring and cod fisheries, thousands gathered at the fishing stations, where there were good harbours, fishermen's shacks and buyers. The fish was salted or dried and transported to Bergen in larger boats. Exports from Bergen were dominated by German merchants, the Hansa, from the 14th until well into the 16th century.

Bergen was for many centuries Norway's most important town, and remained so until the middle of the 19th century. Surrounded by seven mountains, it was very much a shipping community. The sea was the principal, and often only, link with the rural settlements on the islands and in the fjords further inland, as it was with northern Norway, the source of the fish, and the foreign countries to which the fish was shipped. The sea and fjords united, whereas the forests and mountain plateaus divided.

## Inland by sledge

In 1319 Norway and Sweden became subjects to a common ruler, and for over 400 years, from 1380, we shared kings with Denmark and were a part of the Danish kingdom, Copenhagen being the capital and centre of power. Norway's mountains became an important part of the Danish-Norwegian kingdom because the kings and their government officials were obsessed by the search for ore and metal. In 1623, silver was discovered in 'a trackless wilderness, where fed ferocious animals'. King Christian IV journeyed there the following year, accompanied by German miners, and founded the mining town of Konningsberg (Kongsberg). When the Royal Mint took over the silver mine towards the end of the 1600s, coin production was moved from Akershus castle in Oslo to Kongsberg. The town also housed the *Bergseminaret*, Europe's first college for mining students. Mining made Kongsberg the country's second-largest town towards the end of the 18th century, with close to 10,000 inhabitants. A special stagecoach service, known as the *Norwegian Express*, ran between Kongsberg and Copenhagen, but this did nothing to improve communications within Norway itself.

Røros, a copper-mining town, dates from the same period as Kongsberg. What was common to these and other mines, was that they were not located by the sea, but in mountainous areas where the winters were long and snowfalls heavy. The rivers and water systems lent themselves to log flotation, but were not very suitable for goods and passenger traffic. Roads safe for passage were so few that people rode on horseback in summer and travelled by horse-drawn sledge in winter. Goods could be carried on horseback, but sizeable amounts were completely dependent on horse and sledge on the snow. Large quantities of timber and charcoal were transported from the surrounding countryside under harsh conditions. The lives and fates of people in this environment have become part of Norway's cultural history through the novels of Johan Falkberget (1879–1967).

Although the mountainous areas between east and west and between south and north were dangerous, people nonetheless frequented them. Hunters stalked reindeer and other game, and in summer sheep and goats grazed the upland pastures. Dealers and merchants drove herds of cattle and horses across the mountain plateaus, for example along the Nordmannslepa track across the Hardangervidda plateau between Eidfjord in Hardanger and Uvdal in Valdres. By the 1100s, what were known as the King's stone shelters had been built for overnight stays and protection against bad weather.

**Not surprisingly,** when the velocipede first appeared on Norway's primitive roads towards the end of the 19th century, it was dubbed 'velte-Petter' (Topple Peter). Seen here is Røisheim tourist centre in the Bøverdal valley, in the foothills of the Jotunheimen mountains.

The first roads between the different parts of Norway were called the King's roads if they were for administrative or military purposes, or the Priest's roads if they were used for ecclesiastical journeys. The pilgrim road to Trondheim, where Saint Olav was buried, was of the same type. To call them roads was to exaggerate, as they were rough tracks that had been cleared for passage on foot or on horseback. The post roads came about a few centuries later, but neither these were passable by horse and cart, except in towns and population centres in the lowlands and valleys. It was easier to travel by sledge in winter than on bare ground in summer.

When the Norway's mountains and valleys were discovered by English tourists in the 1800s, in their accounts they praised the wildness of the scenery and the friendliness of the people; they never failed to complain about the roads, however.

## The mail must get through

Apart from very locally, communications were organized for the needs of trade and industry and in the military and administrative interests of the political autocracy. For two centuries or so, from its establishment in 1647, this was also the case with the postal service. The delivery of post was a royal monopoly – and a money-making business in a class of its own. Routes were scarce and postage rates high: in 1816 it cost 16 shillings for a letter from Christiania to Bergen and as much as 54 shillings for one to Vardø. People sent letters and messages with incidental travellers, though doing so was illegal until 1827.

In the summer of 1838 an Englishman, Richard C. Smith, travelled from Copenhagen to Christiania on the Norwegian steamer *Prinds Carl*. In his diary he remarks that thirteen years earlier the only regular transport between England and Norway consisted of a cargo ship sailing once a week between Harwich and Gothenburg. Now he could travel by passenger steamer from London, leaving on a Wednesday night and arriving in the Norwegian capital Sunday night. 'What a powerful cultural tool the steamer has become!' Smith wrote. 'It is truly difficult to anticipate the enormous moral and political changes it may bring about in such an undeveloped country.'

The driving force behind the steamer traffic was the state, and the captains were naval officers. In 1827, the paddle-steamer *Constitutionen* provided a regular service between Christiania and Kristiansand (and Bergen in the summer), and *Prinds Carl* between Stavern, Gothenburg and Copenhagen. Ten years later the *Prinds Gustav* was plying regularly between Trondheim and Hammerfest in the summer, a voyage that took eight days. Traffic increased, but the national steamers were too expensive for the general public; the voyage from Christiania to Kristiansand cost more than the annual rent for a cotter's farm, and from the capital to Hammerfest the price was sevenfold. Even so, the state steamers operated at a considerable loss, but the important objective was to strengthen administrative control and improve the postal service for letters and periodicals.

'There shall be liberty of the press . . . Everyone shall be free to speak his mind frankly on the administration of the State and on any other subject whatsoever.' This is the wording of Article 100 of the Norwegian Constitution of 1814. The independent Norway was to cast off the former censorship imposed by an absolute monarch and his government officials. The founding fathers set out to encourage an open and democratic society with an informed and debating public.

Everyone was free to publish newspapers and other printed matter, and the authorities also facilitated distribution. In 1837, Stortinget, the Norwegian parliament, determined that all magazines and periodicals should benefit from permanently reduced postage rates and extra cheap distribution costs. Newspapers and magazines were not afforded these advantages as commercial enterprises, but as channels for distribution of information and political debate. This was considered an important part of the nation building and the cultural integration into written language.

During the Napoleonic Wars in the early 1800s, an optical telegraph had been developed and used for military purposes. However, it was the electric telegraph that became important, most notably, to begin with, for the shipping industry. The first private telegram in Norway was sent in 1854, the same year that the country's first railway line opened. A couple of years later, the telegraph wire had been extended from Christiania to Bergen, and on to Ålesund and Trondheim. In 1864, Norway was connected to the European network, and in the 1870s, northern Norway was also included. In the 1880s Norway possessed a continuous telegraph network with a large number of telegraph stations and an even larger number of employees.

The telegraph reduced the time lag, and through *Norsk Telegrambyrå* (a news agency founded in 1867) it helped to bring news from Norway and abroad, along with political issues at home, to the notice of the general public. In Norwegian politics the telegraph played an important part in the prelude to the dissolution of the union with Sweden, enabling direct contact between the government in Kristiania and the cabinet ministers in Stockholm.

However, the second half of the 1800s was the golden age of the postal service. The long coast was opened up by regular steamship services from the capital all the way north to Vardø. They were state-run, so consequently they were operated by the Postal Service, as post and communications were two sides of the same coin.

In 1855 the stamp was introduced and postage for all ordinary letters reduced to four shillings, regardless of distance. The Storting frequently discussed letter postage, and in 1871 the charge was further reduced, even though the Postal Service was making a heavy loss. The argument was that it was desirable to make it as easy and cheap as possible for people to express themselves in writing, for therein lay 'an educational and edifying element of great importance'. Supporters of the popular-radical Liberal Party, *Venstre*, who were concerned with schools and education as democratizing tools in the advancement of society, regarded the postal service, with its letters and newspapers, more or less as an extension of the public grammar schools that were established in rural areas in 1860.

Many post offices and postal stations were opened, their number increasing from 800 in 1880 to 2,500 at the turn of the century. Together with new mail routes and the rural postal service, this provided the foundation for a communications revolution in an age before the telephone. In the space of 30 years

**Eagerly read and studied,** letters from the many emigrants to America tempted friends and relatives to follow their writers to the 'Land of Opportunity'. This painting from 1847, 'The America Letter', is the work of Adolph Tidemand.

letter volume increased from two million to 16 million; that same year, 1885, 18 million newspapers and magazines were also delivered through the mail. By 1905 these figures had increased to 45 million letters and 70 million magazines and newspapers. It is more than a mere dramaturgic device when Henrik Ibsen's contemporary dramas develop, as they often do, following the receipt of a letter.

The letters that were read most thoroughly, and that were passed from hand to hand and had the greatest impact, were probably the 'America letters'. Emigrants wrote to family and friends, often exaggerating the wonderful prospects offered by the Land of Promise. These letters were in the nature of a call for more people to follow. Towards the end of the 1800s the journey had become less dangerous and exacting than before, not only in

**Norwegian townships,** along with shops and other services, developed at crossroads and railway stations. They are not villages in the European sense of the word. Farmers live on their land. In the 1970s and '80s population centres expanded strongly, and conservation of cultivated farmland became increasingly important. To preserve arable land, new single-family houses were built on large lots on estates in outlying areas. As a result, settlements became more dispersed, making life in the countryside dependent on the car. This aerial photograph is of Stange, Hedmark.

Norway but also on the ocean and in America itself. It was not as irreversible as it had been, either: by transatlantic liner the crossing took no more than a week, so returning home wasn't unrealistic.

### The great moulder of society

Communication is a powerful, relentless and unreliable moulder of society. Each epoch has its own means of transport, creating its own links and networks. Rivers and canals were the very life nerves of industrial Europe until the railway took over, though eventually both ship and railway were superseded by roads and motor vehicles. In Norway, the triumph of the car has been overwhelming.

Most towns and population centres developed where an economic basis existed, and survived when located at transport arteries where people met to trade, worship or contact the authorities. However, the growth and decline of such centres also result from laws, directives and political decisions. Some towns and population centres were planned and built for administrative, ecclesiastical or military reasons. Vardø, on the north coast, which fronts the Arctic Ocean, is Norway's easternmost town and has a long history of fortification. It was accorded town status fifty years after Vardøhus fortress was completed in 1738, to demonstrate Danish-Norwegian dominion in relation to Russia and Sweden

Norwegian municipal borders in coastal and fjord areas are remnants of a communications pattern in which the sea did not divide but united. They tell a story of administrative changes resulting from changes in communications.

The municipality of Karlsøy in Troms is named after a small island on which the main church stood; with its good harbour it was an important stop on the sea route. The same applies to many island municipalities in northern Norway. They are located on both sides of fjords and on parts of several islands, full of impassable mountains. Sea and fjord connected, while mountains separated.

This was also the case with Nærøy, in Nord-Trøndelag. With roads along the coast and tunnels through the mountains connecting places in new ways, the situation has now changed. This former boat-dependent centre has ended up on the periphery, the municipal centre having moved to Kolvereid, a crossroads and traffic junction on the mainland some twenty kilometres away.

The municipality of Leikanger in the county of Sogn og Fjordane covered both sides of the wide Sogne fjord, but its boundaries were adjusted to the changes in traffic pattern after roadless communities on the southern shore of the fjord were connected by road to other municipal centres on the same side of the fjord. Small, roadless Fjærland at the head of the Fjærland fjord beneath the Jostedal glacier was merged with Balestrand, with which it had a ferry connection. Now Fjærland might be included in the municipality of Sogndal, as a new tunnel links the two.

The Directorate for Cultural Heritage has declared Dønnesfjord church in Hasvik on the island of Sørøya, Finnmark, a historic monument. The church was the only building in the municipality still standing after the occupying German forces withdrew in the winter of 1944–45, employing their scorched-earth tactic. The church was first built at the small trading centre of Galten in 1881, but in 1951, when the centre was abandoned, it was moved to a roadless fishing station on Øya in the Dønnes fjord. This station too was later vacated, so the Ministry of Church and Cultural Affairs closed the church. A listed building, the church cannot be demolished, so it stands in the abandoned fishing station as a monument to the changed patterns of trade, communications and habitation – but also to the authorities' desire to preserve such relics of the past.

Some places come into being, and later die, with the means of transport of their age; others are born too late and suffer an equally sad fate. Faded railway halts where trains no longer stop are as desolate as former liner stops after new roads have lured both people and traffic to the mainland.

Other places manage to adapt and create new life when communication patterns change, because in the meantime they have made themselves independent of their original reason for existence. The unending dispute over municipal boundaries also concerns the framework for local affinity and the fear that small places will die if they lose their position as local administrative centres. That is why they appeal to the Norwegian political system's insistence on justice for all.

### Along a country road

The historical basis of the economy, along with the means of transportation of bygone days, has left in its wake a widely dispersed population pattern. Smelting works and other industry were located beside waterfalls and fishing stations near fishing grounds, while farming was carried on in valleys and on islands where the soil was fertile, the grazing good and opportunities existed for hunting and fishing.

The Norwegian pattern of habitation is scattered in a dual sense: distances between population centres are considerable and many centres are not very concentrated. Rural Norway is not dotted with villages, but with farms, each a good distance from its neighbour. It has been jocularly remarked that Norway's farms are so far apart that each needs its own tomcat! This is the result of a deliberate policy dating from the 1800s. Communally owned properties were divided up, small strips of farmland being conjoined to make farming them more rational and commercial. Farmers were subsidized and given cheap loans to enable them to move from the old farming communities that were, in a manner of speaking, small villages, and instead build farmhouses and outbuildings on their land.

Houses in population centres on the coast rarely have a sea view. They face inland. There are, of course, climatic reasons for this: if a house were to have a view of the ocean, it would necessarily be exposed to the vagaries of wind and weather. Instead, houses huddle together where they are protected.

There is, however, another reason why houses so often turn their back on the sea and instead face other houses. Meeting places which provide a basis for social intercourse develop where transport arteries and people converge. When boats were the dominant means of communication, the quay was central. It was protected from the open sea and the rough waters of the fjord. The coastal-steamer quay was the principal meeting place, as it was where the mail and goods arrived, where people departed from and returned to, and where everyone went to meet people and to catch up on the news. After motor vehicles took over transportation of goods and passengers, houses were built along the roads, to be followed by shops and post offices. Houses with a wide, unobstructed view of the sea were for nostalgics, nature lovers and other eccentrics; often newcomers, not locals.

Inland, houses were built along the road, facing it. Here one could ask for news from people passing by – on foot, horse or bicycle. The road was a meeting place for grown-ups, a place for romance for young people and a playground for children. And if a car did crawl by, everyone knew who was out driving. Living by the road gave a social overview and close contact with the rhythm and doings of local society. For a couple of decades after the Second World War the most popular radio request record for birthday greetings to older men and women was a Swedish song, one line of which ran: 'I have lived by a country road all my life, and seen people come and go.'

In rural areas population centres developed at crossroads, where buses stopped for people to get on and off and to pick up milk churns and goods for the shops. That was where people went to pick up mail and newspapers, shop and talk.

But the number of cars on the roads began to increase; they were anonymous, too, and drove faster. Pedestrians lost out, and living by a road grew dangerous. Traditional community centres were ruined by traffic. Some erected stout fences between them and the road as a shield against noise and pollution. Exit roads were closed, and houses turned away from the roads. In some fortunate cases a new road, a bypass, was built to circumvent the old centre. Some such centres gained a new lease of life, but it became more common for shops, public offices and other meeting places to move away to a new and better planned, car-based centre by the new road.

The private car is both a midwife and an executioner. The car increases people's freedom of movement, but also kills people and destroys the environment. Cars also kill places when they become too many, often places which the car itself created in its infancy. Hokksund emerged from the exhaust fog and came to life again after the highway was rerouted away from the main street. Places and local communities die when there are no roads, but they also die when the roads become too congested. In Norway people in towns are less dependent on private cars than people in sparsely populated rural areas without alternative means of transport. For people in the countryside and at smaller centres, cars and rural life are two sides of the same coin.

Also, small towns and rural centres that grew rapidly in the 1970s are no longer densely populated, but areas with a scattered population. New detached houses on quarter-acre plots were built on well-laid-out, outlying estates and on hillsides where they did not conflict with cultivated land. Such housing estates are devoid of integrated workplaces, shops and services: they are built for cars, and cars are instrumental to their survival. For this reason Norwegian population centres and small rural towns have more in common with car-based American suburbs than with European towns and villages. They are too dispersed for both pedestrian traffic and public transport.

## National treasure

Dispersed settlements are regarded as an important Norwegian characteristic and important value: the nation may be portrayed as a diversity of small, scattered settlements. After industrialization, modernization and centralization had been keywords in the years after the Second World War, *decentralization* was the buzz word in Norwegian politics in the closing decades of the 20th century. Although settlement became more centralized on the outskirts and in the country as a whole, it was a common political goal to retain the main elements of the established population pattern and ensure a balance between the regions and different parts of the country. Indeed, the Centre Party, which is particularly well-disposed towards the regions, made the policy statement that no municipality should suffer a population reduction.

It is constantly emphasized in political rhetoric that 'the whole country should be utilized' and sustained. This also means that people living in sparsely populated areas and in the more central parts of the country should be equally entitled to good living conditions. Access to transportation and communications are an important part of what is considered legitimate and fair. Accordingly, the demand for regional harmonization and equal access in all parts of the country has been made and adapted in connection with all changes in communications technology – if not immediately, at least in the long term.

As development of communications is mainly publicly funded and subject to political resolution, demands are directed towards the political system. 'To reduce the disadvantages of distance for people and businesses in the regions' is a recurrent statement in public reports and a valid argument in debates on roads and electronic communications. This is why localization and priorities in the communications sector are such central topics in Norwegian politics, and have been so for two hundred years. They are the only issues in regard to which Norwegian parliamentarians are free to pay attention to local considerations and vote irrespective of party views. Moreover, such issues are a strong political mobilizing force: being given credit for a local stretch of road or a bridge may ensure re-election.

In cases like this, regional and local demands for political justice are more important than questions of socio-economic profitability and business estimates. When delegations of mayors from the regions appear in the Storting to demand a road, it is part of a local fight against strong forces pulling in a different direction. These sentiments correspond to those that have kept Norway outside the EU for 40 years and through two referendums; Oslo may be far away, but Brussels is even further away.

## From water to road

The past one hundred years of communications is the story of how the most important transport arteries have moved from water to land, and hence how the locations of towns and districts have changed. The country increasingly turned its back on the sea, and central locations in the coastal transport network became backwaters.

At Storvågen in Lofoten there are *vågs* everywhere. A *våg* is an inlet which is smaller than a fjord but larger than a cove. Mount Vågkallen provides a majestic background. The name of the municipality is Vågan. Nearby is Kabelvåg, with its overlarge Vågan church, also called the Lofoten Cathedral. Nyvågar is a conference centre where fishermen's shacks are rented out to tourists. At Storvågan we find Lofoten Aquarium, the Lofoten Museum and Kaare Espolin Johnson's art museum.

Vågar, the first town in northern Norway, is now being excavated. It became a town in the early Middle Ages because of its *våg*'s central location in the best area for dried fish. Catholics in southern Europe needed fish for Lent, and merchants from Bergen bought the dried fish and transported it to Bergen, where German Hansa merchants, who had greater power and better boats, shipped it to the Continent.

**Once workhorses** carrying passengers and goods between the towns along the coast, the coastal liners are now tourist ships, floating hotels sailing to and fro on 'the world's most beautiful sea voyage'. Seen here is the 'Nordlys' alongside the quay at Honningsvåg, Finnmark.

Storvågen was big enough and deep enough for the boats of that time. However, as boats grew bigger, the *våg* became too small and surviving business moved to Kabelvåg, where the *våg* was bigger. Now, Kabelvåg, too, with its over-large church, has been left behind. The focal point moved on to Svolvær, a few kilometres away. Here the *våg* was big enough for Svolvær to become the largest fishing station and trading centre in Lofoten, with a coastal-steamer quay and an airport. The town is still surrounded by drying racks for fish, but both salted and fresh fish are now transported in large refrigerated trucks – southwards through the country by road, and across the Skagerrak to Denmark on car ferries.

The shipping route along the coast was perilous. Accordingly, it became an important public task to make it safer, with navigation marks, beacons and pilot services. The harbours in small villages and at fishing stations were located in sheltered coves, but these often became too shallow as the boats got bigger. Only if breakwaters were built could larger fishing vessels and freighters dock alongside the quay. Settlements where government-funded breakwaters were not built faced a dismal future.

**The Telemark Canal** bears testimony to the boldness and skill of the engineers that built it. Magnificent though it is, the canal was a dead letter in Norwegian transport history. The photograph is of the 'Henrik Ibsen' passing through the locks that bypass the 23-metre-high Vrangfossen waterfall.

From time immemorial timber has been floated downriver to sawmills and, later, to pulp mills in coastal towns. In many places stone and log walls were built to prevent log jams. Along some watercourses, locks and canals were built with log flotation in mind rather than passenger and cargo transportation.

The most impressive canal system is the Telemark canal, which dates from 1892. It is 105 kilometres long, with 17 locks, and runs from Skien at sea level to Dalen on Lake Bandak in the mountains, 72 metres above sea level.

The Telemark canal was actually the result of a compromise, a substitute for a railway, but a local parliamentarian entertained great hopes for it, declaring: 'We have before us a magnificent and, by any standards of calculation, profitable enterprise, which will prove of untold value and be a source of advancement for a large area.' In the event, the speaker's hopes were dashed: the canal came too late and was soon ousted by motor roads. Canal building was a dead end in Norwegian communications history, but a trip along the canal by tourist boat is a rewarding experience. The canal is a facet of Norway and a testimony to the great engineering, as the boat is raised through the locks blasted into the mountain to bypass the 23-metre-high Vrangfossen waterfall.

From the late 1800s on steamers in regular service between coastal towns, islands and fjords represented a great communications revolution, puffing along from quay to quay on their daily sailings. When the steamer docked with passengers and mail and cargo, people turned out in force to greet it. These fjord boats disappeared in the latter half of the 20th century, when roads with buses and private cars took over. Elsewhere, stately express vessels, which made fewer calls, came into service.

The coastal liner between Trondheim and Tromsø made its inaugural voyage in 1893. Its departure from Trondheim coincided with the arrival of the express train from Kristiania. These coastal-express liners sailed day and night, summer and winter

**Opened in 1854,** Norway's first railway ran from Christiania to Eidsvoll. Its construction, which took three years, was financed and supervised by British investors and contractors. Timber transportation made it a profitable undertaking.

alike. The voyage became safer, and travelling time was dramatically reduced – from seven days to 48 hours between Trondheim and Tromsø. A letter from the capital to Tromsø took only three days to arrive.

The coastal liner, which eventually went from Bergen to Kirkenes and back, was the very life nerve of communications along the coast. The service peaked in the 1960s, with more than half a million passengers and extensive goods traffic. Thereafter the number of passengers dropped to some 250,000 towards the end of the 1980s. In the 1990s, new and larger ships were introduced, designed for tourists rather than for local transportation of people, animals and cargo. At the turn of the millennium the number of passengers again exceeded half a million. However, by then the onetime workhorse of the coast had been transformed into a cruise ship, the quays were ringed by barbed wire as protection against international terrorism, and the Ministry of Transport had invited international tenders for operation of the 'national treasure' and 'the world's most beautiful sea voyage'.

### The bygone days of the railway

The railway has been an important moulder of society. In the latter half of the 1800s, the 'iron horse' was a craze in Norway, as in the rest of the world. In 1860, 87 per cent of government grants went to communications – half of them to railway systems. Communications were more than economic nation-building; they were a kind of gospel. 'Modern times are invading the country on the railways,' Johan Sverdrup, who would later become prime minister, declared in 1869. The normally so sceptical and ironic poet Aasmund Olavsson Vinje waxed grandiloquent and was full of optimism when, in the summer of 1860, he began his journey by taking the train from the capital to Eidsvoll: 'The wheels carry the spirit of life,' he said.

**Rail transport** reached its peak around 1950, but many branch lines have since been closed down. The network's total length, half of which is electrified, is currently 4,000 kilometres. Less than 5 per cent is double-track. The Bergen line, opened in 1909, traverses extremely rugged and exposed terrain that is subject to heavy snowfalls. Finse station stands at 1,222 metres above sea level.

The canals were a dead end, shipping was confined to the coast, and on land horses were not fast and efficient enough. Large-scale railway construction was the engineering triumph of modern times. The railway was to expand markets, alter population patterns, improve communications and unite the country. Where the rails made their way, capital and power stations, industry and illusions of rapid growth would follow – to roadless hinterlands where people barely knew what a town was. The farmers were sceptical towards these innovations, however – mostly because they would lose income from timber transportation.

The first railway in Norway was opened in 1854 between the capital, Christiania, and Eidsvoll on Norway's largest lake, Lake Mjøsa. It served as a model for the first phase of railway construction, the ideal solution being a line linking a seaport with a lake and carrying goods from the interior to the sea. On the largest lakes iron steamers provided regular services: the paddle-steamer *Skibladner*, which is still in operation, made its maiden voyage on Lake Mjøsa in 1856. The development of railways and steamer routes was organized and financed according to the system that historian Jens Arup Seip called 'the Norwegian system' of 'planned liberalism': local initiative, government funding and engineering work – but all in the shape of private enterprises.

The western line between Christiania and Drammen, which was opened in 1872, was based on a different idea. Linking as it did two major seaports, it was primarily constructed to carry passengers. In 1880 there were three railway connections to Sweden. At this time the Røros line, the first line to link two different regions of the country, was also opened. The day train took two days and, until sleeping berths were introduced a few years later, included an overnight stop at Tynset.

Around 1890, railway construction was resumed according to a more coordinated plan of inter-regional, nationwide lines with the capital serving as the nodal point. In 1894 the Storting adopted the great railway compromise that resulted in the building of the Bergen line and the west-coast line, later renamed *Sørlandsbanen* (the Southern line) to Stavanger, and also paved the way for construction of a line further north from Trondheim to northern Norway. By the turn of the century, Norway had 2,000 kilometres of railway lines – quadrupled since 1875.

In 1895, the Storting determined that, where possible, mail should go by rail. By train to Brevik, steamer to Egersund, the Jæren line to Stavanger and a boat from Stavanger to Bergen, travelling time between Kristiania and Bergen was reduced from three days to 40 hours. After the Bergen line was opened in 1909, the journey took one day. Both the line's construction and operation presented technical challenges. A number of steep gradients had to be surmounted and the line's highest point is 1,301 metres above sea level; what is more, the climate is very harsh and snowfalls are heavy.

The main lines were state-owned, whereas the many local and regional lines were private. They were developed by local initiative, with different gauges and routes that could not be connected to the main network. Many were constructed after the pioneering days of the railway, and ended as loss-making projects and dead ends. Disused railway tracks and derelict factories and workshops bear witness to an industrial and cultural history of towns with a proud past and high hopes for the future. They were defeated by the change in means of transportation and declining trade. After the Second World War most business activities and settlements gravitated to the coastal towns, communication between which became more important than that between the coast and interior. Roads trafficked by buses, private cars and trucks took over. Many local railway lines were turned into roads, these often being promoted as replacements for the closed-down railway.

Although in 1923 the Storting had adopted far-reaching plans for the railways, construction ceased completely in the interwar recession years. Had it not been for the occupying Germans' (1940–45) focus on development of the infrastructure for reasons of military strategy, several railway lines would have remained uncompleted. The Southern line between Kristiansand and Stavanger, a line with many long tunnels, was one of those completed during the war; the 9.6-kilometre-long Kvineshei tunnel on this line was for many years northern Europe's longest. The Germans also speeded up work on the Northern line, *Nordlandsbanen*, which they planned to extend all the way north to Narvik and Tromsø. This line finally terminated at Bodø in 1962, and subsequent proposals for its extension have been more in the nature of ritual political exercises than anything else. On the Continent the railway network is undergoing a renaissance with the introduction of regional and transnational high-speed trains. They do not pollute to the same extent as cars, and between major cities they can compete with aircraft in terms of time and comfort.

In Norway such vistas seem utopian and smack of a come-on for local politicians. Norway's 'big' cities are 500 kilometres apart and have a passenger base that not only cannot support night trains but can barely justify daily express trains; it certainly cannot support frequent services operated by modern high-speed trains. Most lines are single-track, the tracks are much the same as they were a hundred years ago, and travelling time is the same as fifty years ago. The future of railway-based goods traffic is uncertain, as is that of passenger traffic, apart from in the central and urbanized regions round Oslo, Stavanger and Trondheim.

### With roads the nation will be built

In the mid-1800s, Norway had some 15,000 kilometres of poor standard roads, half of which were main highways. In many places they were too steep for heavy loads, and during the spring thaw they were often impassable. Most farmers exchanged goods for services and for them, better roads were not important, because they did not serve their interests. Road building and maintenance only involved work, and they had a duty to transport representatives of the authorities. The farm-

**Linking Åndalsnes** in Romsdal and Valldal in Sunnmøre, Trollstigen ('The Trolls' Ladder') climbs 800 metres in 11.7 kilometres, through eleven hairpin bends, up a steep mountainside, passing many spectacular waterfalls en route. The road is only open in summer.

**Many Norwegian fjords** are spanned by spectacular bridges, many of which are financed by local road tolls. This one, in Møre og Romsdal, is at Hustadvika on the 'Atlantic Route'.

ers' attitude changed towards the end of the 1800s, when self-support was replaced by commercial farming and monetary economy. Roads then became useful as links between the countryside and towns and markets.

By the turn of the century total road mileage had doubled, several major roads had been built and roads across the mountains between eastern and western Norway had been staked out. However, road building did not gain momentum until the automobile made its entry and demanded better conditions. The first two cars were registered in Norway in 1899. Ten years later the number had increased to 215.

In 1901 Highway Commissioner Krag made a trial run by car from Otta to Åndalsnes, a distance of 150 kilometres. A senior engineer went ahead on a bicycle, warning curious people along the route of the approaching car. Krag and the car reached their destination relatively safely after nine hours, but on the return trip, the axle broke on a rock and the car had to be towed by horse to Otta and then transported by train to Kristiania.

In 1920 there were 10,000 cars and 5,000 motorcycles on the road in Norway; by 1939 the total number of motor vehicles had risen to 120,000, 60,000 of them private cars. In the same period the number of buses increased from 500 to 3,000. All motor vehicles were imported, as Norway has never manufactured motor vehicles on any scale: cars were for utility purposes and private luxury.

The road network, which had been built for horse-drawn carriages, was gradually upgraded for motor vehicles – often by the unemployed on relief work. In 1930 there were 18,000 trucks and vans in Norway, but most cargo was still transported by sea and rail.

After the Second World War, motor-vehicle imports were subject to strict limitations for reasons of national economy. One required a permit or hard currency to buy a new private car. The number of private cars in 1950 was the same as it had been ten years earlier, but by 1955 it had doubled. The average citizen's dream for the future was to own a car, and the new age has a starting date: 1 April 1960, which was when restrictions on car sales were lifted. This was the same year that trial television broadcasts started.

With the lifting of controls, car ownership soared, and

after a few years cars were common property, their number increasing from 200,000 in 1960 to 750,000 in 1970 – though road standards and traffic control failed to keep pace with the growth in numbers. One result was that the number of people killed on the roads increased from 133 in 1950 to an all-time high of 560 in 1970. In 1999, out of a total of 3.4 million motor vehicles, 1.8 million were private cars, but because of safer roads and increased focus on driving instruction, the number of fatal accidents had fallen to 277.

The private car has totally permeated society and become decisive to land utilization and communications policy during the last 40 to 50 years. The Norwegian road plan of 1969 for large-scale development of the national road network is a prime example. Roads were rerouted and upgraded, and town and rural centres were adapted to the requirements of the car, for the car had to be able to get there. It has been an endless race between motorists, forecasters, planners and developers.

'With roads the nation will be built,' was the slogan adopted by the patriotic officer and engineer Gabriel Frøholm in a 1970 pamphlet; 'and with bridges and tunnels they will be made shorter and safer', he added. He went a step further, too, saying: 'With roads Europe will be united.'

**Number of private cars**

| | |
|---|---|
| 1945 | 45 723 |
| 1950 | 65 028 |
| 1955 | 122 143 |
| 1960 | 225 439 |
| 1965 | 435 500 |
| 1970 | 694 000 |
| 1975 | 953 657 |
| 1980 | 1 233 620 |
| 1985 | 1 513 950 |
| 1990 | 1 613 040 |
| 1995 | 1 684 660 |
| 2000 | 1 851 930 |
| 2003 | 1 934 000 |

Road builders had a new vision, dreaming of tunnels through mountains and bridges across fjords. The classical solution to the problem of fjords had been ferries, but they represented delays, as they involved waiting and reduced motorists' freedom. Increasingly long bridges were built to span narrow fjords and provide road access to islands, many being locally financed by tolls. The longest bridge in the national road network is Nordlandsbrua, which is 1.6 kilometres long. Where lack of technology stops bridge-building, subsea tunnels take over, provided that the fjords are not too deep. Two of the longest such tunnels are Bømlafjordtunnelen in Hordaland (7.9 kilometres long and 260 metres deep) and Nordkapptunnelen in Finnmark (6.9 kilometres long).

The foregoing notwithstanding, modern Norwegian road construction is primarily characterized by long mountain tunnels. It is more than a coincidence that some of the first tunnels were built for works traffic in connection with hydroelectricity projects. To the developers of hydroelectric power stations, a few kilometres of road tunnels were only a prelude to the really long and advanced tunnels that honeycomb Norwegian mountains to carry water from dams to turbines.

Today there is little call for hydroelectrical engineers, construction workers and contractors, as there are few watercourses left to harness and few rivers to channel through tunnels. This has enabled much such capacity and expertise, together with idle heavy tunnelling machinery, to be devoted to the task of driving road tunnels through the mountains. These tunnels are a triumph of Norwegian engineering skill, and tunnelling expertise has become a recognized export article. Twenty-five of the world's one hundred longest road tunnels are found in Norway. With its 24.5 kilometres, the Tønjum tunnel between Aurdal and Lærdal in the county of Sogn og Fjordane is the world's longest road tunnel. It is equipped with special lighting and decorative effects to keep drivers alert.

In 1992, after much debate, the then Minister of Transport and Communications, Kjell Opseth, who was himself from Sogn og Fjordane, obtained approval for his proposal that the nationally prioritized road between Oslo and Bergen should be built through his county. This route is considerably longer than the shortest alternative, but there are no ferry crossings and in winter it is never blocked by snow. These are important considerations, but the political majority vote was the result of complex horse trading. The Red-Green and rail-friendly party was promised support for a new railway tunnel between Oslo and Hønefoss which would shorten the Bergen line. The people of western Norway are experts at deals of this kind: they are what make and break politicians in that part of the country. Roads, tunnels and ferries are not ordinary topics of discussion: they are hobby horses and represent a demand for justice. This is the way it is bound to be in a region divided up by countless fjords and mountain barriers, but which is now seeing the light at the end of tunnel after tunnel.

In Norway, for both topographical and political reasons, a safe road between east and west, as between north and south, will always be a detour. A direct route would have to cross deep valleys, wide fjords and rugged mountain ranges, which is why roads wind along valley floors and circumvent fjords. If they are to remain passable all year round, they have to snake their way

**The network** of short-runway airports opened in western and northern Norway heralded a communications revolution in the 1970s. Widerøe's small green Twin Otters provided regular services.

through low mountain passes that can be kept open when the snow lies deep and winter storms rage.

Norwegian mountain passes can be great and exhilarating adventures, especially when, as in the west, they wind down to the fjord from an altitude of 1,000 metres over a distance of a dozen kilometres. The argument that it is sad to see an increasing number of mountains from the inside and more and more fjords from below, is a summer tourist view which does not impress the locals, who used to have to depend on ferries or wait to cross a mountain range in convoy behind a snow plough. But although the roads of western Norway now run through mountains and underneath fjords, it is still possible to drive through winding mountain passes and use ferry links if the purpose of one's trip is sightseeing rather than getting from one place to another.

The modern transport dream is the coastal route, though not by sea. It is a road without ferry crossings between Stavanger and Bergen and on to Trondheim – through mountains by tunnel and over and under fjords by bridge and, again, by tunnel. En route the car will resemble an electronic control centre, for nowhere else do we listen more to the radio than there. Many people also make and receive most of their mobile telephone calls while driving. Others say that the car is the place where they most often communicate with their family.

### A flying people

Polar explorer Roald Amundsen, the first person to reach the South Pole, in 1911, was a great believer in aircraft as a means of transportation in polar regions. Together with the Italian Umberto Nobile, in 1926 he flew from Svalbard to Alaska across the North Pole in an airship. Amundsen died two years later when his flying-boat, the *Latham*, crashed during a rescue attempt in the Arctic.

Norwegian aviation pioneers of the interwar period displayed some of Amundsen's daring and enterprise. In 1939 only 29 civilian aircraft were registered in Norway. Airfields were small, and few and far between, and such regular passenger traffic as there was was by seaplane. Ski-planes, which had runners instead of wheels or floats, were also in use.

Between 1940 and 1945 the occupying forces built a number of airfields for military purposes. After the war these were adapted for civilian traffic, though in the early postwar years passenger traffic was on a small scale. In 1950 marginally more than 50,000 passengers flew from Norwegian airports, the majority of them to international destinations. Ten years later 300,000 people took domestic flights and 200,000 travelled abroad.

When SAS (Scandinavian Airlines System) started flying to America across Greenland and the Arctic in 1954, it was marketed as a feat in the spirit of Amundsen. It was also the beginning of the end of the Norwegian America Line, which, with such famous passenger ships as the *Oslofjord*, *Bergensfjord* and *Stavangerfjord*, had been the nation's pride since 1913. When the transatlantic liners docked with emigrants who had come to visit the Old Country, they were greeted by brass bands.

The boom in domestic air travel came in the 1960s, when a network of government-funded airports was built to serve major towns all over the country. The number of passengers doubled from half a million in 1963 to one million in 1966.

The next leap occurred in the mid-1970s with the opening of short-runway airports at several small towns in western and northern Norway. In five years, the number of passengers increased by a million. These airports also became important for carriage of mail and newspapers.

The development of the airport network was a typical example of Norwegian public initiative which needed a broad geographical impact-area in order to gain political acceptance. Not all airports were commercially viable; the argument adduced for their establishment was regional political justice. Also, the country could finally operate a national premier

**Exploration and conquest** of the Arctic were important aspects of Norwegian nation building: if Fridtjof Nansen could ski across Greenland in 1888, it was argued, then Norway could secede from the union with Sweden. Roald Amundsen (1872–1928) failed in his attempt to be the first person to reach the North Pole, but in 1911 won the race for the South Pole. A firm believer in aircraft as a means of transportation in polar regions, he made several unsuccessful attempts to reach the North Pole by air. Together with Italy's Umberto Nobile, he finally succeeded in 1926 in the airship 'Norge'. The flight across the North Pole from Ny-Ålesund on Svalbard to Alaska took three days. Today, the North Pole has become an exclusive, but safe, tourist destination. Skiing there, however, preferably alone, still confers hero status in Norway.

**The Telecommunications Administration's** classical and designer-praised telephone booth has become worthy of preservation after the mobile telephone became common property. This booth is at Leksvik, Nord-Trøndelag. **The Norwegian postal service** is losing out to banks and the Internet. Post offices are being closed down and replaced by rural postal services or 'Post in Shops', with the result that local meeting places, such as this one at Kongsfjord, Finnmark, are rapidly disappearing.

league in soccer which included both Sogn og Fjordane and northern Norway.

Three airlines shared the routes between them in a strictly regulated regime. Braathens, which was privately owned, served most major airports, while Widerøe saw to the needs of the small, publicly subsidized airports. Scandinavian Airlines served the main domestic routes and also handled international traffic. SAS was established because the three Scandinavian countries were each too small to operate an international airline alone. Much of SAS's international traffic from Norway went via Stockholm and, more especially, via Copenhagen, which, strictly speaking, served as Norway's real international airport.

Norwegians became a flying people. Across large distances to remote little towns that could only dream of a railway or fast motor road, air traffic dominated. In 1990, the number of travellers totalled six million on domestic flights and slightly over two million internationally – including half a million by charter. Ten years later, domestic traffic topped 10 million passengers a year and international traffic was up to three million, plus one million charter passengers, half of whom went to Spain and the Canary Islands.

One reason for the growth in air traffic at the beginning of the 21st century was the increase in capacity when in 1998 a new airport was opened at Gardermoen, 20 minutes by high-speed train and 50 kilometres north of Oslo. Gardermoen replaced congested Fornebu, a fifteen-minute taxi ride from the city centre. Norway's principal airport was finally located at Gardermoen after many long rounds of discussion with constantly new proposals and resolutions for an airport close to where the majority of travellers lived. In the end the decisive argument in favour of Gardermoen was that it would be a regional-political instrument to increase commercial activity in the depressed areas north of Oslo.

The second reason for the increase in air traffic at the turn of the millennium was deregulation. Liberalization resulted in the appearance of low-priced competitors. Air travel is no longer a luxury: it can compete with rail, sea and coach travel – not only in terms of time, but also in regard to price.

### Reducing the disadvantages of distance

Norway developed the telephone early, as it was seen as a boon to this sparsely populated country. In 1880 it was in place in Kristiania, and soon after in other towns. In 1895, the Storting resolved to develop a long-distance telephone network, thus launching a national telephone system. At that point, Norway had the highest telephone density in the world, with one telephone device per 140 inhabitants, as compared with 160 in

Denmark and 1,600 in France. In 1899, 38 million local calls were made in Norway. By then, the wireless telegraph, based on radio communication, had been introduced on the islands of Værøy and Røst in the outer Lofotens. If Norway were to have a national telephone network, it would have to benefit the entire nation and reach all parts of the realm.

Later development stagnated as resources were prioritized for other purposes. The telephone was not considered a social benefit for all to enjoy, like daily mail services, electricity and running water. In 1950, Norway had one telephone per 100 inhabitants and there were long waiting lists for subscriptions with the national telecommunications company – especially in the new suburbs around the major cities, which often had only one public telephone booth. The authorities called it a 'distinguished distress'.

In 1950, half of all telephone calls went through manually operated exchanges, and in many places they opposed automatization. These exchanges provided employment and served as local sources of information. There was a certain ambiguity to this, for occasionally the operator would listen in; on the other hand she had an overview, knew who was home and where the taxi or doctor was in case of emergency.

'The postal service is one of the most magnificent of all inventions,' declared economist Oskar Jæger in 1930. Cross-subsidizing was a basic principle, by which profitable services would finance unprofitable and ensure equal domestic postage-rates, no matter how far a parcel or letter was carried. Development of the network continued, and after the Second World War the focus was on rural postal services. Post offices and rural postal services were also agents for the Post Bank, and in this way introduced the entire country to modern banking and payment services.

The number of post offices peaked towards the end of the 1950s at a little below 5,000; by 2003, only 328 were left. Post offices have now been replaced by rural postal services and 1,175 'Post in Shops', services performed by private shops. This system ensures increased accessibility and longer opening hours. Eighty-eight per cent of all first-class (A-class) mail is delivered to the most remote areas of the country the next day, and 99.95 per cent of all households have mail delivered six days a week. Nevertheless, restructuring often meets with vehement local protests, because the post office is regarded as a local cornerstone and meeting place. The reasons for this restructuring are both changes in population patterns and payment services being taken over by banks and the Internet. The number of letters sent is also declining.

### Opinion-forming newspapers

The first Norwegian newspapers printed 'information' and 'addresses' – public announcements and advertisements. The newspaper with the longest history is *Adresseavisen* in Trondheim, which was established in 1767. One hundred years later a new type of newspaper, one with a strong emphasis on social affairs and political agitation, made its appearance. Newspapers and politics were two sides of the same coin, and the newspapers kept up with the tense political dispute between

**Norwegians are** avid newspaper readers. Circulations exploded around 1900, when papers began to include more popular reading matter and invested in more efficient distribution and aggressive selling to non-subscribers, and newsboys became a common sight in towns.

the King and civil service and the radical opposition in the years leading up to 1884. Their expansion was helped by a 50-per-cent reduction in magazine and newspaper postage rates in 1871; there was a connection between postage rates and democracy.

Gradually, the two newspaper traditions merged in a more comprehensive product with extensive domestic and international news coverage. The wealth of subjects increased considerably when the telegraph and telephone became central reporting aids. By the end of the 19th century the major newspapers had some 10,000 subscribers. During the subsequent 20 years, however, circulation exploded with the aggressive sale of single copies by vociferous newsboys. In 1920, with a circulation close to 70,000, Oslo's *Aftenposten* was the country's biggest newspaper.

The Norwegian flora of newspapers includes both national, regional and very local newspapers. The large regional newspapers cover their areas particularly well, but also print comments, national news and international news within the fields of politics, culture, crime and sport.

Norwegian newspapers are special in that no great difference exists between quality and mass-distribution newspapers. Most contain a comprehensive mixture of news, comments, useful information, sport and entertainment. This is also true of the two major national tabloid papers sold mainly to non-subscribers, *Dagbladet* and *Verdens Gang*.

Another special feature of Norwegian newspapers is their historically close association with political parties and interest organizations. Newspapers were either owned by political parties or considered themselves to be party mouthpieces and activists. They campaigned for their parties and supplied information and views based on defined political stances. This was also the basis for the political authorities' organization of financial conditions for newspapers by exempting them from certain taxes and providing them with direct financial support, without binding them to any opinions or contents. Revolutionary *Klassekampen* received the same financial support as the Christian daily *Vårt Land* and the principal organs of the Labour and Centre parties, *Arbeiderbladet* and *Nationen*. The purpose was to maintain 'a differentiated daily press'. This wording aims at political diversity, but also to make it possible for a second newspaper to survive in a town.

Another publishing tradition is provided by periodicals and magazines featuring technical, informative or religiously edifying material and published by voluntary or trade organizations. They existed and exist side by side with more popular weekly magazines with an emphasis on entertainment and articles of practical value. Such publications are not exempt from value-added tax and do not receive public support, which shows that it is the opinion-bearing and -forming aspects of the papers that provide the basis for public support.

In the course of the last 20 years newspapers have severed their political party ties and instead focused on professional, independent journalism. Not everybody agrees that this has increased the diversity: editors often think alike and follow up the same issues. Ownership has been taken over by groups of investors who are more concerned with profits than opinions, and who prefer reading the bottom line of financial statements to editorials. This has hardly added breadth to public debate and undermines the basis of Norwegian media policy.

The number of daily newspapers peaked 50 years ago, falling from 80 in 1960 to 65 in 2000. In addition, about 100 local newspapers are published from one to five times a week. In the same period, overall circulation has more than doubled, to almost four million – two newspapers per adult. We read proportionately more newspapers than any other nation; close to 80 per cent of the population reads a newspaper every day, and readership of electronically-based newspapers is growing rapidly. The largest newspaper is *Verdens Gang*, which has a daily circulation of close to 400,000. The national, non-subscription newspapers have grown parallel with more efficient distribution by air, which allows delivery in the morning all over the country. The finished newspaper is electronically transmitted to printers in different parts of the country and at Norwegian resorts abroad, so that no one need miss his or her daily diet of news.

### Cultural defence measures

In the spirit of national unification that followed the Second World War, distribution of culture became part of the social and regional equality project. Matters of national importance were to be brought to the notice of everyone. Accordingly, a number of national institutions were established to disseminate culture: theatres, pictorial art and concerts. Public libraries were also improved. In the name of regional equality and justice, a travelling cinema, *Norsk Bygdekino*, ensured that people in towns or villages without a permanent cinema were able to see current films.

More recent versions of Norwegian cultural policy have placed greater emphasis on regional cultural expression, without this in any way being seen as a threat to what is common for all Norwegians. On the contrary, the country is so structured that the more Trøndelag- or Telemark-true one is, the more Norwegian one also is.

It gradually emerged that the demand for quality literature was not so great that it could support a broad and viable Norwegian book production. The Arts Council Norway, established in 1964 for cultural purposes, spends half of its funds on buying 1,000 copies of new Norwegian fiction. These books are distributed free of charge to public libraries. Books are also exempt from value-added tax, and the book trade is exempt from normal commercial free price competition. The argument is that this ensures publication of books that appeal to only small readerships and that they sell at the same price in both town and country. Textbooks can only be bought through booksellers, at fixed prices; this is designed to support a broad network of bookshops in rural areas. This system is disputed, and if it collapses it will be an indication that free competition has become more important than national cultural policy.

### The great unifier

When Prime Minister Einar Gerhardsen introduced the first official Norwegian TV broadcast in 1960, he welcomed the new medium as an 'instrument of international understanding'. He foresaw television as 'a new element in education and general enlightenment, and a new means of disseminating knowledge across the country'.

This is the spirit of popular education that had been predominant in the Norwegian Broadcasting Corporation (NRK) since 1933, when it was established as an independent state institution, administratively placed under the Ministry of Church and Education. Earlier, there had been local radio stations financed by advertising, but with few listeners, for a radio was not a common feature in Norwegian homes. NRK was awarded a monopoly on broadcasting and financed by licence fees. The radio was too important a mass medium for the authorities to allow it a free rein without ensuring that it would serve popular education and nation-building purposes.

Ownership of radio sets rocketed, and the radio's pivotal position was clearly demonstrated during the Second World War. Vidkun Quisling announced his assumption of power in a radio speech. Later, the occupying forces confiscated all radios, as they could be used to receive hostile broadcasts. Illegal radios were important to the Resistance movement, which received messages from the Norwegian government-in-exile in London.

The first decades after the Second World War were NRK's boom period as general educator, school broadcaster and cultural common denominator – initially through the country's sole radio channel, later through the only TV channel. Popular programmes united old and young, and radio and television presenters became the country's greatest celebrities. However, education rather than entertainment characterized the 'regular' programmes. One of the major cultural discussions in the country in the 1980s was whether it would be appropriate for NRK to televise the American soap *Dynasty*, which was so far removed from everyday life in Norway.

For 50 years, NRK gathered people and country around a common agenda and common weather forecast, but, this being Norway, a portion of broadcasting time was assigned to local programmes. Local, national and international news broadcasts were gathered under the same umbrella.

As NRK enjoyed a monopoly, it was constantly criticized for a lack of neutrality and for political bias in favour of the dominant social-democratic Labour Party. The Conservative government of the early 1980s therefore opened up for local radio financed by advertising. When NRK prepared itself for tougher competition by establishing three different radio channels directed towards different segments of the listening public, that is, people in general, the cultural élite and the young, protests were

**Norwegians have always** been eager to combine simplicity with modern technology, and even the most outlying areas share in the benefits conferred by new media. Seen here is a holiday cabin at Snillfjord, Sør-Trøndelag, complete with satellite dish.

**Neither Norwegians nor the Sámi** let tradition stand in the way of useful innovations. On the Finnmarksvidda plateau the snowmobile has replaced reindeer-drawn sledges as a means of transportation – for both business and pleasure.

strong. It was asserted that the country's principal radio station ought to present programming that was suitable for everyone and which people all over the country would benefit from.

NRK's television monopoly was rapidly becoming an illusion, as innumerable international channels could be received by cable or satellite dish. In residential areas across the country rows of satellite dishes, usually tilted at the same angle, made their appearance. In the event, however, it was not technical reasons but the argument in favour of greater variety that, in the 1990s, ended the monopoly and led to the introduction of competing national television channels.

The authorities did not relinquish all control, however. A licence was required to broadcast advertising-financed national radio and television. It is demanded of licence applicants that broadcasts be of 'public service' and that the programmes may be received all over the country. In addition, applicants must commit themselves to promotion of the Norwegian language and culture and devote a certain percentage of their programmes to children and other prescribed groups.

The new multi-channel media have fragmented the common, national agenda without investing it with a greater diversity of opinion. News programmes and debates are much the same whatever the channel, and programmes are largely filled with entertainment, which ensures a large number of listeners and viewers and, *ipso facto*, attracts advertising revenue, rather than with information and background material calculated to encourage social involvement. The broadcasting media no longer constitute a nation-building communications community.

### Outpost-modernism

Torjus Pytten was an old man living deep in the heart of Åseral, a mountain valley in southern Norway. From years spent hiking and hunting, summer and winter alike, in the mountains between Ryfylke and Setesdal he knew these trackless wastes like the back of his hand. Year after year he also had marked tracks for the Norwegian Mountain Tourist Association – on skis, carrying only a knapsack, an axe and twigs. He continued marking tracks to the end of his life, but in a different manner; he still stuck twigs into the snow, but to do so he now lay prone on a trailer drawn by a snowmobile.

'Isn't it strange for an old man living deep in a remote valley to have adopted such a newfangled invention?' he was once asked. 'No,' he answered. 'In this valley we do things the old way. But if something new comes along, something we can make use of, then that's what we do'.

Most Norwegians have the same attitude to modern transport and communications as Torjus Pytten. We don't go for anything just because it is new. First we have to be convinced that it is not just nonsense, but something that may be useful. Then we wonder if our neighbour has it or, if he hasn't, when he intends to acquire it, and whether the authorities will promote it in any way. It's important to be quick off the mark, though not too quick; but, above all, not to be too slow.

Once modern gadgets make a breakthrough in Norway, they do so with a vengeance. Such novelties soon become commonplace, for in Norwegian, 'modern' does not mean the newest and latest: it means that which is about to become so common that everybody can have it without standing out from the crowd. What is modern is that which has become so ordinary that you are different if you don't have it.

The Norwegian idea of what is modern is a democratic one quite firmly related to the injunction of the 'Jante law' to be like everone else. We are not very fond of differences and disparities, and we have no need to be a victim of them either. Everybody is so comfortably off that modern appliances do not necessarily create new inequalities. Evenly dispersed wealth and small social and regional differences have made Norway a technologically advanced country.

Because political equality requires that outlying and remote areas should share in the common good, the authorities and private suppliers have had to go to considerable lengths to find solutions. The reason why Norwegian manufacturers of marine cables are so technologically advanced, is that they had to develop such things in order to provide Norwegian island settlements with telephones and electricity.

For the same reasons of equality, little Norway has become a large market for manufacturers of electronic equipment and computer technology. When the video player became modern, when personal computers went from strength to strength, when the mobile telephone made its real breakthrough, and when broadband became available, their spread was incredibly rapid. Seventy-seven per cent of all Norwegians have access to a PC at home, many households have more than one, and most PCs are connected to the Internet. The number of PCs in Norway would take years to sell in countries with greater inequalities between people.

People in the biggest cities are not necessarily the first to gain access to new, technologically advanced devices, with a time lag before they reach remote valleys, fishing stations and other out-of-the-way places. This was once the case, but now the interval is minimal. Indeed, in many areas the situation is quite the opposite. Technically oriented ways of living and thinking often make their first breakthrough in outlying areas, where the distance from technology at work to technology in everyday life is short. Even small fishing boats are equipped with highly sophisticated communications equipment. Technological and electronic devices are simply more natural and useful in many small communities. Besides, they can even out or reduce the disadvantages of distance and mitigate other advantages enjoyed by town dwellers. Such disparities conflict with the politically legitimate and is thus an object of public measures or compensation.

Modern industry and cultural post-modernism may be suffering in Norway, but outpost-modernism is alive and thriving.

### The privatized public administration

The first part of this story about transport and communications in Norway centred on the struggle to unify the nation within a social and geographical community, with the state playing a central role. The other part was about the downsizing of the collective framework and the dissolution of a Norwegian 'room' for reflection in a communicative community. Regional-political values became 'market imperfections'.

In the transport and communications sector regional redistribution is reduced, as is cross-subsidizing and transfer between different projects. The Norwegian Telecommunications Administration, now renamed *Telenor*, has lost its monopoly and public service responsibilities and is expanding on the global mobile telephony market. Each enterprise and each deregulated state company is engrossed in its own cost-benefit analyses. Road construction is contracted out to private enterprise or carried out by public and private companies acting in conjunction, and is often financed by toll revenue from road users. This does away with projects that may be desirable for reasons other than financial profit.

Whereas the physical and technological basis for transport and communications is constantly improving, the national cultural community is disintegrating. Communication in a media-focused society affords the individual greater opportunities for choosing to withdraw from the local and national community through networks, languages and ethnic and cultural subcultures. Anyone can link up directly to global networks without local or national 'doorkeepers'. Distances to other people are shortened, but one is free to choose who the other people are.

Article 100 of the Constitution has remained unchanged for almost 200 years. Because of pressure from changes in means of communication, it is proposed that the term 'liberty of the press' be replaced by 'liberty of expression', and that Article 100 should impose a duty for public commitment: 'National authorities shall facilitate open and informed public discussion'.

Regardless of differing views on Norway's place in Europe, it is a source of cultural and political concern that what has been united is losing out to a variety of special interests and individual freedom of action. This means that the local will not grow into the regional as part of the national, but will disappear in the private and contourless global. If it does, the nation-building project may prove to have been merely an interlude, a 200-year struggle that was nothing more than a passing phase in history.

**Although the fjords** have lost out as local traffic arteries to roads linked by tunnels and bridges, they remain a unique tourist attraction. This photograph is of a tourist ship at Styvi in the Nærøy fjord, Sogn og Fjordane.

**january** fin serck-hanssen **february** rolf m. aagaard

**march** herdis maria siegert **april** janne solgaard

**may** jens hauge **june** vibeke tandberg

**july** dag alveng **august** rune johansen

**september** knut bry **october** asle svarverud

**november** ingvar moi **december** per berntsen

# KIRSTEN FLAGSTAD

'Oh, God!' exclaimed the conductor Arthur Bodenzky when Kirsten Flagstad auditioned at the Metropolitan opera in 1935. The feted, hundred-strong orchestra rose to its feet and applauded her in disbelief. Never had they heard such a magnificent, ethereal voice. At the time, New York's world-famous opera house was in the midst of a financial crisis; its salvation was destined to be a modest women from the small town of Hamar in Norway.

The mystery is how such a divine singer could have remained largely unknown for forty years. The explanation is, in part, that she had grown up in a poor, out-of-the-way agricultural community in Norway, a land that would not have an opera house of its own until almost the end of her life. It was also partly due to her retiring nature: she never went looking for roles – they came to her.

'Haven't you a daughter who sings?'

This was the question the composer Johan Halvorsen asked Kirsten's mother, Maja Flagstad, in 1913. Maja was sorely tempted to say no on behalf of her eldest daughter, as she would have preferred her to train as a doctor – or as a piano teacher. But there was no denying that the eighteen-year-old could sing. She was engaged on the spot to appear in the opera *Tiefland*, with the consequence that she made her stage debut in 1913.

Kirsten Flagstad spent the whole of her first fee on new curtains for her mother. The Flagstads were a musical family in every respect. Kirsten's mother became organist at the local church at the age of nine and her father was an orchestra conductor, violinist and parliamentary stenographer. At Christmas the family used to perform for the inmates of a prison in the capital. One prisoner is reported to have been so moved by Kirsten's singing that he tried to have his sentence extended, provided she came back at Easter.

Kirsten Flagstad never dreamed of becoming famous as a singer. More than anything she wanted a husband, children and a home of her own. At the age of twenty she became engaged to a man from the far north of the country, but after a short time the engagement was broken off. However, her fiancé's disappointed mother treated her to a year's singing studies in Stockholm, where her teacher realized that she would soon be good enough to join the city's opera company. However, shortly before Christmas 1918 Kirsten left the Swedish capital and married Sigurd Hall, a businessman. She gave birth to a daughter, Else Marie, and resolved to give up singing for good.

As it turned out, childbirth greatly improved her already magnificent voice, so she allowed herself to be prevailed upon to return to the stage. She was given a number of lead roles in musical performances of various kinds and toured Norway. One critic wrote that she lacked imagination. She

sang in Copenhagen, where she was acclaimed for the cascading tone of her voice, and in Stockholm people were overwhelmed by her outstanding vocal lustre. In Norway she frittered away her time on musical comedies, revues and light operas. In Oslo, the 'voice of the century' appeared as a belly dancer for 128 nights in a row! 'It is, and will remain, a great shame that we do not have a Norwegian opera for a singer like her,' wrote a Skien newspaper.

Her breakthrough did not come until she appeared at the Stora Teatern in Gothenburg in 1928. By then she was thirty-three and really no more than a housewife who did a bit of singing on the side. However, the Swedish press acclaimed her a goddess. After hearing her perform in *Saul and David*, the composer Carl Nielsen called her brilliant. At about the same time she was formally separated from her husband. At the premiere of *Lohengrin* at Oslo's National Theatre in June 1930, her admirers included one Henry Johansen, a merchant. Three days after the opening-night party he proposed to Kirsten, who accepted.

Her concerts were increasingly attended by influential figures in the musical establishment, all of whom reported glowingly of a voice that was truly miraculous. In 1933 Flagstad sang Wagner in Bayreuth, was engaged by the opera in Brussels, and at the same time was invited to audition for the directors of the Metropolitan. Somewhat reluctantly, she permitted herself to be caught up in the whirl of an international career, while her husband quite happily joined the National Union Party (*Nasjonal Samling*), a Norwegian Fascist movement.

As early as February 1935 leading American newspapers were claiming that a star had been born, and there were reports of 'visionary rapture'. On every street corner news vendors shouted her name, and aeroplanes towed Flagstad streamers across the skies of America's major cities. Following a guest appearance in the star role of Isolde at Covent Garden, Kirsten Flagstad was thirty-eight times brought back on stage by the audience's applause. She created a sensation in Vienna and Prague, Sydney and Honolulu – and in Hollywood she captivated 20,000 people with her renderings of songs by Grieg. 'This is a great artist, who seems to understand all human emotions,' said Eleanor Roosevelt.

In similar circumstances many artists would have become prima donnas or abandoned themselves to the good life; but Kirsten Flagstad spent her time between performances knitting or playing solitaire. Even in her breaks, she sat backstage, knitting garments for her daughter, her husband and herself. She greatly missed family life and more than once resolved to give up her career – not an easy thing to do for a woman who was constantly lauded in the leader columns of the world's major newspapers as 'First Lady of the Opera'.

Kirsten Flagstad had long had a passage booked to return to Norway on the transatlantic liner *Bergensfjord* on 20 April 1940, but eleven days before she was due to leave, Norway was occupied by German forces. However, she missed her family so much that on 19 April 1941 she made the fatal mistake of returning home. Despite her refusal to perform in Norway and in other German-occupied countries, her return was construed as sympathy with the Nazis. Although she gave covert financial assistance to the Resistance and was instrumental in bringing about her husband's resignation from the National Union Party in the summer of 1941, in Sweden she was portrayed as a Nazi. At a festival held in neutral Switzerland she chose to perform Beethoven's opera *Fidelio*, which had become a universal symbol of love and liberty. The American press claimed that she had performed in Germany in the presence of Göring – and that of a person who refused to perform in neutral countries if the conductor was German!

Following Norway's liberation, Henry Johansen was arrested as a major war profiteer, but died in prison before his case came to trial. The Norwegian authorities withdrew Kirsten Flagstad's passport and confiscated her cabin in the country. For nearly two years she was held a virtual prisoner by the country over which she had cast such lustre. Following her release, she returned to America, only to be met in many places by organized protests. Over-zealous Norwegians in authority even took active steps to ruin her career. By 1947 the process of vilification had gone so far that forty Norwegian artists inserted a notice in the press demanding that persecution of Kirsten Flagstad should cease. It was to little avail. We now know that as late as 1953, King Haakon VII refused to open the Bergen Festival if Kirsten Flagstad was performing. She was still the nation's scapegoat.

Nevertheless, slowly but surely she reclaimed her former international reputation. She performed as a guest star on the world's most prestigious stages, made numerous recordings, reconquered the Metropolitan to outstanding acclaim and gave an increasing number of benefit concerts – for causes that included orphaned Jewish children. She contributed to the Save the Children Fund and the Red Cross, and also set up a substantial endowment for destitute Norwegian musicians.

She received admiring letters from Richard Strauss, who asked her to premier four songs he had recently written, and Jan Sibelius, who referred to her as 'the great soulful singer', invited her to his home. But Kirsten Flagstad was an unhappy, lonely and broken woman. Psoriasis, which attacked her joints, led to long spells in hospital, and she missed her husband and her daughter, who had made her home in Montana. It was some compensation for her to be appointed director of the newly established Norwegian Opera Company, but she resigned her post after only a year. Towards the end of her life her repertoire came increasingly to consist of hymns.

Kirsten Flagstad died of bone cancer in 1962, and at her own request was buried in an unmarked common grave. The world-famous star Jessye Norman has claimed that no opera singer in history can compare with Kirsten Flagstad, whom she said would 'always be unique'. The Norwegian Opera did not wish to have a sculpture of Flagstad on its premises, and the Oslo Concert Hall similarly declined. Not until twenty years after her death was a statue to her erected in front of the Norwegian Academy of Music.

'I have experienced the joy of singing,' said Kirsten Flagstad, 'that is enough for me.'

NIELS CHR. GEELMUYDEN

FLAGSTAD, KIRSTEN (1895-1962), opera singer (soprano). Sang in roles all over the world, including at the Metropolitan in New York, 1935-41 and 1949-52. Director-General of Den Norske Opera 1958-60. Made a number of recordings. Widely regarded as 'the voice of the century'.

# EDUCATION AND RESEARCH

# KNOWLEDGE SHALL RULE KINGDOM AND COUNTRY

Tove Bull

FARE YOU WELL, SCHOOLGIRL

*For Unn and the others*

Fare you well, schoolgirl.
With your red satchel like a sunrise
on your back
and pigtails like curtains drawn aside
your neck, this white nun
I always want to say I beg your pardon to,
you go
to your first days at school.
Your face is bursting with an expectation
as explosively fertile
as a newly won field in a rain forest.

Ah, sowers,
go with clean hands and bared heads
when with your seedlip you tread this land.
I doubt the knowledge you broadcast
will fall by the wayside, but I know:
all who without guile,
unsceptical, uncamouflaged
unwittingly artless
go out to meet life wearing a faith
like a precious golden apple in their hands,
are hallowed.

So fare you well, schoolgirl.

Kolbein Falkeid, from *Horisontene*
(The Horizons), 1975

**The highest level of education in the world**

In the autumn of 2003 several newspapers informed us that Norway had gained top place worldwide in education. For many people this came as a surprise, and not a few of them wondered what having the *best* education meant, and whether what we were really talking about was having the *most* education. This led to a debate about education policy that rumbled on in the newspapers throughout the autumn. In our country, public discussion of education policy is hardly a rare event. The background in this case was the report that the OECD publishes every three years, *Education at a Glance*. This report compares levels of education in a number of countries. The basis for the 2003 report was figures from the academic year 1999–2000. The reason Norway awarded itself the gold medal is to be found in statistics that show that for those aged between 25 and 34, it has the highest educational level in the world. As regards people of working age in general, Norwegians are amongst the best educated in the entire OECD area; more accurately, they are among those with the longest education in the world, though not *the* longest. As the figure below shows, 86% of the people in this group had received education at sixth-form college level or higher. As 88% of the same age group in the USA and Switzerland and 87% in the Czech Republic also had this level of education, Norway had to be content with fourth place. The average figure for OECD countries was 64%.

In the group in which Norway scores highest (ages 25–34), fully 94% had received this level of education. This is a very high percentage, but even so, everything suggests that the trend is still upwards.

If we look at the figures for people with education *higher* than the sixth-form college level, for example higher education lasting more than four years, we see that 28% of those between 25 and 64 fall into this category, against an OECD average of 15%. Only the USA has a similar percentage to Norway.

The basis of the OECD statistics is 34 indicators that show educational level, resource distribution, access to education, and school and educational organization.

We can therefore agree that the level of education in Norway is high, and that the prognoses that this level will be maintained or even increased in the future, are good. But length of schooling is one thing, its quality quite something else. *Education at a Glance 2003* also investigates the quality of education. This is something to which we shall return. But first, we will examine educational statistics in terms of real flesh and blood, in the shape of the Everyman family.

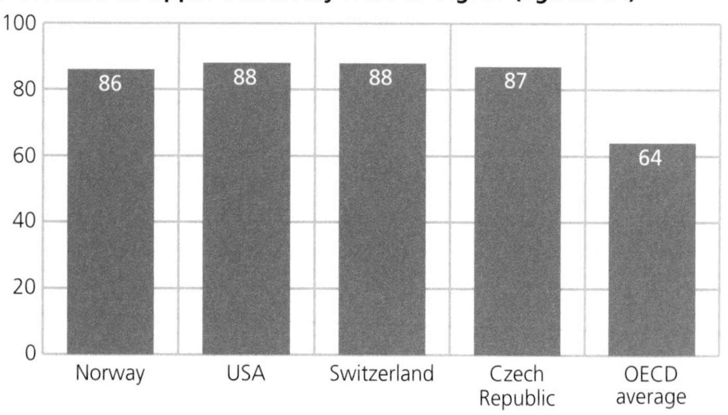


**The Everymans**

For children growing up in Norway in the early 21st century, the chances of receiving higher education are very good. As a result, the contrast in the educational levels of different generations of the Everyman family is rather striking. If we go back a hundred years, everything was quite different. Norway was one of the poorest countries in Europe, with an educational standard to match. To illustrate these developments we will examine the schooling of the individual members of the Everyman family over four generations.

The youngest members of the family, a girl and a boy, each have the most popular name of the year in which they were born, Ida in 2000 and Markus in 2002. They will reach compulsory education age when they are six. Prior to this they will attend playschool, as both parents work outside the home. If families are lucky, their children will get playschool places from the toddler stage, but in 'our' family it is only the elder child that has a regular place at playschool. The parents have had to employ a child-minder for the small boy.

Education, ten years of schooling, is both obligatory and a right in Norway. This is the same for all children and is quite centrally controlled. Curricula and timetables are decided by centralized education authorities. In principle all pupils are supposed to learn the same things: choice is the exception, and English is mandatory for all. A second or third foreign language is, however, optional. Children with Norwegian as their mother tongue learn about their shared Norwegian cultural heritage,

**This may be** the educational reality for Ida and Markus Everyman. This picture was taken at Stovner Sixth-form College, where 120 pupils are being taught in one class and each has their own computer.

especially literature. They must also learn our two official written language variations, Bokmål and Nynorsk. By far the majority (about 85%) take Bokmål as their main written language and Nynorsk as the secondary one. From year nine onwards, training in writing the secondary Norwegian variant becomes compulsory. This is controversial. Children with a mother tongue other than Norwegian learn only one variant of Norwegian. In place of the other they can study Sámi (Lappish), a national minority language (i.e. Finnish) or an immigrant language (i.e. Urdu). Another contentious compulsory subject is known as KRL (Christianity and philosophy). The idea is that KRL study should be so loosely linked to any particular creed as to bring together children from a variety of backgrounds. Critics maintain that the evangelical Lutheran beliefs on which the Church of Norway is founded, are allowed to dominate the subject far too much.

When Ida and Markus start school in 2006 and 2008, it is quite probable that they will be housed in an old and rundown school building with poor temperature control and ventilation. The two risk having to attend a school with few resources for school materials and equipment. This will probably mean that their parents will consider sending them to a private school, the numbers of which are growing each year. Up to now, though, private schools have been viewed as something bordering on the un-Norwegian and an expression of a lack of solidarity and community spirit.

Everyone is entitled to three years' further education. Students can choose which further education course they want, a general studies course or a course of more practical, aesthetic or directly work-related subjects. Even in further education, the material standard is not much to boast about. On completion of a sixth-form college course there is an opportunity for higher education, either at one of the universities or at a scientific institute or national college. In addition there are a few private higher education facilities, for example Handelshøgskolen BI, the Norwegian School of Management, which is in fact one of the largest. The universities and national colleges are dispersed about the country, but the great majority of students apply to universities or colleges in their own locality, unless they go abroad to study. Students are taking this latter option in increasing numbers.

Should Ida and Markus Everyman so wish, they can embark on a lengthy higher education course. Financing for this is assured through loans and bursaries which are available to everyone for educational purposes. Ida might, for example, choose medicine and finish her studies after six years. As a girl, she may well complete her studies in a more focused manner than the majority of boys, and with better results. Were either of them to study science or technology, it would most probably be Markus. Such subjects attract a majority of boys, and the disparity between the sexes is wider in Norway, the land of equality, than in other OECD countries. In general, interest in the natural sciences and technology is badly lacking in Norwegian youngsters, most notably in Norwegian girls. Markus could take a three-year bachelor degree course and then a two-year master's degree. (The old Latin degree names have recently been replaced by the corresponding English ones, in line with general European practice.) After such training, both Ida and Markus could continue with a doctorate, which has been standardized to three years. Norway has joined the so-called Bologna Process and reformed its higher education structure to make it fully compatible with the rest of Europe. The government is very proud of the fact that Norway has introduced nearly all the changes demanded by the Bologna Process. Ambitions are high: Norway wants to be in the lead, and even to be top of the Bologna class.

On the whole, the higher educational institutions are of a much better material standard than the schools and sixth-form colleges, despite consumption being higher the further down the school system one goes. Compared to many countries, Norway's universities and national colleges are fairly recent institutions. This means that much of the building stock around the country is fairly new. In addition, such institutions are funded by the state, whereas local councils are responsible for schools and county councils for sixth-form colleges. Ownership may thus play a part in the material standard of these institutions.

Ida and Markus's parents, Monica and Jan, have both been through higher education. They started school as seven-year-olds and completed nine years of compulsory schooling – like everyone else; then Monica did three years of general studies at sixth-form college, and Jan took a three-year commercial course. Monica, born in 1972, has completed a four-year teacher training course which qualifies her to teach the whole of the ten-year Norwegian school syllabus. Many people believe that Norwegian teacher training is far too lax, and an inadequate qualification for the teaching profession. Monica shares this opinion: she believes there is a direct correlation between this and the drop in social status that teachers have gradually suffered. Jan (b. 1970) took a three-year financial and administrative course at a national college in his home town, where his family now lives. The grandparents live there as well.

Grandfather Arne was born in 1935. He grew up on a farm, and according to the School Act of 1936 for the *folkeskole* system in rural districts, received seven years of elementary schooling. He attended school every other day and never learnt English, for example. After finishing school he went to sea for some years, before returning home to attend agricultural college for one winter preparatory to taking over the farm. Later, the town expanded and the farm fell into disrepair; its old outbuildings are now surrounded by residential blocks. Arne opted for early retirement. Grandmother Bjørg, who was born in the town in 1939 was in an all-girl class at a city *folkeskole*, and went there every day. She literally had twice as many hours of instruction each year as Arne. She was taught English in the final two years, but less maths than in the parallel boys' class, as the girls had to have time for home economics. Afterwards she attended a *realskole* (an old secondary tier) for three years and then started work in an office, but left when she had her first baby. She recently returned to secretarial work, but, like Arne, has now taken early retirement.

Great-grandmother Anna, who was born in 1912, is still alive. When she speaks of her schooldays it is hard for Monica and Jan not to smile. The way she recalls it, you would hardly

**Kroer School** at Ås, photographed in 1913. Great-grandmother Anna might have gone to this school.

have thought she had been to school at all. But Great-grandma has a good memory. She started school at the age of seven in a remote hamlet. A fortnight of school and then a fortnight off, that was the way the school year was organized. Her school was a small, draughty shack which was heated by a wood-burning stove in winter. Whenever she thinks of her school, it always conjures up the smell of damp wool. And she talks readily about the hard, but companionable 'potato-lifting holidays' in the autumn. They only had one teacher in the village; he was responsible for two school districts, so her schooling was somewhat minimal, says Great-grandma, who never received more than a few months' education each year for just seven years. 'But we turned out all right, just the same,' she is fond of adding.

A graphic representation of the school structure in the various periods when the different generations of the Everymans went to school, is as follows:

**Educational structure 1900, 1920, 1935, 1969 and 1997**

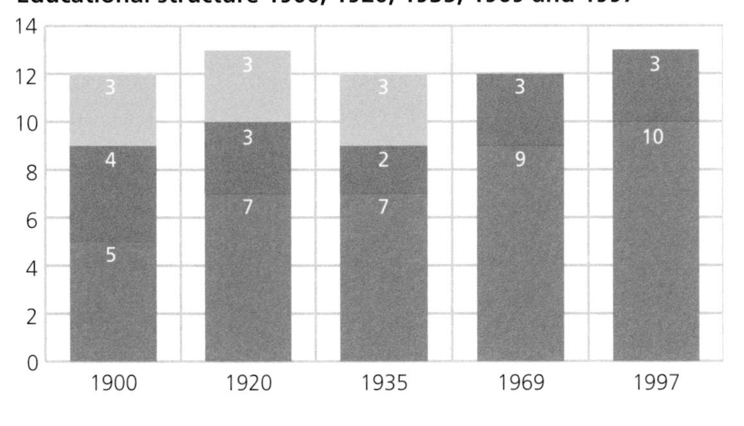


The totals in the columns (number of years) show the foundation for general studentship, what was and what is required for higher education at a university or national college. The column for 1900 illustrates the structure prior to seven-year schooling becoming the universal norm, the one for 1920 the situation after a resolution in the Storting restricted state subsidies to schools that offered a seven-year *folkeskole* (elementary) education. The other three columns show the situation after the reforms of 1935/36, 1969 and 1997.

As we can see, the Norwegian education system has been in a state of constant flux during the 20th century. Reforms have been many and frequent. Viewed like this, the development of the school and educational system reflects the general social development the country has undergone. At the start of the 20th century Norway was one of the poorest countries in Europe; a hundred years later it is amongst the richest in the world. To explain this extraordinary development, evidence from various areas of social life has to be examined, as the causes are clearly complex. But that education and research have played a critical part, there can be no doubt whatsoever. Nor is there any question but that those who thrashed out educational reforms did so out of a strong belief that education is an important factor in the battle against poverty.

When education and education policy are used for explanatory purposes, long historical perspectives are involved. The historical sweep that the generations of the Everyman family provides, is actually not long enough. If we go right back to the earliest schools in Norway, we shall be struck by how anchored the country, including its schools and educational system, was in the rest of Europe. But characteristics unique to Norway will also become apparent as constituents in the development of schools.

### Establishing compulsory universal education

The Norwegian word *skole*, like the English word *school* and the German *Schule*, has its origins in the Latin *schola*, which means 'leisure used for study'. The foreign origins imply that not only the word, but also the activity it describes, is 'borrowed'. The word and the phenomenon arrived with Christianity. We can therefore say that the Norwegian education system, from its inception, is the result of European influence. The oldest school in Norway is Trondheim Cathedral School, Schola Catedralis Nidrosiensis. Its history can almost certainly be traced back to the 1080s. Gradually, five such cathedral schools were established. Originally they were schools for priests and centres of book learning. After the Reformation the cathedral schools were turned into so-called Latin schools, which in turn form the origins of the later *gymnas* (upper secondary) schools and, later still, the *vidaregåande* schools (sixth-form colleges).

It is commonly claimed that it was only long after the Reformation that Norway had anything worthy of the name of universal schools. This was in 1739 and resulted from an Education Act relating to permanent schools and ambulatory schools in rural districts that introduced obligatory school attendance for three months a year for all children between the ages of seven and twelve. This was in response to the introduc-

tion of confirmation as a mandatory rite of passage into adult society in 1736. But even in Catholic times religious instruction had been compulsory for the masses. The Church wanted to make sure that everyone knew their paternoster, creed and Ave Maria, and also after a time the ten commandments. Similarly, other aspects of the Norwegian school have traditions that predate 1739. Generally schools have been – and still are – strongly textbook-orientated and dependent. This is probably because decisions were taken centrally about which textbooks were to be required. This first happened as far back as 1607, when the Norwegian ecclesiastical ordinance prescribed what was known as *Degnbogen* (The Deacon's Book) as a text for sextons who had a duty to instruct children on one day a week. This Deacon's Book was principally a translation of Luther's Small Catechism.

Obligatory school attendance institutionalized the ambulatory school (in which the teacher went from farm to farm to teach). But even this has older roots. Kristian V's Norwegian law of 1687 obliged every parish to have a 'plan of instruction'. In view of the great distances involved it was obvious that the ambulatory school would be the type that would dominate in rural areas, and it lasted right up until the 20th century. The 1739 Schools Act emphasized that Board Schools were to provide a similar education for all. In this way schools helped to stem educational class divisions in the village, in contrast to the development in towns. It was the egalitarian rural schools which set the foundations for the 'unity schooling' system which emerged during the twentieth century, and not the middle-class urban schools. This is unique. The distinction between the urban and rural *folkeskole* lasted right up until the Schools Act of 1959. But by that time the general, seven-year 'unity' *folkeskole* had long since been introduced throughout the country.

The oldest urban Board School is the Christi Krybbe school in Bergen, which was founded in 1737 and began teaching in its own purpose-built premises in 1740. It is also, incidentally, the oldest surviving elementary school in Scandinavia. In contrast to village schools, town schools reflected a class-divided society. For a long time the Board Schools in towns were very neglected. The middle classes preferred the Latin school for their boys, and from the end of the 18th century, the so-called 'civic' school and *realskole* for those who did not see the need for a classical education in Latin and Greek. The name *realskole* reflects that this was a school for material things, for real life. And it was to these schools that girls were eventually admitted. The first female teacher in Norway, Hilchen Sommerschild, was employed by Trondheim's civic *realskole* (now the Gerhard Schøning School) in 1799. She taught French and needlework.

In a European context such civic schools were an expression of the Age of Enlightenment and liberalism. But because towns were relatively few and small, they did not have the same influence as similar schools in other countries where, to a large extent, they were the antecedents of a more extensive private schooling system than ever developed in Norway. The fact that Norway has such a strictly egalitarian education system can partly be explained by the egalitarianism of the system that has always existed in rural areas, where most people lived, and that it was this egalitarian ideology and practice that won through in the reforming work that gained momentum in the 19th and 20th centuries.

From the outset, the job of these new universal schools in the 18th century was to prepare children for confirmation. The syllabus was restricted to the study of the Christian religion. It was a religious knowledge school and nothing more. Its aim was to educate children for a religious purpose. Only later, especially after 1860, was this to alter. Gradually, changes in society demanded space in the school for temporal knowledge and skills development, partly for economic reasons, partly for the purposes of nation-building.

Paradoxically enough, the demand for universal schooling led to an ever greater and faster 'Danicization' of the Norwegian masses. This continued long after the union between Denmark and Norway was dissolved in 1814. The Sámi (Lapps) in the northern regions of Norway were also subjected to these Christian schools – during the 18th century by missionaries who learnt Sámi and who taught using it, but increasingly during the 19th century as part of an attempt at Norwegianization which ultimately proscribed the Sámi language and culture at school. This prohibition was to remain in place for well over a century.

As a result of this development of educational policy, the word 'Norwegianization' has come to mean two diametrically opposite things in the history of Norwegian schooling and language. On the one hand, Norwegianizing of the Danish language and culture to the benefit of Norwegian schoolchildren, who gradually acquired the right to use their own dialect at

**To 'appear** before the priest' was the key to adult society. 'Confirmation', a painting from Hoprekstad in Sogn, by H.A.O. Frigt (1866).

**A Sámi** school at Sandnes, Sør-Varanger.

school. Teachers even had to try to moderate their speech to fit in with the language the children spoke at home. In this way Norwegian dialects assumed a position that is almost unique amongst European societies. On the other hand 'Norwegianization' implied a policy of assimilation with strongly racist overtones for the Sámi and certain people of Finnish stock in the north. And it was the schools that became the most important arena for this assimilation policy.

The early Norwegian school was an authoritarian institution. Don't-want-to was made to! And corporal punishment was often used to coerce him. It was the Education Acts of the 1930s that prohibited the use of such punishments, although in reality they continued long into the postwar period.

This outline description of Norwegian schools of the 18th and early 19th centuries demonstrates that the establishment of obligatory school attendance was not the result of the need of schooling *per se*, or of particular social demands. Obligatory schooling was introduced so that children might be moulded into Christians. They were to learn Christian norms and Christian morals. The subsequent development of Norwegian schools and education can also be interpreted and explained in the light of changing external requirements and ideologies, rather than as the result of internal developments or educationally justified demands.

### School and nation building. The Liberal school

The first Norwegian school statistics date back to 1837. At that time roughly 90% of the population lived on the land and 10% in towns. Ninety-four per cent of rural children went to Board Schools, 87% of these went to ambulatory schools, the remaining 7% to permanent ones. Only one per cent of country children went to private fee-paying schools. Five per cent did not attend school at all. In the towns, 65% went to free schools or poor schools. Around 17% went to private civic schools or grammar schools; 18% of urban children had no schooling at all, either because of insufficient school places, or because of poverty or truancy.

From the middle of the 19th century until well into the 20th was the age of nation building. It was during this time that schools moved away from being purely Christian schools. From now on elementary schools had a double function: the education of Christians and of the nation's citizens. Economic arguments for schooling and education were heard more. The schools' task now included imparting the skills and knowledge that everyone needs to survive in society. Worldly disciplines such as history, geography and science became subjects in their own right. This dual function has characterized Norwegian elementary education to this day, even if its stated Christian objectives have been toned down somewhat. In addition, obligatory school attendance was enforced and the school year extended. Another characteristic trait is that the development moves more and more in the direction of uniform school provision. The private schools the middle classes were so fond of, lost ground. This new departure was formally expressed in continual reforms and statute revisions from the 1840s until the Second World War. These affected both elementary and higher education.

The founding of the first Norwegian university, Det Kongelige Frederiks Universitet (the Royal Frederik University, now the University of Oslo), in 1811, can also be seen as an expression of nation building. This is also true of the foundation of a number of teachers' seminaries throughout the country, which gradually helped give Norway a relatively well educated teaching profession with a high social status.

It is self-evident that these great upheavals aroused controversy. Norwegian schools have developed and changed over time, largely as a result of political upheaval – and from the 1880s, debate between political parties. Such dissent was manifested in many ways, including direct truancy, by parents keeping their children away from school. During the fishing season in the Lofoten Islands, absence increased from about 40% to 80-90%. There can hardly be a clearer illustration of the way parents thought that compulsory schooling affected their ability to make ends meet. What was taught in the 'new' schools was also contentious. Many people wanted to keep the purely Christian school system. P.A. Jensen's *Læsebog for Folkeskolen og Folkehjemmet* (A Reader for Elementary School and for the Home) of 1863 was a particular target for lay opposition to an increasingly secular school.

The education policies of the Liberal (Venstre) government were gradually enacted during the 1880s. The *einskapsskole* ('unity school') was its chief aim; a seven-year comprehensive education that would form the basis for further education for those who were suitable, but at the same time would constitute

**School attendance 1837**

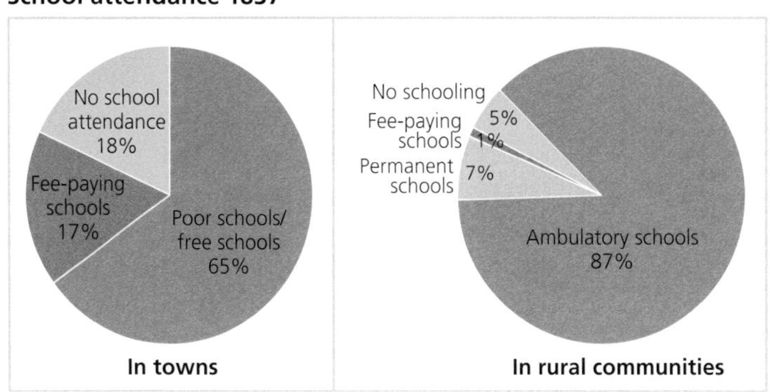


a thorough schooling for those who went straight out to work. The idea was to put so much into state education that private schools would gradually lose their pupil base. Knowledge would rule kingdom and country, and that knowledge would be common to all and to the benefit of all. Norwegianization by means of parity between Landsmålet (the 'country' language) and Dano-Norwegian was an important element in the ideology of the Liberal school; so was the dream of social reconciliation and national identity. This national identity also assumed, as we have already seen, the Norwegianization of the Sámi and Finnish dialect-speaking areas of the north. Sámi and Finnish dialects were consequently banned from use at school. At the turn of the 20th century the school had been consolidated as the cockpit for the dissemination of a national culture, which to a large extent was seen as a rural one. The civic culture of the towns was regarded as un-Norwegian and Danish. This is something quite unique to Norway. Politically, schools could be regarded as an important control mechanism in the welding of this national culture, although it would be wrong to maintain that urban, middle-class culture was not represented within schools. It was rather that schools, well into recent times, found themselves at the interface of the national Norwegian 'peasant' culture and a middle-class city culture.

A peculiarly Scandinavian and deeply national type of school is the *folkehøgskole* (people's college). It is often referred to as the *Grundtvigian folkehøgskole* after its founder, the Danish priest and hymnist Nikolai Frederik Severin Grundtvig (1783–1872). Grundtvig himself saw the *folkehøgskole* as a counter to the Latin school. The Norwegian *folkehøgskole*, which was soon to proliferate, represented a national and popular movement that aimed to bring knowledge and education within everyone's reach. The pupils, who were often boarders at the school, usually took courses lasting six months or a year. The very first Norwegian *folkehøgskole* was Sagatun near Hamar, founded in 1864. Many a young Norwegian has spent the finest year of his or her youth at a *folkehøgskole* together with like-minded fellow students and idealistic, culturally committed teachers. Because these schools did not provide qualifications in the formal sense, they have played a more limited role during the past few decades. But there are still young people who can bear witness to what a year at such a school has given them.

**Bård the schoolmaster and little Marius**

Part of Norway's cultural heritage is understanding the history of schooling through certain selected literary classics. What often characterizes such school portraits is the critical distance of the author, and occasionally nostalgia and sadness. Hardly anyone can have passed through Norwegian elementary and further education without becoming acquainted with, for instance, Bård the schoolmaster and little Marius. Bård is the peripatetic teacher in Bjørnstjerne Bjørnson's *En glad gutt* (A Happy Boy) from 1860. This is how Bjørnson depicts the main character, Øyvind's, encounter with the ambulatory school:

*When they arrived at the pensioner's cabin, a great rushing sound like that of the mill at home assaulted them, and he asked his mother what it was. 'It's the youngsters reading,' she answered, and this made him very happy, because that was just the way he had read before he'd learnt his letters. When he entered, there were so many children sitting round a table that there were no more in church: others sat on their food bowls along the walls, some stood in small groups round a chart. The schoolmaster, an old grey-haired man, sat on a stool directly before the hearth filling his pipe. When Øyvind and his mother entered, everyone looked up, and the chatter of the mill ceased just as it did when they stemmed the headrace. Everyone looked at the newcomers. His mother greeted the schoolmaster, who returned the greeting.*

*'I've come with a little boy who wants to learn to read,' said his mother. 'What's the lad called?' asked the schoolmaster, delving into his leather pouch for tobacco.*

*'Øyvind,' said his mother. 'He knows his letters and he can add up.' 'Oh, ho,' exclaimed the schoolmaster, 'come here, you little whitehead!' Øyvind went to him, the schoolmaster sat him on his knee and took off his cap. 'What a lovely little boy!' he said and patted his hair; Øyvind looked into his eyes and laughed. 'Are you laughing at me?' He knitted his brow. 'Yes, I am,' Øyvind answered with a peal of laughter. At that the schoolmaster laughed as well, his mother laughed, the children knew that they, too, could laugh, and so they all laughed together.*

*And with that, Øyvind had joined the school.*

Bjørnson's schoolmaster Bård is a hero of a teacher, and viewed in a national-romantic light, the ambulatory school in rural areas is the best of all schools. It functions as a class leveller, one of Bjørnson's main messages. The fact that in practice it most certainly was not always as idyllic as in Bjørnson's portrait, is another matter. The contrast between Bjørnson's ambulatory school and the Latin school in Alexander Kielland's *Gift*

**Bjørnstjerne Bjørnson** makes a speech at Sagatun.

(Poison) from 1883 reflects a real contrast of the age. In tune with the prevailing national ideology, the Latin school is precisely that – not national. The very title *Poison* gives a clear indication of what the Latin school means for the young:

*Anything that, here and there, might be found in the instruction that referred directly to life and to the world, as it really is, diminished considerably. And into the driving seat came long processions of dead words about dead things; rules and rigmarole, hammered home into submissive minds, there to take up space for ever; foreign sounds from a foreign life; ancient dust, conscientiously sprinkled everywhere that sap-filled youth showed a moist spot to which the dust could stick.*

This is then illustrated with episodes from the classroom in which teachers of a more or less brutal nature bear down on every weak point in a weak pupil. Some of these descriptions have assumed canonical status in our common national heritage, and words and phrases from the book have almost become proverbs or sayings, as when the teacher Borring again and again demands 'More cities in Belgium' or the quotation: '"Mensa rotunda,"' answered little Marius, and died.' For this is the eventual fate of little Marius, he dies from the lack of life, the poison the Latin school represents, while the pupils who do not die literally, become slowly corrupted.

**The 'Oslo breakfast'.** Schoolchildren having a school breakfast of milk and crispbread with cheese, 1951.

### The social democratic school: the einskapsskole

In every language in the world there are words and expressions which can only be translated with great difficulty. *Einskapsskole* is an example from the Norwegian language. How does one translate it into English or German?

As soon as we come across these 'untranslatable' words and concepts in a language, we know immediately that they spring from a phenomenon which is socially unique to the language area. The 'unity school' is thus something peculiarly Norwegian. And the idea behind the *einskapsskole*, as we have seen, has coloured Norwegian school and educational policies from the very inception of compulsory universal schooling in our country.

The ideology behind the *einskapsskole* is this: everyone has the right and the duty to attend school. The school is unifying, in the sense that all Norwegian pupils have identical rights and obligations. School attendance is the same length for everyone, compulsory subjects are compulsory for everyone, the standards demanded will be the same for everyone. Everyone is entitled to apply for higher education on the basis of what they have achieved in elementary and further education, regardless of social and geographical differences. Schools are open to all and are free.

These fundamental principles are extensions of particular ideas about democracy in an egalitarian society. In the educational context there should be no difference between King Solomon and Joe Bloggs. Equality and justice should prevail.

The idea behind the *einskapsskole* forms the basis of social democratic educational ideology. The school reforms of the late 19th century were driven through by the Liberal Party, but it was to be the Norwegian Labour Party (Det Norske Arbeiderparti) that carried them forward in the new century. So there was a correlation between the decentralized and democratic school of the Liberals and the school policies the Labour Party chose to follow, even though the latter stood for class war-

**The Royal Frederik University** (the University of Oslo) with the students' grounds (Studenterlunden). Coloured lithograph from a painting by Joachim Frisch.

fare in contrast to the conciliatory Liberal line. It must also be admitted that the Labour Party stood for a more centralized schools policy, and that schools under it were more centrally controlled than they had been under the Liberals. The Labour Party also had clear social goals in their schools programme, with free school materials, free school meals in urban areas (including cod-liver oil!), health check-ups and free dental care.

One of the contentious issues in this context concerned the relationship between the seven-year elementary school and the higher schools. Should further education be founded directly on seven-year elementary education (7 + 2 (or possibly 3)), or should one continue to have a special stream (5 + 4) for those who wanted to go on to further education? When an act of Parliament in 1920 made it clear that only higher schools that built on a completed seven-year elementary education would have the right to state subsidy, the seven-year *einskapsskole* was established *de facto*. This was enshrined in law in the School Acts of 1935 (for the higher schools) and in 1936 (for the elementary schools in town and country). Norway now had a seven-year elementary school that was not dependent on social position or class. This was the precursor to the compulsory seven-year rural elementary education Great-grandmother Anna in the Everyman family attended. For those who were suitable for further education, the options were a two- or three-year *realskole*, five-year *gymnas* (secondary school preparatory to university) or four-year *landsgymnas*. Some settled for one or two years of *framhaldsskole* ('continuation' school). The very Norwegian *landsgymnas* were founded by statute in 1914. They were to be a resource for rural youngsters over fifteen years of age who had no more formal education than seven years of elementary school. The initiative came from the Nynorsk movement. The first *landsgymnas* came into operation at Voss in 1916. The *landsgymnas* quickly developed into elite schools, as there was keen competition for places. Many a gifted youth from the country who could not bear the expense of a five- or six-year course after elementary school, applied to them; there he could avoid school fees and even get a bursary. An alternative to *gymnas* was the *yrkesskoler* (vocational schools), which were established in certain places after the guild system was abolished in 1866.

There is thus a correlation and continuity that marks the development of schools under the Liberal and Labour governments. Key characteristics which were common to the values of both parties in the area of schooling can be summed up as follows:

1. Schools were to give everyone a fixed core of general knowledge, whether they were going straight out to work after a seven-year elementary education, or going to a *realskole/gymnas*.
2. Schools were to foster an ideal of equality to reduce class distinctions over the long term.
3. The inculcation of fundamental Christian values and norms remained a key objective.
4. Schools were at the interface of a civic, middle-class culture and an ideological demand for the development of a common national culture, based largely on concepts of the old Norwegian agrarian culture.

Pedagogically speaking there were a number of changes during the twentieth century. A Dewey-inspired working school principle ('learning by doing') got off the ground, in some schools at any rate. Anna Sethne, the head teacher at Sagene School in Oslo, can be cited as an example of one of the principal leaders of this reform. But we are right to question the efficiency of such educational reform movements: they probably have had more influence in theory than in practice.

Educational policy both before and after the Second World War is characterized by reform. *Normalplanen* (the normal timetable) of 1939, which set out national guidelines for timetable and lesson allocation etc. for rural and urban elementary schools, was an epoch-making pedagogic innovation, which the model timetables of 1974 and 1987, as well as the reforms of the 1990s, were heavily based on. An OECD report shows that in 1950, a mere five years after the end of the Second World War, Norway was spending 2.69% of its GNP on the school system. Compared with other European countries, only Sweden, which remained neutral during the war, could show a higher figure, 3.53%. It was under this system, during the 1950s, that Bjørg and Arne Everyman were educated.

The development of the post-war school system can be summed up in the words: more school for more people! And it was much needed. The inconsistencies that still existed can be demonstrated by one simple example: Finnmark got its first *gymnas* in 1948. At that time 20% of the youngsters in the relevant years attended *gymnas* in Oslo.

As early as the 1950s discussions began about extending schooling to an obligatory nine years, in tandem with a considerable increase in the number of lessons, especially in rural elementary schools. The year 1955 saw the start of experiments with secondary schools offering different courses. An Act of 1959 allowed local authorities, under certain conditions, to introduce nine-year compulsory schooling. In 1960 the teaching curriculum for trials of nine-year schooling was put forward. This was a further development of the 'normal timetable' of 1939, now extended to a nine-year course. That same year the Storting passed an Act permitting trials at schools, and this gave the authorities the opportunity to deviate from the Education Acts when the trials were well founded. The nine-year course became compulsory for all with the new Education Act for *grunnskole* (elementary school), as the nine-year schooling was called, in 1969. But even by 1968, 80% of local authorities had adopted nine-year schooling as a compulsory system. In 1975 the law was revised, bringing rules on special schools and remedial teaching within the ambit of the general provisions of the Act. This can certainly be seen as a defining or intensifying of the *einskapsskole* philosophy. Integration of all categories of pupils within the general *einskapsskole* was, and has remained, a highly controversial step.

The next reforms on the agenda concerned the *gymnas*. Once again it is the enlargement of the *einskapsskole* that causes dissent. There was a lot of animosity towards the law, which was passed in 1974. About 50,000 schoolchildren demonstrated against it, and they were joined by students from universities and colleges. The change of name from *gymnas* to *vidaregåande skole* (sixth-form college) gives a clue to the problem. The objective of the new sixth-form college was to prepare students for working life and social responsibility and lay the foundations for higher education for *all* Norwegian youngsters. The ideal of equality that had brought in nine-year compulsory schooling, had now been realized for a further three years. A twelve-year *einskapsskole* had thus become a reality. This is the system in which Monica and Jan Everyman were socialized.

Equality in the school context can mean at least two different things. On the one hand *einskapsskole* can mean that all pupils get the same opportunities within the same school system. The educational policy makers in the Labour Party were thinking along these lines. The Conservatives (Høgre), and

**The University of Tromsø** is the newest of the Norwegian universities and the most northerly university in the world. An interior view of the Norwegian College of Fishery Science (Norges fiskerihøgskole), one of its faculties.

gradually also the intermediate parties, considered that equality implied equal opportunities for all regardless of social background or geographical situation, but with competition between different schools, and separate streams for youngsters with diverse interests. It must be said that in the main it was the education policy of the Labour Party that won through. But there has never been political consensus that the sixth-form college should follow the *einskapsskole* principle, as had slowly happened in the elementary school context.

During the 1980s education policies were taken up by the right wing, in Norway as in the rest of Europe. Gradually an idea formed in most people that schools were suffering from serious problems. It was said that the politics of reform and experiment had made schools 'a place to be' rather than 'a place to learn'. Without abandoning the *einskapsskole* idea, the Labour Party hitched on to liberal currents within European educational policy, and thus largely managed to stem the criticism. With Gudmund Hernes (b. 1941), one of the great educational strategists of our age, as Minister of Education in the Labour government between 1990 and 1995, attainment objectives were explicitly formulated. Hernes initiated and was himself deeply involved in the reforms in elementary school, sixth-form college and higher education. In 1994 he got an Act passed for ten-year elementary school, beginning at the age of six, and this meant that Norway from then on could boast of a thirteen-year *einskapsskole*.

Even though Hernes could in many ways be said to represent the social democratic notion of the *einskapsskole*, he also stood for values which neo-liberal ideologues had espoused for two or three decades. He emphasized that schools should foster the competitive spirit, and wanted to give the academic side better resources. He maintained that there was no incompatibility between knowledge and caring. He went on to insist that schools had the duty of imparting and sustaining a body of common understanding for all Norwegians. Hernes' schools are thus centralized, national schools that guarantee that pupils will learn the same things whichever end of the country they come from. In contrast to those who subsequently took over the development of schools, Hernes also set great store by the school as the repository of culture and good manners, so he had retrospective links to the period of nation building. As Minister he issued unequivocal directives about the curriculum of schools. Naturally this did not happen without resistance. One aspect of the criticism emphasized that in an age characterized by pluralism, multi-ethnicity and multi-culturalism, the attempt to blow on the embers of common national values was totally anachronistic.

It is true that the pupil base of schools is more varied now than it was only twenty years ago. Refugees and immigrants have given education a new face. Because of this there is a body of opinion that maintains it is useless to develop a common curriculum, as Hernes did, when common culture and absolute val-

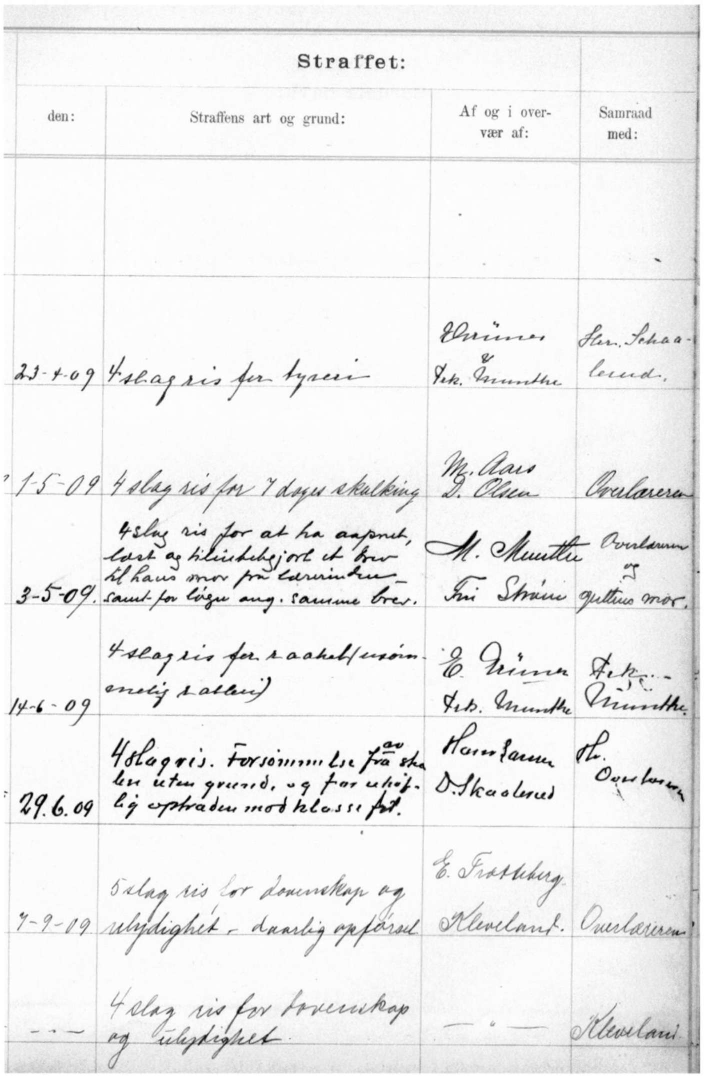

**The punishment book** of Bolteløkka School in Oslo. The punishments given have here been signed by Norway's much-loved writer of children's songs, Margrethe Munthe.

ues have dissipated into all kinds of views and beliefs. Our cultural myths are no longer credible. The nation state and its common values are under constant challenge, partly from pluralism, which has become part of the Norwegian experience, partly from internationalization and globalization.
The Sámi and Finnish speakers of the north have always been part of Norwegian pluralism. For a long time they were seen as a threat, and a policy of assimilation was adopted to eradicate this variety. It failed, and in the postwar period Norwegian Sámi and education policy made a U-turn. Now integration rather than assimilation is the ideal. The Sámi language was officially given equal status with Norwegian in 1991, and Sámi children have gained the right to study and be taught in Sámi. The objective is to make them functionally bilingual, and hopefully also to get them to develop dual cultural competence. So far it looks as if this strategy is yielding better results than the old policies of Norwegianization. The Finnish-dialect speakers were afforded national minority status in 2000. They do not enjoy the same legal protection as the Sámi native people, but by ratifying the European conventions on national minorities and minority languages, Norway has committed itself as regards Finnish language education. Other national minorities are Romanies, Travellers and Jews. Norway also has responsibilities to them in accordance with the ratified conventions. However, it is too early to pass a final verdict on what these conventions will mean for such things as mother-tongue teaching for these minorities.

### Jonas and Herman

A well-known schoolboy from Norwegian literature is young Jonas in Jens Bjørneboe's 1955 novel of the same name. Jonas is dyslexic, and as the school does not understand his condition, he is dismissed as stupid and difficult. His inability to read is not detected until he reaches the second form, and the child must shoulder all the blame himself:

*Jonas found that he was as surprised as Miss when she discovered he couldn't read. He had assumed that things had gone so well at school precisely because he read as ably as he did. He hadn't the faintest idea what he had done, but his teacher had been upset, and she'd said in a voice loud enough for the whole class to hear that he was lying and had brought shame on the entire school. He wasn't too worried about this, but it was obvious that Miss was unhappy – he could see her sorrow on the very tip of her fine nose; it was a tiny bit more arched than usual – and this was a sorrow that he had caused her. It was like a sharp knife inside him, the way he'd given Miss pain.*

*That he now realized he couldn't read was quite a different thing. And he knew just what that meant. He remembered every word that the big boy in the leather cap with the large teeth and ears had said about those who went to Half Wits. They couldn't read. And he remembered exactly how the boy in the leather cap had turned his head and followed them with his eyes. His red freckles and blue eyes looked so mournful that morning in the First Form.*

*Jonas* is a full frontal attack on schools and the school administration. As such, the book is a contribution to the debate. Bjørneboe portrays the school as almost antipathetic to children and its teachers as palpably petty. Where he was almost certainly right, was that the Norwegian *einskapsskole* had for a long time shown little sensitivity towards children with special needs, for example, those with reading and writing difficulties. The special arrangements such children were offered were originally in the form of so-called *hjelpeskoler* (remedial schools), which were highly stigmatizing. Subsequent integration policies were not without their problems, either. Even so, it is not pupils with special learning difficulties who have been the object of most public attention in recent years, but intelligent pupils and high-achievers, who many believe are not sufficiently challenged in Norwegian schools. It is claimed that they have nothing to aspire to.

Lars Saabye Christensen's epoymous protagonist in the novel *Herman* (1988) is one such gifted pupil, but that is not where his problem lies. Herman has contracted a disease that makes all his hair fall out. This overshadows everything else. Here he is, going to school wearing a wig:

*Herman shuts the door and sits down at his desk in the row by the window. The schoolyard is still empty, the blackboard inky as a window at night, and on the teacher's desk is a new box of chalk. It's as if everything is waiting to be used, the silence waiting for the noise, the inkwells for the pen nibs, the wastepaper bins for the rubbish; and this waiting time is like a dream, or maybe a promise.*

Herman is waiting for the lesson to begin. He is sitting with his cap on. His teacher, Tønne, is exaggeratedly kind to him, and lets him off reading out his homework, which he knows like the back of his hand, and which he really wants to read.

*Herman removes his cap.*
*A deep gasp runs through the classroom, a long sigh. Ruby turns and raises her hand to her mouth, as if she's trying to keep her chin in place. Then it turns even quieter than before, it's so hushed that they can hear a snowflake land on a pine needle in Valdres. Tønne turns round, fixes his eyes on Herman's wig and drops his chalk on the floor. It sounds like an aerial bombardment. Tønne smiles helplessly and spends the rest of the lesson listing the differences between sheep and goats at breakneck speed.*

The outsider's problem has not necessarily vanished just because care and concern have entered the classroom.

### Reforms and neo-liberalism

Throughout much of the 20th century the Labour Party was in office. Towards the end of this period the situation changed somewhat, and we had several periods of non-Socialist government. The fight against private schools had been axiomatic for the Labour Party. When it lost power, the Conservatives and intermediate parties saw to it that state subsidies were made available to private schools, which has enabled schools with other philosophies and other educational systems to function in Norway. The private-school niche has been expanded, particularly after the turn of the millennium.

The Right in Norwegian politics has always been critical of the *einskapsskole*. Throughout the entire 20th century they have attempted to slow down its development. They were sceptical of the extension to nine-year *einskapsskole*, just as they were to the founding of the new sixth-form colleges. During this time they have consistently argued for streaming within schools, and have claimed that the *einskapsskole* reduces competitiveness.

The *einskapsskole* concept has few adherents in present-day Europe. Although the *einskapsskole* ideology still generates passable rhetoric in Norway, much points to the fact that ever greater numbers of people want to turn the Norwegian school into a more varied institution offering a greater degree of choice, a school that distinguishes between pupils according to talent and ability. Another marked feature is that there no longer exists such a clear party political division in the debate on educational policy as there was a few decades ago, partly because the centre left appears to have accepted this liberal rhetoric.

### Summary: elementary school and sixth-form college

We could try to summarize the conflicts that have arisen, explicit or implicit, in modern Norwegian educational policy, under four headings:

1. The *einskapsskole* ('unity school') principle has been the lodestar in the development of Norwegian schools. The ideology was fought for and, in all periods of reform, the principle has been challenged. It is now under pressure.
2. The Christian object clause and the place of Christianity as a school subject has also become more of a conflict zone. Norway has adhered to the demand for a Christian aspiration long after other European nations have moved away from it.
3. The question of private schools as an alternative to state provision has always been controversial, and private schools have never had, nor do they enjoy now, a major place in the Norwegian school system. This is changing as it has become easier both legally and financially to set up private schools.
4. Evaluation and marking have been discussed in connection with various reforms, and this too has occasioned debate.

What Norway has gained from her many and frequent reforms is, firstly, a considerable extension of compulsory schooling. Until well into the 20th century, for example, compulsory school attendance was longer in other European countries and the USA than in Norway. We have seen that this is no longer the case. Compared to many countries, Norway has a school system with relatively few pupils per class and relatively many hours of

**Students abroad: main host countries and courses. 2002**

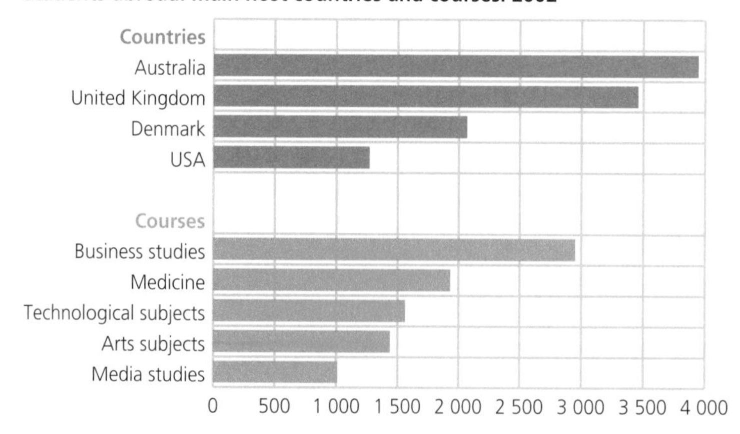

schooling. This means that Norway expends more resources per pupil for elementary schools than most other OECD countries.

Over the past few decades the pupil population of Norwegian schools has become steadily more heterogeneous. More than other parts of society, the school is a multicoloured community: 6.8% of its pupils are from linguistic minorities; in Oslo schools, 31.8%.

The proportion of people who are receiving education continues to increase. Since 1980 the total number of pupils and students has risen from around 850,000 to at least a million. Almost a third of people over the age of 15 are now in the classroom.

### Higher education

Up until the end of the Second World War Norway had only one university, a handful of technical colleges, a fairly large number of teacher training colleges and a few institutions that trained engineers, or what were called technicians and intermediate technicians. In addition there was a kind of 'semi-higher' education in certain health professions, notably nursing.

The postwar period has witnessed formidable growth, also in the number of higher education establishments. Since 1996 there has been collective regulation of all state-run tertiary institutions in the country. The next thing on the agenda is collective regulation of all state-run *and* private higher education institutions.

The building of institutions after the war was necessary to meet the ever increasing pressure on the sector. Student numbers at universities and colleges have grown enormously, with a boom in the 1960s and '70s and a further one in the 1990s. In 1945 there were 5,951 students at the University of Oslo. Now the country has more like 200,000 students. In the same period the population increase in Norway has been well over 20%, from 3.5 million inhabitants to about 4.5 million. The rise in student numbers has been 2,000%! By any standards this is an education explosion. The tertiary stage has changed from being an elite to a mass education. Even if we only go back as far as the 1970s, the changes are considerable. Today, three times as many Norwegians enjoy higher education as then. At the same time the ratio between men and women has evened out, so that there is no longer such an imbalance between them. Women are, in fact, set to overtake men. In the 25-29 age group, 43% of women have higher education as against 31% of men. This trend seems to be growing. Six out of ten students today are women and roughly 60% of graduates are women. At the higher levels and in research, men are still slightly ahead, but even here the proportion of women is increasing. Against this, the female element of scientific personnel at higher education establishments is rather low – lower, in fact, than in many other European countries. Figures that egalitarian Norway can point to are far from impressive: in 2001, 36% of researchers and scientific staff were women; for professors this fell to 13%.

Another clear trend is for more students to study outside Norway. Over the last few years this increase has been explosive. In 2001/2002 there were almost 16,000 Norwegian students abroad, in addition to some 5,000 exchange students. Taken as a whole, this represents 10% of the student population. The numbers are so large that they constitute an entire university, and quite a large one at that. Few countries with a well-developed higher education system can show such a high proportion. The fact that it is English-speaking areas that attract Norwegian students is only to be expected. But that Australia should have overtaken Great Britain, may cause some surprise. The reason is to be found in the aggressive marketing of Australian universities and the numbers of adventure-seeking young Norwegians, who do little to hide the fact that they are heading for Australia more because of its sunny climate and fine beaches than the academic status of their chosen university.

### Educational quality – so so

On 31 December 1986 Professor Gudmund Hernes wrote a feature article in the Oslo newspaper *Dagbladet* provocatively entitled 'Can one nurture ambitions in Norway?'. Hernes' basic assumption was that modern societies have to base themselves on knowledge and expertise. He therefore asked if the country was getting enough out of its talent, and answered his own question by contending that the Norwegian education system was well behind with regard to the demands of a modern knowledge-based society. Throughout an intense and prolonged newspaper debate Norwegian schools were the object of strong criticism for their lack of quality and declining levels of knowledge. Hernes himself said that Norwegian pupils, from primary school to university, require more training, more structure, more standardization and greater subject concentration. And he was given, as we have seen, five years to do something about it.

But accusations of declining standards did not end with Hernes' tenure of the education portfolio. Rather the opposite. Both elementary schools and sixth-form colleges are still targets

**Did these youngsters** get a good enough education? The secondary school situation in Bergen in 1970.

of virulent criticism, for many reasons and from many quarters. Higher education does not escape, either. It is particularly the poor knowledge base that is cited. In many cases it is teachers, and especially lecturers with long experience of schools, who raise the most critical voices. They blame the education authorities for bureaucracy and pedagoguery, and claim that subjects and knowledge have long ago been relegated to the dunce's corner, where, in the old days, naughty children were made to stand, to the scorn and derision of their fellow pupils. In the mouths, pens and keyboards of these lecturers, new teaching methods and the teachers that employ them are the vilest things imaginable. We find interesting documentation for this in three more or less essay-like polemics from recent years: Jon Hustad, *Skolen som forsvann* (The School that Vanished), 2002; Kaare Skagen, *Pedagogikkens elendighet* (The Misery of Pedagogy), 2002; and Jon Severud, *Ubehaget i skolen* (The Unpleasantness at School), 2003. These titles are clear indications of the critical focus each author sets out to propound. All three authors are well-trained lecturers with considerable school experience, mainly from sixth-form college, but also from secondary school. On these grounds their criticisms should be taken seriously. We must nevertheless ask: are they right, all these people who are now so critical of Norwegian schools? We are in fact in the fortunate position of being able to answer this particular question fairly accurately. The OECD survey *Education at a Glance* provides facts and figures that are not so easy to argue away.

One rather disquieting statistic is that Norwegian pupils have only average scores in core subjects like Norwegian and maths. Norwegian nine-year-olds, for example, show very poor results in reading ability, well below the average in other OECD countries. This is somewhat mitigated by the better results amongst 15-year-olds, where we are right on the average. In the same surveys it is the Swedish nine-year-olds and the Finnish 15-year-olds who score best. There is every reason to ask why Norway lags so far behind its neighbours. Norwegian 15-year-olds have only average scores in maths as well; the Swedes and Finns are much better here, too. Japan is right at the top of the table in this subject. Another worrying aspect of the Norwegian school system is that progression in sixth-form college is poor; the same may be said of pupil motivation. In addition, there is the fact that the discipline problem is greater here than in many other countries. We contend with Greece for bottom place in that particular league. Teacher training is also an object of criticism, as student recruitment is poor and the knowledge base low.

When such troubling results are published, they naturally lead to debate. This has partly resulted in a rush to apportion blame for what many see as a failure. Many people are exercized by the fact that we get so little return for the resources that are channelled into the school system. Norwegian schools are costly and bad, critics maintain. But we can also discern trends towards a more constructive discussion in which the focus is on strategies for change. Despite the OECD results, the fundamental divisions that have always existed about the aims and methods of schools are still with us: 'a place to learn' or 'a place to be'? Caring or knowledge? Freedom or discipline? Subjects or teaching methods? Teachers trained at teacher training colleges or universities? Part of the problem is that these dichotomies have largely been accepted as expressions of real disparities. A wise and reasonable education policy maker, teacher, school governor or parent would intuitively understand that it is not a matter of one or the other, but of both together. To give a general answer to how such contrasts should be balanced, is impossible. Each situation and context will of necessity produce different answers. On the other hand, what *is* readily apparent is that early in this new millennium Norwegian schools are grappling with problems that need rapid, effective solutions. Many pupils learn far too little at school, they cannot use their abilities to the full. When, added to this, there are pupils and teachers who show such distaste for school, if nothing is done and the status quo maintained, there is reason to suppose that the prognosis for the Norwegian school of the future is not very good.

**Thomas Hysing** was in charge of the construction of the first Norwegian computer, 'Nusse', which was completed in 1954. The basis for modern programming language and data systems was created a decade later, when Ole-Johan Dahl and Kristen Nygaard developed the programming language 'Simula'.

## RESEARCH

*Anyone who has felt the warm grip of a child's hand around his little finger knows that wonder is built into human nature. How many stars are there up there? Hundreds and hundreds... What is beyond the furthest star? More stars. But still further?*

*A great deal of research springs from this natural and vital curiosity. Like the poets, the physicians and biologists, anthropologists and theologians dream of finding their place in a fantastic world. Who am I, in relation to my fellow men, to nature, to the divine? Questions of this kind have given rise to some of mankind's greatest creations.*

*The purpose of research is to release man from his self-made prisons of ignorance, misunderstandings, obsessions and prejudice. Founded on scientific demands for a critical approach and verifiable methods, science must make its contribution to human development and maturity.*

*But research is more than wonder and examination, inquisitiveness and thirst for adventure. It is also part of the human endeavour to master what is essentially an unknown world. New knowledge and technology will form the foundation for freer lives and relieve suffering and toil.*

### Objectives and use of resources

The quotation above is from the Research Report of 1993. The background to this kind of Storting report is one of its own resolutions that the government should produce a report on Norwegian research in each four-year electoral term. In practice, this happens less often. The first report came out in 1975. In terms of language and style the quotation is untypical. Normally, Storting reports are not so well written, and certainly not couched in such a polished and absorbing style. Parts of the 1993 report show that the then minister, the education and research strategist Gudmund Hernes, was responsible for them.

In all other ways the 1993 report is typical. Its main focus is on the use of resources and research quality. One clear trend over many years is that Norway spends less of its gross national product (GNP) on research than do many other OECD countries. By comparison with education, for example, research comes out badly in terms of resources. Naturally one can question whether the percentage of GNP is a good yardstick of commitment to research. Norway has a high GNP, so we may well be spending more on research in purely monetary terms than other OECD countries. But the proportion of GNP does say something about priorities, and we must therefore conclude that Norway rates research low. This is made even more clear once we realize that Norwegian research is cheaper than research in many other places, because Norwegian researchers are on average cheaper in operation than their colleagues abroad. This is shown by a relatively new study from the Norwegian Institute for Research and Educational Studies (NIFU). It shows that high educational levels and low costs are characteristics of the Norwegian research and development system. And so Norway can point to some of the lowest-cost research in the western world. Norway is generally a high-cost country, so whether this is something to be proud of, is arguable. Those who believe they are underpaid compared with foreign colleagues are unlikely to think so.

The statistics tell us this: in 2001 Norway spent 1.62% of its GNP on research and development work; the OECD average was then 2.3%. In comparison, Sweden spent 4.2%. These figures include both publicly and privately financed research.

In 1985 the Storting decided for the first time that the objective of Norwegian research policy was to come up to the average OECD level. At that time they gave themselves until 1989. In 1985 Norwegian research constituted 1.5% of GNP, whereas the OECD average was 2%. Finland was then roughly on a par with Norway, with Denmark lagging a little way behind. Since that time it has been repeated *ad nauseam* that the aim is to rise to the OECD average, and even to be amongst the leaders.

If we stay with statistics, we can see that the increase between 1985 and 2001 was less than one-hundredth of one per cent annually. So, early in the 1990s we were overtaken by Denmark, and later by Finland. Finland is now far ahead of us. Finland began to increase its investment in research and technology after a severe economic crisis in the first half of the 1990s. This has caused certain Norwegian research strategists to declare that the only thing that can help Norwegian research is an economic downturn or, preferably, a crisis! When, furthermore, we learn that the EU has a target of 3% for collective research in Europe by the year 2010, the road ahead for Norway looks steep and difficult indeed.

Resources and their use have been a recurring theme in Norwegian research policies. One point is that the correlation between state investment and the resources expended by industry is unlike that of other OECD countries. To put it briefly, Norwegian industry invests little in research. This is partly because our companies are mainly small and medium-sized, and such companies do little research, be they located in Norway or elsewhere. Furthermore, Norway's industrial structure is based on raw materials. This is also a contributory factor. We have no Nokia or Ericsson. The size of Nokia's research budget compared, for example, to that of the Finnish universities, shows an asymmetry in favour of Nokia which, at least partly, explains the imbalance between Finland and Norway. However, if we base our international comparisons purely on state-funded research, Norway does not emerge so badly.

Norway's weak investment in research has also been blamed for its poor quality. We shall now consider whether this is correct.

**Research quality**

Two Norwegians have been awarded the Nobel Prize for economics. Ragnar Frisch (1895–1973) won the very first prize for economics in 1969, for his work on market fluctuations. Trygve Haavelmo (1911–99) received his award in 1989 for his work in econometrics. He introduced mathematical statistical methods into economic analyses and proved that existing economic theories were misleading; they took no account of the infinite number of economic factors that feed into economic development. The chemist Odd Hassel (1897–1981) is the only person in this country to have received a Nobel prize for natural science. He was awarded it in 1969 for the development and use of the concept of chemical conformational analysis. What Hassel did was to demonstrate that one and the same organic molecule can occur in several three dimensional geometric forms. In addition to these three, two Norwegian-Americans have received the prize: Lars Onsager for chemistry in 1968 and Ivar Giæver for physics in 1973; but this was after they had moved to America.

Compared with its neighbours, Norway has had few Nobel Prizewinners in the sciences. Is the reason that the quality of Norwegian research is as poor as its resources? Many people believe this. But, at the very least this is debatable. One reason for the paucity of Nobel Prizes may be that Norwegian scientists have excelled in disciplines that do not have their own Nobel Prizes, disciplines that from a geographical point of view could reasonably be expected to interest Norwegians: geology, geophysics, oceanography, meteorology and other sciences linked to arctic conditions in general. Much also indicates that the research profile in our country is characterized by a particular industrial structure that, to a large extent, builds on natural resources and raw-material production. This means that, as a research nation, Norway is different to her neighbours, but not necessarily worse.

Those who argue that Norway is an inferior research nation are supported by results from bibliometric studies which are gaining in importance for research policy. Such bibliometric methods are used to compare research environments, institutions and nations, and they do not cover Norway in much glory. They show, amongst other things, that Norway's share of Scandinavia's scientific papers is about 13%, while its population comprises 18.5%. Norwegian scientists are also less frequently cited than their Finnish, Danish or Swedish counterparts. So Norway gets the wooden spoon in Scandinavia. But at the same time these measurements show that although we produce relatively few papers in physics for reputable international journals, we generate more in geophysics and geology; and though we have relatively few in basic biological research, we have a lot in fishery biology. Once again it is the untypical that stands out.

So the results here are not without their ambiguities. Norway has an untypical research profile – which is not the same thing as poor quality. In talking about Norwegian research in general there is, therefore, a basis for singling the country out as different, rather than as qualitatively weak. There are, for instance, few countries as advanced as Norway in the field of raw-materials-based research. Examples are the fishing industry, fish farming, the shipping industry, the aluminium industry, the light metal and process industries and gradually, too, the oil industry. But in the world of research these fields are not the ones which attract the greatest notice, and that may partially explain that peculiarly Norwegian shame and self-flagellation in the face of our neighbours' high-tech success stories.

### Why must we engage in research?

How is Norwegian research justified? Norway is a small country, and one may well ask if research is necessary at all when we are unwilling to accord it a particularly high priority. Why not simply freeload, harvesting the fruits of research done elsewhere? Of course, we do this to a large extent anyway; innovation and technological development are by definition international activities. One rather banal answer to this question is that without research higher educational institutions would dry up: if education is to remain in the forefront, professors must apply themselves to

**Here the sex** of halibut is being determined at Akvaforsk at the National College of Agricultural Engineering (Noregs landbrukshøgskole), 2002.

research. Other important reasons can be filed under two headings: instrumental and cultural grounds. If we have identified a problem that we wish to have solved or explained by research, we are arguing instrumentally. But we can also maintain that research is a good in itself, that democratic societies need research for the maintenance of freedom of discussion and so that scientific thought will have a place in which to thrive.

Both cultural and instrumental perspectives are represented in most of the Research Reports, but the emphasis may well shift a little according to who is the minister at the time. On the other hand there is every reason to claim that most of what is said and written about research in official circles reflects scientific, technological and medical research. Laboratory research and technical innovation are what most people associate with the term research. The type of activity represented by sociological and humanistic research, which is fundamentally different from the sort that takes place in the laboratory, is easily overshadowed by a man in a white coat surrounded by retorts, test tubes and complex measuring instruments. As such it is *de facto* the instrumental justification that people are most aware of. The desire for more efficient and targeted research, emphasis on consumer control and relevance, points quite unambiguously in the same direction. A further symptom of the same thing is the anxiety and concern many people express about Norwegian scientific and technological research in general, but specifically that recruitment to scientific subjects and technology is faltering, and more so in Norway than in other countries. Whenever this is discussed, disquiet is always expressed that this lack of recruitment will weaken Norwegian scientific and technological research in the long term. This will, in turn, have an effect on economic growth because creativity, entrepreneurial activity and product development will be starved of funds: even now Norway, it is claimed, is the least innovative country in Scandinavia.

## Research structure: how, what and whom?

The Norwegian research establishment can be divided into three parts, corresponding to the authorities, institutions or organizations that have research as a mandatory part of their remit.

1. **Universities and colleges**
   Higher education is supposed to be research-based. This implies, firstly, that its teaching staff must have research expertise, and secondly, that within the sector a specific number of scientific staff posts must be allocated to research. There is thus a close link between higher education and research, not least because the bulk of the research resources granted through the national budget goes to this sector. If we look at the figures for a random year, 1995 for instance, to illustrate this, 45% of public research funds went to universities and colleges and 23% went to the Norwegian Research Council, which in turn channelled 36% of its resources to the universities.

2. **The institutional sector**
   Compared to other countries Norway has a large institutional sector, with applied research as its main activity. In the main this means applied technological and sociological research. This sector has burgeoned in the postwar period. The largest institute is SINTEF (Foundation for Scientific and Industrial Research), with around 2,200 employees. It is the fourth-largest independent institute in Europe, and therefore one of the largest research institutes in Europe for applied technology. SINTEF works closely with Norway's technical and scientific university at Trondheim. In 1995, 27% of public research funds went to the institutional sector. The Norwegian Research Council allotted the sector 58% of the resources at its disposal.

3. **Industry and commerce**
   Roughly 500-600 Norwegian companies conduct research in one form or another. The largest companies, of which Statoil, Norsk Hydro and Telenor are good examples, are the most research-intensive. In 1995, 5% of the budgeted research allocation went direct to industrially-orientated research. Industry and commerce also received 6% of the funds disbursed by the Norwegian Research Council.

The overall picture is, however, rather different to the impression given above when it comes to the use of resources, both in the form of money and expertise. In the final analysis it is commerce and industry that are the most research-intensive, despite their bad showing in international comparisons. The year 1995 saw about NOK 7.3 billion and more than 6,100 man-years spent on industrial research. Comparable statistics for the institutional sector are approximately NOK 4.5 billion and about 4,800 man-years. The universities and colleges spent about NOK 4.1 billion and devoted nearly 5,000 man-years to the purpose.

Norway possesses a research council, the Norwegian Research Council, which is the result of the fusion of five separate research councils. This amalgamation took place in 1992. The research council system can itself be seen as a postwar import from the Anglo-Saxon world. The system is also a result of increased investment in science and research compared to the prewar period, when the state limited its responsibility for research to the funding of universities and colleges and certain research institutions. The structure of research itself has long been an important area of debate for research policy. This involves both the research council structure and the principle of departmental sectors, which is based on the departments granting research funds to their sectors and thus retaining relatively tight control of this money.

One important source of finance for Norwegian research has, right up until recently, been the profits from the Norwegian Pools (founded in 1946), which were divided between research and sport. Pools money is now no longer used for research. Compensation is supposed to be made for this in the national budget.

**The content of Norwegian research**

In the research policy debate, research itself and the objects of research, are often completely invisible. We discuss resources, structures and quality in purely general terms, and quite divorced from concrete research. Because the content of research has not been much discussed, it can be difficult to say anything general about it. Despite this, let us attempt a brief historical overview with a few selected examples, so that its structures can be made vivid and tangible. One way of dividing up the history of research is into three epochs, as is illustrated below:

1. The nation-building period, industrialization
2. The institution-building period
3. The quality-building period, the notion of 'excellence'

The earliest period goes back to the founding of the first scientific institution in the country, Det Trondhjemske Selskab (The Trondheim Society) in 1760, from 1767 called Det Kgl. Norske Selskap (The Royal Norwegian Society of Science and Letters), in Trondheim. When, in 1761, it published its first official proceedings, it was the 'Fishing Trade' and 'Minerals in our Country' that were exemplified as the most important fields of research. From this we can see that it is the way of life in a country that determines its priorities. The same applies to what research there was prior to 1760. Early Norwegian research is characterized by an interest in Norwegian history, topographical conditions and natural history in the locality where the 'researcher' (often a clergyman or other official) resided. The emphasis on natural, national, regional and local background has since then – throughout the whole of Norwegian research history – been a major aspect. According to the science historian Robert Marc Friedman, it has been an ideal for Norway as a research nation to be 'democratic, patriotic and practical'. In his article 'University History in Norway' (2000) he says:

*By the 1920s Norway was perhaps alone in being a nation in which professors were more at home in the field than in the laboratory. Representatives from the Rockefeller Foundation who came to survey European science, expressed surprise at how, rather than the traditional prestige sciences physics and chemistry, Norway supported geophysical and earth sciences.*

This appears to have been a trait of Norwegian research over several centuries, one which today is verified through various bibliometric statistics and the lack of Nobel laureates.

With this kind of perspective on research it is self-evident that Norwegian science, right back to before 1814 when the Danes ruled the country, has contributed to shaping and building our nation, directly or indirectly. It is true of the historical and topographical literature of the 17th and 18th centuries. It is true of J.E. Gunnerus' (1718–73) *Flora Norvegica* (1766–72), and it is true of Christen Jenssøn's (d. 1653) *Den norske Dictionarium eller Glosebog* (The Norwegian Dictionary or Glossary, 1646), and in a slightly wider perspective also of Knud Leem's (1696/97–1774) pioneering works on the Sámi language (*Grammatica* 1748 and *Lexicon* 1768).

The establishment of scientific institutions and the building of the Norwegian nation can be viewed as two parallel developments. The first Norwegian university, Det Kongelige Frederiks Universitet (the Royal Frederik University) was inaugurated in 1811. Since 1939 it has been called the University of Oslo. The reason it came into being when it did was probably largely due to the Danish king's wanting to pre-empt the Swedes. But the time was decidedly ripe for a Norwegian national university. Even so, it should be said that in terms of national and cultural politics the Royal Frederik found itself caught up in the tension between the

urban cultural heritage from Danish rule, which had strongly stamped itself on the official classes, and the newly constructed Norwegian culture, characterized as it was by rusticity and peasant romanticism. The strong roots of the old Dano-Norwegian bureaucratic culture which set its stamp on the civic life of the capital, explains something of the commitment to founding subsequent universities, the University of Bergen in 1946 and the University of Tromsø in 1968. On the other hand, the University of Trondheim, Norway's technical and scientific university, has its roots elsewhere, in the National College of Technology, which was set up in 1910, and in the National University College for Teacher Training of 1922.

Of the early professors at the Royal Frederik, Christopher Hansteen (1784–1873) was probably the only one of international renown. He conducted pioneering research into terrestrial magnetism, but due to lack of money, only the first part of his work was published (in 1819). To Hansteen also belongs the credit for leading the first Norwegian expedition to the far north (Siberia) between 1828 and 1830. The mathematician Niels Henrik Abel (1802–29) must also be mentioned, even though he never held a post at the university. His name still shines out: he was and remains one of the greatest mathematicians in the world. B.M. Keilhau (1797–1858) launched geology as a subject in Norway and mapped the country's geology at about the same time that Michael Sars (1805–69) charted the marine fauna along the coast. Together with his son, G.O. Sars (1837–1927), he also plotted parts of the Arctic fauna in the deep ocean. It can also be claimed that Vilhelm Bjerknes (1862–1951) and his son Jacob ('Jack', 1897–1975) founded modern meteorology through studies of weather conditions on the west coast.

Over time there would be more expeditions to the north – and to the south, the Antarctic. This also shows the strong link between research and the natural conditions with which we are endowed. Fridtjof Nansen (1861–1930) is still regarded as the greatest of the Norwegian polar explorers, but others, like Otto Sverdrup (1854–1930), Roald Amundsen (1872–1928) and Hjalmar Johansen (1867–1913), have their place amongst the Norwegian polar heroes. Some, indeed, were more heroes than actual researchers, if by 'researcher' one means natural scientist. Of the more recent researcher-adventurers must be mentioned Helge Ingstad (1899–2001) who, together with his wife, the archaeologist Anne Stine Ingstad, 'discovered' Vinland in Newfoundland, and Thor Heyerdahl (1914–2002) who, in his many expeditions to destinations much further afield than the Arctic, built up an international reputation the like of which few of his contemporaries achieved.

More recently, Norwegian polar research has been given an institutional face by, amongst others, the Norwegian Polar Research Institute, which is located in Tromsø and also at Ny-Ålesund on Spitsbergen. Ny-Ålesund has now become a centre for international polar research.

In the Norwegian humanistic sciences it is history and archaeology (P.A. Munch (1810–63) and Rudolf Keyser (1803–64)), legal history (Frederik Stang (1808–84) and A.M. Schweigaard (1808–70)) and the Norwegian language (Ivar Aasen (1813–96)) which attracts the greatest interest. The period up to the 1960s saw the flowering of these national disciplines.

The close connection between particular natural conditions and the desire to solve concrete problems is well exemplified by the collaboration of Kristian Birkeland (1867–1917) and Sam Eyde (1866–1940): it led to the founding of Norsk Hydro in 1905. In 1903 Birkeland succeeded in creating a so-called electric plasma arc which was to form the basis of Birkeland-Eyde's electric arc furnace for the industrial manufacture of nitric acid from atmospheric nitrogen. Nitric acid was used in the manufacture of nitrate, especially the fertilizer nitrate of lime. Production took off just as guano exports from South America were decreasing, and thus supplied a large demand for an alternative fertilizer. It was therefore another example of the fairly strong applied perspective of Norwegian research exhibited right up to our own times.

Similar examples can be found in hydroelectric schemes and the oil industry. Norway is famed for its mountains and fjords. Very few people realize that, inside, our mountains look something like Swiss cheese, shot through as they are with holes. More than half the world's subterranean hydroelectric power stations are in Norway, roughly 200 in all. In addition there are about 3,500 kilometres of tunnels linked to these power stations, as well as 750 railway tunnels and 850 road tunnels. All this bears witness to the way Norwegian technological research has been harnessed to useful and practical ends. Traditions like these stood the country in good stead when it faced its greatest technological

**Famous Norwegian** researchers in their true element: Arne Næss out in the countryside, Anne Stine and Helge Ingstad in 'Vinland' and Johannes Moe surrounded by technology.

challenge ever, the construction of an oil industry right from first principles, after vast quantities of oil and gas were discovered in the North Sea. Other traditions, like those of shipbuilding, shipping, navigation and trading also proved useful in this context. After a somewhat cautious beginning Norway is now one of the largest oil- and gas-producing nations in the world. The manufacture of oil-rigs and oil and gas pipelines at great depths requires engineering of an advanced calibre, so advanced, indeed, that the British periodical *The Economist* once called these huge platforms one of the seven wonders of the modern world. Norway is clearly living proof that some of the most successful innovations are based on techniques that have been mastered previously, and which are transferred to new fields.

The head of what was then the National College of Technology (Norges tekniske høgskole), Johannes Moe (b. 1926) took an important initiative in this field when, early in the 1970s, he developed a course in petroleum studies and went to the USA in person to recruit lecturers. He raised money for this through sponsorship from firms like Norsk Hydro, Saga Petroleum and Norske Veritas. This might be called the start of a collaboration between industry and academia, a partnership that has grown closer with time.

On the basis of the skills Norway already possessed in the construction of ships, bridges and dams, and in chemistry and mining techniques, agreements with foreign oil companies and educational centres enabled the country slowly to build up the expertise needed for the running and continued development of an ever more important petroleum industry. If one takes the oil industry and its associated technological developments as a yardstick, it would be hard to maintain that Norway does not shine in research terms. But then Norway has chosen to travel different paths and byways than most other European countries, at least until now.

Research has now become international by definition. And Norway plays her part in an international research community. This is becoming more and more evident. Just as, in international rhetoric, 'excellence' has now become an overwhelming argument for higher education and research, so it has in Norway, too. In a recent initiative from the Norwegian Research Council, several 'centres of excellence' have been set up, linked to universities and other higher educational facilities. We also see a greater tendency than before for Norway to latch on to international fields of research that have a high media profile, like genetic and nanotechological research. Whether anything will come of this gamble for Norwegian research, it is too early to judge. Furthermore, the Norwegian Research Council has now prioritized areas of research more clearly than it used to. Examples of priority areas are marine research, nutritional research and environmentally orientated research.

**Research optimism and research pessimism**

Much scientific and technological research has been motivated by a belief that science and innovation enhance prosperity and growth. This applied to the early, nationally motivated mapping of mineral and marine resources etc., as much as to modern oil technology. There are grounds for believing that this new rhetoric of excellence represents an attempt to inject fresh life into such research optimism. For during the postwar period it has been subjected to sharp criticism, right across the board. In Norway the problematic recruitment situation in the natural sciences and technology has been laid at the door of scepticism about technology and pessimism about civilization. Anti-positivism, which in Norway had its chief spokesman in Hans Skjervheim (1926–99), can be interpreted as an expression of increased scepticism towards certain forms of skills and technological development.

The transformation of the philosopher Arne Næss (b. 1912) from being a Vienna-positivist during the inter-war years to becoming what is known as a 'deep ecologist' now, can be viewed as symptomatic. Skjervheim was once perhaps Næss's principal critic. Now, in retrospect, we can look at the circle around Arne Næss, the debate and criticism their professional activities caused, and see it as fundamental and constitutional for the establishment and further development of Norwegian social science. Another name that must be mentioned in this context is that of Stein Rokkan (1921–79). His importance in both Norwegian and international sociological research is indisputable. Outside the universities, too, there are strong social science milieus, like FAFO, which has conducted remarkable research amongst Palestinians in the Middle East, and the LOS Centre, which has become renowned for research connected with political reforms, democracy and welfare state development. Norwegian electoral research also enjoys a good international reputation. Norwegian social science generally constitutes an uncommonly large sector, compared with other countries. This is yet another example of how Norway, in science and research terms, is untypical.

**january** fin serck-hanssen **february** rolf m. aagaard

**march** herdis maria siegert **april** janne solgaard

**may** jens hauge **june** vibeke tandberg

**july** dag alveng **august** rune johansen

**september** knut bry **october** asle svarverud

**november** ingvar moi **december** per berntsen

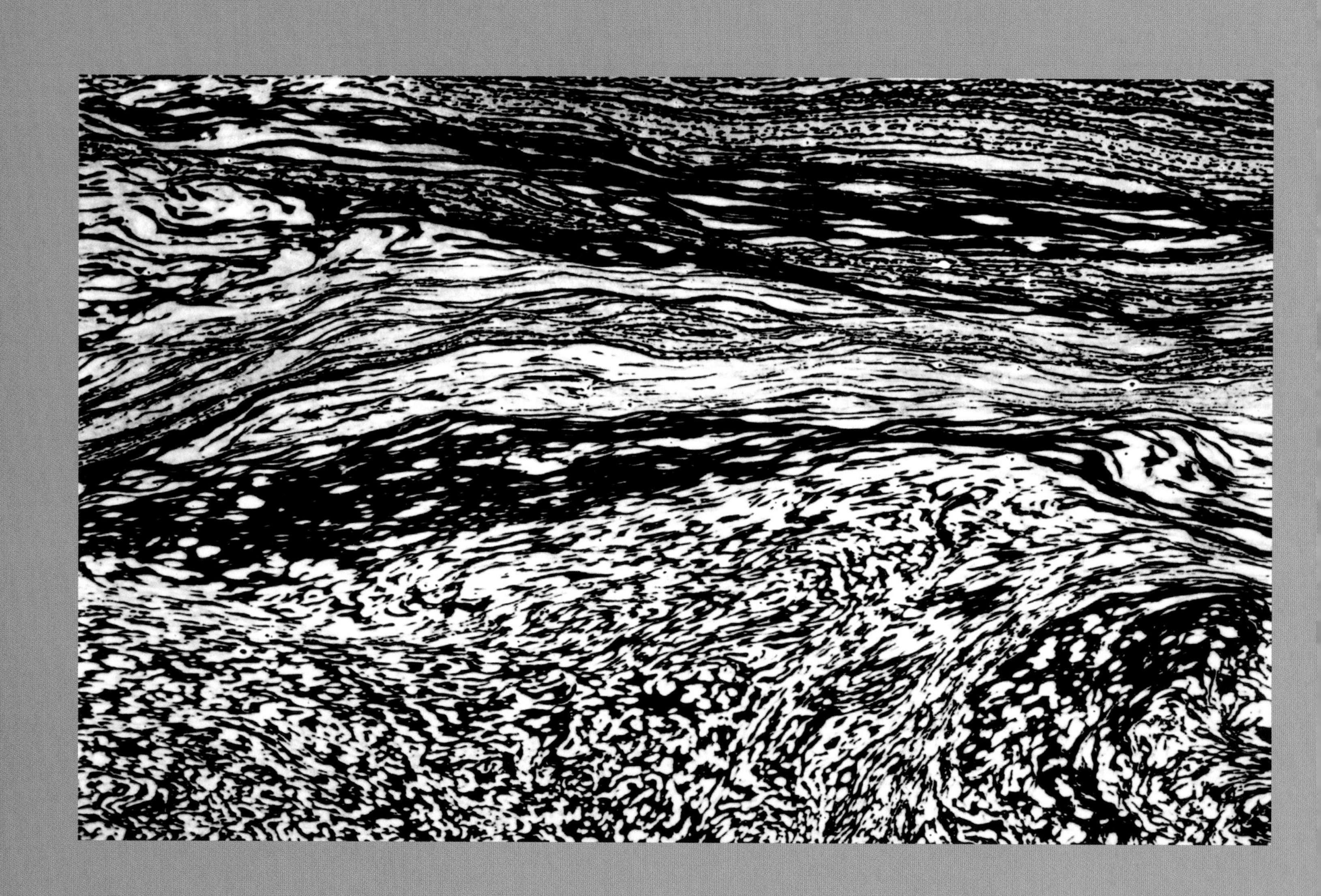

NIELS HENRIK ABEL.

Tegnet af Görbitz.

C Henckels lithogr. Kunstanstalt.

Niels Henrik Abel

# NIELS HENRIK ABEL

It is a sad fate indeed to be born a mathematical genius in a backward agrarian society such as Norway undeniably was in the early nineteenth century, yet that was the lot of Niels Henrik Abel, who was destined to suffer the painful consequences throughout his all-too-brief life. Nor did other circumstances surrounding him do anything to brighten his youthful years. Both his parents were addicted to drink. His father's fall from grace was particularly shameful, as he was both a clergyman and a member of parliament. The nadir was reached when he resorted to selling illicitly distilled liquor to his parishioners from the vicarage – on Sundays, at that! His parliamentary career was in ruins, and it was not long before he effectively drank himself to death. Niels Henrik was then eighteen. Things were no better at the funeral, where Niels Henrik's mother was visibly the worse for drink and all too clearly involved with other men. There were other unpropitious circumstances too: his elder brother was mentally ill, and a younger brother took to the bottle at an early age.

Niels Henrik was marked by his upbringing in that he was always withdrawn and inclined to melancholy, though locally he distinguished himself as a good competitive swimmer and skier. Many people remarked upon his uncanny ability to forecast the weather; he was often called 'the stargazer' because of his predilection for studying the heavens at every opportunity. Another striking feature of his early years was that he earned a reputation as an outstanding card-player.

PORTRAIT

Because of their family circumstances, Niels Henrik and his siblings were offered free places at Christiania Cathedral School. Here the boy was so severely beaten by his teacher that he had to ask to be excused school for a time. The same teacher later maltreated another pupil so badly that the child died, with the result that a man named Holmboe took over the class. This was fortunate for Abel, as Holmboe had a far better grasp of mathematics and was a gentler person altogether. He was a considerable spur to Niels Henrik but soon found himself out of his depth when confronted with the boy's talent for theory. Even in his teens Abel was obsessed with solving the general equation of the fifth degree. A little later he proved that this was impossible by classical algebraic methods, something that is now looked upon as his first breakthrough in equational theory. In other subjects Abel's performance was below average and he twice had to re-sit his exams.

A foundation for poor students provided him with a free place at university, where his friendship with a prominent scientist, Christopher Hansteen, proved of great importance during this period. Mrs Hansteen became something of a surrogate mother for Abel, teaching him how to dress and behave, and in the Hansteen family the young man found the nearest thing to a home he

$$\psi\left(\frac{x}{1+x}\right) = +\int\left(\frac{\partial x}{x} - \frac{\partial x}{x+1}\right)\log(1+x) = \int\frac{\partial x}{x}\log(1+x) - \int\frac{\partial x}{x+1}\log(x+1)$$

Nun aber hat man offenbar $\int\frac{\partial x}{x}\log(1+x) = -\psi(-x)$ und

$\int\frac{\partial x}{1+x}\cdot\log(1+x) = \frac{1}{2}\{\log(1+x)\}^2$ folglich weil die constante gleich null ist

$$\psi\left(\frac{x}{1+x}\right) + \psi(-x) = -\frac{1}{2}\{\log(1+x)\}^2 \quad \ldots\ (7)$$

had ever known. At university it was realized that this budding genius was capable of bringing lustre both to the institution and to Norway; it was also realized that he could learn no more in his native land. A Professor Rasmussen provided funds from his own pocket to send the young man to Copenhagen, where Abel's theses astounded his teachers and where he was given letters of recommendation to leading figures in Europe. It was in Copenhagen that he met Christine Kemp – they were thrown together in a waltz, a dance neither of them mastered. The couple became engaged in 1824.

On Abel's return to Norway the university resolved to send him to Paris, home at the time to the world's foremost mathematicians; and the Cabinet awarded him a two-year government travel grant. Abel was delighted at the prospect of meeting others of the same bent as himself. He gave part of the grant to his brother Peder, who squandered it on drink and frivolous pursuits. Niels Henrik also provided financial support to enable his younger sister to move to the capital.

Five promising young scientists left Norway in the autumn of 1825. Abel, who never liked to be alone, joined the others on their journey through Europe. All five shared the dream that the experience and knowledge they would gain in the world beyond the horizon would ensure them financial security on their return to Norway. For the other four this dream would be realized, but for Niels Henrik Abel, the most gifted of them all, it was not to be. Of particular importance to the young mathematician was his meeting in Berlin with the scientist and engineer August Leopold Crelle. As a direct consequence of this encounter, Crelle founded a mathematical journal that remains one of the world's leading scientific publications to this day. At last someone appreciated the magnitude of what Abel was doing, so the Norwegian's contribution helped to establish the journal's reputation throughout Europe.

Abel accompanied his friends to Dresden, Vienna, Prague, Trieste and Venice before he eventually reached Paris. Here he completed and delivered his *magnum opus* on the integration of differential formulae to France's principal mathematicians. It would later transpire that for some years this treatise remained unread. Abel stayed on in Paris for a while, waiting in vain for a response. The only extant drawing of him was made in this wasted period. Only some years later, after Abel had been laid to rest, was interest evinced in his thesis, and then it was realized that it was one of the most important works in the history of mathematics. This resulted, a year after his death, in his being awarded a French prize of 1,500 francs.

It was a dejected, poor and exhausted Abel who set off for home via Berlin, and there is much to suggest that it was on this journey that he contracted tuberculosis. He had been away from Norway for twenty months. In the meantime, the professorial appointment he had hoped for had gone to his former teacher, Holmboe. Desperately short of money, Abel twice applied to the government for financial assistance, only to be turned down. He longed for a lectureship, but his prayers went unanswered.

Abel's father had left behind debts and commitments that no one else in the family appeared able to discharge. For one thing, he had promised to donate to the university half a barrel of barley from the vicarage annually. This was to prove a heavy burden on Abel. His wild younger brother had also left a trail of unpaid bills all over the capital, which his elder sibling felt obliged to pay. Mathematical genius though he was, Abel was reduced to giving private lessons in elementary mathematics, but even this failed to bring in enough money; at the same time his illness continued to tighten its grip.

Abel has been described by his contemporaries as a happy but sad man. It is likely that he endeavoured to concel his unhappiness by an outward display of cheerfulness. Many of his troubles stemmed from his family and his straitened circumstances. A particular source of distress was that his financial position was never such as to permit him to marry his fiancée. Only rarely did he entertain hopes of a carefree life. It is said that he was only truly happy when immersed in mathematical problems; at such times things would fall into place and the future cease to exist.

Despite his financial and health problems Abel despatched a succession of theses to Berlin. He presented groundbreaking insights into fields such as algebraic equations, elliptical functions and the convergence criteria for an infinite series. Abel's integrals and functions are concepts that are still employed in higher mathematics. Few, if any, have contributed as many innovative ideas and theories as Abel. In 1928, by a lucky chance he was afforded an opportunity to stand in for Hansteen when the professor embarked upon an expedition to Siberia. However, his luck did not last for long: even before taking up the post it became clear that he was suffering from what was then known as galloping tuberculosis.

For the last year and a half Niels Henrik's fiancée had worked as a governess at Froland Ironworks in Arendal. It was with her that Abel wished to be when, around Christmas 1828, he found himself increasingly coughing up blood. After a tiring journey in conditions of extreme cold, he took to his bed at the ironworks, there to remain until death claimed him on 6 April 1829. He was only twenty-seven.

Two days after his death a letter came from his friend Crelle, who was delighted to inform him that he had been awarded a professorial chair in Berlin. Shortly afterwards it became known that leading French mathematicians had taken steps, through the person of King Charles John (Carl Johan), to secure for Abel a prestigious scientific appointment. It reflects little credit on Norway that both Germany and France published commemorative pieces on Abel before his own country followed suit.

After Abel's death the Norwegian authorities came in for severe criticism. The wretched fate of this mathematical genius was cited as an example of something that should never be allowed to happen again. To celebrate the centenary of Abel's birth, King Oscar II held a magnificent banquet at the Royal Palace in Norway's capital and students staged the biggest torchlit parade the capital had ever witnessed. And on a rocky mound in the Palace Park, known ever since as Abelhaugen, the sculptor Gustav Vigeland erected a heroic monument to honour the by then world-renowned mathematician.

NIELS CHR. GEELMUYDEN

ABEL, NIELS HENRIK (1802-29), mathematician. Recipient of a government travel scholarship 1824–26 and university grant 1827. In 1823 proved the impossibility of using radicals to solve the general equation of the fifth degree. His work on the theory of algebraic equations, infinite series and the theory of elliptical functions has assured him a place among the world's most illustrious mathematicians. In 2003, the Abel Prize, the 'Nobel prize for mathematics', as it is called, was awarded for the first time.

# ECONOMY AND BUSINESS

# A LAND OF MILK AND HONEY

Kåre Valebrokk

'Why are you Norwegians always so worried?'

I was asked this question by Terry Macalister, a British financial journalist, when I was editor-in-chief of the daily newspaper *Dagens Næringsliv*. Macalister had spent a week in Norway and was finding it hard to understand why everyone he talked to kept coming back to the question of what Norway and the Norwegians were going to live on, once their North Sea oil wells ran dry. He had been to several government departments, visited banks, industrial companies and stockbrokers, and conferred with most of the financial wizards he had been able to find in Oslo, Stavanger and Bergen. But no matter who he asked, he always got much the same answer: 'The outlook seems reasonably bright for Norway in the short term, that's true. But viewed in a longer perspective the prospects are a lot more dismal. Before long we shall all be living off oil, and no one knows what we are going to live on when it comes to an end.'

I remember embarking upon a rather convoluted review of Norway's economic history and explaining how poor the country had been a century ago, and why most Norwegians believe that a future without the industry that is Norway's principal source of revenue, that is, oil, is synonymous with a parlous and unpredictable future. I eventually realized that I was in danger of reiterating more or less the same arguments he had heard from the pundits, and broke off in mid-sentence.

'But the real reason is that, when opportunity offers, no Norwegian ever says no to a good worry,' I said.

I have thought back on this conversation many times since. My reply was intended as a snappy one-liner of the kind every journalist delights in. But with the passage of time I have come to the conclusion that there was more to it than that. It was really quite a good explanation. At heart, Norwegians are indeed a nation of worriers, a people not easily convinced that the future isn't sure to be worse than they think, but may actually be much brighter. Over the last one hundred and fifty years we have shown ourselves quite adept at exploiting changing circumstances and innovative technologies when the old ones no longer suffice. This notwithstanding, we have brought with us into the twenty-first century limited faith in our own abilities, a strong suspicion that the last bright idea has been and gone, and an innate scepticism that new and exciting opportunities may be just around the corner. Nemesis will catch up with us, we think: when the oil runs out, the party will be over.

This is the story of how we achieved the success we have, of how we came to be what we are; and of how, in the course of barely a century, we were transformed from poor optimists into ultra-rich pessimists. This is the story I shall attempt to tell. When I have done so, I shall send it to my British journalist friend in the hope that he will understand that it is sure to come through all right, this singular little country way up in the north – that in some thirty to forty years' time Norway will be far wealthier than it is at present; and that we Norwegians will be just as worried then as we have been in the past. A deeply rooted national trait cannot be eradicated in the course of only two generations.

**The source of Norway's wealth**: Oil and natural gas have endowed Norway with unprecedented economic freedom compared with other European countries. The oil sector accounts for nearly 20 per cent of the country's wealth creation (GNP). However, only a small portion of the revenue from oil is absorbed into the economy: instead, Norway is building up an oil fund the value of which soon will pass NOK 1,000 billion. This money is invested abroad. But although oil has made Norway one of the world's richest countries, it has brought new concerns in its train. We quickly learned to live off oil, but it is proving hard to live with it.

### Once upon a time there was a country . . .

Winston Churchill said something to the effect that to make sense of the future one must first learn to understand the past. I couldn't agree more. The Norway that greeted a visitor from 'civilized' Europe in the Constitution year of 1814 was a rather depressing sight. For those prepared to see, the poverty was self-evident; those who closed their eyes to it found themselves confronted by it at every turn. The fact is that right up until the last decades of the nineteenth century Norway was one of the poorest countries in Europe, a country of farmers and fishermen, a country living from hand to mouth, as it had since time immemorial; a nation scraping along on small, hard-to-work farms that kept two or three cows alive on a starvation diet through the long, hard winters until the grass again grew lush and green; that salted herring and dried cod, brought ptarmigan down from the mountains and picked berries in the woods; that read the Good Book by the dim light of paraffin lamps, gave birth to far too many children in proportion to the country's resources and despatched those it couldn't feed (after infant mortality had taken its all too heavy toll) across the ocean to America. This was, at any rate, the impression visitors delighted in conveying to the world in the numerous – and generally highly readable – accounts of their travels they published in the first decades following the Napoleonic wars. Such descriptions were not far from the truth, although small, more affluent pockets did exist among the official class, merchants, craftsmen, well-to-do farmers and owners of cargo vessels.

The foregoing notwithstanding, there was a brighter side to the Norway of old, one that tends to be overlooked. In this cold, barren country few people actually starved or suffered so from cold as to endanger their lives; not many countries in the rest of Europe could say the same. And even that early, Norway was well on its way to becoming an egalitarian society. We shared our poverty in much the same way as we now share our wealth: equally. Too equally, perhaps, if economic growth is the aim. Economic growth depends on some people making a profit that can be ploughed back into new activities; but it was hard to make a profit in agrarian Norway.

Visitors to Norway sixty to seventy years later found a wealthier and more contented people than had their predecessors in the first decades after 1814. Something very significant must have happened in a country in which only 3 per cent of a total area of 310 million decares was cultivable, and in which just over 20 per cent is forest, the rest being water or naked rock.

And big changes – or, rather, many small changes – had indeed occurred. It is, at any rate, a fact that despite a marked decline in infant mortality after the long years of privation that were a concomitant of the Napoleonic wars, every year throughout the century the country's farmers managed to increase food production faster than the population grew – and that despite the fact that the population doubled from one to two million in the same period. This is not altogether correct, however, as 'population' includes the several hundreds of thousands of Norwegians whom the country was unable to feed and who for that reason emigrated to America and Canada. Besides, 'to feed' is a relative term: the way in which the rapidly rising population was 'fed' is not without significance. Together with several of her brothers and sisters, my own grandmother was raised by kind, well-meaning relatives because their parents were unable to cope with more children than they already had. Nor must child 'migration' be forgotten. Each spring, ten- to twelve-year-olds from the poor rural areas in the heart of the county of Vest-Agder were sent to tend, all through the summer, livestock on the far richer farms of the adjoining county of Aust-Agder. We know little of what they thought about this, these youngsters who were forced to work for strangers in an alien forest in which bears still roamed. But that the butter and sides of bacon they took home with them in the autumn were a godsend, is a half-forgotten but well-substantiated fact in the history of the south coast and Norway as a whole in these years. This annual transmigration of child labour in the southern counties continued until well into the twentieth century.

The rise in agricultural production that characterized the whole of the nineteenth century was ascribable partly to the importation of new varieties of grain and root crops, partly to improved knowledge of fertilization and drainage, increased mechanization following the introduction of harrows, reapers

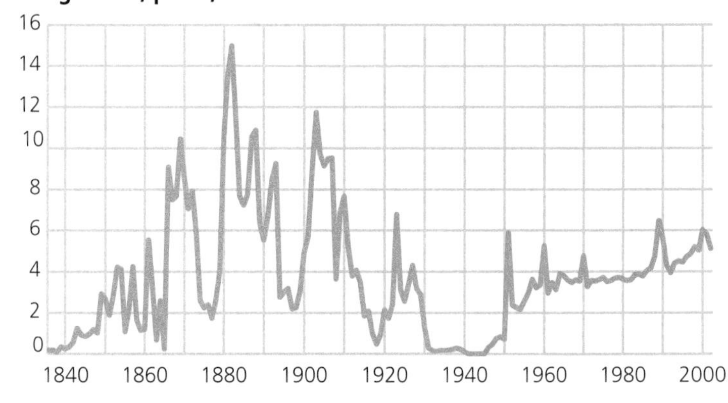


**Emigration to America**: Between 1850 and the outbreak of the Second World War emigration to America was the only alternative open to needy and jobless Norwegians. Over the years, more than one million Norwegians have left the country of their birth to start a new life in the US and Canada – though many of them later returned.

**There was once a country**: The Norway of yesteryear has changed its appearance. Right up to the end of the 19th century many families lived in close-knit communities on a single farm, where they were jointly engaged in agriculture, forestry and tending mountain pastures. Today, the nation's farms are widely dispersed: each is the property of one family and fields and forests constitute distinct legal units. Nevertheless, the number of fulltime farmers continues to fall with every passing year.

and separators, a switch from grain to dairy products, more use of horses for draft and, not least, the authorities' endeavours to put an end to the hopelessly uneconomic practice of strip farming that had for so long bedevilled Norwegian agriculture.

At the beginning of the century, agricultural areas in Norway were characterized by large farmsteads where several families lived in close proximity to each other and together farmed the surrounding arable land, mountain pastures and forests. Not only might individual fields and plots of land have different owners, they were often scattered higgeldy-piggeldy all over the place. In some cases a farmstead could house as many as twelve families, which more or less jointly managed more than five hundred different patches of land. The same held true of woodlands. It was not uncommon for one farmer to own the birchwood and another the spruce and pine wood, while grazing rights were the property of a third. That was the way it had always been, and the country's farmers put up strong resistance – not least because new houses had to be built when families were dispersed – when, between 1850 and 1870, the government made a decisive attempt to end strip farming. An additional problem resulting from joint ownership of land and forests, was that it was difficult, if not impossible, to borrow money for expansion and improvements against a mortgage in property.

As a result of this reform, the rural landscape evolved into something closely akin to that we know today: widely dispersed farms, each the property of one family, and agricultural and forested areas conjoined in clearly defined and well-documented units.

Socially, however, this tidying-up process was by no means without its problems. The sense of a common lot disappeared from rural areas, where people had henceforward to provide for themselves and their families. The writer Inge Krokann has put into words the feelings of many a farmer in these years: 'The strong bands that bound them to their closest relatives were weakened. Even when old houses were moved elsewhere, they seemed lost and out of place in their new settings.'

The role played in this modernization process by the time-worn system of odal tenure of land must not be overlooked. Allodial law, which endowed the eldest son with the right to take over his father's farm at less than its market price, was rooted in age-old custom, but did not become law until 1821 – the same year, as it happens, that Norway's aristocracy was abolished. This right of tenure precluded the buying-up of large adjoining areas of land, and thus contributed greatly to the agricultural structure that is still a feature of present-day Norway. It also helped to ensure that Norway was spared the violent peasant uprisings that took place elsewhere in Europe, and was one reason why the Marcus Thrane movement that sprang up halfway through the nineteenth century soon petered out. Thrane, who had picked up some rather extreme socialist ideas, started a movement that found widespread support among people of humble means in rural areas. But the incentive to revolt was not as great in Norway as in some other countries; nor were there as many wealthy farmers to revolt against. The fact that in the twenty-first century allodial law has outlived its usefulness and ought long ago to have been removed from the statute book, is a different matter altogether.

Throughout the whole of this period of strong population increase, the cotter system was also a pivotal factor. To support himself and his family a cotter would rent, on varying terms, land he could farm under the aegis of a larger farm. In the 1860s, 20 to 25 per cent of the population were, in fact, cotters, but in the years that followed many emigrated to America. In time these smallholders also received help from the government to safeguard their interests, which explains why Norway largely escaped the fate of Sweden's rural proletariat at this time. Nonetheless, as late as 1929 there were still some 6,000 cotters in Norway.

Aid towards modernization of the farming industry was also provided by the many savings banks that sprang up in rural areas from the 1820s onwards. To some extent these banks took over the role hitherto played in the countryside by merchants and the family as a source of finance. The combination of all these factors made Norway's rural population, which, early in the twentieth century accounted for at least 70 per cent of the total population, seem reasonably well-off compared with a generation or two earlier.

**The silver harvest of the sea**: Throughout the whole of the 19th century fishing in Norway was a highly seasonal occupation. It was confined to coastal waters and the gear employed was relatively simple. Not until the years immediately preceding and following the First World War did fishing evolve into a modern, mechanized year-round occupation. Taken in 1911, this photograph is from the herring fishery off Haugesund.

The free owner-farmer was played up for all he was worth in the building of Norway as a nation. To a very great extent he became a legendary figure, a position he was to retain throughout most of the twentieth century and one that greatly overshadowed the real economic importance of farming in the last thirty to forty years. Not least some of the giants of Norwegian literature, most notably, perhaps, Knut Hamsun and Trygve Gulbranssen, have helped to enhance the farmer's status. I do not doubt that rural Norway would have looked quite different had not the farmer, early in the modernization process, been placed on what was as close as this country comes to a political, mythological and economic pedestal. The difference in the way Norwegian and Swedish farming have developed suggests that this interpretation is correct.

Up to the outbreak of the First World War agriculture continued to undergo a steady process of development. The war led to a strong economic upswing and, to some extent, also to soaring prices for agricultural products. On the other hand the postwar years imposed a heavy burden on farmers, not least because of what was known as the parity policy pursued by the government, a policy aimed at restoring the value of the Norwegian krone in relation to gold, the gold standard having been abandoned when war broke out in 1914. The agricultural market collapsed, with the consequence that farmers who had made large capital investments were very hard hit and had difficulty in paying off their debts. Bankruptcies were by no means uncommon in rural Norway all through the 1920s.

But the interwar years were also the heyday of people like the pioneer farmer Isak Sellanraa, protagonist of Knut Hamsun's *Growth of the Soil*, after the government launched a large-scale aid programme to encourage the clearing of new ground and farming of new land. Between 1920 and 1939 government subsidies led to the clearance of 1.2 million decars of new land, to bring the total area of fully cultivated agricultural land in Norway up to 8.3 million decares. To complete the picture it should be added that this pioneer work was continued after the Second World War: the years from 1920 to 1950 saw the establishment of no fewer than 18,000 new farms in Norway.

Right up to the 1970s, when farming revenue received a strong boost, government subsidies designed to encourage the breaking of new ground continued to be provided, despite the fact that both farms and farmers rapidly and inexorably declined in number each year from the 1950s to the end of the century. Throughout the whole of the twentieth century the principal role of farming may well have been to act as an unlimited fount of labour for the economy at large.

Agriculture and forestry currently account for a mere 0.9 per cent of Norway's gross national product (GNP), but both still benefit from substantial government subsidies and aid programmes, as well as restrictions on imports. These measures are partially motivated by, if nothing else, a well-intentioned and consensual wish to keep the countryside populated in order to preserve Norway's characteristic rural landscape. In the course of little more than one hundred years the Norwegian farming community has regressed from being the backbone of the nation to an industry employing only 50,000 full-time farmers. It must be added, however, that farming constitutes the foundation on which thousands of jobs in ancillary trades and processing industries rest.

### The fisherman-farmer

Up to this point in my retrospective look at Norway's first stumbling attempts to find its rightful place in the world, I have confined myself to the nation's farmers and made no mention of the fishermen. This has resulted in a rather lopsided picture of the Norway of the past, as along the entire length of the coast and, more especially, in northern Norway, farming was largely combined with participation in the large-scale herring and cod fisheries. The fisherman-farmer is an established figure in the national consciousness and also a stock character in literature.

From time immemorial fish have been an important export product. As late as the 1860s fish and fish products accounted for 20 per cent of the country's total exports of goods and services. It is harder, however, to provide accurate figures relating to the number of people engaged in fishing, as fishing was very much a seasonal occupation and those who took part in it came by land or sea from all over the country. When, as they did each year, enormous shoals of herring approached the coast of western Norway to spawn, it was not unusual for men from the Setesdal and Hallingdal valleys to make their way on foot across the mountains to take part in the fishery. It is estimated that between 70,000 and 80,000 people, that is, 10 per cent of Norway's working population, were employed in this fishery.

All through the nineteenth century fishing was carried on in coastal waters, so about all that was needed to participate was a line and a hook. This applied only to Norway: in Britain and the Netherlands, for example, the fisheries were much more capital-intensive, as fishing took place on offshore grounds, which necessitated the use of bigger and better boats and gear. Another contributory factor was that in these countries the distinction between capital and labour was more marked than in Norway, where seasonal fishing was largely in the shape of joint projects or local enterprises – the coastal equivalent of communal farming before the system was reformed.

With inshore fishing the rule, in terms of boats and gear modernization came somewhat late to Norway. Nor was the process helped by the fact that city-based merchants monopolized the fish export trade right up to 1882. But towards the close of the century steam engines began to make their appearance, and between 1900 and the outbreak of the First World War the internal combustion engine revolutionized Norway's fishing industry. At this time the changeover from seasonal to year-round fishing had also gained ground, especially in the south. Year-round fishing brought in its train ship-owning companies and, as in Britain and the Netherlands, a greater distinction between capital and labour. For both good and ill, modern capitalism had caught up with fishing in Norway too.

During the First World War Norway's fishermen enjoyed a bonanza in the shape of high, government-guaranteed prices. Fish were an important counter in Norway's endeavours to maintain the country's neutrality. But the good times did not last for ever. During and immediately after the war the fishing fleet expanded rapidly, until, in 1929, the point was reached when it was more than twice the size of what it had been in 1914. In common with the farmers, the nation's fishermen now felt the effects of the government's parity policy and the concomitant steep decline in market prices. And as if that were not enough, it also fell victim to a nationwide temperance campaign, which in 1921 led to Norway's notorious ban on sale of liquor. In retaliation the Mediterranean wine-producing countries placed an embargo on imports of Norwegian fish. Along with widespread smuggling, this was the main reason why prohibition was ended in 1927. In the latter half of the 1920s Norway's fishermen, again in line with the farmers, benefited from a series of new subsidies and aid measures. These

**A global industry**: In the 1920s Norwegian shipowners revolutionized whaling with the aid of Norwegian technology and patents, and in 1927 accounted for 65 per cent of the world's total production of whale oil. The photograph shows a whale being flensed at Grytviken, South Georgia. However, these new methods proved so effective that some species were threatened with extinction.

remained in place in various guises right up until the 1980s, but have now largely been phased out.

The product range of Norwegian fisheries was long mostly confined to herring and cod, first salted or dried, later to an increasing extent fresh, iced, or frozen. After a time, however, other species began to appear in the shops. Large quantities of fish also served to provide raw materials for the extensive herring-oil and canning industries of the western seaboard. No Norwegian over the age of fifty will ever forget the taste of Møller's cod-liver oil, the pre-bedtime bugbear of every Norwegian child. Møller, the manufacturer, enjoyed a leading position on the international market right up until the advent of vitamin pills and similar dietary supplements.

Immediately after the Second World War, for more than 100,000 Norwegians fishing was still their principal source of livelihood. In the 1970s the nation's fishing fleet virtually emptied the sea of herring, and mackerel stocks also came close to exhaustion. This heavy drain on resources led to a complex and highly detailed system of licensing embodying strict limits on the quantities of fish it was permissible to take each year.

Today the number of professional fishermen is about 13,000, and in terms of first-hand value the traditional fisheries' share of Norway's GNP has fallen to only 0.5 per cent.

The fisheries of old are having to contend with greatly varying and possibly also declining resources. On the other hand, the favourable climatic conditions that are a feature of

Norway's extremely long coastline offer rich possibilities for the expansion of fish farming and kindred occupations. Aquaculture really took off in the mid-seventies. It was long strictly controlled, with the intention of favouring local interests and local capital. The industry is still subject to tight licensing, but is now hallmarked by economy of scale and dominated by 'normal' and, to some extent, also stock-exchange-listed capital. In the course of its brief existence this industry has suffered many ups and downs, partly because of over-capacity and problems in selling its products, partly as a consequence of disease among the fish, the proliferation of algae and losses due to escaping fish. Over the years, not a few banks have sustained heavy losses resulting from bankruptcies in the fish-farming industry and the writing-down of loans. The industry is also finding it difficult to cope with the rigid import restrictions imposed by the EU; it would probably have much to gain from Norwegian membership of the Union. Norway's fish-farming industry is exposed to strong competition from countries with similar climatic conditions, most notably Chile and Scotland. In this connection it is worth observing that considerable Norwegian capital has been invested in fish farming in both these countries.

Until recently salmon and trout have been the predominant species of fish farmed in Norway, but more new species, among them halibut and cod, will probably be introduced in years to come; shellfish production is so far only in its infancy. In monetary terms aquaculture is now almost on a par with traditional fishing, although it is only one-third as large in terms of the number of people engaged in it.

In the first half of the twentieth century Norwegian interests built up a world-scale whaling industry. Whaling had always been a time-honoured occupation in Norway, but up to the First World War it was largely confined to the country's own coastal waters and those around the Shetlands, Faeroes and Svalbard. In 1905, however, Chr. Christensen, a Sandefjord shipowner, despatched a pilot expedition to explore the possibilities offered by whaling off the Falkland Islands. The expedition proved a success and aroused considerable interest, particularly in Christensen's home county of Vestfold. This prompted the establishment of a number of specialized new companies, among them Pelagos, Rosshavet and Kosmos, which set about despatching whaling expeditions to the Antarctic. After the hiatus resulting from the First World War, the breakthrough came in the 1920s. This 'new' whaling industry was based almost exclusively on Norwegian-developed technology and patents. But other countries, most notably Japan and Great Britain, soon followed suit, and whereas in 1927 Norway accounted for 65 per cent of world whale-oil production, in the 1930s the country's share fell steeply. Whaling could be an extremely profitable occupation at times, and the older generation still retains fond memories of the way in which whalers, returning from a season in the South Atlantic, gave a welcome filip to restaurants and catering establishments in the small towns of Vestfold. But the whaling industry was very nearly hoist with its own petard. It was so effective, and operated on such a large scale, that it came close to exterminating some species of whale. Most endangered was the blue whale, the largest whale of all. For a time, the whaling nations practised a self-imposed quota system, but as international pressure on the industry increased, in the 1950s and early '60s it became increasingly apparent that commercial whaling was doomed. The last factory ship rounded off the era of Norwegian whaling in 1967, and today scarcely any whaling is done at all.

**Tradition**: Shipbuilding and shipping are time-honoured industries in Norway, but it was the repeal of Britain's Navigation Acts that in the latter half of the 19th century really made Norway one of the world's leading shipping nations. The picture is of the timber-laden barque **Ennerdal**, wrecked just outside its home port of Arendal in 1903.

**A ship in every bay**: A Hardanger sloop in the stocks at Vennesvikfjæra in 1883. In the age of wooden ships, ships were built in every bay and inlet along the Norwegian coast. Norway was slow to change to steam and steel and her shipbuilding yards suffered accordingly. On the other hand, the country's shipowners were quick to replace steam by diesel engines.

### The great leap forward

Many years ago I paid a visit to Selje, a small community on an island – the site of an ancient monastery – off Norway's west coast. There I fell into conversation with a dear old lady, who told me all about the history of the island, recounting it so vividly and concisely as to gladden my journalist's heart. 'This place,' she said, 'was an important centre here in the west – until, that is, they built the roads and isolated us.'

She was right, of course. Before they were linked by roads, the only way of getting from one place to another on Norway's 2,500-kilometer-long coast was by boat; with the advent of roads and cars, Selje and the island on which it stood were forgotten and the population entered into steady decline.

Throughout our long history it was the sea that enabled us to maintain contact with each other, and it was the sea that made it possible to buy and sell our wares. It was the sea, too, that linked Norway with the world at large, making it possible to import grain from Denmark and sell fish to the merchants of Bergen and to the countries bordering the Baltic Sea. Similarly, it was the sea that opened up the markets of Britain, France and the Netherlands for exports of timber. This notwithstanding, in the heyday of merchantilism international trade was very restricted, in Norway's case being confined to the lands rimming the North Sea and the Baltic Sea.

Round about the middle of the nineteenth century, however, a new wind, a wind of change, blew across Europe, bringing with it free trade. This resulted in a general lowering of customs tariffs on a wide range of goods and thus opened wide the doors for Norway's exports of timber. When, on 1 January 1850, Britain repealed her Navigation Acts, which had greatly favoured British shipowners in regard to trade with Britain and her overseas possessions, a whole world suddenly lay open to Norwegian shipping.

A professional historian may disagree, but if there is any point in trying to set a date for Norway's first major break with the agrarian society of yore, it must be 1850. Once the way was clear, Norway was poised to take full advantage of the opportunities thus offered. To judge by developments in the next few years, there must have been a veritable ocean of energy and get-up-and-go pent up behind the dam when it finally burst.

How, it may be asked, was it possible in the course of only thirty years for impoverished little Norway to transform itself from a quite modest maritime nation in 1850 into the third-largest shipping nation in the world, surpassed only by Great Britain and the United States?

Many factors played a part, the most important of them probably being tradition and inherited skills – what we would now call know-how; it could never have come about without them. Norwegians had sailed the seas since time immemorial, and Norway's coastal towns and villages were rich in shipwrights skilled in the art of building ships with the resources they had to hand. Also of significance was the fact that it was easy to finance the building of a ship by one's own labour and from products one produced oneself, something that helped to make shipbuilding and shipping open to every coast dweller, not only to merchants, government officials, wealthy farmers and others with money to invest. It was done through a system of joint ownership, a time-worn way of financing ships that has survived to this day in the shape of limited partnerships. This form of ownership was given a new lease of life with the discovery of oil in the North Sea. The oil companies needed the services of a whole armada of small, purpose-built supply ships. The limited partnership is still a common means of raising capital in Norwegian shipping circles and in the oil industry.

A jointly owned shipping company is, quite simply, a means of sharing expenses – going Dutch, as it were – each participant contributing money, labour or goods as his share in the ship and himself assuming full financial responsibility for his contribution should the ship be lost. In return, each part-owner receives precisely the same share of any profit accruing and has to meet his corresponding share of any loss. A farmer could thus acquire a share in a ship by providing timber for it to be built locally; a nearby sawmill could do its bit by sawing the wood, a captain could contribute by sailing without payment for the first year, a sailmaker could chip in with sails – hardly any combination was impossible for a person wishing to become a part-owner; even junior clerks sometimes joined in. Some companies might have as many as 120 such partners. To spread the risk it was quite common for the more well-to-do to take shares in several ships. The less well-off would take a chance and invest what they could afford. After some years at sea as a part-owner, many a second mate returned a wealthy man; not only wealthy, but also with valuable contacts among London's shipbrokers. As a rule, from there it was but a small step to taking a share in another new company. Part-ownership was long the principal means of financing ships in Norway, and it was not until when, round about the turn of the century, it became possible to borrow money against a mortgage in the ship itself, that joint-stock companies gradually, if somewhat warily, took over the role formerly played by part-ownership.

It was in this manner that Norway became a leading shipping nation. In the early years, ships stuck to trading between Norwegian ports, but later they took to transporting other countries' cargoes between foreign ports. In 1880 Norwegian shipowners owned close on seven per cent of the world's total tonnage and employed more than 60,000 seamen, the vast majority of whom were Norwegian. With the advent of steam, this figure declined: fewer hands are needed to man an engine-room than to handle the sails of a full-rigger.

In his book *Norges økonomiske historie 1815–1970* (The Economic History of Norway 1815–1970) Fritz Hodne reviewed the most important competitive advantages enjoyed by Norwegian shipowners when the country's merchant fleet first came into being. He drew particular attention to the fact that Norwegian seamen were willing to work for low rates of pay and that owners deliberately put their trust in second-rank technology, which meant sailing ships. It was these two factors that for many years enabled us to sail our ships much more cheaply than the foreign owners with whom we had to compete. Between 1840 and 1910 Norwegian wages were 50 per cent lower than British, and lower still compared with what American owners had to pay their men. Conditions on board Norwegian ships were, to put it mildly, nothing to boast about, and many ships were lost. Far too many in comparison with the losses sustained by other countries. In the worst years, some 8 to 10 per cent of the ships in Norway's merchant marine were wrecked. Because of this deliberate concentration on low technology, it was not until 1907 that steam tonnage exceeded sail tonnage.

There were other reasons for this tardy adoption of new techology than lack of capital, however. Norwegian shipowners mostly confined themselves to the timber and bulk trades, and because of this had a greater need to operate cheaply rather than with speed and regularity. For the British, it was the other way round: they needed to sail to India with passengers and mail and return with tea and spices. Moreover, the fortunes of Norwegian owners were strongly bound up with local resources and yards, which rarely possessed the skills required by modern marine engineering, for example the ability to read complicated blueprints and a knowledge of iron and steel rather than of the wood with which they were accustomed to work. But it cannot be denied that conservatism also played an important role. One Arendal shipowner actually went so far as to declare: 'There will be a need for our wooden ships as long as the forest continues to grow and the wind to blow.'

This hidebound owner was soon to be proved wrong. From the close of the 1870s, steam engines, combined with new hull designs and technological advances, offered so many advantages that Norway's sailing ships lost much of their competitive edge. Nor did the opening of the Suez Canal in 1869 help, as it enabled steamships to take a short cut to the East, whereas Norwegian sailing ships were still dependent on the 'long winds' to take them round the Cape. Their tardiness in converting to steam resulted in the bankruptcy of many shipping companies, and not a few south-coast ports found themselves in dire straits as the century neared its end; in fact, the resultant crisis is still very vivid in the memories of many a dweller on the south coast. It affected not only shipowners but also the many yards still building ships of wood, yards whose traditional market vanished before their eyes. But the crisis was not ascribable to the mistakes of the shipping industry alone. The 1880s were a trying time all round for Norway's economic life, as they were for much of Europe, which suffered a similar downturn.

But in Bergen and Kristiania, as Oslo was then called, innovative thinking was more to the fore. Here, the shipping industry was not so closely bound up with local resources, and shipowners were far more willing to adopt new technologies and new business methods. The time charter, a contract providing for hire of a ship on a monthly or yearly basis, and new, creative methods of financing, were developed, as were liner traffic, that is, regular scheduled sailings, and jointly operated services involving several companies. It was mainly in Bergen and the capital that shipping evolved into an industry in its own right, one wholly independent of other aspects of business and commerce. Names dating from this period such as Jebsen, Fearnley & Eger, Otto Thoresen, Wilhelm Wilhelmsen and Fred. Olsen still figure prominently in Norwegian shipping circles.

All in all, however, the switch from sail to steam came too late, with the result that, as the nineteenth century neared its end, Norway's share of world tonnage suffered a sharp decline. Following dissolution of the union with Sweden, however, things began to look up. Nonetheless, when war broke out in 1914, the Norwegian merchant fleet still had a bigger percentage of sailing ships than any other maritime country. In the event, only Finland clung to sailing ships longer than we did.

But when the next great change came, that from steam engine to motor, Norway had learned her lesson and was the first to convert. After suffering heavy losses in the First World War, the country's shipowners rebuilt the country's merchant fleet, tonnage rising from one million gross registered tons (grt) in 1919 to five million in 1939. By then, no less than 62 per cent of Norway's merchant fleet was motor-driven, compared with 26 per cent of the British fleet. This restored Norway to her position as one of the world's foremost shipping nations, a place she retained until the bottom fell out of the market in the 1970s.

It is not by chance that I have devoted so much space to the role played by shipping in the nineteenth century. The shipping industry deserves such detailed treatment, as it not only played a decisive part in the economic development of newly capitalist Norway, but also did much to help build the nation after the humiliation attendant upon its having been casually ceded to Sweden in 1814. Then, as now, the industry produced some extremely astute and enterprising leaders, so it is hardly surprising that it was two shipowners, Christian Michelsen and Gunnar Knudsen, who spearheaded the campaign that culminated in Norway's gaining independence in 1905. In many ways shipping provided Norway with the self-assurance needed to hold one's own in the world. 'Without that,' Michelsen wrote, 'our international and economic position would today have been different and poorer.'

Although it is difficult to determine the political significance of shipping, it is all the easier to assess its economic importance. In 1885 shipping accounted for no less than 43.3 per cent of Norway's total exports, with timber in second place at 19.7 per cent. When, in addition, it is borne in mind that, at the same time, exports and imports made up some 60 per cent of Norway's GNP, there is little more to add.

The foregoing notwithstanding, it is, perhaps, of equal importance that, thanks to part-ownership, shipping offered abundant opportunities for new social classes to save money for investment in other activities. No other trade or industry provided the Norwegian people with more openings for private saving than shipping. A country cannot live from hand to mouth, and the shipping industry did much to create the surplus that was required if Norway were to advance and prosper; both in Norway and abroad, 'shipping money' gradually found its way into many enterprises that had nothing to do with shipping and the sea.

The fact that shipping, with its great need for seamen, also helped to relieve population pressure in rural areas and provide young people with an alternative to emigration to the New World, is another aspect of the matter that must not be forgotten, though it is one shipping shares with the new industries that made their appearance in the run-up to the turn of the century.

After 1850 there was no difficulty in finding cargoes for the rapidly expanding fleet. Free trade, Britain's colonial empire and the rapid rise of the United States in the world market saw to that. New freight markets were opened up and exploited all over the world, from the West Indies to the coasts of Africa and the Far East. But to a great extent shipments of Norwegian timber formed the mainstay of the golden age of Norwegian shipping: shipping and timber made a perfect pair in those first heady years of expansion.

The timber trade had always been largely in the hands of a small coterie who were entitled by royal prerogative to operate sawmills. This anachronistic system was greatly liberalized early in the nineteenth century, and in 1860 it was abolished altogether, enabling anyone who so wished to build a sawmill.

**The breadline**: The opening years of the 20th century were for many people a time of hardship as a result of the 'Kristiania crash' of 1899. The photograph shows a queue for food outside Christiania Dampkjøkken in 1903.

Indgang for Hentende
504 "B"
Eneberettiget 1903
Wilse, Kria

As a result of this new-found freedom, sawmilling technology improved by leaps and bounds. The old sawmills were scattered about all over the country beside randomly chosen waterfalls and employed vertical frame saws with only one blade, a blade so thick that it chewed up half of each log. After a while thinner blades were introduced, the circular saw replaced the frame saw and, with the advent of the steam engine, it became possible to resite mills at river mouths. This enabled sawn timber to be shipped out straight from the mill. When the reform came in 1860, new, steam-powered sawmills were ready and waiting. Transport systems were also improved: linking canals were constructed and small steamships were employed to transport timber across the large inland lakes.

As early as 1840 or thereabouts the British had set about lowering the duty on imported timber. When, in addition, in the following decades the price of timber rose steeply on the world markets, timber soon evolved into Norway's biggest industry, accounting in 1866 for no less than 42 per cent of the country's commodity exports. Britain was far and away the biggest market, followed by France, the Netherlands and Denmark, in that order. The importance of the timber industry is illustrated by the fact that in 1870 it employed 10,000 of the country's 34,000 industrial workers. As in the case of shipping, in the timber industry too, when opportunity offered and there was a market available, enterprising men were to hand, ready and willing to exploit both with the aid of whatever technology was most suitable, be it the best or the next best. It was a matter of choosing what was right for the purpose.

From the timber trade it was but a step to planing mills and what is today known as the wood-processing industry; here too foreign influence – the spread of newspapers in Europe and America – was the determining factor. The principal raw material used to make paper had hitherto been rags, but that industry had reached the limit of its international capacity. Accordingly, when a method allowing for the replacement of rags by wood pulp was invented in Germany, the way stood open for Norway's spruce, a tree too small for the timber trade but ideal for paper production.

An interesting feature of the development of Norway's timber industry is that Norwegian sawmilling expertise became an export product in its own right. To this day Finland's biggest wood-processing company, Enzo-Gutzeit, bears the name of Hans Andreas Meelhus Gutzeit, a Drammen man who emigrated to Finland where, together with a number of his sawmilling compatriots, he made a new start in the south-eastern town of Kotka. Norwegians were very much to the fore in Sweden and Russia, too. Regrettably, much of the money they had invested in Russia was lost in the Bolshevik revolution of 1917, as many were unable to get their money out in time.

### Fireworks herald the dawn of a new century

The building occupied by the Nobel Institute in Oslo is an elegant old patrician villa on the corner of Drammensveien and Parkveien. I live close by, and every day walk past this building, which has a bust of Alfred Nobel, the man behind the Nobel Peace Prize, in its front garden. For a few months, before Norway entered the turbulent century that was to bring with it electricity, industry, war and capitalism, the house was the home of Consul-General Chr. Christophersen.

I occasionally think of Christophersen as I stroll past his onetime home. With interests in shipping, commerce, timber and wood-processing, he was a driving force in the new Norway. He had numerous well-established and reliable business associates abroad and did much to introduce new ideas and establish new projects all over the country. Despite this, it was Christophersen who was responsible for the disastrous Kristiania crash of June 1899.

Few people today have heard of this débâcle, and fewer still are aware of the striking fact that large parts of Oslo appear to have been built between 1890 and 1900. The year these buildings were erected is often to be found written in wrought iron or stucco above the entrance, especially in the more affluent and genteel neighbourhoods, where people were more inclined to spend money on such adornments.

But it is no coincidence. In the closing years of the nineteenth century Norway's capital city was engulfed by a wave of property speculation that has never been matched since, and that cast long shadows well into the twentieth century. The ensuing crash may well have been the reason it was largely foreign capital that eventually financed the strong tide of industrialization that rolled across Norway early in the 1900s. Norwegian banks were quite simply too fearful to invest in anything at all. They can hardly be blamed for holding back as, when the dust from the crash finally settled, not a few of them were left prostrated.

As the nineteenth century neared its close, the capital underwent strong growth. People poured in from all over the country, not least from the rural areas, which were still the nation's principal source of labour. In 1894 the city had 182,000 inhabitants; only four years later this figure had risen to 226,000, and the population continued to increase. Speculators realized that their time had come: money earned from trade, shipping and timber was invested in major building projects and hundreds of joint-stock companies were formed.

The painter Christian Krohg recounts how, in 1898, he arrived back home from a sojourn in Paris to find his favourite restaurant transformed into a madhouse in which everyone was engaged in some wild project or other. But only a few days after his return he himself became a director of a real-estate company. And, as usually happens before things go badly awry, banks lent their support by granting cheap loans to all and sundry against 'security'. Things were bound to go wrong, as the know-alls tend to say – in retrospect – and sure enough, on 11 June 1899, they did.

At the time, Consul-General Christophersen was heavily involved in establishing a number of wood-processing companies. However, these companies were finding it difficult to get started, and Christophersen was so strapped for cash that he ultimately went bankrupt. That was all that was needed to make the bubble burst – because his bankruptcy was far from being an ordinary one. His principal company left behind it a debt equivalent to almost two per cent of Norway's GNP. A corresponding bankruptcy today would result in claims totalling some 30 billion kroner.

This bankruptcy had severe repercussions in several trades and industries, not least in shipping. Numerous real-estate companies collapsed, property and share prices plummeted all over the country, six banks went bankrupt, and growth in the capital suffered a severe setback. Some two years after the crash, almost 9,000 flats still stood empty in Kristiania, 10 per cent of the total number of dwellings in the city. The crash did much to explain why Norway's GNP fell by 0.2 per cent annually between 1899 and 1905.

This was Norway's confrontation with the new century prior to the final settlement with Sweden and the country's independence in 1905. It was a brutal encounter indeed, one that also involved modern capitalism, which revealed a face Norway had until then mercifully been spared. Bankruptcies had, no doubt, long been a normal occurrence: both in the countryside and in shipping circles, it was by no means uncommon for people to lose all they had. But that a single straightforward bankruptcy could have such an overwhelming impact throughout the length and breadth of the country, one that was to make its effects felt for years to come, was something new and totally unexpected. It augured anything but well for the future.

Shipping and timber were the two main growth factors in the latter half of the nineteenth century. Both illustrate the way in which Norway learned effectively to exploit the country's comparative advantages once we were enabled to trade freely and there was a market for our products and services. The need to adopt new technology was never an obstacle. True, we had been exporting timber and fish for centuries, but never had we experienced a boom like the one that occurred in shipping and forestry once the external and internal barriers were removed.

For the first time we had also seen that a Norwegian industry could wrest itself free of Norway and domestic trade and make its own way, as shipping had done in the last few decades. Norwegian ships were now conveying oil from America to France, fruit from the West Indies to America and machinery from Britain through the Suez Canal to India and China.

In the countryside, most people were still relatively poor, but they were decidedly better off than in the past. Renewal, drainage, government educational measures, the reaper, separator and harrow were all contributory factors. In the towns, as in the new urban communities that had grown up in Moss, Strømmen and Mjøndalen when sawmills were moved to river mouths, prosperity was seemingly greater; but life in these places was more of a gamble. The unity and security so typical of country life did not survive transplantation to urban life, where what counted was money. It didn't take much for a man to lose his job, and there was hardly any safety net for those who, through no fault of their own, suddenly found themselves unemployed. Industrial companies were too few and too small to absorb the many young people who fled the countryside in search of work in towns and urban centres, for which reason, as so often in the past, emigration to America was the only escape.

What Norway needed was another powerful boost.

### A bright spark

When the boost that was destined to propel Norway into the Industrial Age finally came, it came on two legs, both of which belonged to a man by the name of Sam Eyde. It is doubtful whether any other Norwegian has had such an impact on the country's economy and development as Eyde. He had the idea, he had the skill, he had the necessary connections – and he had the resolve and drive to see things through.

Sam Eyde was born in the small south-coast town of Arendal in 1866, at a time when the little port boasted some 4,000 inhabitants and a merchant fleet on a par with Denmark's. His grandfather, a former sea captain, had ended his career as a ship- and shipyard-owner, a not uncommon combination on this stretch of coast in the heyday of the sailing ship. His business activities were eventually taken over by Sam Eyde's father, who had likewise spent some years at sea and was German consul. In consequence, Sam Eyde grew up in very comfortable circumstances indeed. He too went to sea for a time, later entering a military training college. He then chose to train as a structural engineer at the technical college in Charlottenburg in Berlin.

On completion of his training, and after having enjoyed a comet-like career with various German engineering companies, while still a young man he soon found himself head of Scandinavia's principal consulting and engineering company, with offices in Oslo and Stockholm. He was responsible for a number of award-winning projects in Norway, Sweden, Denmark and Germany; one of his structures, a boldly conceived bridge, is still to be seen in Lübeck.

At a dinner in Oslo hosted by Gunnar Knudsen, Eyde happened to meet Professor Kristian Birkeland. Birkeland told him of a disastrous experiment he had recently made, an experiment that had resulted in nothing more than a gigantic spark, an arc.

That was it! Sam Eyde needed that spark to extract and fix nitrogen from the air. The two joined forces and already that same year patented what became known as the Birkeland-Eyde method, a process which had only one possible rival, the German Haber-Bosch method.

I am by no means sure that we should take Sam Eyde at his word when he says in his highly self-serving memoirs, *Mitt liv og mitt livsverk* (My Life and My Life's Work), that it was the nitrogen problem he had had in mind when, a year or two earlier, he had taken steps to buy the rights to exploit waterfalls in Vamma and Rjukan. It is quite possible that this striking example of his foresight was more a case of being wise after the event, a not-uncommon occurrence when things turn out well. Whatever the truth of the matter, Eyde had formed two joint-stock companies to manage these rights, and it is a fact that he was looking for means to utilize the enormous industrial potential of the falls. Among those associated with him in these two companies was Knut Tillberg, who was later to put him in touch with Marcus and Knut Wallenberg, directors of the Stockholm Enskilda Bank.

It was an Englishman, Sir William Crookes, who, in an address before the British Association in 1898, had first directed attention to a growing problem: the world was running short of nitrogen. Till then the demand for nitrogen had been met by natural saltpetre from Chile, but if consumption were to continue at the present rate, Crookes said, the world's resources would be exhausted within thirty years. It really was a matter of grave concern: saltpetre was a key product in the manufacture of fertilizers for agriculture and for making explosives.

This was the problem Eyde had set out to solve. He had the idea, he had energy ready to hand in his waterfalls, he had the spark, he had the ability – and now he showed that he also had the connections he needed to realize such a gigantic project.

Following a series of experiments, before long Birkeland and Eyde succeeded in developing a practical method of extracting nitrogen from the air. In parallel with this work Eyde had secured the necessary financial backing, and in January 1904 he founded A/S Det Norske Aktieselskap for Elektrokemisk Industri (Elkem), a company destined to play a central role in Norway's industrialization. The Wallenberg brothers and Knut Tillburg were joint owners of the company. Rights to the Vanna and Rjukan waterfalls were transferred to the new company, along with large tracts of land that Eyde had bought up to augment his waterfall purchases.

The last of the money required to finance Eyde's great project was secured with the aid of the Wallenberg brothers from a big French bank, Banque de Paris. Negotiations were conducted in Paris, in parallel with the inflamed discussions on dissolution of the union with Sweden taking place back home. The latter could have had dire consequences for the outcome of Sam Eyde's own scheme.

Eyde says as much in his memoirs:

*From Paris Wallenberg and I followed the despatches on the dispute over dissolution of the Union while engaged in negotia-*

**Sam Eyde's doing**: The painter Th. Kittelsen's characteristic contribution to the public debate resulting from the harnessing of the Rjukan waterfall. According to the artist, on one side of the fall the painting depicts the stupidity of the project and on the other the envy it aroused.

**Coke is it**: Poverty and a scarcity of goods characterized Norway's capital city after the First World War, prompting Kristiania Kommunale Provianteringsråd, a municipal relief organization, to provide people in need with coke for heating purposes (1919).

*tions with the Banque de Paris, and the day our agreement with the bank was signed, the news came through that Oscar II was no longer king of Norway. 'Let's get back home,' Marcus Wallenberg said to me, 'there's no telling what the French may do now.' How true. We had only got as far as Cologne when we received a telegram from the bank urging us to return to Paris because of the critical state of the talks. However, we had secured our contract, so we continued on our way.*

The contract with the Banque de Paris paved the way for the foundation of Norsk Hydro, which was established on 2 December 1905, the first of Mother Elkem's offspring. Hydro took over the patent rights and falls, and construction of power stations and factories at Rjukan and Notodden commenced. As early as 1916 the isolated rural community that was Rjukan when Sam Eyde bought the falls, had expanded to become a flourishing little town of 10,000 inhabitants. By then Norsk Hydro was already exporting 117,000 tons of fertilizer annually.

Not without justification, what had taken place at Rjukan and Notodden attracted attention all over the industrialized world. Norway, a country hitherto virtually unknown, but of vast natural resources, had abruptly put itself on the map. In the years that followed, a number of large industrial enterprises were established in Norway. Not a few were brokered by Sam Eyde, who also had financial interests in them. Norway's combination of untold reserves of waterpower, an ice-free coast and fjords with deep-water anchorages right up to the shore, made it a tempting object for investment. A number of new industries followed in the wake of the electrochemical plants: nickel and zinc, aluminium, iron and carbide. Even mining, which had long been moribund, enjoyed a new lease of life at this time. Moreover, the electricity produced stimulated the growth of an extensive electrotechnical industry, as well as consumer industries.

Overnight, as it were, Norway elbowed its way into the industrial world. However, most of its industrialization took place under the auspices of foreign investors, we Norwegians having no choice but to stand by, open-mouthed, and watch it happen. The bulk of the capital came from abroad, the initiative came from abroad, the patents, apart from that for the Birkeland-Eyde method, came from abroad, and most of the expertise likewise came from abroad. In 1909, no less than 85 per cent of the shares in Norway's chemical industry were owned by foreigners, as were 80 per cent of shares in the mining industry, nearly 50 per cent of those in the hydroelectric industry and 45 per cent of those in the wood-processing industry; that year, in fact, 39 per cent of the nation's industrial shareholdings were in foreign hands. Norway's role was largely confined to the supply of labour for the enormous amount of construction work involved and to operate the completed plants.

It is understandable that most of the money should have come from foreign sources. Norwegian banks had been badly shaken by the Kristiania crash and were wary of taking risks; many had, in fact, vetoed foreign investments altogether, and some had even blacklisted shipping. What is more, at this time no Norwegian bank had the know-how or experience required to assess the quality of the complex and, to some degree, scientific computations that often formed the basis of new projects. Nor is it likely that private savings in Norway were large enough to enable banks to make investments of such magnitude. It was only to be expected that the initiatives, patents and expertise should likewise have come from abroad. Norway did not possess the level of technoscientific education required to enable it to compete with countries such as Germany, France and Great Britain. That was one of the reasons Sam Eyde had elected to study in Charlottenburg. Norway had no industrial traditions, either, and most certainly none relevant to the kind of industry here in question. However, the wood-processing industry was an entirely different matter. It had sprung from sawmilling, a sphere in which Norway boasted both long traditions and technical know-how second to none.

The new industries soon became a powerful growth factor in Norway's modest economy. In 1900 the GNP stood at NOK 1,115 million. As a direct consequence of the Kristiania crisis, it declined in the next few years, but from 1905 to 1913 the GNP increased from NOK 1,106 million to NOK 1,853 million, a rise of no less than 77 per cent. For what it is worth, in the same period Denmark's GNP increased by 47 per cent.

But not everyone was happy about this foreign influx. After dissolution of the union with Sweden nationalism was very much to the fore, and not a few politicians thought strict limits should be imposed on the right of foreigners to 'buy up Norway'. Whether they really meant that foreign investors should simply pick up the waterfalls and vanish, I cannot say, but there is little reason to doubt that it was Sam Eyde, by his somewhat swashbuckling approach, that had brought matters to a head. Some people were of the opinion that heavy industry would do irreparable harm to the Norwegian landscape, while others feared that it would precipitate the rise of a large and unruly proletariat that might prove disastrous for the country as a whole. But there were others who believed that Norway ought to roll out the red carpet for foreign investors and allow them more or less free access to its waterfalls and other natural resources. Another solution advanced was to permit Norwegian companies to operate without let or hindrance, but to make foreign investment subject to strict licensing. To a great extent the debate followed the same political divisions as the first debate on membership of the EEC almost seventy years later.

On 12 June 1906, shortly before a general election, the prime minister, Christian Michelsen, who was himself in doubt about the wisdom of allowing foreigners a free hand, settled the matter by introducing a provisional law under which all limited companies wishing to purchase forests, mines or waterfalls in Norway had to be licensed. No exemption was made for Norwegian companies: the law applied to all, regardless of nationality, composition of the board and distribution of capital. Time was needed for reflection. The law was immediately dubbed the Panic Act. In September that same year a committee was appointed to consider the matter, and in May 1907 it submitted its report.

Embodied in the resultant Bill was an interesting new proposal for a licensing scheme under which licences would be limited in time and rights would revert to their former owners after a specified number of years. Paradoxically, the idea of reversion originated with Sam Eyde, who had hastened home from Genoa in April 1906 when he learned that Michelsen's government was planning that A/S Tyssefallene, a company of which he was managing director, should be made subject to licensing. But Eyde had other reasons for returning, too: he needed money to expand his Rjukan plant, which in any case would not be affected by the new licensing law as the Act could not be made retroactive. Eyde thought up a creative combination, proposing that the state should advance him NOK 18 million to finance his Rjukan project against a guarantee that the falls, power plants, factories, railway and all appurtenant land should be returned to the state after eighty years at an 'agreeable' price. He also offered to prioritize Norwegian labour and suppliers.

Needless to say, the newspapers found out about the proposed deal; they were no better then than they are now. A critical article in the Oslo newspaper *Dagbladet* immediately dubbed Sam Eyde's offer the 'Falls Gift Package'. The article tore the proposition to shreds, its author putting the boot in by quoting Virgil's famous saying, *Timeo Danaos, et dona ferentes* (I fear the Greeks, even when they bear gifts). True to form, other papers took up the cry. The Storting responded by appointing a special committee which quickly entered into negotiations with Eyde. But after having been offered what he himself acknowledged were generous terms, albeit badly hacked about compared with his original proposal, Sam Eyde felt hard done by. Unaccustomed as he was to knuckling under, he broke off the discussions, went straight to the giant German chemical company BASF, obtained the funding he needed for Rjukan and informed Gunnar Knudsen that he was withdrawing his offer.

With hindsight it is, of course, easy to perceive that the Storting was foolish not to accept Eyde's proposal. On the other hand it is quite understandable that a committee drawn from lay members of the Storting would find it difficult to determine what the power plants, factories and railway would be worth in eighty years' time.

The licensing controversy, which split the Venstre (Liberal) Party, resulted in even more stringent regulations. The dispute was to continue for many years. For one thing, it was claimed that the law fell little short of compulsory purchase and was thus at variance with the Constitution. In 1918 it ultimately received the assent of the Supreme Court.

Development of the country's waterpower resources proceeded at a fairly moderate pace all through the interwar years.

Only in the years immediately following the Second World War did exploitation of Norway's power potential really gain impetus, with the result that the Labour Party's economic policy came to be known as 'power Socialism'.

### Suddenly peace broke out

'I wish things were the way they were before,' was the plaintive cry when, in the 1920s, the country suffered one shock after another. By 'before' was meant before the First World War, the halcyon years leading up to 1914. They may have been hard, but the fact remains that those years were better and more predictable than the ones that followed. Most people were optimistic and the political tumult surrounding dissolution of the union with Sweden was soon forgotten. There was an aura of progress and optimism about the Norway of these years.

The slump that followed the Kristiania crash was succeeded by a long, stable period of growth. New industries brought with them new jobs and new industrial centres, places many people had never previously heard of. But times were good for the 'old' industries too, for the textile, timber, foodstuffs and engineering industries. Shipowners forsook sail for steam, and although the number of vessels in service declined, ships increased in size, with a consequent sharp rise in the cargo-carrying capacity of the country's merchant fleet. Overall, by the outbreak of war Norwegian owners disposed of marginally more than two million gross registered tons of shipping. In these years fishermen switched to motor-powered boats and in rural areas scythe and sickle gave way to reapers and threshing machines. By now machines were a must, as labour had become expensive and the cotters of old were moving to the towns or, failing that, to America. The biggest problem was a rash of labour disputes. Things were not the way they had been for employers: workers had begun to make demands, unequivocal, no-nonsense claims that boded ill for the future.

Norway emerged from the First World war without officially having violated its status as a neutral. But it was a close-run thing, as both the Germans and the British were eager to acquire as much as possible of what Norway had to offer. This meant primarily the merchant fleet, but metals, timber and fish were also strategically important at a time when the great powers were doing their utmost to starve to death all whom they were unable to slay with shot and shell. As a result of strong pressure from Germany on the one side and Great Britain and the USA on the other, for all practical purposes Norway ended up on the side of the Allies. The war cost Norway half its merchant fleet and two thousand seamen lost their lives, largely from sinkings by German U-boats.

The interwar years opened with a boom which, in the late autumn of 1920, gave way to an equally strong depression. Europe was exhausted, both in human terms and economically, and international trade came close to a standstill, with a resultant decline in prices and demand. It didn't help matters that Norges Bank, the central bank, had just appointed a new governor, Nicolai Rygg, the man behind the parity policy. The reasons for introducing this policy were partly economic, partly moral. Rygg, a Liberal, felt that it was highly immoral for people who had scrimped and saved all their lives to see their meagre savings consumed by inflation. He undeniably had a good case and found plenty of support in other parties, though much of it melted away when the effects of the parity policy began to make themselves felt. From today's perspective the monetary policy of the 1920s looks rather foolhardy. It cannot have been much better for people who were heavily in debt to have to abandon home, farm or fishing boat because they were unable to pay the interest and instalments on their mortgages. Industry and the merchant fleet were very badly affected. Factories closed down and ships were forced into lay-up.

Hardest hit of all, however, were the banks. Many were put under public administration, but as a rule such supportive measures came too late or were insufficient. When the time eventually came to take stock, it was found that no fewer than 106 banks had gone under after having had to write off losses totalling NOK 2 billion, almost half of the average GNP in the 1920s. It is hard now to imagine what this really meant, but if a loss equivalent to half the GNP were to be incurred today, it would be the tidy sum of NOK 800 billion, which is considerably more than the national budget. The losses sustained by Norwegian banks in the crisis of the 1990s, which were estimated at NOK 60 to 80 billion, are trifling in comparison.

When, in 1924, the worst was over, inflation set in and industrial production began to pick up. In the blackest periods some 30 per cent of trade-union members had been out of work; unemployment among union members now fell to 10 per cent, though this did not mean that rural debts were a thing of the past. Moreover, there was a new problem. The United States had imposed tight restrictions on immigration, so that the time-honoured Atlantic escape route for the needy and jobless was no longer much of an option.

Additionally, this new period of prosperity was short-lived, as in 1926 Nicolai Rygg reintroduced his policy of parity, with the result that unemployment figures again rose. However, this time he achieved his aim: in the course of two years the Norwegian krone attained full parity with gold. This gave the nation a breathing space of several years, resulting in strong growth in production and, for most people, rapidly increasing earnings. In 1930 production was therefore well above what it had been when the rot set in in 1920.

The respite lasted until 1931, which was when the effects of the Wall Street crash of October 1929 and the concomitant worldwide depression finally reached Norway. This resulted in another economic downturn, and unemployment among trade-union members soared to 35 per cent, though admittedly this was partly owing to a succession of bitter labour disputes and a large-scale lockout.

On this occasion the tide turned early, in 1932. Following conclusion in 1935 of the Basic Agreement (*Hovedavtalen*) between employees and labour, until war came to Norway in April 1940 activity in trade and industry steadily increased.

Throughout the whole of the interwar period the political situation remained unsettled, governments coming and going in rapid succession. But in 1935 Labour formed a government under Johan Nygaardsvold that was to remain in office right through to the end of the war in 1945 (including five years spent in exile in London).

The interwar years are viewed by most people as a time of hardship and strife marked by one economic crisis after another. And so they were for many people, but they were by no means as bad as they are reputed to have been. In particular *de harde tredveåra*, the lean years of the thirties, as they are known, have been unjustly stigmatized as a bad time for Norway. In reality it was the 1920s that were so disastrous; the 1930s, 1931 and 1932 apart, were characterized by uninterrupted growth. Viewed as a whole, the years from 1920 to 1940 were by no means as bad as they are often painted: the fact is that in the course of these two decades Norway's GNP actually doubled.

But for the unemployed these twenty years were bad enough, and social benefits were modest in the extreme. It is difficult to determine how many people actually were unemployed: the figures generally adduced apply largely only to members of trade unions that kept statistics, and by no means all unions did so. Furthermore, union members were mainly employed in industry and in building and construction work, the bulk of the population still being engaged in the primary industries or working as craftsmen, occupations in which unemployment is thought to have been much lower. The 1930 census, which recorded 110,000 unemployed, probably affords the truest picture, though the figure is likely to have been higher in 1933, the worst of the interwar unemployment years. Unemployment between the wars was, in other words, on a par with what it is now, early in the twenty-first century. Even if we allow for the fact that the population round about 1930 was two million less than it is today, the fact remains that most Norwegians had a regular job. This tends to be forgotten in the welter of words surrounding conditions in these turbulent years.

There is a lighter side, too, to the interwar years than unemployment. Admittedly, many companies did fail, but on the other hand thousands of small craft and industrial enterprises were established, some of them in entirely new fields, and never has so much new ground been broken and new farms established as in this period. It was also in these years that Norwegian households came to enjoy the benefits of mains electricity and that rapidly rising car ownership resulted in extensive roadbuilding and a veritable rash of petrol stations and repair shops. The telephone also became an integral part of daily life in these years – at least in homes that boasted a piano.

In the postwar years, when unemployment was virtually non-existent, a refractory myth to the effect that it was Johan Nygaardsvold and the Labour Party that, almost singlehandedly, had brought Norway safely through the critical interwar years, took root. But the reality of the matter was different: the upswing that succeeded the worldwide depression came already at the end of 1932, and once it came, it continued without interruption, bringing in its train regular and healthy growth every year until Norway was occupied in 1940. The Labour Party's economic policy differed little from that pursued by the Venstre (Liberal) government in the preceding two years, and most of the requisite measures were already in place when Nygaardsvold assumed office. If there is any point in discussing this sensitive subject eighty years later, the conclusion must instead be that Norway's economy was more strongly influenced by what happened abroad than by the economic policy pursued at home. What occurred in Norway in 1932 occurred in other western countries also: then, as now, a peculiarly Norwegian economic upswing was very much of a rarity.

## Saved by the Marshall Plan

There are occasions when I find myself rubbing shoulders with people a good deal older than myself. Not infrequently this can be something of a trial, though not because of their greater age. Far from it – I get on admirably with people who don't sport rings in their ears. The trouble is that whenever the conversation turns to politics, senior citizens invariably trot out Einar Gerhardsen. Gerhardsen and the Golden Age, the two decades spanning the end of the Second World War and the time in 1965 when the Labour Party lost government office. The party lost its majority in the Storting as early as 1961.

In a way, I can understand the nostalgia. Those twenty years were indubitably good ones for Norway. Prosperity steadily increased, social security was greatly improved, and unemployment – of which many people had such bitter memories from the 1930s – was non-existent. On the contrary, labour was in short supply. It is true that most commodities were strictly rationed in the first few postwar years, but rationing was gradually phased out, and when, in 1960, even cars again became freely available, the Norwegian people looked to a future bathed in sunshine. Needless to say, all these blessings were credited to Einar Gerhardsen, the rock-steady, anorak-wearing 'father of the nation', the man who could always be relied upon to resolve the country's problems in the best interests of all.

Despite this, it must be observed that the turn taken by Norway's economic policy in the postwar years ran counter to the Labour Party's original intentions and wishes. The country prospered not because Gerhardsen and the Labour Party were able to implement their political ideas but rather for the opposite reason. It prospered because Gerhardsen and the Labour Party were *not* able to implement their political ideas. This can, of course, be expressed more circumspectly by saying that prosperity came because Gerhardsen and those surrounding him were realistic enough to realize that they were heading for disaster, and in consequence elected to change course before it was too late. I leave it to my readers to decide how to phrase it. Moreover, there were moderates in the Labour Party too, men and women who, in the immediate postwar years, advocated a less radical economic policy.

Norway emerged from the ravages of the Second World War in a better state, also in economic terms, than most other European countries. This notwithstanding, a study undertaken after the war revealed that the nation's wealth had been depleted by 18.5 per cent in the course of the five years that Norway was a belligerent. Production facilities were badly run down, the merchant fleet had been almost halved, tonnage falling from 4.5 million to 2.5 million dwt, and Finnmark, the northernmost county, lay devastated, a victim of Hitler's last-ditch scorched-earth policy. Nor did it help that the Germans had succeeded in relieving the central bank of NOK 12 billion in order to sustain their occupation forces, which, by war's end, totalled no fewer than 351,000 men. Despite this, Norway came out of the nightmare that was the Second World War as very much a healthy

**Norway in 1945**: An election poster produced by the Labour Party for the national election held in the autumn of 1945.

**The new Norway**: Årdal Verk, where aluminium poured from 172 melting furnaces, viewed from a surrounding mountainside in 1948. The plant was built by the occupying Germans during the war, but was seized by the state when peace returned.

and united nation, one well prepared for a new working day.

Throughout the whole of its five-year term of office in the interwar years (1935-40), the Labour Party had pursued a policy which was more marked by a willingness to collaborate than by Socialism. The welfare measures inaugurated by the Party were agreeable to the non-Socialist parties and might even (perhaps probably would) have been introduced by them had they been in power.

After five years of war, which the King and government, along with the merchant fleet, had spent in Britain, things were bound to be different. I cannot discount the fact that the Labour Party's primary aim was to avoid the unemployment that had followed in the wake of the First World War, but the measures the party wished to adopt were no less dramatic for that.

Political Norway was united in agreeing that the government needed extensive powers in the extraordinary situation in which the country found itself when the war ended. This view permeated the coalition government in the months preceding Labour's victory in the general election of October 1945, which enabled it to form a government alone in November. But the party wanted to do more than simply form a government: the Norwegian people had taken a step to the left during the war and the more sinister aspects of the Communist regime in the Soviet Union had been somewhat mitigated by the Allied victory. Russia's peaceful withdrawal from Finnmark undoubtedly also contributed towards the positive image many people, not least members of the Labour Party, nurtured of the Soviet Union in the immediate postwar years. That same autumn it was declared at the party conference that the aim was to transform Norway into a Socialist country dedicated to strict centralization and state control of means of production. Backed as it was by a majority of the electorate, the party was now in a position to implement this policy. It even had the legal authority to do so in the shape of what was known as the *Lex Thagaard*, an Act, named after the man whose brainchild it was, passed on 8 May 1945. This Act endowed the Directorate of Prices with extensive power to control prices and economic life in general. The Act, which in 1947 was replaced by an interim Act called *Lex Brofoss*, again after its progenitor, also empowered the government to prohibit the establishment of new activities and enlargement of existing ones, and to order the expansion or closure of business enterprises. Even now I find it hard to understand how the Storting could have sanctioned such measures in a country which, only two years earlier, had still been under German domination. Be that as it may, the fact remains that the law was passed, and that with phraseology and regulations that bore an ominous similarity to those Norway had fought for five long years to wrest herself free of.

Developments in the early postwar years were alarming. The state took over all companies and shares that had been in the hands of the Germans, among them shares in the aluminium plants at Orkdal, Glomfjord and Tyssedal, 47 per cent of Norsk Hydro and German holdings in A/S Sydvaranger. As if this were not enough, it also took over all German shareholdings in a number of small companies; all private telephone companies were bought up and state monopolies were established – for medicaments, grain and fishing gear. At the same time plans were set on foot to build an ironworks, Norsk Jernverk A/S (sanctioned by the Storting in 1946), the first large-scale, state incursion into industry after the war. Calculations show that prewar the state owned 0.4 per cent of the total share capital in Norway; by 1960, after fifteen years of Labour rule, this share had risen to 16 per cent.

I do not wish to paint the Labour Party's intentions in the immediate postwar years as worse than they were. It is quite possible that the party's primary aim was to prevent the Communists gaining a stronger foothold than they already had, and that to that end they wished to appear more radical than they really were. But also in its actions it is difficult to attribute other intentions to the party than a desire to build a society quite different from the one that eventually materialized.

What was it, then, one may ask, that brought about the change? Various reasons have been suggested, but there is no denying that the principal factor was the Marshall Aid, the great American aid programme launched by Secretary of State George Marshall in June 1947 and put into effect the following year. The Americans had clearly learned from their mistake after the First World War, when the Allies deprived the Germans of all means of recovery, thus driving them into the arms of Adolf Hitler. Regardless of what other intentions the Americans may have had with their aid programme, they were determined to help Europe recover before a new generation of revanchists could establish itself.

In Norway, after Marshall had submitted his proposal, things were, to put it mildly, difficult. The vast foreign currency reserves accruing from settlement of the account resulting from the Norwegian merchant marine's contribution to the war effort had been exhausted, and in 1947 the Norwegian krone was written down by 37 per cent against the dollar. The need for imports, not least of new machinery and equipment for run-down industries, and for further development of the hydroelectric network, was acute. The government introduced various measures, among them revocation of all previously granted import licences and strict control of new licences.

One such measure created quite a stir and remains a controversial issue to this day. This was the decision to halt the contracting of new ships. All contracts to build ships abroad were banned for a period of two years unless 100 per cent of the funding came from outside Norway. In all probability this measure severely retarded Norway's shipping industry. Half the fleet had been lost during the war and to recover, replacements were badly needed. In the immediate postwar years new ships were still to be had cheaply, but by the time owners were again free to order newbuildings, prices had risen steeply, not least as a direct consequence of the Korean war. It seems strange that the government should have elected to shackle the very industry that, more than any other, could have directly helped to earn foreign currency.

It was in this precarious situation that the Marshall Aid came to the help of Norway. The government initially estimated that it would need $100 million, but by the time the programme ended, it transpired that Norway had received $400 million, most of it as an outright gift. But for the government – if it really was a shining new Socialist Norway it was aiming at – the Marshall Aid carried with it an unpalatable and effective barb. To qualify for aid, Norway had been compelled to join the OEEC, an organization that presupposed acceptance of market-liberalizing guidelines that ran contrary to the government's controlling intentions and which effectively put paid to all plans for bilateral trade agreements and Norwegian protectionism designed to combat the evil capitalist world beyond her frontiers. For all practical purposes Marshall Aid 'forced' Norway and the Gerhardsen government to make drastic changes in the economic policy the Labour Party seemed set on pursuing.

Following bitter confrontations with the Opposition in 1947, the government appointed a committee to study the possibility of introducing a permanent Price Control Act to replace the provisional Act then in force. When the committee submitted its report in 1952, it was seen to have followed, by and large, the principles enshrined in *Lex Thagaard* and *Lex Brofoss*. But when the Bill was finally tabled, it transpired that the government had quite simply disregarded the most radical proposals, and a majority voted in favour of a relatively moderate Act, one that also the Opposition felt able to accept. The government had retreated.

Today, more than fifty years after Norway benefited from Marshall Aid, it still rankles with some people that the government should have bowed to what they label 'American self-interest'. I personally see no cause for complaint. On the contrary, there can be little doubt that it was Marshall Aid and the conditions attaching thereto that prompted the Labour Party to bite the bullet and curb their ambitions to make Norway a Socialist society.

The idea that the country's economy could be controlled and planned several years ahead with the aid of ecometric models was not new. As early as 1933 Ole Colbjørnsen, an engineer, and Axel Sømme, a geographer, had tried to convert the theories of J.M. Keynes and Professor Ragnar Frisch into practical politics by issuing a treatise they entitled *En treårsplan for Norge* (A Three-Year Plan for Norway). Their ideas were cautiously tried out by the government in the years immediately preceding the outbreak of war, and after the war a large contingent of Frisch's students was ready and eager to build Einar Gerhardsen's New Norway. Or, in the words of the leader of the Conservative Party, C.J. Hambro: 'A whole band of highly intelligent economics graduates stood poised to go to work on a defenceless society.' It was this youthful 'band' that, in the early postwar years, made the national budget into an instrument of central control.

### The industrial boom

On 24 May 1981, a Monday, a bus pulled out from A/S Sydvaranger's brand-new steelworks, Norddeutsche Ferrowerk, in Emden, Germany. In it, longfaced and dejected to a man, sat the Storting's Industrial Committe. On a windswept plain the Conservative's Odd Vattekar summed things up: 'After what we have seen today, there is no reason to stay sober.' I was on that bus as a reporter for my paper, *Verdens Gang*. Vattekar was quite right – there was no reason to stay sober.

The Emden works had been built to process ore from Sydvaranger with the aid of Norwegian gas from the offshore Frigg field. But the ore proved unsuited to the purpose, and a fall in the market for steel coincided with a steep rise in gas prices. Technically, the Emden steelworks was a model of its kind, but it was operative for only a few weeks and went bankrupt in 1982, the year after its completion. When the estate was settled, it was found that NOK 3 billion had gone down the drain.

I mention the case of the Sydvaranger/Emden steelworks because – regrettably – it is rather typical of much that occurred when the Labour Party set out to build and bolster Norway's state-controlled industry. Project after project failed, with the result that in time the appellation 'state enterprise' fell into disrepute. There were many reasons for this, the most important probably being that most such projects were initiated to satisfy Norwegian requirements, not infrequently simply the need to create new jobs in the regions, to utilize Norwegian raw materials or to earn foreign currency. Rarely were such projects embarked upon to satisfy the demands of the market. When the point of departure is a politically agreed desideratum, it becomes all the easier to adduce economic arguments in favour of carrying through a project.

The ironworks at Mo i Rana was a case in point. Norway's last ironworks had closed down in 1906 and it was claimed that a large, modern plant would be of considerable strategic value, both industrially and from a security point of view. At the time, the world was gearing itself for the Cold War.

The new ironworks came on stream in 1955, whereas the aluminium works at Årdal, which was almost ready for production when the Germans were expelled from Norway, did so already in 1946. In 1951 it was resolved to build a new, state-controlled aluminium works at Sunndal. The next big project, in 1961, was a coking plant, Norsk Koksverk, a plant built partly to exploit the coal deposits of the Svalbard archipelago. Again it was to satisfy a purely Norwegian need rather than to meet a market demand. It was Svalbard coal that, following a tragic accident in the King's Bay mine some years later, was to cost the Labour Party its position in power. The state subsequently went on to build large freezing and fish-processing plants in northern Norway, as well as a textile factory, Mosjøen Veveri A/S.

This substantial state involvement in northern Norway was ascribable not least to the government's desire to provide jobs for the many people there who, in the 1950s and '60s, had begun to forsake fishing and farming. In itself this policy may fairly be said to have been successful, at least for a time. In 1945 Mo i Rana had a population of about 2,000; by 1970 this had risen to 21,000. But the ironworks was never to become a profitable concern, and it was closed down in the 1980s, together

**The morning after**: Kåre Willoch, leader of the Høyre (Conservative) Party, is congratulated on his victory in the national election held in the autumn of 1981.

with a number of other state-sponsored projects, among them Kongsberg Våpenindustri, an arms manufacturer. Årdal & Sunndal Verk was ultimately absorbed by Norsk Hydro, Tofte Industrier became a part of the timber company Norske Skog, Sydvaranger was shut down altogether and the Findus fish-processing plant in Hammerfest was sold to Swiss Nestlé . . .

By and large, the winding up and disposal of these state-controlled industrial companies proceeded smoothly: the political sting had already been drawn and the climate had changed. If there was an exception, it was Kongsberg Våpenindustri. Contrary to the assumption of its creditors, most notably foreign investors, when the company was forced into bankruptcy the state refused to assume financial responsibility. The matter attracted much undesirable attention in international financial circles, and it is no exaggeration to say that it did much to diminish confidence in Norway and tarnish the country's reputation. Some years later, however, the strong technical milieu at Kongsberg was to come into its own as supplier to the newly established Norwegian offshore oil industry.

No political party in the last few years has felt inclined to re-establish state-owned industrial enterprises. This change of heart is undoubtedly attributable to the abject failure of such activities in the past, but also to the wave of liberalization that swept across the country in the early 1980s, and which was greatly accelerated and amplified by Kåre Willoch's non-Socialist governments between 1981 and 1986. When the Labour Party under Gro Harlem Brundtland came to power in 1986, it continued to pursue the liberal economic course already staked out by the Willoch governments.

Looking back on the large-scale process of industrialization that was a prominent feature of the first twenty-five postwar years, it is remarkable to what extent the Labour Party – and, in varying degrees, also the other political parties – had lost its former fear of influence from abroad. There was no longer talk of foreigners having robbed us of our right to preside over the fortunes of our own country. Now, foreign capital was welcomed with open arms. In 1959 the Gerhardsen government even went so far as to employ Trygve Lie, a former foreign minister and secretary-general of the United Nations, to front a campaign to present Norway as an attractive source of investment. The bait consisted largely in the well-tried and time-honoured benefits accruing from cheap electric power, an ice-free coast and first-class port facilities. When, seven years later, Lie set out to consider what had been achieved, he could boast of having secured for the country two oil refineries and three large aluminium plants, two of which had been built in collaboration with foreign interests acting together with Elkem and Norsk Hydro. Not a few other valuable links were also forged with Trygve Lie's support. It says something of the extent of foreign participation in the country's industrialization that foreign ownership in Norwegian industry and mining companies increased from NOK 223 million in 1952 to NOK 732 million in 1968, that is, from 15 to 22 per cent.

The foregoing notwithstanding, my emphasis on the role played by the state in the nation's postwar industrialization should not lead the reader to believe that the state was responsible for the industrial growth that occurred from 1945 to the mid-seventies, when the industrial recession really began to bite. The private sector of industry grew rapidly throughout the whole of this period, growth in the mechanical engineering industry, which in 1970 accounted for no less than 20 per cent of industrial exports, being especially impressive. Prior to the shipping crisis of the mid-1970s, which choked the fjords with laid-up ships, there were shipbuilding yards in most large ports, some of them building supertankers of up to 300,000 dwt. Most of these yards are now a thing of the past: only a handful of highly specialized shipbuilding companies are still operative, along with a substantial and healthy substratum of companies manufacturing sophisticated equipment for ships and, not least, the offshore oil industry. The enormous programme of hydroelectric development that distinguished the whole of the postwar period was also in large measure carried through with the aid of Norwegian industry. Some domestic trades and industries have likewise come through with flying colours, among them the graphic and furniture industries. The same cannot be said of the canning, clothing and footwear industries or of that section of the electrotechnical industry engaged in the manufacture of finished products. In the age of branded goods and mass production it is by no means easy to survive in a country whose home market is as small as Norway's. Even after 150 years as an industrialized nation, Norway has not succeeded in producing a single internationally known brand – with the possible exceptions of Mustad fish-hooks, Krag-Jørgensen rifles, Jordan toothbrushes, Møller's cod-liver oil and King Oscar sardines. The Danes, Finns and Swedes, on the other hand, whose domestic markets are little larger than Norway's, have succeeded. However, some specialist products, most notably equipment for the shipping industry, are well known in their own specialized fields.

In retrospect, the 1950s and, more especially, the 1960s have come down to us as the heyday of Norwegian industry. In those days industry was enthusiastically embraced by the whole nation, and some otherwise clear-thinking people still claim in all sincerity that a krone earned in industry is worth more than one earned in some other activity. Norway's political life has similarly long suffered under this bizarre belief in the blessings of industry. It is remarkable that Norwegian politicians seem not to raise an eyebrow when a firm of consultants employing, say, 150 people is forced to close its doors, whereas when a similar closure occurs in industry, those selfsame politicians promise to do all in their power to save the company concerned from going under. Fortunately there is not very much they can do when the market and bottom line dictate otherwise and state aid to crisis-stricken companies is a measure that has long had its day.

In a way one can understand this soft spot for industry. It was, after all, largely industry that staunched the strong flow of emigrants early in the twentieth century, and it was industry again that, after the Second World War, brought about a rapid improvement in living standards, along with shorter working hours, longer holidays, a state pension for all, better education and a Volkswagen, Ford Anglia or Volvo parked outside the door.

Despite my earlier remarks, Norway's Labour Party deserves its fair share of credit for the economic growth the country experienced between 1945 and 1970. But it is worth noting that although the GNP consistently increased at a rate of

**The new world**: The Norwegian oil bonanza began when Phillips Petroleum discovered the enormous Ekofisk field at Christmas 1969. Norwegian-built concrete platforms played a key role in development of the offshore oil industry. Seen here is the Troll platform, one of the biggest and most complex structures ever constructed, being towed out from the Ryfylke yard where it was built to the Troll field in the North Sea.

four to five per cent annually in this period, growth was equally strong in a number of other countries too, and in some cases even stronger. It is also worth noting that growth was largely generated by demand from abroad and probably had nothing to do with political decisions taken at home. It is therefore by no means certain that the result would have been perceptibly different if other political parties had been in office in these decisive years.

The stagnation of industrial development and the downturn that occurred midway through the 1970s were not unexpected. On the contrary, the recession had long been foreshadowed by the unbroken and steep rise of wages and prices. Nevertheless, it still took people a long time to realize that the slump was unlikely to be of brief duration, but that it was, on the contrary, part of a long-term trend.

At this time I was working in Mjøndalen, a small community west of Drammen. Between Drammen and Mjøndalen, like peas in a pod lay a succession of wood-processing plants – seven or eight of them over a stretch of no more than ten to fifteen kilometres. When I moved there, smoke was still belching from their chimney stacks; when I left a few years later, all but one had closed down and the premises they had vacated had been taken over by local service activities. But the closures were effected with a remarkable lack of drama, those who lost their jobs being either pensioned off or absorbed by the public sector or service industries. Today there are as many supermarkets between Drammen and Mjøndalen as there once were wood-processing plants.

More or less the same thing took place all over the country. The changeover proceeded gradually, and the few protests that were heard were in most cases muted. People seemed to accept that that was the way things were and that nothing could be done about it. The process continued too, only at a still faster pace, as pressure on costs increased. Whereas shortly after the war industry surpassed agriculture in terms of numbers employed, in the course of only a few years industry was itself outdistanced by both the service industries and the public sector. The local government sector, in particular, snowballed. It is easy to see the course of events from official statistics: in the decade from 1978 to 1988 the number employed in industry fell from 400,000 to 333,000, while the number employed in the local government sector rose from 286,000 to 402,000. There was a concomitant drain in the farming sector, in which the number employed steadily declined, as it had for the last one hundred and fifty years or so. In the oil industry, on the other hand, the number employed rose from 4,000 in 1978 to 14,400 ten years later, by which time, in monetary terms, the industry was already Norway's most important.

In economic theory there is often talk of the transfer of labour to the most productive sector. This is all very well in theory, but in practice some of those involved must inevitably suffer great hardship.

We have now reached a watershed in this long account: the 1970s marked the transition to a post-industrial Norway, though 'post-industrial' is not wholly apposite. Norway was never an industrial country in the European sense, and when we were poised to become one, oil was found in the North Sea and totally changed the course of our economic development.

### From out the sea an oil rig rose

On 25 February 1958 Svend Foyn, head of *Norges geologiske undersøkelse* (Geological Survey of Norway), wrote a letter to the Ministry of Foreign Affairs that will long be remembered in the Norwegian oil industry. The letter concluded with the following words:

*It may be assumed that the continental shelf off the Norwegian coast is composed of the same rock formations as those in the corresponding area ashore. The possible existence of deposits of coal, oil or sulphur on the continental shelf along the Norwegian coast may be ruled out.*

This letter was prompted by a geological conference in Mexico City two years earlier at which it was suggested that oil might be found in the seabed off the Norwegian coast. Now the Ministry wished to know whether there was any truth in this belief.

Foyn's conclusion will long be remembered as the poorest in Norway's economic history, putting it on a par, to say the least, with the conclusion reached by certain Norwegian car importers when, shortly after the war, Volkswagenwerke sought to persuade them to import its cars. The consensus was that 'such a car would never sell'.

It is only fair to point out that in his letter Svend Foyn referred solely to possible oil deposits 'along the coast', and in that he was correct. What was to be found beneath the open sea, more than one hundred kilometres from land and beyond the deep Norwegian Trench, he had no means of knowing.

At the time no one did expect oil to be found in the sea off the Norwegian coast. However, the discovery in 1959 of enormous quantities of natural gas on what came to be known as the Groningen field in the Netherlands was an eye-opener for the international oilmen. Until then Europe's energy requirements had been met from the continent's own coal deposits and from imported oil. But now new prospects had opened up and a suspicion aroused that was destined to bear rich fruit. If there were hydrocarbons in the North Sea off the Netherlands, it was reasoned, surely it was conceivable that there might be hydrocarbons further north as well. Still, nothing much was done to pursue the matter until the autumn of 1962.

In October that year Trygve Lie was visited by two representatives of Phillips Petroleum, a little-known American oil company based in Bartlesville, Oklahoma. Their mission was to obtain permission to search for oil on Norway's continental shelf. A concrete proposal followed a few days later in which Phillips expressed their wish to secure exploration rights for the whole of Norway's part of the North Sea that lay outside territorial waters, an area in respect of which Norwegian jurisdiction had yet to be clarified. Lie forwarded the proposal to the Ministry of Industry.

It is unclear whether it was the letter from Phillips that prompted the government to act as quickly as it did, but whatever the reason, already in May 1963 the government declared its dominion over the Norwegian part of the continental shelf in the form of an order-in-council. In this order the area concerned was defined as 'as far as the depth of the sea permits exploitation of natural deposits, regardless of other such marine limits as may apply, though not beyond the median line with other states'. June saw the introduction of a law providing for exploitation of natural underwater deposits, and shortly afterwards agreement was reached with Great Britain and Denmark to the effect that the median-line principle should apply. For all practical purposes this meant that the 'Norwegian area' had been enlarged by 1.2 million square kilometres.

I think Norway should be pleased that agreement on the median-line principle was reached before any of the finds in the North Sea were made. Had it not been, it is by no means certain that the result would have been as favourable for Norway as it so demonstratively was. For example, the Ekofisk oilfield was dangerously close to the Danish sector and the Frigg gasfield is almost on the dividing line between the Norwegian and British sectors of the North Sea. The Danish press, in particular, were very disgruntled when the Norwegian finds became known. Like us, the Danes had found it hard to believe that oil would be discovered in the North Sea, and in 1962 they 'gave away' sole right to all future finds to the Danish shipowner A.P. Møller. The agreement was later renegotiated, but even then it remained very much in Møller's favour.

It is not up to me to apportion credit for the good start afforded the Norwegian oil industry. It would be very remiss of me, though, were I not to mention Deputy Under-Secretary of State Jens Evensen of the Ministry of Foreign Affairs. It was he who led the way in ensuring Norwegian sovereignty over these enormous expanses of ocean, and it was he too who was largely responsible for formulating the principle that the shelf should be divided among several companies and not be awarded to one alone.

In May 1965 278 blocks were put on offer, all south of lat. 62 degrees N – the enormous areas north of this were not opened up until 1980. Seventy-eight blocks were allocated and exploration commenced. First off the mark was the drilling rig *Ocean Traveler*, which drilled a well for Esso; the other companies quickly followed suit.

By 1969 thirty wells had been drilled without result and despondency spread. Shell had already thrown in its hand and shut down its exploration unit at Tananger, and the press were continually saying how unlikely it was that oil would be found in the Norwegian sector. One commentator in an Oslo newspaper even went so far as to declare in an editorial that the oil companies might as well start looking for oil in the Jotunheimen mountains. But the pessimists were mistaken and the oil companies' persistence eventually paid off. At Christmas 1969 Phillips Petroleum found the first big field, which was subsequently named Ekofisk. Norway had become an oil-producing nation.

With hindsight it is easy to see that the Norwegian authorities kept a firm grip on developments in the initial phase of the oil era. Things were very different from when Sam Eyde began buying up the country's waterfalls early in the century and the Norwegian authorities failed to realize what was happening until half Rjukan had been developed by foreigners. This time jurisdiction, regulations and control functions were all in place before the first oil reached the mainland. What at the time no one had envisioned was that the state would play such an active role in exploitation of the riches beneath the sea through the medium of its own operative and integrated oil company. It would have been far too risky a proposition to spend the taxpayers' money on such

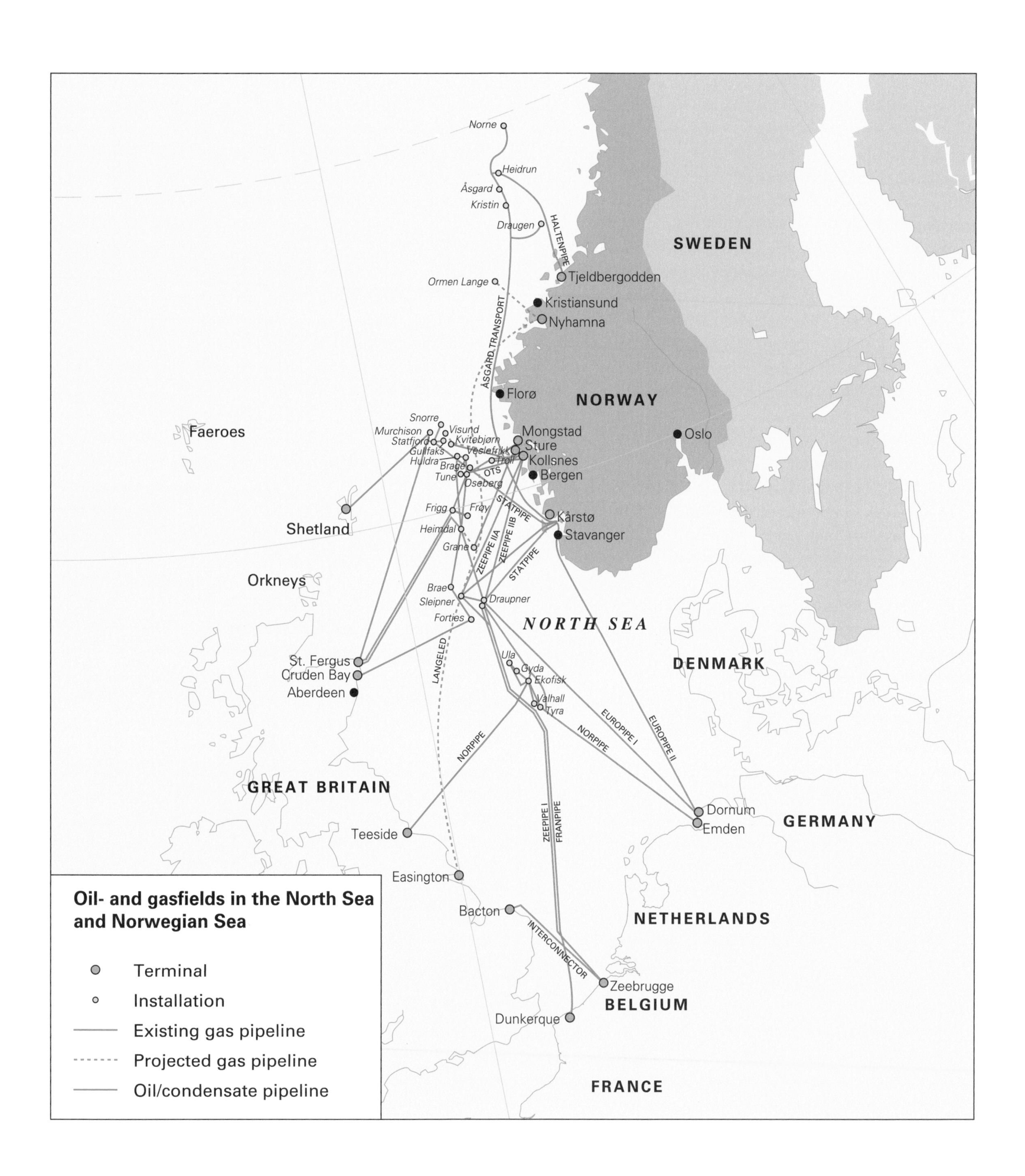
Oil- and gasfields in the North Sea and Norwegian Sea
Terminal
Installation
Existing gas pipeline
Projected gas pipeline
Oil/condensate pipeline
SWEDEN
NORWAY
DENMARK
GERMANY
NETHERLANDS
BELGIUM
FRANCE
GREAT BRITAIN
NORTH SEA
Faeroes
Shetland
Orkneys
Norne
Heidrun
Åsgard
Kristin
Draugen
HALTENPIPE
Tjeldbergodden
Ormen Lange
Kristiansund
Nyhamna
ÅSGARD TRANSPORT
Florø
Oslo
Snorre
Visund
Murchison
Statfjord
Kvitebjørn
Gullfaks
Veslefrikk
Huldra
Troll
Brage
Tune
Oseberg
OTS
Mongstad
Sture
Kollsnes
Bergen
Frigg
Frøy
Heimdal
Grane
STATPIPE
ZEEPIPE IIA
ZEEPIPE IIB
Kårstø
Stavanger
Brae
Sleipner
Draupner
Forties
St. Fergus
Cruden Bay
Aberdeen
LANGELED
Ula
Gyda
Ekofisk
Valhall
Tyra
NORPIPE
EUROPIPE I
EUROPIPE II
Dornum
Emden
Teeside
ZEEPIPE I
FRANPIPE
Easington
Bacton
INTERCONNECTOR
Zeebrugge
Dunkerque

a speculative investment. Nor did Norway possess the expertise required to develop and operate such a company. But once oil had been found, everything changed.

Development proceeded cautiously, one step at a time. When the state's role on the continental shelf first came up for discussion in the Storting, both the conservative Høyre Party and Labour advocated establishment by the state of a holding company which, through affiliated companies, could participate operatively in collaboration or part-ownership with other companies. But then Per Borten's non-Socialist government resigned and the Labour Party's Trygve Bratteli took over. Under Bratteli's brief premiership – he relinquished office after the pro faction lost the vote on Norwegian membership of the EC in 1972 – there was a change of mood in the Labour Party, which now wanted the state to form a fully operative company to take part in every aspect of activity on the shelf. This was what eventually happened. After a long and thorny debate the Storting unanimously resolved to form such a company; named Statoil, it was established on 1 January 1973 with Arve Johnsen as its first CEO.

It is conceivable that the outcome would have been different had the Borten government remained in office. On behalf of the state, Per Borten and the Minister of Industry, Sverre W. Rostoft, had surreptitiously purchased a 51 per cent holding in Norsk Hydro, and Norsk Hydro, large international industrial company that it was, had at least as good a base from which to develop as an operative oil company as the as-yet-unborn company of Statoil.

But if agreement to form Statoil was unanimous, not many years were to elapse before discussion arose as to how the company was to be controlled and how rapidly it was to be allowed to expand. Many on the non-Socialist side feared that Statoil, with options on 50 per cent of all finds, would be a cuckoo in the Norwegian nest. One major source of dissension was whether Statoil should also assume responsibility for management of the state's holdings in blocks on the shelf. The expression 'clipping its wings' was frequently heard – for the first time in the 1980s. Kåre Willoch, who in 1981 became prime minister of a government drawn solely from Høyre, preferred a more urbane expression. He had no desire to clip Statoil's wings, he said, 'only to trim them'.

Looking back, it is hard to believe how quickly and forcefully oil made its impact felt on the Norwegian economy, though this was, of course, linked to the economy's modest size; not much is needed to cause a ripple. But only six or seven years after a massive concrete tank had been towed out and anchored on the Ekofisk field, oil and gas were accounting for nearly 20 per cent of Norway's GNP and their contribution was practically on a par with that of traditional industries. Ekofisk was followed by Frigg, Statfjord and other fields, and for some years Norway could point to stronger economic growth than any other country in Europe.

A special feature of developments on Norway's continental shelf is that the state secured for itself rights in the licences it granted without needing to become actively engaged or help defray expenses until exploitable finds could be commercialized. If a block proved dry, that was the oil company's problem; if, on the other hand, it turned out to be full of oil or gas, the state could then join in as an equal business partner. As if that were not enough, the state also made sure that tax revenue would take the form of oil. Statoil was charged with the task of managing the enormous revenues accruing from this ingenious if somewhat artful arrangement. This gave the new company formidable power over every field on the shelf, a power which, as it continued to grow, caused non-Socialist politicians increasing anxiety. The great political showdown came in 1984.

Bound up with the history of Norwegian oil is the fact that the semi-state-owned company Norsk Hydro was actively engaged on the continental shelf from the outset. Long before the first oil was found, Norsk Hydro set about acquiring a pool of geological expertise, and in the exploratory phase the company took part in all the licensing rounds on the shelf and is cur-

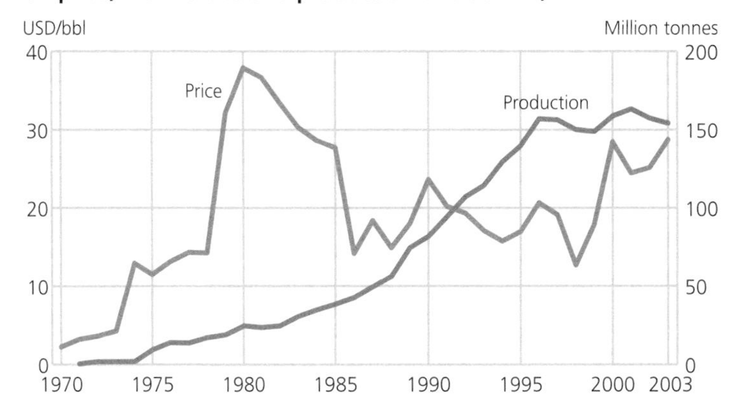


**Up and down**: The price of oil has fluctuated wildly ever since Norway's oil era began. In recent years production has stabilized at about 150 million tonnes annually.

rently operative on a number of major fields, among them Troll, Oseberg, Grane and Heimdal; it also has holdings elsewhere on the shelf. The same year as Statoil, another oil company, Saga, was formed by a consortium of leading Norwegian shipowning and industrial companies and acquired shares in a number of licences, as well as operative responsibility on the Snorre field. Norsk Hydro and Statoil subsequently each acquired a share of this privately owned company, dividing its rights and operations between them.

The problem that arose between the Labour Party and non-Socialist parties in the Storting was primarily ascribable to Statoil's rapidly becoming, thanks to its options and management of the state's interests, incredibly wealthy. The problem was exacerbated by discovery of the vast Statfjord field. When Kåre Willoch succeeded Gro Harlem Brundtland as prime minister in 1981, he immediately shelved the existing plan to transfer operator responsibility on Stafjord from Mobil to Statoil, following up by appointing a committee to consider the possibility of the state's direct participation in the oil activity.

When the issue was placed before the Storting, it ended in a compromise, Statoil being permitted to retain 50 per cent of its holding in the Statfjord field; it was first accorded operative responsibility in 1987. On the other hand the company had to accept the state's direct owner-interests on the shelf being hived off, so that they were no longer a part of Statoil's revenue. True, Statoil would continue to manage these interests, but the state was empowered to instruct the company on how it should vote on its, the state's, behalf in matters relating to the various fields. This represented a substantial weakening of Statoil's overall power in the North Sea. The compromise, or reform as it is also often termed, came into effect on 1 January 1985.

I believe most people today, Statoil employees included, acknowledge that it was necessary to separate the state's interests from Statoil's, especially once it became clear what immense sums would accrue to the country from activities in the North Sea. Statoil was in danger of becoming a state within the state.

After the compromise of 1984 the situation surrounding Statoil normalized; the company now occupied a place in the community that was acceptable to all. In this respect it is characteristic that it was a government drawn from the ranks of the Labour Party that was eventually to take credit for having Statoil go public in 2001. There was nothing dramatic about this move, however – by then Statoil had evolved into a company that had already taken significant and far-reaching steps into the world beyond Norway's frontiers. Now it needed freedom to act and room for further expansion. After twenty-eight years as a controversial political object Statoil had thus become a regular company whose shares were quoted on the stock exchange, a company on a par with Norsk Hydro, Orkla and Norske Skog and one that, though basically Norwegian, in its policies, business activities and geographical range was truly international. It was not a day too soon.

Unsurprisingly, it is the enormous revenues that daily pour into the state coffers from the North Sea that most people associate with Norway's oil and gas activity. But the oil era has resulted not only in untold wealth but also in what is little short of a transformation of Norwegian society. In the early years Norway's role was that of an apprentice, but with astonishing speed Norwegian industry, Norwegian research, Norwegian finance, Norwegian shipping and Norwegian management took over the roles in the North Sea previously played by foreigners. Nowadays, all over Norway, in one way or another the fruits of the Norwegian oil industry are being harvested. Few, if any, would deny that Norwegian engineers and Norwegian technology are the driving forces behind further development of the offshore oil activity.

Within the span of thirty years oil has made Norway a different country.

### The future in the crucible

Is it possible to put a date to the start of the Norwegian oil bonanza? No, not a definite date. Some people will say that it was when oil was first found on the Ekofisk field at Christmas 1969. Others will aver that the start of the recession in the mid-1970s is a better choice. I myself prefer to believe that the oil era began with the motoring-free Sundays of 1973, when OPEC demonstrated to the whole world the power and influence inherent in possession of vast quantities of oil.

When Phillips discovered the Ekofisk field, oil was priced at about $2.00 a barrel. Shortly afterwards the price rose to $10.00; and in 1981, oil cost $30.00 bbl. It was in these years that Norway really became convinced that its oil revenues would be of such magnitude as to bring about a sea of change in the economy and that the nation's future would be totally different from what anyone could have imagined. These years also saw the beginnings of the long decline of the Labour Party; and the foundations were laid for the liberalization that Willoch and

**Our pride and joy**: The Wilh. Wilhelmsen Line, probably the best known of all Norwegian shipowning companies, has from its inception played a leading role in Norway's shipping industry, not least in the liner trade. Seen here off the coast of Korea is the ro-ro vessel M/V **Tamerlane**. The ship is operated by Barber Ship Management for the Wallenius Wilhelmsen Line.

his Høyre, non-Socialist, government embarked upon in 1981 – a process that was to determine the future course of Norway's political and economic development.

By the end of the 1970s the belief that the state of the Norwegian economy could be determined more or less independently of developments abroad had been discarded. Inflation, a steep rise in wages, abortive attempts to introduce state control and incipient unemployment, combined with freer international trade, had effectively seen to that. Gone, too, was the belief that the state could play an active role in business, as was public confidence in the state's knowing what was best for the Norwegian people.

Such changes of attitude were not confined to Norway. Throughout the entire western world John Maynard Keynes's textbooks were replaced by those of Milton Friedman, and in the USA and Great Britain the old leaders were replaced by Ronald Reagan and Margaret Thatcher. A new age had dawned. A well-known saying, possibly wrongfully attributed to Margaret Thatcher, may serve to illustrate the shape of things to come: 'No one would have remembered the Good Samaritan had he only been good. But he had money, too.'

The 1970s were a turning point also in the shipping industry. The industry had greatly expanded following the 1956 closure of the Suez Canal, which forced ships to take the long way round Africa. Norwegian shipowners girded themselves to meet the challenge thus presented, old and small vessels being quickly replaced by new and larger ones. When, early in the 1970s, the introduction of motoring-free Sundays coincided with the oil crisis, tanker freight rates rocketed, prompting owners to order supertankers the way drunken sailors order drinks when ashore. And yards accepted their orders, many of them without having the capacity required to build the ships to the agreed deadline. Nemesis caught up with owners and shipyards alike when, in 1974, the world plunged into an economic recession that resulted in many of the ships delivered in the following years going straight into lay-up. Many Norwegians will remember how, in the mid-1970s, some fjords quickly became choc-a-bloc with superfluous tankers. In 1976 one-third of Norway's merchant fleet was laid up; 40 per cent of these vessels were tankers.

In Norway the shipping crisis led to bankruptcies and collapsing businesses. Not a few veteran shipowning dynasties were dealt a mortal blow, and it must be from these years that the story comes of an owner on the south coast who decided that the only course open to him was to appeal for help to the Almighty. This part of Norway has always been a religious stronghold, and the walls of many old houses are still hung with embroidered psalters. This particular shipowner had one with the words *Jesus, styr du mine tanker* (Jesus, guide thou my thoughts) embroidered on it in black silk. But when he felt the wolves closing in, he took the psalter down and added an 's' to the word *tanker*, thus changing 'thoughts' to 'tankers'. The story may well be apocryphal, but it certainly serves to illustrate the gravity of the situation. Whatever the truth of the matter, it didn't help, as the man went bankrupt.

So too did Bergen's Hilmar Reksten who, more than most

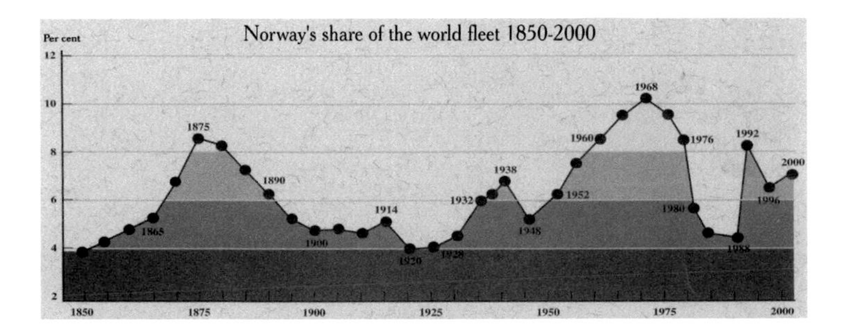


**Growth and crises**: Over the years, Norwegian shipping has had its share of ups and downs. Note the sharp downturn after the crisis years of the 1970s.

Norwegian shipowners, had played the speculative spot market for all it was worth, which made him especially vulnerable when the situation took a turn for the worse. Even substantial aid from the government, which realized that Reksten's bankruptcy might well lead to serious trouble for large sections of the Norwegian economy, failed to save his enormous fleet. Matters were made worse when it was revealed that Reksten had salted away large sums of money abroad, and for many years thereafter he was pursued by lawyers and the tax authorities. Many owners lost their ships in these bleak years. In an attempt to save something from the wreckage the authorities set up a 'Guarantee Institute for Ships and Drilling Rigs'. Well-intentioned though it was, the Institute had little success. It was wound up after sustaining enormous losses and being pilloried by the press all through the 1980s. The shipping crisis was also a disaster for that part of the shipbuilding industry that failed to adapt to new requirements in the oil sector. As usual, the banks had to shoulder much of the burden.

Nor were the years that followed very easy for Norwegian shipping. In an endeavour to cut costs, many vessels were flagged out and not even the Norwegian International Ship Register, which was established in 1986 and conferred considerable crewing advantages on Norwegian owners, could prevent Norway's shipping industry slowly losing some of its time-honoured importance to the nation's economy. Whereas in the years of reconstruction after the war shipping's ability to earn foreign exchange had meant a lot, oil soon took over this role once the North Sea wells came into production in 1975. Since oil entered the economy, the term 'foreign exchange problems' has almost disappeared from the Norwegian vocabulary and the shipping industry has thus lost one of its greatest assets. In recent years tax has been the bone of contention in shipping. EU tax regulations are far more lenient than their Norwegian counterparts, so it is only to be expected that Norwegian shipowners should demand the same treatment as their competitors in member countries. The counter-argument – What does Norway want with shipowners who don't pay tax? – is a specious one. There is more to it than that. For over a century a broad-based environment has grown up around Norway's shipowning companies, possibly one of the strongest and most concentrated in the world. It encompasses one of the world's biggest classification companies, *Det norske Veritas*, an extensive network of shipbrokers, a vibrant research milieu, two marine insurance companies, a substantial supply industry and, of course, a vast body of expertise in ship management and operation. It is significant that no one in Pireus, New York or Singapore considers it at all strange that one of the world's most influential shipping newspapers, *Tradewinds*, should be edited and published in Norway. In time this milieu will probably be undermined and, in the worst case, vanish altogether if the Norwegian flag is no longer flown on ships around the world. Norway's shipowners also play an active role in the oil sector, where they operate supply ships, shuttle tankers, drilling rigs and accommodation platforms. But whereas in 1975 the industry accounted for close on 5 per cent of Norway's GNP, by 2002 its share was down to 2 per cent. Our 'pride and joy' has, in other words, lost much of its former lustre – also in the eyes of the public. In recent years several Norwegian shipping companies have been sold to foreign owners. Best known of these is the Oslo-based Bergersen company, which in 2002 went to the Sohmen family of Hong Kong for NOK 14 billion. A fair share of shipping capital has also found its way ashore, where it has been reinvested in finance and, not least, property.

But if shipping has lost something of its former lustre and importance, oil has more than made up for this by gaining a grip that many people fear is rather too strong. As early as 1980 the oil sector, which in 1975 accounted for 2.5 per cent of Norway's GNP, contributed more than 15 per cent of the nation's earnings. The offshore activity drained other industries of both labour and capital and, in addition, so stimulated public spending that Norwegian industry found itself with a level of costs totally out of step with that of its major competitors. For example, wages rose by 18 and 20 per cent in 1974 and 1975 respectively. The strength of the Norwegian krone subsequently added to the burden. It is little exaggeration to say that the oil sector supplanted large sections of Norwegian industry in the 1970s and '80s, whereas it fell to the service sector, both private and public, to provide new jobs.

The industrial sector's share of Norway's GNP was halved, falling from 18.9 to 9.4 per cent between 1975 and 2002, while in the same period the oil sector's share increased to 17.6 per cent. Not since the years between 1905 and the outbreak of the First World War had Norway experienced such far-reaching and dramatic changes as it did in the 1970s.

In the last two years of Labour Party rule before 1981, the Norwegian economy was close to spinning out of control. The government had abandoned its counter-cyclic policy in favour of a clampdown. A wages and price freeze helped for a time, but when it was lifted, inflation soon returned. When Høyre took over, the government continued to pursue the same restrictive policy – and was compelled to pay for it in the shape of the first wave of unemployment Norway had experienced since the war. When the turnabout in the world economy came in 1983, Norway entered upon a period that can best be described as a bender. Private consumption soared to unprecedented heights and the banks did precisely what they had done prior to the banking crisis of 1923, lending money to all who asked for it, regardless of whether or not the security offered was sound. At this point there were no constraints on the volume of credit, but interest rates were nonetheless kept relatively low. Banks competed to be biggest, and some of them gave their credit departments unequivocal instructions to step up lending. These years have since been dubbed the Yap (Young Aspiring Professionals) years. The growth in loans was further stimulated by a regulation that made all interest paid tax deductible. Again it was inevitable that things would go wrong, and so they did, though not as badly as in 1923. The downturn began with a steep fall in oil prices, from $30.00 bbl to well under $10 bbl; as a result, between 1985 and 1986 the country's balance of payments was impacted by NOK 60 billion. Strong measures were called for, and when restrictions were introduced Willoch's Høyre government fell from office.

I am still at a loss to understand why Kåre Willoch, who on several other issues was in favour of liberalizing the Norwegian economy, could lift controls on credit volume without doing the same on interest rates. He has offered several explanations, none of which stand up to close scrutiny. The time had now come for Gro Harlem Brundtland and the Labour Party to try to sort things out. I am by no means convinced that they did a much better job. As in life, also in financial policy a distinction should be made between shaving and cutting one's throat.

The new government tightened things up considerably, devaluing the krone by 12 per cent and imposing strict controls on wages that eventually brought real wages down. Both measures helped, but they took time to bite, and again the price was a wave of unemployment that left more than 150,000 people out of work.

In the middle of these difficult years, in October 1987, the world was hit by a stock-exchange crash that, as crashes go, was just as bad as the infamous Wall Street crash of 1929. The Oslo Stock Exchange had prospered greatly ever since 1983, so much so that by September 1987 the total index had risen to 442 points; on 10 November, when the overall index stood at 243 points, it hit bottom. In the course of two short months exchange rates were almost halved; and as if this were not enough, property prices also fell following the period of strong growth resulting from the lifting of controls on house prices a few years earlier.

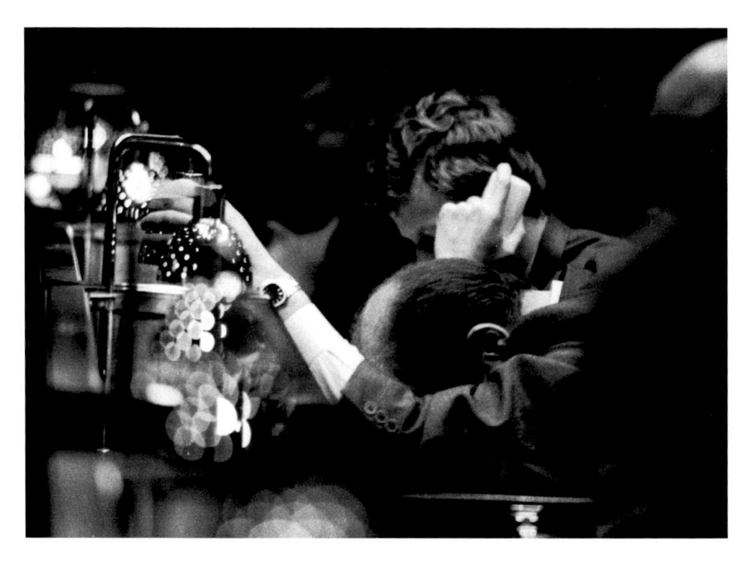

**Black October**: 20 October 1987 was the worst day ever in the history of the Norwegian Stock Exchange. Like the Wall Street crash of 1929, it too occurred in October.

In the next few years the Norwegian economy lurched from one crisis to another. The time had come to repay the easy loans incurred in the 'bender' years, the great spending spree – at a far higher rate of interest than either the public at large or the business sector was accustomed to. The banks panicked and dunned borrowers, who in the meantime had seen the value of their homes and properties reduced and, furthermore, had sustained substantial losses on heavily mortgaged shares. In the years that followed the banks – as they fully deserved to do – had to shoulder much of the blame for the many tragedies resulting from these crisis years. Although the financial policy pursued by the four governments that had to tackle the crisis may not have been all it might have been, it is still hard to excuse the many mistakes that were made. The banks lost an aggregate of between NOK 60 and NOK 80 billion in these years. Some of them went into liquidation, others scraped through by entering into thinly camouflaged mergers, and some were taken over by the state, among them two of the biggest, Fokus Bank and Kreditkassen. In the case of Den norske Bank, the biggest of them all, the state became

**Employment and share of GDP. 1975 and 2003. Per cent**

| | Share of employment | | Share of GDP | |
|---|---|---|---|---|
| | 1975 | 2003 | 1975 | 2003 |
| Agriculture and forestry | 8.7 | 3.0 | 3.5 | 0.9 |
| Fishing/Fish Farming | 1.0 | 0.6 | 0.7 | 0.3 |
| Mining and quarrying | 0.6 | 0.2 | 0.6 | 0.2 |
| Extraction of oil and gas | 0.1 | 1.2 | 2.5 | 17.4 |
| Manufacturing | 22.4 | 12.0 | 18.9 | 9.0 |
| Energy and water | 0.9 | 0.6 | 2.3 | 2.4 |
| Building and construction | 6.8 | 5.7 | 5.5 | 4.2 |
| Shipping (foreign trade) | 2.5 | 1.8 | 4.7 | 1.8 |
| Private services | 6.4 | 43.6 | 37.4 | 38.5 |
| Public administration | 20.6 | 31.3 | 13.8 | 16.4 |
| Undistributed (VAT etc.) | - | - | 10.2 | 9.0 |

**The new Norway**. The years since 1979 have seen radical changes in every sector of Norwegian society.

a majority shareholder. Fokus and Kreditkassen have since been sold to foreign interests.

There was little sympathy for the crestfallen managers who set about picking up the pieces early in the 1990s. Both the corporate sector and the Norwegian people themselves were far too busy licking their own wounds.

Shortly before Christmas 1996 I was seated at my desk at *Dagens Næringsliv*, trying in one of my Saturday editorials to sum up the year that was fast ebbing out. It wasn't at all difficult: 1996 had been a good year for the Norwegian economy, all traces of the years of crisis having been firmly erased in 1994 and 1995. I concluded my article with a quotation from Labour's Thorbjørn Jagland: 'The Norwegian people are wallowing in money.' I then added for my own account: 'And it doesn't seem to be doing them the least harm.'

### Valedictory

Anyone flying over Norway today can see for himself the source of Norway's wealth in the shape of towering oil platforms far out to sea, about midway between the British Isles and Norway. From these platforms and the underwater installations and pipelines that run to Britain and the Continent is derived about 20 per cent of the Norwegian NOK 16 billion GNP and 45 per cent of Norwegian export revenues. Oil and gas have endowed Norway with an economic freedom of action that is unique compared with that of other European countries. Most EU member countries have their work cut out trying to keep the deficit on their national budget down to 3 per cent of their GNP, that being the limit ordained by the EU in what is known as the Stability and Growth Agreement. Norway regularly returns a healthy profit, which this year, thanks to high oil prices, may well run into a two-figure percentage of the GNP. Oil has ensured for Norway a standard of living and economic freedom that most Norwegians could only dream of thirty years ago. As Norway is the third-largest oil exporter (after Saudi Arabia and Russia), our Minister of Finance need not give a thought to the country's balance of payments, and Norway enjoys net wealth. Unemployment is low, running at 3 to 4 per cent, against twice that in the core EU countries

At the start of the new century the Norwegian krone was so strong in relation to other currencies that the country's export industry was beginning to feel the pinch. On the other hand, import prices fell so steeply that fear of permanent deflation impelled the governor of the Central Bank, who aims at an inflation rate of 2.5 per cent, to lower the bank rate to levels that few Norwegian can remember ever having known. Inflation, with which we were once all too familiar and feared, is today a spectre from the past. The only reason the minister may have for concern is that Norway's level of costs is becoming increasingly high and threatens to impose a long-term drag on economic growth. For the time being, however, such macroeconomic problems as do exist are surmountable and in most other European countries would be dismissed as 'luxury problems'. Their presence is very much in evidence in daily life, however. For example, in a country thickly carpeted with forests, it is cheaper to import firewood from Latvia and Finland than to hew it in Norway's own woods, and every day Norwegian fish is sent all the way to China for filleting before it returns to find its way, frozen, into Norwegian shops. That at the same time industrial undertakings are either closing down or transferring operations to countries where costs are lower brings to mind the evils of the interwar years, a skeleton that is still rattled whenever the Labour Party holds one of its 'revivalist' meetings. I have attended some of these myself and know that they are not exactly calculated to strengthen the Norwegian people's belief in a bright future. I have also been to other party meetings, and they are only a tad better. There, talk is mostly of problems that need to be resolved; only occasionally is mention made of opportunities that can be seized and exploited. We do have some problems, though. Despite our having one of the world's highest incidence of doctors per head of population, the health service is bedevilled by waiting lists; and in not a few places so many public swimming pools have been built that the local authorities can't afford to heat them. That's what tends to happen in a country that is so rich that it is bent on resolving every problem there is. I constantly dream of the day when a politician will get to his feet in the Storting and ask what the government intends to do about the fact that people below the age of eighty continue to die in Norway. Three hundred thousand Norwegians of working age are currently in receipt of disability benefits; that is almost seven per cent of the total population.

In my capacity as a journalist I have followed the debate on Norway's economic development throughout the thirty years that may rightfully be termed the oil era. What I remember best is the extensive use that was made of a quite innocent remark by a Danish shipowner who died as far back as 1937. This was H.N. Andersen, a man who assured himself of immortality by concluding a speech with the following words: 'We can't live by shaving one another.'

This postulate, to which the Danes pay scant heed, we Norwegians have borne in our hearts from the start of the oil bonanza – while an increasing number of people have in effect made a living from shaving one another and the economic firmament has grown ever bluer above a country that today boasts the world's next-highest GNP per capita (*c.* NOK 344,000 in 2003) and which, furthermore, in its northern waters possesses oil reserves large enough to last for another generation. Nor does the fact that Norway, in addition, has securely tucked away an oil fund (established after oil prices plummeted in the late 1980s) that soon will pass the size of two national budgets, i.e. NOK 1,000 billion, appear to have made any impression. But this does not alter the fact that we can't live by shaving one another.

Only a very few people are prepared to face the fact that this fund, some of which is invested in international shares, will probably grow fivefold in the course of the next generation, and that it is well on its way towards reindustrializing the Norwegian economy. Norwegian industry nowadays is not confined to Norway, where in any case we have no need of it and most certainly do not have the labour to man it. The labour we have is firmly ensconced in the health service; agriculture, for much of the twentieth century the traditional labour pool, has run dry.

I began this article by citing Terry Macalister's question of why we Norwegians are so worried when we manifestly have so little to worry about. Now, as we near completion of this long history, I think I have some idea of what the answer may be.

Why so many people are worried about the future is probably because we have so quickly grown accustomed to living on our new-found wealth. It will take longer to live *with* it. We feel, in a way, that we have not really deserved it. Maybe we haven't. We may be like the Australians, who, whenever things have looked bad, have found a nugget of gold – in other words, that we have been just plain lucky. It is quite possible. British liberalism saved us after 1850, Sam Eyde and foreign capital gave us a leg-up after that, Marshall Aid and international demand soon put us back on our feet after the last war; and when industry began to find the going hard towards the end of the 1970s, Phillips found the gigantic Ekofisk oilfield. But may not the reverse equally well be true? That new industries invariably cause problems for old-established ones and that the Norwegian economy would have managed quite well had oil never been found? In my opinion it would have. The country's development would in that case probably have been more akin to that of Sweden. We could not have afforded to cling on as long as we have to farming, nor would we have had the means to prioritize regional development the way we have; and we might have had to postpone for a time certain welfare benefits and not been able to retire at sixty. To make up for this, like Sweden we would have possessed more industry. But would it have been any more secure? Who can guarantee the Swedes that Volvos and Saabs will continue to be manufactured in Sweden once Norway runs out of oil? To my mind, no one, and certainly not General Motors and Ford, who have bought up the Swedish automobile industry. Would we today be willing to exchange Norwegian oil for shares in Volvo, as Prime Minister Odvar Nordli once tried to do? I don't think so. I most certainly don't.

What I do believe is that we Norwegians have shown ourselves quite adept at grasping new opportunities, at replacing old industries by new and at adopting the best technology available at the earliest possible moment. We did so in shipping and we did so in wood-processing; the proof was there in the heyday of industry, and it was there again when oil first was found on the Norwegian continental shelf. Moreover, I believe we shall prove ourselves equally capable when the time comes for another all-out effort, as come it will.

When the banks found themselves up against it in the 1990s, a Labour government was forced to take over the nation's three biggest banks. This gave the party a commanding position in the economy, one on a par with that it had dreamed of in the immediate postwar years. But on this occasion it voluntarily relinquished its dominant power. Today Focus Bank is owned by Denmark's Den Danske Bank and Swedish Nordea has taken over Kreditkassen; however, the state is still a minority shareholder in the biggest of the three, Den norske Bank. Statoil has been partly privatized, as has the state-owned telecommunications company Telenor; and state-owned industrial undertakings have largely been sold or wound up without undue controversy. Political agreement on economic policy has generally been widespread in the last twenty-five years. Many of the liberalization measures for which Høyre deserves most of the credit, among them opening-up of the housing market and the lifting of credit restrictions in the 1980s, were planned by the Labour Party but implemented by Willoch's non-Socialist Høyre government. It is obvious that, when the time has come for a change, whoever happens to be in power is of minor significance. The Norwegian krone floats freely in relation to other currencies, which would have been unthinkable only a few years ago, and, although the electorate has twice voted against membership, to all intents and purposes Norway is just as closely linked to the EU as it would have been had it been a full-blown member. Capital flows freely, and banks determine levels of interest, both on lendings and on borrowings, themselves. Most subsidies have been done away with and all political parties have ceased advocating prioritization of certain industries, with the possible exception of shipping. The determinant factor today is the market. The enormous changes that have taken place in Norwegian politics, the economy and the life of the community in the age of oil are readily apparent in the daily life of the people.

None of this has occasioned the Norwegian people misgivings. If they do have any, it must be in regard to the role played by the *nouveaux riches* in a modern private-capitalistic society. That an individual like Kjell Inge Røkke, a young man who came back from America with a fortune made from fishing, can act on a whim and do as he likes with such key industrial concerns as Aker and Kværner and, furthermore, permit himself to realize his jet-set ambitions in the full glare of publicity, is harder to swallow.

Now we have come to the end of our journey. We have made our way through most of Norway's modern history, a history characterized by sudden squalls and unforeseen events, by wars and down trips, but also by growth and steady progress. The most remarkable thing of all is that there have been no major political crises or grave social disturbances. Basically, the Norwegian people are still a united people, and it would be hard to find a greater compliment than the 'Norwegian model'.

What, fundamentally, has happened? Is it, as some claim, that the ideologies of yesteryear are no more? Have we, as others maintain, surrendered to the market and forsaken the traditional virtues of frugality and material equality? Or is it simply that our new-found wealth has enabled us to pave over the pitfalls, all the things that could have gone so terribly wrong, in a way that, despite everything, makes us feel at home with this novel, individualized, urbanized and globalized world? That, in fact, we are happy in it? I think so. No, I know so. It's just that we are taking a long time to admit that, quite simply, we like the Norway we have created.

What it doesn't mean is that we are any the less worried.

**Sørlandet**: The Lindesnes lighthouse on the south coast at dusk.

**january** fin serck-hanssen **february** rolf m. aagaard

**march** herdis maria siegert **april** janne solgaard

**may** jens hauge **june** vibeke tandberg

**july** dag alveng **august** rune johansen

**september** knut bry **october** asle svarverud

**november** ingvar moi **december** per berntsen

# KRISTIAN BIRKELAND AND SAM EYDE

It is hard to imagine two more diametrically opposed personalities than Kristian Birkeland and Sam Eyde. But perhaps it was this very lack of similarity that made it possible for the two to lay, at the start of the twentieth century, the groundwork for what would become Norway's biggest industrial concern. Birkeland was a pale and introverted theoretician, in poor health and with only a modest financial flair. A keen student, he was appointed a professor in physics at a young age. He married a minister's daughter, but the couple remained childless. Nothing preoccupied him more than his attempt to solve the mystery of the Northern Lights.

His first major Northern Lights expedition at the turn of the century ended in a death and failure to keep within his budget, so the Storting refused to finance his next expedition, forcing Birkeland to obtain funding himself. With Sweden and Norway on the verge of war, he directed his efforts towards inventing an entirely new kind of weapon – an electromagnetic canon capable of hurling projectiles weighing ten kilograms over a distance of 100 kilometres. He believed that, with some minor adjustments, it would be possible to bombard Stockholm from the Norwegian border. While trying out his invention he more than once managed to wreck his study, but things really went seriously wrong when he gave a promotional demonstration of his wonder weapon before a formal gathering in the University's old auditorium. The canon short-circuited, spanning the hall with a tremendous arc, and the shocked guests from Norway and abroad had to be evacuated. What no one knew at the time was that this accident would eventually result in 38,000 jobs and profits running into billions of kroner: Birkeland realized that the arc could be employed to extract and fix the nitrogen in the air to manufacture artificial fertilizer in the shape of saltpetre.

PORTRAIT

From childhood Eyde was an extrovert, a spirited young rascal who climbed to the mastheads of the ships in harbour in his home town of Arendal. With his olive skin and brown eyes, he was unlike the other children in his family, something that was explained locally as his being the outcome of an extramarital affair. Eyde was bottom of the class at school and twice failed his exams. He was eventually packed off to sea, where he was roughly handled and even locked up. Life at sea would, however, encourage him to resume his education. Having passed his science exams he considered a military career, but his grades at the Norwegian Military Academy were not good enough for him to continue.

Hopeless case though he seemed to be, he made his way to Germany instead, there to train as a structural engineer, followed by six years of work on major German engineering projects, including a number of bridges, several of which are still standing. Most importantly, he was involved in the development of railway stations in Germany – work that he would continue to pursue on his return to Norway in 1898. His newly established engineering company designed railway stations in Kristiania (now Oslo), Stockholm and Gothenburg. Eyde's ties to Sweden were

**Kristian Birkeland** (right) and Eivind Bødtker Næss at work on the production of nitrogen fertilizer from air. The photograph is thought to be from 1903.

strengthened when he married a Swedish noblewoman, with whom he had three children.

Alongside his work as an engineer, Eyde, ever the entrepreneur, speculated in the building of Norway's first warehouse, a coal silo and a city canal – projects that all ended in failure. Convinced that the railway station market was nearing saturation point, he began buying up mines and waterfalls. Among his purchases was Rjukanfossen, a waterfall he acquired for 40,000 kroner in the belief that he could sell it on to foreign interests for six million – but nobody wanted it and Eyde was in danger of running out of funds.

The circumstances of the first meeting between Birkeland and Eyde, at a dinner party on 13 February 1903, were somewhat farcical: Birkeland had an electric canon that no one wanted to buy and Eyde had a waterfall and no idea of what to do with it. So the two joined forces and manufactured artificial fertilizer using what would come to be known as the 'Birkeland/Eyde method'. Eyde applied himself to the raising of foreign capital: he organized everything and nurtured visions of a large future industry, while Birkeland attended to the technical side of the business. Both were operating in fields far removed from their specialist areas, the physicist working as a chemist and the designer as an electrical engineer.

In reality neither Birkeland nor Eyde was greatly impressed with the other. The Swedish Nobel Committee considered awarding the prize for chemistry to Birkeland for his discovery, as it was seen as a major contribution to the fight against a worldwide food shortage. Eyde, however, was disappointed at being omitted from the nominations and used his influential circle of friends in Sweden to prevent the prize being awarded to Birkeland alone – despite the fact that the professor held the patent.

With the foundation of Norsk Hydro in 1905, Eyde became Norway's first managing director and promptly received the highest annual salary in the entire country. Outwardly he gave the impression of being a harnesser of waterfalls and an industrial miracle-worker, using his boundless energy to develop one industrial site after another. The small towns of Rjukan and Notodden, in particular, are regarded as Eyde's work, as is the town that bears his name, Eydehavn. Only six years after it was founded Norsk Hydro was employing a workforce of 2,500. Eyde bought a magnificent house with a servants' wing and a dining room that seated fifty guests. With the king beside him in the rear seat, he would draw up before his Notodden residence in his bright-

EYDE, SAMUEL (SAM) (1866-1940), engineer and industrialist. Founded the nitrogen industry together with Kristian Birkeland and, in 1904, together with the Swedish Wallenberg family, formed Det Norske Aktieselskab for Elektrokemisk Industri (Elkem) and, in 1905, Norsk Hydro-Elektrisk Kvælstofaktieselskab (Norsk Hydro). Managing director of Norsk Hydro until 1918 and Conservative member of the Storting (parliament) 1918-20.

red Mercedes, which was driven by his private chauffeur, a German. There was a popular joke during the First World War that goes some way towards illustrating the vanity and occasional self-importance displayed by Eyde: 'The German Kaiser has gone power-mad – he thinks he's Sam Eyde'.

As with most entrepreneurs, Eyde was no administrator or bookkeeper, and he spread himself too thinly. This insatiable and grandiose man then went into the iron and steel industry, concentrating on titanium, nickel and sulphuric-acid production. In the First World War he also went into explosives, a morally dubious business in the eyes of many.

In practice Hydro's founder and first managing director was dismissed in 1917, but being the pioneer that he was in most walks of life, he made sure that he got Norway's first ever severance deal. The agreement was that he would be paid a quarter of a million kroner every year for ten years. Eyde tried to prepare the ground for a political career, though without much success. While it is true that he became a Member of Parliament for the Norwegian Conservative party in 1919, he never became a cabinet minister, though he was given an appointment as the Norwegian minister in Poland. Three years later his name and reputation suffered irreparable damage as a result of the so-called Nickel scandal, in which it was claimed that there was proof that Eyde had benefited to the tune of several millions of kroner at the shareholders' expense. So great was the scandal that he had to give up his post as a minister in Poland. The resultant opprobrium explains why, in 1923, he took up residence abroad, primarily on the French Riviera.

This failure to bow to convention was also a feature of Sam Eyde's private life. As a husband he was unfaithful, in 1906 fathering a child by one of his mistresses. To spare her the shame, he arranged a nominal marriage for her with a French count. When his wife left him, taking their three children with her to Sweden, he married his lover and adopted his own son. Eyde devoted his last years to the writing of his autobiography, a controversial document intended to buttress his by then crumbling reputation as Norsk Hydro's big man. The hostility between Eyde and his successors at Hydro was such that he was not even invited to attend the company's 25th anniversary celebrations.

Birkeland, for his part, suffered from nerves and insomnia, depression, radiation injuries and deafness, and was living in straitened circumstances. His wife left him and Eyde squeezed him out of Hydro. The professor took to drinking heavily, combining alcohol with a high intake of sleeping pills. In a letter he once wrote he complained of 'years of outrageous baseness on the part of Eyde'. His twilight years were spent in the Sudan and Egypt, studying the zodiacal light. Increasing paranoia led him to protect himself with two guard dogs, a rifle and a revolver. Emaciated and alone, Kristian Birkeland died from a drug overdose in a hotel room in Tokyo at the age of forty-nine.

Not until a full generation after his death in 1917 did the world realize that in many fields of study Kristian Birkeland had been well ahead of his time: for example, America's Star Wars weapons programme would come to be based on his technology. Above all, however, satellites launched in 1966 would prove his theories about the Northern Lights to have been correct in every respect. Eyde, who died in 1940, has streets and squares all over Norway named after him; Birkeland would give his name only to a crater on the moon. Viewed in this light, the two remain worlds apart to this day.

NIELS CHR. GEELMUYDEN

BIRKELAND, KRISTIAN OLAF BERNHARD (1867–1917), professor of physics at Oslo University, 1898, inventor. Formulated a theory on the Northern Lights (1896) and established Northern Lights observatories. Demonstrated the existence of electrical currents in the upper atmosphere (Birkeland currents). Designed an electromagnetic canon which, together with Sam Eyde, he employed to oxidize nitrogen in the air to produce nitric acid and calcium nitrate. This invention led to the establishment of Norsk Hydro in 1905.

# SPORT

2:32:31
NEW YORK CITY
FINISH
MARATHON '78
FINISH
ERS HANOVER · RUDIN FAMILY · PERRIER · NEW YORK TELEPHONE · NEW TIME
MANUFACTURERS
1173F
HANOVER

# READY, STEADY, GO...

Grete Waitz and Kristen Damsgaard

When, in New York in 1978, I stood at the starting line ready to take part in my first marathon, I already had behind me a 10-year career as a track athlete. I had been a middle-distance runner since my teens and took part in my first Olympic Games before I was 20. As I stood there on that beautiful October day, I had no idea that it would mark the start of my 'second career'.

So why did I choose to participate? It was because my husband, Jack, had persuaded me to do so. The organizers of the New York Marathon had invited me in the belief that I would make a good pacemaker for the favourites. As I had never run further than 20 kilometres at the time, I can only assume that they thought that was all I could manage. However, I accepted the offer, as I had never been to the States and Jack and I wanted to see the sights.

To my own, and everyone else's amazement, I not only won the New York Marathon that year, in my debut as a long-distance runner I also set a world record. But the race did not exactly whet my appetite. I was ill-prepared to run the whole 42 kilometres, so I was in a terrible state when I passed the finishing line, and determined never to run another marathon.

However, the following year, there I was again at the starting line by the Verrazano Bridge; once more Jack had convinced me that I should take part. This time, however, I was better prepared, and as a result set another world record and became the first woman to run the distance in less than 2 hours 30 minutes. This success encouraged me to continue, and I eventually won the New York Marathon nine times.

The key to my success was to be found in the past, on the other side of the Atlantic, at home in Norway. I started my career in a local athletics club in Oslo. It was an important period in my life, one in which were laid the foundations for my later success as a middle- and long-distance runner. In many ways I am a product of Norwegian sports culture and the way it has developed – and, not least, of the position occupied by sport in Norway. In the course of my career I have competed all over the world and have learned a great deal about sport elsewhere. In the light of my experience, I dare to claim that, compared with that of many countries, the history of Norwegian sport is in many respects unique. Political and cultural influences over the years have helped to make sport in Norway what it is today.

**From upper class activity to mass movement**

Over a thousand years ago, in the Viking Age, sporting activities and competitions were already popular; but it was not until the 1850s that specialized sports organizations were established. Different disciplines started to form clubs – gymnastics was the first, followed by skating and skiing. All clubs were members of the Confederation of Sports for the Promotion of Physical Exercise and Weapons Use, a forerunner of the present Norwegian Olympic Committee and Confederation of Sports. When the Confederation was established in 1861, it was one of the first such confederations in any country. In its early years, marksmanship was an issue much to the fore.

Towards the end of the 1890s, sport began to change. Great Britain exerted a considerable influence, and gradually British sporting traditions were adopted. Competition became the driving force and with it came specialization, timekeeping/measurement and record lists. The British concept of 'amateurism' also became an ideal. I think it is interesting to note that earning money from sport is not a modern phenomenon – prize money was already being awarded for sports events a hundred years ago. But this stopped with the introduction of 'amateurism', at the same time as such people as gymnastics teachers

**A ski meet** in Fjelkenbakken, 1898 – a painting by Gustav Wentzel.

and gunsmiths were no longer allowed to compete in the disciplines with which they were associated.

The increased focus on competition and the establishment of many new clubs for different disciplines naturally resulted in the formation of specialized national federations. In the 1900s, sport in Norway was governed by such specialized federations. But in 1919, with the support of the Storting (parliament), the Confederation of Sports was reorganized and renamed the Norwegian National Confederation of Sport.

Norwegian athletes took part in the modern Olympic Games for the first time in Paris in 1900, and went on to win a number of gold medals in subsequent Games. Following reorganization of the Confederation in 1919, and the advent of Winter Olympics in 1924, interest in sport grew rapidly. The Norwegians' performances caused something of a sensation, with the result that public enthusiasm rocketed. However, certain senior officials wanted sport to be more health-oriented and of greater practical value, and they very nearly succeeded in preventing Norwegian participation in the 1928 Winter Olympics.

The industrialization of Norway in the early 1900s fostered a growing and more politically aware working class that gradually gained influence in Norwegian society. Workers formed their own athletics, boxing, wrestling, football, skiing and skating clubs. Subscriptions and charges for equipment were kept as low as possible to put membership within the reach of all. However, these workers' clubs felt that they had no say in the newly formed National Confederation, which was dominated by the social elite, so in 1924 they established their own organization, the Workers' Confederation of Sports (AIF).

AIF believed sport should be accessible to all and that it should be broadly based. They fought for new facilities to be multi-sport complexes and not specialized facilities for competitive sports. They wanted to make sport available to the masses and to this end focused on the benefits of engaging in sports. The AIF therefore lobbied for sports to be included in the remit of the Ministry of Social Affairs rather than the Ministry of Defence, as was then the case. The interwar period was a time of class struggle and social unrest. Sport was also marred by political extremes, as middle-class athletes often acted as strikebreakers in industrial disputes. As a result, workers' clubs started to organize their own national and international competitions, introducing cross-country skiing and walking competitions, relay races through the streets, swimming and gymnastics events. These AIF-sponsored championships proved very popular. For the first time in Norwegian sporting history, corporate sport was included and women were allowed to participate, most notably in athletics. As was to be expected, some exceptional athletes emerged from this mass movement. At its peak, the AIF had about 100,000 members and was the second-largest workers' sports movement in the world, after that of the Soviet Union.

With the passage of time, the gap between the two organizations narrowed. A more moderate board took over management of the AIF and the National Confederation adopted some resolutions that were more in line with AIF policy. Gradually it became accepted that women could engage in sport, and mass events, such as the Birkebeiner ski race, were introduced.

In 1935 the Labour party came to power and sport was placed under the umbrella of the Ministry of Social Affairs, which put pressure on the two organizations to merge. Around this time there was an increasing focus on top sports events, largely thanks to a new mass medium, radio; major championships were now broadcast and sports stars were lauded as heroes. The two organizations were close to becoming one confederation when war broke out. They finally merged in 1946 and the Norwegian Confederation of Sports was born.

The notion of corporate sport was developed by the AIF, it being an important part of the Federation's work to promote sport for all. This laid the foundation for what was later to become the Norwegian Federation of Corporate Sport, which was founded in 1957.

Shortly after the Germans occupied Norway in 1940, leading figures in the sports world decided that international competitions should be banned and that Germans would not be allowed to join Norwegian sports organizations. The occupying forces and Norwegian Nazis tried to subjugate the sports organizations by establishing a new Ministry of Sport. But the Federation board members stood down, as did the majority of regional and club representatives. Athletes left their clubs when Nazi leaders took over. Some of the finest athletes of the day, among them skiers, skaters and wrestlers, were summoned before the authorities in an attempt to force them to continue competing. When they refused outright, they were 'disqualified'

**The Labour movement** long held its own sporting contests. This poster advertises the Winter Games held in Oslo in 1928.

for life – which later came to be regarded as a badge of honour.

The 'sports strike' lasted throughout the Occupation, and very few meets were held. On the rare occasions that the Germans and their Norwegian accomplices did try to hold a meet, no one came to watch. Athletes went 'underground', continuing to train and hold meets in secret. To be fair, not all events were clandestine in the strictest sense, as hundreds of participants and up to several thousand spectators would often show up at illegal football matches. Many young people who were involved with sport lost the opportunity to compete, but these circles were important recruiting grounds for the Home Front (the civilian underground movement) and the military Resistance movement. Many sports officials and athletes were imprisoned by the Germans and their Norwegian henchmen. Speaking at the constitutional General Assembly of the Confederation of Sports in February 1946, Rolf Hofmo, the Confederation's vice-president, said the 'test' passed by Norwegian sport in forming a united front during the Second World War was the 'greatest sporting achievement in the history of Norway'.

The years following the war were characterized by frugality and reconstruction. It was a difficult time, one when athletes had to apply, through their local club, for the means to buy, for example, tennis balls, tracksuits or ski boots – and it was up to individual federations to decide whether to grant the money. Eventually footballs and football boots were exempted, but things like ski boots and tracksuits continued to be rationed.

The two most important events in Norwegian sport in this period were the establishment in 1946 of the Government Office for Youth and Sport and of Norsk Tipping A/S, a state-sponsored football pool. A unique feature of the latter (which brought in far more than had been envisaged) was that profits were divided equally between sport and science and research. The bulk of the money allocated to sport went to build sports centres all over the country.

New areas of activity in the postwar period included company sports, sports for the disabled, and the organization of sports events and provision of sports facilities for the men and women of Norway's merchant marine. In the first twenty years after the war, growth in the membership of sports organizations was slow and remained more or less at a standstill. But the development in the two decades that followed could justifiably be termed a 'sports revolution', membership figures rising from roughly 400,000 to around 1.6 million. The main reasons for this rapid growth were:

- Increased focus on children and young people
- More participation in sports by women
- The introduction of new activities (keep fit) and inclusion of new disciplines in the Confederation of Sports
- Greater awareness among leading figures of the need for diversity and access for all
- Growing interest and a more positive attitude to sports among politicians; sport was integrated into cultural policy and given more financial support and improved facilities
- An improvement in people's personal finances that allowed them to participate more

These trends have continued from the mid-1980s into this century. Several other trends have also made their appearance:

- Greater, more focused and better coordinated investment in elite sports
- Improved commercialization in many areas of sport
- Extensive anti-doping measures
- New 'favourites' such as golf, snowboarding, training in commercial gyms with no affiliation to sports clubs, etc.

### Sport in Norway today

When I was twelve years old, I joined Sportsklubben VIDAR in Oslo to take part in athletics. At the time, I had no ambitions to be a world champion, but the club became my most important social arena outside the home. The atmosphere there was good and VIDAR became more than just a place to train and compete: it was also where I made most of my friends, found a boyfriend and got married – and it is still the core of my social circle at home in Norway.

The local sports club is the cornerstone of all sport in Norway, be it the only such facility in a small rural community or one of many in a town or built-up area. There are 11–12,000 such local sports clubs and teams in Norway. Half of them have fewer than 100 members and only 2-3 per cent can boast of more than 1,000 members. Altogether, Norwegian sports clubs have a total of 1.85 million members. Women account for a 40 per cent share, but this is gradually rising. Some people are members of several clubs, so it is estimated that about a third of the Norwegian population belongs to a sports club. It will come as no surprise to learn that football enjoys the most widespread support and is also the fastest-growing sport. The number of sports disciplines included in the Norwegian Confederation of Sports has also increased in recent years and now stands at 60.

Active sport is, of course, the most important element of a club's activities and external image. But behind the scenes, work is carried out at many levels. I have already mentioned the social significance of these clubs, but of equal importance is the fact that they provide an excellent training ground for voluntary work. Teamwork is a fundamental factor in the success of most sports clubs. Everyone can gain valuable experience from sitting on boards and committees and from helping out with training, competitions and social events. Many people benefit from this in later life – in their personal and working lives, or in connection with politics. It is no exaggeration to say that sport is an important democratic arena for the people, a kind of school for democracy.

### Organization of Sport

The Norwegian Olympic Committee and Confederation of Sports is the umbrella organization in which is vested overall responsibility for policy in relation to all sports in Norway. It is governed by a board, which is elected for a four-year period by the general assembly, where the participants are mostly representatives of sports clubs and individual federations.

I am often asked how sport is financed in Norway, particularly in the USA, where local sports clubs are virtually non-existent, as college and professional sports dominate. Naturally, financial circumstances vary greatly in the different areas of Norwegian sport. At a local level, the majority of clubs have an annual revenue of less than NOK 200,000 or thereabouts. Funds usually come from sponsors, the profits accruing from sporting events, jumble sales, raffles and other communal projects. Membership fees account for the second largest item of revenue, followed by public grants. It is a generally accepted principle that membership fees for children and young people should be kept at a level where everyone can afford to enjoy sport, and this has largely been successfully achieved.

**A bevy of determined** young girls vie with each other in friendly competition at Holmenkollen. This children's ski race is a popular annual event.

At a local level, the division of roles is such that the local authorities seek to build and run the larger sports facilities and make these available to clubs, whereas the clubs themselves are responsible for their own activities. The standard and quality of facilities vary considerably from one municipality to another.

As has been said, Norwegian sport depends heavily on voluntary work. Most clubs are run by unpaid elected representatives and have no salaried administration. As a rule, coaches are not paid – and parents provide enormous support in this area. I am myself a 'product' of this system: my first coaches worked on a voluntary basis and spent untold hours coaching every week, in addition to attending the many weekend meets in and around Oslo. My husband later assumed responsibility for my coaching.

The Confederation of Sports' central administration and regional branches are largely financed by lottery money and from public funds. The financial circumstances of individual federations vary enormously. But as sponsorship, lottery funds, TV contracts and membership fees are the main sources of revenue, it will come as no surprise that the football, handball and ski federations take the lion's share.

### Into the Big Time

The fact that a small country like Norway, which has just over 4 million inhabitants, can perform so well in international sports events has attracted some attention. It is not due simply to coincidence or good luck. Over the last twenty years, the Norwegian Confederation of Sports has invested heavily in elite sport and given it clear priority. My own running career was coming to an end when the Olympiatoppen project really took off, so my time following an Olympiatoppen training programme was limited.

The reason for this massive investment in elite sports was Norway's poor showing at both the summer and winter Olympics in 1984. Norway has always had great expectations of its sports stars, not least because of our success in winter sports as a result of favourable natural conditions and first-class training opportunities. Prosjekt 88 was established as a forerunner to what is today called Olympiatoppen, which is responsible for the development of elite sports in Norway. Olympiatoppen provides financial support for athletes and individual federations, but demands in return commitment and effort. Regular training, augmented by medical and planning reports, is required. Professionals cannot benefit from this support scheme, though they do have the same rights as everyone else when it comes to using the services and facilities of Toppidrettssenteret (Elite Sports Centre).

An important centre of elite sport in Norway, Toppidrettssenteret adjoins the Norwegian University of Sport and Physical Education in Oslo. It is an important venue for elite sport in Norway. Specialists and sports personalities meet there, and professional athletes are tested and studied. Nothing is left to chance in terms of training, diet and medical check-ups. Of course, this focus on elite sport costs millions of kroner a year and is financed by income from sponsors, and state gaming funds.

Olympiatoppen also pioneers research and development in, for example, high-jump training, ski-sole and waxing projects, and equipment improvements.

### Combating Cheating

Before drugs testing was introduced in athletics, the only check that was required was a gender test. I received a certificate, which I had to show at all international competitions, to verify that I was a woman. I was called in for a drugs test for the first time after winning the bronze medal in the 3,000-metre race at the European Championships in Prague in 1978. It was quite usual then for medal winners to be tested.

Among the commonest and best-known drugs at that time were anabolic steroids, synthetic male hormones that increase strength and endurance. The drug is normally associated with bodybuilders and people out to increase their muscle mass, but in small quantities it can also help to improve endurance, speed up recovery from injury and reduce body fat; users can also train more, as they recover faster. As a track athlete in the 1,500- and 3,000-metre class, I saw some of my keenest competitors caught out for using anabolic steroids. The list of banned substances now runs to several pages.

I well remember the many rumours about substance abuse among female athletes that were rife at the Olympics in Montreal in 1976. At the time they were largely linked to eastern European athletes, but now it no longer matters which country you come from – Norwegian athletes have been discovered cheating too. Today we have to acknowledge that drug use is a serious problem everywhere.

Norway was the first country to introduce testing outside competitions. I remember being called in while I was training, to give a urine sample. In those days we were given several days' warning, but nowadays athletes risk unannounced tests at any time, up to several times a year. Norway was a driving force behind the establishment in 1999 of the World Anti-Doping Agency (WADA), a kind of trans-frontier 'drugs police'.

**Trine Hattestad**, Olympic javelin champion, 2000, is one of Norway's many eminent women athletes.

### From Kitchen Sink to Sports Stadium

Women in sport have generally had to put up with poorer facilities and long received less media recognition than men. In the latter half of the 1960s, however, Norway boasted a world-class women's cross-country ski team which, in 1968, brought home an Olympic gold medal won in a relay race. This led to a higher level of recruitment in women's cross-country skiing and greater interest in women's sporting events.

As a female athlete, I faced obstacles and ran into difficulties from the outset. My first problem was that the club I wished to join did not accept female members. In my experience, the organized sports world was seen as a male domain until the 1970s. For this reason women encountered considerable resistance when they wanted to run longer distances or start playing football; it was men who set the parameters for women's sport. Long-distance running for women is a good example of this.

In 1928 the International Olympic Committee dropped the 800-metre race from its programme, as several runners collapsed after crossing the finishing line, and thirty-two years were to pass before the race was again included in the Olympic programme. A further twenty-four years were to elapse before women were given the opportunity to run distances of more than 1,500 metres in the Olympics. I was personally engaged in this historic event in the history of women's sport when I ran the marathon in Los Angeles in 1984.

Norway has faced the same problems as other western countries in terms of equality in sport. When I started to be successful as a runner, conditions for men and women were far from equal. Major international meets at Oslo's Bislett stadium featured very few events for women. And, in relative terms, to gain equal recognition from the press and public, female competitors had to be much better than their male counterparts. Only when I made my international breakthrough did I receive appropriate coverage in the press.

Until the late 1970s, I had the impression that women's athletics was basically seen as 'entertainment' at men's meets. But towards the end of the decade we were given a helping hand by the general equal rights campaign, which lobbied for equal terms and conditions for men and women. Feminists demanded, among other things, that women should be allowed to run in the traditional Holmenkollen relay. In the wake of this struggle, longer distances were introduced in running, skiing and skating. All this happened around the time that I was making significant progress as an athlete, including winning the bronze in the 1,500-metre race at the European Championships in Rome in 1974.

I have always seen myself first and foremost as an athlete, not as a female athlete. Nonetheless, I do think that my career has contributed to greater equality for women. An illustration of the development in women's sport that gives me enormous pleasure is the growing number of women who participate in the annual Grete Waitz Run. In 1983 I took the initiative to organize a race for women only through the streets of Oslo. Participation in this race has since rocketed, with an all-time high of 48,000 entrants.

**A time-honoured** international event, the annual Holmenkollen Ski Meet always attracts thousands of spectators.

### Skiing – Norway's Gift to the World

*Skiing is the most national of all Norwegian sports, and a wonderful sport it is. If anything deserves to be called the sport of sports, it is in truth skiing.*

These are the words of the renowned polar explorer and scientist Fridtjof Nansen. His 1888 crossing of the Greenland icecap, in conjunction with Roald Amundsen's conquest of the South Pole in 1910–12, proved to the world that skis were, first and foremost, a valuable means of travel.

All the same, skiing as a sport has long traditions in Norway. In Old Norse mythology, the winter god Ull was 'so good that no one could compete with him' and the goddess of skiing, Skade, 'had mastered the art of running on skis and shooting with a bow'.

The legendary Viking kings who ruled between 900 and 1100 – Håkon the Good, Olav Tryggvason, Harald Hardråde, Sigurd Jorsalfar ('The Crusader') and his brother, Øystein – are all portrayed as extremely good skiers.

The oldest skis found in Scandinavia were discovered in Sweden and are 4,500 years old. Skis were used to get about on, not least when hunting and in battle. It was said of the Sámi in the early 900s that they 'were so nimble on skis that no beast could outrun them'. There are reports of skis being used in battles from the ninth century, when the Sámi defeated the Norwegians on skis, until the thirteenth century. In the seventeenth and eighteenth centuries skis acquired greater military significance with the establishment of specialist ski troops. Competitions were organized in which contestants had to fire at a target while on the move, weave their way downhill through trees, or ski down slopes and on the flat; as a prize, the winners received cash prizes.

By the mid-1800s, skiing competitions were being organized for the civilian population. In 1843, ski-jumping competitions were held in Tromsø, but it was not until 1860 that things really started to move. At the time there were no set standards for competitions – runs often involved just a few turns and jumps. Skiers from Telemark dominated competitions in the vicinity of the capital, and their skills, technique and equipment were therefore used to set standards for everyone participating in competitions. Sondre Norheim (1825–97) from Morgedal in Telemark was a leading pioneer, and Morgedal is often referred to as 'the cradle of skiing'.

Skis were originally thick, wide and heavy and up to three or four metres in length. One ski was often longer than the other to improve gliding, while the shorter ski, which was leather-bound, was used to steer with. Skis were attached to the feet by toe-straps; only one pole was used, for balance and thrusting forward. As skis and equipment were made in villages and rural areas, they varied widely. Telemark skis, which gradually became the national norm, were the same length and shaped, being widest

**In 1869 Knud Bergslien** painted this picture of the infant prince Håkon Håkonssøn being borne to safety across the mountains from Lillehammer to Rena. To commemorate this historic event, a ski race, Birkebeinerrennet, is held annually in the same region.

at the shovel, narrowest at the waist and a little wider at the tail. This, combined with a heel binding, meant that they were better suited to turning and jumping. In the 1890s, an even better and more stable metal binding was introduced.

As has been said, regulations for ski competitions were not very well developed. Requirements often included the ability to jump, turn, go uphill and ski cross-country. Specialization in different skiing disciplines did not really come in until the 1880s. Around this time, people also started to use two poles and special cross-country skis were developed. In 1888, a 50-km ski race was organized in conjunction with a jumping competition (Husebyrennet). It was won by Torjus Hemmestveit from Telemark, who later went on to pioneer skiing in the USA.

From 1879 onwards, until it was superseded in 1892 by the annual ski-jumping contest held nearer the capital at Holmenkollen, Husebyrennet was Norway's principal skiing competition. It was at this period that skiing really developed as a sport and spread to many other parts of the world. Not without reason, it has been claimed that skiing is Norway's gift to the world. Skis did not exist in central Europe or America until they were 'introduced' by Scandinavians. Even the word *ski* is derived from the Old Norse word 'skid', which means a split length of wood. *Slalom* is from the same source and means tracks through even, sloping terrain. Turns on the outer ski and landings from jumps are called Telemark turns and Telemark landings, while a turn on the inner ski, a classic alpine turn, pays tribute to Oslo's former name and is known as a Christiania or Christie.

When Norwegians emigrated, they took their skis with them and pioneered the sport in many countries. 'Snowshoe' Thompson was a legendary figure in the 1850s who carried the mail across the Sierra Nevada in winter to the mining communities of California. His real name was Jon Torstein Rui and he originally came from Telemark. For fifteen years he carried mailbags weighing 30-40 kilos across the mountains. He made his own skis and never took with him a sleeping-bag, weapon, map or compass. A statue in memory of 'Snowshoe' stands in Genoa, Nevada. Other skiing pioneers include the brothers Torjus and Mikkel Hemmestveit in the Midwest and, later, Olav Engen in Utah.

Norwegian students were often great ski ambassadors in central Europe. Skiing was introduced into Austria and Switzerland, and competitions held there, as early as the 1880s and '90s.

**This depiction of a skier,** found on the island of Rodøy, Nordland, is proof that the history of skiing extends more than 4,000 years into the past.

In the course of the twentieth century, skiing as a sport spread to many countries and developed rapidly. Norwegians and other nationals contributed to the changes. In fact, Norwegian traditions may at times have even been an obstacle to progress, as is illustrated by Norway's initial scepticism towards plastic skis, pursuit starts and the skating technique.

Today, the sport is divided into different disciplines and specialized to an incredible extent. Some years ago the V-style was introduced into ski jumping and competitors of both sexes now jump well beyond the 200-metre mark. These days, everyone uses the skating technique in cross-country and biathlon events, as it is much faster than the diagonal stride. Mass starts, pursuit races and sprints have all made competitions more media- and spectator-friendly. Wooden skis have been replaced by plastic skis and waxing has become a science. Skiers used to wax their own skis, but elite-class skiers now have a waxing team and a dozen pairs of skis at their disposal. Alpine events now include slalom, giant slalom, Super G, downhill, telemarking, off piste and freestyle. Biathlon events have attracted more attention and snowboarding, which is different from skiing though there are some similarities, has become a popular alternative for many young people.

People often say that Norwegians are born with skis on their feet, but this is, to put it mildly, an exaggeration: after all, I was three before I learned to ski. But like many Norwegians, I am still a keen skier. Skiing has been a popular sport in Norway since the start of the last century, even for those living in towns, not least the capital. If you consider that women have generally

**Norway's Crown Prince Haakon** lights the Olympic flame at the opening of the XVII Winter Games in Lillehammer in 1994.

engaged in this activity too, you may safely say that skiing has been a national sport for over one hundred years.

### Winter Olympics in Norway

The Winter Olympics in Oslo in 1952 were a great success – not only in terms of sport, but also in terms of the event as a whole. It was the first time the Winter Olympics had been held in a large town where the local population was genuinely interested. In the course of four days, over 93,000 spectators packed Bislett Stadium in Oslo, where the skating events took place, and as many as 23,000 people watched the women's figure skating.

The ski jumping and cross-country events were held at the Holmenkollen arena, and on the last day some 130,000 spectators made their way up to the jump to cheer their compatriots on to victory. No less impressive was the fact that 23,000 people bought tickets to see participants in the 50-km cross-country ski race start, only to vanish from sight in the woods and reappear at the finishing line some three hours later.

Having taken part in several Olympic Games myself, I find it interesting that such a major competition could be organized without any advertising or sponsors and with non-existent security. It was also the first time that nearly 1,000 contestants were housed together in a so-called Olympic village; the press were accommodated in a hotel specially built for the purpose. Another innovation was Norway's first artificial ice rink, Jordal Amfi, where the ice-hockey matches were played.

Norway emerged as the best nation, so the Games were a huge success also in terms of sport. And with a total of more than 530,000 paying spectators, they returned a healthy profit.

Another forty-two years were to pass before Norway would once again host the Winter Olympics. The Games in Lillehammer in 1994 were on a completely different scale from those held in Oslo. The host town may have been very small by international standards, with only 25,000 inhabitants, but the fact that there were nearly 2,000 participants in 61 disciplines and 8,000 media representatives present indicates how much sport and people's interest in sport had expanded, and demonstrates the revolution that has taken place in arena construction and technology, not least, in new media.

I may as well say it straight out: the Norwegian people and I were, and indeed still are, extremely proud of the Winter Olympics in Lillehammer. And we hope that IOC President Juan Antonio Samaranch was not just being polite at the closing ceremony when he said that the Lillehammer Games were the best in the history of the Olympics. The joy and satisfaction derived from the Games was, of course, enhanced by Norway's amazing achievements, which included beating Russia to become the best nation with no fewer than ten gold medals.

But the biggest winner at Lillehammer was the public – and I do not mean the two billion people throughout the world who watched the Games on television. No, I want to pay tribute to the 1.2 million who bought tickets and cheered participants on so enthusiastically at outdoor events in temperatures of between 10 and 30 degrees below zero. The ski jumping attracted 120,000 spectators and 110,000 people went to watch the men's cross-country relay. In considering attendance figures it is important to bear in mind how few people actually live in

**The Olympic Winter Games** held in Oslo in 1952 were an outstanding success.

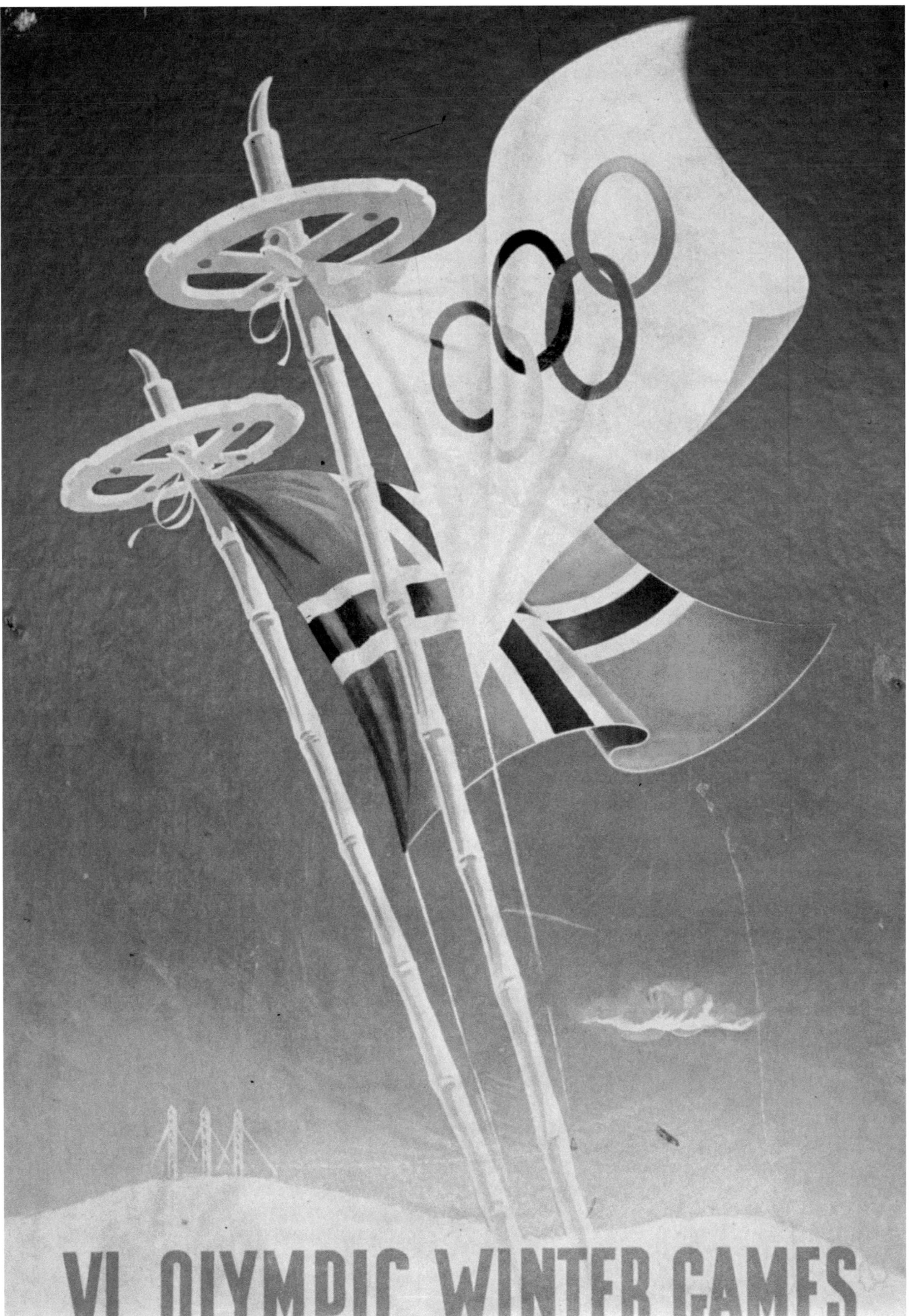
VI OLYMPIC WINTER GAMES
14.-25. FEBRUARY OSLO NORWAY 1952

the Lillehammer area. It may have been very cold, but we were extremely fortunate with the weather – two weeks of brilliant sunshine and blue skies was more than even the greatest optimist could have hoped for.

Needless to say, before the Games voices were raised questioning whether it was right of the Norwegian government to expend so much public money – NOK 11–12 billion – on a sports event. But this has barely been mentioned since and now, ten years on, I still meet people from other countries who remember the fantastic Games in Lillehammer and, not least, the enthusiastic crowds.

## SPECIAL NORWEGIAN SPORTS EVENTS

### The Norway Cup

This football tournament, the world's largest and Norway's biggest sports event, encompasess scores of football matches in and around Oslo over the course of several days and attracts 27,000 boys and girls from 40 countries. Girls have been allowed to participate in the tournament since it started in 1972, and 30 per cent of the players are now girls, which shows just how popular women's football has become. The tournament can therefore take much of the credit for the strong position of women's football in Norway today. The Norway Cup has also been dubbed the 'Colourful Community', as from the outset the organizers have invited teams from Third World countries to participate. In fact, the tournament was awarded the Young People's Peace Price and UNICEF's special prize for this very reason. The Norway Cup is a media event on a par with other major international championships. Over 600 journalists, photographers and TV people were accredited to it in 2003.

### Skarverennet

Every year, thousands of dedicated skiers set off on the 'last ski race of the season' along Hallingskarvet, a mountain ridge between Oslo and Bergen. The course, from Finse to Ustaoset, is 'only' 36 km long and within the capacity of most fit people. It is a popular race, attracting between 10,000 and 12,000 participants each year, nearly half of them women.

### Inga-Låmi

According to the sagas, Inga from Varteig was the mother of Håkon Håkonsson, the heir to the throne, who as a child was borne across the mountains between Lillehammer and Østerdalen on skis in January 1206. The Inga-Låmi ski race, which is for women only, is held annually in her honour; it was established in 1993 as an alternative to the Birkebeiner, which many women find too challenging. The event has been a great success from the outset, some 5,000 women making their way to Lillehammer each year to take part in either the 15- or 30-km race. Cultural events are also staged in the town, making it a great weekend for women.

### Ridderrennet

This, Norway's most famous cross-country race for the handicapped, was first held in 1964. It has gradually evolved into an international sports week at Beitostølen that draws some 500 contestants each year. The event was originally only for the blind or partially sighted, but now other disabled people can participate. Entrants come from all grades of sport, from the untrained to the elite.

**No one can fail** to be impressed by the enthusiasm and proficiency of contestants in Ridderrennet, an annual competition for the handicapped held at Beitostølen. Seen in action here is Harald Guldahl, winner of a gold medal in the Giant Slalom.

### Birkebeinerrennet

Like the Inga-Låmi race, Birkebeinerrennet is based on the story of Håkon, the infant Crown Prince who, in 1206 was carried across the mountains between Lillehammer and Rena to escape the King's enemies. Two loyal Birkebeiners, Torstein Skjevla and Skjervald Skrukka, needed all their stamina and strength to save the future king and bring him to safety. The first Birkebeiner race, as we know it today, was held in 1932 and contestants had to carry a rucksack weighing 3.5 kg, the weight of the Crown Prince. Although initially only men participated in this gruelling 54-km race, women now make up 10 per cent of entrants. In 2004, nearly 10,000 skiers completed the course.

### Birkebeinerrittet

Although it does not have such a long history as the original Birkebeiner ski race, with its well over 10,000 participants, this mountain-bike race, first held in 1993, is now the biggest such race in the world. Participants have to cycle both off-road and on unmade roads. It does not follow quite the same route as the ski race, but both races start in Rena and finish in Lillehammer. The race is open to both men and women, but as with the ski race, women account for only marginally more than 10 per cent of the participants. As elsewhere in Europe, mountain biking is a fast-growing sport in Norway.

### Den Store Styrkeprøven

This cycle race runs from Trondheim to Oslo and is the world's longest single-leg race. Keen cyclists, be they keep-fit enthusiasts or professionals, have set out on the close to 600-km ride every year since 1967. Contestants ride racing or mountain bikes. Unsurprisingly, nearly all (95 per cent) of the 2,000 who take part are men.

### Holmenkollstafetten

This is the biggest athletics event in Norway and attracts thousands of runners, both men and women, from all over the country. A relay race based on a Swedish model, it was first run in 1923; then, as now, it started from Oslo's Bislett Stadium. The event attracted Norwegian athletes at all levels. In 1928 the number of legs was increased from ten to fifteen. Although women were eventually allowed to take part in athletic events, they were still excluded from Holmenkollstafetten. In 1975 the organizers were more or less forced to open the event for women, and within a few years the women's class had become an important category in the race. I have had the pleasure of taking part in this great race myself, and my club has several times won the women's class. From its inception, Holmenkollstafetten has been open to both serious athletes and the general public; today there are a number of different classes, such as elite, keep-fit, corporate, junior and military.

## KINGS OF SPORT

In Norway it is usual to designate a sports personality who is a leader in his or her field as a king or queen. We have thus had 'ski kings', 'skating kings', 'running queens' and 'skiing queens', and those accorded this accolade are, of course, held in high esteem by the public. But the appellation 'king of sport' can also be applied to some of the great Viking kings, as well as to the three 'modern' kings who have occupied Norway's throne since independence in 1905.

A thousand years ago, for example, Snorri Sturluson, chronicler of the sagas, described King Olav Tryggvason as 'the greatest master of all sports' – he was expert at skiing, running, swimming, archery, fencing (with both hands) and throwing two javelins at once.

King Haakon VII (1872–1957) and Queen Maud were of Danish and British extraction respectively. Shortly after taking up residence in Norway they were photographed on skis, which, of course, immediately won the hearts of the Norwegian people. In 1906, only a year after their arrival, they both attended the Holmenkollen ski festival. Throughout his reign, King Haakon followed Norwegian sport with keen interest. He was an attentive spectator at many sporting events and presented a cup, the King's Cup, to be awarded to the winners of a number of Norwegian championships.

King Olav V (1903–91) was an enthusiastic skier from an early age. But it was ski jumping that was closest to his heart, and he once took fourth place in the Norwegian Junior Championships. Norwegians are extremely proud of his having jumped at our national ski jump, Holmenkollbakken. He enjoyed other sports too, but sailing was undoubtedly his greatest passion. A highly proficient yachtsman, in 1928 he won an Olympic gold medal. King Olav remained interested in sports all his life. Each year he would attend many sports events and he was very knowledgeable, as I discovered for myself when he presented me with the St Olav medal in 1981. The audience was only supposed to last for fifteen minutes, but in the event we talked about sport for over half an hour.

**Taken in 1907,** this photograph of Norway's newly adopted Royal Family shows how quickly they took to the national sport of skiing. The little boy in the lead subsequently ascended the throne as King Olav V.

Our present king, Harald V (1937–), has inherited his father's interest in sport. Sailing is his first choice, as it was his father's. He has won several World Championships and more than once competed in the Olympic Games. He has also made his mark in the administrative side of sport, among other things as president of the Norwegian Sailing Federation. He was honorary president of the Lillehammer Olympic Organizing Committee and did much to ensure that Norway won its bid for the 1994 Winter Olympics. As a fellow member of the Committee, I was privileged to observe his dedication at close hand.

## OUTSTANDING ATHLETES

Norway has nurtured many great sportsmen and -women over the years, so it is no easy task to decide who to include and who not. Some people are sure to disagree with the names I have chosen, as many have had to be left out. We have numerous world record holders and Olympic champions deserving of a mention, but as space is limited I have decided to focus on men and women who have been pioneers in their sport and whose achievements are recognized abroad as well as at home.

**Mons Monsen Øyri** (1795–1843) from Leikanger in Sogn, one of Norway's more unconventional sporting heroes, was better known as the champion runner **Mensen Ernst**. This former sailor became a courier for some of Europe's royal houses and noble families, walking and running over a large part of Europe. In those days physical prowess in the shape of speed and stamina was valued very highly, and those who achieved fame were viewed as both athletes and entertainers. Mensen Ernst was famous all over Europe for his incredible long-distance runs, in one of which, in 1832, he covered the distance from Paris to Moscow in 14 days. His greatest achievement, however, must be his 8,600-km Constantinople-Calcutta-Constantinople run, which he completed in only 59 days.

As a winter nation, it is natural that Norway should have fostered many great skiers and skaters. There are plenty of ski and skating 'kings' and 'queens' to choose from, but in skating I have elected to concentrate on the following:

**Oscar Mathisen** (1888–1954) held all the world speed-skating records in the course of his career. His best time for the

**The holder of countless medals,** speed-skating ace Oscar Mathisen rounded off his career by turning professional.

**Birger Ruud** displays the classic 'Kongsberg style' to perfection at Holmenkollen in 1947.

1,500 metres (2.17.4) remained a world record for 23 years! He turned professional in 1916, attracting thousands of spectators whenever he competed. Not surprisingly, Oscar Mathisen was the great sporting hero of his day.

His successor was **Ivar Ballangrud** (1904–69), undisputed skating king of the 1930s. He won four Olympic gold medals and was four times world champion.

**Sonja Henie** (1912–69), the figure skater, was undoubtedly Norway's greatest sports star ever, winning as she did the Olympics in 1928, 1932 and 1936 and holding ten world championship titles. Following her sporting career, from 1937 on, thanks to her touring ice shows and many films, she became internationally known and loved as a queen of the ice. She and her husband, Niels Onstad, a shipowner, donated their valuable art collection and considerable sums of money to the Henie-Onstad Art Centre on the western outskirts of Oslo.

**Hjalmar Andersen** (b. 1923), who is affectionately known as 'Hjallis', was extremely popular and maintained his popularity long after he gave up skating. 'King Happy', as he was called, won three gold medals for speed skating at the Olympic Games in Oslo in 1952. He was also three times world champion (1950, 1951, 1952).

From the ranks of successful speed skaters in more recent times, it is natural to make mention of **Johann Olav Koss** (b. 1968). In the course of his brief career, the Winter Olympics at Lillehammer in 1994 were undeniably the high point. Few people will ever forget his three gold medals and world record series. Following his skating career, Koss has gone on to do a lot of humanitarian work, in particular in connection with the 'Right to Play' movement.

It would be difficult to find a more all-round sportswoman than **Laila Schou Nilsen** (1919–98). In a class of her own in a number of disciplines, she was in many ways ahead of her time. In the 1930s and '40s scant attention was paid to women's sport, but Laila Schou Nilsen's accomplishments were always spoken of with respect. She broke several world speed-skating records and at the 1936 Olympics took bronze in the downhill event. On a national level, she won 73 individual championships in tennis and played in the national handball team. She also made her mark in motor racing, participating more than once in the Monte Carlo Rally. She was a truly outstanding sportswoman.

No list of our pre-eminent skiers would be complete without **Birger Ruud** (1911–98). A member of a great sporting family, he was a world-champion ski jumper, as were his two brothers. Only Birger, however, was also an Olympic champion (1932 and 1936); what is more, he was a top-ranking alpine skier too – though many people probably remember Birger and his brothers better for what can only be described as their ski acrobatics. He was equally famous in central Europe, where he was a great ambassador for Nordic skiing. His career could have been more illustrious still had it not been interrupted by the Second World War. Birger himself considered his greatest achievement to have been his winning, at the age of 37, of the silver medal at the 1948 Olympics.

The expression 'to jump after Wirkola' has entered the Norwegian language to mean that it is not easy to follow up a great performance. **Bjørn Wirkola** (b. 1943) began his career as a combination skier and ended it in 1966 as a double ski-jumping champion. He dominated international ski jumping in the mid-1960s and was the first person to win both jumping events (large and small hills) in the World Championships or Olympic Games. Following his success as a ski jumper, he went on to become a football player, helping his club, Rosenborg, to win the Norwegian Championship.

From its infancy, alpine skiing has been dominated by the central Europeans. But there was one exception, Norway's **Stein Eriksen** (b. 1927), who caused a sensation when he won Olympic gold and silver medals at home in 1952. Two years later he became world champion in slalom, giant slalom and combined slalom/downhill. Stein Eriksen was an expert in technique and introduced several stylistic improvements. Following his success in the World Championships, he emigrated to America, where he became a professional skier and instructor. He has contributed to the spread of alpine sports in the US, where he is still a well-known personality in skiing circles.

For many years alpine skiing was not accorded the same priority in Norway as were cross-country skiing and ski jumping. As part of the focus on elite sports following the Olympic Games in Sarajevo, work began on the development of a strong alpine tradition. **Ole Kristian Furuseth** (b. 1967) proved that it was possible to achieve success when he won the Giant Slalom Cup in 1989 and came second overall in the World Cup in 1990.

**Kjetil André Aamodt** (b. 1971) took up where Furuseth left off and dominated alpine skiing in the 1990s. He won his first Olympic gold in 1992, following up with two more golds in Salt Lake City in 2002. In between he won a number of World Championships. He holds no fewer than 19 Olympic and World Championship medals, making him the current holder of most alpine titles. An exceptional all-rounder, he has also won gold medals in Super-G and combined downhill/slalom.

**Lasse Kjus** (b. 1971) won the gold in combined slalom/downhill in Lillehammer in 1994. Four years later he won a silver medal at the Nagano Winter Olympics. Kjus' strongest discipline is downhill skiing, in which he won silver medals in 1998 and 2002. His greatest achievement was, however, his winning of medals in all five disciplines in the World Championships in Vail in 1999; with two gold and three silver medals, he was crowned 'King of the Rockies'. Altogether he has 16 championship medals and many victories in World Cup competitions to his credit. Kjus and Aamodt have paved the way for a number of outstanding young Norwegian alpine skiers, all of whom have helped make Norway a leading country in alpine skiing.

Cross-country skiing has always occupied first place in Norway. At the first Winter Olympics in Chamonix in 1924, Norwegians won a host of medals in skiing. Since then, we have had many exceptional cross-country skiers, but I am sure most people will agree that the best of them all is **Bjørn Dæhlie** (b. 1967). Dæhlie totally dominated cross-country skiing in the 1990s and was voted top Winter Olympics sportsman of his day. No one can match his eight Olympic golds and four silvers – to which must be added nine gold, four silver and two bronze medals in the World Championships. He was a fantastic competitor who gave his all; it was not unusual for him to collapse from exhaustion on crossing the finishing line. He mastered the skating style and diagonal stride and was a top achiever in all distances from 10 km to 50 km.

When it comes to women I should like to mention **Bente Skari** (b. 1972), who was a leading figure in international women's cross-country skiing at the end of the 1990s and early in the present century. She won five Olympic medals, with the gold in the 10-km race in Salt Lake City as a high point. In addition to her Olympic medals she holds five gold medals from World Championships and has won more World Cup races than any other female skier – 44!

**Kjetil André Aamodt** goes airborne to win a gold medal at the Winter Olympics in Salt Lake City in 2002

**Top to bottom, from left:** Ole Kristian Furuseth, Stein Eriksen, Lasse Kjus, Hjalmar Andersen, Johann Olav Koss, Laila Schou Nilsen, Ole Einar Bjørndalen, Bjørn Wirkola, Liv Grete Skjelbreid Poirée.

**Top to bottom, from left:** Vebjørn Rodal, Knut Holmann, Jan Stenerud, Ingrid Kristiansen, Ole Gunnar Solskjær, Kirsten and Espen Salberg, Norway's women's football team, Petter Solberg, Norway's women's handball team.

The biathlon is a popular sport and makes excellent television entertainment, so interest only increased when **Ole Einar Bjørndalen** (b. 1974) made his breakthrough. A first-class cross-country skier, he is faster than most biathletes; he is also an excellent marksman. He won four gold medals in Salt Lake City, which made him the best-ever Norwegian sportsman in any one Olympic Games. He had earlier won medals for individual races and the relay at the World Championships and the Olympic gold in the 10-km event in 1998. As he is still competing, he is likely to add to his harvest of medals.

**Liv Grete Skjelbreid Poirée** (b. 1974) has made her name as biathlon queen. She won four medals in the 2001 World Championships, including a gold, and the silver in the 2002 Winter Olympics. Her greatest achievement to date was the winning of four gold medals in the 2004 World Championships after having had a baby the year before. Like Ole Einar Bjørndalen, she is set to continue competing and will doubtless bring home still more medals and titles.

In the 1990s snowboarding became a very popular winter sport with the young. One of those who helped to popularize the sport internationally was **Terje Håkonsen** (b. 1974). Having won European and World Championship titles in halfpipe, he has become a leading figure in this somewhat special milieu.

**Champion cross-country skier** Bjørn Dæhlie was always at his best when the chips were down.

No other sport commands as much attention in Norway as football. Matches are broadcast on TV and radio for hours on end, and football takes up page upon page in the press. It is questionable whether interest in the sport really is so great as to justify the wide coverage it gets, but there is no doubt that Norwegians do love to follow both their own and international matches. British football is very popular in Norway, and many Norwegians are eager supporters of British teams. But first let us take a look at American football.

When he was five, **Knute Rockne** (1888–1931) emigrated with his family from Voss to the USA, where thirty years later he became as famous as any other public figure of his day. He is looked upon as the father of modern American football. As a coach at Notre Dame University, he revolutionized American football. His team won many championships, earning him the nickname of 'the Wizard'. He also fostered more All- American players than anyone else of his generation. The name of Knute Rockne, that short, bald Norwegian, is still highly revered in American football circles.

**Jan Stenerud** (b. 1942) is also legendary, being credited with transforming the art of kicking in professional American football. He played for several teams in the elite series over the course of nineteen years. Interestingly, Stenerud was originally awarded a ski scholarship to go to the USA from Fetsund, but he eventually dropped all thought of a ski career when his talent for kicking earned him a place in the university team in Montana.

On this side of the Atlantic, the Berlin Olympics in 1936 marked the first international breakthrough for Norway's national football team. Known as the **'Bronze Team'**, it beat Germany 2–0 in the quarter-finals. This particular match is remembered more than the bronze match itself, in which Norway beat Poland 3–2, the reason probably being that in the grandstand, confidently expecting Germany to wipe the floor with little Norway, was Adolf Hitler, surrounded by his satraps.

In more recent times Norway has twice – in the 1994 and 1998 World Championships – fought its way through to the finals. Our 1998 victory over Brazil was one of our greatest achievements. Another great moment was when we beat England in the World Cup qualifier in 1981.

Many Norwegian football players play professional football abroad. Norwegian players have achieved success in the UK, in particular, but there are also Norwegian players in such major football nations as Germany and Italy. As far back as the 1950s, **Per Bredesen** (b. 1930) was a famous player in Italian football and **Rune Bratseth** (b. 1961) was a major star in Germany in the 1990s. The most highly profiled Norwegian players abroad today are **Ole Gunnar Solskjær** (b. 1973), **Tore André Flo** (b. 1973), **John Arne Riise** (b. 1980) and **John Carew** (b. 1979).

And as we are talking about leading sportsmen and women who have been pioneers in their field, we have to mention our **football girls**. They have fought hard to be accepted by the Norwegian public. To begin with nobody took them seriously, neither sports journalists nor coaches (men's), and they were laughed at. Lots of people thought that only boys could play football. The road from the 1970s, when the first women's football match took place, to the present day has been long and arduous. Today, however, football is the biggest sport for girls in Norway and the Football Federation has over 100,000 female members. What is more, the popularity of women's football continues to grow. In the run-up to the Sydney Olympics, the Norwegian women's football team played the USA, with around 15,000 spectators in the stands. After winning a silver medal in their first World Championship in 1991, the team was honoured with the 'Name of the Year' title in Norway. As a result of this well-earned token of public recognition, women's football has gone from strength to strength and now receives much more attention than in the past. The biggest breakthrough came in 1995, when Norway beat the United States to win the World Championships. The following year, the girls took the bronze at the Olympic Games in Atlanta, and four years later went on to win the gold in Sydney.

I think the **women's handball team** also deserves a place among our outstanding sportsmen and -women. Handball has been a popular sport for girls in Norway for many years. I played it myself, long before I started to concentrate on running. But as with so many other sports at the time, male players got all the attention. Not until the mid-1970s was it decided that there should be equal investment in women's handball. More women were then given better training, with the result that in 1986 they made their first breakthrough with a bronze in the World Championships. After winning the silver medal at the Seoul Olympic Games in 1988, the women's handball team had all Norway behind them. With new sports personalities as role models, young girls flocked to the clubs and handball is now a highly popular sport for girls.

In the 1990s, the women's handball team won several medals in international competitions, putting the Norwegian men's handball team in the shade. After winning a gold medal in the European Championships in 1998, expectations were high for the World Championships in Norway the following year. Whether their winning the gold in the European Championships gave them the confidence they needed, I would not like to say, but the fact remains that their performance in the final was unparalleled.

Norwegians, men and women alike, have made their mark in other areas of sports too. In motor racing, I must mention rally driver **Petter Solberg** (1974–), who in recent years has earned himself a place among the world's top drivers. Norway also has some major international stars in ballroom dancing, a pursuit affiliated to the Norwegian Confederation of Sports. **Kirsten and Espen Salberg** (1947– and 1952–) were pioneers in the 1970s and '80s, winning the gold in both the European and World Championships as amateur and professional dancers. Norway has also harvested many gold medals in such Olympic events as boxing, wrestling, throwing the javelin, shooting, weightlifting and cycling – and, not least, rowing and canoeing.

We have a history of big names in athletics, but in conclusion I must say that it was a very special occasion indeed when **Ingrid Kristiansen** (1956–) and I found ourselves among the world elite at the same time. I started my international career before Ingrid, and in the time that I was at the top I was five times world champion in cross-country running and won the gold in the marathon at the World Championships and silver in the Olympics. However, what I am best remembered for is winning the New York Marathon nine times and for being the first woman to run the distance in less than 2 hours 30 minutes, which I did in 1979. Like me, Ingrid has several times been world champion and has set the world record for the 5,000- and 10,000-metres, as well as for the marathon.

**Snowboarder** Terje Håkonsen in action.

**january** fin serck-hanssen **february** rolf m. aagaard

**march** herdis maria siegert **april** janne solgaard

**may** jens hauge **june** vibeke tandberg

**july** dag alveng **august** rune johansen

**september** knut bry **october** asle svarverud

**november** ingvar moi **december** per berntsen

# SONJA HENIE

There are many who forcibly assert that Sonja Henie was the first female athlete in history. Until she proved otherwise, sport for women was largely viewed as a diversion from the daily round, some doctors even claiming that women could be become physically and spiritually deformed by engaging in it. Understandably, no woman dared entertain serious hopes of a career in sport – not, that is, until little Sonja Henie came along to sweep the board at international figure-skating events between the wars and in so doing blaze the trail for all women's sports.

Six thousand Norwegians turned out to welcome their 'Skating Princess' at Oslo's main railway station when, aged only fifteen, Sonja returned from the 1928 Olympics in St Moritz with the gold medal she had won in the only event open to women. Behind her, peacock proud, stood her father. Sonja was Daddy's little girl if ever there was one. A well-to-do furrier who in his youth had been a world champion track-cyclist, he more or less dedicated his life to encouraging his daughter's talent. Even as a seven-year-old Sonja was obsessed with skating. She also played football, practised ski jumping and beat up boys older than herself. She was the apple of her father's eye, and he used to reward her with a little something whenever she won a competition – which was often. Her elder brother was pale and ungainly, so Sonja became the child prodigy whose medals and trophies were displayed in her father's shop window. Father and daughter were very much alike: their handwriting, for example, was so similar that the father often signed his daughter's autographs to enable her to devote all her time and energy to skating practice.

Sonja was nine when she gave her first public skating display. Two years later, in 1924, she was parading through the Olympic village in Chamonix. The organizers of the Games had wanted to bar her, but her father fought for his daughter and won; in the event, Sonja came last. 'Child prodigies like that never come to anything,' declared the winner of the gold, which goes to show how wrong an Olympian can be. From 1928 onwards Sonja Henie won all there was to be won in figure skating. She was world champion on ten consecutive occasions and three times in succession Olympic figure-skating champion. She will always be the reigning prima ballerina of the ice.

Sonja Henie was once described as the Pavlova of the ice: she turned figure skating into ice ballet and developed a technique so consummate as to be invisible. She was in a class of her own, though this was due in part to her having trained harder than her competitors. Training was not the norm in those days, being regarded as something of an American fad. Sonja trained so intensively and so often that it interfered with her schooling; in effect, she never enjoyed a proper child-

hood. The unparalleled grace she displayed on the ice was not infrequently in contrast to her conduct off the rink. For one thing, she was in the habit of swearing, both vehemently and often. She once made the mistake of referring to Britain's Prince of Wales as 'damned cute'. Many were surprised at how such a demure little girl could behave like a hoyden.

'Bunny', as she was called, did more than win medals and prestige; she also won the heart of the public. In Copenhagen, a display she gave drew 50,000 spectators, and in Gothenburg 35,000 people paid to see her. She was almost trampled underfoot by fans and had to have a police escort. Despite her having trained and performed to the level of an athlete, a condescending press could still say things like, 'this little enchantress executes some neat flourishes'. Her costumes, several of which she designed herself, often occasioned as much comment as her performances. It is clear that she was never taken really seriously as an athlete, though her fame knew no bounds. It is quite conceivable that no other Norwegian has ever achieved such international renown. In 1935 an American newspaper asserted that she was the third most popular person in the world, surpassed only by Charlie Chaplin and the Prince of Wales.

Regrettably, she also won the heart of Adolf Hitler. At the start of the free-skating event at the 1936 Olympic Games, which were held in Berlin, Sonja stood to attention and gave the Nazi salute. A photograph of her greeting a smiling Führer went round the world. It transpired that she had paid Hitler a visit on the eve of the Games and that he had phoned to wish her luck just before the competition. The Führer presented her with a self-portrait, complete with dedication, which Sonja ordered should hang in her palatial home on the western outskirts of Oslo during the Occupation, with the result that the house was left alone by the occupying forces.

In Berlin she was accused of breaching the amateur rules. As a result, instead of returning to Norway with her compatriots, at the age of twenty-four she simply dropped out of competitive skating and took up residence in America, there to make a career for herself in films. She was immediately given one of Hollywood's most lucrative contracts, earning as much as Marlene Dietrich. Her teeth were polished and capped, her nose reshaped, her face lifted and her hair ruined by bleaching, which was why, from the age of twenty-six, she always wore a wig. Her employers, Twentieth-Century Fox, built an ice rink especially for her. Sonja's films were released in rapid succession and were smash box-office hits, albeit less so with the passage of time. At the height of her career she received more fanmail than Shirley Temple. It has often been said that it was Sonja Henie who taught Americans to skate. From 1940 onwards she lived in Beverly Hills and was formally regarded as an American citizen. She was pictured arm in arm with Edith Piaf, Judy Garland and Ginger Rogers, but few people took her seriously as an actress.

After the war Sonja Henie donated what was in those days the large sum of two million kroner to

*Norgeshjelpen* (Norwegian Relief Fund), but the picture of her with Hitler was etched in the minds of her fellow countrymen. It was felt that she should have done more than she did to help her homeland, with the result that in the immediate postwar years Sonja Henie was largely a *persona non grata* in Norway. She received no invitation to attend the Winter Olympics when they were held in Oslo in 1952, but the following year she performed in Norway for the first time in eighteen years. Four hundred thousand tickets were sold for the thirty-three ice shows she put on in the city of her birth – an impressive turnout, given that at the time the population of Oslo was only 300,000. There were also long queues that same year to buy her newly published autobiography, *Wings On My Feet*. There was probably still some residual bitterness at her having left her own country to become an American. 'I wouldn't have had the opportunity to develop in Norway,' she said.

Following her father's death in 1937 Sonja showed that she had also inherited his business acumen. The Oslo newspaper *Dagbladet* proclaimed her the world's most astute businesswoman. With her film career on the wane, Sonja toured the world with her spectacular ice shows, spin-offs from which included Sonja skates, Sonja dolls and Sonja dresses. The latter half of her life was spent in unimaginable luxury; she was so weighed down with diamonds and other jewels that she described herself as looking like a Christmas tree. One marriage after another ended on the rocks. One husband introduced Sonja to an evening whisky-and-soda, a habit that eventually led to alcoholism. When she stumbled and fell at an ice show in Rio, the state she was in was clear to all. She was too drunk to complete her act and this was to be her last show. Twenty years of performing in ice spectaculars were at an end.

In 1960 Sonja Henie was believed to be one of the world's wealthiest women. She owned skyscrapers in Chicago, fifty kilograms of jewels, a ranch in California, several luxurious homes, a chain of sports stadiums and one hundred and sixty valuable paintings.

However her story is also a story of the cold and loneliness that so often accompany fame. It was as though the ice she had reigned over for so many years was now exacting revenge and engulfing its former mistress. Sonja was increasingly seen shivering in her father's cast-off fur coats. Towards the end of her life she even broke all ties with her mother and brother, which resulted in a harrowing court case. At forty-four she married a Norwegian shipowner, Niels Onstad. They were both keen art lovers and together owned the most valuable art collection in the Nordic region. They sought to donate their collection to the city of Oslo, but the offer was turned down on the grounds that it was too large; and so what was unquestionably Norway's biggest private art collection went to a neighbouring district. Sonja's old friend Trygve Lie, the first secretary-general of the UN, arranged for a suitable site, but both the building and its location provoked fierce protests, many people claiming that the building would spoil the look of the countryside. 'Norwegians have enough countryside,' was Sonja's retort. Since it opened in 1968 the Henie-Onstad Art Centre has been visited by more than 100,000 people annually.

It has often been said that fame at a young age is a heavy burden to bear, and few people have had to shoulder a burden greater than that borne by Sonja Henie. Norway's first female patron of the arts died from advanced leukemia on a flight home from Paris to Oslo on 10 October 1969. The skating legend was only fifty-seven.

NIELS CHR. GEELMUYDEN

HENIE, SONJA (1912-69), figure skater. Olympic champion 1928, 1932, 1936. Toured the world with her ice shows from 1937. Starred in several films. Together with her shipowner husband Niels Onstad (1909-77), donated a valuable art collection and large sums of money to the Henie-Onstad Art Centre.

# FOOD AND BEVERAGES

# AT THE TABLE IN NORWAY

Astri Riddervold, Torkjell Berulfsen and Bent Stiansen

The Norwegian culinary tradition is inextricably linked to the basic ingredients provided by nature and to the changing seasons. From time immemorial, Norwegians have been hunters, dependent on cod and herring from the sea, birds and small game from the forests, reindeer from the uplands and salmon and trout from the rivers. This rich supply of basic ingredients is, however, limited to brief seasons, so it was essential to devise ways of storing the food throughout the rest of the year. A great many traditional Norwegian meals would probably never have been developed if we had had access to fresh ingredients all year round, as is the case further south in Europe. The distinctive qualities of Norwegian food are therefore the result of two decisive factors: we used local, naturally available basic ingredients and we developed means of preservation that have resulted in unique dishes and flavours.

In discussing Norwegian food it is important to remember that, as with the culinary tradition of every country, it evolved in a rural rather than an urban setting. Genuine cuisine is almost always *peasant* cuisine. As early as the eighteenth and nineteenth centuries, well-to-do people in the towns adopted continental eating habits, dining in the same way as did their fellows in Copenhagen and Paris. It was in the rural communities along the coast and in the interior of the country that a uniquely Norwegian style was developed – albeit with considerable local variations, depending on the natural surroundings. On the southern coast there were a great many recipes that were inspired by foreign culinary traditions, mainly those of England and the Netherlands, due to the extensive contact provided by maritime links. But just ten kilometres inland there was an entirely different culinary tradition. To understand Norwegian food, it is therefore necessary to understand Norway's climate and geography, the difference between country and town, and the need to process food using methods that would enable it to keep for several months.

Flavour is something that develops over time in all foods. The various methods that were used throughout the country for preserving food have therefore provided us with a range of distinctive taste experiences – experiences from which we would not otherwise have benefited had we not had access to fresh basic ingredients the whole year round.

**The table is set** – with herring, butter, leavened rye bread and beer. Dating from c. 1650, this painting is probably the work of an unknown Bergen artist.

***Rakefisk***, which can be documented in Norway from 1348, is fish that has been fermented, or has been preserved by fermentation. In hot countries this process is stabilized by adding large quantities of salt, whereas we use little salt and low temperatures. Along the coast, fermented herring was a staple food, while in the upper valleys of eastern Norway trout, char and common whitefish were used. *Rakefisk* was supposed to be ready for Christmas and was eaten without further preparation, though it could also be boiled or fried.

***Lutefisk*** has been eaten for dinner on Christmas Eve in many parts of the country from Catholic times, and still is. The dried cod was first left to soak in running water (often in a stream) for several days. In the meantime about a litre of pure birch ash was boiled up in a bucketful of water. This mixture was then left to cool and strained through a sieve. Next, the fish was left to soak for a few days in this liquid (called birch lye, though it was actually potassium carbonate), before being returned to the stream to rinse out the taste of lye. Then it was boiled and served with melted butter and dry mustard, melted mutton fat and browned onions. In Trøndelag it was often served with goat's cheese, and in northern Norway with syrup and lingonberries. These days it is most often served with creamed peas, bacon fat and bacon, and the fish is usually prepared using soda lye or caustic soda. Pollock, ling and pike can be prepared in the same way.

**Herring**, or 'Norwegian silver', has always been an important food source for both man and beast. The economy of the western coastal region was to a large extent dependent on herring, in the same way that northern Norway was dependent on cod. The oily herring was dried on the north-facing walls of outhouses or salted in barrels, and was one of the country's first exports. When potatoes were introduced in the nineteenth century, herring and potato became a daily meal, at first as salt herring or herring soup, but then also fried, boiled or smoked. Variants of salt herring, marinated in wine, herbs, cream and various sauces, would be served to visitors. In the inland regions, where herring was an important dietary source of iodine, amongst other things, it prevented goitre.

**Salmon** were taken both in the sea and in rivers, and were an important source of food, as well as an export product. In olden days salmon were preserved cured, and from the nineteenth century also in smoked form – the Norwegian equivalent of France's foie gras and Russia's caviar. Smoked salmon is only slightly salted because the smoke preserves, in particular, the surface, so inhibiting the formation of mould and preventing the fish turning rancid. Even less salt is added to *gravlaks*, which can only be kept for a relatively short time. With *gravlaks*, the fillets are marinated with two parts coarse salt and one part sugar, plenty of coarsely milled pepper and fresh dill, and preferably also with an eggcupful of cognac. These ingredients are then stored for two or three days under light pressure in a cool place. It is often served with mustard sauce. It is said that Crown Princess Märtha introduced *gravlaks* to the menu at the royal palace after the Second World War, with her own personal mustard sauce.

**Shellfish** are plentiful in the natural aquarium that is Norway's coastal waters. The water is so clean and so cold that it gives the shellfish a quality rarely found in more southerly parts of Europe. Although shellfish have never occupied a central position in the Norwegian culinary tradition, a good Norwegian meal ought to include scallops, marine crayfish or lobster – all of which have their own unique flavour.

***Sodd*** is a broth that has been a regular Sunday meal for centuries the length and breadth of the country. Salted meat and whatever vegetables were available were boiled up together over an open fire. Pearl barley was also added to *sodd*.

***Kumle*** (also known as ***raspeball***) is a kind of potato dumpling – a more recent variant of the combination of salt or smoked mutton, barley flour and grated, raw potato. The flour, potato and water were kneaded together to form a dough and rolled into large balls, often with a piece of meat in the middle. These dough balls were then boiled up with meat and slices of swede, and served with hot fat skimmed from the surface of the stock. This was a regular Thursday dinner in many parts of the country.

***Pinnekjøtt***, or cured mutton, has been served on Christmas Eve, especially in the northwest of the country, ever since the Reformation in 1536. Salted, and sometimes slightly smoked, spareribs from a young sheep were steam-cooked in a large pot on a rack of birch twigs from which the bark had been stripped. Once the water had boiled off, fat dripped down into the pot, where it would boil and spit, almost grilling the meat. Nowadays this is done using a roasting tin of water in an oven, with the meat on a rack above. The grill is then put on full for a short time just before serving. *Pinnekjøtt* is served with mashed swede.

***Smalahove***, which is made from a sheep's or lamb's head, is an example of how important it was to use every part of an animal when it was slaughtered. The head was first scorched, after which it was salted in order to draw out the moisture so that it would keep. In some parts of the country it was also common for the meat to be smoked, so that it would develop a skin that would allow it to keep for even longer. *Smalahove* is served boiled and cut in half, often with swede and potatoes.

**Reindeer** have been domesticated on the mountain moors of Finnmarksvidda in the north, and roam wild on Hardangervidda in the south. The Sámi had little access to salt for preserving the meat, but they did have access to natural deep-freeze facilities. Meals such as *finnbiff* or *reinsdyrskav* were prepared simply by cutting slices from the fresh, half-frozen meat, preserved in nature's own freezer.

**Fowl** from the inland forests, for example ptarmigan, capercaillie and black grouse, were not dried, but eaten fresh. They therefore formed more of a supplement, to than a main feature, of the diet.

**Berries** are plentiful in Norway, lingonberries and cloudberries being particularly abundant. The latter are to be found only in boggy areas in the northern hemisphere. Both lingonberries and cloudberries contain a natural preservative, which means that they keep well.

**The proof of** the pudding is in the eating – but who can resist a foretaste? Brown cheese in the making.

***Geitost***, or goat's cheese, is the most distinctive Norwegian cheese – though, strictly speaking, it is not really a cheese. It is made from whey, the clear liquid left over after the curd has been separated from the milk. The whey is cooked until the water content has boiled away, leaving a caramelized residue. While the curd from the goat's milk is used to make the more familiar yellow cheese, *geitost* is an example of how all the constituent parts of a basic food resource are used.

***Gammalost***, a mature sour milk cheese, and ***pultost***, which is similar to cottage cheese, are our traditional cheeses. They are both made from sour, skimmed cow's milk. Once they have matured, they are supposed to have an aroma similar to traditional, mature *rakefisk*.

Nowadays there is no need to preserve the basic ingredients that perpetuate interest in traditional Norwegian foods. It would seem, however, that the old methods resulted in the basic ingredients developing qualities that cannot be achieved in any other way. Food matures over time and flavour is created, and it is thanks to processes such as drying, salting and smoking that the Norwegian culinary tradition has developed a broad spectrum of characteristic flavours.

The fact that we continue to be proud of these foods and that they still represent an important feature of Norwegian cuisine has something to do with a sense of national identity and a clear understanding that this is something that is uniquely ours. National dishes are an essential part of the identity of every country. Seen in this way, Norwegian chefs have an important role to play as custodians of tradition and cultural heritage. It is our food that tells the story of who we are.

But as an old adage has it: *Food is only half the meal*; the other half is drink.

**Vikings raise** their drinking-horns aloft. A woodcut by Halfdan Egedius to illustrate Snorri Sturluson's Sagas of the Kings, 1899.

## NORWEGIAN DRINKING CULTURE: BEER, COFFEE AND AQUAVIT

Being a Norwegian is no problem, as long as there is beer – and that's the way it has been as long as this country has been populated.

We have shared the joys of beer with people the world over ever since an anonymous hero, some 8,000–10,000 years ago, started brewing beer to honour the gods in the culture that flourished between the Euphrates and the Tigris, in what is now Iraq. This was the drink that would change mankind, according to the American anthropologist Solomon H. Katz. He believes that beer was invented *before* bread, and that it was the desire for beer that impelled the nomadic hunters to stay put: they had to tend their cereal crops, so they settled down, became farmers and, eventually, a civilization.

The art of brewing spread out like ripples on the surface of this very beer, from culture to culture, and as early as a few millennia ago, our ancestors who lived in what would one day be Norway, were sitting round an open fire praising the host's beer.

It had to be beer in our country. We could not cultivate grapes, as vines do not grow well north of 50 degrees of latitude. When wine made its cautious appearance, like some exotic bird, in the twelfth century, it was prohibitively expensive. A tankard of wine in the fourteenth century cost the same as half an ox. Only aristocrats and kings could afford that kind of excess. But beer, whether we are talking about small beer, malt beer, light beer, strong beer, second-ferment beer or weak beer – that was the Norwegian way.

Or it could have been mead, made from diluted honey that was fermented and flavoured with herbs. We know that honey was introduced from countries further to the south as early as the ninth century. Sweet mead, however, could not compete with beer for everyday use, or for banquets or drinking sessions. Mead became the favoured drink of women, eventually dying out in daily use during the sixteenth century.

We learned the art of brewing from the gods, from Odin himself, who committed the first act of industrial espionage in our history in order to learn the art, which was jealously guarded by a giant, Suttung. When the giant was away, the mead, the drink of scalds, was watched over deep within a mountain by his daughter, Gunnlød.

Odin transformed himself into a serpent and succeeded in making his way in to Gunnlød at her post. There, he resumed his normal form and, in time-honoured fashion, seduced her. As a token of her love, she allowed him to drink from the precious source she was guarding.

It is common knowledge that love is blind, so Gunnlød should have known better. Odin drank the source dry, then fled. He managed to get clear of the mountain, transform himself into an eagle and, unsteady on his feet and heavily weighed down by the liquid he had consumed though he was, to take off. But suddenly he found another bird of prey close behind him, and a very angry one at that. It was Suttung. Fathers do not take kindly to intruders who first seduce their daughter and then steal their most valuable possession.

Speed was the answer and weight was what was holding Odin back. He had to lighten his load in a hurry, and accordingly discharged it fore and aft without a thought to where it might land. That was how beer came to rain down on mankind. But in Asgarth, home of the gods, the other gods, seeing that Odin was in trouble, raced outside with whatever buckets, tubs and bowls they could lay their hands on to save what little beer Odin had left.

And so it was that beer became a traditional part of everyday life among the Germanic and Nordic peoples. At times it became abundantly clear that one could have too much of a good thing. As early as 99 AD the Roman historian Tacitus wrote of how the Germanic tribes would often spend every waking moment drinking and carousing, be it to celebrate a wedding, an election or the signing of a contract or in sheer delight at the joy of living. A Danish writer once described the later Viking raids in the light of his own attitude to beer:

*Like fearless, ruthless murderers in the 'dark' Middle Ages, the Nordic warriors plundered and fought like beer-drunk berserkers. In this deranged state, the Norsemen reduced parts of Europe to ashes. In return, they gave the world a gift in the form of beer. With hindsight, it was perhaps no bad thing.*

The winter solstice was a natural high point, when beer would be drunk in earnest. The 21st of December provided a wonderful excuse for getting together and celebrating the brighter days ahead. The ale bowl was sent round the table, and people drank to each other and to the gods, first and foremost Odin, then Freya, the goddess of fertility and love. They drank a toast to a good year and to peace. *Skål*, the Norwegian equivalent of 'cheers', comes from the ale bowl, the *skål* that was passed around.

Then came Christianity – but not as in Iceland, where the new faith was adopted without any fuss by the Althing, the Icelandic parliament. Far from it. The introduction of the White Christ and everything He stood for was in Norway to be a long

**A beer ladle** from the Setesdal valley. Note the comical, if slightly risqué, three-part handle.

**A country wedding** at Kinsarvik, Hardanger. Men and women alike cast inhibitions aside as they ate and drank on equal terms. A painting by Niels Hertzberg, a local clergyman, c. 1820.

and bloody affair. Traditions harking back to Odin and the whole pantheon of gods were long and firmly established. And the new priests were not to everyone's liking: sobriety in good company was considered a sign that the household was possessed by evil spirits, and the new priests did not get drunk! There was only one thing to do with devils like these, who sailed under false colours: kill them.

It did not take long for the men of the cloth to work out where salvation in this life lay: in the drinking horn.

And the men of the Church learned fast. Not only did they accept many of the old customs more or less tacitly, they even adopted them. For example, there was an old duty to brew beer for the midwinter sacrifice. With the stroke of a pen, the provision was changed to honour Christmas and the birth of Christ. In other words, Christ and the Virgin Mary took over the positions previously occupied by Odin and Freya. The drinking of toasts, fertility and peace were retained in their original form.

According to the old calendar, the *primstav*, the first Christmas ale was supposed to be ready on 21 December, on Thomas Bryggerens (Thomas the Brewer's) day. In *Gulatingsloven* (a mediaeval law dating from *c.* 1200), paragraph one, chapter seven reads as follows:

*There is another brewing that is required by law, with an equal amount of malt in weight for man and wife, that is to be blessed on Christmas Eve in honour of Christ and St Mary, for a good year and peace. If this is not done, a fine of three marks shall be paid to the bishop. If someone has omitted to brew or pay the fine for the sake of our Christianity for three years and he is found guilty of this, then he shall forfeit every penny of his estate. Our king shall own half and the bishop shall own half. If he has the occasion, he shall go to confession and atone [literally: church fine] and then he can remain in Norway. If he does not wish to do this, then he must leave our king's realm.*

This was straight talking indeed: Fail to brew ale for the church for three years and you will lose your house and land and be exiled. All your possessions would be divided equally between Church and state. I have no idea when this regulation was repealed, but the modern state Church would need a good lobbyist to get chapter seven of *Gulatingsloven* re-introduced now.

Beer was not just a drink, it was a ritual, a factor in social cohesion. Agreements were made, disputes settled and friendships sealed over the beer tankard, the ale bowl and the drinking horn. The rules were to be followed to the last detail; failure to do so could have serious consequences. As Øystein Øystå says in his book *Øl til glede* (Beer for Enjoyment):

*In the same way that you toasted marriage to a woman, thereby drawing her into your circle, you would also drink to your neighbour. In this way, he would also be brought into your circle, into the peace. It was very difficult to bear arms against someone whose hospitality you had enjoyed. Just one drink could, at a fateful moment, be sufficient to set the future on a decisive new course.*

And there was a beer for each of the significant moments in a person's life. The Norwegian word *barsel* (meaning *birth* or *confinement*) comes from the word *barnsøl* (children's beer), drunk to celebrate a new human life. As the child grew up, an engagement was celebrated with the *festarøl* (betrothal beer) and the wedding with the *samgongoøl* (conjugal beer). The English word *bridal* is derived from *brudeøl*, bride ale. But that was not all – life was full of toasts, and *brottfararøl* (seagoing beer) was just as self-evident when someone was to set off on a voyage as *heimkomarøl* (homecoming beer) was when they returned; finally, when life came to an end, there was *gravøl* (literally grave beer).

They were no small amounts that people were downing. In his *Daglig liv i Norden* (Daily Life in Scandinavia), Troels Lund tells us that one nun was entitled to four *potter* of beer a night. That's four litres! One cannot help but wonder when she found time to sleep, in between consuming and disposing of so much liquid.

The benefit to health was almost the most important thing, even if it was as yet unknown. At a time when the distinctions between sewer, well and river could be, to put it mildly, vague, especially in towns and cities, beer was the only sensible drink, alongside different varieties of milk. In fact, beer was water that had been made more healthy and better-tasting by the addition of herbs and seeds. Even the brewing process itself could have an antibacterial effect, and cleanliness was important in order to prevent contamination and sour beer. The Swedish botanist Carl Linneus wrote a short essay in 1749 on drinking habits, in which he stated that milk and wine had their good points, but that beer was the best drink for people and for the nation. It does not excite the blood, as wine does, and it provides more nourishment, especially for those who do physically demanding work.

Long before vitamins made their appearance, beer was a nourishing dietary supplement that must have safeguarded the lives of generations. A tankard of beer was supposed to be downed in one, so as not to bite a gift from God. It was fine to get drunk on special occasions, of which there were plenty, but drinking also involved responsibility. One was supposed to be able to 'take one's drink' – to *have the capacity* to drink, in other words. And whereas today some local district councils still deny their constituents in old people's homes the right to a beer with their meal, it was expressly stated in *Gulatingsloven* that an estate should never be divided up as long as those involved were still able to ride a horse and drink beer. In other words, you had to be able to sit on a horse and have a drink without falling off.

Things could get a bit tricky at Christmas, when people were supposed to drink at least one pot of beer to be assured of peace and tolerance. In present-day terms, a pot is about two litres. On the other hand, it was not fitting to be drunk until after the day after Christmas – something that required a fine sense of balance.

Moderation was the watchword in daily life. As it says in *Håvamål* ('Sayings of the High One', a traditional poem containing proverbs and good advice): 'Better gear than good sense a traveller cannot take with him; a worse burden than too much drink a traveller cannot carry.' The basic message is exactly the same today: 'Don't drink on an empty stomach.'

Nowadays Norway is not exactly a world leader with regard to this admonitory point. Much can be said about boisterous behaviour during the summer months involving half litres at open-air restaurants and rowdiness at marinas, or young people buying in crates of beer for the weekend. But as beer-drinkers go, Norwegians are below average compared with other nationalities. We have barely a dozen breweries, supplying 4.5 million Norwegians with 53 litres each per year. The Danes drink 124 litres each. Even the Swedes beat us with their

65 litres. But we are all amateurs compared to the Czechs, each of whom downs 160 litres over the year – at a price that is laughable seen through the eyes of our social democratic, health-focused and tax-obsessed authorities.

### Al-qohl

Beer certainly did a lot of good, but where there was a need for medicine, something stronger was required, along with a little help from classical Arab culture.

This was a culture based on logic and analysis. The Arabs developed the principles of mathematics and a knowledge of the nature of things. They strove to find the purest and finest of substances, the very essence: *al-qohl*, alcohol. Their logic was that if a grape was good and wholesome, then its innermost nature, stripped of the skin and pips, its very soul, must be even more wholesome. They were about to stumble upon the fifth of life's building blocks: air, water, fire, earth . . . and alcohol.

The Arabs used alcohol as a disinfectant, to release the magical properties of plants and to create ethereal oils and perfumes. But it was not for drinking – Mohammed had already decided that.

In the ninth century, the Arabs took the art of distilling with them when they crossed the Straits of Gibraltar. Here they met Irish monks travelling around the Mediterranean and these monks took their newly acquired knowledge back home with them to the Emerald Isle. There was no grape juice in Ireland with which to distil alcohol, so they used what they had, beer. When their effort proved successful, they called the product *uisge beatha*, Gaelic for 'the water of life'. It was probably the soldiers of Henry II who shortened this to *whiskey*. They probably learned to appreciate it when they invaded Ireland in the thirteenth century, though their pronunciation would certainly have suffered progressively with each swig.

The rest of Europe learned the art of making brandy from the school of medicine in Salerno, south of Naples, as early as 1050. They called this wonderful new medicine *aqua ardens*, burning water, and soon it became known throughout the civilized world. In 1250, Thaddæus, who lectured at the university in Bologna, wrote a monograph on *aqua ardens*, the queen of medicines.

Eventually France got its *eau de vie* and Scandinavia its *aqua vitae*, water of life. Wherever it was made, the drink of immortality was a result of geography and basic ingredients: grapes or cereals. Regardless of what it was made from, it tasted dreadful; but it was good for you. The idea was that if you could find the right dosage (*quantum satis*) you would live for ever – and there are still plenty of people working hard to find it.

**Unwilling to risk** drinking what might be contaminated water from the fountain in Christiania's main square, two coachmen share one for the road instead. A painting by Johannes Flintoe, 1820.

Brandy was used solely as a medicine, and the apothecaries, who were holders of a royal charter, guarded their growing monopoly. They could, after, all interpret and act as intermediaries for Our Lord's textbook, known as the Doctrine of Signatures, where the Almighty ordained which remedy was good for which illness. Just take a look at a foxglove flower and you will see that it resembles the cut-off fingertip of a glove. It is tempting to try it on one's finger. It was reasoned that an extract of foxglove had to be good for arthritis. Similarly, kidney-shaped fruits and leaves were thought to be good for the kidneys, anything that was heart-shaped would help the heart, and anything red was good for the blood. It does not, therefore, take much imagination to work out what sort of miracles asparagus could work.

However, collecting herbs and making brews and potions was women's work. The first person to give a face to all these wise women was Anna von Sachsen, who lived in Sweden and was untiring in her zeal and research. When, still without having solved the mystery of the water of life, she died in 1585, she left behind her more than 181 suggestions and recommendations; she still died, though.

It is believed that there was brandy in Norway at the time of the Black Death (1349), though this is not certain. The first Norwegian reference we have to the secret production of seasoned brandy is in a letter from Eske Bille, castellan at Bergenhus castle. In 1531 he sent a greeting and a gift to Olav Engelbrektson, our last Catholic archbishop in Trondheim, in which he wrote:

*I am sending Your Grace some water with John Teiste that is called Aqua Vitae, and that is good for all manner of internal diseases from which a person may suffer.*

In his letter he also uses the word *brennevin* (literally 'distilled wine'), in other words, a spirit based on distilled grapes. The obvious assumption would be that the distilled wine came from abroad, while the seasoning and the herbs were home produced. If this is the case, then Eske Bille was the first person we know of who made *aqua vitae* in Norway – and he was Danish.

Brandy might not be the water that gives promise of immortality, but it did at least give a moment's joy, a sense of well-being and relief at a time when daily life could be very hard and the average life expectancy was but a fraction of what it is now. It was no easy matter getting up on a bitterly cold winter morning. Everything froze: beer froze, milk (which was not available all year round) froze, and so too did water. Coffee and tea were still in the future, and wine was unobtainable for anyone other than the wealthy ruling classes. What was needed was a good, healthy brandy to enable one to cope with the dullness and hardships of everyday life – but the country could not afford to import expensive drinks from France, the Netherlands or Germany.

This was a challenge for Christopher Blix Hammer (1720–1804), because if anyone is to be honoured as the father of Norwegian aquavit as we eventually came to know it, then it is 'the Counsellor and true Justice of the Supreme Court, Christopher Blix Hammer'.

There is scarcely one area in which Hammer did not conduct research, investigation and experimentation. He wrote cookery books, he was a surveyor, a cartographer, a hydrologist, a fish breeder, a botanist, a patriot and, at the same time, a gastronomic archaeologist preoccupied with the social problems of his day. Whether the subject be popular education, science, new or imported ideas or cultural history in the eighteenth century, Christopher Hammer crops up everywhere. He even concerned himself with the national economy, describing the Norway of his day as a poor and impoverished country in which living conditions were hostile to the hard-working farmer. In 1776, Hammer wrote a 'Chemical and Economical Treatise on Norwegian Aquavit and the Tinctures and Juices of Berries', which was nothing less than a textbook for home distilling. It was even written at a time when distilling was prohibited in Norway due to a shortage of cereals. His intention was, however, clear and unequivocal:

*. . . all kinds of simple and blended Aquavits shall be distilled from unflavoured and odourless Norwegian Cereal Brandy [raw spirits], and similarly the Appearance of the Aquavits can be coloured using Norwegian Berry Juices, Berries and Herbal Tinctures . . . thus saving the Expense of French Brandy and allowing Money to be Saved for other necessary Expenses.*

He went on to provide a clear definition of where it should be used:

*Norwegian Brandy is essential for the Farmer's Domestic Necessities: 1) for his Travels in Winter, since Ale freezes, and it is expensive to buy Ale or Brandy at his Destination, and often there is insufficient Money for this; because it is detrimental to the Traveller to drink only cold Water in the worst Cold. 2) When doing Timberwork. 3) When Coal-Mining. 4) With all other Forest and Winter Journeys, where a moderate Drink of Brandy is both good and healthy for a Person working in Severe Cold . . .*

His diatribe continues, castigating those well-off people who could afford to drink punch, coffee and tea, and stuff themselves with 'mandelade' (marzipan), chocolate and suchlike: *'Many of these people are lucky to see their fortieth year, they contract Gout and many other Diseases, and then they die.'*

The good, healthy townsman and farmer should stick to brandy, beer and whey drinks, leaving the ruling classes to suffer of their own doing from gout and die young. In those days a good swig of brandy served as a wonderful 'pick-me-up' when the working day became too arduous – we are talking about a time when the district governor of Nordland in the north of Norway claimed that almost a quarter of the region's revenue went on brandy.

So along comes the counsellor insisting that there must be an alternative to be found in our own national larder. The answer was a good brandy from nature's own kitchen:

*. . . but it must be made from wholesome and healthful Herbs that are good for the Stomach and the Character. Our own Flora contains plenty of Herbs and Plants that are good for both Body and Spirit: Fennel, Caraway, Gale, Cumin, Aniseed, nothing from our Norwegian Countryside is in any way inferior to foreign Seasoned Brandy . . .*

When Hammer distilled his brandy, however, he used cereals – largely imported from Denmark and therefore subject to duty charged by a grain monopoly. Availability was also dependent on harvest and yield. Just when Hammer was most intensely involved with his experiments, times were very bad, for which reason a prohibition on distilling brandy was introduced in 1756. This was, in fact, our first intoxicating-drinks law. Its aim was not just to limit the deleterious effects of a poor harvest, but also to curb abuse amongst farmers and townsmen. The nation's thirst was not to be slaked at the cost of hunger.

Hammer, nevertheless, continued to work tirelessly on his experiments: this was after all nationally beneficial research for the good of land and country, and the local bailiff, Anders Lysgaard, was certainly not the kind of person to harass the counsellor by constantly visiting him to check that the unadulterated flour in a sack was used only to make bread, not brandy.

But we found an alternative to cereals. The potato began its migration to Norway at the end of the eighteenth century. It was a difficult tuber to manage. There was little knowledge of potato cellars and frost-free storage through the winter, and it did not take much for the tubers to freeze and turn sweet, watery and inedible. Here, however, was just the answer to at least one future use of the potato, which was eventually to become Scandinavia's grape.

Potatoes contain about 17 per cent starch. When they freeze, this starch turns into nearly 17 per cent sugar. Just add brewer's yeast and a little water, and the mash will soon be bubbling away. After a few days, the stage is set for large-scale production. Add to this the fact that a given area planted with potatoes could produce three times as much brandy as the same area planted with cereals, and the problem was solved. It was simply a matter of distilling away to one's heart's content – and that is precisely what people did. A survey from 1840 was able to report 6,400 'brandy pans', or distillation stills. Stills bubbled away on every other farm, but by now Norway was fast approaching a new problem. Distilling took over completely, and the country plunged headlong into the nationwide binge of the 1840s, with an average per-capita consumption of 22 litres of pure spirit annually. Nowadays, consumption is officially put at nine litres.

Eventually there were four distillery towns in Norway: Moss, Drammen, Christiania (now Oslo) and Trondheim. In Moss alone, in the peak year of 1851, 2.5 million litres of spirit were produced by 14 distilleries, 9 per cent of it being sold out of town. This means that the town's 3,000 inhabitants were responsible for putting away the 250,000 litres that were sold from 74 retail outlets. And in addition to this must be added large quantities of beer!

**Coffee and tea**

This coincided with a period during which any nation worth its salt had to have colonies. Most things were admittedly produced at home, but spices, sugar, coffee and tea had to be purchased from far-off countries and were sold in 'colonial stores'.

There was one product in particular from these colonies that would halt the unrestricted consumption of alcohol: coffee. It made its first serious appearance in Europe in the seventeenth century, when it was regarded as a panacea.

Coffee was supposed to help with trapped air in the bowels; it was said to fortify the liver and the gallbladder, purify the blood, settle the stomach, sharpen the appetite, keep the drinker awake, calm violent temperaments, warm a cool nature – in short, it was supposed to be a cure for all ills.

In Norway, the introduction of coffee led to a blissful liberation from drunkenness and mayhem. Out in the countryside, beer was in practice the only alternative to brandy, but now there came these exotic beans that allowed the drinker to think more clearly and that promoted sobriety. We know that the men who drafted

Norway's constitution at Eidsvoll had access to coffee when they were deliberating the various articles and sections of the law, and in both town and country coffee and bread were served to children and adults as a second breakfast and at the afternoon meal (*eftasverd*). Eventually the custom evolved of having people over for coffee, usually with many different kinds of cake.

However, coffee was not cheap and the writer Aasmund Olavsson Vinje scoffed at the excessive coffee drinking that was as great a threat to the national economy as brandy. Among his stories is one about a farmer who had become so hooked that he sold his last cow to buy coffee. Nevertheless, coffee caught on and became an alternative beverage for the working class. It is no coincidence that when the workers' movement took shape in the second half of the nineteenth century, close collaboration developed with the budding temperance movement.

Coffee really has become a permanent feature of our modern daily life, especially now that Norway has become caught up in the coffee-bar wave, with its lattes, cappuccinos and espressos served from hissing machines by local baristas. Ironically, it is a wave that originated not in Italy, but in the United States.

**In the 19th century,** children and adults alike breakfasted off light loaves and coffee. A painting by Gustav Wentzel, 1882.

Today's Norwegians consume close to 160 litres of coffee per person per year. In general, people in the Scandinavian countries may be said to be heavy coffee drinkers. We import generally better quality coffee than, for example, Germany, France and Spain. In Scandinavia, however, a lot of coffees that in other countries are sold as speciality coffees go straight into proprietary blends. We lightly roast our coffee, in order to bring out its exciting, fruity flavours, something that goes well with our soft, calcium-poor water. Further south in Europe coffee is roasted to a darker colour. This naturally produces a more burnt flavour, but also one that is more bitter, so people use more milk and sugar in their coffee; but, then, coffee consumption there is about half of what it is in the north.

**Aquavit**

There are lot of good things to be said about coffee, but no drink is more characteristically Norwegian than our aquavit, which is emphatically different from Swedish and Danish aquavits. This distinctiveness has its origin in the crews of sailing ships on long journeys, who took with them local brandy with added caraway. One swig was enough to keep the drinker healthy and agile.

There are two stories that explain how *linie* (line – here, the Equator) aquavit came into being. One has to do with Jørgen B. Lysholm of Trondheim. His close relative Catharina Lysholm, together with her brother, had the brig *Trondhiems Prøve* built. It is well documented that the ship sailed to the East Indies in 1805 with a new product, potato spirit, on board. According to the ship's log, the brig crossed the Equator on 24 October. The purpose of the voyage was to find new markets for dried fish, salt fish and cured ham – and, more especially, for the five barrels of hard liquor. The sales campaign was a failure and in 1807 the ship returned with the liquor unsold. However, when the rejected cargo was tasted, it did not take long to realize that the liquor had changed completely – for the better. The reason for its improvement was to remain a family secret for a long time. When young Jørgen B. Lysholm took over the family soap factory in 1821, he converted it into a distillery. He had studied chemistry and the art of brewing in Berlin and now he set about developing his aquavit. When, in 1840, the Nordenfjeldske Steamship Company started regular sailings taking dried cod from Trondheim to Rio de Janeiro, Lysholm aquavit was sent out with the ships as an export item. On one occasion, one of the barrels was sent back. Once again, when it was tasted it was found to have improved. The interaction between oak barrels and the aquavit gave it near-symphonic qualities. Lysholm then began systematically sending out barrels all the way across the Equator – and linie aquavit was born.

The other story is the one that Wilh. Wilhelmsen's shipping company swears to. Just before the age of the sailing ship came to a close, Wilhelmsen was sending ships to Australia on a regular basis. Following one trip to Australia, the captain went to see the shipowner with a barrel of aquavit that they had not managed to empty during the voyage. The two of them tasted the noble liquid and found it to be absolutely first-class. But why? The matter required some research.

The shipowner had a barrel of aquavit slung in a harness underneath his desk, where he would regularly and steadily rock it with his foot. The captain, for his part, left for Australia with a barrel that was to be rocked by the sea. Upon his return, the contents of the two barrels were thoroughly tasted. The captain and shipowner soon agreed that the experimental batch that had stayed at home was a wasted effort compared with that entrusted to the motion of the waves.

Knowledge of this discovery was to have historic consequences. When the newly established Vinmonopolet (the Norwegian state liquor monopoly) began the manufacture of liquor in 1927, it conferred the exclusive right to transport linie aquavit on the shipowner Wilh. Wilhelmsen. The first barrels were shipped out in 1927 on the 7,000-ton liner *Tungsha*. To this day, these barrels (only ever sherry barrels) are always carried on the deck of Wilhelmsen's ships in order to achieve the full effect of heat and the rolling motion. Much is lost through evaporation, with as much as 5 per cent of what starts out on the 81,000-kilometre, four-and-a-half month voyage never coming back; this percentage is known as the 'angels' share'.

Today's successor to Vinmonopolet, Arcus, despatches on

average 12 to 15 containers with each ship. Each container holds 20 barrels, so there are at least 100,000 litres onboard. There are plenty of sceptics who look upon all this as nothing more than a sales gimmick that adds a full krone to the cost of each bottle. However, chemists at the Norwegian Centre for Industrial Research have been able to use advanced equipment to establish that a change really does occur in the aquavit on its round-the-world trip. Isoprenoids (substances such as vitamins A and D, menthol and camphor), chemical double bonds, are transferred or oxidized – producing new substances with different flavours and aromas. The chemists describe the process as maturation, with some of the substances present in the raw aquavit simply disappearing – something that can be expressed quite simply as an improvement in the aroma.

But it is not absolutely essential to send the noble liquor all the way around the world. The real secret is that the aquavits produced in Norway are, without exception, matured in old sherry barrels for anything from a few months to years. In the case of *Gilde Non Plus Ultra*, we're talking about 12 years, with the addition of products that are 15 and 20 years old – a storage time that is almost twice as long as that required before a cognac can carry the designation 'XO'.

This is the main difference between Norwegian aquavits and those made in Sweden or Denmark. Without wishing to say anything unkind about our neighbours' efforts, their aquavits can *in principle* be made at nine and be in the shops by ten. And if their aquavits have the same golden colouring as their Norwegian competitors, this is the result of adding caramel.

Next there is the question of whether aquavit should be drunk cold or at room temperature. This is an easy one to answer: half the flavour of aquavit is from the herbs and spices that have been added, while the other half is from the oak barrels, just as it is with cognac – and you would need your head examined if you put cognac in the freezer. The lower the temperature, the less taste there is. So, let's agree on a slightly cool room temperature.

To sum up, we may safely say that our power and glory have brought us more than white sails and linie aquavit. We also can also boast of the world's finest 'medicine', a cure for absolutely anything. It will suffice to quote Per Degn, protagonist of Ludvig Holberg's comedy *Erasmus Montanus*, as an excuse for raising a glass: '*I do not usually drink brandy unless I have a stomach ache, but I do generally have a bad stomach.*'

But, then, is a better pretext required than the taste?

## NORWEGIAN FOOD: A CULTURAL HISTORY

It is said that you are what you eat – though for inhabitants of the industrialized world, where supermarket shelves offer endless rows of tins, bags and boxes, often of indeterminate content and origin, it's not always easy to know who one is.

By the same token Norway, too, is currently suffering from something of an identity crisis. The food we eat is increasingly made from basic ingredients that have been grown elsewhere and undergone a variety of industrial processes before reaching our shelves. The name often gives a clue as to which regional tradition the product is supposed to represent, but only by reading the list of ingredients can one really tell what one is eating. Up until the period following the Second World War, food was predominantly produced locally, whereas today's international food industry and revolutionary advances in technology, economics, commerce and the travel industry have to a large extent swept away regional, national and international differences.

Nevertheless, traditional foods and meals have not disappeared completely. In recent years various attempts have been made in the fields of politics, research and education to document and utilize certain elements of our traditional culinary culture. These include time-honoured methods of preservation and the preparation of traditional preserved foods such as *lutefisk* (lyed fish), *rakefisk* (fermented fish), *spekekjøtt* (cured meat), *smalahove* (preserved lamb's or sheep's head), *raudsei* (salted saithe preserved with blood and salt in the intestines) and *gamalsteik* (cured, roast lamb), to name but a few.

The difference between then and now is that, in times gone by, these meals were firmly established in various regional culinary traditions. Now, however, they have spread to new areas, where they have assumed a collective role and become symbols of identity. This new tradition is practised partly at home, as in the past, but has also become an important feature of the modern café and restaurant culture.

Up until the eighteenth century there had been little change in the daily diet. With the drastic fall in population after the Black Death in 1349 and almost no increase in population until the mid-seventeenth century, a lot of time and thought during this period went into producing food with the sole aim of keeping body and soul together. During the growing season, which lasted only three months, food had to be produced for both man and beast and also preserved for consumption over the following nine

months. Of course we harvested fish from the sea throughout the year, but herring and cod arrived in large numbers over short periods in the winter, so they had to be preserved.

The Norwegian climate favours the preservation of food and we became masters at exploiting this. The old-fashioned preserved raw foodstuffs continue to occupy an important position in our traditional food culture: they let nature do most of the work. The exception is salt, which is now imported, but we learned early on to produce our own salt by boiling seawater. Olaus Magnus, who published his book *Historie om de nordiske folkene* (A History of the Nordic Peoples) in 1555, gives a detailed description of how Norway's coast dwellers produced salt. The one requirement was that there had to be enough wood to boil off the seawater. There are reports from Trøndelag that the seawater was allowed to freeze three times in a large, flat salt pan, the ice being removed each time in order to increase the concentration of salt in the water, and in this way also save fuel.

Only a small amount of fresh fish and meat was eaten – meat only in the slaughtering season and fish mainly during the summer. Fresh milk was not drunk until the twentieth century, apart from a few drops that were often given to a family's youngest child. However, dairy products were an important staple in the shape of butter, cheese and sour whey; the milk of reindeer, sheep and goats was also used. These products could also be stored for use in winter. The cows largely freshened only in the spring, as did the other animals, so they did not provide milk in winter; neither calves nor milk arrived until Easter. Sour whey mixed with water was called *blande* or *bleng*, and this was our daily drink as long as the supply of whey from the summer months lasted. Once it had run out, which was usually about Christmas time, small beer, second-ferment beer and weak beer became the daily drink until Easter.

Small beer was made by brewing a second batch from the same malt used to make strong Christmas ale, a large bunch of dried herbs generally being added to the mash. Ove Arbo Høeg, a professor of botany, refers to these herbs as the kings of beer. Small beer was a kind of herbal drink that could be drunk cold, unlike the hot herbal teas that had also been a daily drink for centuries, especially in the mornings. In the north, the most commonly used herb was caraway; in the south it was sage, while dried lingonberry leaves were used throughout the country.

**Inland, freshwater fish** occupied an important place in people's diet and working life. Lightly salted, fermented fish – rakefisk – was a popular item of food. This painting is from Lake Sølen in Rendalen, Hedmark.

**In ancient times** grain was venerated as a 'loan from God'. Oats and barley did ripen this far north, but crops were poor. The photo is from 1905.

We did not drink water that had not been boiled. We were afraid of the water – after all, it could have been contaminated by the human or animal excrement that was left more or less everywhere before the old-fashioned outside privy came into use in the countryside towards the end of the nineteenth century and byres were built with dung cellars.

### Cereals, bread and flatbread

Cereal products have the longest continuity in the history of our food culture, but cereals were expensive. They were called *God's loan*, or just *the food*. Cereals were the source of food and drink, porridge and gruel, *braudiskr* (a bread trencher) and flatbread, as well as strong beer for celebrations and small beer for daily consumption.

These ingredients continue to play an important role in our modern food culture, though people may not be aware of how old they really are.

Snorri Sturluson, chronicler of the sagas, describes the Vikings' bread trencher, or *braudiskr*, as a flattened cake of coarse barley flour, ground with a hand-operated mill and mixed with water to make a stiffish dough that was baked on both sides using a bread pan. Archaeologists have found 132 such bread pans, including those found on the Oseberg ship, a Viking longship. These trenchers were put directly on the table, and anything else that was going to be eaten (fish, meat, etc.) was simply piled on top. Everyone, even women, carried a knife in their belt. The other culinary utensils used were Our Lord's fork, i.e. fingers. The whole thing is reminiscent of the modern pizza, the only difference being the type of flour used. Whereas we used to use barley or oats, modern pizzas are made from wheat.

Flatbread is often thought of as our 'original bread', but it actually only came into being with the arrival of the watermill around the turn of the thirteenth and fourteenth centuries.

Our bread culture is based on the knowledge that grain must be kept free from mould – something that has been known for many centuries. Modern science has revealed that one of the moulds that grow on grain produces a dangerous toxin, aflatoxin.

Women were responsible for ensuring that the grain remained free from mould, and as this was easier with un-milled grain rather than flour, they used a hand-operated mill to grind just enough flour for two days' use. They then baked with this, cooking their bread trenchers for that day and perhaps the next day too.

Sometime in the thirteenth and fourteenth centuries, the watermill was introduced in Norway and men took over the task of milling the grain. As there was not always enough water in the stream, it was important to get as much grain milled as possible when the mill was turning. This meant that the women had to keep a flour bin free from mould instead of a grain bin, which was far from easy. This explains why flatbread came into being. The thin, dry loaves were not prone to infection by mould and could be stored for a long time without any problem. We know that it was common to bake two or three times a year. A blacksmith made the large, round iron griddle, which was then put on an iron stand over an open fire, and whereas before the bread was flattened by hand, this was now done using a rolling pin. This flat bread became an important part of the diet, along with porridge and gruel.

In olden times the Norwegian word 'food' was actually used only for food made from grain and the word 'bread' only for flatbread. A great many mistakes in old accounts can be traced back to the person asking the questions not being aware of this.

Although flatbread took over as the daily bread, the bread trencher did not disappear. Instead it just changed its name to *klappkake*, *skeibladkak* (used in Trøndelag) and *nevabrød* (Fana). During the British blockade in the early nineteenth century, the absence of cereals prompted the Norwegians to experiment with mashed boiled potatoes, resulting in the potato cake, or *lompe*, which proved a popular emergency solution to the *klappkake* problem. Along with the potato pancake, this has now become a highly regarded tradition.

Oats and barley are the cereals that grow best in the far north, but they do not contain gluten, so they cannot be used in a product leavened with yeast, for which rye or wheat are needed. Rye could be bought from Hanseatic merchants in Bergen from the Middle Ages onwards, but it was expensive and we find only small imported amounts in the customs records.

From the mid-eighteenth century, large enclosed baker's ovens started to appear in some regions, in addition to the open fire in the hearth. This suggests that leavened rye bread was being baked, though it was not called bread. It was referred to as *stump* along the northern coast and in western Norway, and as *kaku* in Finnskogene, the densely forested area on the Swedish frontier, and in the region around Sandefjord. It is here that we find the oldest baker's ovens. Nowadays the distinction between these terms is somewhat blurred.

The rye found in these areas came from various sources. In northern Norway, from 1742 to 1914 it came from what was known as the Pomor trade, the summer catch off the Finnmark coast being sold to the Russians, who paid with rye flour. The people of Finnskogene had their own method of cultivation, burning off forests and sowing rye in the ashes, while the Sandefjord region got its rye through trade with eastern Germany.

## The revolution in nutrition

So, throughout the eighteenth century our food culture underwent a slow process of revolution that gained momentum in the nineteenth and twentieth centuries, right up today, when we could be said to have reached a temporary zenith.

The Industrial Revolution brought major changes in terms of basic ingredients. In the Netherlands and Great Britain, people started to cultivate vegetables, berries and fruit, some of them introduced from more southerly climes; these began to

**Grain products** of all kinds were referred to as mat (food), but only flatbrød (flatbread), introduced in the 13th or 14th century, was designated brød (bread). Rolled thin and baked on an iron griddle, it kept virtually for ever. Taken in 1912, this photograph is from Nesflaten in Suldal.

appear in Norway in the nineteenth century. Life expectancy improved and scientists discovered that something could be done to alleviate poverty. The end of the eighteenth century also saw the development of the sciences of chemistry and chemical analysis. German scientists investigated the chemical composition of foods and human excrement, and found discrepancies between the substances present in what was consumed and the excreted waste. Welded as they were to the traditional medical belief that 'like replaces like', they claimed that, when it didn't, the human body could derive no benefit from food. Together with French social scientists, they advanced the theory that poverty was caused by a wrong diet, instead of the reverse.

So, in order to do something about poverty, something had to be done about diet. Previously this had been the domain of women who had been taught by their mothers and grandmothers. Now that this traditional knowledge had been found wanting, as the scientists proclaimed, women had to learn everything over again, but based on scientific principles.

This in turn led to a steadily increasing interest throughout the nineteenth century in food and the role of women in society. Along with new basic ingredients and new technology, these attitudes came to have important consequences for our culture.

The ideas and publications of the originators of this theory arrived in Norway with the storyteller Peter Christen Asbjørnsen, who ceased collecting folk tales in the 1840s when he travelled to Germany to train as a forester. It was here that he became familiar with the works of the physician Herman Klencke and the scientists Liebig and Koch, originators of the theory.

Asbjørnsen blindly accepted Klencke's theories and teachings on both diet and women, and presented them, admittedly with due reference to Klencke's work, in his later books on food preservation and in the foreword to a cookbook, *Fornuftig Madstel* (Sensible Cookery) published in 1864. The book was critically reviewed by Eilert Sundt, a social scientist, thus triggering a bitter, two-year-long public controversy that came to be known as the *Porridge Dispute* (1864–66).

Eilert Sundt called the book an insult to Norwegian women. The point at issue was whether traditional Norwegian food was good enough, and whether or not Norwegian women could cook. The conclusion proposed by Asbjørnsen, with reference to Klencke, was that the traditions did not hold up, so now women had to go to school and learn cookery that was based on scientific principles. At the same time Lous, the superintendent of schools in Bergen, submitted an application, supported by four physicians, to the Storting for funding to run just such a school in Romsdal.

As far as Asbjørnsen was concerned, Klencke's theories were entirely self-evident, and they were presented uncritically in relation to both food and to women. In Klencke's many books about women (which were not translated into Norwegian) he presents Rousseau's philosophical system from the eighteenth century as science's portrayal of the female as having been created by nature to complement the autonomous male, a dependent creature who functioned solely within the confines of the home.

In her 1970s doctoral thesis Else Viestad provides an excellent analysis of Rousseau's ideas, ideas that Klencke and Asbjørnsen had swallowed hook, line and sinker. But not Eilert Sundt, nor most Norwegian women, who traditionally carried the key to the storeroom on their belt – a symbol of their role as the family's financial manager in an economy based on self-sufficiency.

## New dietary elements

The nineteenth century was characterized by imperialism. During the Crimean War (1853–56) more soldiers died from contaminated food than from enemy fire. Florence Nightingale and a master chef named Soyer were despatched from England to sort out the problem, and the Academy of Science in Paris announced that it was commissioning research into possible methods of making food non-perishable and safe.

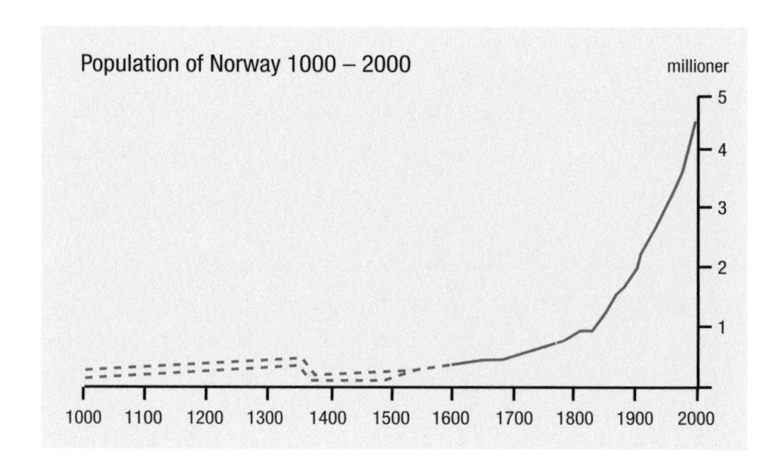


**A graph illustrating** population growth in Norway. It provides quite a dramatic picture of the way the population rose and fell. Sources prior to 1660 are open to doubt, but henceforward they are deemed reliable.

At the time science was still in its infancy and bacteria were as yet unknown. Many impractical suggestions were put forward, for example adding arsenic to food, but one suggestion was practical and has been of worldwide benefit ever since. This was the Appert method of hermetic sealing invented by a French chef, Nicolas-François Appert, in 1809. It is the only method of preservation to which a name and a date can be put, though even that is open to question as a number of researchers had already touched upon the method – in England, for example, where the boiling of fruit and berries with sugar added was a prestigious fashion on large country estates in the late eighteenth century.

Throughout the nineteenth century a near-endless stream of new elements entered Europe's food culture. It all started in the eighteenth century, a century marked by favourable economic conditions for many, lively commerce and fairly long periods of peace. New basic ingredients such as spices and dried fruit from the colonies were sold in Norway in exchange for dried fish and timber. Coffee came from Turkey, tea from India, cocoa from Africa, sugar from sugar cane, which was now also being cultivated in Europe, and cheap grain, both rye and wheat, from Odessa.

But by far the most important item for everyone, rich and poor alike, was the potato, which had been imported from South America and was eventually to become a staple ingredient of the daily diet all over northern Europe.

In early nineteenth-century Norway, especially on the west coast, the potato saved a great many people from starvation during the Napoleonic Wars, when England blockaded all grain imports into Norway. Together with the large herring that spawned in the spring, the potato had a profound impact on living conditions in Norway in terms of longevity, health and especially fertility; this was thanks to the vitamins A, D and C and the fatty acid omega-3 this diet contained, though this was not known at the time.

The population curve shows explosive growth in both the nineteenth and twentieth century. The increase was actually sharper than the graph suggests, as it does not include the many who emigrated to America.

The rise in population was too great to be absorbed by the countryside, and throughout the nineteenth century there was steady growth in towns and in industrial activity. In 1860 a ban was imposed on keeping animals in the towns and cities, thus creating a market for fresh agricultural products. The first dairy was set up in 1851 and the purpose of farming changed in part from self-sufficiency to the sale of agricultural products.

This is where the old-fashioned outside privy became a significant production factor. Its products helped to reduce the great disparity between cultivated areas and the amount of manure available in most places. Now that the aim was to produce as much as possible for sale, the old custom of leaving land fallow every third year was gradually discontinued.

In the capital, there was an organized collection of the population's waste, which was taken to a newly established composting plant (a night soil factory); the product was then sent by the new railway to Eidsvoll to fertilize the arable land and potato fields in the surrounding flat countryside.

The mid-nineteenth century saw the arrival of the cast-iron range, with its oven and multiple cooking apertures, which slowly spread throughout the country. Fire-insurance assessments reveal that by the beginning of the twentieth century such ranges were to be found everywhere, having replaced the fireplace where 'Ma's pot' once hung in a recess over an open fire and meals were few and much of a muchness. On the whole, everything was cooked in the same pot, or eaten uncooked as salted, cured, fermented raw ingredients straight from the barrel – along with flatbread, gruel or porridge.

It was now that the really big changes came. Professor Anni Gamerith of Graz in Austria has shown that when basic ingredients are not used in industrial production, meals are determined by where they are cooked. The cooking apertures in the iron range meant that a meal could be divided into a number of smaller dishes. Now we have soup intended only as a starter or a final course, and we have dessert, a brand new dish and one to which a certain prestige was attached. Old recipes show that desserts, mostly jellies, were largely wine-based. Gelatine was made at home from calf bones and was called *husblas*. The oven could be used for baking the most mouth-watering fruit pies using newly imported wheat flour, butter from the dairy, or margarine, and refined cane sugar from the colonial store, the grocer's. There were steady improvements in the cultivation of berries and fruit and in preserving the crop with the aid of sugar to make jam or wine. It was also recommended that some of the sugar in the jam should be replaced by cognac

The oven also paved the way for biscuits, with recipes being presented by Hanna Winsnes in 1845 as 'biscuits to serve with jam'. In time, these were to become the now-so-familiar Christmas cookies, joining the old traditional Christmas bread, a sweet, round bread containing raisins, and thin, round, rolled wafers and waffles baked in special irons, dating from the seventeenth and eighteenth centuries. The deep-fried cakes known as *fattigmann* (poor man) and *hjortetakk* (stag's antlers) are more recent fancy cakes.

By far the most important oven-cooked product was the fresh, oven-roasted meat that was served with gravy on Sundays and to guests. It was about now that roasted rack of pork was introduced to the dinner table on Christmas Eve to compete with *lutefisk*, while *pinnekjøtt* (cured lamb ribs cooked in a pot over an open fire) had been eaten on Christmas Eve in northern and western Norway for some time longer.

Norwegian women were sure of themselves and confident of their culinary skills, though they were well aware that their knowledge of the new dietary science was sadly lacking. The first school of home economics, a private establishment, was opened in the 1860s, and in the 1880s female activists founded *Kvinnesaksforeningen* (The Feminist Association), which campaigned not only for equal rights to education for men and women but also for women's right to specialist training in home economics. The organizers applied for funds to set up a school at Stabekk on the western outskirts of Oslo for training home economics teachers.

Knowledge of this new science was then disseminated to pupils all over the country with the introduction of home economics in schools, and to adults and young women, who were taught at free, state-funded schools of home economics everywhere, as well as at many private establishments.

**Introduced** into elementary schools in the 1890s, the teaching of home economics rapidly spread throughout the country. This photograph was taken at Kampen School in Kristiania (Oslo) in 1890.

It was mainly the same women who instigated all these activities. They were supported by some prominent men, but also publicly opposed by others, men who had adopted the views on women advanced by Rousseau, Klencke and Asbjørnsen.

In 1896, some of these women established *Norske Kvinders Sanitetsforening* (Norwegian Women's Public Health Association), which set up autonomous women's groups throughout the country devoted to spreading information about diet and health for both young and old.

In accordance with the traditional role of the Norwegian woman, that of a partner entrusted with the key to the storehouse, it was stated in the articles of association that the intention was to stand shoulder-to-shoulder with Norwegian men in the task of building a strong and healthy nation.

The significance of all this activity for Norwegian food culture cannot be overestimated. Via the home economics teachers trained at Stabekk, knowledge of both traditional food culture and the results of research were passed on to Norwegian women of all ages, in the school kitchen and home economics schools, and to young and older mothers through the activities of the *Sanitetsforening*. The entire population of Norway benefited from this knowledge through two wars and the years of depression in between.

And so the revolution continued into the twentieth century, embracing the roles of food and of women. It is still too early to say what the results will be, because it is an ongoing process. On the contrary, in recent decades a new dimension has been added to our food culture: in Norway, as in many other countries, a lot of people now eat the main meal of the day out, at a café or restaurant. And like people in most other European countries, we have developed a very global food culture. Pizza, spaghetti, tacos and other imported dishes now feature regularly on Norwegian dinner tables and when we go out to eat, we are as likely to eat Chinese or Indian food as traditional Norwegian fare. Nevertheless, local traditions have recently received support from some county authorities, who have issued instructional food guides listing regional eating establishments where customers can enjoy local cuisine.

Another exciting feature of our food culture in recent years has been the impressive placings achieved in international competitions by Norwegian chefs using classic Norwegian basic ingredients. Let us then conclude this chapter by presenting a menu for an eight-course meal, composed by our first world champion of the culinary art, Bent Stiansen.

# A taste of Norway

BENT STIANSEN'S IDEAL NORWEGIAN MEAL

This menu is based on the excellent and distinctive basic ingredients that are available in Norway, and that are a source of such pride to chefs in this country. Food is prepared on the basis of Norwegian traditions, though it is presented with the aid of techniques that are an integral part of modern cooking. History tells us that food is often prepared in the same way for several hundreds of years, the only improvement being in the way in which it is presented as a result of changing fashions. Bon appetit!

'LEFSE' ROULADE WITH CURED LEG OF MUTTON, SOUR CREAM AND MUSTARD

SMOKED SALMON WITH SALMON CAVIAR SAUCE

CREAMED DRIED COD TART WITH RAW EGG YOLK

SAUTÉED MARINE CRAYFISH TAILS SERVED IN THEIR OWN LIGHT CRAYFISH SOUP
WITH HAMBURG PARSLEY

BOILED COD WITH BUTTER-GLAZED CARROTS AND MUSSEL SAUCE

'A SYMPHONY OF GAME'
REINDEER FILET AND MEDIUM-RARE BREAST OF PTARMIGAN
SERVED WITH BUTTER-GLAZED BRUSSELS SPROUTS WITH BACON, HARDANGER PEARS
STEWED WITH LINGONBERRIES AND GRILLED FOREST MUSHROOMS
JUNIPER-BERRY CREAM SAUCE

CLOUDBERRY AND ALMOND BRITTLE ICE CREAM WITH 'KRUMKAKER'
AND CLOUDBERRY SAUCE

'TILSLØRTE BONDEPIKER' (BROWN BETTYS) WITH GRAVENSTEIN APPLE PURÉE
AND ALMOND BREADCRUMBS

Bent Stiansen
Chef de cuisine
Statholdergaarden
2004

## 'Lefse' roulade with cured leg of mutton, dairy cream and mustard

A 'lefse' is a thin, soft griddle cake made from boiled potatoes and flour. This thin cake is spread with butter, mustard and sour cream, and covered with thin slices of 'fenalår', which is leg of mutton that has been salted, smoked and dried – delicious summer food.

**Serves 4**

**2 'lefser'**
**2 tbs butter**
**2 tbs sweet mustard**
**4 tbs sour cream**
**200 g cured leg of mutton**

Butter the lefser, then spread with the mustard. Add thin slices of the mutton, then spread sour cream on the mutton. Roll the lefser together and cut into slices. It is a good idea to hold the slices together with cocktail sticks if the roulade is to be eaten as an hors-d'oeuvre before a meal.

If the lefser are to be eaten as a first course, arrange them on a plate with more mustard and sour cream.

## Smoked salmon with salmon caviar sauce

Smoked salmon is the best basic ingredient that Norway produces. We may safely say that we are world champions at smoking salmon. Serve simply, with scrambled eggs or, as here, with a butter sauce with salmon caviar.

**Serves 4**

**400 g smoked salmon, preferably from the middle of the filet**

**Salmon caviar sauce**

**200 ml fish stock**
**100 ml white wine**
**2 tbs chopped shallots**
**2 tbs cream**
**200 g unsalted butter**
**50 g salmon caviar**
**2 tbs finely chopped chives**
**salt and pepper**

Remove the bones from the smoked salmon and cut into thin slices. Take a quarter of the salmon slices, lay them out in a row and roll them together. Spread out one end of each of the rolled slices to make a nice rose. Store the roses at room temperature.

Place the fish stock, white wine and shallots in a pan and reduce to 50 ml. Add cream and whisk in small pieces of unsalted butter to form a smooth sauce. When serving, heat up the sauce without bringing to the boil, then add the salmon caviar, chives and salt and pepper as required.

Arrange the salmon roses on a plate and pour the sauce around them.

## Creamed dried cod tart with raw egg yolk

I call this dish 'Midnight Sun'. We start by baking a puff-pastry tart base in the shape of the sun and filling it with the world's finest filling of freshened and boiled dried cod, cream and capelin roe. Dried cod, known as klippfisk or bacalao, is our second-best-selling fish product and has helped to establish Norway's worldwide reputation as a fish-producing nation. Bacalao is synonymous with quality fish from Norway. Klippfisk is a salted and dried cod filet that must be left to stand in water for a minimum of twenty-four hours before it is used.

**Serves 4**

**200 g dried cod**
**200 ml cream**
**2 tbs capelin roe, uncoloured**
**a little lemon juice**
**salt and pepper**
**2 sheets of puff pastry**
**1 egg yolk for brushing on the puff pastry**
**4 egg yolks for the tarts**
**8 chive leaves**

Leave the salt cod to soak in water for 24 hours.

Allow the puff pastry to thaw and divide the sheets into two. Cut out a star pattern and mark out a circle in the middle of the four tarts. Brush with egg yolk, then bake at 180°C for 20 minutes until the tarts have turned a golden brown and risen. Allow to cool, then cut a hole in the tops of the tarts to form a cavity for the filling.

Transfer the cod to a pan of cold water, bring to the boil and simmer for 5 minutes. Take out the fish and leave to cool. Remove the skin and bones and put in a pan with the cream. Boil the mixture until it begins to thicken. Add salt, pepper and lemon juice to taste. To serve, add the capelin roe and fill the tarts with the mixture. Place a raw egg yolk in the centre of the filling, replace the pastry circle that you previously cut out and decorate with a few chives.

## Sautéed marine crayfish tails served in their own light soup with Hamburg parsley

Norway's extensive coastline, with its pure, cold and unspoiled ocean waters, is the world's best environment for shellfish. Marine crayfish can weigh up to 400 grams and have a wonderfully clean, sweet shellfish flavour. This dish makes full use of the crayfish in the form of a soup boiled from the shells and sautéed tails.

**Serves 4**

**1 kg marine crayfish**
**1 tbs sunflower oil**
**salt and pepper**
**1 tbs finely chopped parsley**
**100 g Hamburg parsley**

Cut the crayfish in two and remove the tails from the shells, as you would with shrimps. Take out the alimentary canal. Salt and pepper the tails and fry them for a minute on each side. Keep hot. Peel the Hamburg parsley and dice it finely. Sauté in the remainder of the oil and add the ordinary parsley. Arrange the crayfish tails and Hamburg parsley in deep plates and pour on the soup.

### MARINE CRAYFISH SOUP

**shells from the crayfish**
**2 tbs sunflower oil**
**1 onion**
**1/2 carrot**
**30 g celery root**
**2 tomatoes**
**1 tbs tomato purée**
**3 cloves of garlic**
**1 tsp thyme**
**4 star anises**
**2 dl white wine**
**3 dl fish stock**
**3 dl cream**
**salt, pepper and lemon juice**

Sauté the crayfish shells in oil together with the chopped onion, carrot and celery root. Add chopped tomatoes, tomato purée, garlic, thyme and star anises. Fry for a little longer, then add the white wine, fish stock and cream. Bring to the boil and leave to simmer for 20 minutes, then strain through a sieve. Add salt, pepper and lemon juice to taste and whisk with a hand mixer.

## Boiled cod with butter-glazed carrots and mussel sauce

Whether you use local coastal cod or the cod that comes into Lofoten to spawn in March, you still have an extremely high-quality basic ingredient. I have chosen to boil it and serve it with a cream sauce of mussel stock and parsley.

**Serves 4**

**500 g cod dorsal filet**
**33 ml salt per litre water**
**300 g crisp carrots**
**100 ml water**
**50 g butter**
**1 tbs sugar**
**1 tsp salt**

Divide the cod filet into four equal pieces. Boil up plenty of water, adding 33 ml salt per litre. Add the cod and leave for 6 minutes.

Peel the carrots. Place them in a pan of water, add butter, sugar and salt and bring to the boil.

Leave to boil uncovered for 5 minutes, so that the water boils off and the carrots are glazed in the butter and sugar. Arrange the fish on a bed of carrots and dress with the mussel sauce.

### MUSSEL SAUCE

**500 g mussels**
**1 tbs butter**
**2 tbs chopped onion**
**1 clove of garlic**
**100 ml white wine**
**200 ml cream**
**1/2 tsp cornflour**
**1 tsp lemon juice**
**salt and pepper**
**1 tbs chopped parsley**

Wash the mussel shells and remove the beards. Discard any shells that float. Fry the chopped onion and garlic in butter and add the mussels. Add white wine, cover the mussels and steam for two minutes until they open. Remove from the pan and take out the flesh. Reduce the stock by a half and add the cream. Bring to the boil and thicken the sauce with a little cornflour mixed in cold water. Add salt, pepper and lemon juice to taste. Before serving, add the mussels and the chopped parsley.

## 'A symphony of game.'

**Reindeer filet and medium-rare breast of ptarmigan served with butter-glazed Brussels sprouts with bacon, Hardanger pears stewed with lingonberries, grilled forest mushrooms and juniper-berry cream sauce**

The autumn hunting season is sacred to many Norwegians: we have hunted reindeer and ptarmigan since time immemorial. Reindeer meat is tasty and extremely tender. Ptarmigan is a bird that lives at 700 metres above sea-level and higher. It has a flavour that is very gamy, but at the same time delicate, and one of the finest foods a host can serve in Norway is ptarmigan shot by himself. Game is usually served with cream-based sauces that provide a contrast to the somewhat sharp, gamy taste. A sweet-and-sour garnish, such as pears stewed with lingonberries, also gives an excellent flavour to balance the game. Our forests are full of mushrooms – a natural accompaniment to game dishes.

Serves 4

**400 g reindeer steak, filet or loin; you can also use beef rump steak**
**2 ptarmigan**
**1 tbs chopped fresh thyme**
**salt and pepper**
**2 tbs butter**

Clean the meat, removing any membrane, and cut the breasts from the ptarmigan. Season the meat with salt and pepper and sprinkle with the finely chopped thyme. Heat up a frying pan, add the butter and brown the meat. Remove the meat and place it on a roasting tray and roast in the oven for 5 minutes at 180°C. Remove the meat and leave to rest on a plate for 10 minutes. To serve, slice the meat.

### BUTTER-GLAZED BRUSSELS SPROUTS WITH BACON

**400 g Brussels sprouts**
**3 tbs butter**
**50 ml water**
**salt and pepper**
**100 g bacon**
**1 tbs butter**

Remove any soiled leaves from the Brussels sprouts and slice thinly. Place in a pan with the water, butter, salt and pepper and bring to the boil. Simmer for 5 minutes until soft. Cut the bacon into thin strips and fry in a little butter until brown and crisp. To serve, strain the Brussels sprouts and sprinkle the bacon on top.

### HARDANGER PEARS STEWED WITH LINGONBERRIES

**2 Hardanger pears**
**200 ml water**
**50 ml sugar**
**100 ml lingonberries**

Peel and quarter the pears and remove the cores. Purée the water, sugar and lingonberries in a food processor or with a hand blender. Place the pear segments in a pan and pour on the lingonberry sauce. Bring to the boil and simmer for 3 minutes until the pears are tender. Serve half a pear per person.

### GRILLED FOREST MUSHROOMS

**300 g forest mushrooms, chantarelles, ceps or hedgehog fungi**
**1/2 onion**
**2 tbs sunflower oil**
**1 tbs butter**
**salt and pepper**
**1 tbs. parsley**

Clean the mushrooms and cut into pieces. Heat some oil in a frying pan and sauté the mushrooms until the liquid from them has boiled off. Add finely chopped onion and butter and season with salt and pepper to taste. Fry gently for a few more minutes before adding the chopped parsley. The mushrooms are now ready.

### JUNIPER BERRY CREAM SAUCE

**400 ml game stock made from reindeer scraps and ptarmigan carcass**
**100 ml white wine**
**50 ml port**
**1 tbs white wine vinegar**
**1/2 tbs crushed juniper berries**
**2 tbs lingonberries**
**1 tbs redcurrant or rowanberry jelly**
**1/2 tsp thyme**
**200 ml cream**
**1 tsp cornflour**
**salt and pepper**

Place the game stock, white wine, port, vinegar, juniper berries, lingonberries, redcurrant jelly and thyme in a pan and reduce to 200 ml. Strain through a sieve and add the cream. Bring back to the boil and thicken the sauce with cornflour mixed in a little water. Add salt and pepper to taste.

## Cloudberry and almond-brittle ice cream with 'krumkaker' and cloudberry sauce

Cloudberries are yellow berries that resemble raspberries in shape, though they have an entirely different flavour.

They grow in bogs in forests and high in the mountains. They ripen in August, when they have a rich, sweet flavour faintly reminiscent of ripe mango. Cloudberries keep well when fresh due to their naturally high benzoic-acid content. They are often served mixed with whipped cream in krumkaker, which are thin wafers baked on a *krumkakejern,* a kind of waffle iron, then rolled into a cone.

**Serves 4**

### ALMOND BRITTLE

**100 g sugar**
**100 g blanched almonds**

Brown the sugar in a non-stick pan and add the blanched almonds. Leave to cool on greased baking paper. Once the mixture has cooled and gone hard, blend to a fine almond-brittle powder in a food processor.

### CLOUDBERRY ICE CREAM

**5 egg yolks**
**100 g sugar**
**2 tbs Lakka-likør (cloudberry liqueur) or cognac**
**500 ml whipping cream**
**200 g cloudberries**

Whisk the egg yolks together with the sugar and liqueur. Next add the whipped cream and mix well. Purée the cloudberries using a hand blender, pass the cloudberry purée through a sieve and then mix it into the rest of the mixture. Pour into a bread tin and leave overnight in a freezer. To serve, roll the ice cream in the finely chopped almond brittle before slicing. Serve with krumkaker and cloudberry sauce.

### CLOUDBERRY SAUCE

**100 g cloudberries**
**50 g icing sugar**
**50 ml water**

Mash the cloudberries together with the water and icing sugar and pass the purée through a sieve.

### KRUMKAKER

**90 g sugar**
**100 g butter**
**2 eggs**
**1/2 tsp cardamom**
**125 g flour**
**1 tbs butter for cooking**

Cream the sugar and softened butter. Add an egg and mix thoroughly. Add half of the flour, then the second egg before mixing in the rest of the flour with the ground cardamom. Heat the krumkake iron and brush with butter. Bake small krumkaker. When they turn golden brown, wrap round a wooden pin until they harden. They keep well if stored in an airtight box.

## 'Tilslørte bondepiker' (brown Bettys) with Gravenstein apple purée and almond breadcrumbs

Some parts of southern Norway are particularly suitable for growing apples. Our long, light summer evenings make our apples very tart and very sweet. This is a traditional dish, used in thousands of homes, which here has been given a rather more modern slant.

**Serves 4**

**4 Gravenstein apples**
**100 ml white wine**
**100 ml sugar**
**300 ml whipping cream**
**2 tbs sugar**
**1 tsp vanilla sugar**
**4 rusks**
**70 g almonds**
**1 tbs butter**
**1 tbs sugar**
**1 tsp cinnamon**

Peel the apples and chop into small pieces. Stew with the white wine and sugar to produce a purée. Leave to cool. Whip the cream with sugar and vanilla sugar. Grind up the rusks and finely chop the almonds. Melt the butter in a frying pan and sauté the rusks, almonds, sugar and cinnamon until the mixture turns a light brown. Leave the almond breadcrumbs to cool.

Once all the ingredients have cooled, begin to assemble the dish. Layer the apple purée, almond breadcrumbs and whipped cream in a dish or glass bowl. Add as many layers as you like, and decorate the top with whipped cream.

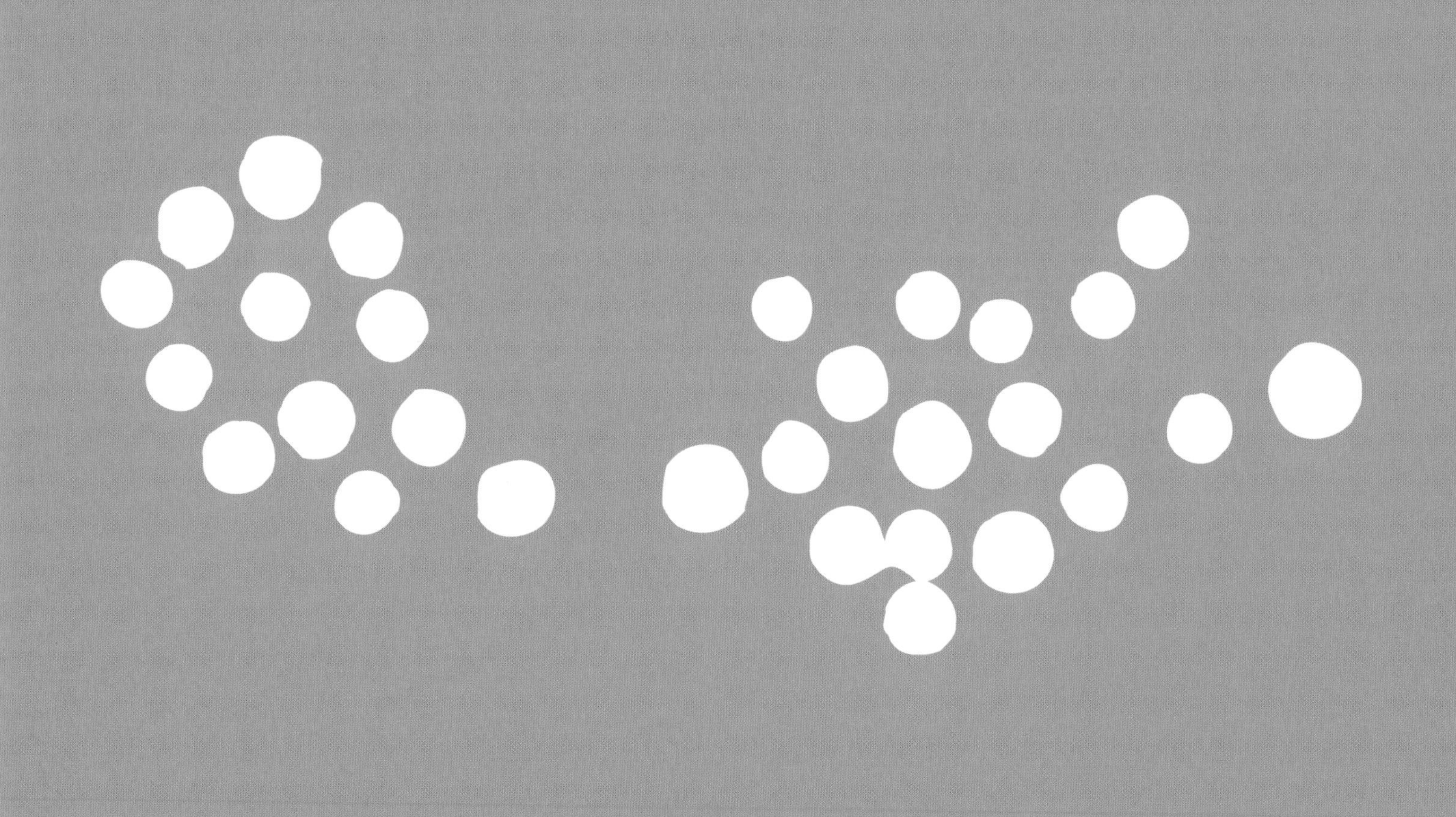

# A STATISTICAL PORTRAIT

Jan Erik Kristiansen
Statistics Norway

# GEOGRAPHY

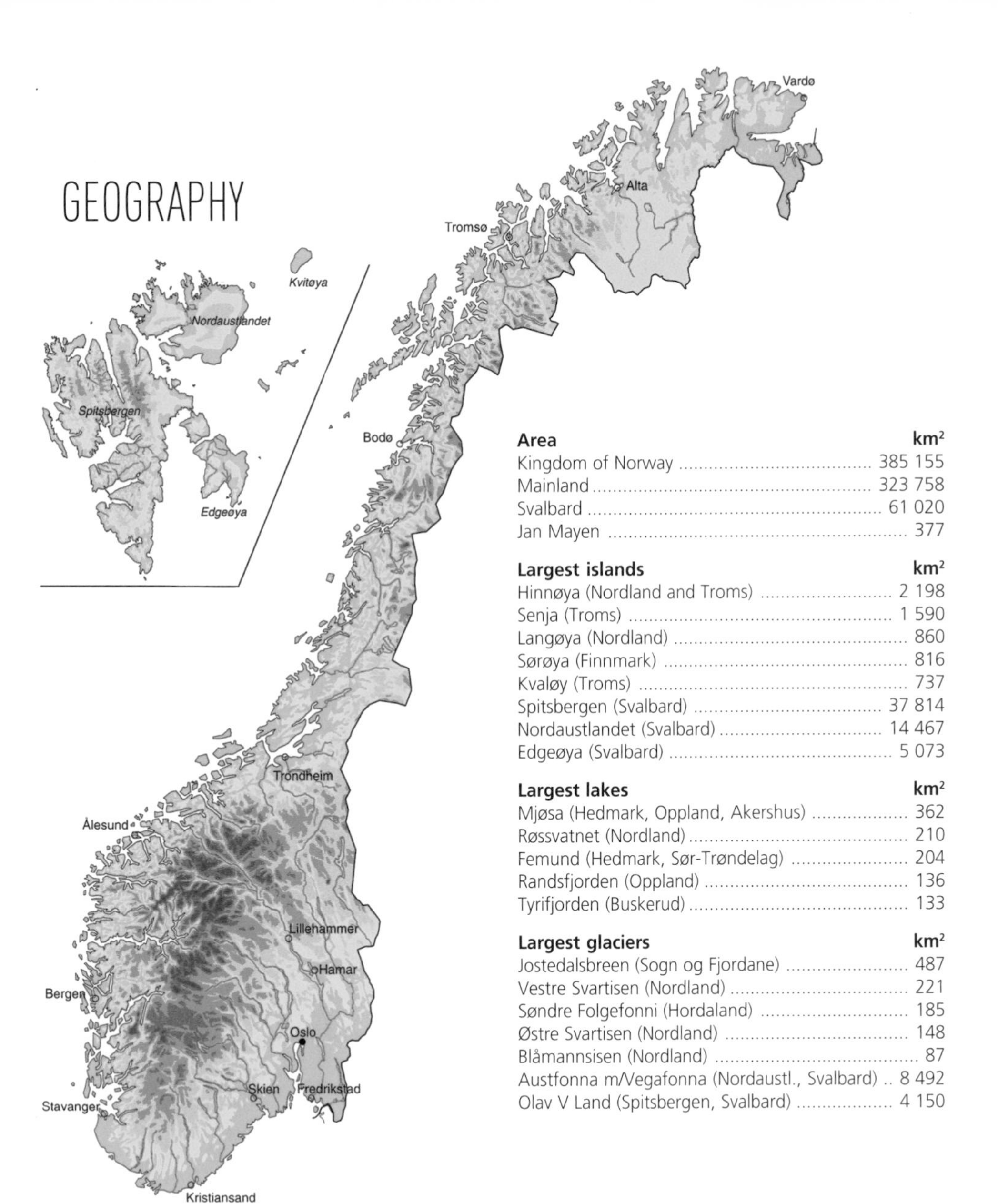


| Area | km² |
|---|---|
| Kingdom of Norway | 385 155 |
| Mainland | 323 758 |
| Svalbard | 61 020 |
| Jan Mayen | 377 |

| Largest islands | km² |
|---|---|
| Hinnøya (Nordland and Troms) | 2 198 |
| Senja (Troms) | 1 590 |
| Langøya (Nordland) | 860 |
| Sørøya (Finnmark) | 816 |
| Kvaløy (Troms) | 737 |
| Spitsbergen (Svalbard) | 37 814 |
| Nordaustlandet (Svalbard) | 14 467 |
| Edgeøya (Svalbard) | 5 073 |

| Largest lakes | km² |
|---|---|
| Mjøsa (Hedmark, Oppland, Akershus) | 362 |
| Røssvatnet (Nordland) | 210 |
| Femund (Hedmark, Sør-Trøndelag) | 204 |
| Randsfjorden (Oppland) | 136 |
| Tyrifjorden (Buskerud) | 133 |

| Largest glaciers | km² |
|---|---|
| Jostedalsbreen (Sogn og Fjordane) | 487 |
| Vestre Svartisen (Nordland) | 221 |
| Søndre Folgefonni (Hordaland) | 185 |
| Østre Svartisen (Nordland) | 148 |
| Blåmannsisen (Nordland) | 87 |
| Austfonna m/Vegafonna (Nordaustl., Svalbard) | 8 492 |
| Olav V Land (Spitsbergen, Svalbard) | 4 150 |

| Longest fjords | km |
|---|---|
| Sognefjorden (Solund-Skjolden) | 204 |
| Hardangerfjorden (Bømlo-Odda) | 179 |
| Trondheimsfjorden (Agdenes-Steinkjer) | 126 |
| Porsangen (Sværholtklubben-Brennelv) | 123 |
| Storfjorden (Hareidlandet-Geiranger) | 110 |
| Wijdefjorden (Spitsbergen, Svalbard) | 105 |
| Isfjorden (Spitsbergen, Svalbard) | 100 |

| Longest watercourses | km |
|---|---|
| Glomma | 600 |
| Pasvikelva | 360 |
| Numedalslågen | 352 |
| Gudbrandsdalslågen/Vorma | 351 |
| Tana | 348 |

| Largest waterfalls | m |
|---|---|
| *Total fall:* | |
| Kjelsfossen (Aurland) | 840 |
| Søndre Mardalsfoss (Nesset) | 705 |
| Mongefossen (Rauma) | 700 |
| Vedalsfossen (Eidfjord) | 650 |
| Opo (Ullensvang) | 650 |
| *Near-perpendicular waterfalls:* | |
| Tyssestrengene (Odda) | 300 |
| Ringedalsfossen (Odda) | 300 |
| Skykkedalsfossen (Eidfjord) | 300 |
| Vettisfossen (Årdal) | 275 |
| Austerkrokfossen (Sørfold) | 256 |

| Highest mountains | m |
|---|---|
| Galdhøpiggen (Lom) | 2 469 |
| Glittertind (Lom) | 2 464 |
| Store Skagastølstind (Luster, Årdal) | 2 403 |
| Styggedalstind (Luster) | 2 387 |
| Skarstind (Lom) | 2 373 |

**The 20 largest municipalities**

| | Population 1 Jan. 2003 | Area, km² |
|---|---|---|
| Oslo | 517 401 | 454 |
| Bergen | 235 423 | 465 |
| Trondheim | 152 699 | 342 |
| Stavanger | 111 007 | 70 |
| Bærum | 102 529 | 192 |
| Kristiansand | 74 590 | 276 |
| Fredrikstad | 69 288 | 290 |
| Tromsø | 61 182 | 2 558 |
| Drammen | 56 444 | 138 |
| Sandnes | 55 729 | 303 |
| Asker | 50 290 | 101 |
| Skien | 50 272 | 779 |
| Sarpsborg | 49 044 | 407 |
| Bodø | 42 186 | 921 |
| Larvik | 40 877 | 530 |
| Sandefjord | 40 696 | 122 |
| Skedsmo | 40 676 | 77 |
| Ålesund | 39 695 | 98 |
| Arendal | 39 502 | 272 |
| Karmøy | 37 199 | 228 |

**Norway's counties: Inhabitants and area**

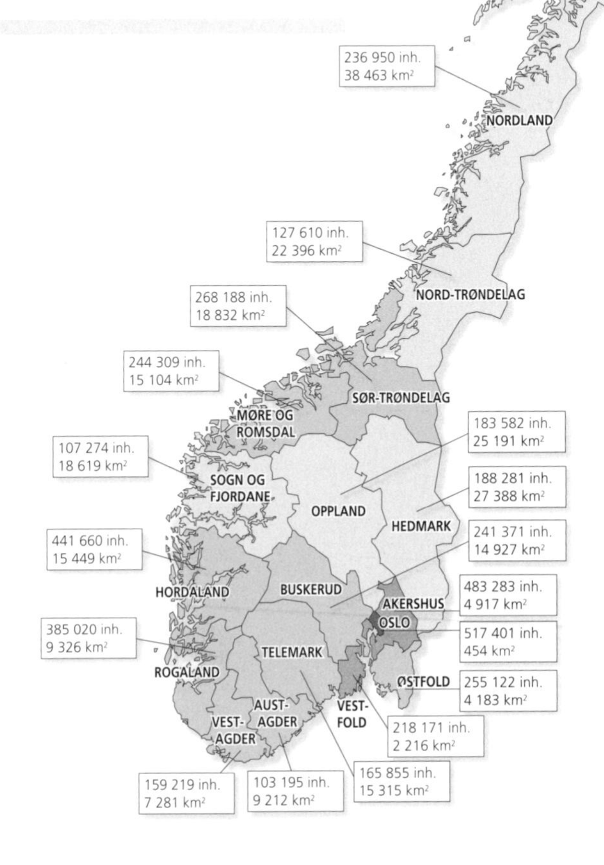


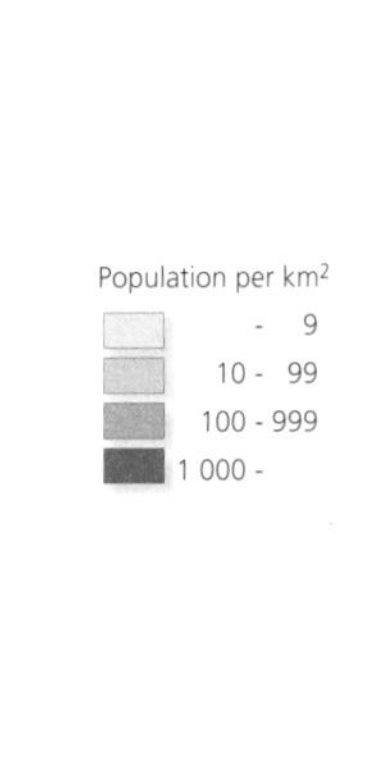

# NATURE AND CLIMATE

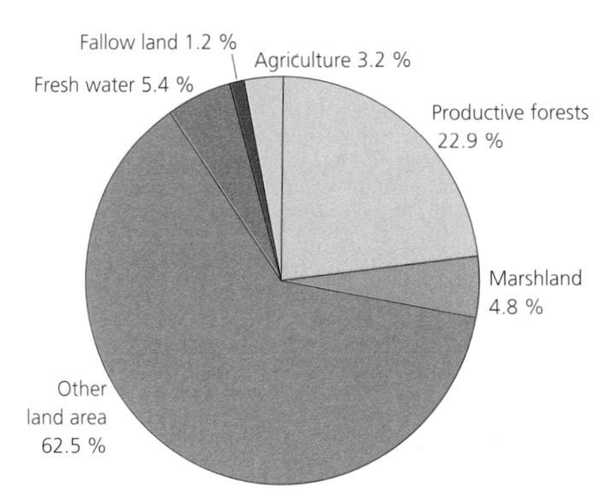


Source: Norwegian Mapping Authority and Statistics Norway.

**Mountains and forests**

With an area of 324 000 km² and 4.5 million people, Norway – after Iceland – is Europe's most sparsely populated country, with 14.8 inhabitants per km².

Only slightly over one per cent of Norway's total area is built-up (including roads). Three per cent is agricultural land and 23 per cent productive forests. Non-productive forests account for 15 per cent and lakes five per cent. The rest, just over 50 per cent, consists of mountains, plains and marshland.

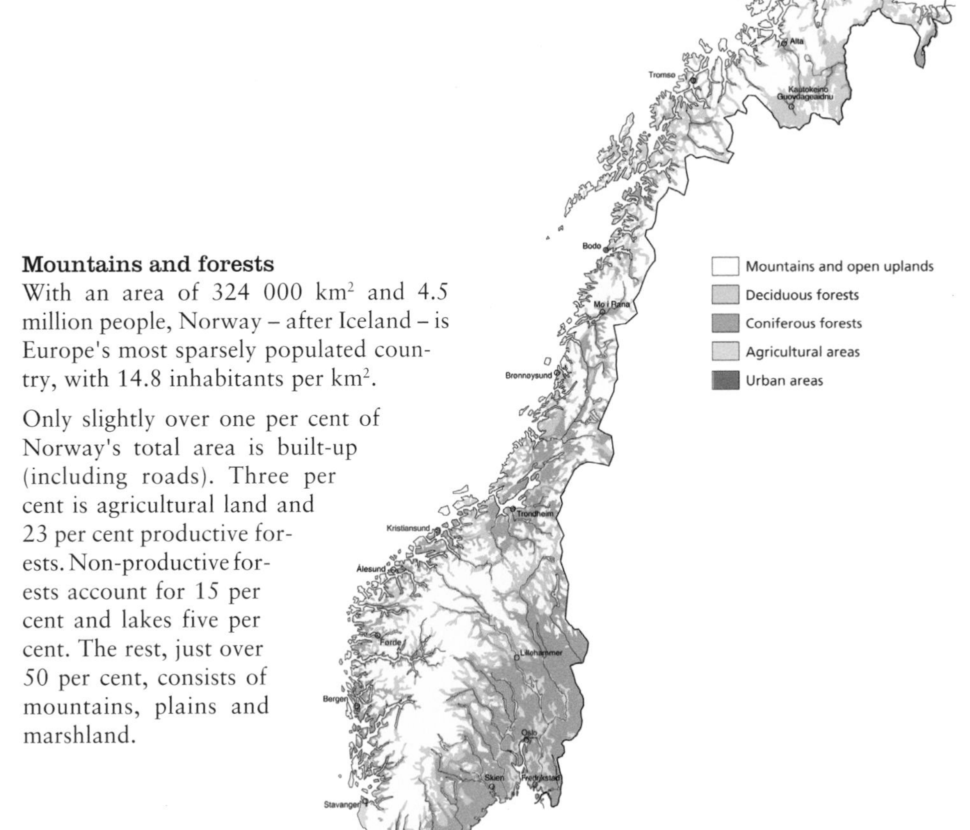


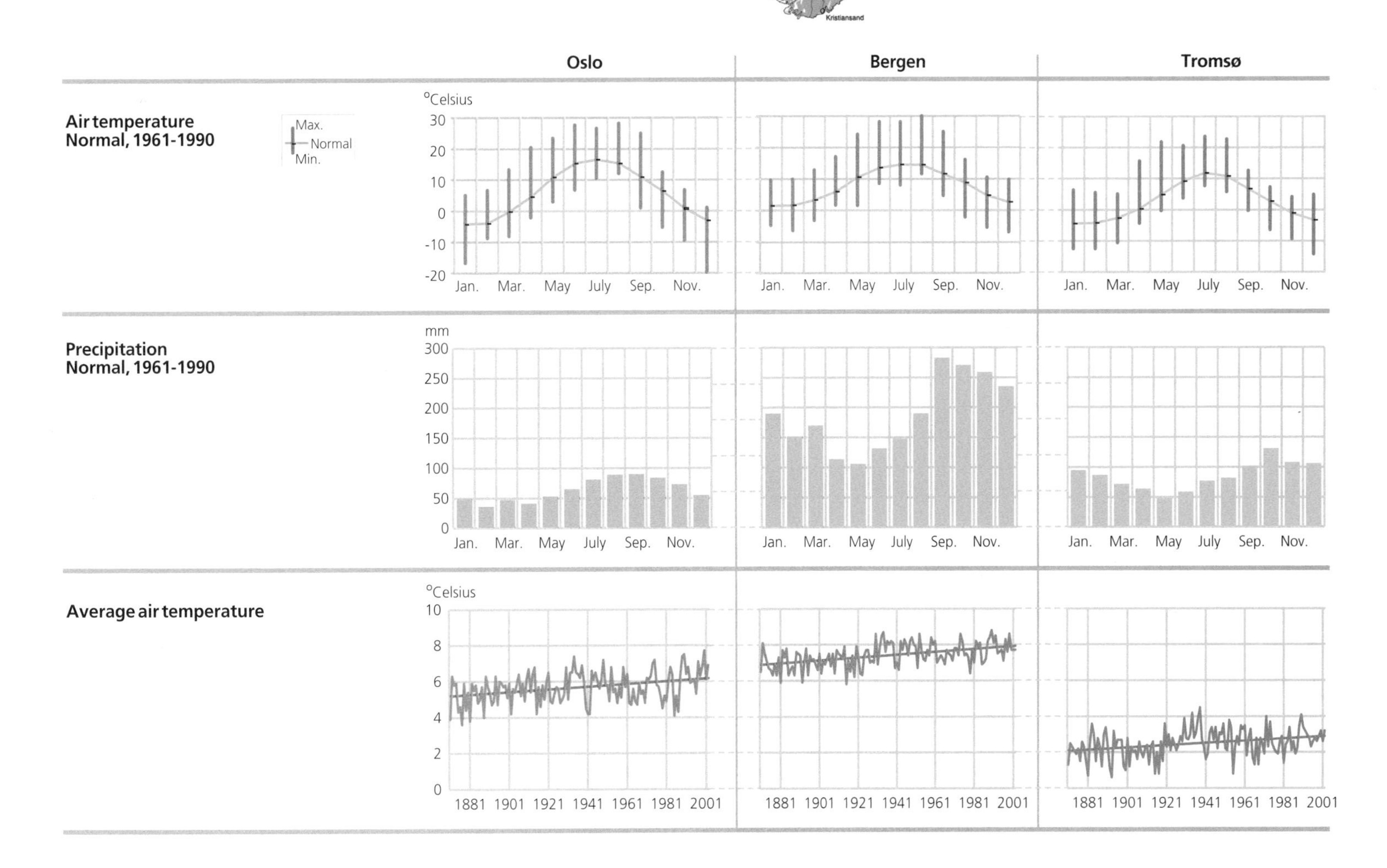

# POPULATION

**Continued population growth ...**

Norway's population exceeded 4.5 million in 2000, an increase of 1.25 million since 1950. The first years after the Second World War, the annual growth in population was about 1 per cent, mainly as a result of high birth rates. Growth declined to a third of a per cent in the 1980s and has since increased slightly. Today, net immigration is as important as births for the growth in population.

**Population 1 January**

| | Population | Annual growth in % |
|---|---|---|
| 1950 | 3 250 000 | |
| 1960 | 3 568 000 | 0.98 |
| 1970 | 3 863 000 | 0.83 |
| 1980 | 4 079 000 | 0.56 |
| 1990 | 4 233 000 | 0.38 |
| 2002 | 4 525 000 | 0.57 |
| *Projected* | | |
| 2010 | 4 724 000 | 0.55 |
| 2020 | 4 975 000 | 0.53 |
| 2030 | 5 244 000 | 0.54 |
| 2040 | 5 440 000 | 0.37 |
| 2050 | 5 591 000 | 0.28 |

**... also in the next fifty years**

What we predict for the future obviously depends on our assumptions. One prognosis, with average fertility and life expectation, centralization and net immigration, gives continued growth during the next 50 years, but at a far lower rate than in the last 50 years. The population will exceed 5 million in 2020 and by 2050 the number of inhabitants will be close to 5.6 million, with annual population growth approaching a quarter of a per cent.

A significant proportion of future growth will probably result from net immigration. If net immigration is low, Norway's population will reach a maximum of about 5.1 million around 2050.

**Senior boom on the way**

We have been hearing about the senior boom for a long time now. However, the situation is very similar to a day at the beach, waiting for the large wave. We think we see it approaching, but most often it flattens out long before it reaches us.

**Proportion of children/young people and seniors in the population**

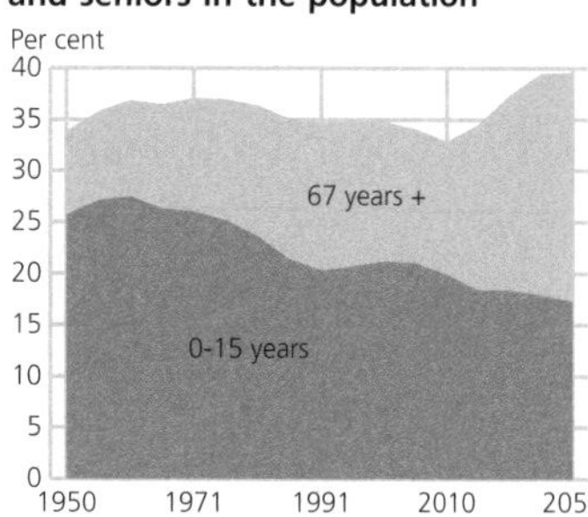


To a certain extent we could say that the senior boom has already hit us. While in 1950 slightly over 8 per cent of the population was over the age of 67, today's figure is in excess of 13 per cent. However, not until after 2010 (when the baby-boomers of the post-war period reach retirement), will this proportion increase further, to 19 per cent in 2030 and 22 per cent in 2050. The proportion of children and young people under 15 will continue to decline, to about 17 per cent in 2050.

**Population according to age and gender, registered and projected**

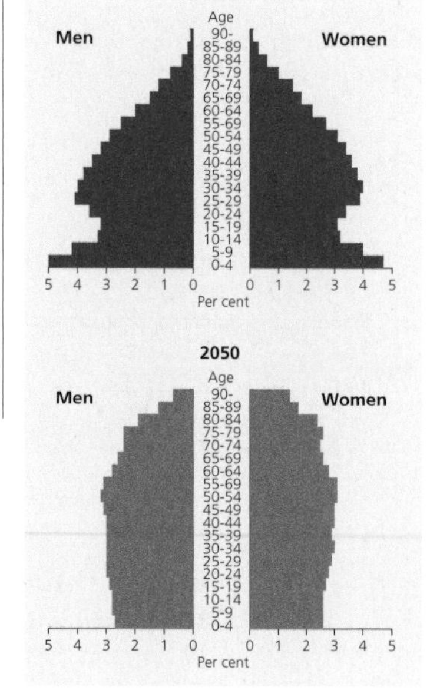


The senior boom is only partly due to the fact that we live longer, which means that there are more people at the top of the pyramid. More important is the low birth rate, meaning that there are fewer at the bottom of the pyramid. The reason the senior boom has not yet fully reached us, is that fertility rates in Norway are still (relatively) high and immigrants are young.

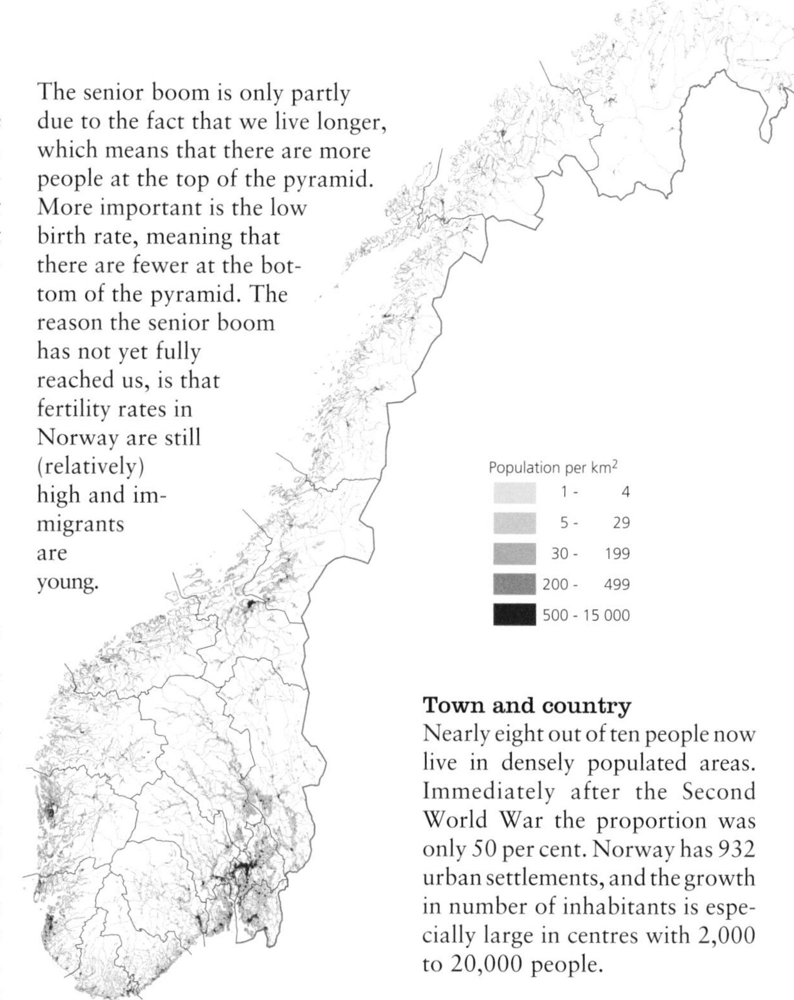


**Town and country**

Nearly eight out of ten people now live in densely populated areas. Immediately after the Second World War the proportion was only 50 per cent. Norway has 932 urban settlements, and the growth in number of inhabitants is especially large in centres with 2,000 to 20,000 people.

**7.6 per cent 'immigrants'**

The number of 'immigrants' obviously depends on how we define an immigrant. Statistics Norway uses the term immigrant population for persons with two foreign-born parents: i.e. both first-generation immigrants and children born in Norway to two foreign-born parents (often called second-generation immigrants). At the beginning of 2003, the immigrant population consisted of 349,000 people. This is 7.6 per cent of the total population, triple that in 1980. Slightly over 70 per cent have backgrounds from non-western countries, i.e. Eastern Europe, Turkey, Asia, Africa, South and Central America. The size of Norway's immigrant population roughly corresponds to that of Denmark (8 per cent) and is far smaller than for example Sweden's (14 per cent) and the Netherlands' (12 per cent).

**Immigrant population in per cent of the total population**

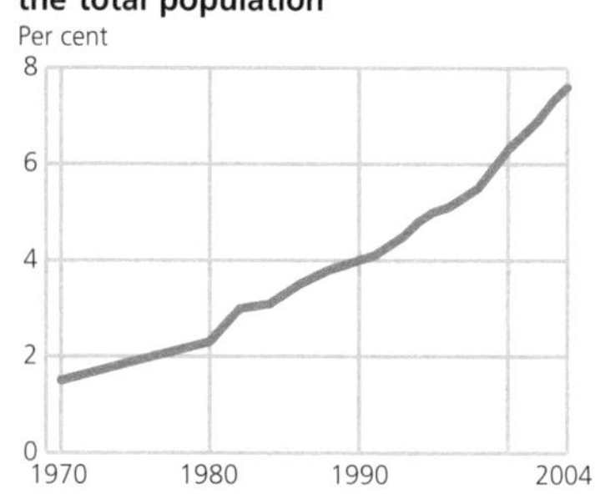


**Immigrant population by national background, major countries, 2004**

| Country | Number |
|---|---|
| Pakistan | 26 300 |
| Sweden | 22 900 |
| Denmark | 19 300 |
| Vietnam | 17 400 |
| Iraq | 17 300 |
| Somalia | 15 600 |
| Bosnia-Hercegovina | 15 200 |
| Iran | 13 500 |
| Turkey | 13 000 |
| Sri Lanka | 11 900 |

# FERTILITY

### Low fertility ...

The baby boom after the Second World War lasted until the mid-1960s, to be followed by a decline that hit bottom around 1985. Thereafter, fertility again increased slightly, but indications are now that it is on its way down again; in 2003, the total fertility rate was 1.80.

**Total fertility rate***

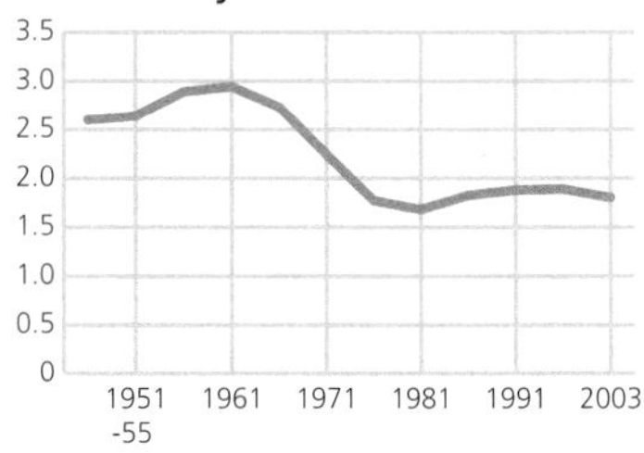


*Average number of live births per woman during her life, provided that the fertility pattern of the period applies to the woman's complete fertile period and no deaths occur.

If we exclude immigration and emigration, the total fertility rate in a country must be at least 2.1 in order to avoid a long-term decline in population. In Norway, the rate has been less than this since the middle of the 1970s..

**Total fertility rate in selected countries, 2002**

|  |  |
|---|---|
| Ireland | 2,01 |
| Iceland | 1,93 |
| France | 1,88 |
| **Norway** | **1,75** |
| Denmark | 1,73 |
| Sweden | 1,65 |
| United Kingdom | 1,64 |
| EU average | 1,47 |
| Portugal | 1,42 |
| Germany | 1,40 |
| Russia | 1,31 |
| Italy | 1,26 |
| Spain | 1,25 |
| Greece | 1,25 |

Source: Eurostat.

### ... but high compared with other countries

The decline in fertility during the past decades is a general phenomenon in the western world. In fact, Norway has been one of the countries with the highest fertility rate in recent years. For example, the average fertility rate of the EU countries is now about 1.5, with Italy and Spain almost down to 1.2. The countries with the highest fertility rates are Iceland and Ireland.

### Half outside marriage

Half of all children are now born outside marriage, compared with only three per cent in the 1950s. The largest increase took place in the 1970s and '80s, an increase that has now slowed down. The great majority of children born outside marriage, however, have cohabiting parents. Only 10 per cent are born to single mothers. Of first-borns, 48 and 16 per cent had cohabiting or single mothers respectively. When the second child arrives, the parents are more often married.

### Most in the north

Most of the children born outside marriage are in the three northernmost counties and in Trøndelag, while the Agder counties and Rogaland have the lowest numbers. There is a clear north-south pattern in Europe too, with Iceland at the top of the list, followed by Sweden and the other Nordic countries. The countries in northern Europe come next. In southern Europe, this is still a relatively rare phenomenon.

### Older mothers

With a rising level of education and occupational activity, mothers are becoming increasingly older. Since the early 1970s, the average childbearing age has increased by about 4 years, to 30.1, the age of first-time mothers being 27.9 years.

### More multiple births

For a long time, the proportion of multiple births (mainly twin births) remained at 1 per cent. From the end of the 1980s, this proportion has increased, and the figure is now close to 2 per cent. This development is assumed to be associated with the increase in the age of childbearing mothers and more frequent use of the test-tube method.

### Falling abortion figures since 1990

Abortion figures increased strongly at the beginning of the 1970s. After the Abortion Act was adopted in 1978, figures have remained relatively stable between 14,000 and 16,000, with 13,836 abortions being carried out in 2003. This corresponds to about 25 per cent of all live births. The abortion frequency is especially high among young women between 18 and 24 years old, and every year between 2 and 3 per cent of this age group undergo an abortion. In the 15 to 19 age group, the number of abortions is now twice as high as the number of births.

**Number of abortions**

### More foreign adoptions

Since the 1960s, the annual number of adoptions has been between 800 and 1,000. There has, however, been a marked change as regards the backgrounds of adopted children. At the end of the 1960s, nine out of ten adopted children were Norwegian. Subsequently, this proportion declined strongly, and today only two out of ten adoptions are Norwegian children, and most of these are adopted stepchildren.

**Number of adopted children, Norwegian and foreign***

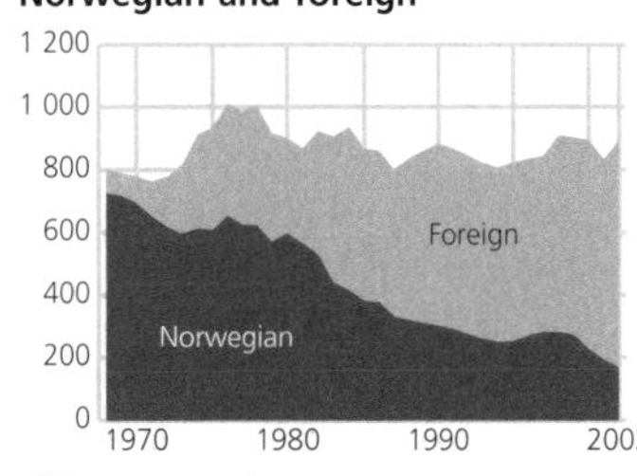


*Three-year moving average

China is now the dominating 'supplier' country, followed by South Korea and Colombia. While a small majority of the children adopted from most countries are boys, nearly all the children adopted from China are girls, and this is assumed to be related to China's one-child policy.

**Percentage of children born outside marriage in selected countries, around 2000**

|  |  |
|---|---|
| Iceland | 65.8 |
| Sweden | 55.3 |
| **Norway** | **49.6** |
| Denmark | 44.6 |
| France | 47.7 |
| United Kingdom | 39.6 |
| The Netherlands | 24.9 |
| Germany | 22.1 |
| Spain | 16.3 |
| Italy | 10.2 |
| Greece | 3.9 |

Source: Eurostat.

### What, then, will be the child's name?

Whether the children are born inside or outside marriage, are twins or adopted, they must all have a name. In 2003, Mathias and Emma were the most popular names in Norway.

Naming fashion seems to go in waves, and many of today's names were very popular about a hundred years ago. Furthermore, many of the names are 'international', that is, names we also see at the top of the list in other countries (in other words, 'Norwegian' names with the letters æ, ø and å are disappearing).

A third trend is that children are no longer given several names; double names or hyphenated names (such as JanErik and Ole-Petter) are on the decline.

**Most popular first names, 2003**

| | Boys' names | Girls' names |
|---|---|---|
| 1 | Mathias/Matias | Emma |
| 2 | Tobias | Ida |
| 3 | Andreas | Thea/Tea |
| 4 | Martin | Sara/Sarah |
| 5 | Kristian/Christian | Julie |
| 6 | Jonas | Nora |
| 7 | Markus/Marcus | Emilie |
| 8 | Sander | Maria |
| 9 | Kristoffer/ Christoffer | Ingrid |
| 10 | Daniel | Hanna/Hannah |

# THE FAMILY

### More people live alone ...

The postwar period saw the golden days of the nuclear family. Marriage frequency was high, with a slight decrease in the proportion of one-person households. From the beginning of the 1970s, however, marriage figures declined, at the same time as the number of divorces increased. In combination, this has resulted in a more than doubling of single-person households. Today, 38 per cent of all households consist of singles, and singles make up 17 per cent of the population. Single-person households are especially common in the inner-city areas of the major towns and in sparsely populated areas.

**Proportion of one-person households**

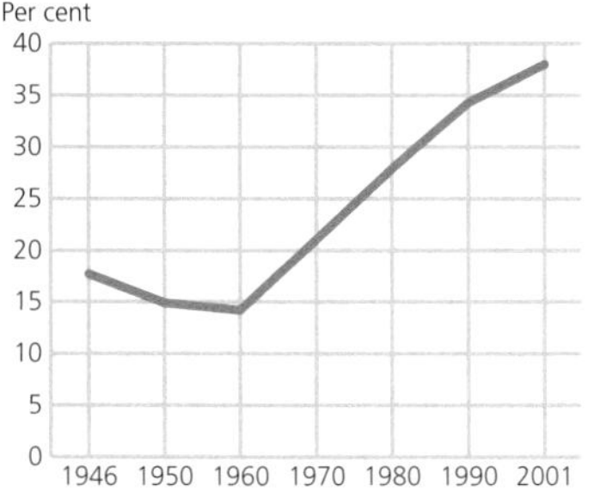


**Number of married couples and cohabiting couples with and without children**

| | 1990 | 2001 |
|---|---|---|
| Total no. of couples | 973 000 | 1 039 326 |
| Total number of married couples | 871 000 | 834 969 |
| Without children | 467 000 | 485 468 |
| With children | 404 000 | 349 501 |
| Total no. of cohabiting couples | 102 000 | 204 357 |
| Without children | 52 000 | 86 856 |
| With children | 50 000 | 119 501 |

### ... and more people cohabit

The decline in the number of existing marriages in recent years is not only due to more people divorcing and living alone. There is also an increasing proportion choosing to live together without getting married. Unmarried cohabitants entered the statistics already towards the end of the 1970s, but it is only during the past decade that this form of cohabitation has become more common. Unmarried cohabiting couples now account for 20 per cent of all couples, an increase from 10 per cent in 1990. And while, previously, cohabitants normally did not have children, the majority now have children.

Among young people (under 30) it is now more common to cohabit than to marry. Oslo and the counties of Trøndelag northwards have the highest proportion of cohabiting couples. Nine of the ten municipalities with the lowest number of cohabiting couples are found in Rogaland and Vest-Agder, while seven of the ten municipalities with the highest proportion are located in Finnmark.

**Cohabiting couples in per cent of all couples**

Per cent
6.1 - 17.3
17.4 - 21.1
21.2 - 32.0

### One of three marriages is civil

After the number of new marriages bottomed out in the early 1990s, the number increased again for a few years. In the 1970s, the proportion of civil marriages increased strongly, peaking in the early 1980s, when 38 per cent of all marriages entered into were civil. Later this proportion declined slightly, only to increase again in recent years.

The large proportion of civil marriages is assumed – among other variables – to be associated with the fact that over 20 per cent of the people getting married, are doing so for the second or third time around. It has furthermore become popular to get married abroad; almost 15 per cent of all marriages are entered into abroad.

**Civil marriages and marriages entered into abroad**

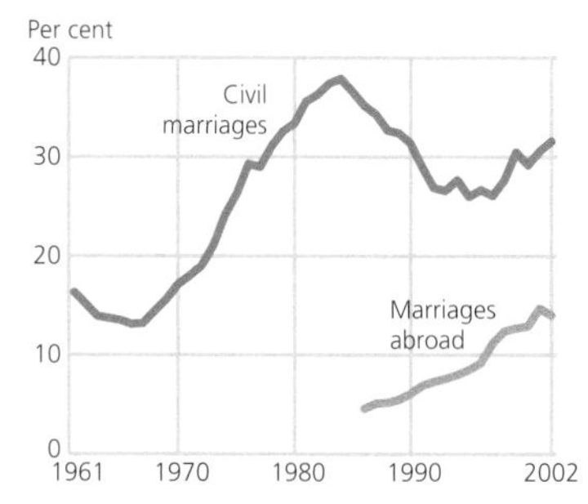


### Close to 200 same-sex partnerships a year

In 1993, same-sex partnerships as a form of cohabitation also became part of the statistics; since then, slightly over 1,400 partnerships have been registered. Initially, same-sex partnerships were predominantly entered into between men. Gradually, this situation has changed, but men still make up the majority.

**Number of same-sex partnerships contracted. Men and women**

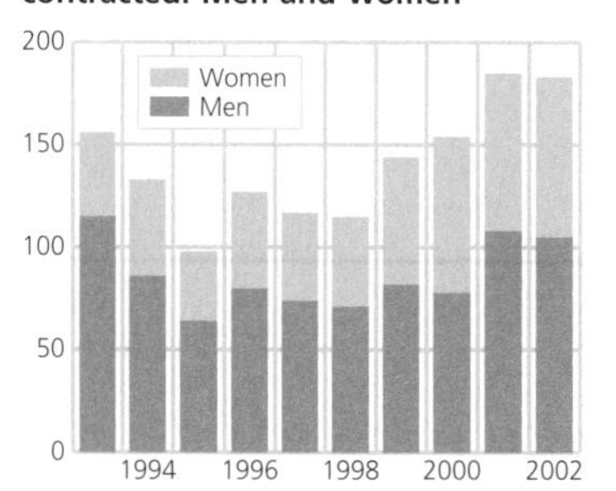


### Many divorces, but ...

After a sustained and marked increase in the number of divorces until the beginning of the 1990s, the number now seems to have stabilized at about 10,000 per year. This means that between 40 and 45 per cent of all marriages will probably end in divorce.

With a large and increasing proportion of cohabiting couples, divorce figures will gradually become less representative as an indicator of couple break-ups.

**Number of divorces**

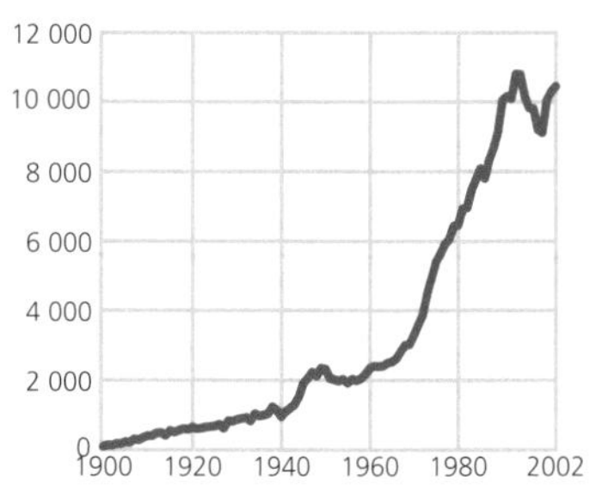

# HEALTH

## A long life

Life expectancy is frequently used as an indicator of the health of the population. A new-born boy can now expect to become 77.0 years old, a girl 81.9. This is a marked increase since the period 1946-50, when the figures were 69.3 and 72.7 years respectively.

**Life expectancy at birth for men and women**

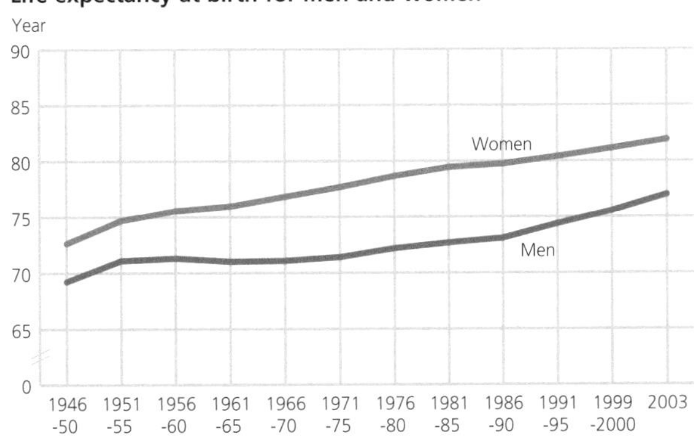


In the 1950s and '60s, the difference between men and women increased, mainly because of a rise in deaths caused by cardiovascular diseases among men. During the past ten years this difference has diminished.

In the same way as there are large differences in life expectancy from country to country, there are also distinctive regional differences in Norway. For example, women in Sogn og Fjordane may expect to live for almost 83 years, while a woman in Finnmark can expect to live for slightly less than 80 years.

**Life expectancy at birth for certain selected countries. Around 2000**

| | Men | Women |
|---|---|---|
| Japan | 77.4 | 84.8 |
| Spain | 75.5 | 82.7 |
| Switzerland | 76.9 | 82.6 |
| France | 75.2 | 82.7 |
| Sweden | 77.4 | 81.7 |
| Austria | 77.0 | 82.4 |
| Canada | 77.1 | 82.2 |
| Italy | 76.3 | 82.4 |
| **Norway** | **77.0** | **81.9** |
| Iceland | 77.4 | 82.0 |
| Denmark | 74.5 | 79.3 |

Source: Eurostat.

**Remaining life expectancy at different ages. 2002**

| | Men | Women |
|---|---|---|
| 0 | 76.5 | 81.5 |
| 10 | 66.9 | 71.9 |
| 20 | 57.1 | 62.1 |
| 30 | 47.6 | 52.3 |
| 40 | 38.2 | 42.5 |
| 50 | 28.9 | 33.0 |
| 60 | 20.2 | 24.1 |
| 70 | 12.7 | 15.8 |
| 80 | 6.9 | 8.7 |

**Causes of death, in per cent**

| | Men | | | Women | | |
|---|---|---|---|---|---|---|
| | 1951-1955 | 1971-1975 | 1996-2000 | 1951-1955 | 1971-1975 | 1996-2000 |
| All causes | 100.0 | 100.0 | 100.0 | 100.0 | 100.0 | 100.0 |
| Violent deaths | 8.6 | 7.5 | 6.4 | 3.7 | 4.4 | 4.2 |
| *Deaths due to sickness:* | | | | | | |
| Tuberculosis and other infectious diseases | 3.9 | 0.8 | 1.0 | 2.6 | 0.8 | 1.2 |
| Cancer | 18.1 | 18.6 | 25.4 | 19.2 | 19.1 | 21.9 |
| Diabetes | 0.7 | 0.5 | 1.4 | 1.0 | 0.9 | 1.4 |
| Cardiovascular diseases | 40.1 | 50.5 | 42.0 | 45.0 | 51.3 | 44.2 |
| Respiratory diseases (e.g. pneumonia) | 6.5 | 8.0 | 8.8 | 7.8 | 10.1 | 9.8 |
| All other diseases | 22.1 | 14.2 | 14.9 | 21.0 | 13.5 | 17.2 |

**Life expectancy for men and women, 1996-2000**

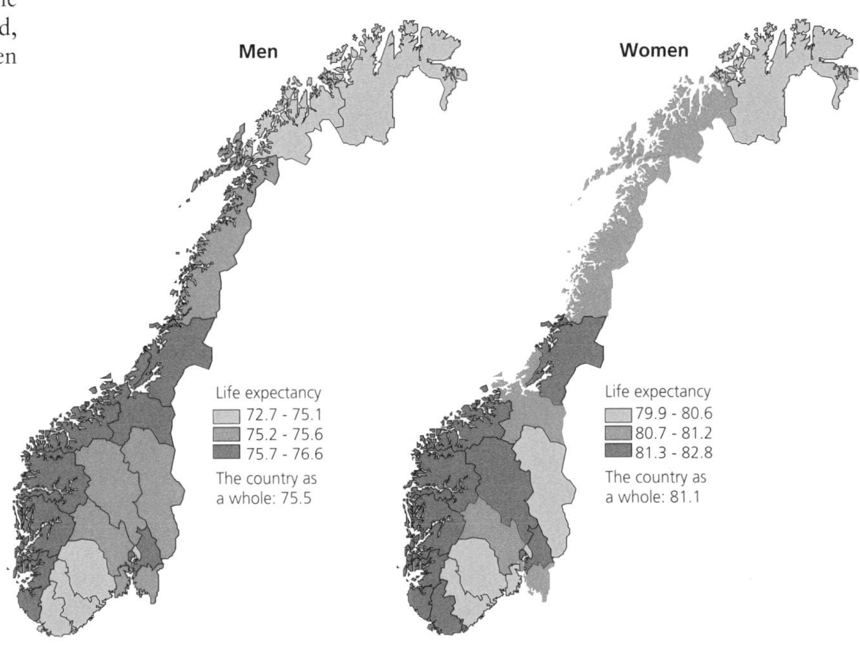


## What we die of

Before, during and just after the Second World War, tuberculosis and other infectious diseases were important causes of death, but these have played a minor role since 1960. At the same time, the importance of cardiovascular diseases grew, and at the beginning of the 1970s caused more than fifty per cent of all deaths. Their significance has since declined somewhat. Cancer mortality, on the other hand, has shown a continuous increase, especially for men.

The number of violent deaths has remained relatively stable since the Second World War. However, while drowning and accidents in the fishing and shipping industries previously dominated the statistics, falls, traffic accidents and suicides are now predominant.

## Fewer daily smokers

Since the early 1970s, the proportion of daily smokers has declined considerably. The percentage of male smokers has sunk from over 50 to 27. For a long time, the figure for women smokers remained stable at slightly over 30 per cent, but this has now declined to 25 per cent. An additional 11 per cent report that they are occasional smokers.

**Daily smokers. Women and men, 16-74 years old***

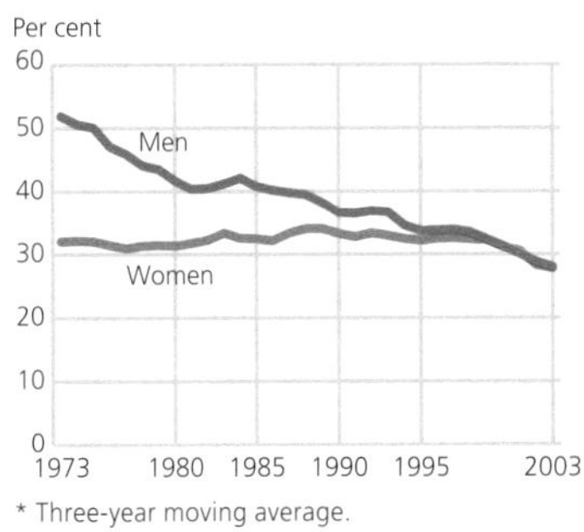


* Three-year moving average.

Parallel with the decline in the proportion of male smokers, the proportion of men taking snuff has increased in recent years. Of men between 16 and 74, six per cent state that they take snuff daily, and an additional six per cent state that they take snuff 'occasionally'. Whereas snuff was previously most common among older men, its popularity is now highest among younger men under 45.

# EDUCATION

**Women and men with higher education**

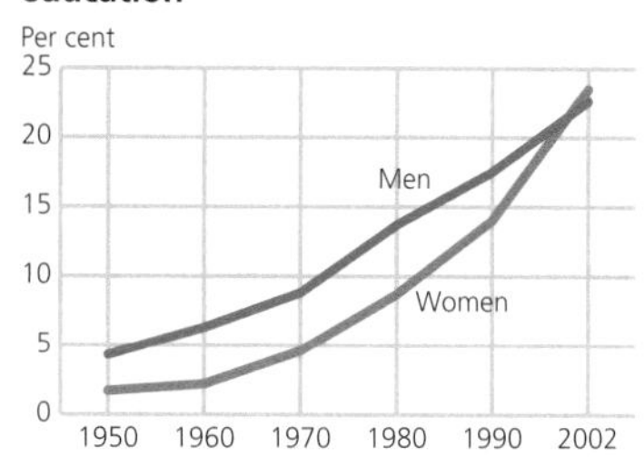


### Women on the go

Since the mid-1980s, the majority of students in higher education have been women, and today, nearly six out of 10 students are women. The female dominance is particularly noticeable at the university colleges (63 per cent). The majority (almost 60 per cent) of graduates from universities and colleges are women. 50 per cent of students completing graduate education were women, whereas the portion of women completing undergraduate education amounted to 63 per cent.

### As many women as men have higher education

Compared with 1970, three times as many Norwegians have now completed higher education. And there is no longer a difference between men and women; about 22 per cent of both men and women over 15 years old have college or university education. However, men still take a longer higher education than women. Among the youngest age group (under 50), there are now far more women than men with higher education; the dominance is especially large in the 25-29 year age group, where 43 per cent of women have a higher education, compared with 31 per cent for men. Since 1955, the total number of pupils and students has increased from about 550,000 to slightly over 1 million, and more than one-fifth of all Norwegians are now studying.

### Primary and lower secondary education

After the change from 7 to 9 years of compulsory primary and lower secondary education, the number of pupils increased in the 1960s and early 1970s. Thereafter, the number of pupils declined until the mid-1990s, when it increased strongly when school for 6-year olds was introduced in 1997 (Reform 97). In the autumn of 2003, there were 617,000 pupils in primary and lower secondary school in Norway.

**Number of pupils and students in primary and lower secondary school, upper secondary school and at universities and colleges**

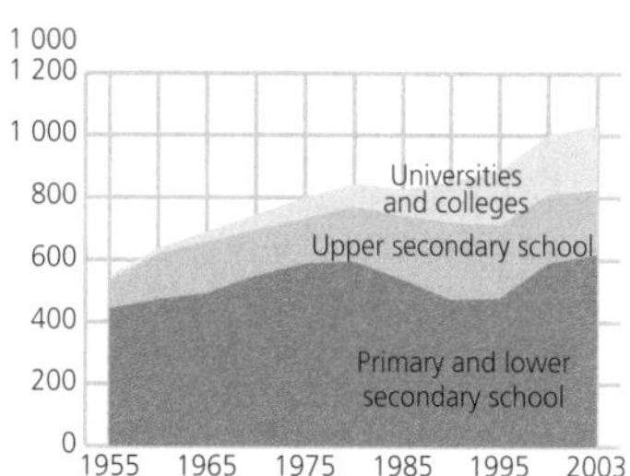


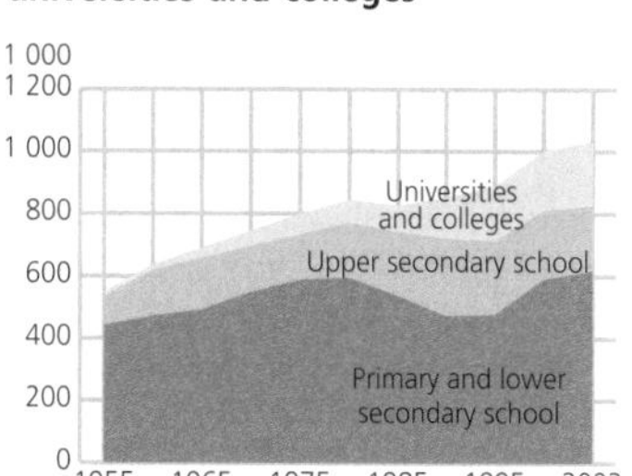

### High school

The number of students increased until the beginning of the 1990s, but has subsequently experienced a slight decline. Slightly over 90 per cent of all 16-18 year olds now attend high school, compared with 65 per cent in 1980.

### Universities and colleges

The marked growth in university and college education flattened out towards the end of the 1990s. The total number of students is now 210,000, and more than every fourth Norwegian between 19 and 24 years old completes a higher education. In other words, there are as many college/university students as there are students in upper secondary school.

### Research and development

In 2001, the cost of research and development (R&D) amounted to NOK 24.5 billion. This constituted 1.6 per cent of Norway's gross domestic product (GDP), a percentage that has remained quite stable during the last ten years. In comparison, the average for OECD countries was 2.3 per cent and for the EU 1.9 per cent. Of the Nordic countries, Sweden spent 4.3 per cent of its GDP on R & D, Denmark 2.4 and Finland 3.4 per cent.

Slightly more than half of the R&D expenses (NOK 12.6 billion) related to trade and industry, NOK 6.3 billion was spent by universities and colleges, while research institutions accounted for NOK 5.6 billion.

**Proportion of population with higher education, 2002**

Per cent
17.1 - 18.1
18.2 - 21.2
21.3 - 37.7
Total, country: 23.0

### Out and about

An increasing number of young people study abroad. Since 1960, the number has quintupled, and the increase has especially been high in the last decade.

In the 2002/2003 academic year, 16,000 Norwegian students studied abroad. Around 6,000 students on exchange programmes come in addition to this. In all, this represents over 10 per cent of all students.

Here, too, women have gradually become the majority (almost 57 per cent of students studying abroad are women).

**Number of students abroad**

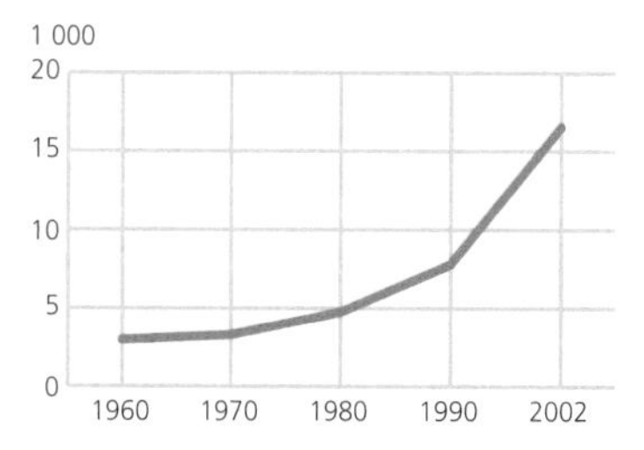


### Nynorsk on the decline

After a marked decline from 1950 to 1976, the proportion of pupils speaking Nynorsk (one of the two official Norwegian languages) in primary and lower secondary school stabilized at about 17 per cent. However, during the last 5 – 6 years, the proportion has further declined, and in 2003 was 14.5 per cent..

**Nynorsk-speaking primary and lower secondary school pupils**

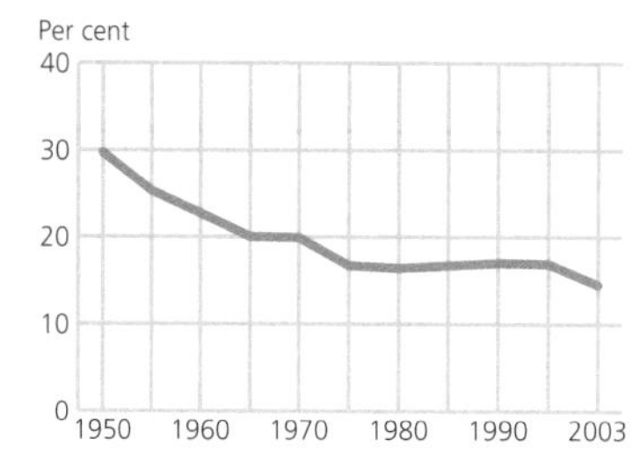


**Students abroad: The most important countries and subjects, 2002**

| | Number of students |
|---|---|
| **Country** | |
| Australia | 3 946 |
| United Kingdom | 3 458 |
| Denmark | 2 068 |
| USA | 1 269 |
| Sweden | 973 |
| **Subjects** | |
| Commerce | 2 952 |
| Medicine | 1 934 |
| Engineering/Technology | 1 563 |
| Arts | 1 439 |
| Media | 1 011 |

Source: State Education Loan Fund

# EMPLOYMENT

**Labour force participation rate for women aged 15-64. and proportion working part-time. 2002**

| | Partici-pation rate | Proportion working part-time |
|---|---|---|
| Iceland | 81.9 | 44.7 |
| **Norway** | **74.2** | **42.9** |
| Denmark | 72.6 | 31.1 |
| Sweden | 72.5 | 32.3 |
| Switzerland | 71.6 | 56.2 |
| Finland | 67.3 | 16.9 |
| United Kingdom | 65.3 | 43.3 |
| Germany | 58.8 | 39.2 |
| France | 56.4 | 29.6 |
| Ireland | 55.2 | 36.2 |
| Spain | 44.0 | 16.9 |
| Italy | 41.9 | 16.7 |

Source: Eurostat

**Labour force participation rate, women and men aged 16-74**

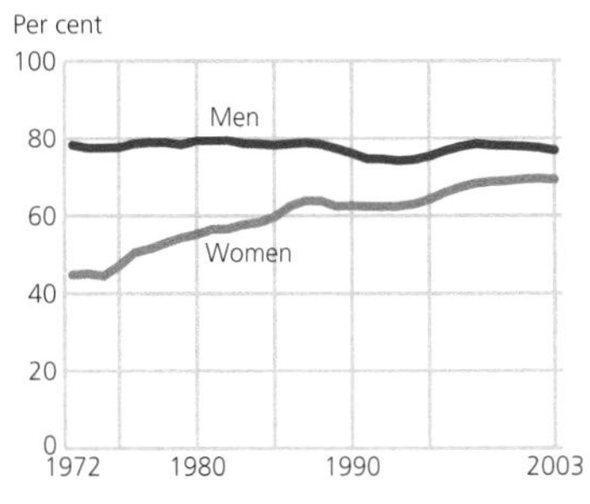


**Weekly working hours for employed women and men**

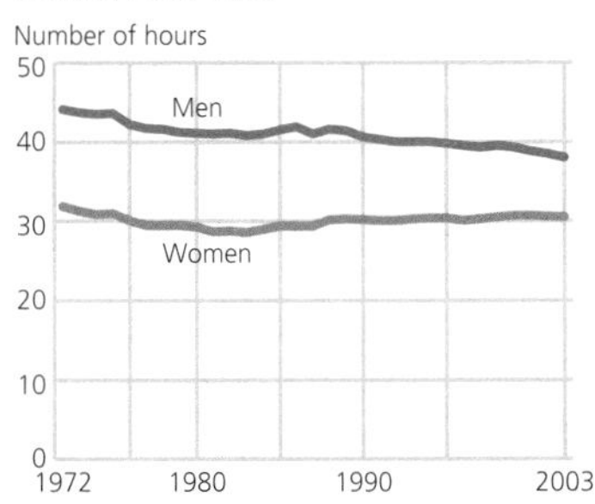


**Unemployed men and women aged 16-74. In per cent of the labour force**

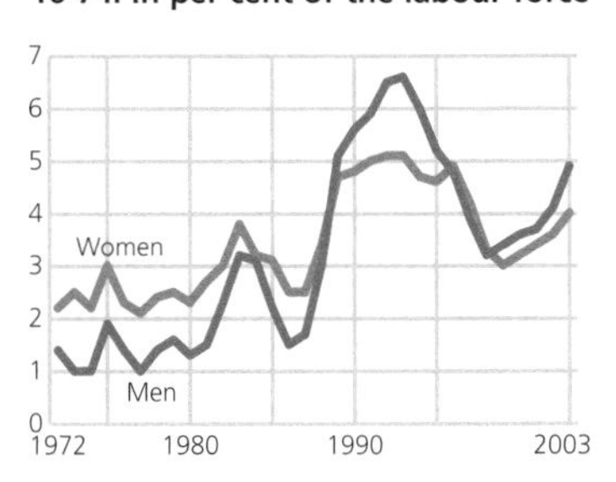


## Women's employment frequency is almost as high as that of men ...

In 2003, the number of employed people was almost 2.3 million, corresponding to 50 per cent of the population. Of this figure, women now account for 47 per cent. From the mid-1970s until 1986, women's occupational activity increased markedly. During the economic recession from 1987 to 1993, women's employment frequency remained stable, while it declined slightly for men. After 1993, it has increased somewhat for both men and women, but most for women. In 2002, the labour force included 69.6 per cent of all women and 77.4 per cent of all men aged 16 to 74.

## ... but they work shorter hours

Many women still work part-time, although the proportion is declining: in 1980, 47 per cent worked full-time; in 2002 the proportion had increased to 56 per cent. The proportion of men working full-time remains stable at about 90 per cent, and part-time work is largely reserved for students. Since 1972, men's actual weekly working hours have been shortened by almost six hours, from 44.1 to 38.4. Women's working hours declined slightly until 1983, because at that time the increase in their employment was largely in the form of part-time employees. Since then, growth has increasingly been in the form of full-time employment, and women's average working hours have increased by about two hours, to 30.4.

## Unemployment on the increase again

From the early 1970s until the recession in 1983-1984, unemployment remained stable at about 2 per cent of the workforce, consistently about one percentage point higher for women than for men.

When unemployment rose in the 1980s, gender differences evened out, and from 1988 to 1995, unemployment among men was higher than among women. One reason was that women are more frequently employed in the public sector, and thus less exposed to cyclical fluctuations. Unemployment for men still remains somewhat higher than for women.

**Number of employed men and women in selected occupations, 2001**

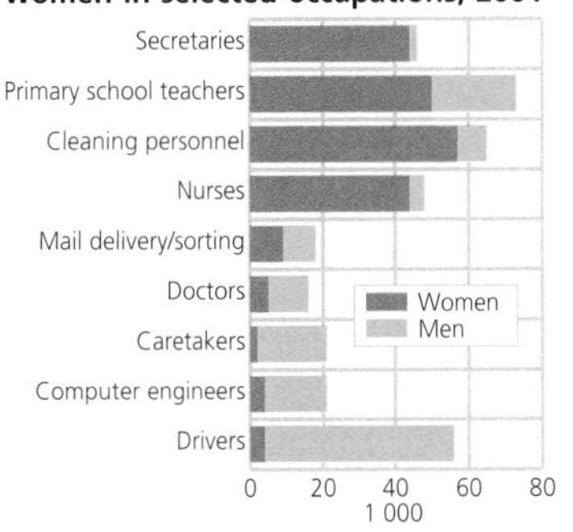


*Labour force* = employed and unemployed. In per cent of the population this is called economic activity rate.

*Working hours*: Full-time = 37 hours +, and 32-36 hours when this is said to correspond to full-time

**Monthly pay for full-time employed men and women in selected occupations, 2001**

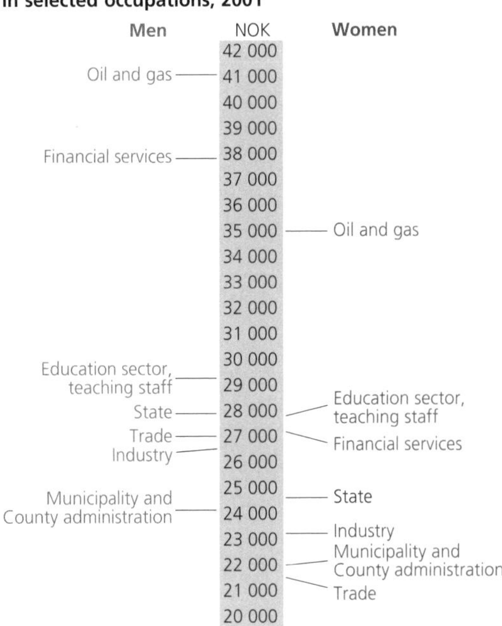


## Still women's and men's professions

Despite an increasing level of education, both men's and women's career choices remain rather traditional. Typical female occupations are nursery and primary school teachers, nurses, cleaning personnel and secretaries. Typical male occupations are craftsmen, construction workers, drivers and engineers.

In some occupations, for example, within post delivery, marketing and consultancy services, there are about as many men as there are women.

## Large pay differences

The pay for a normal work-year increased from NOK 30,900 in 1970 to NOK 320,200 in 2002. Adjusted for inflation, the real increase in pay was 68 per cent. The increase was especially high at the beginning of the 1970s and towards the end of the 1990s.

In 1991, the average monthly pay for full-time employed men and women was NOK 26,937 and NOK 23,134 respectively. In other words, women's monthly pay amounted to 86 per cent of the men's. This difference has not changed much in recent years. In the long term, however, the difference has decreased. Around 1960, women were paid only 60 per cent of what men were paid. The situation varies between different industries: in the financial services industry women's pay constitutes only 76 per cent of that of men, while within the education sector it is almost 95 per cent.

# INCOME AND ASSETS

### Increased social security

In 2002, the average Norwegian household income was NOK 444,800, more than twice that in 1986. About 71 per cent of this is earned income, that is, income from employment and self-employment. This proportion has declined slightly in recent years, while social security benefits, such as pensions and child benefits, now constitute a larger proportion than before.

Capital income, such as interest on capital and share dividends, tripled during the period.

**Composition of household income**

| | 1986 | 1990 | 1992 | 1994 | 1996 | 1998 | 2000 | 2002 |
|---|---|---|---|---|---|---|---|---|
| | | | | *NOK* | | | | |
| **Total income** | **207 700** | **255 800** | **274 100** | **282 700** | **311 800** | **357 500** | **405 100** | **444 800** |
| Earned income | 161 800 | 191 000 | 196 600 | 202 800 | 223 800 | 262 200 | 286 700 | 316 800 |
| Capital income | 10 900 | 15 600 | 14 800 | 15 100 | 19 400 | 19 200 | 34 200 | 33 500 |
| Social security benefits | 35 000 | 49 200 | 62 700 | 64 800 | 68 600 | 76 100 | 84 200 | 94 500 |
| | | | | *Per cent* | | | | |
| **Total income** | **100.0** | **100.0** | **100.0** | **100.0** | **100.0** | **100.0** | **100.0** | **100.0** |
| Earned income | 77.9 | 74.7 | 71.7 | 71.7 | 71.8 | 73.3 | 70.8 | 71.2 |
| Capital income | 5.2 | 6.1 | 5.4 | 5.3 | 6.2 | 5.4 | 8.4 | 7.5 |
| Social security benefits | 16.9 | 19.2 | 22.9 | 22.9 | 22.0 | 21.3 | 20.8 | 21.3 |

### Women's income 61 per cent of men's

In 2001, the average gross income for all adults was NOK 243,900, and the average assessed tax was about 25 per cent.

Although full-time employed women's average monthly pay is about 84 per cent that of men, women's annual gross income is only 60 per cent that of men. In 1984 the corresponding proportion was 47 per cent.

The difference in income between men and women is far greater than the pay difference because of the lower employment frequency of women and the fact that they more often work part-time.

### Larger income differences

The tenth of people with the lowest household income per consumption unit had their share of the total income reduced from 4.2 per cent in 1986 to 3.6 in 2002. At the same time, the tenth with the highest income increased their share, from 18.6 to 23.6 per cent. The increased difference, in other words, is primarily due to the rich having become richer.

**Average gross income in 2001 NOK**

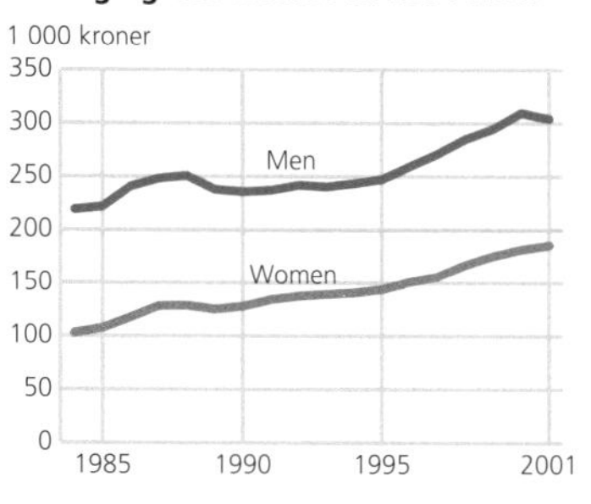


### More people own shares

The survey of household assets and liabilities shows that both real assets and financial assets have increased since 1986, but it is especially 'other financial assets' (shares, mutual funds, etc.) that have grown. In 1986, the value of bank deposits was twice as high as the value of other financial assets. In 2000, the value of shares and bank deposits was almost the same, but since then bank deposits have increased strongly while the value of shares has dropped.

Like other average figures, these too cover up large inequalities, and the distribution of financial assets is very uneven: the tenth of households with the largest financial assets accounted for as much as two-thirds of these assets.

### Heavy debt burden for many, but interest rates less important

The debt of the average household has increased strongly in recent years, and in 2002 amounted to NOK 495,000. Slightly over 80 per cent of all households are in debt, a proportion that has declined somewhat in recent years. The proportion with a large debt burden, twice the annual income or higher, rose to 16 per cent in 1992. Thereafter, it declined a little, but now seems to be on the increase once more.

The significance of the interest expenses, however, has lessened; until the beginning of the 1990s, interest expenses accounted for 13 - 14 per cent of the income of a household. Because of a lower interest level, this proportion has later decreased to 6-7 per cent.

### Four per cent are poor

The proportion of people with household incomes after tax per consumption unit below 50 per cent of the median income is often used to define a low income or poverty limit (OECD). This proportion was about 4 per cent for the country as a whole. The highest number of people with a low income is found in Oslo and in non-central municipalities.

**Proportion of total income after tax per consumption unit earned by people with the highest/ lowest incomes**

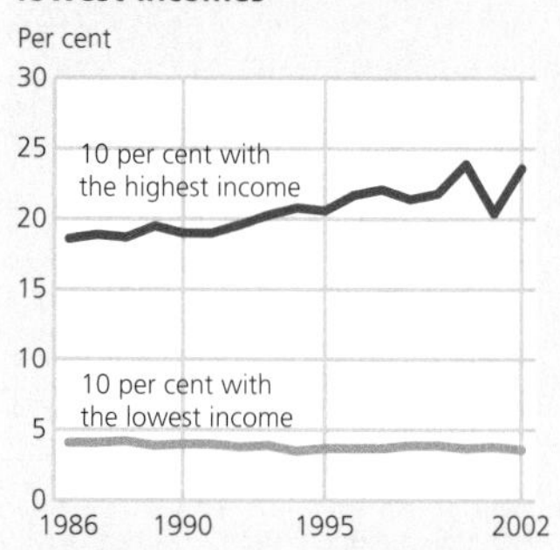


**Proportion of households with debt twice their annual income or higher**

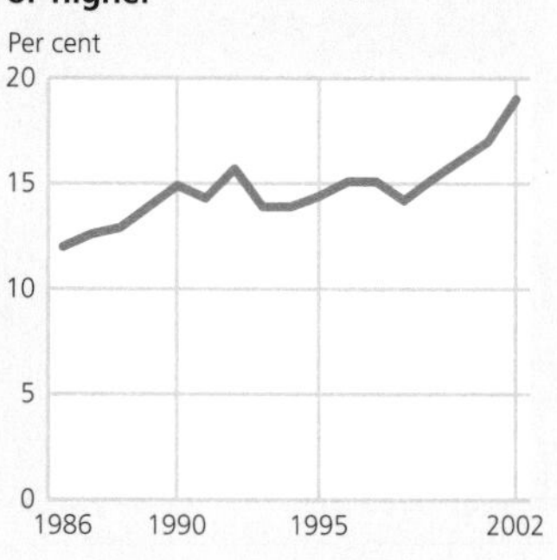


**Household assets and liabilities**

| | 1986 | 1990 | 1992 | 1994 | 1996 | 1998 | 2000 | 2002 |
|---|---|---|---|---|---|---|---|---|
| Real assets | 147 900 | 182 900 | 200 300 | 202 000 | 226 400 | 240 200 | 260 600 | 302 000 |
| Total financial assets | 135 800 | 176 300 | 172 900 | 192 800 | 217 000 | 284 200 | 352 800 | 363 700 |
| Bank deposits | 89 900 | 123 600 | 127 500 | 129 700 | 136 400 | 145 800 | 172 900 | 205 800 |
| Other financial assets | 45 800 | 52 700 | 45 400 | 64 100 | 80 600 | 138 400 | 179 900 | 158 000 |
| Debt | 217 800 | 284 200 | 288 200 | 281 500 | 316 200 | 353 900 | 415 000 | 495 500 |
| Net assets | 65 900 | 75 000 | 85 000 | 113 400 | 127 200 | 170 500 | 198 400 | 170 200 |

# CONSUMPTION

## Consumption has almost tripled since 1958

From 2000 to 2002, average annual consumption expenditure per household was NOK 299,300. In 1958, the corresponding amount was NOK 11,088, which in 2002-kroner equals about NOK 108,000. Taking into consideration that during this period, households became smaller, real consumption has more than tripled.

**Portion of household expenditure spent on food, housing and transport**

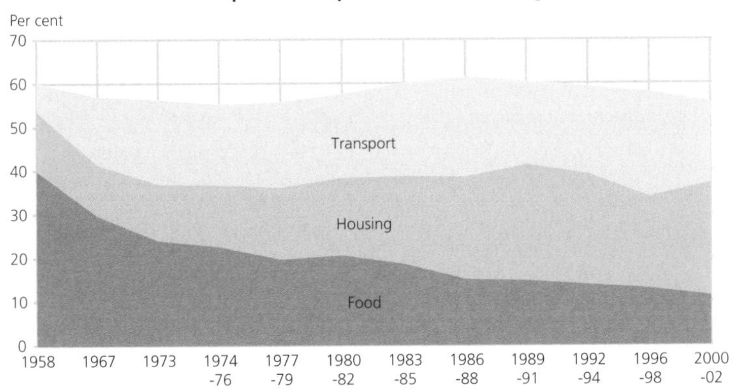


### Less on food ...

There have been two main trends in the development of consumption during the last 40 years. The proportion spent on food and non-alcoholic beverages has been declining throughout the period (at the same time as we are becoming more concerned about the price of food), and today, an average household spends only slightly more than 11 per cent of its annual consumption expenditure on food, compared with 40 per cent in 1958.

### ... and more on housing and transport

On the other hand, we spend an increasing proportion on housing and transport: 26 and 19 per cent respectively. Most of the transport expenses relate to the purchase of cars, their maintenance and operation. Food, housing and transport together account for almost 60 per cent of total consumption expenditure, a proportion that has remained relatively unchanged since 1958.

**Price increase, selected goods and services, 1979-2002**

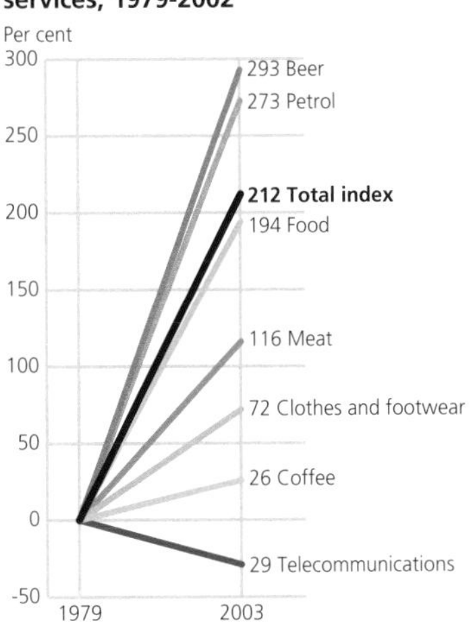


**Percentage of household expenditure on food, alcohol and tobacco in selected countries. 1999**

|  |  |
|---|---|
| Ireland | 22.4 |
| Spain | 21.0 |
| Italy | 20.9 |
| France | 18.9 |
| Sweden | 18.3 |
| Denmark | 17.3 |
| Finland | 17.1 |
| **Norway** | **14.9** |
| United Kingdom | 13.4 |
| The Netherlands | 12.6 |
| Germany | 11.1 |

Source: Eurostat.

### Less on clothes and footwear ...

It is perhaps somewhat surprising that we also spend less on clothes and footwear – a little under 6 per cent, less than half of what we spent in 1958.

The reason is not that we buy fewer clothes and shoes today, but rather that these products have become relatively cheaper because the price increase has been lower than for most other products.

### ... but more on mobile telephones

Telecommunications, too, have become cheaper in recent years. Even so, the proportion spent on telephone services has increased to about 2 per cent, and annual spending now averages NOK 6,500.

### We drink more wine

Since 1945, the total consumption of alcohol has more than tripled and each adult Norwegian now drinks an average of 6 litres of pure alcohol a year.

**Consumption of liquor, wine and beer per inhabitant aged 15 and over**

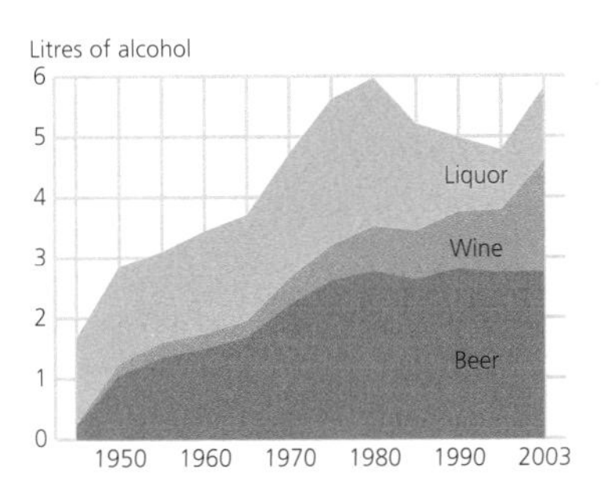


Alcohol consumption increased steadily until about 1980, primarily because of higher consumption of beer and liquor. Thereafter, liquor consumption dropped by more than 50 per cent at the same time as beer consumption stabilized. In spite of this, the total alcohol consumption has risen in recent years due to increased consumption of wine. There has also been an increase in the consumption of alcoholic soft drinks, to 0.2 litres per inhabitant.

Despite the increase in consumption, we do not spend more on alcohol: during the last 30 years beer, wine and liquor have accounted for about 2 per cent of household expenditure.

### Changed food habits ...

Not only do we spend a smaller proportion of our money on food, we also spend it on different foods.

**Consumption of selected foods per person per year**

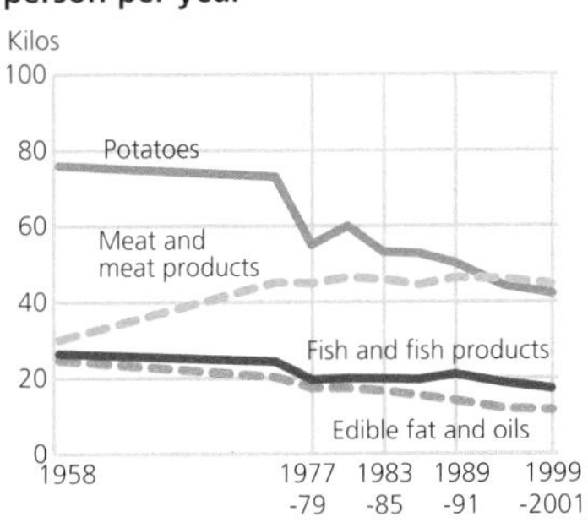


Norway is no longer a 'potato country'. Since 1958, potato consumption has almost halved, to 43 kilos per person (including a little over 4 kilos in the form of crisps, chips, etc.). Consumption of butter, margarine and oils is down by more than 50 per cent.

While meat consumption has remained relatively stable during the past 25 years, we eat progressively less fish and fish products. Consumption of fruit and vegetables, on the other hand, has risen.

### ... and drinking habits

It is not only with regard to alcohol that our drinking habits have changed. Milk consumption has dropped from almost 170 litres per person to slightly over 90 litres: and while we previously drank mostly whole milk, we now drink mostly semi-skimmed and skimmed milk.

**Consumption of milk and mineral water/soft drinks per person per year**

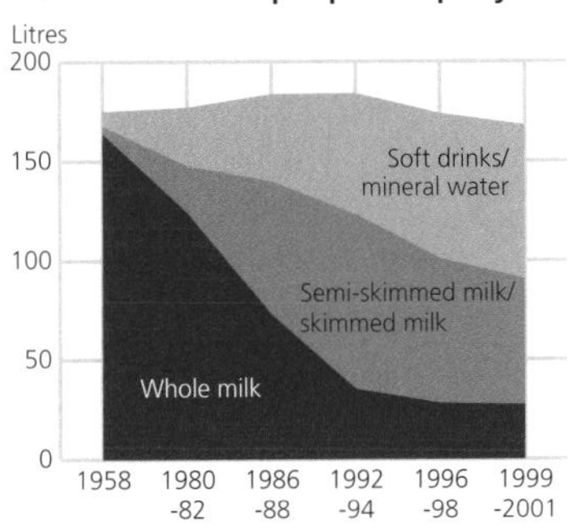


However, our consumption of non-alcoholic beverages (mineral water and soft drinks) has increased tenfold since 1958. We now drink 77 litres a year on average. This increase corresponds quite accurately to the drop in milk consumption.

# HOUSING

### Nearly two of three in detached houses

In 2001, there were about 1,962,000 dwellings in Norway; almost twice as many as in 1950. Of these units, 57 per cent are detached houses (or farmhouses), accommodating 64 per cent of the population. 21 per cent are semi-detached, terraced or other small houses, whereas 18 per cent are blocks of flats or apartment buildings. Seven of ten households have accommodation units with gardens.

### Nearly eight of ten own their own housing

77 per cent of all households live in owner-occupied housing, while 23 per cent live in rented accommodation. The proportion renting their accommodation has increased since 1990, and this increase is mainly in urban areas. In Oslo, close to 30 per cent of all households rent their accommodation. The corresponding figure for 1990 was 24 per cent. The increase in people renting accommodation is most prominent among young people and singles, a development that, among other things, reflects the rise in house prices, especially in the major cities.

Compared with the rest of Europe, Norwegian households more often live in small owner-occupied units. Whereas almost eight out of ten Norwegian households live in small owner-occupied units, this is only the case for four out of ten German households, for example.

### Larger dwellings ...

Norwegian dwellings are getting larger and larger. In 2001, the average home had 4.1 rooms, an increase from 3.6 rooms in 1980, when each person had 36m² at his/her disposal. Twenty years on we have a little over 50 m² each to bounce about in.

**Floor area per person**

**Dwellings, 2001**

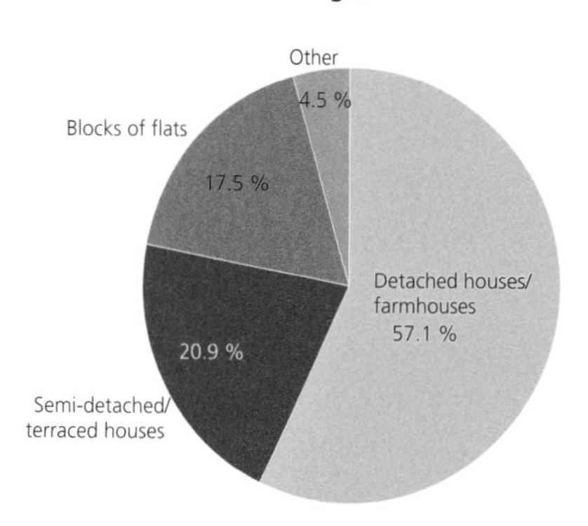


**Portion of households living in small owner-occupied housing units, selected countries, 1998**

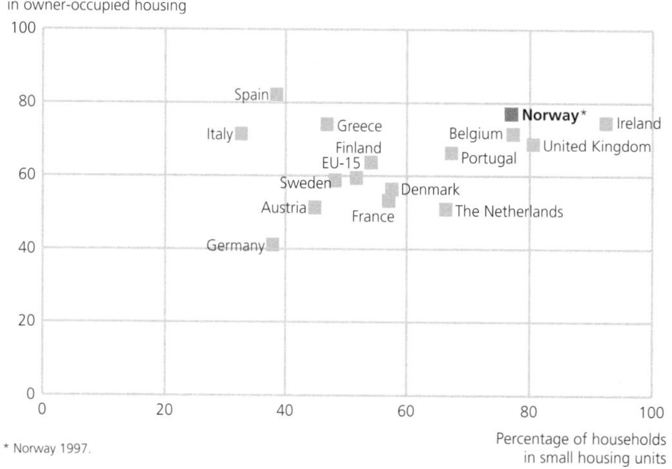


* Norway 1997.

### ... and a higher housing standard

In 1980, 10 per cent of the population still did not have a bathroom or a shower, but by 1990, this had been reduced to 1 per cent. At the same time, the proportion of people with two or more bathrooms has increased from 18 per cent in 1988 to slightly over 30 per cent in 2001.

**Floor area per dwelling, selected countries. 2002**

| | m² |
|---|---|
| **Norway** | **114.0** |
| Denmark | 108.9 |
| The Netherlands | 98.0 |
| Italy | 90.3 |
| Sweden | 89.8 |
| France | 88.0 |
| Spain | 85.3 |
| United Kingdom | 85.0 |
| Portugal | 83.4 |
| Finland | 76.5 |

Source: Housing statistics in the European Union.

### 369,000 holiday homes

At the beginning of 2004, there were 369,000 holiday homes (cabins, summer houses) in Norway, with the counties of Oppland (40,900) and Buskerud (40,000) having the most.

More than 20 per cent of all households own holiday homes, a proportion that has remained practically unchanged since 1980. In addition, many have access to holiday homes. Four out of ten people now say that they have access to a holiday home.

### High cost of accommodation

In the 1980s, household accommodation expenses increased, because of the increase in both debt and interest rates. At the beginning of the 1990s, the accommodation expenses (including lighting and heating, but excluding loan instalments) of more than half of all households exceeded 25 per cent of their consumption expenditure. During the 1990s, the proportion with high accommodation expenses sank to about 40 per cent because of sinking interest rates.

**Households with accommodation expenses exceeding 25 per cent of total consumption expenditure**

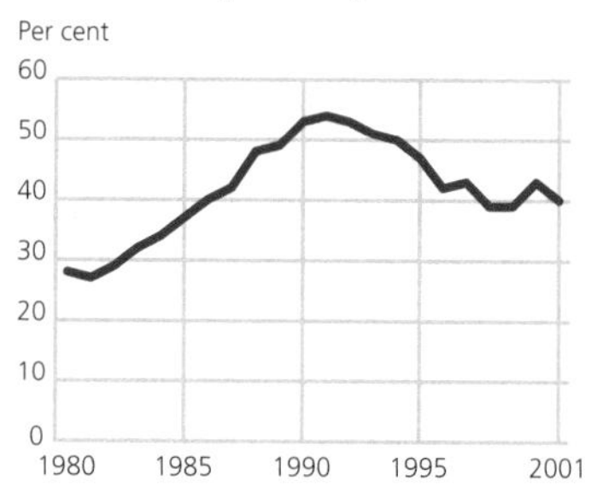


### House prices doubled in ten years

From 1991 to 2002 the price of resale housing increased by more than 100 per cent. In comparison, the general price increase during the period was about 26 per cent.

The price of flats in blocks increased far more than the price of detached houses, and especially in the Oslo area, the increase was extremely high. The price of resale housing in Oslo and Bærum almost tripled.

**Price development, resale housing, Index 1991 = 100**

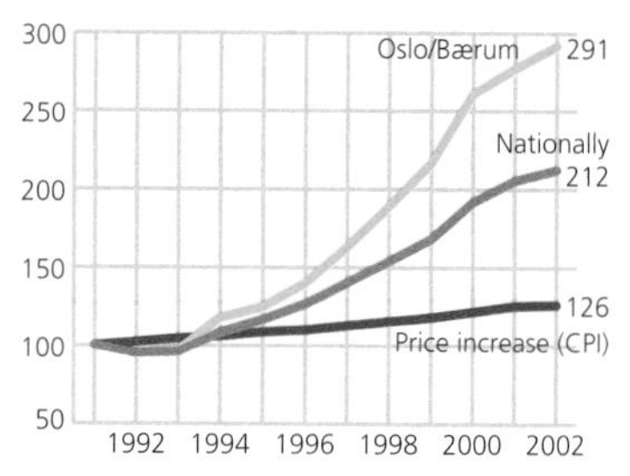

# CARE AND SOCIAL SECURITY

## The development of the welfare state

The main tasks of the welfare state, in addition to being responsible for the health and education of the population, are to take care of children, old people and other people in need of care and financial security. The development of the welfare state has generally been in the direction of public authorities taking over the responsibility for care and welfare benefits previously provided by the family.

The development of the welfare state is reflected in different ways in statistics, for example, when we look at government expenditure as a percentage of the gross domestic product. Around 1960, government expenditure constituted approximately 30 per cent of the gross domestic product (GDP). Then the proportion gradually increased to over 50 per cent in the early 1990s, but has subsequently declined to a little over 40 per cent. The decline is partly due to the strong growth in petroleum revenues and GDP in recent years.

The bulk of this expenditure is spent on education, health care and social benefits and welfare. In comparison, in countries such as Sweden and Denmark the percentage of GDP is more than 50 per cent.

**Government expenditure in per cent of GDP. 2001**

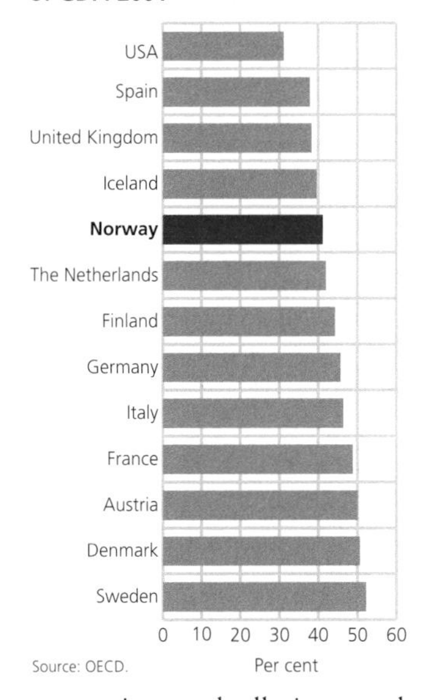


Source: OECD.

## Soon full day care coverage?

There were just over 5,800 day care centres in Norway in 2002. Almost half of them were privately owned, offering a little over 40 per cent of all day care places.

A total of 198,200 children are currently in day care and the coverage for all children aged 1-5 is 66 per cent; coverage has more than tripled since 1980. The Ministry of Children and Family Affairs estimates that coverage of 80 per cent means full coverage of demand. Eight of ten older children (3-5 years) are now in day care, while coverage for the youngest children has stabilized at about 40 per cent. This reflects the introduction in 1998 of a cash benefit when a parent stays at home with their child/ children; in 2002, more than 70 per cent of all children aged 1 to 3 received this cash benefit.

## Child protection: No increase in number of children in care

During the last 50 years, the number of children under protection of the social services has more than quadrupled, from 6,000 to 26,000. The number of children receiving some form of help during the year is even higher, 34,400 in 2002. This corresponds to 3 per cent of all children aged 0-17.

Most of the children under protection are given different forms of support and services, for example a visiting home, a support child-minder or a place in kindergarten. Only about 20 per cent of these children are in care – mostly in foster homes. The number of placements, however, has been very stable during the last fifty years (about 5,000), whereas the number of children given preventive support has greatly increased.

## Social security

The number of social security benefit cases increased rapidly in the 1980s: from 60,000 to 178,000 in the peak year of 1994. Then the number declined until 1999, and has now levelled out at about 138,000 cases, comprising 128,000 people, or almost 3 per cent of the population. If we also include dependents supported by people on social benefit, close to 5 per cent of the population, directly or indirectly, receive social support.

The proportion of people receiving social benefits is particularly large among young people, singles and single parents.

**Number of people on social benefit**

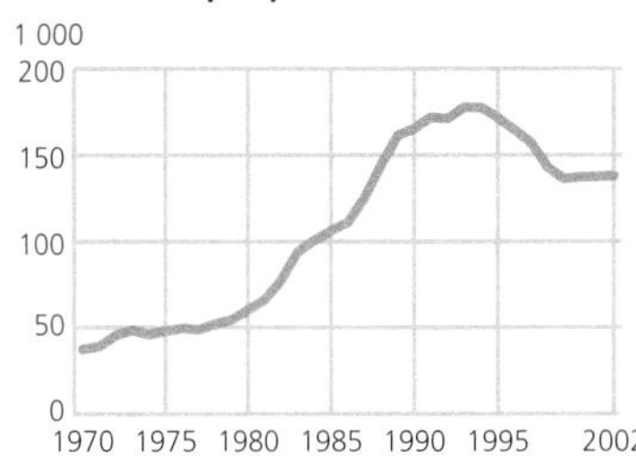


## Number of people on disability benefit again on the increase

In the mid-1970s, the number of people receiving disability benefits was about 140,000, equally distributed among men and women. During the 1980s, the number increased, especially among women. In the early 1990s, growth flattened out and for some years the number declined, before it rose again after 1995.

In 2003, the total number of people on disability benefit was 301,200: 173,000 women and 128,000 men. This is approximately 10 per cent of the working population aged between 16 and 66.

**Number of people receiving disability benefits. Men and women**

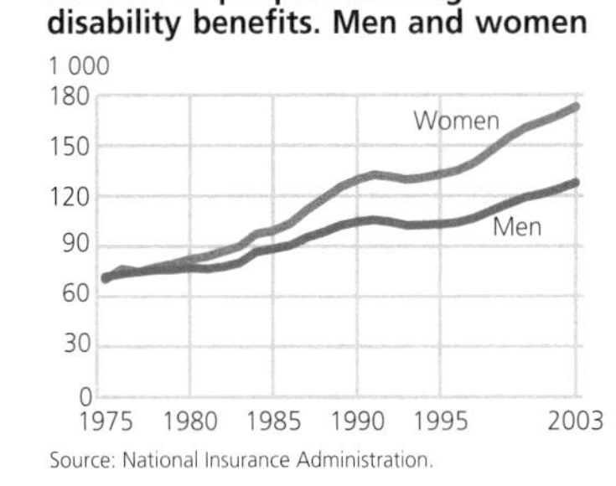


Source: National Insurance Administration.

**Day care coverage**

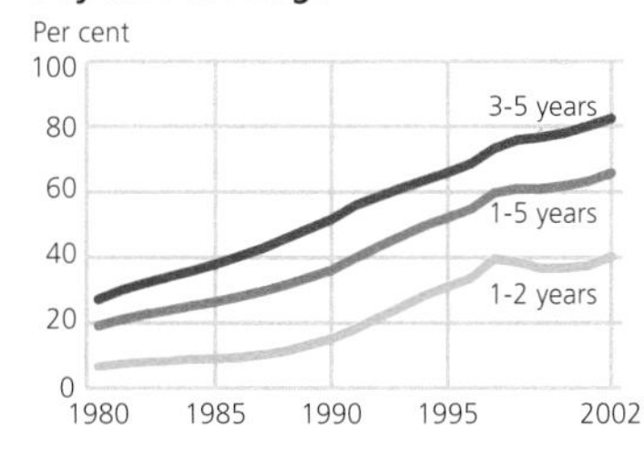


**Number of children in child care**

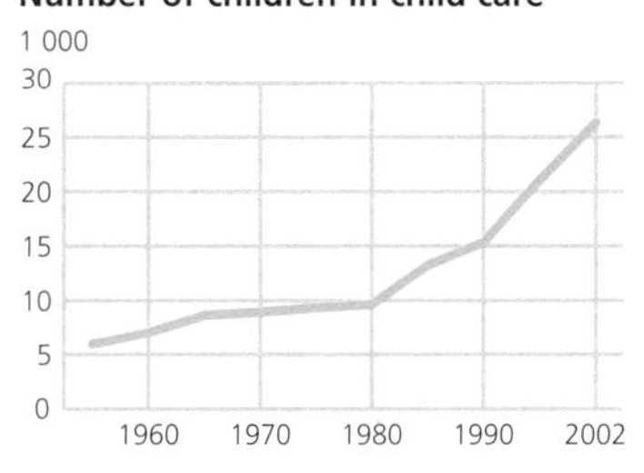


## Care for the aged: from institution to dwelling

Public care for the aged can roughly be divided into three main sectors: institutions, housing for seniors, and home support services.

Since the mid-1990s, there has been a clear growth in users of municipal nursing and care services, the main reason being that more people are now given support at home. In particular, the number of people being nursed at home has risen, but also the number of nursing and care housing units adapted for old people has increased considerably.

The number of places in old people's homes and nursing homes has declined slightly in recent years, one reason being rebuilding to increase the number of single rooms (now constituting 89 per cent).

**Users of various nursing and care services**

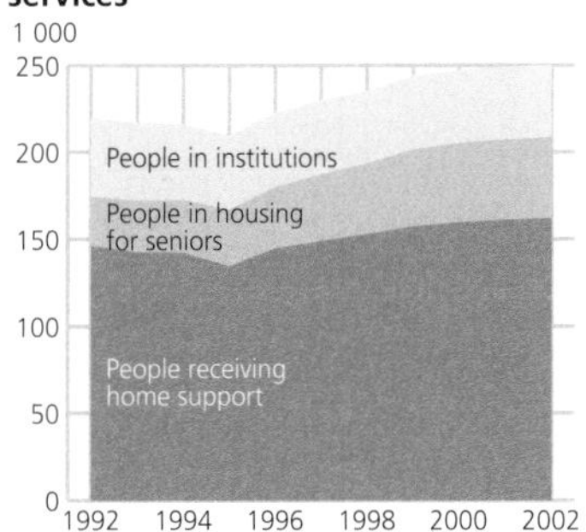

# CULTURE

## Cinema renaissance

In Norway, as in the rest of Europe, the 1950s were the golden age of the cinema. In 1960, cinema visits reached about 35 million, corresponding to almost ten cinema visits per inhabitant.

In the early 1960s, TV was established in Norway, and by 1970 cinema visiting numbers had almost halved. In the 1970s, however, there was only a small reduction. Then, in the 1980s, the cinemas experienced another period of decline, the bottom being reached in 1992 with about 9.5 million visits. This corresponds to 2.2 visits per inhabitant. Later, visiting numbers increased again, to 12 million in 2002. In recent years, the proportion seeing Norwegian films has been about 10 per cent.

In 2003, 66 per cent of the population aged 9-79 had been to a cinema during the last 12 months, and the average number of visits was 4.3 per person.

**Number of cinema visits**

## More people to theatres and opera houses ...

Theatre and opera visits also declined for a long time. However, from the middle of the 1980s, the situation improved, and after a stagnation around 1990, visiting numbers have increased strongly again to about 1.5 million.

**Number of theatre and opera goers**

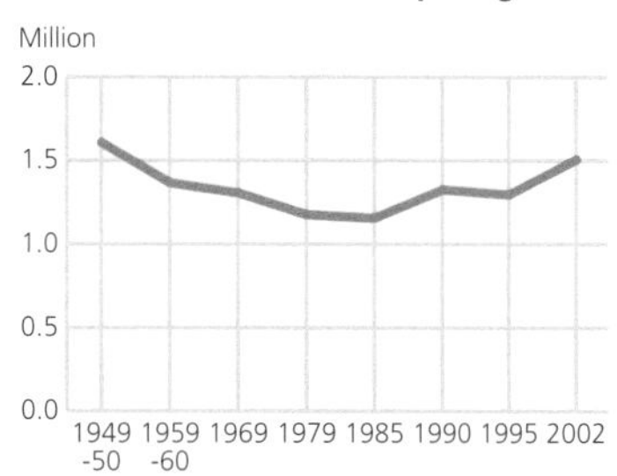


Half the population state that they have been to the theatre during the last year, 6 per cent have been to an opera, and 11 per cent have been to a ballet.

## ... and to concerts, exhibitions and museums

The proportion who have been to a concert during the year has increased sharply during the last decade; the proportion who have been to a classical concert increased from 27 to 37 per cent, and the proportion to other types of concerts increased from 32 to 39 per cent from 1991 to 2000.

About 45 per cent attended an art exhibition and/or visited a museum in 2000. These numbers have also increased somewhat.

**Number of people aged 9-79 who visited different cultural institutions last year. In per cent.**

| | 1991 | 1994 | 1997 | 2000 |
|---|---|---|---|---|
| Cinema | 58 | 61 | 60 | 65 |
| Theatre/musical/show | 44 | 45 | 44 | 50 |
| Opera/operetta | 5 | 5 | 6 | 6 |
| Ballet/dance performance | 8 | 9 | 8 | 11 |
| Classical concert | 27 | 34 | 37 | 37 |
| Popular concert | 32 | 38 | 38 | 39 |
| Art exhibition | 41 | 44 | 43 | 44 |
| Museum | 41 | 45 | 44 | 45 |
| Public library | 49 | 51 | 52 | 52 |
| Sports event | 57 | 59 | 54 | 57 |

## Libraries more than books

Book loans from public libraries have increased throughout the postwar period, from 3.3 million in 1945-46 to more than 20 million in the early 1990s. After that, loans have fallen to 18 million in 2002.

Towards the end of the 1980s, libraries also began lending out music, audio books, videos and CDs. These loans constitute more than 6 million items a year, and total loans from libraries now exceed 24 million. Half the population visits a public library in the course of a year.

**Number of loans from public libraries**

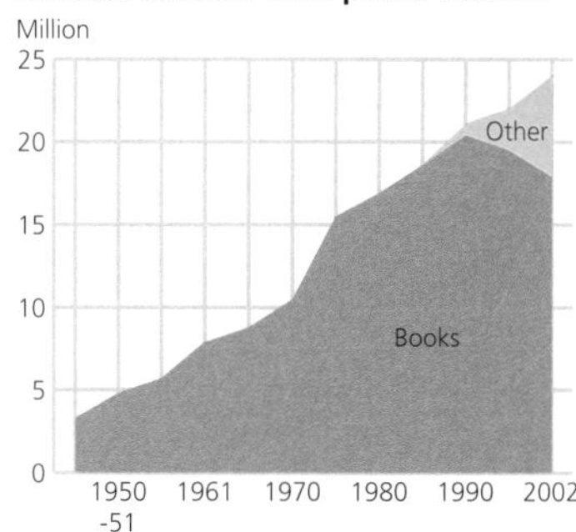


## Culture: Mostly for women – and the highly educated

When asked how interested they are in different cultural activities, women far more often than men reply that they are 'very or quite interested'. This is most clearly seen in connection with ballet, opera and theatre, but women are also far more often interested in classical concerts, art exhibitions and libraries. As regards cinemas, museums, and popular concerts, the men's interest almost equals that of women. Only with regard to sports events are men far more interested than women.

Gender differences as regards interest expressed generally correspond to the proportion actually attending the various cultural activities, although the differences are slightly smaller.

In addition to the gender differences, the differences between the different levels of education are more striking. Most cultural activities are attended far more often by people with higher education.

The increased cultural activity in recent years must be viewed in connection with other aspects of social development. A higher level of education leads to increased interest in different cultural activities. At the same time, more leisure and an improved financial situation make it easier to make use of the offers. In addition, a constantly increasing proportion of the population lives in towns and population centres, where the offer of cultural activities is the best.

**Proportion of women and men aged 9-79 who say they are 'very/quite interested' in attending ..., 2000**

## Fewer spectators at sports events?

Throughout the 1990s, between 50 and 60 per cent were spectators at a sports event in the course of the year. From 1994 to 2000, however, the number of sports events attended sank from 6.7 to 5.2. Football is the sport with the highest number of spectators, followed by handball. Most sports have stable numbers of spectators, with the exception of skiing, where the proportion of spectators has halved since 1994 (however, this year was probably special, because of the Winter Olympics which were held at Lillehammer).

# MEDIA

### Screen media take over

Television's dominating position is, of course, not something new: ten years ago we already spent almost twice as much time in front of the TV as we did on reading.

**Number of minutes spent on screen and print media in an average day**

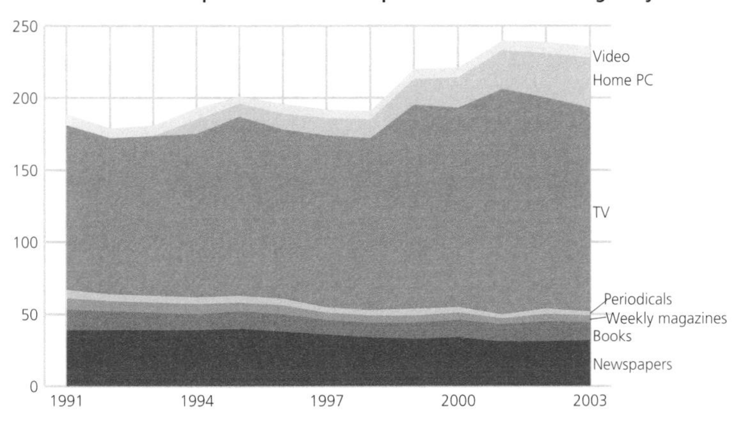


During the 1990s, the time we spend reading continued to decline, at the same time as we watched far more TV. In addition, more people acquired (and used) personal computers (PCs) at home. Now we spend on average slightly over half an hour in front of the PC every day. In other words, we spend nearly four times as much time in front of a screen as we do reading. It is a paradox, perhaps, that the higher the education level becomes, the less we read. This is the case for all types of printed publications, not only weekly magazines.

### TV dominates

The proportion watching TV remained relatively stable during the 1990s, at a little over 80 per cent, but the time we spent in front of the TV has increased to two hours and twenty minutes per day. Videos, however, are only used by a small minority, and this proportion has remained stable throughout the period.

**Number of minutes spent on screen and print media in an average day**

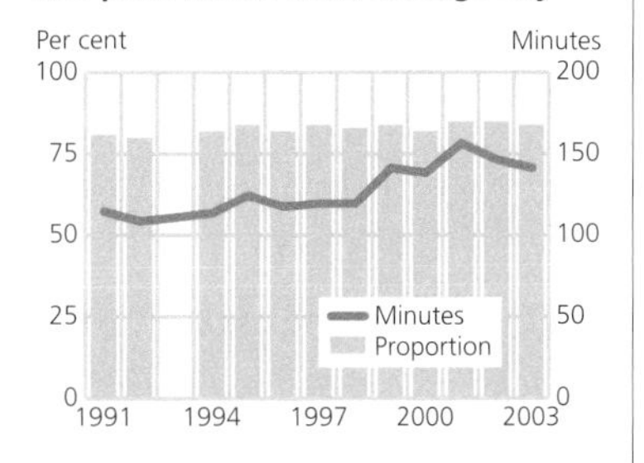


The most enthusiastic TV-viewers are found among the oldest (67 and over) and the youngest (aged 13-15).

### The arrival of the PC

Since the middle of the 1990s, the proportion of daily home-PC users has increased from about 10 to 36 per cent, and we now use the PC slightly over half an hour every day (the proportion who have home-PCs, however, is far higher: 77 per cent).

**Proportion using home-PCs and time spent in an average day**

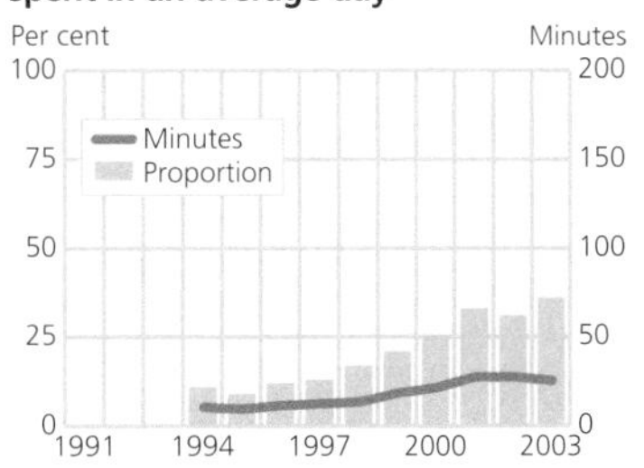


There are large variations in use of the PC. For example, one out of two young boys uses a PC daily, whereas this is the case for only one out of twenty elderly women.

### Radio = music?

In ten years, the proportion listening to the radio every day has declined from 71 to 58 per cent, but in recent years it would seem that the time spent listening to the radio has stabilized at about half an hour per day (those listening to the radio, in other words, spend more time doing so than before).

**Proportion of radio listeners and time spent in an average day**

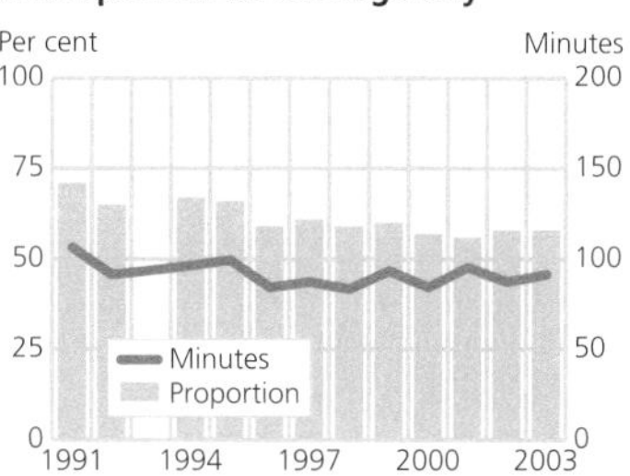


It is primarily news, district and entertainment programmes that have lost listeners. The same applies to information programmes and weather forecasts. Religious programmes and classical music programmes, too, have fewer listeners. Programmes with popular music, on the other hand, remain popular.

Radio is first and foremost the medium of middle-aged men. In the 45-66 age group, the proportion of listeners is 71 per cent.

### Newspapers

Newspaper circulation increased up until about 1990, but has since stagnated. Circulation per 1,000 inhabitants declined during the 1990s, but in 2002 is still higher than in the other Nordic countries (543 in 2002, compared with 435 in Finland and 411 in Sweden).

**Proportion of newspaper readers and time spent in an average day**

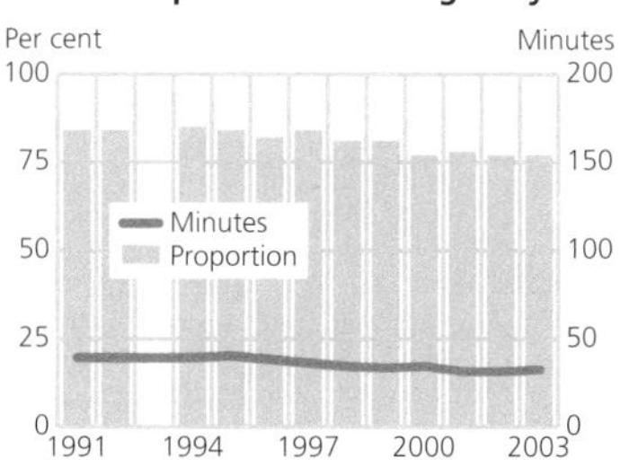


At the same time, the proportion of people reading newspapers every day has sunk somewhat since the mid-1990s: from 85 to 77 per cent. We also spend less time on newspapers: half an hour per day on average. Newspaper reading has become less common especially among the youngest age groups.

### Books

The number of fiction publications doubled from 1983 to 1994 (from 900 to 2,000 publications), but has since dropped to 1,700. Book loans from public libraries also dropped, from 4.7 per inhabitant in 1992 to 4.0 in 2002.

**Proportion of book readers and time spent in an average day**

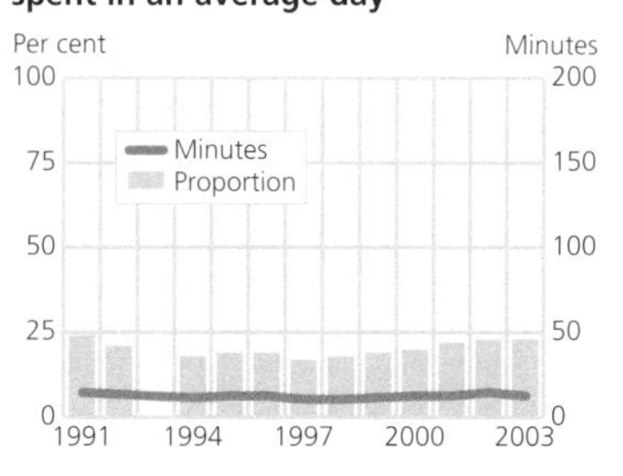


The proportion reading books during their spare time has not followed the same trend; after some years of decline, the proportion reading a book daily again rose to 23 per cent. The proportion reading books daily is somewhat higher for women than for men, 30 and 17 per cent respectively.

### Weekly magazines

The proportion of weekly magazine readers has declined considerably during the last five to six years, and 16 per cent of the population now read weekly magazines on an average day. This decline is not reflected in a corresponding decline in circulation; on the contrary, the total circulation increased slightly in the 1990s.

Women read weekly magazines far more often than men. This is especially the case for older women aged 67-79, of whom 39 per cent read weekly magazines on an average day.

# TIME USE

## More free time

On average Norwegians have 75 minutes more free time per day compared with 1970, and we now have almost 6 1/2 hours free to spend on different leisure activities. The time we spend on education and paid employment has not changed much, and the increase in free time is mainly due to us spending less time on domestic work (50 minutes) and personal care (30 minutes).

The amount of free time has increased slightly more for women than for men, which, among other things, reflects the fact that women have reduced domestic work by two hours. One of these hours is spent on paid employment, the second on leisure. Men, on the other hand, have reduced the amount of time spent on paid employment, but at the same time have increased the time they spend on domestic work.

Despite women having increased the time spent on paid employment during the last decade and reduced the time spent on domestic work, it has not become more common to buy cleaning services; the proportion with such help is 4 per cent, roughly the same as in the early 1990s. It is especially highly educated families with children who buy cleaning services.

**Time use in an average day. Minutes**

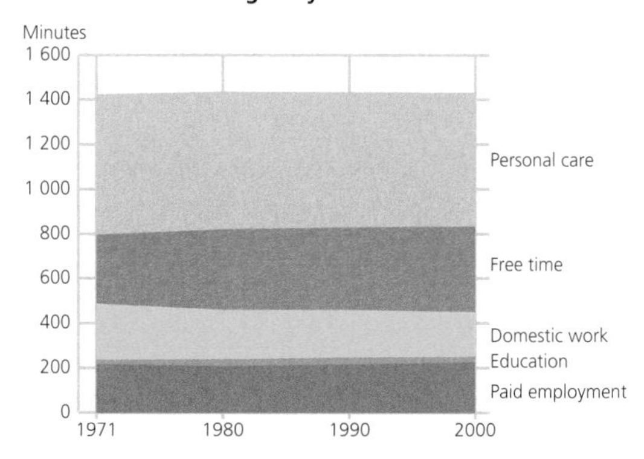


**Change in time spent on various main activities from 1971 to 2000, age group 16-74**

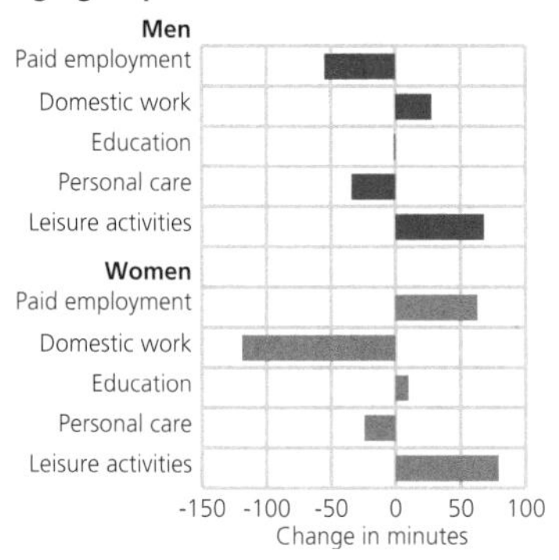


**Change in time spent on domestic work from 1971 to 2000, by gender and age**

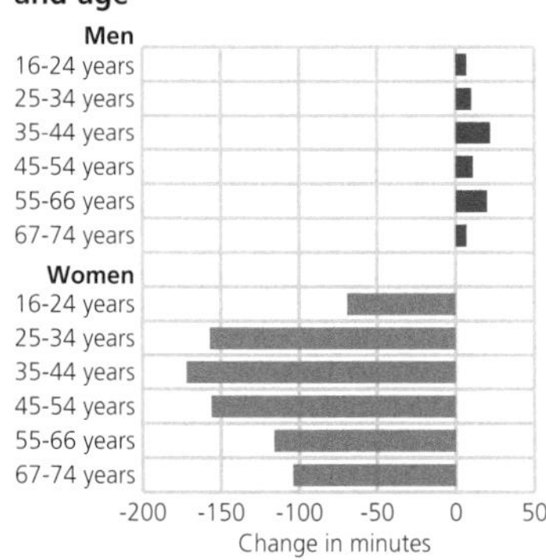


**Change in time spent on watching TV from 1971 to 2000, by gender and age**

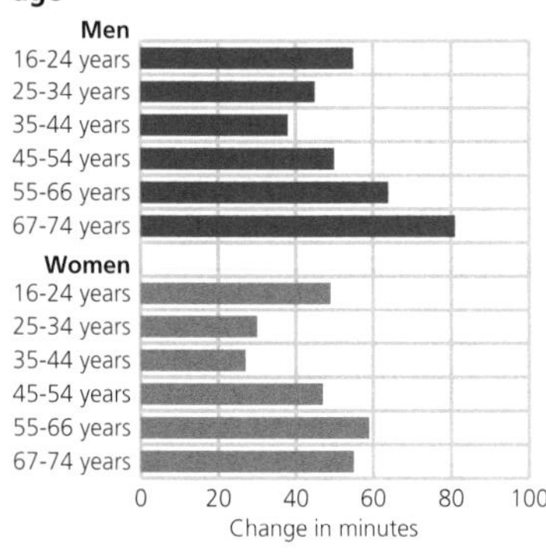


## More time in front of the TV set

The increase in free time is largely spent in front of the TVset. Time spent watching TV has increased significantly, and compared with 1980, the TV night starts earlier and ends later.

## Eight hours of sleep

We sleep 8 hours a day on average, and there has been only a slight increase since 1970.

However, there has been a change as regards at what time we sleep at night; we both go to bed and get up later. In 1980, for example, 72 per cent of the population was asleep by 11.30 pm. This proportion had sunk to 62 in 1990 and 55 per cent in 2000. Similarly, in 1980, 6 per cent were still asleep at 9 am in the morning, compared with 12 per cent in 2000.

The need for sleep seems to be virtually unchanged, both over time and between the different groups of the population. While other activities often vary with, for example, gender, education or place of residence, most people sleep about 8 hours: only the youngest and oldest sleep a little longer.

**Time spent on cooking and meals**

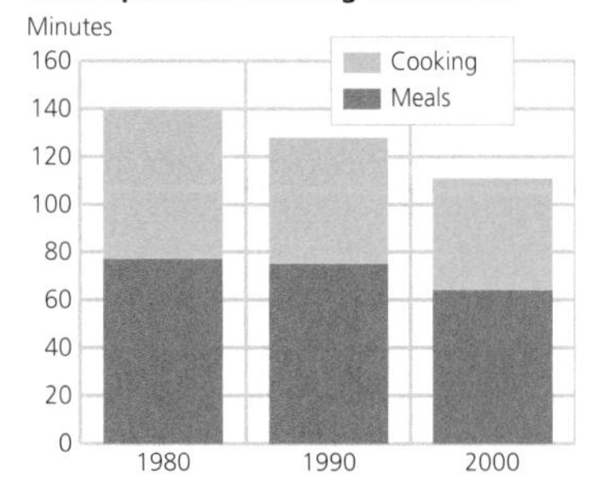


**Proportion watching TV at different times. Monday-Friday**

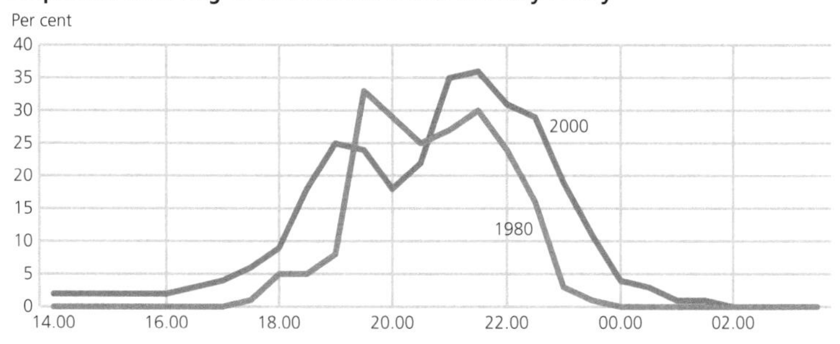


**Proportion sleeping at different times. Monday-Friday**

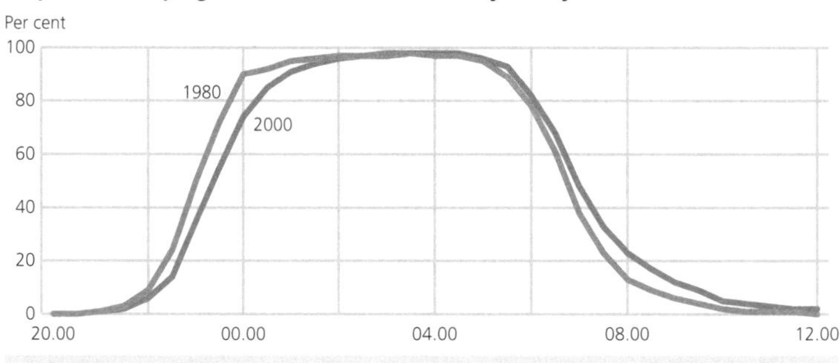


## Fast food

The extreme interest in cookery books and TV cooks in recent years does not seem to have resulted in our spending more time in the kitchen. True, more men cook today, but we spend 30 minutes less on cooking and meals than in 1980. The reduction is roughly equally distributed between cooking and meals.

There is also a tendency to move the main meal further into the evening. Although most people still have dinner between three and half past five in the afternoon, an increasing number now eat later.

## '... only out shopping for a few minutes'

While an increasing number of people spend time shopping for goods and services, we spend less time in the shops. In the course of an average day, more than half of us do some kind of shopping, as compared with four out of ten twenty years ago. At that time we spent an average of 54 minutes on shopping, compared with 44 minutes in 2000. One in three buys groceries on an average day, and we spend 24 minutes doing so.

# TRANSPORT

## Mile after mile

In 1946, Norwegians travelled an average of 4 km a day (domestically) and almost half of that distance (1.8 km) by train. Today, we travel ten times as far: 40 km a day. The increase has primarily been in the use of private cars and aircraft. The figures for railway and sea transport have not changed much in 50 years (we actually travelled more by train in 1960 than in 2001). Today, domestic air traffic also seems to have stabilized, whereas our car use is still increasing.

**Number of private cars**

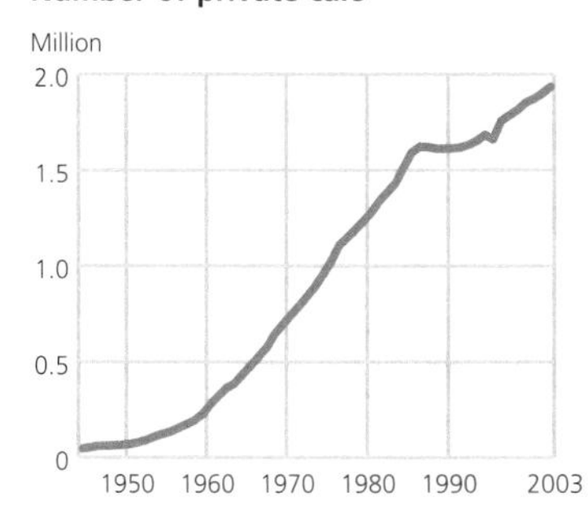


## Car after car

The number of motor vehicles (including vans, trucks and buses) now totals 2.4 million units, of which a little over 1.9 million are private cars. From 1960, when restrictions on car sales were removed, until 1987 the number of cars increased continuously, and during the latter half of the 1990s, we experienced strong growth once more.

More than 70 per cent of all households now own a car and almost a quarter have two or more cars.

The car density is 422 private cars per 1,000 inhabitants. The density is highest in Akershus (474), lowest in Finnmark (365) and Oslo (357). Another way of measuring 'car density' is to look at the number of cars in relation to available road. In 1945, each car had almost half a kilometre of road at its disposal. Today each car only has slightly over 30 metres. In Oslo, each car, if all were on the road at the same time, would only have a little over 5 metres at its disposal.

**Most common car makes. Registered private cars. 2003**

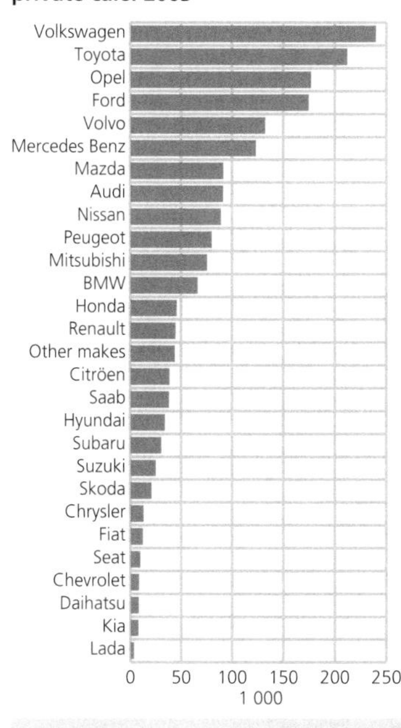


**Number of private cars per 1,000 inhabitants in selected countries. 2002**

| | |
|---|---|
| Italy | 586 |
| Germany | 545 |
| France | 490 |
| USA | 476 |
| Spain | 469 |
| Sweden | 458 |
| **Norway** | **422** |
| Finland | 421 |
| Portugal | 370 |
| Denmark | 351 |
| Greece | 344 |

Source: The Norwegian Road Federation

**Metres of road per motor vehicle**

| | |
|---|---|
| 1945 | 452 |
| 1960 | 97 |
| 1970 | 65 |
| 1980 | 48 |
| 1990 | 38 |
| 2000 | 33 |
| 2003 | 31 |

**Passenger kilometres per inhabitant per day**

| | Total | Personal car | Other passenger traffic on road | Air traffic | Railways* | Sea traffic |
|---|---|---|---|---|---|---|
| 1946 | 4.05 | 0.93 | 0.88 | 0.00 | 1.83 | 0.40 |
| 1952 | 5.40 | 1.31 | 2.04 | 0.01 | 1.86 | 0.45 |
| 1960 | 8.94 | 3.65 | 3.51 | 0.08 | 1.99 | 0.49 |
| 1965 | 12.84 | 7.43 | 3.93 | 0.25 | 1.78 | 0.50 |
| 1970 | 18.31 | 12.61 | 3.44 | 0.45 | 1.37 | 0.45 |
| 1975 | 24.14 | 17.99 | 3.45 | 0.70 | 1.55 | 0.45 |
| 1980 | 27.30 | 20.41 | 3.61 | 0.99 | 1.84 | 0.44 |
| 1985 | 31.44 | 24.34 | 3.57 | 1.42 | 1.69 | 0.42 |
| 1990 | 34.80 | 27.58 | 3.49 | 1.72 | 1.57 | 0.45 |
| 1995 | 35.28 | 27.44 | 3.49 | 2.24 | 1.68 | 0.43 |
| 2000 | 38.37 | 28.52 | 4.64 | 2.70 | 2.00 | 0.52 |
| 2002 | 39.91 | 29.73 | 4.42 | 2.43 | 1.80 | 0.52 |

*Including trams/suburban lines

## The price of mobility

Mobility has its price. Every year about 300 people now lose their lives in traffic and more than 1,000 are seriously injured. An additional 10,000 people are less seriously injured.

The number of road fatalities increased throughout the postwar period, reaching a peak at the beginning of the 1970s, when more than 500 people were killed every year. The development in numbers of seriously injured shows a similar trend: from 4,500 in 1970, the number has subsequently declined to about 1,000 a year. The number of people suffering less serious injuries seems to have stabilized at a little over 10,000 per year.

The stable injury figures for the most recent years disguise a changed distribution: the number of killed and injured car drivers and motorcycle drivers is increasing, while the number for moped drivers, cyclists and pedestrians is declining.

**Number of people injured in traffic**

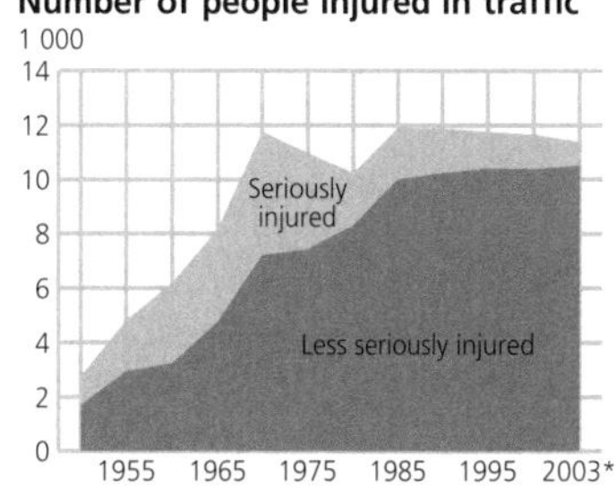


## Safest in the Nordic countries

In relation to population, six people per 100,000 inhabitants are killed annually in Norway. This is roughly the same as in the other Nordic countries.

The further south we get in Europe, the more the numbers increase: traffic mortality is highest in Greece with 18 people killed per 100,000 inhabitants. This is despite car density being only half of Norway's. Italy, which has the highest car density in Europe, has a traffic mortality rate equal to the average.

**Number of people killed in traffic**

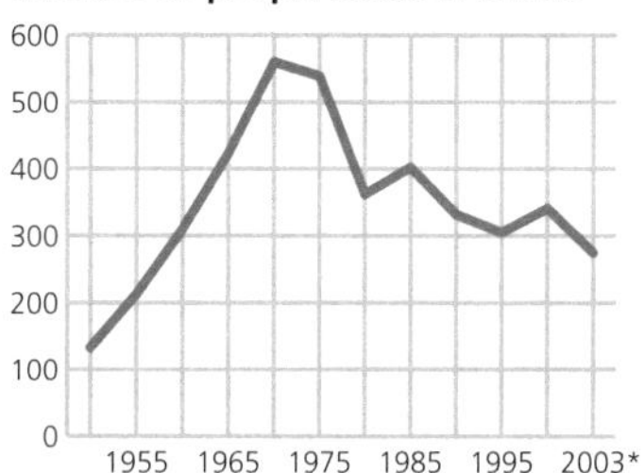


**Number of people killed in traffic accidents per 100,000 inhabitants in some European countries. 2001**

| | |
|---|---|
| Greece | 18 |
| Portugal | 16 |
| Spain | 14 |
| France | 14 |
| Italy | 12 |
| Germany | 9 |
| Denmark | 8 |
| Finland | 8 |
| Sweden | 7 |
| **Norway** | **6** |
| United Kingdom | 6 |

Source: CARE.

# HOLIDAYS

## Three out of four on holiday

After an increase at the beginning of the 1970s, the proportion going on holiday every year has been stable. Every year about 75 per cent go on holiday. On average we make 1.6 holiday trips a year, a figure that has also remained stable during recent years.

The length of the holiday trip has also remained relatively stable at about 15 - 16 days. Among the people who actually go on holiday, the average number of trips is 2.1, and they spend a total of 20 days on holiday; this represents only a slight increase during the last 10 years.

The fact that these figures have not risen more is probably due to the increased popularity of so-called weekend trips, for example city trips involving two to three nights' stay. Since holiday surveys only include trips of four nights or more, short trips are not included in the statistics.

**Proportion of Norwegians making holiday trips during a year**

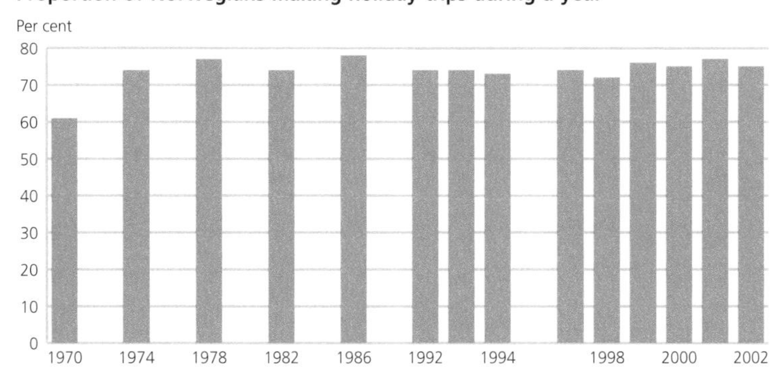


## Norway on the holiday top

Norwegians and Germans are the most frequent holidaymakers, followed by the Dutch, Swedes and British. In Italy, less than half the population goes on holiday every year, and in Spain and Portugal only about one-third go on holiday.

## More often abroad

An increasing number of people go abroad during their holidays. At the beginning of the 1990s, almost one-third of holiday makers went abroad to countries outside Scandinavia.

This proportion is now approaching 40 per cent. In addition, about 20 per cent travel to other Nordic countries.

Of all holiday trips, 49 per cent of holidaymakers go abroad, and as international holidays often last longer, they make up 55 per cent of all overnight stays. In this respect, we now holiday more abroad than in Norway.

Danes, Germans and the Dutch are the holidaymakers who are most eager to go abroad, spending as they do between 60 and 70 per cent of their holidays abroad. In comparison, only 5 and 10 per cent of Greek and Spanish holidays respectively are taken abroad.

## Spain most popular

Spain is clearly the most popular foreign destination, and every year Norwegians make close to 500,000 trips to Spain. Then follow Denmark, Greece and Sweden. For a long time these four countries (in a somewhat varying order) have clearly been the most popular destinations.

Further down on the list, however, changes are taking place: The United Kingdom and Germany were very popular destinations some years back, but have now been overtaken by France. Italy, too, is becoming an attractive holiday destination for Norwegians.

**Proportion of people on holiday in selected countries. Around 2000.**

Norway
Germany
The Netherlands
Sweden
United Kingdom
Denmark
Greece
Finland
Italy
Spain
Portugal
0 20 40 60 80
Per cent

Source: Eurostat.

**Number of holiday trips to the main destinations abroad. 2002**

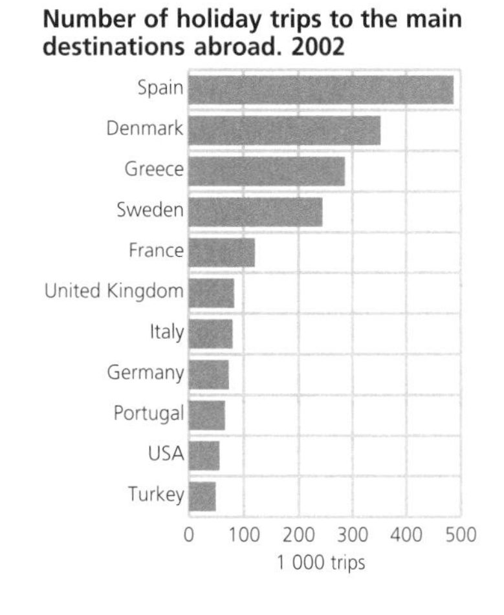


## 2.3 million foreign tourists

Every year, about 2.3 million foreign tourists visit Norway. Most come from Sweden (28 per cent), followed by Germany and Denmark (both 19 per cent). Then follow Finland (7 per cent) and the USA and United Kingdom (both 5 per cent). Foreign tourists on average spend 7 nights in this country.

**Proportion of holidays taken abroad in selected European countries. Around 2000. Per cent**

| | Proportion of holidays abroad |
|---|---|
| Greece | 4.5 |
| Spain | 10.3 |
| Portugal | 18.0 |
| Italy | 22.8 |
| Finland | 28.6 |
| Sweden | 30.1 |
| United Kingdom | 45.0 |
| **Norway** | **46.7** |
| The Netherlands | 63.0 |
| Germany | 66.0 |
| Denmark | 69.1 |

Source: Eurostat.

## The affluent are the most frequent holidaymakers

Going on holiday costs money, so it comes as no surprise that financial situation is of great significance to holiday activities. Whereas only one of two persons in households with incomes of NOK 100,000 or less went on holiday in 2001, nine out of ten persons in households with incomes exceeding NOK 500,000 went on holiday.

People with high incomes are also more frequent holidaymakers. However, sound finances do not lead to longer holidays. On the contrary, it is those with the lowest incomes who make the longest trips (on average 36 nights). This is because this group includes students and old-age pensioners, two groups that often stay away for a long time when they finally go on a holiday.

Older people and people with a low education/income, in particular, do not go on holiday.

# CRIME

## From violation of the law to punishment

Of the 430,000 reported infringements of the law in 1997, we are able to follow 420,000 through the court system; and five years later, we can take stock as follows. Three per cent of the cases were dropped because there was no case to answer. An additional 60 per cent were dropped as being unsolved (including 6 per cent with unknown decisions), and thus 37 per cent of the offences were solved. A majority of these were settled by deciding not to bring criminal charges or by imposing fines (this applied especially to minor offences). Slightly over 17 per cent of the infringements ended in indictment, 16 per cent resulted in conviction and 10 per cent of the infringements ended in unconditional imprisonment.

**From violation to punishment: the course of violations through the court system**

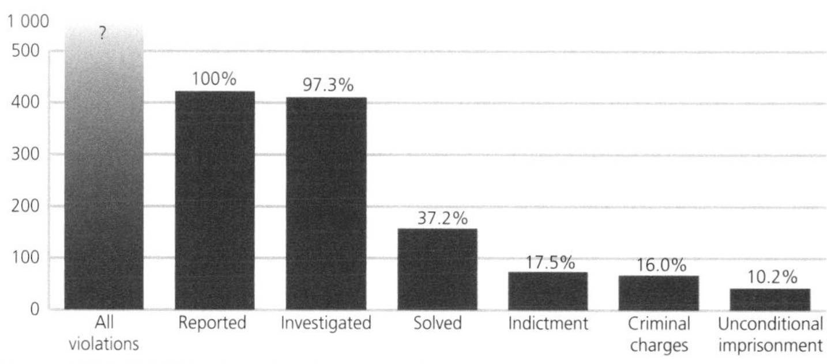


## More than 1,200 offences reported every day

Some 450,000 violations of the law are reported every year. Of these, slightly over 320,000 are indictable offences (criminal acts which according to Norwegian law are punishable by a suspended or unconditional prison sentence of more than three months) and over 120,000 are minor offences (e.g. traffic offences). This corresponds to more than 1,200 reported offences every day. How many crimes are actually committed, is not known, but the hidden figures are assumed to be large.

## Strong increase

The number of investigated crimes has octupled since 1960: from 38,700 in 1960 to 310,000 in 2001. If we take into account that the population has increased by about one million people during this period, the increase represents a sextupling. Investigated crimes now comprise 70 per 1,000 inhabitants. Part of the increase is assumed to reflect a greater inclination to report some law infringements today, for example theft, and to more efficient police registration and reporting routines.

**Number of investigated crimes**

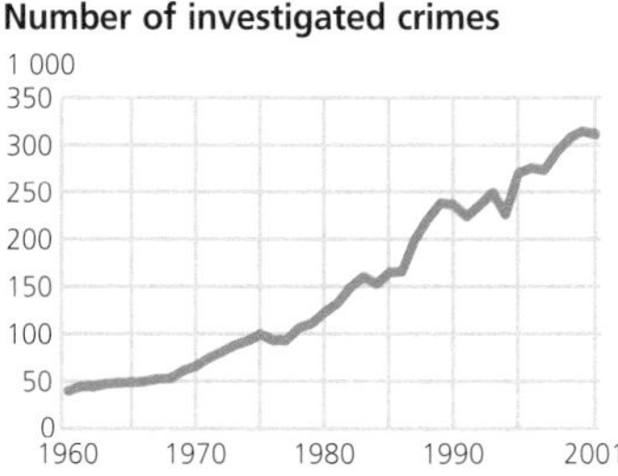


## Thefts dominate

180,000 to 190,000 thefts are reported every year, and these represent the dominant type of crime. Thefts and other financial crimes now account for two-thirds of all crimes. Thus, the strong increase in number of thefts largely explains the increase in crime since the mid-1900s. Car theft and theft from cars account for between 50,000 and 60,000 thefts annually. Including about 60,000 minor traffic offences, the car is directly or indirectly involved in about 25 per cent of all law infringements.

**Most common thefts. 2001**

| | Number |
|---|---|
| Thefts from cars and other vehicles | 33 200 |
| Thefts from firms and public institutions | 32 700 |
| Thefts from housing/cabins | 25 200 |
| Bicycle thefts | 19 600 |
| Thefts of cars and other vehicles | 20 600 |

**Number of reported homicides, attempted murders and cases of grievous bodily harm**

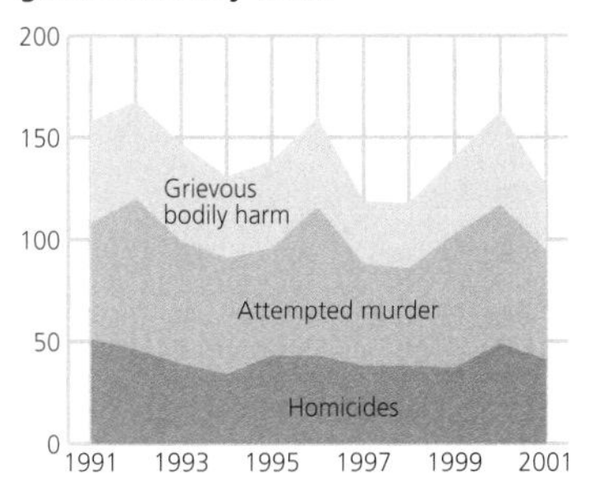


## More drugs

Drug offences account for about 15 per cent of all reported crimes. The number exploded from 200 at the end of the 1960s to 48,000 in 2001. However, this increase must be viewed in light of changes in drugs legislation and the police's increased efforts in this field. It is especially less serious drug offences (use and possession) that have increased in number. Serious drug offences make up only 2 per cent of the total number of drug-related crimes.

## No increase in serious violence

Violent crime has increased significantly, now accounting for almost 6 per cent of all reported infringements. Here, too, the less serious crimes dominate: i.e. threats and bodily harm.

In interview surveys about 5 per cent of the population say that they have been exposed to violence or threats of violence during the year. This percentage has remaind stable since the beginning of the 1980s.

## One-third solved

In 1960, four out of ten crimes were solved. By the end of the 1980s, the number of crimes solved had dropped to less than 20 per cent. Since then the situation has changed once more, and in 2001, 33 per cent of all crimes were solved (about eight of ten minor offences are solved). The percentage of crimes solved varies considerably, depending on the type of crime. Almost all murder cases are solved, and the same applies to drug-related crimes, while only about 10 per cent of all thefts are solved.

## Young men dominate

The people charged with an offence are often young: in 2001, 40 per cent of all the people charged were under 25; most of them were between 18 and 20 years old. In this age group, about 7 per cent are charged with an offence every year.

**Number of people charged with offences per 1,000 inhabitants in different age groups. 2001**

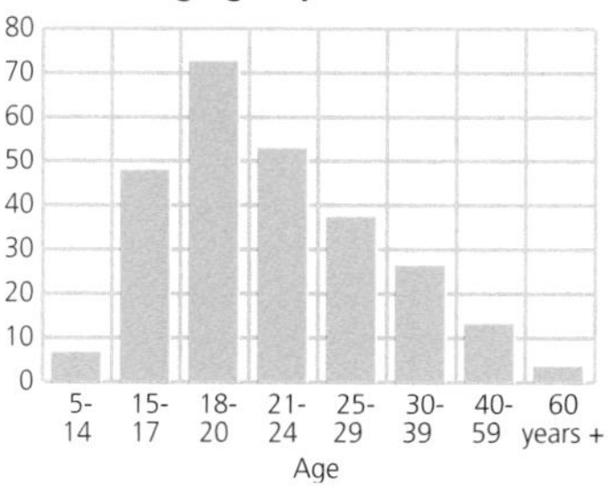


The majority of the people charged are men; women still make up less than 20 per cent of those charged. 20 per cent of all simple thefts, drugs-related offences, frauds, forgeries and embezzlements are committed by women.

## International comparisons

International comparisons of crime levels are difficult because of different definitions and terms. The main impression, however, is that Norway is still far down on the list with regard to serious crimes such as murder and robbery with violence. The exception is rape, where Norway, Sweden and Denmark are far above the European average. This may, of course, have to do with the threshold for reporting such violations being lower in the Nordic countries. Norway, together with other wealthy nations where there is much to steal, is also above average with regard to crimes of gain.

# ELECTIONS

**Turnout**

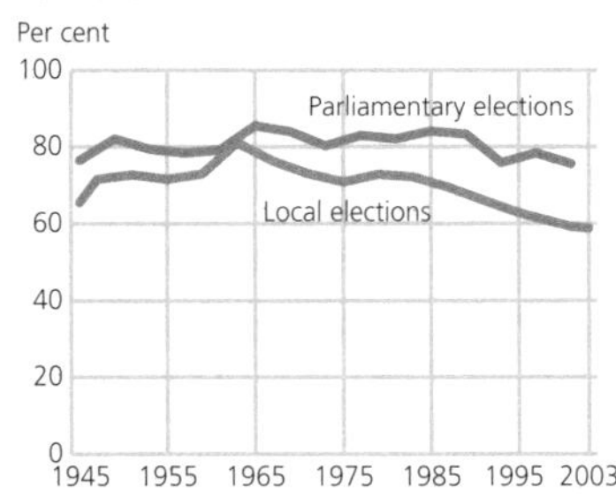


**Percentage of persons aged 16-79 who are members of a political party**

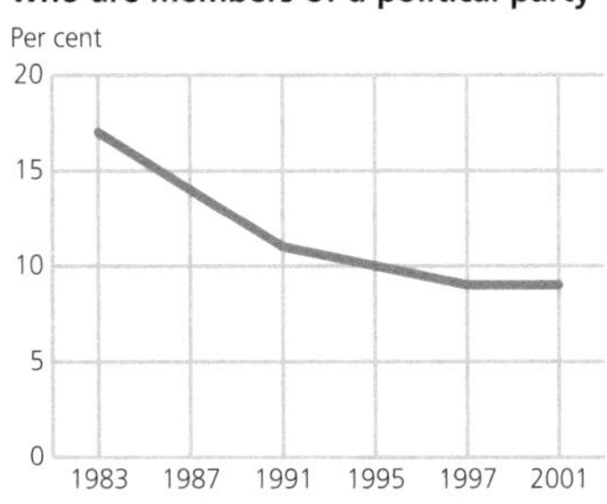


**Turnout at parliamentary elections in some European countries. Around 2000. Ca. 2000**

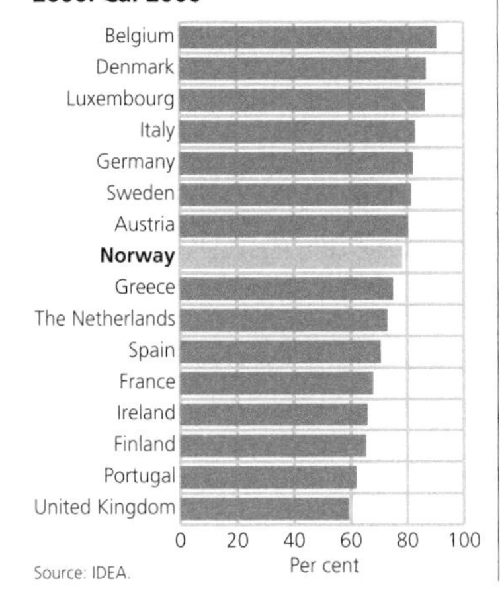


Source: IDEA.

## Falling turnout ...

The group of abstainers is continually growing, both at parliamentary and local elections. Parliamentary election turnout peaked in 1965, when 85.4 per cent of all qualified voters voted. The turnout has subsequently declined – to 75.5 per cent in 2001.

The decline has been even more marked at local elections. In 2003, abstainers represented the largest 'party'. Only six out of ten voted, compared with slightly over eight out of ten in 1963, a decline of about 25 per cent.

The declining interest in politics is also confirmed by the falling numbers of political party members. From 1983 to 2001 the proportion of political party members dropped by almost half, from 16 to 9 per cent.

## ... especially among men

Traditionally, there has been a higher election turnout of men than women. At the first elections after the Second World War, the turnout of men was 6 to 7 per cent higher than that of women. In the 1980s this difference diminished, and in subsequent years women have more often made use of their right to vote. This is the case for women of all ages, with the exception of women over 50. Older men still go to the polls more often.

## Average turnout in Norway

In an international context, the turnout at Norwegian parliamentary elections is not particularly high. Our Nordic neighbours, Denmark, Iceland and Sweden, all have a turnout of about 80 per cent or more. Only in Finland is participation lower than in Norway.

In a European context, Norway's turnout is about average. The highest turnouts are found in Belgium (90.6 per cent), the lowest in the UK (59 per cent).

**Turnout of different age groups. Parliamentary election 2001**

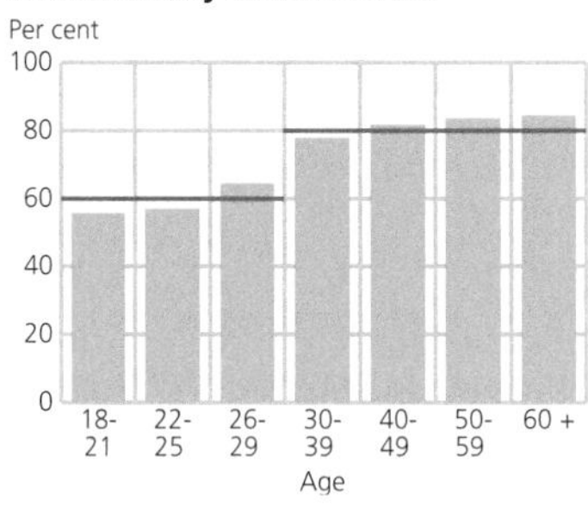


## Young people often non-voters

Turnout increases with age. Whereas only just under 56 per cent of those voting for the first time make use of their voting rights, more than 84 per cent of electors aged 60 and over do so.

A distinct change in turnout seems to take place around the age of 30. Those under 30 have a turnout of plus/minus 60 per cent, while about 80 per cent of the over-30s vote.

**Female members of parliament and local councils**

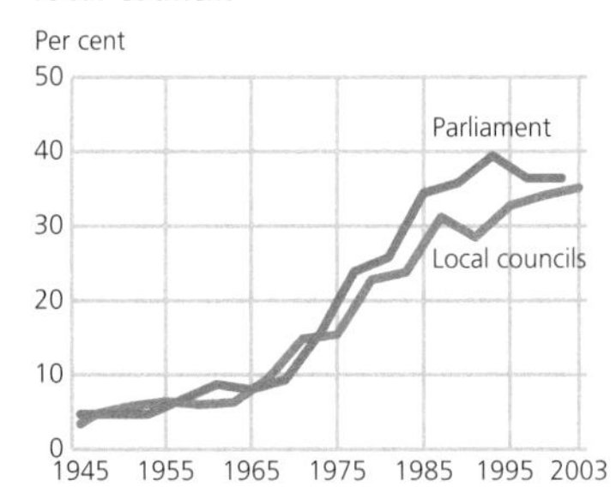


## More women – both in parliament and local councils

From the beginning of the 1970s, the proportion of women members of both parliament and local councils has increased significantly. In recent years the increase in the share of women parliamentarians seems to have come to a standstill at a little over 35 per cent, while the share of women on local councils is still increasing. In parliament, the proportion of women in the Labour Party, Socialist Left Party and Centre Party is about 50 per cent. In the Conservative Party and the Christian Democratic Party one-third of the representatives are women, while in the Progress Party there are around 10 per cent.

Compared with other countries, Norway nevertheless is high up on the list. Only in the other Nordic countries do we find a larger proportion of women in legislative assemblies; Sweden has 43 per cent, Denmark and Finland have 37 per cent. In comparison, Germany has 31 per cent, the United Kingdom 18 and France only 11 per cent.

**Percentage of votes cast for the main parties at parliamentary elections**

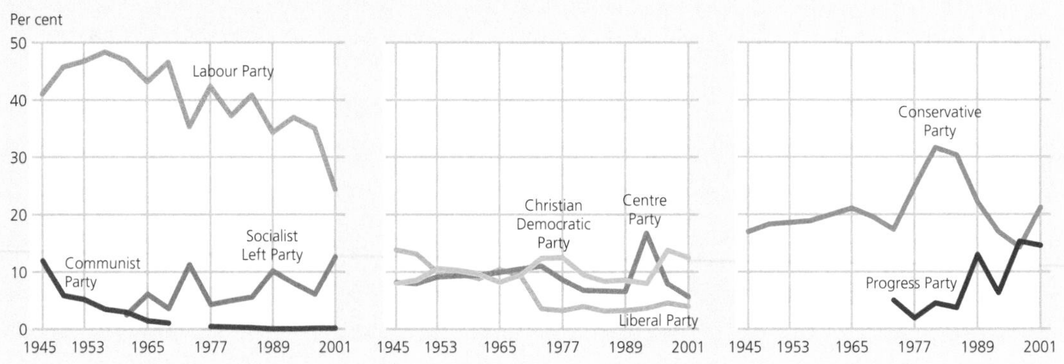

# ECONOMY

### 1 531 159 000 000

The gross domestic product (GDP) is a measure of a country's total output of goods and services and is often used as an indicator of the development in a country's prosperity. In 2002, Norway's total value creation amounted to NOK 1,531 billion.

**GDP according to use. 2002**

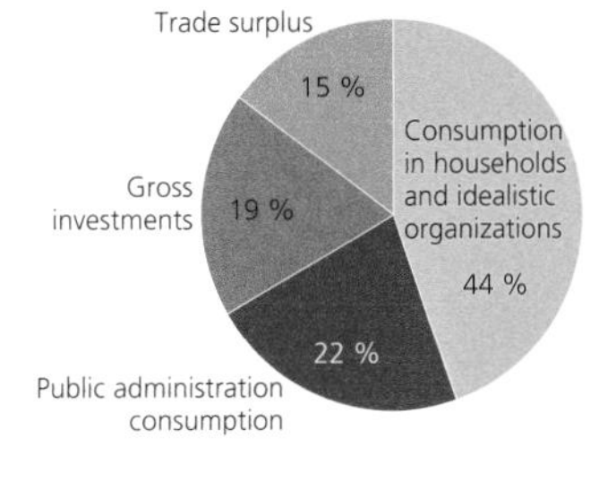


Of this, 44 per cent was spent on household consumption, 22 per cent on consumption in public administration, and 19 per cent was invested. The remaining 15 per cent represents Norway's trade surplus, which means that the value of our production exceeds the value of our consumption.

In 1970, GDP per inhabitant was NOK 23,500. In 2002, this figure had increased to NOK 337,400, more than a tenfold increase in 30 years. Most of the increase, however, relates to the general price inflation: converted to 2002-prices, GDP in 1970 was NOK 128,700. In other words, the real growth was a little over 160 per cent, that is, an average annual growth of more than 3 per cent.

### High GDP ...

Norway has gradually become one of the richest countries in the world. In a European context, Norway's GDP per inhabitant is 43 per cent above the EU average (differences in price levels between the various countries having been taken into account).

Only Luxembourg has a higher GDP per inhabitant, largely because many of Luxembourg's employees are residents of its neighbouring countries. Thus, they contribute to the wealth creation, but are not included in the 'per inhabitant' calculations. In addition there is a significant border trade.

**GDP per inhabitant and consumption in selected countries. Adjusted for price-level differences. 2001. EU15=100**

| | BNP | Household consumption | Personal consumption |
|---|---|---|---|
| Luxembourg | 188 | 149 | 142 |
| **Norway** | **143** | **98** | **108** |
| Switzerland | 117 | 118 | 108 |
| Denmark | 116 | 92 | 105 |
| Ireland | 117 | 91 | 91 |
| Iceland | 113 | 102 | 111 |
| The Netherlands | 115 | 99 | 104 |
| Austria | 111 | 112 | 109 |
| Belgium | 108 | 100 | 103 |
| Finland | 104 | 82 | 88 |
| Germany | 103 | 108 | 105 |
| France | 103 | 98 | 102 |
| Italy | 102 | 101 | 100 |
| Sweden | 102 | 81 | 93 |
| Spain | 84 | 85 | 83 |
| Portugal | 71 | 74 | 72 |
| Greece | 64 | 74 | 69 |

Source: Eurostat.

**GDP per inhabitant, current and fixed prices (2002-NOK)**

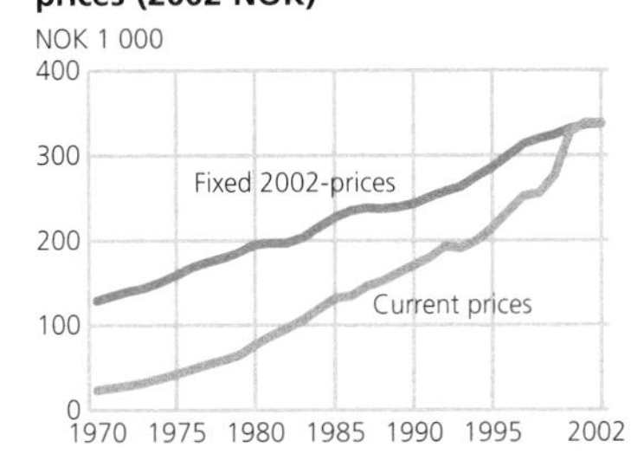


### ... average consumption

A high GDP, however, does not indicate high consumption: in 2002, the consumption of Norwegian households roughly corresponded to the average consumption of the then 15 EU states. However, as regards personal consumption (which includes the sectors of public consumption used by the individual, e.g. health and education services), Norway is somewhat above average.

**Exports and imports, traditional goods. 2002**

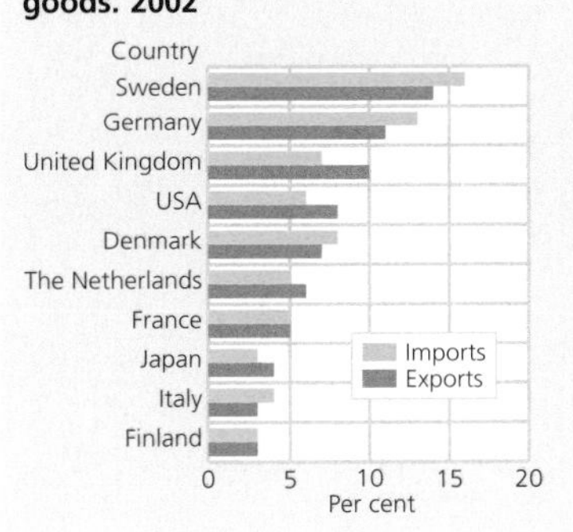


### Changed industrial structure

During the last 50 years, the industrial structure in Norway has changed dramatically. Generally, there has been a movement away from primary and secondary industries towards tertiary industries. The agriculture and manufacturing industries have had to yield to the service sector. We work less in the fields and on the factory floor and increasingly more often in shops and offices.

Whereas primary industries now account for slightly less than 4 per cent of the workforce and secondary industries about 21 per cent, tertiary industries employ as much as 75 per cent of the workforce.

Another way of illustrating the significance of industries is to look at their contribution to the GDP, which paints a slightly different picture: primary industries contribute less than 2 per cent, secondary industries close to 40 per cent (oil contributes far more in terms of value than in terms of employment) and tertiary industries contribute 59 per cent.

**Labour force by primary, secondary and tertiary industries***

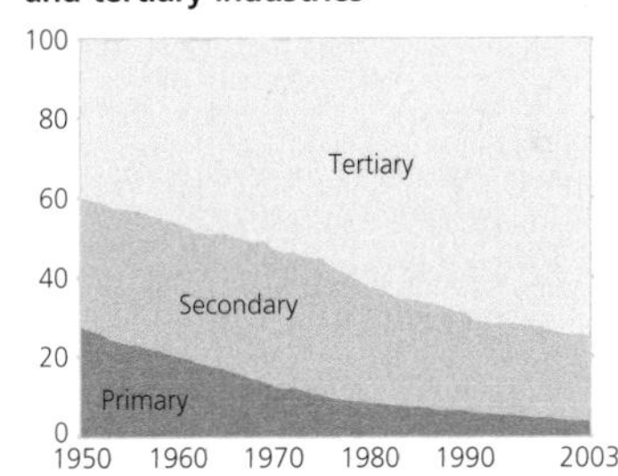


*Primary industries include agriculture, forestry, fisheries and fish farming.

Secondary industries include the manufacturing industry, petroleum production and mining, construction activity, electricity and water supply.

Tertiary industries include remaining activities such as wholesale and retail trades, hotels and restaurants, transportation and communications, public and private services.

**Exports and imports of goods (incl. oil and gas)**

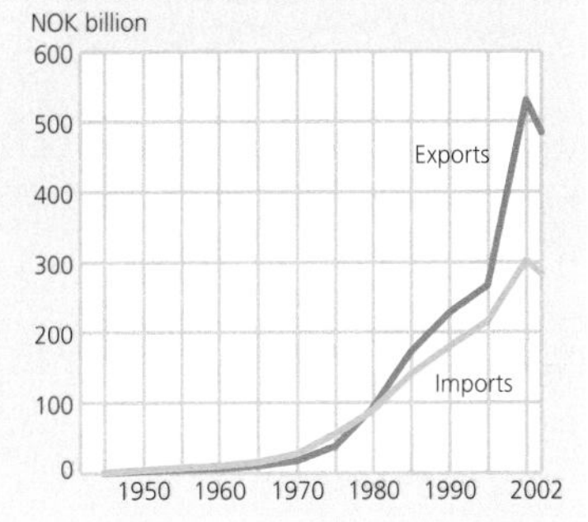


### Trade surplus since 1979

The postwar period was characterized by reconstruction and development, and for a long time imports of goods exceeded exports.

Not until exports of oil began towards the end of the 1970s, did we gradually secure a trade surplus. Apart from in the years 1986-1988, we have since enjoyed a foreign trade surplus, which in 2002 amounted to NOK 200 billion.

Exports of oil and gas in 2002 amounted to a little over NOK 270 billion, which means that we had a foreign trade deficit for traditional goods. Although the service industries dominate both in terms of employment and value, exports of services are relatively modest. In 2002, we exported NOK 156 billion worth of services, which represents almost a quarter of total exports.

The relatively low level of trade in services is due to the dominating service sectors being public. The ongoing GATS (General Agreement on Trade in Services) negotiations may deregulate the international trade in services, including public services.

### Trade with Sweden

Norway's trade with Sweden is more than just the border trade at Svinesund. Sweden is our most important trade partner as regards both imports and exports. 16 per cent of our imports come from Sweden, while 14 per cent of our exports go to Sweden. Then follow Germany (where we also have an import surplus) and the United Kingdom, where our exports exceed imports.

### Oil and motor vehicles

Our predominant export article, by a clear margin, is oil (and increasingly gas). Then come metals (especially aluminium) and fish. Imports are dominated by motor vehicles (cars and buses) and other means of transportation (aircraft and ships).

# PRIMARY INDUSTRIES

### Large structural changes in agriculture

From 1949 to 2003, the number of farms dropped by more than two-thirds, from 213,000 to 58,800: on average, 8 farms closed down every day.

Total agricultural land being utilized nevertheless remains unchanged, because land from the abandoned farms has become supplementary land for the remaining farms. Thus the average area of the remaining farms more than tripled during this period, from about 12 acres to over 44 acres.

**Number of farms**

1 000

250
200
150
100
50
0

1949 1959 1969 1979 1989 2003

The number of people employed in agriculture has also fallen. In 1950, more than 20 per cent of the workforce was employed in agriculture. In 2003, the proportion was 2.8 per cent. Moreover, agriculture's share of the GDP today is less than one per cent.

### Fewer horses and cows – and fur-bearing animals

In addition to the horse almost disappearing from Norwegian agriculture, the number of cattle has declined by more than 50 per cent (328,000 animals in 2003). On the other hand, milk production per cow has increased considerably, from about 2,000 litres in 1949 to 5,700 litres in 2001. Stocks of pigs and sheep, however, have increased.

**Number of fur-bearing animals**

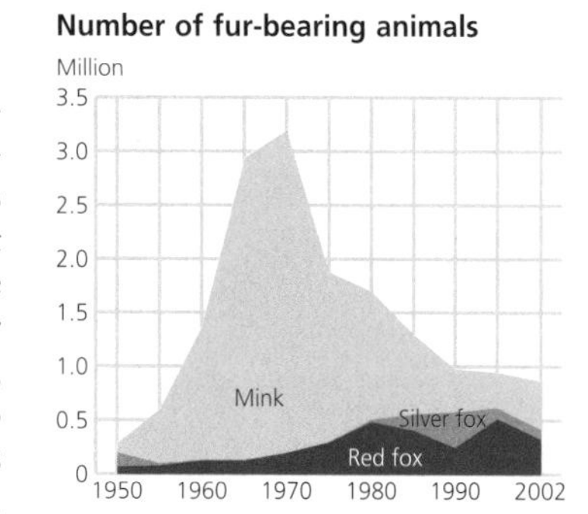


The fur industry had its golden age towards the end of the 1960s, with more than 3.2 million animals; of these, 95 per cent were mink. In recent years the decline has come to a halt and the stock now comprises slightly fewer than 1 million animals.

### Less potatoes – more grain

Agricultural crops vary significantly from year to year. In a somewhat longer perspective, however, the trend is clear. Since 1950, potato production has sunk to almost one-third, while grain production has tripled. Meadow crops are at about the same level as 50 years ago.

**Agricultural crops**

1 000 tonnes

6 000
5 000
4 000
3 000
2 000
1 000
0

Hay
Grain
Potatoes

1950 1960 1970 1980 1990 2002

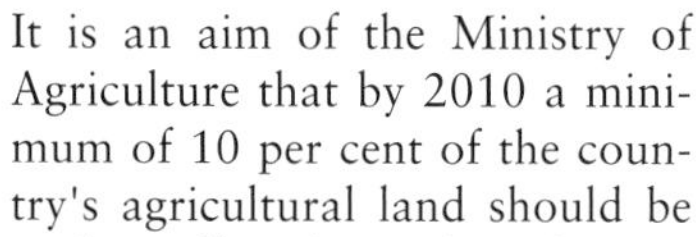

It is an aim of the Ministry of Agriculture that by 2010 a minimum of 10 per cent of the country's agricultural land should be ecologically cultivated. Today, ecological production in terms of acreage accounts for 2.6 per cent, compared with 6-7 per cent in the other Nordic countries.

### Norwegian wood

The economic importance of forestry has been significantly reduced. In 1950, forestry accounted for 2.5 per cent of the GDP, whereas in 2000 it contributed only 0.2 per cent. Felling quantities during the period have varied between 6.6 and 11 million cubic metres of sales timber per year. While in 1950 all the timber was cut and lopped manually by means of saws and axes, the chain-saw gradually took over. Today, felling machinery dominates, and thus the number of people employed has been greactly reduced.

### Fewer fishermen, but heavier catches

Around 1950, there were about 100,000 fishermen in Norway. In 2001, the number was 19,000, of whom 13,700 had fishing as their main occupation.

**Catches, Norwegian fisheries**

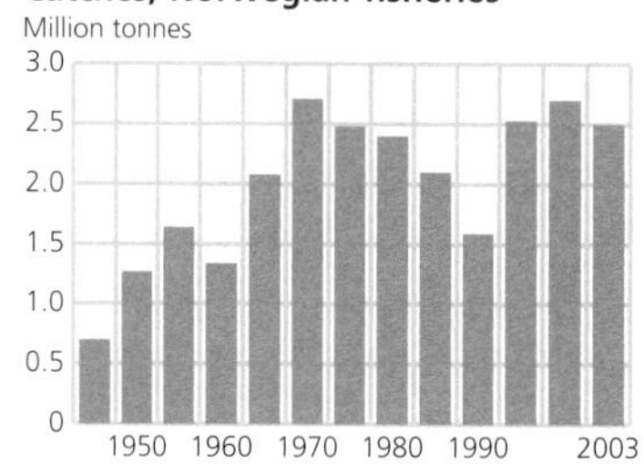


Fish catches vary considerably from one year to the next. From 1945 to the peak year of 1977, catches more than quadrupled, rising from 0.7 to 3.4 million tonnes. Since then, catches have declined, totalling in 2001 2.5 million tonnes.

This places Norway as number ten on the list of the world's largest fishery nations. China tops the list (17.2 million tonnes), followed by Peru, Japan, Chile and the USA.

In terms of economic value, cod is the most important, followed by herring and brisling, mackerel, prawns and mussels.

### Salmon; our newest livestock

Fish farming has expanded greatly since it began in the 1970s, and in 2002 produced almost 550,000 tonnes of fish. In recent years growth has levelled off, mainly because of production regulations that are partly the result of dumping accusations.

**Fish farming. Quantities of salmon and trout sold**

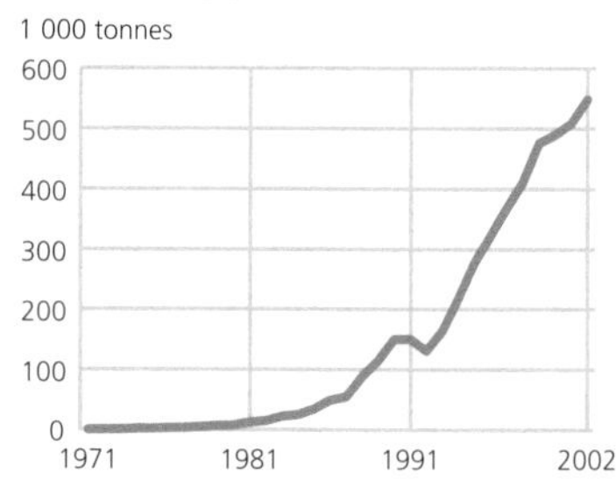


Salmon dominates the fish-farming industry, but trout production is increasing. Other species, too, are on the verge of becoming commercial; in 2001, slightly over 900 tonnes of mussels were farmed, and cod is also on the increase with over 600 tonnes.

### Few people employed – high values

The fish-farming industry employs fewer than 4,000 people on about 1,300 farms. However, the industry's economic significance is far greater. Although the prices in the export market (i.e. the EU) were especially low in 2001, the landed value of the fish-farming industry was nearly as high as that of the traditional fisheries, NOK 9.2 and 11.4 billion respectively.

**Landed value of fish farming and traditional fisheries**

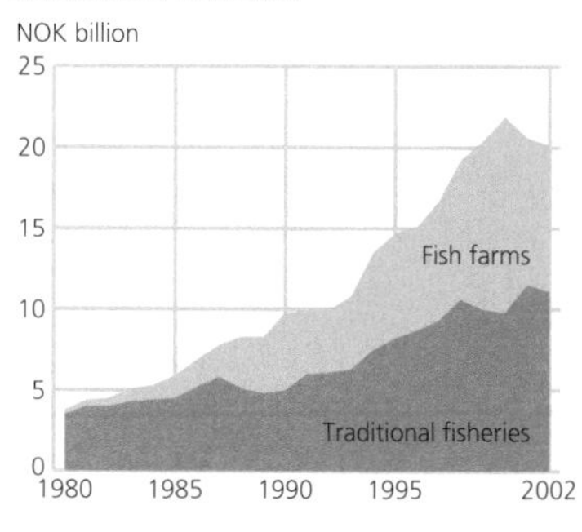

# SECONDARY INDUSTRIES

### The rise and fall of manufacturing industry

Secondary industries as a whole (manufacturing industry and mining, petroleum production, construction, and electricity and water supply) have declined slightly during the last 30 years, and now employ some 490,000 people. Relatively speaking, however, the decline is far greater. From employing almost a third of all employed people until about 1970, secondary industries today account for only 21 per cent.

Since the peak year of 1974, the number of jobs in manufacturing and mining has fallen by almost one-third from 400,000 to 273,000. This decline took place at the end of the 1970s and in the 1980s. After an increase in the 1990s, numbers have again declined in recent years. The proportion of people working in the manufacturing industry today is 13 per cent. The decline in employment has been especially high in the textile and clothing industry, the wood-processing, pulp and paper industry, and the engineering industry.

Despite the decline in employment, the output value (in fixed 2002-NOK) increased from NOK 260 billion in 1972 to over NOK 500 billion in 1999. In subsequent years the output value has been somewhat lower. The increase in output value was especially large within machinery and equipment, petroleum and chemical products, and electrical and optical products.

**Number of people employed and output value in the manufacturing and mining industries**

### Oil and gas: Increased production ...

Apart from a decline towards the end of the 1990s, oil production has increased steadily since it started in 1971. For a long time gas production, which commenced towards the end of the 1970s, remained stable, between 20 and 30 million Sm³ of oil equivalent. From the middle of the 1990s, gas production has increased, and today accounts for more than 20 per cent of the total petroleum production, a proportion that is expected to rise in the years ahead.

**Total production of oil and gas**

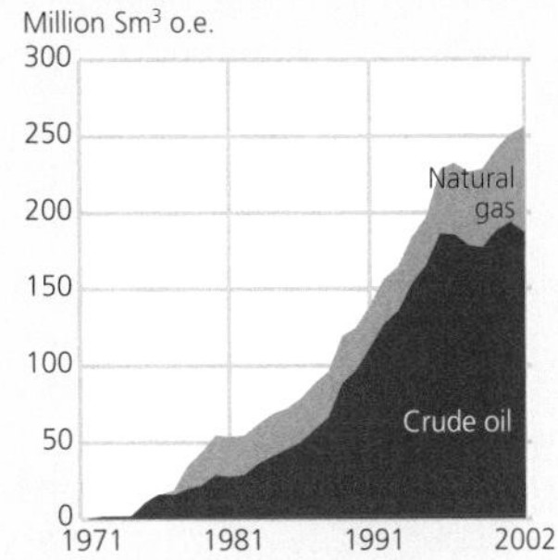


### ... but relatively few employees

From the start in 1972, employment in oil and gas production gradually increased until the end of the 1990s, when about 16,000 people were working in the industry. In addition there are 8,000-9,000 employees in various services relating to the petroleum industry.

**Employment in oil and gas production**

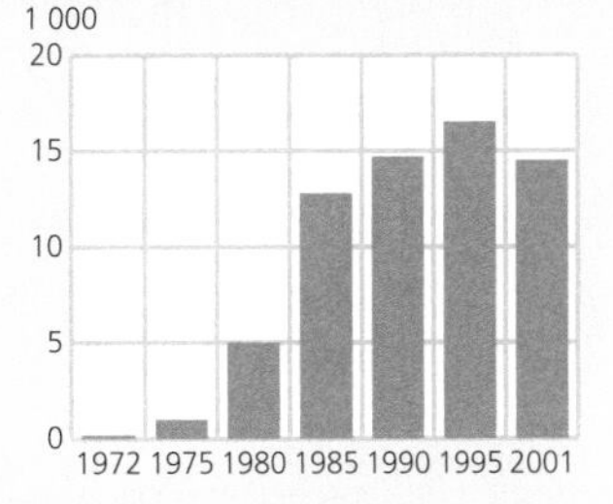


If we also include drilling activity and employment in various contractor industries, the total number of employees related to oil and gas activity is about 75,000. In other words, there are about as many employees in the industry as a whole as in the primary industries.

### Large values

The significance of the petroleum industry, however, is far greater than is reflected in the number of people employed. In terms of value, this is Norway's number one industry, currently accounting as it does for more than 20 per cent of the country's GDP. The petroleum industry's proportion of export revenue is now about 45 per cent.

The economic importance of the petroleum industry is obviously associated with production volumes, and it also reflects the relatively high oil prices during this period.

**Oil and gas production. Share of GDP and employment**

1 Sm³ (standard cubic metre) oil equivalent (o.e.) = 6.29 barrels

1 barrel = 159 litres

### Oil prices

The oil price curve shows that oil production in Norway started at a very favourable point in time. After having remained stable at about USD 2 per barrel throughout almost the entire century, the oil price rose at the beginning of the 1970s, and in connection with the first oil crisis in 1973-1974, it tripled. It later increased again around 1980. From the middle of the 1980s, it has generally fluctuated between USD 13 and 30.

**Oljepris. Brent blend**

Source: IMF and Petroleum Intelligence Weekly.

### Short life for oil?

The remaining oil and gas reserves on the Norwegian shelf are estimated at 10.2 billion Sm³ oil equivalent. In comparison, total production to date (2002) has been 3.5 billion Sm³ of oil equivalent.

Whereas Norway's share of the world's oil and gas resources is less than 1 per cent, we now contribute respectively 4.5 and 2.3 per cent of the world's annual oil and gas production. This means that the life of the Norwegian reserves is considerably shorter than the life of the world's total reserves, especially as regards oil.

**Largest oil producers. August 2002. Million barrels/day**

| | |
|---|---|
| Former Soviet Union | 9.5 |
| Saudi-Arabia | 7.7 |
| USA | 7.7 |
| Mexico | 3.6 |
| Iran | 3.4 |
| China | 3.4 |
| **Norway** | **3.1** |

Source: Petroleum Economist

### Money in the bank

Because oil revenues will gradually decline and the increasing number of elderly people will lead to higher pension, nursing and care expenditure, the Norwegian state has established a petroleum revenue fund, which is managed by Norway's central bank and comprises the share of the petroleum revenues that are not used in the state budget. From 1996 until the end of November 2003, this fund increased from NOK 48 billion to NOK 845 billion.

**The Government Petroleum Fund**

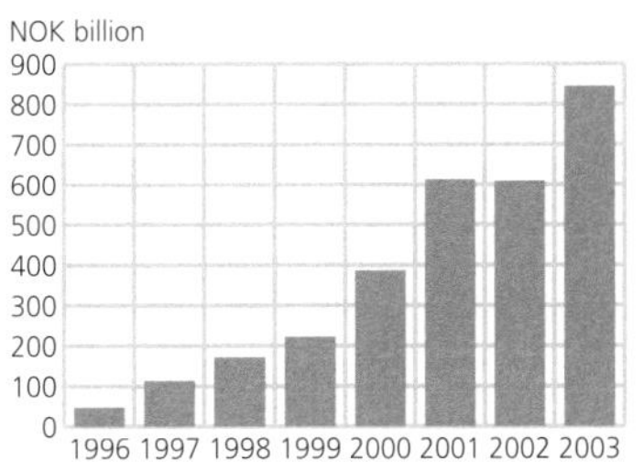

# TERTIARY INDUSTRIES

### Three out of four in the service sector

In all, employment in the tertiary industries, or the service sector, rose from 750,000 at the beginning of the 1960s to 1,760,000 today and now constitutes almost 75 per cent of the labour force. The dominant position of the tertiary industries has led to the labelling of today's society as 'the post-industrial society', 'the information society' or the 'service society'.

**Number of people employed in different tertiary industries. 2002**

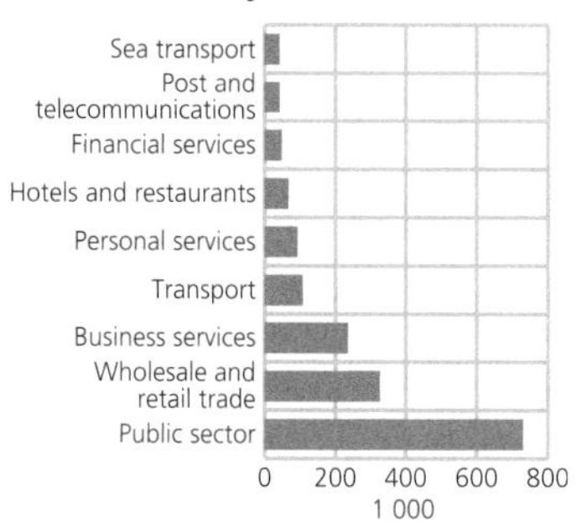


The tertiary industries comprise many varied sectors, for example, wholesale and retail trade, hotels and restaurants, transport, financial services, and tourism. The largest and most dominant service sector is nevertheless the public sector, that is, municipal and state services, including social services, health services, education, administration, etc.

### Strong growth in the public sector

During the last decades, the public sector has seen strong growth, and now employs about 730,000 people, compared with only 200,000 in 1962.

**Public sector employment in per cent of total employment**

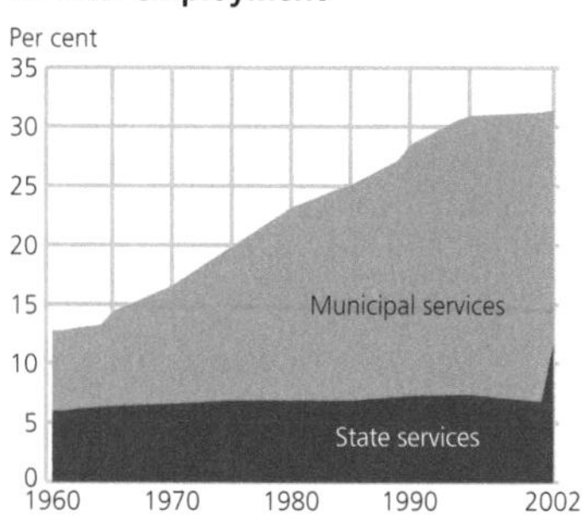


Public sector employment has risen from 13 to slightly over 30 per cent, which corresponds to 27 per cent of all hours worked (part-time work is rather more common in the public sector).

Employees in the municipal services constitute the large majority. Because of the state's takeover of county hospitals, employment in the state administration rose by 114,000 people in 2002.

The strong growth in recent years has primarily taken place in health and social services and education. Public administration has undergone the weakest growth.

### Many public sector employees in northern Norway

As stated earlier, a little over 30 per cent of all employed people work in the public sector. There are wide variations between counties, however. The highest proportions are found in Troms and Finnmark, where more than 40 per cent are employed in the public sector (due both to the presence of the Norwegian armed forces and to sparsely populated municipalities requiring a relatively large number of employees to maintain the various municipal services).

The lowest proportion of employees in state or municipalities is found in Oslo and Rogaland, with only 24-25 per cent. In Oslo, many people work for the state, but there are fewer in the municipal administration.

**Number of public sector employees. 2001**

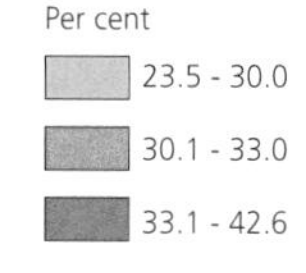


### ICT: a new growth sector

Information and Communication Technology (ICT), includes a number of industries mainly involved in information and communication technology, such as manufacturing of computers and computer accessories, ICT trade, telecommunications and consultancy. This sector crosses traditional industrial sector boundaries in that it includes both production of goods and services.

**Number of employees in the ICT sector**

| Year | Employees |
|---|---|
| 1995 | 59 500 |
| 1996 | 63 234 |
| 1997 | 68 100 |
| 1998 | 73 700 |
| 1999 | 80 300 |
| 2000 | 85 500 |
| 2001 | 88 700 |
| 2002 | 86 900 |

In 2002, the ICT sector employed 87,000 people, which corresponds to 4 per cent of the total employment.

Consultancy services account for 45 per cent of the total employment in ICT, and is the branch that is growing fastest.

### Important in our everyday lives

Despite the economic significance of the ICT sector, this technology's significance is far more visible on the consumer side, both in industry and in households. During the 1990s, modern means of communication such as PCs, mobile telephones and the Internet became an important part of both working life and daily life at home.

In trade and industry, nine out of ten companies (with more than ten employees) now have access to the Internet, compared with four out of ten in 1998. Half of the companies have their own website. In this area, Norwegian businesses seem to be somewhat behind their Nordic neighbours.

However, it is perhaps in private households that the significance of modern communications technology is most evident. In 2001, 75 per cent had access to PCs and 60 per cent had access to the Internet at home. One out of three used a PC and the Internet on an average day.

Norway and the other four Nordic countries top the world list as regards access to and use of ICT equipment, and, for example, access to the Internet. The same is the case for home PCs and mobile telephones.

# ENERGY AND THE ENVIRONMENT

### Norway number one as regards electricity

In a mountainous country like Norway, with its abundant hydroelectric power, electricity is an important energy source. We have the world's highest electricity consumption per capita: 27,300 kWh. This is almost five times the average in Europe, which is about 5,700 kWh. (This figure includes electricity consumption in all sectors, not only private households.)

**Electricity consumption per inhabitant in selected countries. 1998**

| | |
|---|---|
| **Norway** | **27 277** |
| Iceland | 22 759 |
| Canada | 17 486 |
| Sweden | 16 629 |
| Finland | 15 420 |
| USA | 14 089 |
| Denmark | 7 927 |
| France | 7 613 |
| Germany | 6 785 |

Source: IEA.

**Price of unleaded petrol (95 octane) and electricity to households in selected countries. 2000**

| | Petrol (NOK/litre) | Electricity (NOK/kWh) |
|---|---|---|
| **Norway** | **10.57** | **0.50** |
| Denmark | 9.09 | 1.73 |
| Finland | 9.20 | 0.69 |
| The Netherlands | 9.43 | 1.15 |
| Italy | 8.80 | 1.18 |
| United Kingdom | 10.64 | 0.95 |
| Switzerland | 7.29 | 0.98 |
| Austria | 7.64 | 1.06 |

Source: IEA.

Compared with other countries, electric power constitutes a relatively large share of energy consumption in Norway – almost 50 per cent. This obviously reflects the relatively low price of electricity. In 2000, the price per kWh was roughly half that of many European countries.

### Average energy consumption

The high electricity consumption does not mean that Norway has an unusually high total energy consumption, however.

From 1976 to 2001, energy consumption increased by 45 per cent, from slightly over 600 petajoules to almost 900. Measured per inhabitant, Norway is slightly above the average for western countries, and is on about the same level as Sweden and Finland.

Whereas Norway has produced increasingly more oil, paradoxically there has been a transition from the use of oil products to electricity during this period. Electricity now accounts for about 50 per cent of the total energy consumption. However, while stationary oil consumption (for example, for heating) has declined sharply, oil used for transport has increased a little. The use of gas, district heating and solid fuel has also increased. The growth in energy consumption has been highest within the private services sector and in households.

**Energy consumption per inhabitant in selected countries. toe 1999**

| | |
|---|---|
| Iceland | 12.2 |
| USA | 8.4 |
| Canada | 8.2 |
| Finland | 6.4 |
| **Norway** | **5.7** |
| Sweden | 5.4 |
| The Netherlands | 4.8 |
| France | 4.3 |
| Denmark | 3.6 |

Source: OECD/IEA.

**Energy consumption according to energy type*. Petajoule**

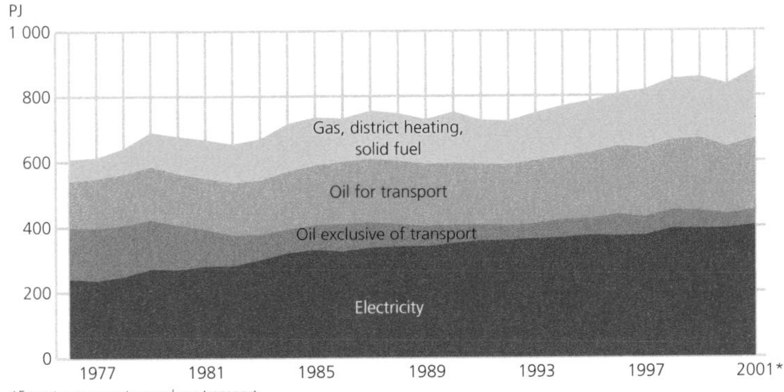


*Except energy sectors and sea transport.

**Emission of greenhouse gases. Million tonnes of $CO_2$ equivalents**

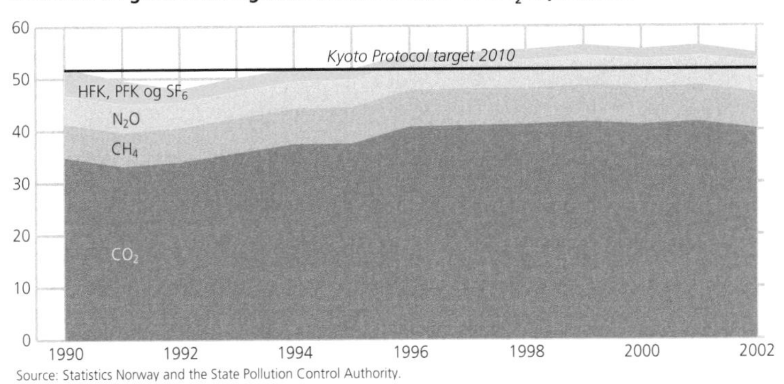


Source: Statistics Norway and the State Pollution Control Authority.

### Increased emissions to the air ...

Increased production and use of oil and gas result in higher emissions to the air. Norwegian emissions of greenhouse gases have increased by more than 8 per cent from 1990, the base year for the Kyoto Protocol, to 2001, when emissions were the highest ever. The growth in emissions was lower than the economic growth (measured as GDP in fixed prices). In 2002, emissions declined a little, and are now 5 per cent above the level in 1990.

$CO_2$ accounts for almost three-quarters of the total greenhouse gas emissions. The most important sources of $CO_2$ emissions are road traffic, oil and gas production, industrial combustion and processing emissions from metal production.

According to the Kyoto Protocol, Norwegian emissions, including the so-called Kyoto mechanisms, may only increase by a total of 1 per cent in the twenty years starting from 1990.

### ... and more waste

Economic growth and wealth also generate large amounts of waste. In 2000, we generated in excess of 8.5 million tonnes of waste, that is, almost 2 tons per inhabitant. Since 1995 the increase has been 1 million tonnes. The increase in waste in the 1990s was still lower than the economic growth, measured in GDP.

Industrial waste accounts for 40 per cent of the total, while the remaining sectors together generate about the same amount. The remaining 18 per cent relates to household waste, which is increasing in volume more than other types of waste.

In 2002, each inhabitant on average generated 354 kilos of household waste. Household waste has increased more than household consumption.

**Household waste. Kilos per inhabitant**

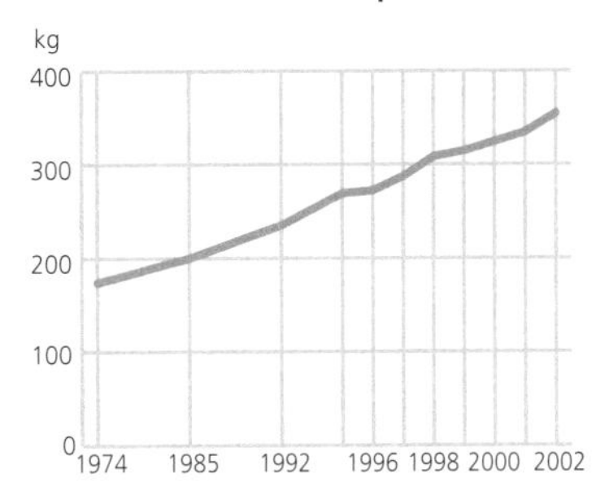

# HISTORICAL TIME CHART

- **10,000 BC** Ice Age nears its end. First hunters and gatherers. Palaeolithic Age.
- **4000 BC** Agriculture reaches Norway. Neolithic Age.
- **1800 BC** Bronze Age with chieftainships.
- **500 BC** Iron Age and colder climate.
- **400 – 600** Period of migrations, petty kingdoms and hill forts.

0

- **600 – 800** Merovingian Period. Viking ships developed.
- **793** Start of the Viking Age with attack on Lindisfarne monastery in England.
- **800 onwards** Emigration to Iceland, the North Sea islands and Greenland.
- **About 900** Harald Hårfagre (Fairhair) unites coastal Norway.
- **900s** Ting and Leidang – larger legislative areas and new defence system.
- **About 1000** Leiv Eiriksson reaches North America.

1000

- **1000s** Christianity introduced in Norway. Churches built. Latin alphabet introduced.
- **1030** Olav Haraldsson falls at Stiklestad. Later canonized.
- **1066** Harald Hardråde (the Ruthless) falls at Stamford Bridge after an unsuccessful attempt to conquer England. End of the Viking Age.
- **1130** Civil wars after the death of Sigurd Jorsalfare (the Crusader).
- **1152-53** Nidaros (Trondheim) becomes an archbishopric.
- **1163** A new Act of Succession increases the power of the Church.
- **1177** Sverre declares himself king. Birkebeiners against Baglers (the Church party).

1200

- **1247** Håkon Håkonsson crowned. Norway's golden age. Norwegian dominion: control of Iceland, the North Sea islands and Greenland.
- **1270s** Magnus Lagabøte (the Law-Mender) introduces a new national legislative code.
- **1300** The Roman Catholic Church is the biggest landowner in Norway.
- **1319** Håkon V dies without male issue. Norway in union with Sweden.
- **1349** The Black Death ravages Norway, wiping out more than one-third of the population.
- **1300s** The Hanseatic League gains control of Norway's foreign trade. Bryggen (Hanseatic houses) in Bergen built.
- **1397** Queen Margaret I negotiates the Kalmar Union between Denmark, Norway and Sweden.

1400

- **1537** Norway becomes a Danish province. The King seizes Church properties. Danish becomes Norway's written language.
- **1500s** Timber trade and mining in progress. Population increases.
- **1644-60** Wars with Sweden. Denmark-Norway forced to cede territory.
- **1600s** Denmark-Norway establishes colonies in America, Africa and Asia.
- **1600s** Witch trials in Norway.
- **1660-61** Autocracy introduced in Denmark-Norway.
- **1700–20** Great Nordic War. Karl XII falls at Fredriksten in 1718.
- **1736** Confirmation introduced – first school system in 1739.
- **1700s** Population increase and scarcity of land, resulting in the development of a system of smallholdings.
- **1780s – 1790s** Christian Lofthus and Hans Nielsen Hauge revolt against the state and receive long prison sentences.

- **1807–1814** Denmark-Norway sides with Napoleon. War with Sweden and Great Britain. Years of hardship.
- **1811** Norway's first university established in Christiania.
- **1814, January** Denmark forced to cede Norway to Sweden by the Treaty of Kiel.
- **1814, 17 May** Norway declares itself an independent kingdom with its own constitution and king.
- **1814, July/August** Following a brief war, King Karl Johan of Sweden compels Norway to negotiate.
- **1814, November** Union with Sweden.

1820

- **1825** Emigration to America begins.
- **1829** 'Battle of the Marketplace' in Christiania. Dispute over 17 May celebrations.
- **1837** Local council legislation. Municipal self-government.

1840

- **1840s –1850s** National Romanticism in art and culture strengthens Norwegian nationalism. Ivar Aasen introduces New-Norwegian as a written language.
- **1845** First industrial activity in Christiania and Bergen.
- **1845 –1851** Marcus Thrane's labour movement suppressed. Thrane is sentenced to several years' imprisonment. Emigrates to America in 1858.

1850

- **1851** The Norwegian parliament grants Jews access to Norway.
- **1852** The Kautokeino revolt. Five Sámi sentenced to death and two executed.
- **1850s** First railway to Eidsvoll, regular coastal steamer routes, telegraph system and postage stamps.
- **1850s –1860s** Scandinavianism – the idea of a unified Nordic region gains ground.

1870

- **1870s –1880s** Mass emigration to America. Enormous growth in the merchant fleet.
- **1884** Parliamentarism. The first political parties, the Liberal Party and the Conservative Party.
- **1880s** Dispute surrounding bohemians Hans Jæger (author) and Christian Krohg (painter).
- **1887** Labour Party established.
- **1888 – 1889** Fridtjof Nansen crosses Greenland. Skiing becomes the national sport.

1890

- **1890s** Spearheaded by Bjørnstjerne Bjørnson, Henrik Ibsen, Edvard Munch and Edvard Grieg, Norwegian culture blooms.
- **1895** Norway demands its own consular service and foreign minister. Union crisis and threat of war.
- **1896** Fridtjof Nansen returns from his North Pole expedition on board the 'Fram'.
- **1898** Full suffrage for men introduced.

1905

- **1900** Norway builds fortifications along the border with Sweden.
- **1903** Bjørnstjerne Bjørnson is awarded the Nobel Prize for Literature.
- **1903** The Labour Party is elected to parliament.
- **1904 –1905** Norwegian-Swedish negotiations on a separate Norwegian consular service.
- **1905, 7 june** Norway breaks with Sweden. The Storting rejects King Oscar II.
- **1905, August** Referendum results in an overwhelming majority for dissolution of the union.
- **1905, September** Karlstad negotiations avert war.
- **1905, November** Haakon VII becomes King of Norway following a referendum.

# HISTORICAL TIME CHART

- **1905** Norsk Hydro established. Start of the hydroelectric industry, based on the harnessing of waterfalls.
- **1906** First licensing legislation to limit foreign control of Norway's natural resources.
- **1912** In the 'Start' Hans Dons makes the first Norwegian flight, flying from Borre via Horten/Moss to Fredrikstad.
- **1913** Full suffrage for women.
- **1914** First World War. Norway declares itself neutral.
- **1914–1918** Period of boom and high prices. 2,000 seamen lose their lives.
- **1918** The Spanish influenza epidemic claims over 10,000 lives in Norway.
- **1918–1919** The Labour Party goes revolutionary and joins the Communist International (Comintern).

1920

- **1920** Norwegian Agrarian Party (Bondepartiet) formed.
- **1920** Norway awarded dominion over Svalbard. Sovereignty in 1925.
- **1920** Norway joins the League of Nations.
- **1920** Knut Hamsun awarded the Nobel Prize for Literature.
- **1922** Fridtjof Nansen awarded the Nobel Prize for Peace.
- **1923** The Labour Party withdraws from the Comintern. Comintern supporters establish the Communist Party of Norway (NKP).
- **1920–1927** Bank crisis, bankruptcies and parity politics. Conservative minority governments.
- **1928** Sigrid Undset is awarded the Nobel Prize for Literature.

1930

- **1931** Repercussions of the world economic crisis reach Norway. Mass unemployment.
- **1931** The Menstad battle. National police and military protect strikebreakers.
- **1931** Norwegians occupy eastern Greenland. Norwegian Arctic Ocean imperialism. The Hague Court supports Denmark (1933).
- **1933** Vidkun Quisling forms Nasjonal Samling (NS) (National Union) Party.
- **1933** Dispute over liberal theology. Breakaways from the Liberal Party establish the Christian Democratic Party.
- **1934** First laws on eugenics and compulsory sterilization introduced. Employed against the gypsies and mentally retarded.
- **1935** Trade Unions (LO) and Employers' Confederation (NAF/NHO) sign a main agreement. The right to strike, organize, and control is accepted.
- **1935** Labour Party government under Johan Nygaardsvold, supported by the Agrarian Party.

1940

- **1940, April** German attack on Norway. Vidkun Quisling carries out the world's first coup d'état by radio.
- **1940, June** Norway abandons military resistance. King and government flee to London. The merchant fleet enters the service of the Allies.
- **1940, September** Josef Terboven bans all political parties apart from the NS and appoints commissary ministers from the NS.
- **1941** The Home Front is organized. Labour leaders Viggo Hansteen and Rolf Wickstrøm executed.
- **1942** Quisling named 'Minister President'.
- **1942** Action against teachers. Church protests. Norwegian Jews transported to Germany.
- **1943** Quisling takes action against students and officers.
- **1944** The Germans employ scorched-earth tactics in Finnmark and northern Troms. The Soviet Union liberates eastern Finnmark.
- **1945** Germany capitulates on 8 May. Norwegian coalition government and joint programme.

- **1945** The Labour Party wins the election and forms a majority government under Einar Gerhardsen. (Labour retains its majority until 1961.)
- **1945–1952** Strict rationing of imported consumer goods.
- **1948** Norway receives Marshall Aid from the USA. Cultural Americanization.
- **1949** Norway joins NATO after a Labour Party majority supports the Atlantic Treaty.

1950

- **1957** King Haakon VII dies. Olav V becomes king.
- **1959** The Agrarian Party changes its name to the Centre Party (SP).
- **1960** Motor-vehicle imports freed. The Norwegian Broadcasting Corporation (NRK) starts television broadcasts.
- **1961** Socialist People's Party (SF) established in protest against nuclear policy and NATO membership.
- **1961** The Labour Party loses its absolute majority in parliament.
- **1965** The conservative parties win a majority in parliament. Coalition government under Per Borten (SP).
- **1967** National Insurance Act comes into effect.
- **1968** Dawn of youth revolts, student protests, Women's Lib and the 'green' movement.

1970

- **1970** Pakistani immigrant workers come to Norway. The Ekofisk field is declared commercially exploitable. Norway becomes an oil nation.
- **1971** The Borten government resigns over the EEC issue. Laobour government under Trygve Bratteli.
- **1972** Opponents of Norwegian EEC membership win the referendum. Trygve Bratteli's Labour government resigns.
  Conservative government under Lars Korvald (KrF) completes negotiations for trade agreement with the EEC.
- **1973** Anders Lange's Party (later renamed the Progress Party) and AKP(m-l) (Workers' Communist Party (Marxist-Leninist)) are established.
- **1973–1974** Oil crisis. Car-free weekends. Counter-cyclical policy in Norway staves off unemployment.
- **1975** Socialist Left Party established by SF, factions of NKP and breakaway faction from the Labour Party.
- **1978** Abortion on demand legalized. Equal Rights Act.

1980

- **1980** Alexander Kielland offshore oil platform collapses, with the loss of 123 lives.
- **1981, January** Police confront demonstraters protesting against damming of the River Alta.
- **1981, February** Gro Harlem Brundtland (Labour) appointed Norway's first woman prime minister.
- **1981, October** Conservatives win parliamentary election. Kåre Willoch forms a government.
- **1980s** Banking, broadcasting and housing policy liberalized. Beginning of the so-called YAP (Young Aspiring Professionals) period.
- **1989** Sámi National Assembly formed in Kautokeino.

2005

- **1991** King Olav V dies. Harald V becomes king.
- **1994** Norway signs EEA agreement, hosts Winter Olympics in Lillehammer and says 'No' to the EU in a referendum.
- **1996** Gro Harlem Brundtland resigns after three periods as prime minister.
- **1997** Conservative coalition government under Kjell Magne Bondevik (KrF).
- **2005** Celebration of Norway's 100th anniversary as an independent nation.

# CONTRIBUTORS

Photo: Johannes Haugan/Samfoto

**H.R.H. CROWN PRINCE HAAKON**
b. 1973. H.R.H. Crown Prince Haakon has written the introduction, and has been an active member of the editorial committee.

Photo: Vegar Andreassen/UiT

**EDITOR-IN-CHIEF Tove Bull**
**EDUCATION AND RESEARCH**
b.1945, linguist, Professor at the University of Tromsø, University Vice President 1990–95, President 1996–2001.

Photo: Janne Møller-Hansen/Scanpix

**EDITOR-IN-CHIEF Harald Norvik**
b.1946, Bachelor of Commerce, adviser to Prime Minister Odvar Nordli 1976–79, Under-Secretary, Ministry of Petroleum and Energy 1979–81, Financial Director Aker Group 1981–1988, CEO Statoil 1988–99, Chairman and partner in ECON Management. Chairman of the Supervisory Board of DnBNOR, Chairman of, *inter alia*, Oslo Stock Exchange and Aschehoug Publishers.

Photo: Knut Falch/Scanpix

**Niels Chr. Geelmuyden 15 PORTRAITS**
b. 1960, cand.polit. (philology). Writer, lecturer and author. Has published 15 books and worked as columnist for *Henne*, *Kapital*, *Bergens Tidende* and *Tønsbergs Blad*. He also gives talks on NRK Radio.

Photo: Tine Poppe

**Erling Lægreid NORWEGIAN HISTORY UNTIL 1814**
b.1939, cand. philol. (philologist), producer, NRK News Department. Worked in several departments at NRK Radio and NRK Television. Extensive experience as a speaker, lecturer and writer.

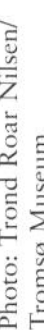

Photo: Trond Roar Nilsen/ Tromsø Museum

**Marit Anne Hauan THE NORWEGIAN PEOPLE**
Associate Professor of Folklore, University of Tromsø. Editor of the two-volume work *Nordnorsk kulturhistorie* and of the periodical *Tradisjon*. Has focused on subjects such as regional identity, masculinity, hunting culture in polar regions and folklore narrative traditions in northern Norway.

Photo: Birgitte Aasen/Scanpix

**Per Egil Hegge ADMINISTRATION AND INTERNAL AFFAIRS**
b. 1940, journalist on the staff of *Aftenposten* since 1962 and the newspaper's correspondent in London, Moscow and Washington. Cultural Editor of *Aftenposten* 1992–98. Author of several biographies.

Photo: Tor Richardsen/Scanpix

**Geir Lundestad THE NOBEL PEACE PRIZE**
b.1945. Director of the Norwegian Nobel Institute and secretary of the Norwegian Nobel Committee since 1990; he is also Professor of History at the University of Oslo. He has published numerous books and articles on international relations since 1945. His latest book is entitled *The United States and Western Europe since 1945* (Oxford University Press, 2003).

Photo: Tine Poppe

**Espen Barth Eide FOREIGN POLICY**
b.1964, senior researcher. Employed by NUPI (Norwegian Institute of International Affairs) since 1993. Under-Secretary, Ministry of Foreign Affairs 2000–01. Head of the Department of International Politics, NUPI, since 2002.

Photo: Martial Trezzini/AP Photo/ Keystone/Scanpix

**Gro Harlem Brundtland NATURE, RESOURCES AND ENVIRONMENTAL PROTECTION**
b.1939, physician and politician. Minister of Environmental Protection, 1974–79, Member of Parliament 1977–97, Leader of the Norwegian Labour Party 1981–92. Head of UN's Special Commission for Environmental and Development Issues 1984–87. Prime Minister in 1981, 1986–89 and 1990–96. Director General of the World Health Organization (WHO), 1998–2001.

Photo: Tine Poppe

**Ole Mathismoen NATURE, RESOURCES AND ENVIRONMENTAL PROTECTION**
b.1961, educated as a journalist in the UK. Political journalist on the staff of *Aftenposten* since 1984. Special areas include environmental issues, energy and defence. *Aftenposten*'s correspondent in Brussels 1995–97. Has published several books about environmental protection.

Photo: Bjørn Sigurdsøn/Scanpix

**Gunnar Stålsett FAITH AND PHILOSOPHIES**
b.1935, theologian, writer, former politician. Secretary General of the International Church Council 1970–77, Under-Secretary 1972–73, Chairman of the Centre Party 1977–79, Secretary General of The Lutheran World Association 1985–1994, Head of Practical Theological Study, University of Oslo, 1994–98. Bishop of Oslo since 1998.

Photo: Tine Poppe

**Håvard Rem** 200 YEARS OF NORWEGIAN POETRY
b.1959, writer and translator. His *Selected Poems* were published in Norwegian (1996), Arabic (2000) and Russian (2003). He has published numerous poetic works, essays, plays and biographies.

Photo: Dagbladet/All Over Press

**Hege Duckert** ARTS AND CULTURE
b.1962, journalist, on the staff of *Dagbladet* since 1982. Founded *Magasinet* in 1999. Cultural Editor of *Dagbladet* since 2002.

Photo: Astrid Vannebo /Programbladet/Scanpix

**Gunnar Danbolt** ART GALLERY
b.1940, Professor of European Art History at the University of Bergen. He has published books and articles on paintings and sculptures from ancient Greece and Rome, the Middle Ages and the Renaissance, modern art, art theory, handicrafts and children's culture.

Photo: Dagbladet/All Over Press

**Andreas Hompland** TRANSPORT AND COMMUNICATIONS
b.1946, sociologist, journalist, researcher and writer.
On the staff of *Dagbladet* since 1971, first as a journalist in the Political Department, then as Cultural Editor. Regular columnist in the same newspaper since 1980.

Photo: Bjørn Erik Larsen/Scanpix

**Kåre Valebrokk** ECONOMY AND BUSINESS
b.1940, economist, columnist and journalist for *Morgenbladet* and *VG*. Editor-in-Chief of *Dagens Næringsliv* 1985–89, Editor-in-Chief and Managing Director of *Dagens Næringsliv* 1989–99. Editor-in-Chief and Managing Director of TV2 since 1999.

Photo: Erlend Aas/Scanpix

**Grete Waitz** SPORT
b.1953, athlete. World Champion, marathon gold medallist 1983, silver medallist at the 1984 Olympic Games, World Champion and gold medallist in cross-country running in 1978–81 and 1983. Nine times winner of the New York City Marathon and twice winner of the London Marathon.
Two 3000-metre world records.

Photo: privat

**Kristen Damsgaard** SPORT
b.1938, graduate in Norwegian, history and sports. Extensive background in teaching. Former National Coach/Manager of Sports. National/international experience in the fields of fitness/exercise and quality control coaching.

Photo: Bjørn Brøymer/Scanpix

**Astri Riddervold** FOOD AND BEVERAGES
b.1925, ethnologist, one of Norway's leading experts on cuisine. Has published a number of books.

Photo: Berit Roald/Scanpix

**Torkjell Berulfsen** FOOD AND BEVERAGES
b.1943, philologist and journalist. On the staff of NRK since 1970. Well known for numerous entertainment and cultural programmes. Has published several books on, for example, culinary delights, the history of tobacco, and wines and spirits.

Photo: Signe Dons/Scanpix

**Bent Stiansen** FOOD AND BEVERAGES
b.1963, chef and owner of the Statholdergaarden gourmet restaurant in Oslo. Awarded gold medal in Bocuse d'Or, the World Championship of Chefs, in Lyons, 1993.

Photo: privat

**Jan Erik Kristiansen** A STATISTICAL PORTRAIT
b.1945, sociologist, Senior Adviser in Statistics Norway, Department of Communication.

# PETROGLYPHS

David Vogt of the Museum of Cultural History, the University of Oslo

**NORWEGIAN HISTORY UNTIL 1814**
Løberghaugen in Gjerpen, Skien municipality, Telemark. Rock carving from the late Bronze Age (1100–500 BC). A highly stylized horseman, not an especially common rock-carving subject.

**THE NORWEGIAN PEOPLE**
Lille Borge in Borge, Fredrikstad municipality, Østfold. Rock carvings from the late Bronze Age (1100–500 BC). This photo shows a detail of three human images from one of Norway's largest and most impressive rock-carving sites. Two of these figures are probably carrying bronze lures.

**ADMINISTRATION AND INTERNAL AFFAIRS**
Borgen in Skjeberg, Sarpsborg municipality, Østfold. Rock carving from the late Bronze Age (1100–500 BC). Circular image consisting of concentric rings. Meaning unknown.

**FOREIGN POLICY**
Begby in Borge, Fredrikstad municipality, Østfold. Rock carving from the late Bronze Age (1100–500 BC). Human figures standing on a ship, the stem and stern of which bear decorative elements, probably horses' heads.

**NATURE, RESOURCES AND ENVIRONMENTAL PROTECTION**
Solberg in Skjeberg, Sarpsborg municipality, Østfold. Rock carving from the late Bronze Age (1100–500 BC). It depicts a tree or large plant, a very rare image almost without parallel in Scandinavia.

**FAITH AND PHILOSOPHIES**
Løberghaugen in Gjerpen, Skien municipality, Telemark. Rock carving from the late Bronze Age (1100–500 BC) depicting two soles of the foot with lace bound under the sole and a circular figure. The meaning of the sole symbol is not known.

**ARTS AND CULTURE**
Evjestien at Rolvsøy, Fredrikstad municipality, Østfold. Rock carving from the late Bronze Age (1100–500 BC). The figure is called a triskelion, from Greek, meaning three-legged or –lined. The symbol is occasionally found on objects and as a carving symbol. Its meaning is unknown.

**TRANSPORT AND COMMUNICATIONS**
Begby in Borge, Fredrikstad municipality, Østfold. Rock carving from the late Bronze Age (1100–500 BC). A two-wheeled cart, not drawn in perspective but 'laid out' on the rock. The two-wheeled chariot was a valuable asset in war and an important symbol for chieftains.

**EDUCATION AND RESEARCH**
Fossum in Gjerpen, Skien municipality, Telemark. Rock carving from the late Bronze Age (1100–500 BC). The figure is called a 'wheel cross'. It may depict either a round shield or a cart wheel, both of which may have been important symbols of power.

**ECONOMY AND BUSINESS**
Skjellin in Borge, Fredrikstad municipality, Østfold. Rock carving from the late Bronze Age (1100–500 BC). Two stalwart warriors, both with swords, horned helmets and possibly leg protection. One of the men with a phallus.

**SPORT**
Skjellin in Borge, Fredrikstad municipality, Østfold. Rock carving from the late Bronze Age (1100-500 BC). Several hundred carved figures are found here. This image shows a so-called vaulter. Similar cast bronze figures also exist from this period.

**FOOD AND BEVERAGES**
Skogerveien in Drammen municipality, Buskerud. Rock carving from the Neolithic Age. The image was most probably carved between 6400 and 4500 BC. It depicts a halibut.

**A STATISTICAL PORTRAIT**
Onsøy rectory, Fredrikstad municipality, Østfold. Rock carving, probably from the late Bronze Age (1100–500 BC). Cup marks are round, shallow depressions carved in the rock. It is not unusual to find many cup marks at the same place. Their meaning is unknown.

# BIBLIOGRAPHY


**200 YEARS OF NORWEGIAN POETRY**

**Andersen, Astrid Hjertenæs** (1915–85): 'The Horses Stand in the Rain', in *De unge søylene*, Aschehoug, Oslo 1948

**Bjørneboe, Jens** (1920–76): 'Iscariot', in *Dikt*, Gyldendal, Oslo 1951

**Bjørnson, Bjørnstjerne** (1832–1910): 'Song for Norway', in *Samlede Digte I*, Gyldendal, Oslo 1926.
Bjørnson won the Nobel Prize for Literature in 1903. 'Song for Norway' is the Norwegian national anthem, published for the first time in 1859 and set to music by Rikard Nordraak (1842–66).

**Boine, Mari** (b. 1956): 'Boadan nuppi beadle' from *Eight Seasons*, *Gávcci Jahkejuogo*, Universal, 2002. Winner of the Nordic Council Music Prize, 2002.

**Boyson, Emil** (1897–1979): 'Rest by Running Water', in *Sjelen og udyret*, Gyldendal, Oslo 1946

**Brekke, Paal** (1923–93): 'As in a Cinema', in *Det skjeve smil i rosa*, Aschehoug, Oslo 1965

**Bull, Olaf** (1883–1933): 'Metope', in *Samlede Digte*, Gyldendal, Oslo 1959

**Christensen, Lars Saabye** (b. 1953): 'Stamps V', in *Stempler*, Cappelen, Oslo 1989.
Saabye Christensen won the Tarjei Vesaas Prize for the Best Debut in 1976 and the Nordic Council Literature Prize in 2002.

**Dahl, Henning Kramer** (b. 1962): 'Hoarfrost', in *Barfrost*, Solum, Oslo 1983

**Eidslott, Arnold** (b. 1926): 'Hymn', in *Veien til Astopovo*, Gyldendal, Oslo 1976

**Ellingsen, Svein** (b. 1929): 'The Darkness around us is the Dark before Dawn', in *Det skjulte nærvær*, Aschehoug, Oslo 1978

**Falkeid, Kolbein** (b. 1933): 'There is a Locked Room', in *En annen sol*, Cappelen, Oslo 1989

**Gill, Claes** (1910–73): 'Maria', in *Fragment av et magisk liv*, Cappelen, Oslo 1939

**Grøndahl, Cathrine** (b. 1969): 'The Sundial's Philosophy', *Det har ingenting med kjærlighet å gjøre*, Gyldendal, Oslo 1998.
Grøndahl won the Tarjei Vesaas Prize for the Best Debut in 1994.

**Hagerup, Inger** (1905–85): 'A little Verse' in *Videre*, Aschehoug, Oslo 1945

**Hamsun, Knut** (1859–1952): 'The Island', in *Det vilde Kor*, Gyldendal, Copenhagen 1904.
Hamsun won the Nobel Prize for Literature, 1920.

**Hauge, Olav H.** (1908–94): 'Kuppern skating in Squaw Valley', in *På ørnetuva*, Noregs Boklag, Oslo 1961

**Hofmo, Gunvor** (1921–95): 'From Another World', in *Fra en annen virkelighet*, Gyldendal, Oslo 1946

**Ibsen, Henrik** (1828–1906): 'The Miner', in *Digte*, 1871. *Samlede verker*, Gyldendal, Oslo 1937

**Jacobsen, Rolf** (1907–94): 'The Silence Afterwards', in *Stillheten efterpå*, Gyldendal, Oslo 1965

**Johannesen, Georg** (b. 1931): 'Jewish Partisans' Song', in *Nye dikt*, Gyldendal, Oslo 1966

**Jonsson, Tor** (1916–51): 'Then rise up in me, loneliness', in *Ei dagbok for mitt hjarte*, Noregs Boklag, Oslo 1951

**Lunden, Eldrid** (b. 1940): 'The Museo Academico in Florence', in *Til stades*, Aschehoug, Oslo 2000

**Mehren, Stein** (b. 1935): 'I hold your head', in *Mot en verden av lys*, Aschehoug, Oslo 1963

**Narvesen, Kurt** (b. 1948): 'Frost', in *Steppene*, Gyldendal, Oslo 1975

**Nilsen, Rudolf** (1901–29): 'The Call of the Revolution', in *På gjensyn*, Gyldendal, Oslo 1926

**Nygard, Olav** (1884–1924): 'To My Son', in *Dikt*, Gyldendal, Oslo 1934

**Næss, Kate** (1938–87): 'Terreo', in *Mørkerommet*, Aschehoug, Oslo 1964

**Obstfelder, Sigbjørn** (1866–1900): 'I See', in *Digte*, John Grieg, Bergen 1893

**Opstad, Steinar** (b. 1971): 'Prohibited Area' in *Synsverk*, Gyldendal, Oslo 2002.
Opstad won the Tarjei Vesaas Prize for the Best Debut in 1996.

**Paus, Ole** (b. 1947): 'Kajsa's song', in *Zarepta*, Zarepta, Oslo 1974

**Prøysen, Alf** (1914–70): 'On the Rocky Slope on the Hillside', in *Drengstu'viser*, Tiden, Oslo 1948

**Stenberg, Lars Lillo-** (b. 1962): 'Is There A Woman', in *Så lenge det er tvil er det håp*, Tiden, Oslo 2001. First published on the LP *Suser avgårde*, Sonet, 1986.

**Stueland, Espen** (b. 1970): 'At Random', in *Å si om seg selv*, Oktober forlag, Oslo 2003

**Torvund, Helge** (b. 1951): 'If We're Making a Woodpile', in *Lyssmeden*, Gyldendal, Oslo 1983

**Ulven, Tor** (1953–95): '(Test)', in *Samlede dikt*, Gyldendal, Oslo 2000

**Vesaas, Halldis Moren** (1907–95): 'Words Over A Gate', in *I ein annan skog*, Aschehoug, Oslo 1955

**Vinje, Aasmund O.** (1818–70): 'Back to Antiquity', 'Dølen', 1868, in *Skrifter i samling* V, Cappelen, Kristiania 1921.

**Vold, Jan Erik** (b. 1939): 'December Light (silent film on Wergeland's Way)', in *Mor Godhjertas glade versjon. Ja*, Gyldendal, Oslo 1968.
Vold won the Tarjei Vesaas Prize for the Best Debut in 1965

**Vaa, Aslaug** (1889–1965): 'Waiting and Watching', in *Villarkonn*, Gyldendal, Oslo 1936

**Wergeland, Henrik** (1808–45): 'To the Spring', *Morgenbladet*, Oslo, 24 May 1845.

**Yttri, Nils** (1947–80): 'The Peace of the Private Life is an Open Wound', in *Når min fantasi berører dine drømmer*, Gyldendal, Oslo 1981

**Øverland, Arnulf** (1889–1968): 'Here, Wandering', in *På Nebo bjerg*, Aschehoug, Oslo 1962

**Aasen, Ivar** (1813–96): 'The Norseman', in *Symra*, 1863

## NORWEGIAN HISTORY UNTIL 1814

*Aschehougs Norgeshistorie*, vol. 1, Aschehoug, Oslo 1994

*Norges historie*, Cappelen, Oslo 1976–79
*Norges kulturhistorie*, Aschehoug, Oslo 1984

**Andersen, Per Sveaas:** *Vikings of the West*, Universitetsforlaget, Oslo 1971

**Brønsted, Johannes:** *Vikingene*, Gyldendal, Oslo 1961

**Bagge, Sverre & Mykland, Knut:** *Norge i dansketida*, Cappelen, Oslo 1987

**Danielsen, Rolf et al.:** *Grunntrekk i norsk historie*, Universitetsforlaget, Oslo 1991

**Fladby, Rolf:** *Samfunn i vekst – under fremmed styre 1536–1660*, Universitetsforlaget, Oslo 1986

**Hagen, Anders:** *Norges oldtid*, Cappelen, Oslo 1983

**Helle, Knut:** *Norge blir en stat 1130–1319*, Universitetsforlaget, Oslo 1974

**Henriksen, Rian, Hjort & Grev:** *Norges konger*, Grøndahl, Oslo 1987

**Holtan, Inger:** *Ekteskap, frillelivnad og hor i norsk høgmellomalder*, Samlaget, Oslo 2003

**Luthen, Eyvind:** *I pilegrimenes fotspor til Nidaros*, Cappelen, Oslo 1992

**Seip, Jens Arup:** *Utsikt over Norges historie*, Gyldendal Oslo 1981

**Steinsland, Gro & Sørensen, Preben Meulengnacht:** *Menneske og makter i vikingenes verden*, Universitetsforlaget, Oslo 1994

## THE NORWEGIAN PEOPLE

**Alhaug, Gulbrand:** 'Endringar i fornamnsmønstret i Norge på 1900-talet (1900–1975)', in *Namn gjennom 2000 år – namn i år 2000*, the 9th National Onomastics Conference

**Andersen, Benny:** 'Jeg ved lidt om Norge', in Erling Nielsen (ed.): *Buket til Norge*, Gyldendal Norsk Forlag, Oslo 1975

**Berggren, Brit:** *Da kulturen kom til Norge*, Aschehoug, Oslo 1989

**Bjørklund, Ivar:** *Sapmi – en nasjon blir til*, catalogue for an eponymous exhibition, TMU, University of Tromsø, Tromsø 2002

**Blehr, Barbro:** *En norsk besvärjelse. 17. maj-firande vid 1900-talets slut*, Nya Doxa, Falun 2000

**Bomann-Larsen, Tor:** *Den evige sne*, Cappelen, Oslo 1993

**Drivenes, Einar-Arne, Hauan, Marit Anne & Wold, Helge A.** (eds): *Nordnorsk kulturhistorie*, vols I & II, Gyldendal, Oslo 1994

**Elstad, Åsa:** 'Å kle seg nordnorsk', trial lecture for doctorate/history 2002, unpublished manuscript

**Eriksen, Anne:** *Historie, minne og myte*, Pax, Oslo 1999

**Eriksen, Thomas Hylland:** *Veien til et mer eksotisk Norge*, Ad Notam, Oslo 1991

**Eriksen, Thomas Hylland:** 'The nation as a human being – a metaphor in a mid-life crisis?', in Eriksen, Trond Berg, Hompland, Andreas & Sørensen, Øystein: *Et lite land i verden*, vol VI in *Norsk idéhistorie*, Aschehoug, Oslo 2003

**Frykman, Jonas and Löfgren, Orvar:** *Svenska vanor och uvanor*, Natur och Kultur, Stockholm 1991

**Gaunt, David and Löfgren, Orvar:** *Myter om svensken*, Liber, Stockholm 1985

**Goksøyr, Matti:** 'Idretten og det norske: aktivitet som identitet', in Sørensen, Øystein (ed.): *Jakten på det norske*, Ad Notam Gyldendal, Oslo 1998

**Gullestad, Marianne:** *Kitchen-table society: a case study of the family life and friendships of young working-class mothers in urban Norway*, Universitetsforlaget, Oslo 1984

**Hauan, Marit Anne:** 'Helten min heter Henry Rudi', in *Tradisjon* no. 24, 1994

**Hauan, Marit Anne:** 'Folkloristikken og den mangfoldige kulturelle kommunikasjonen', in *Tradisjon* no. 28, 1998

**Helland, Amund:** *Norges land og folk. Beskrivelse over Finnmarkens amt II*, Aschehoug, Kristiania 1906

**Hertzberg Johnsen, Birgit:** 'Tradisjon og samfunn – et kvinneperspektiv', in Hodne, Bjarne et al. (ed): *Muntlige kilder. Om bruk av intervjuer i etnologi, folkeminnevitenskap og historie*, Universitetsforlaget, Oslo 1981

**Hodne, Ørnulf 1998:** 'Sagn og eventyr som nasjonalkultur', in Sørensen, Øystein (ed.): *Jakten på det norske*, Ad Notam Gyldendal, Oslo 1998

**Hoel, Sigurd:** 'Eventyrene våre' (1949), in Lie, Nils (ed.): *Essays i utvalg*, Gyldendal, Oslo 1962

**Hompland, Andreas:** 'Vi viser verden vinterveien', in Eriksen, Trond Berg, Hompland, Andreas & Sørensen, Øystein: *Et lite land i verden*, vol VI of *Norsk idéhistorie*, Aschehoug, Oslo 2003

**Hompland, Andreas:** 'Annerledeslandet', in Eriksen, Trond Berg, Hompland, Andreas & Sørensen, Øystein: *Et lite land i verden*, vol VI in *Norsk idéhistorie*, Aschehoug, Oslo 2003

**Ibsen, Henrik:** *Digte*, 1871 in *Samlede verker*, Gyldendal, Oslo 1937

**Knudsen, Knud:** *Unorsk og norsk eller Fremmords Avløsning*, Cammermeyer, Kristiania 1881

**Langeland, Nils Rune:** 'Feministisk wonderboy', in *Aftenposten*, Oslo, 7 January 2004

**Mathisen, Stein R.:** 'Real Barbarians Eat Whales. Norwegian Identity and the Whale Issue', in Anttonen, Pertti J. (ed.): *Making Europe in Nordic Contexts*, NIF Publications, Turku 1996

**Nielsen, Reidar:** *Folk uten fortid*, Gyldendal, Oslo 1986

**Nordland, Odd:** 'Mellom tater og andre farande folk', in *Norsk kulturhistorie*, vol. 4, Aschehoug, Oslo 1980

**Olwig, K.F. & Hastrup, Kirsten (eds):** *Siting culture. The shifting anthropological object*, Routledge, London and New York 1997

**Opsahl, Erik:** 'Del I, 900–1814', in Kjeldstadli, Knut (ed.): *Norsk innvandringshistorie*, Pax, Oslo 2003

**Stenersen, Øivind & Libæk, Ivar:** *Norges historie*, Dinamo Forlag, Bærum 2003

**Sørensen, Øystein (ed.):** *Jakten på det norske*, Ad Notam Gyldendal, Oslo 1998

**Sørensen, Øystein:** 'Kampen om Norges sjel', in vol. III, *Norsk idéhistorie*, Aschehoug, Oslo 2001

**Thomassen, Ivar:** *Attmed havet*, privately released CD, Alta 2003

**Thuen, Trond:** *Quest for Equity. Norway and the Saami Challenge*, St Johns, Newfoundland 1995

**Aasen, Ivar:** *Ordbog over det norske Folkesprog*, Werner, Carl C., Kristiania 1850

## ADMINISTRATION AND INTERNAL AFFAIRS

**Bergsgård, Arne:** *Ole Gabriel Ueland og bondepolitikken* vol. I, Aschehoug, Oslo 1932

**Danielsen, Rolf, Hambro, C.J., Kaartvedt, Alf & Greve, Tim (eds.):** *Det norske storting gjennom 150 år*, vols I, II, Norges Storting 1964

**Fuglum, Per:** *Norge i støpeskjeen 1884–1920*, vol. 12 in Mykland, Knut (ed.) *Norges historie*, Cappelen, Oslo 1976–80

**Kjeldstadli, Knut (ed.):** *Norsk innvandringshistorie*, vol. III, Pax, Oslo 2003

**Smith, Carsten:** *Loven og livet: foredrag, artikler, taler*, Universitetsforlaget, Oslo 1996

**Smith, Carsten:** Press release from the Chief Justice, 2 May 2000

**Tschudi-Madsen, Stephan (ed.):** *Norges Høyesterett*, Aschehoug, Oslo 1998

## FOREIGN POLICY

The primary reference work on Norwegian foreign policy is the six-volume series *Norsk Utenrikspolitikk* edited by Professor Olav Riste and published by Universitetsforlaget, Oslo. Historical data and the definition of periods in this chapter draw on this series, which consists of:


**Berg, Roald:** *Norge på egen hånd 1905–1920*, Universitetsforlaget, Oslo 1995

**Bjørgo, Narve, Rian, Øystein & Kaartvedt, Alf:** *Selvstendighet og Union. Fra middelalderen til 1905*, Universitetsforlaget, Oslo 1995

**Eriksen, Knut Einar & Pharo, Helge Øystein:** *Kald Krig og Internasjonalisering 1945–1965*, Universitetsforlaget, Oslo 1997

**Fure, Odd-Bjørn:** *Mellomkrigstid 1920–1940*, Universitetsforlaget, Oslo 1996

**Riste, Olav:** *Norway's Foreign Relations*, Universitetsforlaget, Oslo 2001

**Sverdrup, Jacob:** *Inn i Storpolitikken 1940–1949*, Universitetsforlaget, Oslo 1996

**Tamnes, Rolf:** *Oljealder 1965–1995*, Universitetsforlaget, Oslo 1997


The leading political science 'standard text' on Norwegian foreign policy is:


**Knutsen, Sørbø & Gjerdåker (eds):** *Norsk Utenrikspolitikk*, Cappelen, Oslo 1997


The chapter otherwise draws on the following sources:


**Annan, Kofi:** Speech to the World Economic Forum in Davos, 24 January 2004

**Claes, Dag Harald:** 'EØS-avtalen – mellom diplomati og demokrati' in *Internasjonal Politikk*, vol. 61, no. 3, 2003

**Claes, Dag Harald & Tranøy, Bent Sofus (eds):** *Utenfor, annerledes og suveren? Norge under EØS-avtalen*, Fagbokforlaget, Bergen 1999

**Cooper, Robert:** *The Breaking of Nations – order and chaos in the twenty-first century*, Atlantic Monthly Press, New York 2003

**Corbin, Jane:** *Gaza first: The secret Norway channel to peace between Israel and the PLO*, Bloomsbury, London 1994

**Dale, Geir:** *Grenser for alt. Kritiske perspektiver på norsk utenrikspolitikk*, Spartacus, Oslo 2000

**Egeland, Jan:** *Impotent superpower, potent small state: Potentials and limitations of human rights objectives in the foreign policies of the United States and Norway*, Universitetsforlaget, Oslo 1988

**Eide, Espen Barth:** 'Adjustment Strategy of a Non-Member: Norwegian Foreign and Security Policy in the Shadow of the European Union', in *Cooperation and Conflict*, vol. 31, no. 1, 1996

**Eide, Espen Barth:** 'Norsk Multilateralt Militærsamarbeid i en ny epoke', in Neumann, Iver B. & Ulriksen, Ståle (eds) *Sikkerhetspolitikk*, TANO, Oslo 1996

**Eide, Espen Barth et al.:** *EF, EFTA, Norge – tilpasning eller mistilpasning?*, NUPI-rapport no. 140, Oslo 1990

**Eide, Espen Barth & Støre, Jonas Gahr:** 'Stakkars EØS-avtalen' in *Aftenposten*, Oslo, 14 February 2002

**Eide, Espen Barth, Claes, Dag Harald, Ulrichsen, Hanne & Toje, Asle:** *Norge og EU: Medlemskap, EØS eller 'sveitsisk løsning'*, NUPI, Oslo 2003

**Frydenlund, Knut:** *Lille land – hva nå?*, Universitetsforlaget, Oslo 1982

**Frydenlund, Knut:** *En bedre organisert verden: foredrag, innlegg og taler*, Tiden, Oslo 1987

**Godal, Bjørn Tore:** *Utsikter. Store lille Norge i en ny verden*, Aschehoug, Oslo 2003

**Holst, Johan Jørgen:** *Norsk sikkerhetspolitikk i strategisk perspektiv*, NUPI, Oslo 1967

**Holst, Johan Jørgen & Heradstveit, Daniel (eds):** *Norsk Utenrikspolitikk*, TANO, Oslo 1985

**Jagland, Thorbjørn:** *Vår sårbare verden*, Aschehoug, Oslo 2002

**Jagland, Thorbjørn:** *Ti teser om EU og Norge*, Aschehoug, Oslo 2003

**Leonard, Mark:** *Public diplomacy*, Foreign Policy Centre, London 2002

**Lodgaard, Sverre:** 'Helhetsperspektiver på norsk utenrikspolitikk', in *Internasjonal Politikk*, vol. 60, no. 1

**Lundestad, Geir:** *Øst, Vest, Nord, Sør: hovedlinjer i internasjonal politikk 1945–1990*, Universitetsforlaget, Oslo 1991

**Lundestad, Geir:** *Empire by Integration. The United States and European Integration 1945–1997*, Oxford University Press, Oxford 1998

**Matlary, Janne Haaland:** *Verdidiplomati – kilde til makt? En strategisk analyse av norsk utenrikspolitikk*, Unipub forlag, Oslo 2002

**Neumann, Iver B:** *Norge – en kritikk. Begrepsmakt i Europa-debatten*, Pax, Oslo 2001

**Neumann, Iver B. (ed.):** *Ny giv for nordisk samarbeid*, Tano, Oslo 1995

**Neumann, Iver B. & Ulriksen, Ståle (eds):** *Sikkerhetspolitikk*, Tano, Oslo 1996

**Neumann, Iver B. (ed.):** *Global politikk: krig, diplomati, handel og nyhetsformidling i praksis*, Cappelen Akademisk forlag, Oslo 2002

**Neumann, Iver B.:** *Hva så lille land – essays om Norges alminnelighet*, Spartacus, Oslo 2003

**Rieker, Pernille:** *Europeanization of Nordic Security. The EU and the Changing Security Identities of the Nordic States* (doctoral thesis), University of Oslo, Institutt for statsvitenskap, Oslo 2003

**Skogrand, Kjetil:** *Fryktens likevekt: atombomben, Norge og verden 1945–1970*, Tiden, Oslo 2001

Stortingsmelding no. 12 (2000–2001): *Om Norge og Europa ved inngangen til et nytt århundre*

**Tamnes, Rolf & Eriksen, Knut Einar:** 'Norge og NATO under den kalde krigen', in *NATO 50 år. Norsk sikkerhetspolitikk med NATO gjennom 50 år*. See www.atlanterhavskomiteen.no

'The National Security Strategy of America 2002'. See www.whitehouse.gov

**Tvedt, Terje:** *Utviklingshjelp, utenrikspolitikk og makt: den norske modellen*, Gyldendal Akademisk, Oslo 2003

**Ulriksen, Ståle:** *Den norske forsvarstradisjonen – militærmakt eller folkeforsvar?*, Pax, Oslo 2002

Utenriksdepartementet (2001): *Norsk USA-strategi*. See http://odin.dep.no/ud/norsk/publ/handlingsplaner/032001-120015/index-dok000-b-n-a.html

**Waage, Hilde Henriksen:** *Peacemaking is a risky business: Norway's role in the peace process in the Middle East, 1993–96*. PRIO Report 1/2004, PRIO, Oslo 2004


For further sources, see 'Bibliografi over norsk utenrikspolitikk' in www.nupi.no

## NATURE, RESOURCES AND ENVIRONMENTAL PROTECTION


***Aftenposten:*** Articles from 1984–2004 (www.aftenposten.no)

**Bellona:** Reports 'Sources to radioactive contamination in Russian counties of Murmansk and Arkhangelsk' (1994) and 'The Russian Northern Fleet' (1996), and later updates on Bellona's website (www.bellona.no)

**Berntsen, Bredo & Hågvar, Sigmund (eds):** *Norsk naturarv – Våre naturverdier i internasjonalt lys*, Andresen & Butenschøn, Oslo 2001

**Brundtland, Gro Harlem:** *Mitt liv 1939–1986*, Gyldendal, Oslo 1997

**Brundtland, Gro Harlem:** *Dramatiske år 1986–1996*, Gyldendal, Oslo 1998

***Dagbladet:*** Articles/press releases 1994–2004 (www.dagbladet.no)

**Directorate for Nature Management:** Norwegian Red List (www.dirnat.no)

**Helberg, Claus:** *De første vandrere*, The Norwegian Mountain Touring Association, 1994

**Mathismoen, Ole:** *Verdens Miljøstatus*, Scanbok, Oslo 1992

**Ministry of the Environment:** State of the Environment Norway, 2003 and 2004 (www.miljostatus.no)

**Ministry of the Environment and Ministry of Agriculture:** Press releases 2002–04 (www.odin.dep.no)

**Nature and Youth:** Articles and press releases (www.nu.no)

**NINA (Norwegian Institute for Nature Research) and NIKU (Norwegian Institute for Cultural Heritage Research):** Facts sheets 2000–03 (www.nina.no)

**NINA (Norwegian Institute for Nature Research):** *Natur i endring, Terrestrisk naturovervåking 1990–2002*. Temahefte no. 24, 2003 (www.nina.no)

**Norges Skogeierforbund:** Articles and press releases (www.skogeierforbundet.no)

**Norsk Telegrambyrå:** Articles/press releases 1994–2004 (www.ntb.no)

**Norwegian Mountain Touring Association:** Press releases and background information (www.turistforeningen.no)

**Norwegian Pollution Control Authority:** Various press releases and articles (www.sft.no)

**Norwegian Society for the Conservation of Nature:** Articles and press releases (www.naturvernforbundet.no)

**Nøttestad, Øyvind:** *SFTs historiebok*. Norwegian Pollution Control Authority 2002 (www.sft.no/om_oss/historie/)

**Statistisk sentralbyrå:** Natural resources and the environment 2003 (www.ssb.no)

**Stortingsmelding no. 25 (2002–2003):** *Regjeringens miljøvernpolitikk og rikets miljøtilstand* (www.odin.dep.no)

**Tormodsgard, Sigbjørn:** *Årboken Gamle Hallingdal*, Hallingdølen AS, 2002/2003

**WWF Norway:** *Norges korallrev*, 2003 (www.wwf.no)

**Aanderaa, Rune,** biologist and general manager of Samarbeidsrådet for biologisk mangfold (SABIMA): Written and oral material (www.sabima.no)


## FAITH AND PHILOSOPHIES


**Elstad, Hallgeir and Halse, Per:** *Illustrert norsk kristendomshistorie*, Fagbokforlaget, Bergen 2002

**Gullaksen, Per-Otto:** *Stat og kirke i Norge. Kirkerett mellom teologi og politikk*, Verbum, Oslo 2000

**Henriksen, Jan-Olav and Krogseth, Otto (eds):** *Pluralisme og identitet. Kulturanalytiske perspektiver på nordiske nasjonalkirker i møte med religiøs og moralsk pluralisme*, Gyldendal, Oslo 2001

**Schjørring, Jens Holger (ed.):** *Nordiske folkekirker i opbrud*, Aarhus Universitetsforlag, Århus 2001

**Stålsett, Gunnar:** *Hva er da et menneske?*, Gyldendal, Oslo 2002


## ARTS AND CULTURE


**Ambjørnsen, Ingvar:** *Utsikt til paradiset*, Cappelen, Oslo 1999

**Beyer, Anders:** 'Maris magiske musikk', from the journal *Ballade*, June 2003

**Boine, Mari:** *Gávcci Jahkejuogu/Eight Seasons*, Universal Music, 2001

**Brundtland, Cecilie Malm:** *Nicolaus Widerberg*, Labyrinth Press, Oslo 2000

**Buresund, Inger & Gran, Anne-Britt (eds):** *Frie grupper og Black Box teater 1970–1995*, Ad Notam Gyldendal, Oslo 1996

**Bø, Ola E.:** 'Innafor og utafor' in Scenekunstmeldingen NOU 2002: 8, *Etter alle kunstens regler*, Kirke- og Kulturdepartementet, 2002

**Cowie, Peter:** *Straight From the Heart: Modern Norwegian Cinema 1971-99*, Kom Forlag, Kristiansund 1999

**Ebbestad Hansen, Jan-Erik:** *Fenomenet Nerdrum*, Gyldendal, Oslo 1996

**Eide, Harriet:** 'Sverre Fehn, arkitekturens dikter', in *Dagbladet*, Oslo 2003

**Eriksen, Trond Berg, Hompland, Andreas & Tjønneland, Eivind:** 'Et lite land i verden' in *Norsk idéhistorie*, vol. VI, Aschehoug, Oslo 2003

**Ermacora, Beate:** 'Bjarne Melgaard, Interface to God', catalogue, Kunsthalle zu Kiel, 2002

**Fosse, Jon:** *Nokon kjem til å komme*, Samlaget, Oslo 1996

**Haga, Sverre Gunnar:** 'Et åndsforlatt næringsliv', *Dagbladet*, Oslo 2003

**Hamer, Bent:** *Salmer fra kjøkkenet*, Bul-Bul film/SF Norway, 2003

**Huijts, Stijn:** 'Bjarne Melgaard, Back Again from Down Under', catalogue, Stedelijk museum, Amsterdam 1997

**Haavardsholm, Espen & Øverland, Janneken:** *Litteraturhistorie for den videregående skolen*, Gyldendal, Oslo 1993

**Johnsen, Kai:** 'Nokon kjem til å komme, noen punktvise nedslag i Jon Fosses teaterspråk' in *Vinduet* 2/2002, Gyldendal, Oslo 2002

**Kittang, Atle:** 'Makelaus roman', review of Dag Solstad's *Genanse og verdighet* in *Bergens Tidende*, 30 November 1994

*Kunst* no. 4, 2003

**Lien, Jens:** *Jonny Vang*, Universal 2003

**Løchen, Kalle:** 'Finnmarks filmpoet' in *Dagbladet*, Oslo 2004

**Mangset, Per:** *Norsk Kunstnerpolitikk – organisasjonsmakt og statlig styring*, Norges Forskningsråd, Oslo 1995

**Melgaard, Bjarne:** *Skam*, exhibition, Bergen kunsthall 2003

**Osland, Lidvin M. & Mangset, Per:** *Norwegian Cultural Policy, Characteristics and Trends*, Norsk kulturråd, Oslo 1995

**Paasche, Marit:** *Video vides videmus*, Riksutstillinger 2003

**Régy, Claude:** 'Jon Fosse' in *Norsk Shakespeare- og teatertidsskrift* 2, 2003

**Ruth, Arne:** *Den nordiska femklövern – kulturpolitisk odling i efterkrigstidens välfärdssamhälle*, Nordiska kulturfonden 2003

**Rød, Johannes:** *Kunstneren i atelieret*, Gyldendal fakta, Oslo 1998

**Sandberg, Lotte:** 'Mari Slaattelids visuelle spill: Blikk for sammenstillinger', in *Aftenposten*, Oslo 2003

**Solstad, Dag:** *Genanse og verdighet*, Oktober forlag, Oslo 1994

**Stang, Ragna:** *Edvard Munch, mennesket og kunstneren*, Aschehoug, Oslo 1989

**Stortingsmelding** no. 48 (2002–2003): *Kulturpolitikk fram mot 2014*

**Sørheim, Sarah:** 'Kunst til folket' in *Tidsskriftet Kultur* 2004

**Tøjner, Poul Erik:** *Verdenskunst*, Geelmuyden.Kiese forlag, Oslo 1997


## TRANSPORT AND COMMUNICATIONS


**Aspenberg, Nils Carl:** *Glemte spor. Boken om sidebanenes tragiske liv*, Baneforlaget, Oslo 1994

**Bastiansen, Henrik G. & Dahl, Hans Fredrik:** *Norsk mediehistorie*, Universitetsforlaget, Oslo 2003

**Brekke, Nils Georg:** *Kulturhistorisk vegbok, Hordaland*, Nord 4/Vestkyst, Bergen 1993

**Broch, Just:** *Av Norges statsbaners historie II: Gjennom 70-årenes lys inn i 80-årenes mørke*, Cappelen, Oslo 1936

**Børrehaug Hansen, Trond, Gundersen, Håkon & Sando, Svein:** *Jernbanen i Norge*, Pax, Oslo 1980

**Baalsrud, A. (ed.):** *Norske Rutebileieres Forbund 1929–1954*, NRF, Oslo 1954

**Christensen, Arne Lie:** *Den norske byggeskikken*, Pax, Oslo 1995

**Christensen, Arne Lie:** *Det norske landskapet*, Pax, Oslo 2002

**Enzensberger, Hans Magnus:** *Norsk utakt*, Universitetsforlaget, Oslo 1984

**Frøholm, Gabriel:** *Med veg skal landet byggjast. Med bru og tunnel skal vegen kortast og tryggjast*, Frøholm-forlaget, Oslo 1970

**Furre, Berge:** *Norsk historie 1914–2000*, Det Norske Samlaget, Oslo 1999

**Hasle, Geir:** *Veg i Norge – alle tiders utfordring*, Vegdirektoratets informasjonskontor, Oslo 1993

**Huitfeldt, Carl:** *Norge i andres øyne. Utdrag av utenlandske reisebeskrivelser gjennom 2000 år*, C. Huitfeldt Forlag, Oslo 1970

**Jacobsen, Rolf:** 'Anderledeslandet', in *Alle mine dikt*, Gyldendal, Oslo 1990

**Johannessen, Finn Erhard & Thue, Lars:** *Alltid underveis. Postverkets historie gjennom 350 år*, vols I & II, Elanders forlag/Posten, Oslo 1997

**Lange, Even:** 'Samling om felles mål. 1935–1970', *Norges historie*, vol. 11, Aschehoug, Oslo 1988

**Nerbøvik, Jostein:** *Norsk historie 1860–1914*, Det Norske Samlaget, Oslo 1999

**Norges Offentlige Utredninger:** 'Ytringsfrihed bør finde Sted', NOU 1999: 27

**Ottosen, Rune, Røssland, Lars Arve & Østbye, Helge:** *Norsk pressehistorie*, Det Norske Samlaget, Oslo 2002

**Pryser, Tore:** *Norsk historie 1814–1860*, Det Norske Samlaget, Oslo 1999

**Rødland, Kjartan:** *Bergensbanen. Livsnerven over fjellet*, Alma Mater, Bergen 1999

**Seip, Jens Arup:** *Tanke og handling i norsk historie*, Gyldendal, Oslo 1968

**Slagstad, Rune:** *De nasjonale strateger*, Pax, Oslo 1998

**Smith, Richard Carter:** *Reise i Norge 1838*, Universitetsforlaget, Oslo 1976

EDUCATION AND RESEARCH

**Bjørneboe, Jens:** *Jonas*, Aschehoug, Oslo 1955

**Bjornson, Bjørnstjerne:** *En glad gutt*, 1860, from Bjørnstjerne Bjørnson: *Samlede verker*, 11th ed., Gyldendal, Oslo 1995

**Christensen, Lars Saabye:** *Herman*, Cappelen, Oslo 1988

**Clemet, Kristin:** 'The Norwegian school can get better', feature in *Aftenposten*, Oslo, 19 January 2004

**Eriksen, Trond Berg, Hompland, Andreas & Tjønneland, Eivind:** 'Et lite land i verden 1950–2000', in *Norsk idéhistorie*, vol. VI, Aschehoug, Oslo 2003

**Falkeid, Kolbein:** *Horisontene*, Cappelen, Oslo 1975

**Friedman, Robert Marc:** 'University History in Norway', *Uppsala Newsletter*, Spring 2000

**Grankvist, Rolf:** *Utsyn over norsk skole*, Tapir, Trondheim 2000

**Hustad, Jon:** *Skolen som forsvann*, Det Norske Samlaget, Oslo 2002

**Jensen, Eivind Bråstad:** *Vegen inn i utdanningssamfunnet*, Cappelen, Oslo 1999

**Kielland, Alexander:** *Gift*, 1883, from Kielland, Alexander: *Samlede verker*, 11th ed., Gyldendal, Oslo 1995

**Kveseth, Kari:** 'Myths and facts in Norwegian research', feature in *Dagbladet, Oslo,* 31 December 2003
OECD: *Education at a Glance*. OECD Indicators 2003

**Olsen, Tore:** 'A presentation of the scientific and technological potential, and the R&D policy of Norway', a lecture given in Antwerp 26 October 1994. Manuscript

**Sand, Gunnar:** 'Fine words and forgotten promises about Norwegian research', feature in *Aftenposten,* Oslo, 18 January 2003

**Sand, Gunnar and Skretting, Kathrine:** *Fortellinger om forskning*. Tapir, Trondheim 2002

**Severud, Jon:** *Ubehaget i skolen*, Universitetsforlaget, Oslo 2003

**Sivertsen, Gunnar and Aksnes, Dag W:** 'What kind of research nation is Norway?', *Forskningspolitikk* 1/2000

**Sivertsen, Gunnar and Aksnes, Dag W.:** 'Norway as a research nation', *Forskningspolitikk* 3/2000

**Skagen, Kaare:** *Pedagogikkens elendighet. Ukorrekte artikler på randen av litteratur*, Høyskoleforlaget, Kristiansand 2002

**Skoie, Hans:** 'An overview of the Norwegian R&D system'. From Hans Skoie: *Norway – A Province of Science in a Changing World*, Norwegian Institute for Research and Educational Studies (NIFU), STS report no. 32, 1997

**Skoie, Hans:** *Norsk forskningspolitikk og forskningspolitisk rådgivning – hovedtrekk fra etterkrigstiden*. Institute for Studies in Research and Higher Education, report 9/1991

**Skoie, Hans & Såtvedt, Øyvind:** *Forskning, kultur og autonomi*, Norwegian Institute for Research and Educational Studies (NIFU) report 17/1998

**Skoie, Hans & Såtvedt, Øyvind:** 'The cultural bases for research', *Forskningspolitikk* 4/1998

**Skoie, Hans &Såtvedt, Øyvind:** 'Research and culture', *Forskningspolitikk* 1/1999

**Slagstad, Rune:** *De nasjonale strateger*, Pax, Oslo 1998

**Slipersæter, Stig, Wendt, Kaja & Sarpebakken, Bo, (2003):** *Instituttsektoren i et internasjonalt perspektiv belyst ved FOU-statistiske data*. NIFU report 30/2003

**Statistisk sentralbyrå:** *Dette er Norge. Hva tallene forteller*, Oslo 2003

**Stortingsmelding no. 35:** *Forskning for fellesskapet. Om forskning*

**Telhaug, Alfred Oftedal:** *Norsk skoleutvikling etter 1945*, Didakta, Oslo 1982

**Telhaug, Alfred Oftedal:** 'The crisis in teacher training', *Horisont* no. 3/2001

ECONOMY AND BUSINESS

**Anker Olsen, Kr.:** *Wilh. Wilhelmsen i hundre år*, Wilh. Wilhelmsen, Oslo 1962

**Brundtland, Gro Harlem:** *Mitt liv: 1938-1986*, Gyldendal, Oslo 1997

**Eyde, Sam:** *Mitt liv og mitt livsverk*, Gyldendal, Oslo 1939

**Furre, Berge:** *Vårt hundreår: norsk historie 1905-1990*, Samlaget, Oslo 1991

**Gerhardsen, Einar:** *I medgang og motgang: erindringer 1955-65*, Tiden, Oslo 1972

**Hanisch, Tore Jørgen, Søilen, Espen & Ecklund, Gunhild:** *Norsk økonomisk politikk i det 20. århundret*, Høyskoleforlaget, Kristiansand 1999

**Hodne, Fritz:** *Norges økonomiske historie 1815-1970*, Cappelen, Oslo 1981

**Hodne, Fritz & Grytten, Ola Honningdal:** *Norsk økonomi 1900-1990*, Tano, Oslo 1992

**Imset, Geir & Stavrum, Gunnar:** *Bankerott: det norske bankvesens vekst og fall*, Gyldendal, Oslo 1993

**Kjelstadli, Knut (ed.):** *Norsk innvandringshistorie 1-3*, Pax, Oslo 2003

**Kleppe, Per:** *Kleppepakke: meninger og minner fra et politisk liv*, Aschehoug, Oslo 2003

**Lange, Even:** *Samling om felles mål, Aschehougs Norgeshistorie,* vol. 11, Aschehoug, Oslo 1998

**Lerøen, Bjørn Vidar:** *Dråper av svart gull*, Statoil 2002

**Norges Rederiforbund:** Statistical/historical material

**Slagstad, Rune:** *De nasjonale strateger*, Pax, Oslo 1998

**Statistisk sentralbyrå:** Historisk statistikk 1968

**Statistisk sentralbyrå:** Norges økonomi etter krigen

**Statistisk sentralbyrå:** Various statistics and surveys

**Willoch, Kåre:** *Myter og virkelighet*, Cappelen, Oslo 2002

**Willoch, Kåre:** *Utfordringer*, Cappelen, Oslo 2004

***Aftenposten*, Oslo:** Various articles

***Dagens Næringsliv*:** Oslo: Various articles

***Dagsavisen*, Oslo:** Various articles

***Kapital*, Oslo:** Various articles

## SPORT

**Bjørnsen, Knut & Jorsett, Per:** *Store norske sportsbragder i 1000 år*, J M Stenersens Forlag, Oslo 1995

**Bø, Olav:** *På ski gjennom historia*, Det norske Samlaget, Oslo 1992

**Foreningen til Ski-Idrettens Fremme:** Holmenkollen Skimuseet, 1996

**Larsen, Petter:** *Med AIF-stjerna på brystet,* Tiden, Oslo 1979

**The Norwegian Olympic Committee and Confederation of Sports and the Ministry of Culture and Church Affairs,** annual 'Status Reports'

**Olstad, Finn & Tønnesen, Stein:** *Norsk idretts historie*, vol. 1, 1861–1939 and vol. 2, 1939–1986, Aschehoug, Oslo 1987

**Vaage, Jakob:** *Skiens Verden*, Hjemmets Forlag, Oslo 1979

## FOOD AND BEVERAGES

### FOOD

**Gamerith, Anni:** *Feuerstättenbedingte Kochtechniken und Speisen*, Ethnologia Scandinavica, 1971

**Grøn, Fredrik:** *Om kostholdet i Norge fra omkring 1500-tallet og op til vår tid*, Dybwad, Oslo 1926

**Höegh, Ove Arboe:** *Planter og tradisjon*, 3rd ed., Universitetsforlaget, Oslo 1976

**Norske Kvinners Sanitetsforening:** *Vekst og Virke i 50 år 1896-1946*, Oslo 1946

**Oleaus, Magnus:** *Historien om de Nordiska Folken* (1555), Swedish translation, 2nd ed., part 3, 1951-76

**Riddervold, Astri & Ropeid, Andreas:** *Popular Diet and Development of Science 19th Century. The Porridge Feud*, Ethnologia Scandinavica, 1984

**Riddervold, Astri:** *Lutefisk, Rakefisk and Herring in Norwegian Tradition*, Novus Press, Oslo

**Riddervold, Astri:** *Konservering av mat*, Teknologisk forlag, Oslo 1993

**Riddervold, Astri:** *Silda og potetens rolle i norsk kultur*, Årbok for Nordmøre Museum, Kristiansund 1995

**Riddervold, Astri:** *Drikkeskikk, Nordmenns drikkevaner gjennom 1000 år*, Teknologisk forlag, Oslo 1997

**Riddervold, Astri & Andresen, Kasper:** *Middelalderens matkultur*, Stiklestad Book, p. 157, 2003

**Torstenson, Inge:** *Fra nattmann til renholdsverk, avfall og renovasjon i Oslo gjennom tusen år*, ProArk, Oslo 1997

**Viestad, Else:** 'Kjønn og ideologi. Om Rousseaus undertrykkingsstrategi', *Materialisten*, 1, 82, 1982

**Watson, L.:** *Lightning Bird*, London 1982

### BEVERAGES

**Alm, Jens M.:** *Den norske dram*, Brennerienes forening, Oslo 1979

**Dege, Hroar:** *Historian om de norske akevitter*, Kilden forlag, Arendal 1997

**Dega, Hroar:** *Christopher Hammer*, Landbruksforlaget AS, Oslo 1994

**Heuch, Halvor:** *Akevitt, en norsk brennevinshistorie*, Cappelen, Oslo 2002

**Øystå, Øystein:** *Øl til glede*, Bergsnov, Mellbye & Rosenbaum Forlag, Oslo 1996

## PORTRAITS

ABEL, NIELS HENRIK:
**Ore, Øystein:** *Niels Henrik Abel: Et geni og hans samtid*, Gyldendal, Oslo 1954
**Stubhaug, Arild:** *Et foranskutt lyn: Niels Henrik Abel og hans tid*, Aschehoug, Oslo 1996

BIRKELAND, KRISTIAN AND EYDE, SAM:
**Grimnes, Ole Christian:** *Den grenseløse gründer*, Aschehoug, Oslo 2001
**Jago, Lucy:** *Nordlysets gåte – beretningen om Kristian Birkeland*, Gyldendal, Oslo 2002

THE MEN OF EIDSVOLL:
**Fure, Eli:** *Eidsvoll 1814: Hvordan Grunnloven ble til*, Dreyer, Oslo 1984

FAIRHAIR, HARALD:
**Sturluson, Snorri:** *Kongesagaer*, J.M. Stenersens Forlag, Oslo 1930

FLAGSTAD, KIRSTEN:
**Gunnarson, Torstein:** *Sannheten om Kirsten Flagstad*, Flagstadselskapet 1985
**Solbakken, Ingeborg:** *Stemmen: Kirsten Flagstad: Verdensstjerne og syndebukk*, Genesis, Oslo 2003

GERHARDSEN, EINAR:
**Hjelle, Egil:** *Einar Gerhardsen*, Tiden, Oslo 1975
**Olstad, Finn:** *Einar Gerhardsen: En politisk biografi*, Universitetsforlaget, Oslo 1999

GRIEG, EDVARD:
**Andersen, Rune J.:** *Edvard Grieg: Et kjempende menneske*, Cappelen, Oslo 1993
**Benestad, Finn & Kortsen, Bjarne:** *Brev til Frants Beyer 1872-1907*, Universitetsforlaget, Oslo 1993
HAMSUN, KNUT:
**Braatøy, Trygve:** *Livets cirkel*, Cappelen, Oslo 1954
**Ferguson, Robert:** *Gåten Knut Hamsun*, Dreyer, Oslo 1988

HENIE, SONJA:
**Andersen, Alf Gunnar:** *Som i en drøm: Sonja Henies liv*, Schibsted, Oslo 1985
**Stenset, Bodil:** *Kvinne på is*, Pax, Oslo 2002

HEYERDAHL, THOR:
**Evensberget, Snorre:** *Oppdageren*, J.M. Stenersens Forlag, Oslo 1994
**Ralling, Christopher:** *Thor Heyerdahl: Eventyret og livsverket*, Gyldendal, Oslo 1989
Author's interview with Heyerdahl, 1995

IBSEN, HENRIK:
**Gran, Gerhard:** *Henrik Ibsen: Liv og verker*, Aschehoug, Oslo 1918
**Heiberg, Hans:** *Født til kunstner – Et Ibsen-portrett*, Aschehoug, Oslo 1967
**Ibsen, Bergliot:** *De tre*, Gyldendal, Oslo 1948

MICHELSEN, CHRISTIAN:
**Nanseth, Finn:** *Veien til unionsoppløsningen i 1905*, Libretto, Oslo 2001
**Wyller, Thomas Christian:** *Christian Michelsen – Politikeren*, Dreyer, Oslo 1975

MUNCH, EDVARD:
**Stang, Nic.:** *Edvard Munch*, Tanum Forlag, Oslo 1971
**Stang, Ragna:** *Edvard Munch: Mennesket og kunstneren*, Aschehoug, Oslo 1984
**Stenersen, Rolf:** *Nærbilde av et geni*, Gyldendal, Oslo 1945

NANSEN, FRIDTJOF:
**Hegge, Per Egil:** *Fridtjof Nansen: Bare én vilje*, J.M. Stenersens Forlag, Oslo 2002
**Sørensen, Øystein:** *Fridtjof Nansen – Mannen og myten*, Universitetsforlaget, Oslo 1993

UNDSET, SIGRID:
**Anderson, Gidske:** *Sigrid Undset – et liv*, Gyldendal, Oslo 1989
**Ørjasæter, Tordis:** *Menneskenes hjerter: Sigrid Undset – et kunstnerliv*, Aschehoug, Oslo 1993

# PICTURE CREDITS

SCANPIX

28l (Werner Formann/Corbis), 63 (Jon Eeg/AP), 66 (Jan Greve), 88 (Erik Thorberg), 90, 91 Håkon Gullvåg, Portrett av Carsten Smith (c) Håkon Gullvåg/BONO 2004 (Photo: Mattis Sandblad), 99 (Erik Berglund), 101, 103 (Paul Audestad), 104 (NTB), 121 (Bettmann/Corbis), 122 (Erik Johansen), 136 (Erik Berglund), 141, 143, 144 (Kjell Lynau / Aktuell), 145 (NTB), 147 (Erik Thorberg/NTB), 148, 149, 151 (NORAD), 153 (Per Svensson), 154 (Harald Henden), 158 (Harald Henden), 159 (Svein Tornås), 160 (Odd Steinar Tøllefsen), 162 (Dag Grundseth), 165 (Arash A. Nejad), 167 (Ole Magnus Rapp), 169 (Jon Eeg), 171, 178 (Aktuell), 180 (Aage Storløkken/Aktuell), 185 (Erik Thorberg / NTB), 185l (Grete Sandberg/NTB), 192 (Ingeborg Hauglid), 209 (Ole Magnus Rapp), 214 (NTB), 218l (NTB), 218r (Knut A. Nilsen), 226 (AP), 240tl (Per Frogner), 240tr (Lise Åserud), 240b ( Hans O. Torgersen), 246 (Bjørn Sigurdsøn), 251, 252 (Bjørn Sigurdsøn), 262, 286, 294 (Knut Fjeldstad), 295 (Karin Beate Nøsterud), 296 (Torbjørn Grønning), 297 (Jon Hauge), 299 (Cornelius Poppe), 302 (Trygve Indrelid), 303 (Terje Gustavsen), 304t (Rolf M. Aagaard), 304bl (Trond Bø), 304br (Rolf M. Aagaard), 307bl (Norsk Designråd / HANDOUT), 307br (Per Svein Reed), 308 (Espen Sjølingstad Hoen), 309tl (Heiko Junge), 309bl (Tor Richardsen), 309r (Mattis Sandblad), 311 (Knut Fjeldstad), 354, 370 (Terje Mortensen), 386, 390 (NTB), 393 (Dan Petter Neegaard), 401 (NTB), 409 (Aktuell), 411 (Nils Bjåland), 414tl (Veronica Melå), 414b, 449, 461 (Janne Møller Hansen), 470r (NTH), 472, 482 (Cornelius Poppe), 483, 486, 487 (Lise Åserud / NTB / Scanpix Spandols), 488 (Jan Greve), 491 (NTB), 492 (NTB), 493 (Tor Richardsen), 494tl (Ruben Sprich/Reuters), 494tc (Knut Edv. Holm), 494tr (Alessandro Trovati/AP Photo), 494cl, 494c (Lise Åserud), 494cr (TOPHAM), 494bl (Tor Richardsen), 494bc (Jan Greve), 494br (Heiko Junge), 495tl (Erik Johansen), 495tc (Erik Johansen), 495tr, 495cl, 495c (Tor Richardsen), 495cr (NTB), 495bl (Calle Törnstrøm), 495bc (Erlend Aas), 495 br (Jerry Lampen/Reuters), 496 (Gunnar Lier), 498 (Erik Johansen), 504 (Sverre A. Børretzen/Aktuell), 506, 513 (Knut Snare), 573 cl (Sverre A. Børretzen/Aktuell)

## OTHER ILLUSTRATIONS:

Akershus fylkesmuseum: 57 (Asker museum) All Over Press, Norge: 93 (Eliot Press), 451 (Johan Brun) Andreassen, Frank/Nettfoto: 14/15 Arbeiderbevegelsens arkiv og bibliotek: 448, 479 Aschehougs bildearkiv: 50 Bergen skolemuseum: 408 Bergen Sjøfartsmuseum: 435, 436 Brun, Christian: 532, 535, 536, 539, 540, 543 Det Nationalhistoriske Museum på Frederiksborg, Hillerød: 32 (Hans Petersen) Det norske nobelinstitutt: 119, 125 (Arne Knudsen) Det norske misjonsselskap: 170 Edvard Grieg Museum, Troldhaugen: 348, 351 Eide, Per: 13, 51, 184, 188, 193, 206/207, 212, 464 Fjellanger Widerøe Foto A/S: 360 Forsvarets mediesenter: 163 Havran, Jiri: 235 Hedmarkmuseets fotoarkiv, Hamar: 384 Helgestad, Asgeir: 194, 197 Hvalfangstmuseet, Sandefjord: 434 Ibsenmuseet: 264 Ingstad, Helge (heirs): 26, 414tr Kon-Tiki Museet: 228 Maihaugen - De Sandvigske Samlinger: 72, 75 Maipo Film og TV-produksjon: 291 Nasjonalbiblioteket i Oslo, Billedsamlingen: 82, 84, 85, 86, 87, 94 (Worm-Petersen), 114, 117 (J. C. F. Hilfing-Rasmussen), 130 (A. B. Wilse), 133, 139, 284 (A. B. Wilse), 371, 400 (E. Hammerstad), 402, 422 (Johan Gørbitz), 424, 431 (Ole Tobias Olsen) Nasjonalmuseet for kunst: 29 (Kunstindustrimuseet i Oslo), 46 (K. Ø. Nerdrum/Nasjonalgalleriet), 52 (J. Lathion/Nasjonalgalleriet), 521 (J. Lathion/Nasjonalgalleriet) Norges Hjemmefrontmuseum: 142 Norsk Filmstudio A/S: 290 (Mona Haug) Norsk Folkemuseum: 217t, (Arild Berg), 357 (Axel Lindahl), 394 (A. B. Wilse), 396, 398 (Elisif Wessel), 432 (A. B. Wilse), 490 (A. B. Wilse), 510, 515, 516, 525 (A. B. Wilse), 527 (A. B. Wilse), 530 Norsk Hydro: 470l Norsk Jernbanemuseum: 365 Oslo kommune, Byarkivet: 404, 444 (Narve Skarpmoen), Oslo Bymuseum: 373 (A. B. Wilse), 439 (A. B. Wilse), 519 Oslo kommune, Kunstsamlingene, Munch-museet: 318, 320 O. Væring Eft. A/S: 40, 80, 83, 97 (Reidar Aulie: *freske i Oslo Rådhus (C)*, Reidar Aulie/BONO 2004), 359, 443, 478, 484, 570c Poppe, Tine: 60 ((c) Gustav Vigeland/BONO 2004), 78, 572 Puschmann, Oskar / NIJOS: 200 Samfoto: 9 (Johannes Haugan), 10 (Trym Ivar Bergsmo), 24 (Bård Løken), 25l (Espen Bratlie), 25r (Bård Løken), 30 (Marianne Grøndahl/BAM), 31 (Bård Løken), 49t (Espen Bratlie), 49b (Espen Bratlie), 53 (Fred Friberg), 56 (Espen Bratlie), 62 (Espen Bratlie), 64t (Trym Ivar Bergsmo), 64b (Trym Ivar Bergsmo), 105 (Bård Løken), 106 (Henrik Sørensen / BAM), 187r (Steve Halsetrønning), 203 (Asgeir Helgestad), 208 (Tore Wuttudal), 217b (Trym Ivar Bergsmo), 232 (Bård Løken), 234 (Per Eide), 236t (Arne Strømme), 236bl (Bård Løken), 236br (Bård Løken), 239 (Kim Hart), 245 (Bernt Eide), 247 (Fredrik Naumann), 250 (Espen Bratlie), 255 (Stig Tronvold), 298 (Bård Løken), 305 (Bård Løken), 312 (Trym Ivar Bergsmo), 363 (Espen Bratlie), 364 (Bård Løken), 366 (Helge Sunde), 367 (Jan Arve Dale), 368 (Bård Løken), 372t (Bjørn Rørslett), 372b (Ole A Buenget), 375 (Steve Halsetrønning), 376 (Trym Ivar Bergsmo), 378 (Per Eide), 428 (Dag Jenssen), 481 (Espen Bratlie), 485 (Steinar Myhr), 524 (Steinar Myhr) Sjømannskirken, Norsk kirke i utlandet: 248 Snorre Sturlasons kongesagaer: 16 (Erik Werenskiold: *Harald Hårfagre* (c) Erik Werenskiold/BONO 2004) Snøhetta A/S: 306t (Gerald Zugmann) Sports Illustratet: 476 (George Tiedemann) Stavanger Aftenblad: 453 Stortingsarkivet: 43 Svensen, Rudolf/UWphoto: 201 Sæbø, Håvard: 249 Universitetet i Tromsø: 403 (Marit Karlstad) Universitetets kulturhistoriske museer: 18 (Ove Holst), 22 (Ove Holst), 27 (Ove Holst), 28r (Ove Holst), Vefsn museum: 59 (Wilhelm Walle) Wilh. Wilhelmsen: 459 Østfold fylkes billedarkiv: 140 Aavatsmark, Erik: 300 Bull, Tove: 395 Direktoratet for naturforvaltning: 186 IMF og Petroleum Intelligence Weekly: 457 Miljøverndepartementet: 196 Nasjonalregnskapet, Statistisk sentralbyrå: 462 Norges Rederiforbund: 459 Norsk samfunnsvitenskapelig datatjeneste og Kirkerådet: 238t Riddervold, Astri: 528 Statens lånekasse for utdanning: 406 Statistisk sentralbyrå: 238b, 369, 392, 399,430 Statistisk sentralbyrå og Statens forurensningstilsyn: 205, 216 Steigan, Geir Tandberg: 47, 161, 456 Utslippsregnskapet til Statistisk sentralbyrå og Statens forurensningstilsyn: 213

## PHOTO OF THE MONTH

January: **Fin Serck-Hanssen.** From the series «Isbre», 1994 February: **Rolf M. Aagaard.** Lofoten March: **Herdis Maria Siegert.** 1)»Eggum, Lofoten 2002», 2) «Utakleiv, Lofoten 1999», 3) «Rørvik, Lofoten 1999», 4) «Hauklandsand, Lofoten 1997» April: **Janne Solgaard.** No. 1 og No. 2 May: **Jens Hauge.** 1)»Vårlandskap 1983», 2) «Vårlandskap 1982», 3) og 4) from the series «Utsiktspunkt og gøymestad» 2003 og 2002 June: **Vibeke Tandberg:** From the series «Living Together», picture No. 12, No. 2, No. 19 og No. 17, 1996 (c) Vibeke Tandberg/BONO 2004 July: **Dag Alveng.** From the series «Sommerlys» 1) Kirsebær i øret (Matilda og Frida), 1987, 2) Kirsebær, 1981, 3) Beth og Matilda, 1987, 4) Stien med skygge, 1996 August: **Rune Johansen.** 1) «Gi oss i dag vort daglige brød», 2) «Min blomstrende bestemor» , 3) «Villy», 4) «Lofotveggen» September: **Knut Bry.** 1) fra Jæren, 2) fra Tvedestrand, 3) fra Hardanger, 4) fra Hallingdal October: **Asle Svarverud.** 1) Skummønster i vann, Sigdal, 2) Strå i vann, Nøklevann, Oslo, 3) Hesjestaur, Vossastrand, 4) Speiling, Eggum, Lofoten November: **Ingvar Moi.** From the series «Ventar i vinden», picture XVII, XIV, XVIII og V December: **Per Berntsen.** 1) Sognefjellet 3, 1997, 2) Sognefjellet 2, 1997, 3) Strynefjellet 1, 1997, 4) Strynefjellet 3, 1997

## ART GALLERY CREDITS

Peder Balke, photo: **J. Lathion/Nasjonalgalleriet/Nasjonalmuseet for kunst**, 1999 Johan Christian Dahl, Rasmus Meyers samlinger/Bergen Kunstmuseum Anonymous artist, photo: **Eirik Irgens Johnsen/Universitetets kulturhistoriske museer** Adolph Tidemand, photo: **J. Lathion/Nasjonalgalleriet/Nasjonalmuseet for kunst**, 1995 Christian Krohg, Rasmus Meyers samlinger/Bergen Kunstmuseum Ludvig Karsten, photo: **J.Lathion/Nasjonalgalleriet/Nasjonalmuseet for kunst, 2004** Olaf Tostrup, photo: **TeigensFotoatelier/Kunstindustrimuseet i Oslo/Nasjonalmuseet for kunst** Gustav Gaudernack, photo: **TeigensFotoatelier/Kunstindustrimuseet i Oslo/Nasjonalmuseet for kunst** Edvard Munch, Solen 1916 (c) Munch-museet/Munch-Ellingsen gruppen/BONO 2004 Frida Hansen, Museum für Kunst und Gewerbe, Hamburg Edvard Munch, Portrett av Sigbjørn Obsfelder, 1897 (c) Munch-museet/Munch-Ellingsen gruppen/BONO 2004 Synnøve Anker Aurdal, Rommet og ordene, 1977 (c) Synnøve Anker Aurdal/BONO 2004. Photo: **O. Væring Eft. A/S** Gro Jessen, Sidsels landskap, 1980 (c) Gro Jessen/BONO 2004 Jakob Weidemann, Tåke i Getsemane, 1965 (c) Jakob Weidemann/BONO 2004 Carl Nesjar, Vann- og isfontene, 1971 (c) Carl Nesjar/BONO 2004. Photo: **Landbrukshøgskolen, Ås** Per Kleiva, Blad frå imperialismens dagbok, 1971 (c) Per Kleiva/BONO 2004. Photo: **J. Lathion/Nasjonalgalleriet/Nasjonalmuseet for kunst**, 1999 Kristian Blystad, Badende, 1991 (c) Kristian Blystad/BONO 2004 Mikkel McAlinden, Den onde hytta, 2000 (c) Mikkel McAlinden/BONO 2004 Erik Pløen, Krukke, 1968 (c) Erik Pløen/BONO 2004 Niclas Gulbrandsen, Beethovens Frülingsonate, 1998 (c) Niclas Gulbrandsen/BONO 2004 May Bente Aronsen, Bølge, Korall, 1999 (c) May Bente Aronsen/BONO 2004. Photo: **Guri Sandvik** Olav Christopher Jenssen, The thinking Bells, 2002 (c) Olav Christopher Jenssen/BONO 2004. Photo: **Stein Jørgensen/Courtesy Galleri Riis** Børre Larsen, Fjærball, 1999-2002 (c) Børre Larsen/BONO 2004 Sigurd Bronger, Ring, 1994 (c) Sigurd Bronger/BONO 2004. Photo: **Kyrre Andersen**

# INDEX OF NAMES

# INDEX OF PLACE NAMES

**Endpapers photo:**
Detail of the pulpit of Lesja church, Gudbrandsdalen. It was carved by Jakob B. Klukstad between 1743 and 1749.

Picture editor: Tone Svinningen
Jacket and design: Tine Poppe
Production consultants: Arne Olsen and Rune Samuelsen

Typeset in Sabon 10/14

Paper: Furioso 130 gr.
Typeset, printed and bound by PDC Tangen

First printing

ISBN: 82-8071-086-8

**The editors wish to express their gratitude to the following:**
Stein Bjørlo, Cecilie Malm Brundtland, Johnny Evang, Ivar Libæk, Ivar Liseter,
Geir Thomas Risåsen, Øivind Stenersen, Stig Storhaug, Terje Svabø, Jan R. Tislevoll.

Published with the support of Norge 2005.



Enquiries relating to this book may be addressed to:
Dinamo Forlag, Pb 442, NO-1327 LYSAKER, Norway
Tel.: +47 67 200 000

www.dinamoforlag.no